# Exploring Youth Studies in the Age of AI

Zeinab Zaremohzzabieh
*Insitute for Social Science Studies, Universiti Putra Malaysia, Malaysia*

Rusli Abdullah
*Universiti Putra Malaysia, Malaysia*

Seyedali Ahrari
*Faculty of Educational Studies, Universiti Putra Malaysia, Malaysia*

A volume in the Advances in Human and Social
Aspects of Technology  (AHSAT) Book Series

Published in the United States of America by
    IGI Global
    Information Science Reference (an imprint of IGI Global)
    701 E. Chocolate Avenue
    Hershey PA, USA 17033
    Tel: 717-533-8845
    Fax:  717-533-8661
    E-mail: cust@igi-global.com
    Web site: http://www.igi-global.com

Library of Congress Cataloging-in-Publication Data

CIP DATA PROCESSING

2024 Information Science Reference

ISBN(hc):  9798369333501
ISBN(sc):  9798369349533
eISBN:  9798369333518


British Cataloguing in Publication Data
A Cataloguing in Publication record for this book is available from the British Library.


The views expressed in this book are those of the authors, but not necessarily of the publisher.

For electronic access to this publication, please contact: eresources@igi-global.com.

# Advances in Human and Social Aspects of Technology (AHSAT) Book Series

Mehdi Khosrow-Pour, D.B.A.
Information Resources Management Association, USA

ISSN:2328-1316
EISSN:2328-1324

## Mission

In recent years, the societal impact of technology has been noted as we become increasingly more connected and are presented with more digital tools and devices. With the popularity of digital devices such as cell phones and tablets, it is crucial to consider the implications of our digital dependence and the presence of technology in our everyday lives.

The **Advances in Human and Social Aspects of Technology (AHSAT) Book Series** seeks to explore the ways in which society and human beings have been affected by technology and how the technological revolution has changed the way we conduct our lives as well as our behavior. The AHSAT book series aims to publish the most cutting-edge research on human behavior and interaction with technology and the ways in which the digital age is changing society.

## Coverage

- Public Access to ICTs
- Cultural Influence of ICTs
- ICTs and social change
- Cyber Bullying
- Human Rights and Digitization
- Technology Dependence
- Information ethics
- Human Development and Technology
- ICTs and human empowerment
- Activism and ICTs

IGI Global is currently accepting manuscripts for publication within this series. To submit a proposal for a volume in this series, please contact our Acquisition Editors at Acquisitions@igi-global.com or visit: http://www.igi-global.com/publish/.

# Titles in this Series

For a list of additional titles in this series, please visit: www.igi-global.com/book-series

*Bridging Human Rights and Corporate Social Responsibility Pathways to a Sustainable Global Society*
Maja Pucelj (Faculty of Organisation Studies, University of Novo Mesto, Slovenia) and Rado Bohinc (Scientific Research Centre Koper, Slovenia)
Information Science Reference • copyright 2024 • 324pp • H/C (ISBN: 9798369323250) • US $245.00 (our price)

*Driving Decentralization and Disruption With Digital Technologies*
Balraj Verma (Chitkara Business School, Chitkara University, India) Babita Singla (Chitkara Business School, Chitkara University, India) and Amit Mittal (Chitkara Business School, Chitkara University, India)
Engineering Science Reference • copyright 2024 • 322pp • H/C (ISBN: 9798369332535) • US $325.00 (our price)

*Considerations on Cyber Behavior and Mass Technology in Modern Society*
Paolo Beneventi (Independent Researcher, Italy)
Engineering Science Reference • copyright 2024 • 271pp • H/C (ISBN: 9781668482285) • US $240.00 (our price)

*AI and Emotions in Digital Society*
Adrian Scribano (CONICET, University of Buenos Aires, Argentina) and Maximiliano E. Korstanje (University of Palermo, Argentina)
Information Science Reference • copyright 2024 • 321pp • H/C (ISBN: 9798369308028) • US $240.00 (our price)

*Adoption and Use of Technology Tools and Services by Economically Disadvantaged Communities Implications for Growth and Sustainability*
Alice S. Etim (Winston-Salem State University, USA)
Information Science Reference • copyright 2024 • 383pp • H/C (ISBN: 9781668453476) • US $225.00 (our price)

*Philosophy of Artificial Intelligence and Its Place in Society*
Luiz Moutinho (University of Suffolk, UK) Luís Cavique (Universidade Aberta, Portugal) and Enrique Bigné (Universitat de València, Spain)
Engineering Science Reference • copyright 2023 • 439pp • H/C (ISBN: 9781668495919) • US $215.00 (our price)

701 East Chocolate Avenue, Hershey, PA 17033, USA
Tel: 717-533-8845 x100 • Fax: 717-533-8661
E-Mail: cust@igi-global.com • www.igi-global.com

# Table of Contents

*Seyedali Ahrari, Women and Family Studies Research Center, University of Religions and Denominations, Iran*

*Zeinab Zaremohzzabieh, Women and Family Studies Research Center, University of Religions and Denominations, Iran*

*Rusli Abdullah, Faculty of Computer Science and Information Technology, Universiti Putra Malaysia, Malaysia*

*Ismi Arif Ismail, Faculty of Educational Studies, Universiti Putra Malaysia, Malaysia*
*Nor Wahiza Abd Wahat, Faculty of Educational Studies, Universiti Putra Malaysia, Malaysia*
*Jeffrey Lawrence D'Silva, Institute for Social Science Studies, Universiti Putra Malaysia, Malaysia*
*Mohd Faiq Abd Aziz, Faculty of Educational Studies, Universiti Putra Malaysia, Malaysia*
*Hayrol Azril Mohammed Shaffril, Institute for Social Science Studies, Universiti Putra Malaysia, Malaysia*
*Dzulhailmi Dahalan, Institute for Social Science Studies, Universiti Putra Malaysia, Malaysia*

*Fakhroddin Noorbehbahani, Faculty of Computer Engineering, University of Isfahan, Isfahan, Iran*
*Zeinab Zaremohzzabieh, Women and Family Studies Research Center, University of Religions and Denominations, Qom, Iran*
*Hooman Hoghooghi Esfahani, Faculty of Computer Engineering, University of Isfahan, Isfahan, Iran*
*Soroush Bajoghli, Faculty of Computer Engineering, University of Isfahan, Isfahan, Iran*
*Mahboobeh Moosivand, Women Research Center, Alzahra University, Tehran, Iran*

*Mudasir Rahman Najar, SRM University, India*

*Puspita Dash, Department of Information Technology, Sri Manakula Vinayagar Engineering College, Puducherry, India*
*N. Kalaiselvi, Department of Information Technology, Sri Manakula Vinayagar Engineering College, Puducherry, India*
*K. Bhavani, Department of Information Technology, Sri Manakula Vinayagar Engineering College, Puducherry, India*
*M. Lakshmiprabha, Department of Information Technology, Sri Manakula Vinayagar Engineering College, Puducherry, India*
*E. Valarmathi, Department of Information Technology, Sri Manakula Vinayagar Engineering College, Puducherry, India*
*V. Padmapriya, Sri Manakula Vinayagar Engineering College, India*
*C. Vanaja, Sri Manakula Vinayagar Engineering College, India*

*S. C. Vetrivel, Kongu Engineering College, India*

# Detailed Table of Contents

**Chapter 1**

*Nita Beluli Luma, Mother Teresa University, North Macedonia*
*Arta Xhelili, Mother Teresa University, North Macedonia*
*Elisabeta Bajrami Ollogu, Mother Teresa University, North Macedonia*
*Diturije Ismaili, Mother Teresa University, North Macedonia*

Keywords Adolescent, digitalization, mental health, parenting style, social media

**Chapter 2**

*Huma Zaidi, Ras Al Khaimah Medical and Health Sciences University, UAE*
*Omar Turkey AlJadaan, Ras Al Khaimah Medical and Health Science University, UAE*
*Mahmoud Yousef Al Faress, KSA Ministry of Education, Saudi Arabia*
*Ahmad Omar Jabas, Shaqra University, Saudi Arabia*

This chapter delves into the real impact of our digital dependence on our lives – how it affects our minds, and connections with others. Shedding light on the challenges faced in balancing digital and offline worlds, especially in today's fast-paced society. We see the dangers of spending a lot of time glued to screens and the signs of digital addiction that we overlook. But there's a silver lining filled with practical advice and inspiring tales of people who have found a healthier relationship with technology. From simple tricks like setting screen time limits to embracing offline activities and mindfulness, we discover ways to reclaim control over our digital lives. Looking ahead, we glimpse a promising future where technology supports our well-being, thanks to innovations like AI and 5G that foster positive digital experiences. Whether you're navigating your digital habits, teaching others about digital wellness, supporting patients in healthcare, or shaping policies, this chapter serves as a trusted guide on the journey to a more mindful and fulfilling tech experience.

**Chapter 3**

*Ruqia Safdar Bajwa, Bahauddin Zakariya University, Pakistan*
*Asma Yunus, University of Sargodha, Pakistan*
*Hina Saeed, The Women University, Multan, Pakistan*
*Asia Zulfqar, Bahauddin Zakariya University, Pakistan*

This chapter explores the evolving dynamics of parenting in the age of artificial intelligence (AI), emphasizing the dual roles of parents as both guardians and facilitators in the digital realm. With the integration of AI into everyday life, parenting transforms, confronting new challenges, and harnessing opportunities to influence child development positively. Drawing on recent studies, this work highlights the early engagement of children with AI, revealing that children as young as six years old formulate their own metaphors and perspectives on AI, and utilize it in ways that significantly impact their learning processes and emotional well-being. The chapter discusses how AI revolutionizes education by providing personalized learning experiences and monitoring children's emotional and physical states, while also examining the potential pitfalls, including digital addiction, privacy concerns, and the risk of technology interference in parent-child interactions.

## Chapter 4

*Ruqia Safdar Bajwa, Bahauddin Zakariya University, Pakistan*
*Asma Yunus, University of Sargodha, Pakistan*

This chapter explores the relationship between screen time and identity formation, specifically for adolescents and young individuals. It discusses how digital media can benefit and challenge personal expression and social connectivity. The chapter examines the dynamic interplay between screen time and identity development, highlighting the potential risks related to cyberbullying, privacy concerns, and mental health issues. It emphasizes the important role of educators and parents in guiding youth through their digital engagement and advocates for a balanced approach to digital consumption that fosters positive digital citizenship and well-being. The chapter also explores the impact of emerging technologies, such as virtual and augmented reality, artificial intelligence, and personalization algorithms, on the evolving concept of digital identity.

## Chapter 5

*Wang Fei, Faculty of Human Ecology, Universiti Putra Malaysia, Malaysia*

Digital natives, surrounded by technology since birth, face a unique landscape shaped by artificial intelligence (AI). While AI unlocks a world of connection, information, and personalization, it can also present challenges for their mental well-being. This chapter explores this intricate relationship. The authors will delve into potential sources of anxiety, stress, and isolation linked to AI, like social media algorithms and constant connectivity. But it won't all be concerns. They will also explore solutions, like critical thinking skills, mindfulness practices, and fostering positive online communities. This chapter aims to equip readers with insights and strategies to navigate the digital world in the AI age, promoting a healthy mental landscape for young people.

## Chapter 6

*Ruqia Safdar Bajwa, Bahauddin Zakariya University, Pakistan*

This chapter explains the impact of digital devices and the responsible use of technology. It analyses the harmful effects of prolonged screen time on our physical, mental, and social health. The chapter explores the benefits of digital detox interventions and their challenges. It concludes with a call for a mindful, personalized approach to technology use. It emphasizes the need for a balanced and conscious approach to technology use, highlighting the potential risks of excessive screen time as evidenced by empirical research. However, it also showcases the significant advantages of digital detox interventions, such as enhanced sleep quality, mood, productivity, creativity, and improved personal relations. The chapter offers strategies for adapting to diverse lifestyles, needs, and responsibilities.

*Seyedali Ahrari, Women and Family Studies Research Center, University of Religions and
    Denominations, Iran*
*Zeinab Zaremohzzabieh, Women and Family Studies Research Center, University of
    Religions and Denominations, Iran*
*Rusli Abdullah, Faculty of Computer Science and Information Technology, Universiti Putra
    Malaysia, Malaysia*

In today's world of continuous learning, there are challenges in providing accessible career guidance to young people that connect education and employment. However, there has been limited research into using artificial intelligence (AI) to improve guidance in professional life. This chapter discusses the progress made in leveraging AI to enhance and advance youth career guidance. One innovative solution to this challenge lies in the use of AI technology. AI can revolutionize the way career guidance is delivered by offering personalized and data-driven recommendations tailored to each individual's unique skills, interests, and goals. Despite the immense potential of AI in transforming the way career guidance is provided, there has been limited research on how this technology can be effectively utilized in higher education and professional life. This lack of exploration is a missed opportunity to leverage AI to its fullest potential in empowering individuals to make informed decisions about their education and career paths.

*Wasswa Shafik, School of Digital Science, Universiti Brunei Darussalam, Gadong, Brunei
    Darussalam & Dig Connectivity Research Laboratory (DCRLab), Kampala, Uganda*

Recent technological developments influence different daily human activities, including education and lifestyle. This chapter explores the significance of mobile learning and bringing your own device to enhance education in the digital age. It highlights the growing use of mobile devices in educational settings and their advantages and drawbacks. The literature review analyses existing research, frameworks, and best practices for utilizing mobile devices and smartphones in educational settings. The study examines pedagogical approaches, mobile resources, and educational applications that utilize mobile technology for personalized and engaging learning. It also discusses related policies, implementation difficulties, and successful case studies of technology adoption. The chapter offers best practices for maximizing the benefits, such as management strategies, and a safe learning environment. The chapter also speculates on the future developments and effects of mobile learning in the classroom, exploring new technologies and innovations that may influence education.

*Potchong M. Jackaria, Tawi-Tawi College of Technology and Oceanography, Mindanao
    State University, Philippines*
*Bonjovi H. Hajan, Tawi-Tawi College of Technology and Oceanography, Mindanao State
    University, Philippines*
*Al-Rashiff H. Mastul, Tawi-Tawi College of Technology and Oceanography, Mindanao State*

*University, Philippines*
*Fatima Zahra Sali, Tawi-Tawi College of Technology and Oceanography, Mindanao State*
*University, Philippines*

This chapter aims to conduct a review of existing literature on the artificial intelligence applications in education in the context of generation AI students. Particularly, this chapter looks into opportunities and challenges through the systematics literature review. Challenges identified include the risk of youth over-reliance on AI, and the widening of the digital divides between the privilege and the underprivilege youth. Educators and practitioners are concerned on the potential bias of AI algorithm, privacy, and the ethical issues, especially when children use AI. On the other hand, some opportunities emerged including the automation of many routine tasks, the delivery of personalized learning tailored to students' abilities and interest and the giving of real-time feedback. This chapter suggests for the inclusion of AI literacy in schools as this will be needed in the future workplace. Ethical, privacy and safety issues should also be freely discussed in schools involving youth so that they can make better decisions.

## Chapter 10

*Dwijendra Nath Dwivedi, Krakow University of Economics, Poland*
*Ghanashyama Mahanty, Utkal University, India*
*Shafik Khashouf, University of Liverpool, UK*

Higher education institutions face a problem with student turnover that has many aspects and affects both students and universities in different ways. Using predictive analytics and machine learning, this study shows a new way to deal with this problem. The main goal is to create predicting algorithms that can predict which students are most likely to drop out, so colleges can get involved in their lives in a timely and effective way. As part of this method, the authors collect and preprocess a large dataset from different university records. This dataset includes information about academic success, socioeconomic background, participation in campus activities, and psychological health. The study uses advanced machine learning methods to look at all of these different data points. It focuses on feature selection and engineering to find the most important factors that predict student dropout. Rigid validation methods are used to test how well the model works, making sure that it can accurately and reliably predict the future.

## Chapter 11

*Ali Saad Kadhim, School of Arts, Department of Psychology, Mustansiriyah University, Iraq*
*Hanan Yousif Mousa, Mustansiriya University, Iraq*

The most important outcome of the Fourth Industrial Revolution is artificial intelligence due to its multiple uses in various fields. It is expected to be the cause of limitless innovations, and to lead to more industrial revolutions, bringing about a radical change in human life. With this (massive and rapid) technological development and the industrial transformations the world is witnessing, artificial intelligence will be the reason for progress, growth, and prosperity in most areas of life over the next few years, and it can establish a new world that may now seem like a fantasy, but current innovations confirm the possibility of creating this world.

## Chapter 12

The Role of Artificial Intelligence in Teaching Turkish to Foreigners and Chat GPT Assessment

There are many benefits of adapting artificial intelligence to foreign language teaching. In this study, the adaptation of ChatGPT to teach Turkish to foreigners is discussed. The aim of the study is to evaluate the effect of using ChatGPT against traditional methods in developing writing skills in foreign language teaching. Experimental and control groups were formed to investigate the importance of ChatGPT in teaching Turkish to foreigners. The groups were exposed to A2-B1 level writing activities for six weeks. At the end of the activities, students were given feedback by both ChatGPT and teachers. Which of the feedbacks was more effective was evaluated. It was determined which of the ChatGPT and traditional methods was more effective in developing writing skills.

## Chapter 13

This survey study reports findings on information technology and artificial intelligence among two types of youth: youth aged 15–30 and youth aged 31–40 in Selangor, Malaysia. Data were collected from 1000 youth from 9 districts of Selangor (Gombak, Petaling, Kuala Langat, Hulu Langat, Kuala Selangor, Hulu Selangor, Sabak Bernam, Klang, and Sepang). The study findings for information technology and artificial intelligence show eleven items. As expected, overall respondents from youth categories recorded the highest mean score of 4.04, and the youth adult mean score is 3.99. In conclusion, the digital age presents both opportunities and challenges for youth in Selangor, Malaysia. Understanding the implications of information technology and artificial intelligence on youth is crucial for promoting their well-being and harnessing the benefits of digital advancements in education, health, and social interactions

## Chapter 14

*Soroush Bajoghli, Faculty of Computer Engineering, University of Isfahan, Isfahan, Iran*
*Mahboobeh Moosivand, Women Research Center, Alzahra University, Tehran, Iran*

This study aimed to explore the connections between digital disorder, socio-demographics, physical health outcomes, and artificial intelligence (AI) on decision-making loss. The study relied on data from 550 people in Isfahan, Iran. The results showed that while decision-making loss was slightly more prevalent in females than males, this difference was not statistically significant. However, individuals aged between 26-35 showed a significant correlation with decision-making loss, while other age groups did not. Neither education level nor employment status demonstrated significant associations with decision-making loss, nor did the frequency of device use affect it either. Participants who experienced decision-making loss scored significantly higher on digital disorder overall score and specific indicators, such as addiction to social media and the internet, compared to those who did not. They also reported higher scores on various physical health outcomes related to device usage.

## Chapter 15

*Mudasir Rahman Najar, SRM University, India*

The chapter is a journey interior into the nuances of the magnificent technological pursuits. While talking in general, numerous case studies around the world attest to the enormous potential that young people have to drive AI innovation for social impact, like youth-led initiatives utilizing AI have surfaced to address urgent global issues like environmental sustainability, healthcare, and poverty. AI algorithms are used in India as part of the "smart village" effort, which is being led by young entrepreneurs, to improve crop yields, optimize agricultural methods, and reduce rural poverty. Similar to this, young-led businesses are using AI-powered healthcare platforms to lower maternal death rates and increase access to other social activities. In addition, young activists around the world use AI to track environmental data, forecast natural disasters, and promote sustainable policies—all of which help combat climate change and save biodiversity. So, these illustrations highlight the revolutionary potential of youth-driven AI innovation in for the societal benefits.

## Chapter 16

*Puspita Dash, Department of Information Technology, Sri Manakula Vinayagar Engineering College, Puducherry, India*
*N. Kalaiselvi, Department of Information Technology, Sri Manakula Vinayagar Engineering College, Puducherry, India*
*K. Bhavani, Department of Information Technology, Sri Manakula Vinayagar Engineering College, Puducherry, India*
*M. Lakshmiprabha, Department of Information Technology, Sri Manakula Vinayagar Engineering College, Puducherry, India*
*E. Valarmathi, Department of Information Technology, Sri Manakula Vinayagar Engineering College, Puducherry, India*
*V. Padmapriya, Sri Manakula Vinayagar Engineering College, India*
*C. Vanaja, Sri Manakula Vinayagar Engineering College, India*

The contemporary landscape underscores the critical importance of virtual environments for organizations, educational institutions, and various other entities. To address the challenges of this digital era, we have come to rely heavily on video conferencing and communication systems that facilitate seamless remote interactions. However, in this digital realm, we often overlook the needs of individuals who are mute and deaf, for whom sign language is the primary means of communication. This includes American Sign Language (ASL) and Indian Sign Language (ISL), both of which involve intricate hand gestures. Sign language recognition has emerged as a rapidly evolving field of research, and in response to the unique needs of this community, the authors have developed a video chat application tailored to mute individuals. This project's primary focus centers on Indian Sign Language. To accurately recognize and interpret the diverse hand gestures made by users, the authors harness the power of deep learning convolutional neural network (CNN) algorithms. As users convey their messages through hand gestures to the camera, this CNN-based algorithm swiftly identifies the corresponding phrase, number, or letter, seamlessly relaying it to the frontend. This real-time gesture detection and sentence formation process enhances the overall user experience. Recent advancements in this field have introduced novel techniques that hold promise for transforming the way we understand and facilitate communication through sign language. The overarching objective is to develop a video call model capable of recognizing and interpreting hand gestures and signs. Through rigorous training, the authors intend to create a model that facilitates the conversion of sign language into text or speech, bridging the communication gap and enabling meaningful interactions with individuals who are inherently deaf or have cognitive mentally disabilities.

## Chapter 17

S. C. Vetrivel, Kongu Engineering College, India
K. C. Sowmiya, Sri Vasavi College, India
V. P. Arun, JKKN College of Engineering and Technology, India
T. P. Saravanan, Kongu Engineering College, India
R. Maheswari, Kongu Engineering College, India

As artificial intelligence (AI) technologies continue to evolve, there is a growing recognition of the need for ethical considerations in their development, particularly when targeting younger demographics. "Ethical AI: Guiding Principles for Youth-Centric Development" explores the ethical dimensions of AI with a focus on creating a framework that prioritizes the well-being and development of young users. This chapter investigates the intersection of technology, ethics, and the unique vulnerabilities associated with youth engagement in AI-driven systems. The study begins by outlining the current landscape of AI applications in various sectors that directly impact the lives of young individuals, including education, entertainment, social media, and healthcare. It delves into the potential risks and benefits associated with these applications, highlighting the ethical challenges that arise when designing AI systems for youth consumption.

## Chapter 18

Asma Yunus, University of Sargodha, Pakistan
Shahzad Khaver Mushtaq, University of Sargodha, Pakistan
Ruqia Safdar Bajwa, Bahauddin Zakariya University, Pakistan

Artificial intelligence (AI) has emerged as a powerful force, revolutionizing industries worldwide. Its transformative capabilities extend beyond mere automation, shaping the way we work, innovate, and make decisions. In this chapter, the authors explore how AI is reshaping healthcare and financial sectors, driving efficiency, accuracy, and customer satisfaction. AI is undoubtedly revolutionizing industries globally, providing innovative solutions that enhance productivity, stimulate innovation, and push the boundaries of decision-making.

>    Wang Xiaodan, Universiti Putra Malaysia, Malaysia
>    Aini Azeqa Ma'rof, Institute for Social Science Studies, Universiti Putra Malaysia, Malausia
>        & Faculty of Educational Studies, Universiti Putra Malaysia, Malausia
>    Haslinda Abdullah, Institute for Social Science Studies, Universiti Putra Malaysia, Malausia
>        & Faculty of Educational Studies, Universiti Putra Malaysia, Malausia
>    Wei Wang, Universiti Putra Malaysia, Malaysia

The rise of artificial intelligence has brought profound changes to society and brought new challenges and opportunities to adolescents. With the development of artificial intelligence, adolescents are facing unprecedented social pressure and changes and need to adapt to new roles and responsibilities. This requires them to have a full understanding of their own abilities and characteristics, as well as good communication and collaboration skills. In addition, adolescents need to pay attention to the impact of artificial intelligence on their own development and social development and strive to promote positive changes. Therefore, this chapter will provide feasible strategies for role reconstruction in the artificial intelligence era, helping adolescents better adapt to social changes and seize more opportunities.

>    Asma Yunus, University of Sargodha, Pakistan
>    Ruqia Safdar Bajwa, Bahauddin Zakariya University, Pakistan
>    Shahzad Khaver Mushtaq, University of Sargodha, Pakistan

This chapter sheds light on the AI networks' capabilities as agents of positive change, emphasizing creative applications of AI that foster youth engagement, education, and social activism. Combining empirical studies, expert opinions, and real-life examples, this chapter sets out a moderate view of the challenges and benefits of AI networks in the lives of young people. The current chapter is tipped to scrutinize how AI through social networks extends from the seemingly simple models of interactions such as 'likes' as well as 'shares,' to directly or indirectly and complex machineries that influence and even determine young people's perceptions, actions, and interactions.

>    Avni Avdiu, Mother Teresa University, North Macedonia
>    Agron Kurtishi, Mother Teresa University, North Macedonia
>    Arta Xhelili, Mother Teresa University, North Macedonia
>    Agron Vrangalla, Mother Teresa University, North Macedonia

The use of digital display devices has grown and continues to expand significantly over the past few years. Since contents in online media are numerous, more intense, and without space and time limitations, compared to face to face interactions, their influence is much greater than other social agents'. Taking into consideration that youth use digital media frequently and for a longer duration, they have a considerable contribution to the formation of new generations' identities. This study analyzes the impact of digital media use on youth in terms of identity formation. A quantitative study was conducted based on 312 respondents' self-reports. The findings showed that a positively significant relationship exists between social media exposure and identity formation. The stronger the social media exposure, the less certain respondents are in regard to themselves and their values and beliefs.

    *Vijay Bhutani, Amity University, Greater Noida, India*
    *Preeti Singh Bahadur, Amity University, Greater Noida, India*
    *Sunil K. Sansaniwal, The Energy and Resources Institute, New Delhi, India*
    *Pratima Bais, Dr. C.V. Raman University, India*

The rapid advancement of Artificial Intelligence (AI) has significantly transformed various facets of contemporary society, and the impact on youth is particularly profound. The chapter will delve into the impact of AI on social interaction and identity formation among youth. Social media platforms powered by AI algorithms have revolutionized the way young people connect, communicate, and express themselves, shaping not only their social interactions but also their sense of self and identity. Furthermore, the chapter will explore the ethical implications of AI for youth, examining questions of privacy, autonomy, and agency in an increasingly data-driven world. With AI systems capable of collecting, analyzing, and interpreting vast amounts of personal data, concerns about surveillance, manipulation, and control loom large, raising profound questions about the rights and freedoms of young people in the digital age.

    *Ismail Baydili, Firat University, Turkey*

Artificial intelligence, one of the significant developments of our era, has a profound impact on many areas. These new companions frequently encountered in our daily lives facilitate many aspects of our lives. However, beyond the conveniences they provide, they also affect our identity and personality. The impact of digital tools is particularly significant for 'digital natives,' who were born in the digital age and have grown up using them. It is more inevitable and crucial for them than for other individuals. Young people who lack sufficient life experience and have not had enough human-to-human interaction may develop a communication pattern devoid of emotions and empathy by transitioning to human-machine experiences. This could have a profound impact on both individuals and society. Rather than creating machines that think and feel like humans, we may end up with humans who think and live like machines. This study examines the effects of artificial intelligence on human interaction, identity, and personality.

# Preface

In an era defined by the relentless march of technology, the seamless integration of Artificial Intelligence (AI) into our daily lives has ushered in a transformative landscape. At the forefront of this evolution are the Digital Natives of Generation AI, navigating the complexities of a digital world where algorithms are integral to their daily experiences. This juncture presents a dual influence, marked by the continuous progression of technological advancements and the dynamic ways the youngest members of our society engage with and adapt to the digital environment. As we stand at the crossroads of youth studies and AI, there arises a pressing need to comprehend the profound impact of this convergence on the future leaders of our world.

Addressing this imperative, *Exploring Youth Studies in the Age of AI* emerges as a comprehensive solution to unravel the complexities and opportunities within this evolving landscape. This book, meticulously crafted for academics, researchers, educators, policymakers, and technology ethicists, serves as a guiding beacon in understanding how AI shapes the experiences of today's youth and, in turn, how youth culture influences the development and application of AI technologies. With a collection of enlightening chapters covering topics from "Data-Driven Pedagogies" to "Ethical AI: Guiding Principles for Youth-Centric Development," the book investigates into the diverse dimensions of this intersection, providing actionable insights and fostering a nuanced understanding for those invested in the ethical, social, and educational implications of AI within the context of youth.

As the reader embarks on this intellectual journey, *Exploring Youth Studies in the Age of AI* beckons as an active participant in shaping the future, not only an observation of the current state of affairs. From uncovering the intricacies of AI's influence on education to exploring the socio-economic implications, the book serves as a visionary guide, offering insights into the present and the potential and responsibilities that come with molding the future in the crucible of innovation. With each chapter serving as a gateway into a specific facet of the intersection, this book stands as an indispensable resource for those seeking to navigate the transformative power of AI in the field of youth studies, promising a richer and more informed engagement with the challenges and opportunities of the digital age.

The chapters within this book cover three main topics: digital well-being and mental health, educational and career development, and socio-demographic diversity and ethical considerations. Each chapter provides a detailed exploration of these themes, offering a holistic view of the intricate relationship between AI and youth. The insights presented here are not only intended to inform but also to inspire and empower readers to actively contribute to shaping a future where technology serves the greater good of society, particularly its youngest members.

It is our hope that *Exploring Youth Studies in the Age of AI* will serve as a cornerstone for ongoing discussions and research, guiding readers towards a deeper understanding and a more thoughtful engagement with the rapidly evolving digital world. Together, let us embark on this journey to explore, understand, and shape the future of youth studies in the age of AI.

## ORGANIZATION OF THE BOOK

The book is organized into twenty-two chapters. A brief description of each of the chapters follows:

### Section 1: Digital Well-being and Mental Health

"Chapter 1: Adolescents Mental Health in Digital Era: Exploring the Effects of Parenting Styles," Nita Beluli Luma, Arta Xhelili, Elisabeta Bajrami Ollogu, and Diturije Ismaili investigate the impact of social media and parenting styles on adolescents' mental health. Through a survey of 573 participants from secondary schools in Skopje, North Macedonia, this chapter reveals significant correlations between parenting styles, social media usage, and adolescent mental health, providing insights into fostering a positive social media experience for adolescents.

"Chapter 2: Navigating Digital Detox: A Journey towards Mental and Physical Well-Being," Huma Zaidi, Omar Turkey AlJadaan, Mahmoud Yousef Al Faress, and Ahmad Omar Jabas explore the effects of digital dependence on mental and physical well-being. The chapter discusses practical strategies for digital detox, including setting screen time limits and embracing offline activities, and examines how AI and 5G innovations can support well-being.

"Chapter 3: Parenting in the Age of Artificial Intelligence: Digital Guardians," Ruqia Safdar Bajwa, Asma Yunus, Hina Saeed, and Asia Zulfqar examine the dual roles of parents in guiding and facilitating their children's digital engagement in an AI-driven world. The chapter highlights the benefits and challenges of AI in education and its impact on children's emotional and physical well-being, advocating for balanced and mindful use of technology.

"Chapter 4: Screentime and Identity Formation as a Digital Dilemma: Identity in the Screen Age," Ruqia Safdar Bajwa and Asma Yunus analyze the relationship between screen time and identity formation among adolescents. The chapter discusses the benefits and risks of digital media on personal expression and social connectivity and emphasizes the role of parents and educators in guiding youth towards positive digital citizenship and well-being.

"Chapter 5: The Mental Well-being of Digital Natives in the Age of AI: Challenges and Solutions," Wang Fei explores the unique mental health challenges faced by digital natives in an AI-driven world. The chapter discusses sources of anxiety, stress, and isolation linked to AI and social media, and offers solutions such as critical thinking skills, mindfulness practices, and fostering positive online communities to promote mental well-being among young people.

"Chapter 6: Digital Detox by Balancing Screen Time and Offline Experiences: Balancing Digital and Real Worlds," Ruqia Safdar Bajwa discusses the impact of excessive screen time on physical, mental, and social health. The chapter highlights the benefits of digital detox interventions, such as improved sleep quality, mood, productivity, and personal relations, and provides strategies for achieving a balanced and conscious approach to technology use.

### Section 2: Educational and Career Development

"Chapter 7: AI-Enhanced Youth Career Guidance by Mapping Future Employment Paths with Theory and Practical Application," Seyedali Ahrari, Zeinab Zaremohzzabieh, and Rusli Abdullah examine how AI can revolutionize youth career guidance by offering personalized, data-driven recommendations tailored to individual skills, interests, and goals. The chapter addresses the potential of AI to transform career guidance and the need for further research to fully leverage this technology in education and professional life.

"Chapter 8: Enhancing AI-Enabled Education through Mobile Learning and Bring Your Own Device (BYOD) Integration," Wasswa Shafik explores the integration of mobile learning and BYOD in education. The chapter reviews existing research, frameworks, and best practices, highlighting the benefits and challenges of mobile technology in personalized and engaging learning, and speculates on future developments in mobile learning.

"Chapter 9: Generation AI in a Reimagined Classroom: Challenges, Opportunities and Implications to Education," Potchong M. Jackaria, Bonjovi H. Hajan, Al-rashiff H. Mastul, and Fatima Zahra Sali conduct a literature review on AI applications in education for Generation AI students. The chapter discusses the challenges and opportunities of AI in education, including personalized learning, real-time feedback, and the need for AI literacy and ethical considerations in schools.

"Chapter 10: Predictive Analytics for Reducing University Dropout Rates: A Machine Learning Approach," Dwijendra Nath Dwivedi, Ghanashyama Mahanty, and Shafik Khashouf present a machine learning approach to predict and reduce university dropout rates. The chapter details the use of predictive analytics to identify at-risk students and implement timely interventions, focusing on feature selection, data preprocessing, and model validation.

"Chapter 11: The Role of Artificial Intelligence in Improving the Quality of Education," Ali Saad Kadhim and Hanan Yousif Mousa explore the transformative potential of AI in education. The chapter discusses how AI can enhance educational quality through personalized learning, automation of routine tasks, and real-time monitoring of student progress, emphasizing the need for ethical considerations in AI development.

"Chapter 12: The Role of Artificial Intelligence in Teaching Turkish to Foreigners and Chat GPT Assessment for Writing Skills," Cemile Uzun investigates the use of ChatGPT in teaching Turkish to foreigners. The chapter compares the effectiveness of AI-driven feedback versus traditional methods in developing writing skills, highlighting the benefits of AI in foreign language education.

## Section 3: Socio-Demographics, Diversity, and Ethical Considerations

"Chapter 13: A Survey on Information Technology and Artificial Intelligence among Youth in the Digital Age in Selangor, Malaysia," Nur Raihan Che Nawi, Mohd Mursyid Arshad, Ismi Arif Ismail, Nor Wahiza Abd Wahat, Jeffrey Lawrence D'Silva, Mohd Faiq Abd Aziz, and Hayrol Azril Mohammed Shaffril report findings from a survey of youth in Selangor, Malaysia. The chapter examines the implications of information technology and AI on youth well-being, highlighting opportunities and challenges in education, health, and social interactions.

"Chapter 14: AI on Loss in Decision-Making and Its Associations with Digital Disorder, Socio-Demographics, and Physical Health Outcomes in Iran," Fakhroddin Noorbehbahani, Zeinab Zaremohzzabieh, Hooman Hoghooghi Esfahani, Soroush Bajoghli, and Mahboobeh Moosivand explore the connections between digital disorder, socio-demographics, physical health outcomes, and AI-related decision-making loss. The chapter analyzes data from 550 participants in Isfahan, Iran, revealing significant correlations and highlighting the impact of digital disorder on physical health.

"Chapter 15: Diffusive Dynamics of an AI in the Contemporary Society of Techno-Educational Era," Mudasir Rahman Najar examines youth-driven AI innovation for social impact. The chapter presents case studies from around the world, showcasing how young entrepreneurs use AI to address global issues such as environmental sustainability, healthcare, and poverty, emphasizing the transformative potential of youth-led AI initiatives.

"Chapter 16: Gesture-Driven Communication and Empowering the Deaf-Mute Community using Deep Learning Algorithm," Puspita Dash, Kalaiselvi N., Bhavani K., Lakshmiprabha M., Valarmathi E., and Padmapriya V. focus on the use of deep learning algorithms to enhance communication for the deaf-mute community. The chapter details the development of a CNN-based model for real-time gesture recognition and translation, highlighting the potential of AI to bridge communication gaps.

"Chapter 17: Guiding Principles for Youth-Centric Development: Ethical AI," Vetrivel SC, Sowmiya KC, Arun VP, Saravanan TP, and Maheswari R. explore the ethical dimensions of AI development for youth. The chapter investigates the intersection of technology, ethics, and youth engagement, proposing a framework for ethical AI that prioritizes the well-being of young users in various sectors, including education and social media.

"Chapter 18: Impact of AI on Diversity and Inclusion," Asma Yunus, Shahzad Khaver Mushtaq, and Ruqia Safdar Bajwa discuss how AI is reshaping industries and impacting diversity and inclusion. The chapter explores the transformative capabilities of AI in healthcare and finance, emphasizing the need for ethical considerations to ensure equitable outcomes.

"Chapter 19: Role Reconfiguration among Adolescents in the Age of AI," Wang Xiaodan, Aini Azeqa Ma'rof, Haslinda Abdullah, and Wei Wang analyze the impact of AI on adolescents' roles and responsibilities. The chapter provides strategies for role adaptation, emphasizing the importance of communication, collaboration, and understanding of AI's influence on personal and social development.

"Chapter 20: Social Dynamics of AI Networks for Impacting Youth Asma Yunus, Ruqia Safdar Bajwa, and Shahzad Khaver Mushtaq examine the social dynamics of AI networks and their impact on youth. The chapter discusses how AI-powered social networks influence perceptions, actions, and interactions, highlighting both challenges and benefits of AI in fostering youth engagement and social activism.

"Chapter 21: Youth Identity Formation in the Age of Digitalization: Exploring Digital Dilemmas in the North Macedonian Context," Avni Avdiu, Agron Kurtishi, Arta Xhelili, and Agron Vrangalla investigate the impact of digital media on youth identity formation in North Macedonia. The chapter presents findings from a quantitative study, revealing significant relationships between social media exposure and identity formation, and discussing the implications for youth development.

"Chapter 22: Youth Studies in the AI Era: Navigating Uncharted Territory," Vijay Bhutani, Preeti Singh Bahadur, Sunil K. Sansaniwal, and Pratima Bais explore the impact of AI on youth social interaction and identity formation. The chapter examines ethical implications, privacy concerns, and the transformative effects of AI on young people's lives, advocating for informed discussions on AI's role in youth development.

"Chapter 23: Screen Time and Identity Formation: A Digital Dilemma," Ismail Baydili examines the effects of artificial intelligence on human interaction, identity, and personality.

**Zeinab Zaremohzzabieh**

*Women and Family Studies Research Center, University of Religions and Denominations, Qom, Iran*

**Rusli Abdullah**

*Faculty of Computer Science and Information Technology, Universiti Putra Malaysia*

**Seyedali Ahrari**

*Women and Family Studies Research Center, University of Religions and Denominations, Iran*

# Section 1
# Digital Well-Being and Mental Health

# Chapter 1
# Adolescent Mental Health in the Digital Era:
## Exploring the Effects of Parenting Styles

**Nita Beluli Luma**
*Mother Teresa University, North Macedonia*

**Arta Xhelili**
https://orcid.org/0000-0001-5345-9948
*Mother Teresa University, North Macedonia*

**Elisabeta Bajrami Ollogu**
https://orcid.org/0000-0002-9993-7156
*Mother Teresa University, North Macedonia*

**Diturije Ismaili**
*Mother Teresa University, North Macedonia*

## ABSTRACT

*Living in the age of digitization brings with it many facilities in terms of enhancing massive information and communication when people efficiently employ technology, but at the same time the digital era brings with it challenges which when it comes to mental health seem to be increasing, in particular for adolescents. Therefore, this research aims to explore adolescents' mental health under the influence of social media and in addition, the impact that parenting style can have on adolescents' mental health. More in specific, the research examines quantity the correlation between parenting styles, social media usage, and mental health as imperative to foster a positive social media experience for adolescents. Our survey involved 573 participants who were selected from seven randomly chosen secondary education schools in Skopje, North Macedonia. The results of this survey provide strong evidence that there are linked patterns between parenting style, social media use and mental health.*

DOI: 10.4018/979-8-3693-3350-1.ch001

## INTRODUCTION

Social media has become an integral part of growing up in today's digital world, by having a great impact on society and influencing numerous aspects of our daily lives. Research has shown that engaging in various forms of social media is beneficial for children and adolescents since it enhances communication and social connection (O'Keeffe & Clarke-Pearson, 2011; Ito, et al., 2008). However, there are also several risks involved, particularly regarding the excessive use of social media and its potential impact on mental and somatic health for everyone, particularly for the youngsters (Sturm, 2010).

The impact of social media on the mental health of young individuals is a multifaceted issue, shaped by various complex factors. These factors include, but are not limited to, the amount of time children and adolescents spend on social media platforms, the type of content they consume or are otherwise exposed to, and the activities and interactions social media allows (American Psychological Association, 2023). It is noteworthy that the influence of social media on different individuals varies based on their individual strengths and vulnerabilities, as well as socio-economic, cultural, and historical factors (Beyens et al., 2020; Hollis et al., 2020). But other that these numerous factors which have been already widely investigated, we have come to another critical factor, that is the parenting style, which we assume to be positively correlated to how the youngsters use the social media and how they altogether influence and affect adolescent's mental health. Parenting plays a more significant role in determining children's wellbeing (Hung, 2022).

Although the field of parenting styles and their impact on children's virtual consumption is still in its nascent stages, recent studies have revealed that it not only affects the parent-child interaction but also the amount of time children spend online, as well as their attitudes, beliefs, habits, and personality traits (Mupalla et al., 2023; Hale & Guan, 2015). These findings suggest that the way children consume virtual data can have a significant impact on their overall development, and as such, it is important for parents and educators to consider the role of parenting styles in shaping their children's virtual consumption habits.

Applying appropriate parenting is seen as unprecedentedly important, as such a parental approach tremendously impacts youths' mental health, regarding stress, anxiety, and depression symptoms (Dwairy, 2004; Ramesh et al., 2022; Lipps et al., 2012; Romero-Acosta et al., 2021).

Despite the need for further research, these initial findings provide valuable insight into the potential impact of parenting styles on children's psychological wellbeing and virtual consumption and underline the importance of responsible and supporting parenting in the digital age.

The Covid19 pandemic limited contact with friends, peers, and brought additional stress to young people at crucial developmental period for adolescents. While spending time in social media increased, educational institutions lost the opportunity to monitor the mental health of young people. A study conducted in 2021, revealed that the biggest challenges related to mental health and young people in North Macedonia were: depression (64%), stress (55%), anxiety (58%), suicide (56%) and general mental health care (67%) (Национален младински советна Македонија, 2021). A study on adolescents' mental health and their caregivers revealed that 30% of adolescents had moderate to severe symptoms of depression and 42.1% of adolescents had moderate to severe symptoms of anxiety (Bajraktarov, et al., 2023). According to Bajraktarov et al. (2023), the consequences of the pandemic on the mental health of young people will be furthermore visible in the following period, which increases the importance of examining the adolescents' mental health in the country and all factors that could contribute in it.

In this book chapter we highlight, the examination of the correlation between parenting styles, social media usage, and mental health as imperative to foster a positive social media experience. It is essential to comprehend the adverse effects of specific parenting styles and social media on mental health. By addressing these detrimental influences, we can facilitate the promotion of overall psychological well-being in children. Therefore, it is crucial to identify and evaluate the impact of parenting styles and social media utilization on mental health and optimize the psychological welfare of children.

## LITERATURE REVIEW

An expanding corpus of research suggests that teenagers' use of social media may have an impact on their mental health (Khalaf,A et al., 2023). Many studies on social media's effects have been conducted. O'Reilly M., & Dogra N., & Whiteman N., & Hughes J., & Eruyar S., & Reilly P. (2018)propose that prolonged use of social media sites may be linked to negative manifestations and symptoms of depression, anxiety, and stress.In this study, we discuss about how social media usage exposes adolescents to different risks compared to other groups. Children, compared to adults, engage in more risky behaviors, value danger less, and seek more novelty and stimulation (Fuentes et al., 2020; Steinberg L., & Morris A.S 2001).

Duerager and Livingstone (2012) stressed that the role of parents in mediating their children's Internet use is crucial. Parenting styles have a significant impact on how children perceive the world and themselves, is associated with childhood development in areas including physical fitness, psychological well-being, social behavior, and behavioral difficulties (Brockmann et al., 2016; Zhaoet al., 2018; Limtrakul et al., 2017). They play an essential role in determining children's media use, given their considerable amount of time spent with them and the establishment of the household climate associated with children's media exposure (Lee et al., 2022).

Research indicates that parents with permissive and neglectful parenting styles are more likely to allow their children to spend more time on media, while parents with authoritarian and authoritative parenting styles are less likely to do so (Coyne at al., 2017; Jago et al., 2011; Padilla-Walker & Coyne, 2011). Therefore the research have come to findings that suggest that permissive parenting significantly predicted adolescents internet addiction (Setiawati et al., 2021), while another has come to a conclusion that neglectful parenting has the strongest relationship with addictive internet use by adolescents (Tur-Porcar, 2017). A third study concluded that the authoritarian parenting style is a significant predictor of children's internet use (Ihmeideh&Shawareb, 2014).

## AI IMPACT IN PARENTING AND SOCIAL MEDIA USE ON ADOLESCENTS MENTAL HEALTH

The literature suggests that artificial intelligence technology (AI)is rapidly being used in various contexts for learning, entertainment, and other purposes, among youth and its impact on adolescent's development is increasing.

Studies indicate that over 95% of teenagers have access to a smartphone, and nearly 45% are online 'almost constantly' (Vaterlaus, Aylward, Tarabochia, & Martin, 2021). This digital revolution, while offering unparalleled access to information and social connection, also raises concerns about mental health (Pandya &Lodha,2021). The unrestricted exposure to AI-driven social media content can worsen existing mental health issues (Razzak&Yousaf, 2022), leading to increased rates of depression, anxiety, isolation and other psychological issues (Ormel&VonKorff,2024; Kashif et al., 2024). Huang et al., 2024 have pointed out how the use of AI can lead to AI dependence, which can threaten mental health. The emergence of new technologies, such as artificial intelligence (AI), may manifest as technology panic in some people, including adolescents who may be particularly vulnerable to new technologies (Huang et al., 2024). For instance, technology panic is the fear that emerging new technologies, such as AI, will encourage adolescents to become addicted to them, just as radio addiction did in an earlier era (Orben, 2020). Other studies show that social media can affect adolescents' self-view and interpersonal relationships through social comparison and negative interactions, including cyberbullying; moreover, social media content often involves normalization and even promotion of self-harm and suicidality among youth (Abi-Jaoude et al., 2020).

Research examining the impact of AI in the enhancement of social media content and adolescents' wellbeing (Kashif, et al., 2024) had come to findings that suggested that parental monitoring of social media use was positively associated with adolescent's mental wellbeing, referring to the parental supervision as the balance that would calculate the needed virtual social connectivity and the potential harm that derives from it. Encouraging parents to be proactively involved in limiting children's and teens' use of smartphones and social media may be helpful (Abi-Jaoude et al., 2020).Parental limits may be effective at reducing the amount of media use by younger children and may prevent negative effects on their mental wellbeing. In the same line, (Beyens et al., 2022) suggest that parents may manage adolescents' social media use and social media-induced well-being and ill-being through media-specific parenting: parental actions to restrict, regulate, and discuss adolescents' social media use.

On the other hand, Artificial Intelligence is a helpful tool for empowering parents with personalized tools and tailored recommendations through evidence-based methods and time solutions to enhance their parenting skills as well as their parent-child interaction. Even though the importance of the impact of AI as the most influential technology of the future is foreseen to have far greater impact than what the internet revolution had to the older generation, yet the research studies are on nasal stages.

Innovation in artificial intelligence seems to be rapid, and more research is needed to confirm and evaluate the impact of AI use on adolescents' mental health and other implications it can bring in their social life.

In this digital era, we are living in, it is crucial that these issues are addressed and investigated.

The present chapter aims to assess the impact of different parenting styles on social media use and mental health among adolescents in North Macedonia. This study represents a novel contribution to the field, as no previous research has examined this combination of variables in our region. By undertaking this investigation, we hope to enhance our understanding of the complex interplay between parenting styles, social media use, and mental health issues in this population. Our analysis will be based on robust statistical methods, and we will draw on a range of relevant literature to ensure that our findings are situated within the broader context of research in this field. Therefore, the following objectives and hypothesis are provided:

## OBJECTIVES

1. To analyze the correlation between parenting styles, social media use and mental health outcomes in adolescents
2. To investigate the potential risk associated with different parenting styles and excessive screen time
3. To explore the impact of virtual media-related stressors and adolescents psychological wellbeing
4. To investigate the impact of each parenting style and their correlation to adolescents' anxiety, depression levels

## HYPOTHESIS

H1. There is a statistically significant correlation between parenting styles, adolescents' social media use and mental health

H2. There is a significant difference between parenting styles and adolescent's social media use and mental health

H4. Children who spent more time on social media are those who have higher levels of anxiety and depression

H5. Adolescents who excessively use social media have higher social dysfunction issues

H6. Adolescents who excessively use social media have higher somatic issues

H7. Children who have parents with permissive parenting style will have higher levels of media use.

H8. Children who have parents with authoritative and authoritarian parenting styles will have lower levels of media use.

H9. Permissive parenting styles are associated with an increased risk of mental health issues in children, such as higher levels of anxiety, due to unrestricted access to digital media.

H10. Authoritarian parenting styles are associated with higher levels of anxiety and depression in adolescents, as a result of strict control and limited autonomy in digital media use.

## METHODOLOGY

This chapter will draw on quantitative data to provide a comprehensive overview of the relationship between parenting styles, children's social media use, and mental health outcomes.

## PARTICIPANTS

The study utilized simple random sampling for data collection. It involved a total of 573 participants (N=573) who were selected from seven randomly chosen secondary education schools in Skopje, North Macedonia. The adolescents surveyed included 142 (24.8%) males and 431 (75.2%) females, and their age ranged from 14 to 22 years (M= 16.17, SD= 1.17). In terms of study year, 35.1% of the participants were in their third year of middle school, 32.5% in their first year, 17.8% in the second year, and 14.7% in their fourth year. With regard to place of residence, 60.7% (N=348) of the participants lived in urban areas and 39.3% (N=225) in rural areas. The majority (N=361, 63%) lived in a nuclear family, followed by 33.9% (N=194) in an extended family, and only 2.1% (N=12) in a single-parent family. As for birth order, most of the participants were the oldest child (38.2%), followed by the middle child (32.3%), the youngest child (25.3%), and the only child (1.7%).

## MEASUREMENTS

Social media use questionnaire was created to find out about adolescent's social media usage. The questionnaire consisted questions in regard to the time adolescents' spend on social media, which social media platforms they use the most, what's the main reason they use social media, Likert scale alternatives in regard to social media use and their self-perception of social media addiction.

A Perceived Parenting Style Scale (PPSS) and a General Health Questionnaire (GHQ-28) scale were used to collect data. The PPSS measures the subject's perceived parenting style regarding three dimensions: authoritarian, authoritative, and permissive (Divya & Manikandan, 2013). It consists of 30 items rated on a five-point Likert scale, ranging from 1 (strongly disagree) to 5 (strongly agree).

The GHQ-28 measures adolescent mental health and is divided into four sub-scales: somatic symptoms, anxiety/insomnia, social dysfunction, and severe depression (Goldberg & Williams, 2013). Each item is scored from 0 to 3, with higher scores indicating higher levels of distress.

The internal consistency of the PPSS subscales was found to be reliable with Cronbach Alpha coefficients of .906, .806, and .870. The internal consistency of the GHQ-28 was found to be $\alpha=.903$. Three variables based on the mean of all related items were computed by grouping the items of the PPSS into three subscales: Authoritative, Authoritarian, and Permissive. Five subscales were computed based on the mean of related items in the GHQ-28 resulting in: Mental_Health, Somatic, Anxiety, Social Dysfunction, and Depression. The questionnaires were translated and adapted to the Albanian language by bilingual researchers and reviewed by an expert in the field of clinical psychology.

These questionnaires have been widely used to investigate the impact of parental style on adolescents' development and have been found to be reliable and valid across different cultural contexts.

## DATA ANALYSIS

Data were analyzed using SPSS 20.00 data system.

After inserting the data in the system, tests were conducted for reliability, descriptive statistics and inferential statistics. The associations between socio-demographic data, parenting style, social media use and mental health are analyzed with parametric tests. The Pearson correlation coefficient was used to establish the association between different parenting styles, social media use and mental health symptoms. Independent T-test, ANOVA tests and regression analysis were used to examine differences in dependent measures as a function of specific demographic variables including sex, age and child order.

# RESULTS

## Descriptive Statistics

Descriptive statistics were run on the independent variable social media usage and dependent variable mental health.

It was found that the average time spent on social media was 4 hours per day. 34.6% of the respondents spent 2-4 hours, followed by 23.1% spending 4-6 hours and 8.9% up to 6 hours per day. The prevalent social media platforms used by the respondents were: TikTok (35.4% of the respondents), Snapchat (29.2%), Instagram (16.4%), Youtube (9.35) and WhatsApp (7.7%). The majority of the respondents used social media for communication and friendship connection (39.1%), information and learning (32.2%), entertainment (22.3%) and only 1.2% for network.

*Table 1. Descriptive statistics for social media use questionnaire social media use items*

| Table 1. Descriptive statistics for Social Media Usequestionnaire Social Media use items | Strongly disagree | Disagree | Neutral | Agree | Strongly agree | Mean | Std. D |
|---|---|---|---|---|---|---|---|
| Use social media 15 minutes before going to sleep | 12.8 | 10.9 | 19.2 | 33.0 | 20 | 3.3794 | 1.29860 |
| Use social media more than you planned | 14.4 | 23.6 | 15.7 | 20.9 | 25.3 | 2.9979 | 1.28611 |
| Use social media within the first 15 minutes of waking up | 16.9 | 26.3 | 17.7 | 23.2 | 15.9 | 2.9478 | 1.34421 |
| Your parents complain about the time you spend on social media | 24.0 | 24.0 | 16.0 | 22.3 | 13.8 | 2.7792 | 1.38783 |
| Don't feel the need for social media | 20.9 | 23.7 | 29.8 | 12.6 | 8.1 | 2.6141 | 1.20655 |
| Feeling annoyed when you don't have access to social media | 29.2 | 26.7 | 20.3 | 13.6 | 10.2 | 2.4885 | 1.31270 |
| Use social media while eating breakfast/lunch/dinner | 34.1 | 25.0 | 12.6 | 15.1 | 13.2 | 2.4835 | 1.42506 |
| Neglecting lessons due to the use of social media | 34.3 | 31.2 | 17.6 | 9.4 | 7.5 | 2.2469 | 1.23104 |
| Feeling anxious if you don't have access to social media | 48.1 | 27.6 | 13.1 | 7.3 | 3.9 | 1.9129 | 1.11905 |

Table 1 provides descriptive statistics for each item.

The results put on a descending format show that 53% of the respondents agree that they use social media 15 minutes before going to sleep, 46% use social media more than they planned, 39.1 use social media within the first 15 minutes of waking up. 44.5% disagree that they do not need social media and 41.1% are not sure if they are addicted followed by 26% that they admit of being addicted to social media (Table 1).

With those items, a new scale was compound for perceived social media usage on the mean of all related items. Descriptive statistics were run on the new scale and revealed that on average respondents rated their exposure to social media (SD=.83) as 2.62 which is moderate.

Descriptive statistics on the dependent variable are shown in separate tables for each factor of analysis, somatic symptoms (Table 2), anxiety (Table 3), social dysfunction (Table 4) and depression (Table 5).

*Table 2. Somatic symptoms means for each item*

| Somatic symptoms | Not at all | No more than | Rather more than usual | Much more than usual | Mean | Std. D |
|---|---|---|---|---|---|---|
| 1 Been feeling perfectly well and in good health | 9.9 | 0 | 26.3 | 63.8 | 2.7747 | 1.19927 |
| 2 Been feeling in need of a good tonic | 22.3 | .2 | 29.2 | 48.2 | 2.2648 | 1.41597 |
| 3 Been feeling run down and out of sorts | 29.1 | .2 | 24.9 | 45.8 | 2.1008 | 1.51420 |
| 4 Been feeling that you are ill | 40.5 | .2 | 25.1 | 34.2 | 1.6581 | 1.49577 |
| 5 Been getting any pains in your head | 28.1 | 0 | 27.1 | 44.9 | 2.1186 | 1.50174 |
| 6 Been getting a feeling of tightness or pressure in your head | 39.1 | 0 | 23.3 | 37.5 | 1.7708 | 1.55774 |
| 7 Been having hot or cold spells | 57.3 | .2 | 21.1 | 21.3 | 1.1403 | 1.41354 |

*Table 3. Anxiety/insomnia means score for each representative item*

| Anxiety/Insomnia | Not at all | No more than | Rather more than usual | Much more than usual | Mean | Std. D |
|---|---|---|---|---|---|---|
| 8 Been losing much sleep over worry (2) | 44.3 | .2 | 17.4 | 38.1 | 1.6877 | 1.62570 |
| 9 Been having difficulty in staying asleep once you fall asleep (7) | 45.8 | 0 | 18.0 | 36.2 | 1.6502 | 1.64171 |
| 10 Been feeling constantly under strain (12) | 56.7 | .2 | 18.2 | 24.9 | 1.2174 | 1.49195 |
| 11 Been getting edgy or bad tempered (16) | 30.8 | .2 | 28.3 | 40.7 | 1.9901 | 1.50046 |
| 12 Been getting scared or panicky for no reason (20) | 43.9 | 0 | 19.2 | 37.0 | 1.7036 | 1.63594 |
| 13 Been feeling everything is getting on top of you (24) | 48.2 | 0 | 23.5 | 28.3 | 1.4783 | 1.55701 |
| 14 Been feeling nervous and strung-out all the time (28) | 37.7 | 0 | 25.3 | 37.0 | 1.8123 | 1.56266 |

*Table 4. Social dysfunction means score for each representative item*

| Social Dysfunction | Not at all | No more than | Rather more than usual | Much more than usual | Mean | Std. D |
|---|---|---|---|---|---|---|
| 15 Been managing to keep yourself busy and occupied (3) | 9.3 | 0 | 24.1 | 66.6 | 2.8340 | 1.18577 |
| 16 Been taking longer over the things you do (6) | 19.2 | .2 | 31.0 | 49.6 | 2.3123 | 1.33251 |
| 17 Been feeling on the whole that you were doing things well (10) | 16.0 | 0 | 24.3 | 59.7 | 2.5711 | 1.34086 |
| 18 Been satisfied with the way you have carried out your tasks (13) | 11.9 | 0 | 21.9 | 66.2 | 2.7549 | 1.24885 |
| 19 Been feeling that you are playing a useful part in things (19) | 16.0 | 0 | 21.9 | 62.1 | 2.6166 | 1.35385 |
| 20 Been feeling capable of making decisions about things (25) | 7.7 | 0 | 22.7 | 69.6 | 2.9407 | 1.14859 |
| 21 Been able to enjoy your normal day do day activities | 22.9 | 0 | 35.2 | 41.9 | 2.1166 | 1.33951 |

*Table 5. Depression means score for each representative item*

| Severe depression | Not at all | No more than | Rather more than usual | Much more than usual | Mean | Std. D |
|---|---|---|---|---|---|---|
| 22 Been thinking of yourself as a worthless person (4) | 54.7 | .2 | 17.0 | 28.1 | 1.3241 | 1.56246 |
| 23 Been feeling that life is entirely hopeless (8) | 49.4 | 0 | 18.4 | 32.2 | 1.4980 | 1.59485 |
| 24 Been feeling that life is not worth living (11) | 57.1 | .2 | 13.6 | 29.1 | 1.3202 | 1.62538 |
| 25 Been thinking of the possibility that you may do away with yourself (15) | 21.7 | .2 | 19.0 | 59.1 | 2.4644 | 1.47713 |
| 26 Been feeling at times that you could not do anything because your nerves were too bad (17) | 38.3 | 0 | 24.5 | 37.2 | 1.7945 | 1.56105 |
| 27 Been finding yourself wishing you were dead and away from it all (21) | 61.5 | .2 | 13.6 | 24.7 | 1.1700 | 1.57668 |
| 28 Been finding that the idea of taking your own life keeps coming into your minds (23) | 67.0 | .2 | 14.6 | 18.2 | .9308 | 1.41322 |

It was found that the average score for a mental health survey was a total score of 54 out of 84, with a mean 1.9, which indicates that there is a presence of distress.

H1. There is a statistically significant correlation between parenting styles, adolescents' social media use and mental health

The output in the form of a correlation matrix showing the relationships between all variables, including the correlation of a variable with itself (Table 6), reveals that the relationship is statistically significant ($p<.000$) and positive for social media use and parenting style. The correlation between mental health and parenting style is low ($r=0.061$, $p>0.05$), the correlation of social media use and parenting style is ($r=0.19$, $p<0.05$) and social media use and mental health do not correlate with one another ($r=.07$, $p>0.05$). This suggests that parenting style correlates with adolescents' social media use but there is not a significant correlation with adolescents' mental health. Thus, parenting style matters in adolescents' social media usage.

*Table 6. Correlation test among parenting style, mental health, and social media use*

| Correlations | | Parenting_Style_Sum1 | Mental_health_sum | Social_M_Sum |
|---|---|---|---|---|
| Parenting_Style_Sum1 | Pearson Correlation | 1 | .061 | .191** |
| | Sig. (2-tailed) | | .172 | .000 |
| | N | 506 | 506 | 506 |
| Mental_health_sum | Pearson Correlation | .061 | 1 | .074 |
| | Sig. (2-tailed) | .172 | | .096 |
| | N | 506 | 506 | 506 |
| Social_M_Sum | Pearson Correlation | .191** | .074 | 1 |
| | Sig. (2-tailed) | .000 | .096 | |
| | N | 506 | 506 | 506 |

**. Correlation is significant at the 0.01 level (2-tailed).

*Hypothesis 2.* There is a significant difference between parenting styles and adolescent's social media use and mental health. Levenes test was used to test if there are differences among adolescents' social media use and perceived parenting styles. When comparing means (Table 7) of these variables we can see that there is a noteworthy difference among the means (p<0.01) which brings us to a conclusion that there is a statistical important difference among perceived parenting style and social media use by adolescents.

*Table 7. Inferential statistics in regard to perceived parenting styles and social media use*

| One-Sample Test | | | | | | |
|---|---|---|---|---|---|---|
| | Test Value = 0 | | | | | |
| | T | df | Sig. (2-tailed) | Mean Difference | 95% Confidence Interval of the Difference | |
| | | | | | Lower | Upper |
| Parenting_Style_Sum1 | 142.752 | 505 | .000 | 83.085 | 81.94 | 84.23 |
| Social_media_use | 70.460 | 498 | .000 | 2.61932 | 2.5463 | 2.6924 |

*There is a significant difference between parenting styles and adolescents mental health, is the second part of this hypothesis.* We came into a conclusion that there is a significant statistical difference between the perceived parenting style and adolescents mental health (p<0.01) therefore we reject the null hypothesis.

*Table 8. Inferential statistics in regard to perceived parenting styles and mental health*

| One-Sample Test | | | | | | |
|---|---|---|---|---|---|---|
| | Test Value = 0 | | | | | |
| | T | df | Sig. (2-tailed) | Mean Difference | 95% Confidence Interval of the Difference | |
| | | | | | Lower | Upper |
| Parenting_Style_Sum1 | 142.752 | 505 | .000 | 83.085 | 81.94 | 84.23 |
| Mental_health_sum | 56.006 | 505 | .000 | 54.01581 | 52.1209 | 55.9107 |

H3. Children who spent more time on social media are those who have higher levels of anxiety and depression.

Based on the ANOVA test, it is shown that for the value of significance is: > 05, which presents that the groups are homogeneous (Table 9 and 10). These results indicate that social media use is not significantly related to anxiety/insomnia nor depression. Therefore, the hypothesis is rejected.

*Table 9. Means through ANOVA test for time spent on social media and presence of anxiety/insomnia and depression*

| Descriptives | | N | Mean | Std. Deviation | Std. Error | 95% Confidence Interval for Mean | | Min | Max |
|---|---|---|---|---|---|---|---|---|---|
| | | | | | | Lower Bound | Upper Bound | | |
| Severe_depression | 10-30 min | 34 | 10.8235 | 8.81621 | 1.51197 | 7.7474 | 13.8996 | .00 | 28.00 |
| | 30 min - 2 h | 135 | 10.2593 | 8.90326 | .76627 | 8.7437 | 11.7748 | .00 | 28.00 |
| | 2-4 h | 175 | 10.3086 | 8.55386 | .64661 | 9.0324 | 11.5848 | .00 | 28.00 |
| | 4-6 h | 117 | 10.8291 | 8.82032 | .81544 | 9.2140 | 12.4441 | .00 | 28.00 |
| | + 6 h | 45 | 10.8889 | 9.17809 | 1.36819 | 8.1315 | 13.6463 | .00 | 28.00 |
| | Total | 506 | 10.5020 | 8.75254 | .38910 | 9.7375 | 11.2664 | .00 | 28.00 |
| Anxiety_insomnia | 10-30 min | 34 | 11.5588 | 9.24151 | 1.58491 | 8.3343 | 14.7833 | .00 | 28.00 |
| | 30 min - 2 h | 135 | 11.3037 | 9.07043 | .78066 | 9.7597 | 12.8477 | .00 | 28.00 |
| | 2-4 h | 175 | 11.6743 | 8.88639 | .67175 | 10.3485 | 13.0001 | .00 | 28.00 |
| | 4-6 h | 117 | 11.4359 | 8.74089 | .80810 | 9.8354 | 13.0364 | .00 | 28.00 |
| | + 6 h | 45 | 11.9778 | 8.82272 | 1.31521 | 9.3271 | 14.6284 | .00 | 28.00 |
| | Total | 506 | 11.5395 | 8.88783 | .39511 | 10.7633 | 12.3158 | .00 | 28.00 |

*Table 10. ANOVA test for time spent on social media and presence of anxiety/insomnia and depression*

| ANOVA | | Sum of Squares | Df | Mean Square | F | Sig. |
|---|---|---|---|---|---|---|
| Sever_depression | Between Groups | 37.268 | 4 | 9.317 | .121 | .975 |
| | Within Groups | 38649.230 | 501 | 77.144 | | |
| | Total | 38686.498 | 505 | | | |
| Anxiety_insomnia | Between Groups | 20.598 | 4 | 5.149 | .065 | .992 |
| | Within Groups | 39871.112 | 501 | 79.583 | | |
| | Total | 39891.709 | 505 | | | |

H4. Adolescents who excessively spent time in social media have higher social dysfunction issues.

Regarding this hypothesis we have conducted the T-Test (table 11.) which reveals that the time spent in social media and adolescents social dysfunction have a significant relation, with a p value < 0.05, thus the hypothesis is accepted.

*Table 11. T-Test for time spent in social media and adolescents' social dysfunction*

| One-Sample Test | | | | | | |
|---|---|---|---|---|---|---|
| | Test Value = 0 | | | | | |
| | T | Df | Sig. (2-tailed) | Mean Difference | 95% Confidence Interval of the Difference | |
| | | | | | Lower | Upper |
| Time spent in social networks | 63.800 | 505 | .000 | 3.00791 | 2.9153 | 3.1005 |
| Social_dysfunction | 76.882 | 505 | .000 | 18.28458 | 17.8173 | 18.7518 |

*Figure 1. Line chart regarding time spent in social networks and adolescents social dysfunction*

Figure 1. Line chart regarding time spent in social networks and adolescents social dysfunction

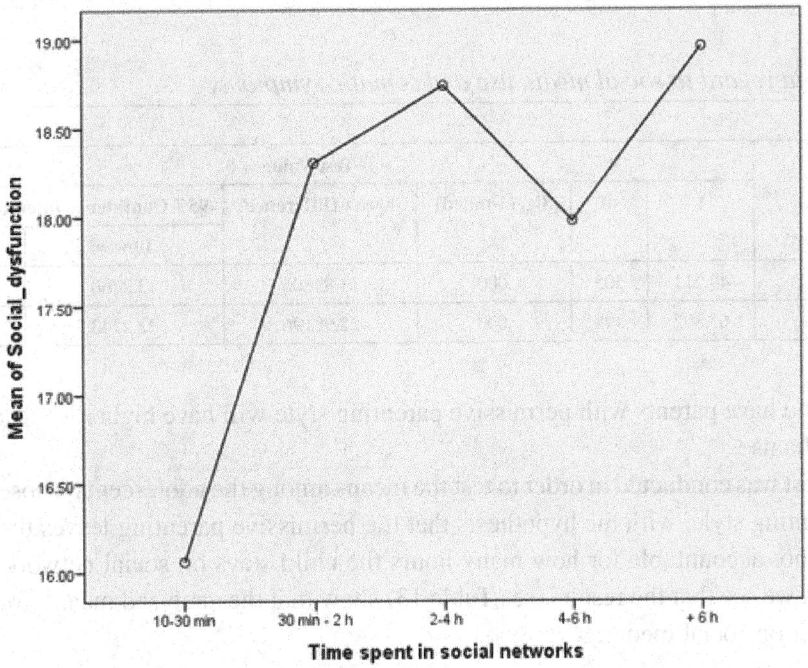

Figure 1. visualizes the findings from the T-Test, where it can be seen that as the time spent in the social networks grows, so does the social dysfunction in adolescents.

H5. Adolescents who excessively use social media have higher somatic issues.

The study aimed to investigate whether there is a significant difference between social media use and somatic issues among adolescents. In order to test this, a T-Test was conducted to compare means of the two variables. The results (as shown in Table 12) revealed a noteworthy difference in means, with a p-value of less than 0.01, indicating that the means of the two groups are heterogeneous. Based on these findings, there is enough statistical evidence to reject the null hypothesis.

*Table 12. T-test in regard to social media use and somatic symptoms*

| One-Sample Test | | | | | | |
|---|---|---|---|---|---|---|
| | | | | Test Value = 0 | | |
| | t | df | Sig. (2-tailed) | Mean Difference | 95% Confidence Interval of the Difference | |
| | | | | | Lower | Upper |
| Somatic_symptoms | 49.211 | 505 | .000 | 13.82806 | 13.2760 | 14.3801 |
| Social_Media_S | 63.802 | 498 | .000 | 22.98196 | 22.2743 | 23.6897 |

H6. Children who have parents with permissive parenting style will have higher levels of time spent in social media use.

An Anova Test was conducted in order to test the means among the adolescents whose parents exhibit permissive parenting style, with the hypothesis that the permissive parenting leaves the adolescent not supervised and not accountable for how many hours the child stays on social networks. Regarding to such assumption we see that the results (see Table 13) show that the analyzed means grow higher as the child stays longer on social media.

*Table 13. Descriptive means regarding to permissive parenting style and adolescents time spent in social media*

| Descriptives | | | | | | | | |
|---|---|---|---|---|---|---|---|---|
| Permissive_PS | | | | | | | | |
| | N | Mean | Std. Deviation | Std. Error | 95% Confidence Interval for Mean | | Min | Max |
| | | | | | Lower Bound | Upper Bound | | |
| 10-30 min | 34 | 19.1471 | 8.54270 | 1.46506 | 16.1664 | 22.1277 | 10.00 | 48.00 |
| 30 min - 2 h | 135 | 19.0074 | 8.05624 | .69337 | 17.6360 | 20.3788 | 10.00 | 47.00 |
| 2-4 h | 175 | 17.9257 | 6.76707 | .51154 | 16.9161 | 18.9353 | 10.00 | 42.00 |
| 4-6 h | 117 | 20.2479 | 8.00744 | .74029 | 18.7816 | 21.7141 | 10.00 | 43.00 |
| + 6 h | 45 | 23.1778 | 10.85501 | 1.61817 | 19.9166 | 26.4390 | 10.00 | 48.00 |
| Total | 506 | 19.3004 | 8.06169 | .35839 | 18.5963 | 20.0045 | 10.00 | 48.00 |

The One-way ANOVA test (Table 13) revealed that children of parents who exhibit permissive parenting style are more prone to excessively use social media. The P value of significance is < 0.05, which indicates that permissive parenting style is significantly related to excessive time the adolescents spend in social media use. We accept the hypothesis since there is enough supporting evidence.

*Table 14. ANOVA test in regard to permissive parenting style and adolescents time spent in social media*

| ANOVA | | | | | |
|---|---|---|---|---|---|
| **Permissive_PS** | | | | | |
| | **Sum of Squares** | **df** | **Mean Square** | **F** | **Sig.** |
| Between Groups | 1124.659 | 4 | 281.165 | 4.444 | .002 |
| Within Groups | 31695.681 | 501 | 63.265 | | |
| Total | 32820.340 | 505 | | | |

H7. Children who have parents with authoritative and authoritarian parenting styles will have lower levels of media use.

In the clustered bar we have compared the means of the authoritarian and authoritative parenting style and the time spent in social media by youngsters. By an inspection of the group means, we hereby come to understanding that this hypothesis has not solid ground to be supported. The One-way ANOVA test (see Table 14.), revealed that the p-value for perceived parenting styles and time spent in social media is significant only for the authoritarian parenting style, $p < 0.05$, but the data are homogeneous for the authoritative parenting style where the p value is > 0.05, thus the hypothesis is partly rejected.

*Figure 2. Clustered bar chart for mean comparison among authoritarian, authoritative parenting style and time spent in social media*

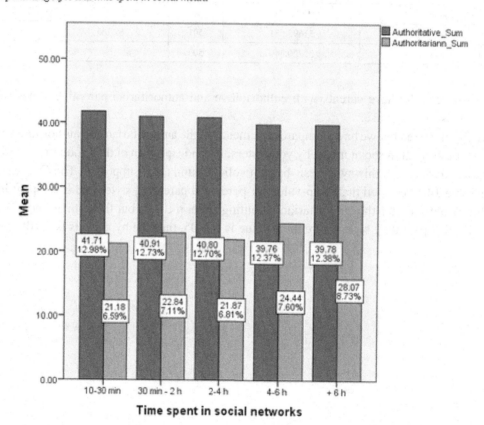

Figure 2. Clustered bar chart for mean comparison among authoritarian, authoritative parenting style and time spent in social media

While the data is somewhat significant, we must reject the hypothesis due to the evidence presented in Figure 2. It appears that adolescents with authoritative parents tend to spend more than 6 hours on social media, which contradicts our hypothesis that they would spend less time.

*Table 15. ANOVA test for authoritative and authoritarians perceived parenting styles and time spent in social media*

| ANOVA | | | | | | |
|---|---|---|---|---|---|---|
| **Time spent in SM** | | **Sum of Squares** | **Df** | **Mean Square** | **F** | **Sig.** |
| Authoritariann_Sum | Between Groups | 1711.414 | 4 | 427.853 | 7.942 | .000 |
| | Within Groups | 26988.902 | 501 | 53.870 | | |
| | Total | 28700.316 | 505 | | | |
| Authoritative_Sum | Between Groups | 173.652 | 4 | 43.413 | .585 | .674 |
| | Within Groups | 37195.069 | 501 | 74.242 | | |
| | Total | 37368.721 | 505 | | | |

H8. Permissive parenting styles are associated with an increased risk of mental health issues in children, due to unrestricted access to digital media.

The One-way ANOVA test (table 16) shows that for perceived permissive parenting style and general mental health the value of significance is 0.05 which is in limit of the permitted degree of freedom. These results indicate that permissive parenting style is not significantly related to general mental health. Thus, the hypothesis is rejected.

On the other hand, we have found statistically significant differences between the means of permissive parenting style and the means of anxiety/insomnia, where the p values is <0.05 and therefore we reject null hypothesis.

*Table 16. ANOVA test regarding permissive parenting style and adolescents' mental health overall and anxiety/insomnia in particular*

| ANOVA | | | | | | |
|---|---|---|---|---|---|---|
| **Permissive parenting** | | **Sum of Squares** | **df** | **Mean Square** | **F** | **Sig.** |
| M_H_2_Sum | Between Groups | 16358.412 | 36 | 454.400 | 1.433 | .053 |
| | Within Groups | 148685.564 | 469 | 317.027 | | |
| | Total | 165043.976 | 505 | | | |
| Anxiety_Insomnia | Between Groups | 81.295 | 36 | 2.258 | 1.445 | .049 |
| | Within Groups | 732.822 | 469 | 1.563 | | |
| | Total | 814.117 | 505 | | | |

H9. Authoritarian parenting styles are associated with higher levels of anxiety and depression in adolescents, as a result of strict control and limited autonomy in digital media use.

To come to such findings, we see the Multivariate Tests table 17. in which we see that we have a sig. value of.000, which means that p<0.01. Therefore, we conclude that adolescents' anxiety and depression are significantly dependent by the perceived authoritarian parenting style.

*Table 17. MANOVA test regarding authoritarian parenting style and levels of anxiety and depression in adolescents*

| Multivariate Tests[a] | | | | | | | |
|---|---|---|---|---|---|---|---|
| **Effect** | | **Value** | **F** | **Hypothesis df** | **Error df** | **Sig.** | **Partial Eta Squared** |
| Intercept | Pillai's Trace | .410 | 161.951[b] | 2.000 | 467.000 | .000 | .410 |
| | Wilks' Lambda | .590 | 161.951[b] | 2.000 | 467.000 | .000 | .410 |
| | Hotelling's Trace | .694 | 161.951[b] | 2.000 | 467.000 | .000 | .410 |
| | Roy's Largest Root | .694 | 161.951[b] | 2.000 | 467.000 | .000 | .410 |
| Authoritarian_Sum | Pillai's Trace | .170 | 1.174 | 74.000 | 936.000 | .157 | .085 |
| | Wilks' Lambda | .836 | 1.183[b] | 74.000 | 934.000 | .146 | .086 |
| | Hotelling's Trace | .189 | 1.192 | 74.000 | 932.000 | .135 | .086 |
| | Roy's Largest Root | .139 | 1.761[c] | 37.000 | 468.000 | .005 | .122 |

a. Design: Intercept + Authoritarian_Sum

b. Exact statistic

c. The statistic is an upper bound on F that yields a lower bound on the significance level.

To determine how the dependent variables differ for the independent variable, we need to look at the **Tests of Between-Subjects Effects** (Table 18). A separate ANOVA was conducted for each dependent variable, on which we have come to understanding that when separately there is no significant difference between the independent variables and the dependent ones, for anxiety,insomnia F(2.46)=0.64, p>0.05, patial$\eta^2$ = 0.048 and for severe depression F(2.46)=1.13, p>0.05,patial $\eta^2$ = 0.082.

*Table 18. Test of between subject effect*

| Tests of Between-Subjects Effects | | | | | | | |
|---|---|---|---|---|---|---|---|
| **Source** | **Dependent Variable** | **Type III Sum of Squares** | **df** | **Mean Square** | **F** | **Sig.** | **PES** |
| Corrected Model | Anxiety_insomnia | 1923.185[a] | 37 | 51.978 | .641 | .952 | .048 |
| | Sever_depression | 3180.372[b] | 37 | 85.956 | 1.133 | .276 | .082 |
| Intercept | Anxiety_insomnia | 24511.023 | 1 | 24511.023 | 302.123 | .000 | .392 |
| | Sever_depression | 21241.644 | 1 | 21241.644 | 279.982 | .000 | .374 |
| **Authoritariann_Sum** | **Anxiety_insomnia** | **1923.185** | **37** | **51.978** | **.641** | **.952** | **.048** |
| | **Sever_depression** | **3180.372** | **37** | **85.956** | **1.133** | **.276** | **.082** |

continued on following page

*Table 18. Continued*

**Tests of Between-Subjects Effects**

| Source | Dependent Variable | Type III Sum of Squares | df | Mean Square | F | Sig. | PES |
|---|---|---|---|---|---|---|---|
| Error | Anxiety_insomnia | 37968.525 | 468 | 81.129 | | | |
| | Sever_depression | 35506.126 | 468 | 75.868 | | | |
| Total | Anxiety_insomnia | 107271.000 | 506 | | | | |
| | Sever_depression | 94494.000 | 506 | | | | |
| Corrected Total | Anxiety_insomnia | 39891.709 | 505 | | | | |
| | Sever_depression | 38686.498 | 505 | | | | |

a. R Squared = .048 (Adjusted R Squared = -.027)
b. R Squared = .082 (Adjusted R Squared = .010)

Considering these findings, we conclude that authoritarian parenting style is significantly determinant for the manifestation of anxiety and depression in adolescents when considered jointly but is not statistically significant when considered separately.

## DISCUSSION AND CONCLUSION

The purpose of this study was to assess the relationship between parenting style and social media use on adolescents' mental health. A quantitative method approach was used to explore these relationships. A survey asking adolescents to self-report about their perceived parenting style and social media use was conducted. The survey also measured adolescents' mental health. When combined, the results of this survey provide strong evidence that there are linked patterns between parenting style, social media use and mental health. Adolescence is a critical development period and as such, it is crucial that factors that could contribute to adolescents' wellbeing are substantially examined.

Parenting style comprises various patterns of parents' attitudes and behaviors that parents utilize when interacting and raising children, and that altogether create an emotional climate in which the parents' behaviors are expressed (Darling and Steinberg, 1993). Baumrind (1971) divided parenting styles into authoritarian, authoritative, and permissive parenting. This typology was used to measure perceived parenting style.

Social media use is growing among adolescents. Taking into consideration the time spent with social media, it is significant to deeply investigate their use among adolescents and inspect its impact on adolescents wellbeing.

Parenting styles not only affect the parent-child interaction but also the amount of time children spend online, as well as their attitudes, beliefs, habits, and personality traits (Mupalla et al., 2023; Hale & Guan, 2015). Applying appropriate parenting is seen as outstandingly important, as such a parental approach tremendously impacts youths' mental health, regarding stress, anxiety and depression symptoms (Dwairy, 2004; Ramesh et al., 2022; Lipps et al., 2012; Romero-Acosta et al., 2021). Studies in regard to adolescents' mental health in the Republic of North Macedonia, have shown that the mental scores have increased substantially during pandemic (Министерство за здравство, 2018; Национален младински совет на Македонија, 2021; Bajraktarov, et al., 2023). This critical period has been recognized with increased social media use, which set a ground for our hypothesis in regard to parenting style, social media use and adolescents' mental health.

This study's objective was to analyze the correlation between parenting styles, social media use and mental health outcomes in adolescents. Findings suggest that parenting style correlates with adolescents' social media use but there is not a significant correlation with adolescents' mental health. Thus, parenting style significantly matters in adolescents' social media usage. This is consistent with previous findings, which stated that parenting style plays an essential role in determining children's media use (Lee et al., 2022).

The study examined the impact of each parenting style and excessive screen time and found that there is a significant difference between parenting styles and adolescents social media use.

This has been supported by previous studies which indicated that there is a difference in social media use by parenting style (Coyne at al., 2017; Jago et al., 2011; Padilla-Walker & Coyne, 2011; Ihmeideh & Shawareb, 2014; Tur-Porcar, 2017). In the same direction it was found that there is a significant statistical difference between the perceived parenting style and adolescents mental health. In regard to mental health factors the study revealed that adolescents who excessively spent time in social media have higher social dysfunction and somatic issues, however time spent was not found to be related with anxiety and depression.

In regard to permissive parenting style, the study revealed that children of parents who exhibit permissive parenting style are more prone to excessively use social media. This is in accordance with previous studies that indicated that parents with permissive and neglectful parenting styles are more likely to allow their children to spend more time on media, while parents with authoritarian and authoritative parenting styles are less likely to do so (Coyne at al., 2017; Jago et al., 2011; Padilla-Walker & Coyne, 2011).Therefore the research have come to findings that suggest that permissive parenting significantly predicted adolescents' internet addiction (Setiawati et al., 2021). The study did not find support in regard to authoritative and authoritarian parenting style and lower social media use, in contrary to studies that showed authoritarian parenting style as a significant predictor of children's internet use (Ihmeideh & Shawareb, 2014).

In regard to parenting style and mental health examination, the study found that permissive parenting style was not related to the adolescents' general mental health. On the other hand, the study found that adolescents' anxiety and depression were significantly dependent on the perceived authoritarian parenting style. This is in line with previous research that have shown that parental approach has had a tremendous impact in youths' mental health, regarding stress, anxiety and depression symptoms (Dwairy, 2004; Ramesh et al., 2022; Lipps et al., 2012; Romero-Acosta et al., 2021).

## Limitations

Several limitations in respect to internal and external validity should be noted. First, the participants were adolescents from one ethnicity and municipality in the Republic of North Macedonia. Taking into consideration the multinational nature of the country, generalizing those results to the whole population should be done with caution. Since social media use is a growing trend, a longitudinal study would be recommended to see how the relationship between these variables might change with time. The study relied on adolescents' self-reports and other reports. Jensen and Dost-Gozkan (2015) have found that there is an inconsistency between parents' and adolescents' perceptions on parenting style, thus our findings might be different of what would have been found if parents' were reporting on their style. The study might be a question to social desirability bias. Since the participants were recruited through their school, despite guaranteeing anonymity they might have been biased when responding in an intimate and private topic.

## Implications

Findings highlight the fact that different parenting styles have a different impact on adolescents' mental health and social media use. Thus, incorporating healthy practices in parenting style might considerably positively influence the general mental health and constructive use of social media in adolescents. This is a first study to examine the effect of parenting style on social media use and mental health in the context of North Macedonia. The findings of this study target the reduction of permissive parenting and the promotion of acquiring a healthy parenting style.

In general, this study contributed to the understanding of how parenting style influences adolescent social media use and mental health. The chapter was tailored for parents, educators, mental health professionals, and researchers interested in understanding how parenting styles influence children's mental well-being in the digital era.

# REFERENCES

Министерство за здравство (2018). Националнастратегија за унапредување на менталнотоздравје во РепубликаМакедонијасептември 2018 - 2025 година со акциски план (септември 2018 – 2025).

Национален младински совет на Македонија (2021). *Застапувачко-нормативен документ за менталноздравјекајмлади.*

Abi-Jaoude, E., Naylor, K. T., &Pignatiello, A. (2020). Smartphones, social media use and youth mental health. *CMAJ: Canadian Medical Association journal = journal de l'Association medicale canadienne, 192*(6), E136–E141. 10.1503/cmaj.190434

American Psychological Association. (2023). *Health Advisory on Social Media Use in Adolescence.* American Psychological Association.

Bajraktarov, S., Kunovski, I., Raleva, M., Kalpak, G., Novotni, A., Stefanovski, B., & Hadzihamza, K. (2023). *Mental health of adolescents and their caregivers during the Covid-19 pandemic in North Macedonia.* University Clinic of Psychiatry.

Baumrind, D. (1971). Current patterns of parental authority. *Developmental Psychology, 4*(1, Pt.2), 1–103. 10.1037/h0030372

Beyens, I., Keijsers, L., & Coyne, S. M. (2022). Social media, parenting, and well-being. *Current Opinion in Psychology, 47,* 101350. 10.1016/j.copsyc.2022.10135035561563

Beyens, I., Pouwels, J. L., van Driel, I. I., Keijsers, L., & Valkenburg, P. M. (2020). The effect of social media on wellbeing differs from adolescent to adolescent. *Scientific Reports, 10*(1), 10763. 10.1038/s41598-020-67727-732612108

Brockmann PE., Diaz B., Damiani F., &Villarroel L., Núñez F., & Bruni, O. (2016). Impact of television on the quality of sleep in preschool children. *Sleep Med.* .10.1016/j.sleep.2015.06.005

Darling, N., & Steinberg, L. (1993). Parenting style as context: An integrative model. *Psychological Bulletin, 113*(3), 487–496. 10.1037/0033-2909.113.3.487

Divya, T. V., & Manikandan, K. (2013). *Perceived Parenting Style Scale.* Department of Psychology, University of Calicut.

Duerager, A., &Livingstone, S. (2012). *How can parents support children's internetsafety?* EU Kids Online.

Dwairy, M. (2004). Parenting Styles and Mental Health of Palestinian–Arab Adolescents in Israel. *Transcultural Psychiatry, 41*(2), 233–252. 10.1177/136346150404356615446722

Fuentes, M., Garcia, O., & Garcia, F. (2020). Special Issue Psychosocial Risk and Protective Factors for Sustainable Development in Childhood and Adolescence. *Sustainability (Basel), 12*(15), 5962. 10.3390/su12155962

Goldberg, D., & Williams, P. (1991). *General health questionnaire (GHQ).* NferNelson.

Hale, L., & Guan, S. (2015). Screen time and sleep among school-aged children and adolescents:A systematic literature review. *Sleep Medicine Reviews, 21,* 50–58. 10.1016/j.smrv.2014.07.00725193149

Hollis, C., Livingstone, S., & Sonuga-Barke, E. (2020). Editorial: The role of digital technology in children and young people's mental health - a triple-edged sword? *Journal of Child Psychology and Psychiatry, and Allied Disciplines*, 61(8), 837–841. 10.1111/jcpp.1330232706126

Huang, S., Lai, X., Ke, L., Li, Y., Wang, H., Zhao, X., Dai, X., & Wang, Y. (2024). AI Technology panic-is AI Dependence Bad for Mental Health? A Cross-Lagged Panel Model and the Mediating Roles of Motivations for AI Use among Adolescents. *Psychology Research and Behavior Management*, 17, 1087–1102. 10.2147/PRBM.S44088938495087

Hung, J. (2022, June). Digitalisation, Parenting, and Children's Mental Health: What Are the Challenges and Policy Implications? *International Journal of Environmental Research and Public Health*, 19(11), 6452. 10.3390/ijerph1911645235682037

Ihmeideh, F. M., & Shawareb, A. A. (2014). The Association Between Internet Parenting Styles and Children's Use of the Internet at Home. *Journal of Research in Childhood Education*, 28(4), 411–425. 10.1080/02568543.2014.944723

Ito, M., Horst, H., & Bittani, M (2008). Living and learning with new media: Summary of findings from the digital youth project. *Catherine T. MacArthur Foundation Reports on Digital Media and Learning*. MacArthur Foundation.

Jago, R., Davison, K.K., Brockman, R., Page, A.S., Thompson, J.L., & Fox K.R. (2011). Parenting styles, parenting practices, and physical activity in 10- to 11-year olds. *Prev Med. Jan;52*(1), 44-7. 10.1016/j.ypmed.2010.11.001

Jensen, L. A., & Dost-Gözkan, A. (2015). Adolescent-parent relations in Asian Indian and Salvadoran immigrant families: A cultural-developmental analysis of autonomy, authority, conflict, and cohesion. *Journal of Research on Adolescence*, 25(2), 340–351. 10.1111/jora.12116

Kashif, A. (2024). Examining the Impact of AI-Enhanced Social Media Content on Adolescent Well-being in the Digital Age. *Kurdish Studies*, 12(2), 771–789.

Khalaf, A., Alubied, A., Khalaf, A., & Rifaey, A. (2023). The Impact of Social Media on the Mental Health of Adolescents and Young Adults. *Systematic Reviews*. 10.7759/cureus.4299037671234

Lee, H. E., Ji Young, K., & Changsook, K. (2022). The Influence of Parent Media Use, Parent Attitude on Media, and Parenting Style on Children's Media Use. *Children (Basel, Switzerland)*, 9(37), 1–12. 10.3390/children901003735053662

Limtrakul, N., Louthrenoo, O., Narkpongphun, A., Boonchooduang, N., & Chonchaiya, W. (2017). Media use and psychosocial adjustment in children and adolescents. *Journal of Paediatrics and Child Health*, 54(3), 296–301. 10.1111/jpc.1372528948669

Lipps, G., Lowe, G. A., Gibson, R. C., Halliday, S., Morris, A., Clarke, N., & Wilson, R. N. (2012). Parenting and depressive symptoms among adolescents in four Caribbean societies. *Child and Adolescent Psychiatry and Mental Health*, 6(1), 31. 10.1186/1753-2000-6-3122998793

Muppalla, S. K., Vuppalapati, S., Reddy Pulliahgaru, A., & Sreenivasulu, H. (2023). Effects of Excessive Screen Time on Child Development: An Updated Review and Strategies for Management. *Cureus*, 15(6), e40608. 10.7759/cureus.4060837476119

O'Keeffe, G. S., & Clarke-Pearson, K. (2011). The impact of social media on children, adolescents, and families. *Pediatrics*, 127(4), 800–804. 10.1542/peds.2011-005421444588

O'Reilly, M., Dogra, N., Whiteman, N., Hughes, J., Eruyar, S., & Reilly, P. (2018). Is social media bad for mental health and wellbeing? Exploring the perspectives of adolescents. *Clinical Child Psychology and Psychiatry*, 23(4), 601–613. 10.1177/135910451877515429781314

Orben A. (2020). The Sisyphean Cycle of Technology Panics. *Perspectives on psychological science: a journal of the Association for Psychological Science, 15*(5), 1143–1157. 10.1177/1745691620919372

Padilla-Walker, L. M., & Coyne, S. M. (2011). "Turn that thing off!" parent and adolescent predictors of proactive media monitoring. *Journal of Adolescence, 34*(4), 705–715. https://doi.org/10.1016/j.adolescence.2010.09.002

Ramesh, N., Vijay, C., &Gonsalves, K. (2022). Parenting styles and mental health of adolescents: A cross-sectional study in South India. *Journal of Mental Health and Human Behaviour*. 10.4103/jmhhb.jmhhb_176_20

Razzak, A., & Yousaf, S. (2022). Perceived resilience and vulnerability during the pandemic-infused panic buying and the role of COVID conspiracy beliefs. Evidence from Pakistan. *Journal of Global Marketing*, 35(5), 368–383. 10.1080/08911762.2022.2051156

Romero-Acosta, K., Gómez-de-Regil, L., Lowe, G. A., Garth, E. L., & Gibson, R. C. (2021). Parenting Styles, Anxiety and Depressive Symptoms in Child/Adolescent. *International Journal of Psychological Research*, 14(1), 12–32. 10.21500/20112084.470434306576

Setiawati, Y., Hartanti, D. T., Husada, D., Irwanto, I., Ardani, I. G. A. I., & Nazmuddin, M. (2021). Relationship between Paternal and Maternal Parenting Style with Internet Addiction Level of Adolescents. *Iranian Journal of Psychiatry*, 16(4), 438–443. 10.18502/ijps.v16i4.723135082856

Steinberg, L., & Morris, A. S. (2001). Adolescent Development. *Annual Review of Psychology*, 52(1), 83–110. 10.1146/annurev.psych.52.1.8311148300

Sturm, S. (2010). *Social networking psych studies: research shows teen Facebook users prone to depression*. Trend Hunter.

Tur-Porcar, A. (2017). Parenting styles and Internet use. *Psychology and Marketing*, 34(11), 1016–1022. 10.1002/mar.21040

Vaterlaus, J. M., Aylward, A., Tarabochia, D., & Martin, J. D. (2021). "A smartphone made mylife easier": An exploratory study on age of adolescent smartphone acquisition and well-being. *Computers in Human Behavior*, 114.

Zhao, J., Zhang, Y., Jiang, F., Ip, P., Ho, F., Zhang, Y., & Huang, H. (2018). Excessive Screen Time and Psychosocial Well-Being: The Mediating Role of Body Mass Index, Sleep Duration, and Parent-Child Interaction. *The Journal of Pediatrics*, 202, 157–162.e1. 10.1016/j.jpeds.2018.06.02930100232

# Chapter 2
# Disconnect to Reconnect:
## Your Path to Physical and Mental Wellbeing

**Huma Zaidi**
https://orcid.org/0000-0002-3259-2448
*Ras Al Khaimah Medical and Health Sciences University, UAE*

**Omar Turkey AlJadaan**
https://orcid.org/0000-0003-1504-6442
*Ras Al Khaimah Medical and Health Science University, UAE*

**Mahmoud Yousef Al Faress**
https://orcid.org/0009-0001-8949-024X
*KSA Ministry of Education, Saudi Arabia*

**Ahmad Omar Jabas**
*Shaqra University, Saudi Arabia*

## ABSTRACT

*This chapter delves into the real impact of our digital dependence on our lives – how it affects our minds, and connections with others. Shedding light on the challenges faced in balancing digital and offline worlds, especially in today's fast-paced society. We see the dangers of spending a lot of time glued to screens and the signs of digital addiction that we overlook. But there's a silver lining filled with practical advice and inspiring tales of people who have found a healthier relationship with technology. From simple tricks like setting screen time limits to embracing offline activities and mindfulness, we discover ways to reclaim control over our digital lives. Looking ahead, we glimpse a promising future where technology supports our well-being, thanks to innovations like AI and 5G that foster positive digital experiences. Whether you're navigating your digital habits, teaching others about digital wellness, supporting patients in healthcare, or shaping policies, this chapter serves as a trusted guide on the journey to a more mindful and fulfilling tech experience.*

DOI: 10.4018/979-8-3693-3350-1.ch002

# DIGITAL ADDICTION-EFFECTS ON PHYSICAL AND MENTAL WELL-BEING

## The Era of Digital Technology

Technology has shaped the way individuals, families, and societies operate as there is an unprecedented reliance on technology for every activity. There is a proliferation of smartphones, social media platforms, and cloud computing that enables instant communication, access to information, and above all entertainment. In the professional world, there is a revolution in the work environment, with the popularity of remote work with the advancement in digital infrastructure. However, research (Basu, 2019) focused on the effects of digital detox on individuals' work performance. A survey of 70 employees who had already undergone digital detox confirmed that it helped them to identify more with their work and increase their motivation to work. In the field of education, we have witnessed an evolution with e-learning and educational apps for all subjects including professions like engineering and medicine. According to research (Ugur & Koc, 2015), conducted to examine the distraction caused by mobile phones in the classroom, 100% of students confessed to owning a mobile phone, with 98% texting while waiting for the class to begin, 60% checking WhatsApp messages, and were not willing to refrain from using the phone unless there were strict guidelines. Hence, there is an increased need for a digital detox in educational environments to avoid students getting distracted by social media.

Another longitudinal experimental study was conducted (Hunt, Marx, Lipson, & Young, 2018) with a randomized controlled trial (RCT) design with 143 participants to examine social media use in relation to well-being. The participants were allowed to Smartphones at the beginning of the experiment, but after a week they were randomly divided into an experimental group (limiting media use to ten minutes per day) and a control group (unlimited media use). The restriction of social media use led to a significant decrease in perceived loneliness and depression in the experimental group compared to the control group after three weeks. Also, participants were generally more aware of their social media consumption, which was due to digital detox. However, the results did not show any significant differences between the two groups in terms of fear of missing out, perceived anxiety, perceived self-esteem, perceived social support, and psychological well-being.

## Definition of Digital Detox

Keeping the urge and the lack of control of using digital gadgets, the World Health Organization (WHO) in 2020, formally recognized and labeled digital device addiction as a widespread problem as online activities and compulsive internet use (or problematic usage of the internet) can affect a significant proportion of the population worldwide (Dresp-Langley & Hutt, 2022). Digital detox is defined as a "period of time during which a person refrains from using their electronic devices, such as smartphones, regarded as an opportunity to reduce stress or focus on social interaction in the physical world" (Dictionaries, 2019). Both, the public and scientific community use different terms when it comes to the non-use of electronic devices. Usually, terms like abstinence, detox, timeout, or unplugging are used (Brown & Kuss, 2020). In the era of technology, where digital devices have become an extra organ on our bodies, we have become dependent on this organ to the extent that it has started affecting our mental and physical health. It has permeated our lives so much that it has become an almost indispensable part of our personal and professional activities. A digital detox involves practicing an abstinence from digital devices to mitigate these negative effects

A study revealed that 33.1 million Germans use the Internet "multiple times a day", and 11 million even use it "constantly, almost the whole time" (Most popular social networks worldwide as of April 2024, ranked by number of monthly active users (in millions), 2022). Scholarship clearly suggests that this compounded screen time can be detrimental to the well-being of individuals (Pflügner, Maier, Mattke, & Weitzel, 2020). Using IT can lead to technostress. The term Technostress was coined by the American psychologist Craig "Technostress: the human cost of the computer revolution". The psychologist referred for the first time to the stress associated with the use of technologies and their impact on the psychological level. In the definition of Brod, the Technostress was "a modern disease of adaptation caused by the inability to cope with new computer technologies in a healthy manner" (Technostress, 1984). The working environments where the risk is high technostress are many; however, the most at-risk workers are networkers (who work in the network), the ICT professions (Information and Communications Technology), call center operators, journalists, community managers and web content editors, accountants, lawyers, advertising, financial analysts, business people, and programmers (Mirbabaie, Stieglitz, & Marx, 2022).

*Figure 1. Use of digital technology*

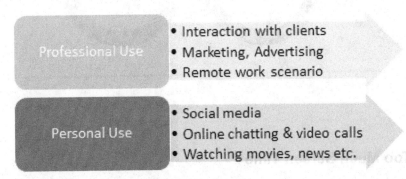

We cannot imagine surviving in this world without mobile phones, computers, laptops, iPads, earphones, smart watches, and other gadgets. This digital deluge has made our lives easier, no doubt, but at the same time the endless scrolling, responding immediately to messages or waiting for a response, notifications, one-minute tik-toks, rewinding and forwarding videos, and the sheer amount of information on the internet has left us overwhelmed and anxious. There is a lot of information, less knowledge, and no wisdom. This has become the predicament of the present generation and a cause of frustration for the generation that is in their forties and fifties as they have to deal with technology at this age. Children prefer to play digital games rather than with their human counterparts. As a result, their social skills are deteriorating, which is detrimental to society. Human interaction has decreased, and people are disconnected from the people around them and have become more involved with the virtual. The rise of digital dependence mirrors our increasing reliance on technology, driven by the ubiquitous presence of smartphones and their multifaceted roles in our lives. Consider how smartphones have evolved from mere communication tools to indispensable companions, aiding us in tasks ranging from communication and navigation to entertainment and accessing essential services. In business, digital tools like data analytics and AI have enhanced communication, bridged distances, and eased connectivity. This dependence deepened significantly during the COVID-19 pandemic, with digital platforms becoming lifelines for remote work, online learning, telehealth services, and virtual social interactions (Gonçalves LL, 2023).

According to an article on Social Media Addiction Statistics 2024, written by Branka, on Truelist, (updated February 18, 2024) the following figures have emerged regarding internet addiction among adults in the US:

*Figure 2. Taken from Social Media Addiction Statistics 2024 by Branka from Truelist*

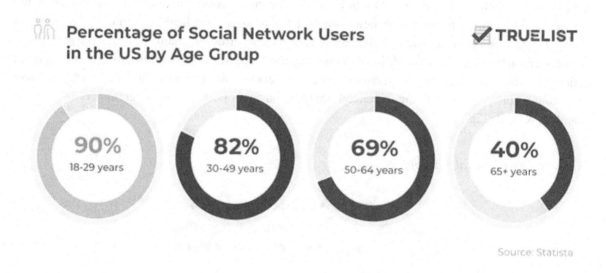

## The Toll of Too Much Screen Time

However, the overuse of digital technology also manifests as psychological and physiological risks. A recent review, for example, examined the scientific literature on the risk of Facebook use (Stangl, Riedl, Kiemeswenger, & Montag, 2023). The results indicated that excessive and uncontrolled use of Facebook, the most used social networking site in the world (Most popular social networks worldwide as of April 2024, ranked by number of monthly active users (in millions), 2022), may be associated with various negative psychological (e.g., perceived depression) and physiological effects (e.g., human brain alteration). Excessive screen time, especially on devices like smartphones, tablets, computers, and TVs, takes a toll on both our mental and physical well-being. Take, for instance, the impact on sleep quality due to prolonged screen exposure emitting disruptive blue light. This disruption can lead to difficulties falling asleep or maintaining restful sleep patterns, affecting overall sleep quality. Moreover, sedentary behaviors associated with excessive screen time contribute to physical health concerns like obesity, cardiovascular issues, and musculoskeletal disorders, leading to discomfort and health complications (Muppalla SK, 2023).

In terms of mental health, excessive screen time, particularly on social media, has been linked to heightened feelings of anxiety, depression, loneliness, and low self-esteem. We pay heavily in terms of meaningful family and social connections and end up feeling isolated from the world around us. The constant exposure to curated online personas can fuel negative comparisons and unrealistic expectations, straining mental health (Nakshine VS, 2022).

Some very interesting, but at the same time alarming statistics updated in 2024 can be found on a blog written by Mathew Woodward on Search Logistics "Social Media Addiction Statistics for 2024" According to this information, if someone opens an account on social media at the age of 16 and lives till the age of 73 years they spend about 2,995,920 minutes on social media. This equates to 5.7 years of his/her life.

*Figure 3. Taken from Social Media Addiction Statistics for 2024 by Mathew Woodward on Search Logistics*

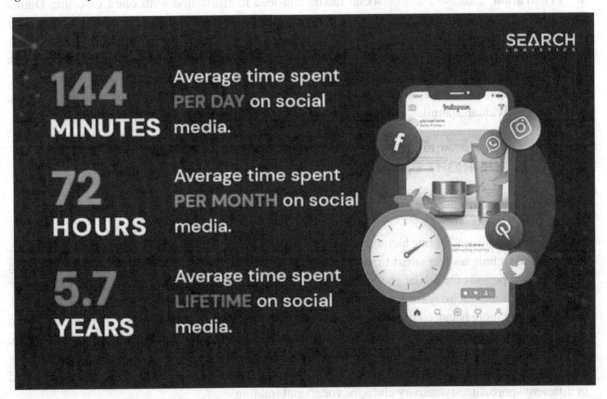

## Identifying Digital Addiction Red Flags

Characterized by compulsive and unhealthy digital device use, red flags, that can be identified early for intervention, manifest in various ways. It is crucial to recognize the red flags of digital addiction which start popping up when screen time crosses the boundary of a healthy use of gadgets. These most common signs can be any or all of the following:

1. **Checking the device all the time**: The urge to check/use the device during meetings, dinner tables, public gatherings and even carrying it to the washroom.

2. **Neglecting family/Social responsibilities**: Not giving enough time or not attending to the needs of the spouse/ children/ parents and neglecting other professional/social responsibilities.

3. **Adverse effects on physical health**: Weight gain due to a lack of physical activities is the most obvious sign along with headaches, eyestrain (glasses for children), and sleep disturbance leading to a feeling of tiredness and irritability. Some of the users also experience cervical pain and pain in parts of the hands due to holding the device for a long time in one particular position

4. **Frustration**: Excessive use of social media can lead to frustration with one's own life. Digital addicts have even gone to the extent of committing suicide if they don't get validation from their digital community.

5. **Decreased productivity**: Productivity at the workplace is affected as people don't focus on the task at hand due to their involvement with their virtual world.

Recognizing these signs is crucial for timely intervention and promoting healthier technology habits, benefiting individuals, families, educators, and healthcare professionals alike (Karakose T, 2023).

## STRIKING THE RIGHT BALANCE

## Finding Harmony

In today's digital age, finding harmony between our online and offline lives is key to overall well-being. Some of the techniques like smart time management strategies can be adopted, which means carving out dedicated periods for digital engagement and offline pursuits. For instance, setting aside specific "screen-free" hours each day for activities like reading, exercise, or socializing can help us reduce screen time and lead a more balanced lifestyle (Seyed Amin Mirlohi Falavarjani, 2019). It is also a good idea to allot "tech-free zones" in the house, like the living room or the dining area for family time and relaxation.

Parents can also make it mandatory for the children to spend some time on offline activities to promote connection with the real world, for example, pursuing hobbies, traveling together, getting enrolled in different sports/literary/activity clubs, or vocational training.

Furthermore, integrating mindfulness into our daily routines can heighten our awareness of digital habits and encourage intentional technology use. Mindfulness practices, such as mindful breathing or eating, can foster focused attention and being fully present in the moment rather than getting lost in endless scrolling or multitasking on devices (Cameron Guthrie, 2021).

## The Benefits of Moderation

Limiting screen time brings about a host of advantages for our mental, emotional, and physical well-being and interpersonal relationships. For instance, scaling back on excessive screen exposure can significantly improve sleep quality by reducing blue light exposure and avoiding stimulating content before bedtime. Research indicates that individuals who curb screen time before sleep tend to enjoy better sleep duration and quality, leading to enhanced overall health and daytime functioning. We cannot ignore the vital contribution of physical activities in promoting better cardiovascular health, weight management, and overall fitness.

According to Falavarjani (Seyed Amin Mirlohi Falavarjani, 2019), moderation in screen time can sharpen our focus and boost productivity. By minimizing digital distractions, we free up more time and mental energy to tackle tasks efficiently, particularly in academic or professional settings where concentration and productivity are paramount (Seyed Amin Mirlohi Falavarjani, 2019) and be more stress-free and emotionally resilient. Moreover, the consumption of social media and digital content can stifle creativity and imagination in children, it is known for exacerbating peer pressure and can be the cause of mental stress and even suicide among children and adolescents as they seek validation from the virtual family in the form of likes and comments. There have been cases of cyberbullying, harassment, and body shaming which have had negative impacts on children. However, limiting screen time will lead to finding innovative ways to utilize their potential. There are numerous benefits of controlled use of social media for children. It gives them a platform for expressing their thoughts and getting their own identity. Positive feedback and validation from peers can boost their confidence and expose them to diverse viewpoints.

## Benefits of Offline Living

Diving into offline experiences plays a pivotal role in enhancing well-being and nurturing meaningful connections, both with ourselves and others. Whether it's immersing ourselves in nature, pursuing hobbies, or cherishing face-to-face moments with loved ones, offline activities promote relaxation, creativity, and emotional fulfillment. Scientific studies underscore the stress-relieving, mood-lifting, and mental health benefits of activities like hiking, gardening, painting, or making music.

Furthermore, these offline adventures contribute to a sense of equilibrium and satisfaction in life. By diversifying our activities beyond screens, we uncover new passions, hone skills, and forge genuine connections that infuse our lives with purpose and joy. Prioritizing offline experiences empowers us to disconnect from the digital noise and rediscover the beauty of being present in our lives and the world around us (mynameisajo, 2012). This is bound to increase self-regulation, improve the quality of sleep, and mood, reduce anxiety and stress, and decrease procrastination in personal and professional work.

## DIGITAL DETOX-HOW TO DO IT

### The Most Vulnerable Group

School and college-going students are the most vulnerable group among all. They need to focus more on their curricular and extra-curricular activities. They should set up SMART goals, (Specific, Measurable, Achievable, Relevant, Time-bound) and not be affected by peer pressure. A good idea would be to block the websites that consume more time. For medical students, the pressure of studies, clinical rotations, and exams leads them to find solace in digital devices and procrastinate on their work. Integrating technology into medical education has made students more dependent on technology for their studies and research. They need to be continuously updated with the latest information and advancements in medical research, diagnostic techniques, etc. This overwhelming information makes them check their emails, websites, and social media leading to digital addiction. Medical students need to understand the risks of anxiety, depression, and ADHD (Attention Deficit hyperactivity Disorder), adopt healthy coping strategies for themselves, and guide their patients.

### Setting Attainable Goals

Setting achievable goals, such as reducing screen time by a manageable increment each day or dedicating certain days to screen-free activities, lays the foundation for lasting change (Newport, 2019) (Carr, 2011).

Leveraging technology tools like screen time tracking apps can be your compass on this voyage. Apps like Moment or Screen Time act as trusty companions, offering insights into your daily screen usage, allowing you to set limits, and nudging you with notifications if you veer off course from your screen time goals (Price, 2018).

Setting realistic goals that suit your lifestyle before starting a digital detox journey is paramount. Understand that it is a slow process that cannot be completed overnight. So, start with the following small steps initially:

1. Give yourself time
2. Start by reducing your screen time every day. Try to shift your means of entertainment to reading magazines and fiction instead of watching TV and mobile. But watching a movie on TV or theater occasionally is a healthy habit.
3. Counsel yourself that you don't have to know what is happening in the other person's/ celebrities' life, where they are spending their vacation, and which designer they are wearing
4. Start taking more interest in your immediate relations and try to help people around you more often.
5. Understand that you don't need all the information available online. Most of it is useless for you.
6. Give more importance to the opinion of people close to you rather than your virtual community. In fact, getting constructive feedback from family and friends is a good idea.

## FACING THE CHALLENGES

Navigating the challenges of digital detox requires resilience and adaptability. People encounter withdrawal symptoms like restlessness or anxiety as they cut back on-screen time. Employing coping strategies such as deep breathing exercises, staying physically active, or seeking support from loved ones can help weather these storms and keep you anchored to your detox plan (Mirbabaie, Stieglitz, & and Marx, 2022).

Creating a supportive environment around you can be your guiding star. Communicating boundaries with family, friends, or colleagues about your tech use expectations, fostering shared offline activities, and nurturing a culture of mindfulness in digital interactions contribute to a smooth-sailing digital detox journey (Shankar, 2023).

By weaving together these strategies tailored to your needs, you chart a course toward reduced screen time, healthier tech habits, and the rewards of a harmonious digital lifestyle.

## DIGITAL HARMONY

### Guiding the Gen Z and Millennials Towards Healthy Tech Habits

In today's digital world, guiding children and adolescents toward healthy screen habits is paramount. The onus to instill responsible technology use from an early age lies equally on schools, parents, and educators.

According to Social Media Addiction Statistics 2024, more than half of the children aged 11 and 12 have their own social media accounts, though most social media platforms have put up an age requirement of 13+ years.

Schools should integrate digital literacy programs into their curriculum, teaching students about the benefits and pitfalls of technology like mental health issues and decreased productivity, cybercrime, online safety, and responsible social media conduct (Dienlin T, 2020). Their seniors or mentors, like the educators or parents should be role models for them. Their successes and achievements should be celebrated to boost their morale. At home, parents set the tone by modeling positive tech behavior and establishing clear screen time guidelines. This includes creating zones free from screens, setting reasonable device limits, and encouraging offline endeavors like sports, arts, and family bonding moments. By fostering healthy screen habits early on, young ones learn to strike a harmonious balance with technology (Wies B, 2021).

### Attaining Mindfulness Amid Digital Distractions

Incorporating mindfulness techniques into our daily lives can be very effective in managing digital distractions. Let us accept the fact that we can't survive without technology in this era, but we can try to limit its use and be more mindful of our surroundings, whether we are indoors or outdoors, and be grateful.

Embracing mindfulness in the digital era means practicing self-awareness, being present, and using technology with intention by focusing on one task at a time instead of multitasking and switching between apps. We can incorporate mindfulness techniques like mindful breathing, mindful eating, meditation, or valuing moments into our digital interactions. Before diving into social media or tackling emails, taking a mindful pause to breathe and reflect on your intentions and emotions can lead to more conscious and meaningful engagement (Mohammad Hossein Jarrahi, 2023).

To support this journey, mindfulness apps like Headspace or Calm offer guided practices and gentle reminders, making mindfulness accessible in our daily routines. By weaving mindfulness into our digital habits, we can limit mindless scrolling, sharpen our focus, and nurture overall well-being (Nina B. Eduljee, 2022).

## Creating Meaningful Bonds With Technology

Building bonds with technology means utilizing it to create a positive impact on our lives. It can be used by scientists in different fields to solve complex global issues, employ computer simulations to find answers, and use AI to analyze data. Similarly, healthcare professionals can make the best use of technology to enhance patient care by using medical imaging technologies like MRIs and CT Scans and conducting research in areas like genomic sciences to aid treatment. Telemedicine platforms are the best ways to reach out to remote underserved areas. We can also integrate technology to strengthen our relationships and simplify daily chores. The world has become a global village and family members stay away from each other. We can use technology to stay in touch with our loved ones through video calls.

Wearable devices like fitness trackers and smartwatches can be beneficial in promoting healthier habits. Digital devices come equipped with features like tracking the time spent on screen by giving an alert to the user on exceeding the set limit. Some devices send a notification to the user to take a break. This reminds the user to get up and do some physical exercise, practice mindfulness and relax. There are also sleep-tracking options to set bedtime routines.

Building healthy relationships with technology involves setting boundaries, practicing moderation, and valuing genuine interactions. Imagine carving out specific times for digital tasks, limiting unnecessary screen time, and creating tech-free reservations at home.

## Balancing Connectivity and Well-Being With 5G

Imagine you're a student in a world where downloading study materials or joining virtual classes happens instantly, thanks to the lightning-fast 5G networks. It's a game-changer, offering incredible connectivity and unlocking new educational possibilities. However, with this speed comes the challenge of finding the right balance between online productivity and offline well-being. You can use 5G technology to make your study sessions more motivating and productive. 5G opens up a whole new world of immersive learning experiences through virtual reality (VR) and augmented reality (AR). Instead of staring at screens all day, you can dive into virtual field trips, simulations, or interactive lessons that make learning fun and engaging. It's like stepping into a different reality where you can explore ecosystems, historical events, or scientific concepts without feeling glued to your devices.

You set specific study goals and tasks, and once you achieve them, you reward yourself with quality offline relaxation time. It's like turning your online work into a game where efficient studying earns you well-deserved offline breaks (Fioravanti, Prostamo, & Casale, 2019).

Moreover, nurturing offline connections and experiences is crucial. This includes cherishing quality time with loved ones, pursuing screen-free hobbies, and immersing ourselves fully in face-to-face interactions. By cherishing real-life connections and experiences, we cultivate a balanced and gratifying relationship with technology.

In essence, promoting digital wellness requires a holistic approach encompassing education, mindfulness practices, and intentional shifts in behavior. By embracing these strategies, we can navigate the digital realm mindfully, enhance our well-being, and enjoy the rewards of a harmonious digital lifestyle (Wiederhold., 2020).

## INSPIRING STORIES OF DIGITAL TRANSFORMATION

### Real-Life Digital Detoxes

Within the next paragraphs, you'll find inspiring narratives of individuals and families who embarked on transformative digital detox journeys. These stories unveil how they successfully reduced screen time, redefined their tech relationships, and embraced positive changes in their lives (Haddock, Ward, Yu, & ODea, 2022).

A family (name not disclosed) that embraced a weekly "tech-free day," immersing themselves in outdoor adventures, board games, and heartfelt conversations without digital distractions. Their bond grew stronger, communication flourished, and stress levels dwindled, showcasing the profound impact of disconnecting from screens.

Then there's another real-life story of an individual (name not disclosed) who embraced a month-long digital detox challenge, prioritizing essential tasks over mindless scrolling, stepping away from social media, and embracing offline passions. The outcome? Heightened productivity, improved sleep patterns, and an enriched sense of fulfillment in daily life.

These real-life triumphs echo the transformative power of digital detoxes, inspiring others to embark on their journeys toward a more balanced digital existence (Radtke, 2022).

### Insights and Epiphanies: Lessons From Digital Detox Successes

Reflecting on these triumphs unveils valuable lessons and key takeaways for those venturing into their own digital detox endeavors.

1.  One lesson is the importance of setting clear goals and boundaries when reducing screen time. Defining specific objectives, such as cutting social media use or integrating more offline activities, provides a roadmap for focused and sustained progress.

2.  Another revelation lies in the significance of accountability and support systems. Whether through accountability partners, digital wellness communities, or support groups, having a network fosters encouragement, motivation, and resources for navigating challenges and staying committed to detox goals.

3.  These success stories highlight the profound benefits of mindfulness, self-care, and immersive offline experiences. By embracing mindfulness practices, prioritizing self-care rituals, and indulging in enriching offline pursuits, individuals unlock a treasure trove of well-being and resilience against digital distractions.

In essence, the tales and insights shared in this chapter underscore the transformative potential of intentional tech use, supportive communities, and holistic well-being. By embracing these lessons, individuals can embark on sustainable journeys toward digital wellness and craft mindful and fulfilling lifestyles in the digital age (Nguyen, 2022). However, another research by Radke says that most of the studies showed either no effects or mixed findings regarding digital detox efficacy. In contrast, all three studies that investigated depression symptoms found a decline in such symptoms after a digital detox intervention. Nevertheless, no effect across studies was found consistently among cognitive and physical performance measures after a digital detox intervention. For all other presented outcomes in this review, the included studies revealed mixed and contradictory findings. Thus, the answer to our main research question of whether digital detox interventions are effective in improving outcomes such as duration of use, performance, self-control, health, well-being, or social relationships is that mixed findings exist, and no clear answer can be given yet" ((Radtke, 2022),

## EMBRACING THE DIGITAL LANDSCAPE OF THE FUTURE

### Innovations Paving the Way for Digital Wellness

The future of digital detox is intertwined with exciting technological innovations aimed at promoting digital wellness and empowering individuals to manage their screen time effectively. Picture smartphone features like screen time tracking, app limits, and bedtime modes that give users insights into their digital habits, set boundaries, and promote healthier bedtime routines by reducing blue light emissions.

Wearable devices, such as fitness trackers and smartwatches, take digital wellness a step further by offering mindfulness reminders, activity tracking, and stress management tools. Imagine a smartwatch nudging you to take a mindful break or guiding you through breathing exercises to combat screen fatigue and foster well-being throughout the day.

Emerging technologies like augmented reality (AR) and virtual reality (VR) hold immense potential in the realm of digital wellness. AR applications enhance real-world experiences by blending digital elements into our surroundings, encouraging mindful engagement. Similarly, VR simulations offer immersive experiences promoting relaxation, stress relief, and mindfulness, offering alternatives to screen-centric entertainment. According to De Witte, selective and targeted use of technology within care and welfare can have several advantages including improved quality of care and active user involvement. (De Witte NAJ, 2021).

### Shaping Tomorrow's Digital Landscape

The ripple effects of digital detox extend beyond individual well-being, influencing societal norms and shaping future generations' tech relationships. Imagine a cultural shift where face-to-face interactions, nature experiences, and meaningful connections take precedence.

In educational realms, digital detox practices foster digital literacy, critical thinking, and healthy tech habits among youth. Schools championing digital wellness education and mindful practices equip students to navigate the digital world responsibly and embrace a balanced tech approach.

Furthermore, a heightened awareness of digital detox benefits may drive policy changes and industry shifts toward ethical tech design. Imagine tech solutions prioritizing user well-being, privacy, and accessibility, leading to a more mindful and user-centric digital landscape.

In essence, the future of digital detox promises a harmonious blend of innovative tech solutions, mindful practices, and societal shifts toward a healthier relationship with technology. Embracing digital detox empowers individuals, communities, and societies to thrive in the digital age while prioritizing well-being and balance (Zhenjun Yan, 2023).

## NAVIGATING THE DIGITAL WELLNESS ECOSYSTEM

### A Treasure Trove of Knowledge and Guidance

Dive into a sea of resources beckoning further exploration into digital wellness. Books like "Digital Minimalism" by Cal Newport, where he discusses Digital minimalism and offers practical tips about how to reduce screen time, reclaim attention, and create meaningful offline experiences. "How to Break Up With Your Phone" by Catherine Price, where she offers a 30-day plan with practical tips exercises, and mindfulness techniques to guide us in developing healthier and meaningful relationships with our devices, and "The Shallows: What the Internet Is Doing to Our Brains" by Nicholas Carr where He argues that the constant bombardment of information and distractions online is reshaping our brains, making it more difficult for us to focus deeply, think critically, and retain information. Carr draws on research from neuroscience, psychology, and history to support his thesis, illustrating how the medium of the internet, with its hyperlinks, multimedia content, and constant interruptions, is altering our cognitive processes. Another very interesting book is "The Tech-wise Family: Everyday Steps for Putting Technology in its Proper Place" by Andy Crouch. The author discusses how families can get closer and develop strong relationships in the digital age.

These books serve as beacons, offering insights into technology's impact and practical strategies for fostering a healthier screen-life balance.

Delve deeper with reputable articles from journals like the Journal of Computer-Mediated Communication and Cyberpsychology, Behavior, and Social Networking. These scholarly works provide evidence-based insights into digital wellness trends, screen time effects, and interventions for healthier tech use.

There are a lot of online platforms like Digital Detox and the Center for Humane Technology, where a wealth of resources, tools, and community support await. Newport suggests that we should engage in forums, challenges, and discussions on Screen-Free Parenting and other dedicated platforms to exchange experiences and strategies for mindful tech use (Newport, 2019). However engaging in online forums will again become addictive, so it is better to read books and articles.

### Tools for Managing Screen Time

Artificial Intelligence (AI) has become a helpful companion for students, offering personalized learning experiences, instant access to information, and efficient study tools. However, spending too much time with AI-powered educational platforms and apps can sometimes mean spending more time staring at screens. This could make students worry about how much time they're spending online and how it might affect their well-being. One way students can handle this is by using AI-powered time management tools, sort of like having a digital assistant to help organize their day. These tools can create schedules that mix study time with breaks for exercise, socializing, and relaxation. Imagine a smart calendar that suggests when it's time to take a break from screens and do something offline.

Discover a plethora of apps designed to help manage screen time effectively. Apps like Forest, Flipd, and Offtime gamify focus and limit distractions by temporarily blocking access to distracting sites and apps. Track your progress with screen time tracking apps such as Moment or RescueTime, gaining insights into your digital habits and setting goals for a balanced approach.

For parents, parental control apps like Qustodio (mention it or Family Link provide peace of mind, offering features to manage children's screen time, block inappropriate content, and monitor online activities. These tools empower parents to create a safe digital environment for their kids and instill responsible tech use habits from an early age (Siamack Zahedi, 2021).

## Building Connections and Finding Support

Forge connections and seek support through digital wellness communities and support groups. Organizations like Offline Camp and Screen-Free Week host events and workshops, fostering mindfulness and promoting offline experiences.

Join online communities such as the Digital Wellbeing Community on Reddit or Screen-Free Parenting groups on social media, where individuals come together to share experiences and tips for managing screen time. Participate in digital wellness challenges like the "National Day of Unplugging" to embark on collective journeys toward mindful tech use.

For those grappling with digital dependencies, specialized support groups and therapy programs offer professional guidance and interventions. These resources equip individuals with personalized strategies, coping mechanisms, and behavior changes for healthier tech habits and overall well-being.

By embracing these resources, individuals can navigate the digital landscape mindfully, cultivate digital wellness, and nurture a balanced and fulfilling relationship with technology (Jeunemaître, 2023).

## EMBRACING THE DIGITAL JOURNEY

## Reflecting on the Highlights

Before we conclude, let's take a moment to revisit the key landmarks we've explored throughout this journey. We've defined digital detox and the predicament of the present generation and delved into the detrimental effects of excessive screen time on our well-being, emphasized the importance of setting boundaries and goals for digital detox, and uncovered the profound benefits of integrating offline experiences and mindfulness into our daily lives. Most importantly, we have given tips to identify the red flags in digital addiction and how to implement control in the use of electronic devices. Moreover, responsibility at different levels has also been discussed. These key points serve as guideposts, reminding us of the significance of digital wellness and the need for a balanced relationship with technology (Philippe Doneys, 2024).

## Embracing Change, One Step at a Time

We encourage you to embark on your quest for a balanced digital lifestyle. Set realistic goals, craft digital detox plans, and weave mindfulness practices into your daily routines. Each small step you take towards mindful tech use and offline engagement is a stride toward a healthier and more fulfilling life. Draw inspiration from success stories, absorb motivational quotes, and implement actionable tips to fuel your digital wellness journey (Bradley, 2023).

## Paving the Path to a Brighter Digital Future

We can envision a brighter future at various levels.

1. **At the personal level**, firstly we have to realize that we are addicted to technology and then make a conscious effort and take practical measures to detoxify ourselves of technology. We may get apps or devices encouraging breaks from screen time to support digital detox.
2. **In the workplace**, corporate offices may create policies that encourage employees to take digital detox breaks to prevent burnout and manage their work-life balance. An environment where employees can take a break without the fear of consequences would be an ideal setup.
3. **The next level is creating public awareness** about the detrimental consequences of digital addiction, and highlighting the merits of digital well-being. Schoolchildren can be made the ambassadors of this project. Social organizations and healthcare professionals can conduct workshops and spread awareness on digital detoxing and mindful tech consumption.
4. **Lastly, the highest level is the policymakers at the government level**. Guidelines that protect consumers from digital overuse should be included and measures to promote responsible use of technology should be introduced. Technology companies can be stakeholders by designing products that support digital well-being.

Looking ahead, let's envision a digital landscape where well-being thrives, connections deepen, and individuals flourish. Embrace emerging technologies that promote digital wellness, advocate for ethical tech design, and champion digital literacy in education and policy. Together, we can create a future where technology enhances our lives, fosters meaningful connections, and empowers us to thrive in a digital age (Stefano Za, 2021).

## ACKNOWLEDGMENT

The authors would like to acknowledge the support of the management in writing, and Prof. Rajani Dube (RAKMHSU) for reviewing the chapter.

## REFERENCES

Basu, R. (2019). Impact of digital detox on individual performance of the employees. *International Journal of Research and Analytical Reviews*, 6(2), 378–381.

Bradley, J. (2023, Jan 7). *Embracing Change: Transforming Your Life One Step at a Time*. Medium. https://medium.com/lampshade-of-illumination/embracing-change-transforming-your-life-one-step-at-a-time-63781bd0f63b

Brown, L., & Kuss, D. J. (2020). Fear of missing out, mental wellbeing, and social connectedness: A seven-day social media abstinence trial. *International Journal of Environmental Research and Public Health*, 4566(12), 4566. 10.3390/ijerph1712456632599962

Cameron Guthrie, S. F.-W. (2021). Online consumer resilience during a pandemic: An exploratory study of e-commerce behavior before, during and after a COVID-19 lockdown. *Journal of Retailing and Consumer Services*, 61, 102570. 10.1016/j.jretconser.2021.102570

Carr, N. (2011). *The Shallows: What the Internet Is Doing to Our Brains*. W. W. Norton & Company.

De Witte, N. A. J., Joris, S., Van Assche, E., & Van Daele, T. (2021, December 23). Technological and Digital Interventions for Mental Health and Wellbeing: An Overview of Systematic Reviews. *Frontiers in Digital Health*, 754337, 754337. 10.3389/fdgth.2021.75433735005695

Dienlin, T. J. N., & Johannes, N. (2020). The impact of digital technology use on adolescent well-being. *Dialogues in Clinical Neuroscience*, 22(2), 135–142. 10.31887/DCNS.2020.22.2/tdienlin32699513

Dresp-Langley, B., & Hutt, A. (2022). Digital Addiction and Sleep. *International Journal of Environmental Research and Public Health*, 19(11), 6910. 10.3390/ijerph1911691035682491

Eduljee, N. B., Murphy, L., & Croteau, K. (2022). Digital Distractions, Mindfulness, and Academic Performance With Undergraduate College Students. In S. Gupta (Ed.), Handbook of Research on Clinical Applications of Meditation and Mindfulness-Based Interventions in Mental Health (pp. 319-336). IGI Global. https://doi.org/10.4018/978-1-7998-8682-2.ch02010.4018/978-1-7998-8682-2.ch020

Fioravanti, G., Prostamo, A., & Casale, S. (2019). Taking a short break from Instagram: The effects on subjective well-being. *Cyberpsychology, Behavior, and Social Networking*. 10.1089/cyber.2019.040031851833

Gonçalves LL, Nardi AE, King ALS. Digital Dependence in Organizations: Impacts on the Physical and Mental Health of Employees. Clin Pract Epidemiol Ment Health. 2023 Jan 25;19:e174501792212300. doi: 10.2174/17450179-v19-e230109-2022-17. PMID: 37275437; PMCID: PMC10161397.10.2174/17450179-v19-e230109-2022-1737275437

Haddock A, Ward N, Yu R, O'Dea N. Positive Effects of Digital Technology Use by Adolescents: A Scoping Review of the Literature. Int J Environ Res Public Health. 2022 Oct 27;19(21):14009. doi: 10.3390/ijerph192114009. PMID: 36360887; PMCID: PMC9658971. 10.3390/ijerph19211400936360887

Hunt, M. G., Marx, R., Lipson, C., & Young, J. (2018). NO MORE FOMO: LIMITING SOCIAL MEDIADECREASES LONELINESS AND DEPRESSION. *Journal of Social and Clinical Psychology*, 37(10), 751–768. 10.1521/jscp.2018.37.10.751

Jeunemaître, A. M. (2023). The Future of Wellbeing: Value Creation in Digital Mental Health Services. *The Future of Consumption*, 233–249. 10.1007/978-3-031-33246-3_15

Karakose, T. Y. B., Yıldırım, B., Tülübaş, T., & Kardas, A. (2023, February 8). comprehensive review on emerging trends in the dynamic evolution of digital addiction and depression. *Frontiers in Psychology*, 14, 1126815. 10.3389/fpsyg.2023.112681536844332

Mirbabaie, M., Stieglitz, S., & Marx, J. (2022). Digital Detox. *Business & Information Systems Engineering*, 64(2), 239–246. 10.1007/s12599-022-00747-x

Mohammad Hossein Jarrahi, D. L. (2023). Mindful work and mindful technology: Redressing digital distraction in knowledge work. *Digital Business*, 3(1), 100051. 10.1016/j.digbus.2022.100051

*Most popular social networks worldwide as of April 2024, ranked by number of monthly active users (in millions).* (2022). Statista. https://www.statista.com/statistics/272014/global-social-networks-ranked-by-number-of-users/

Muppalla, S. K., Vuppalapati, S., Reddy Pulliahgaru, A., & Sreenivasulu, H. (2023, June 18). Effects of Excessive Screen Time on Child Development: An Updated Review and Strategies for Management. *Cureus*, 15(6). Advance online publication. 10.7759/cureus.4060837476119

Nakshine VS, Thute P, Khatib MN, Sarkar B. Increased Screen Time as a Cause of Declining Physical, Psychological Health, and Sleep Patterns: A Literary Review. Cureus. 2022 Oct 8;14(10):e30051. doi: 10.7759/cureus.30051. PMID: 36381869; PMCID: PMC9638701. 10.7759/cureus.3005136381869

Newport, C. (2019). *Digital Minimalism: Choosing a Focused Life in a Noisy World*. Portfolio.

Nguyen, V. T. (2022). The perceptions of social media users of digital detox apps considering personality traits. *Education and Information Technologies*, 27(7), 9293–9316. 10.1007/s10639-022-11022-735370441

Pflügner, K., Maier, C., Mattke, J., & Weitzel, T. (2020). Personality profiles that put users at risk of perceiving technostress. *Business & Information Systems Engineering*, 63(4), 389–402. 10.1007/s12599-020-00668-7

Philippe Doneys, K. K. (2024). Gender, technology and development: reflections on the past, and provocations for the future. *Technology and Development*, 285-294. 10.1080/09718524.2022.2153459

Price, C. (2018). *How to Break Up With Your Phone*. Trapeze.

Radtke, T. A., Apel, T., Schenkel, K., Keller, J., & von Lindern, E. (2022). Digital detox: An effective solution in the smartphone era? A systematic literature review. *Mobile Media & Communication*, 10(2), 190–215. 10.1177/20501579211028647

Seyed Amin Mirlohi Falavarjani, F. Z. (2019). The reflection of offline activities on users' online social behavior: An observational study. *Information Processing & Management*, 56(6), 102070. 10.1016/j.ipm.2019.102070

Shankar, V. (2023). *Disconnect to Reconnect: Guide to Digital Detoxificatiom*. Independently published.

Siamack Zahedi, R. J. (2021). A systematic review of screen-time literature to inform educational policy and practice during COVID-19. *International Journal of Educational Research Open*, 2, 100094. 10.1016/j.ijedro.2021.10009435059672

Stangl, F. J., Riedl, R., Kiemeswenger, R., & Montag, C. (2023, August 3). Negative psychological and physiological effects of social networking site use: The example of Facebook. *Frontiers in Psychology*, 14, 1141663. 10.3389/fpsyg.2023.114166337599719

Stefano Za, R. W. (2021). *Sustainable Digital Transformation: Paving the Way Towards Smart Organizations and Societies*. Springer International Publishing.

Technostress, B. C. (1984). *The human cost of the computer revolution*. Addison Wesley Publishing Company.

Ugur, N. G., & Koc, T. (2015, July 3). Time for Digital Detox: Misuse of Mobile Technology and Phubbing. *Procedia: Social and Behavioral Sciences*, 195, 1022–1031. 10.1016/j.sbspro.2015.06.491

Wiederhold, B. K. (2020). Forging Stronger Bonds Through Technology: How Virtual Reality Can Instill Empathy. *Cyberpsychology, Behavior, and Social Networking*, 577-578(9), 577–578. 10.1089/cyber.2020.29193.bkw32845732

Wies B, Landers C, Ienca M. Digital Mental Health for Young People: A Scoping Review of Ethical Promises and Challenges. Front Digit Health. 2021 Sep 6;3:697072. doi: 10.3389/fdgth.2021.697072. PMID: 34713173; PMCID: PMC8521997.10.3389/fdgth.2021.69707234713173

Zhenjun Yan, L. J. (2023). Intelligent urbanism with artificial intelligence in shaping tomorrow's smart cities: Current developments, trends, and future directions. *Journal of Cloud Computing (Heidelberg, Germany)*, 197(1), 179. 10.1186/s13677-023-00569-6

## DIGITAL DETOX RESOURCES

Below is a list of books and links that extensively discuss digital detox. Some of them have been mentioned in this chapter. Pick up/go to any of these and start your detox journey.

1. Bored and Brilliant: How Spacing Out Can Unlock your Most Productive and Creative Self (by Manoush Zomorodi)
2. Reclaiming Conversation: The Power of Talk in a Digital Age (by Sherry Turkle)
3. Off: Your Digital Detox for a better Life (by Tanya Goodin)
4. The Rise of Addictive Technology and the Business of Keeping Us Hooked (by Adam Alter)
5. The Tech-Wise Family: Everyday Steps for Putting Technology in its Proper Place (by Andy Crouch)
6. Digital Minimalism (by Cal Newport)
7. How to Break Up with Your Phone (by Catherine Price)
8. Irresistible: The Rise of Addictive Technology and the eBusiness of Keeping Us Hooked (by Adam Alter)
9. Digital Detox: https://www.digitaldetox.com/
10. Center for Humane Technology: https://www.humanetech.com/
11. Forest app: https://www.forestapp.cc/
12. Flipd app: https://www.flipdapp.co/
13. Offtime app: https://www.offtime.app/
14. Moment app: https://apps.apple.com/us/app/in-the-moment-mindful-eating/id807652328
15. RescueTime app: https://www.rescuetime.com/
16. Qustodio: https://www.qustodio.com/
17. Family Link (by Google): https://families.google.com/familylink/
18. Offline Camp: https://offlinefirst.org/camp/
19. Screen-Free Week: https://www.screenfree.org/
20. Digital Wellbeing Community on Reddit: https://www.reddit.com/r/digitalwellbeing/
21. Screen-Free Parenting groups on social media platforms.

# Chapter 3
# Parenting in the Age of Artificial Intelligence:
## Digital Guardians

**Ruqia Safdar Bajwa**
https://orcid.org/0000-0002-4460-2025
*Bahauddin Zakariya University, Pakistan*

**Asma Yunus**
*University of Sargodha, Pakistan*

**Hina Saeed**
https://orcid.org/0000-0002-8954-2492
*The Women University, Multan, Pakistan*

**Asia Zulfqar**
https://orcid.org/0000-0001-9435-128X
*Bahauddin Zakariya University, Pakistan*

## ABSTRACT

*This chapter explores the evolving dynamics of parenting in the age of artificial intelligence (AI), emphasizing the dual roles of parents as both guardians and facilitators in the digital realm. With the integration of AI into everyday life, parenting transforms, confronting new challenges, and harnessing opportunities to influence child development positively. Drawing on recent studies, this work highlights the early engagement of children with AI, revealing that children as young as six years old formulate their own metaphors and perspectives on AI, and utilize it in ways that significantly impact their learning processes and emotional well-being. The chapter discusses how AI revolutionizes education by providing personalized learning experiences and monitoring children's emotional and physical states, while also examining the potential pitfalls, including digital addiction, privacy concerns, and the risk of technology interference in parent-child interactions.*

DOI: 10.4018/979-8-3693-3350-1.ch003

## INTRODUCTION

The integration of artificial intelligence (AI) in everyday life poses new challenges and, at the same time, opens new opportunities for parents to control the direction of child development in the digital environment. According to modern researchers, children as early as six years old may create their metaphors and views on AI and use it at an evolving level (Sacan et al., 2022). Li (2022) illustrates this early engagement by showing how AI could enhance the experiences of children's learning, such as piano lessons. In the digital age, parents play a complex and challenging role, especially in the context of AI. Scholars such as Singler (2020) and Croeser (2019) argue for an updated form of parenting in this regard, considering the challenges and opportunities that AI presents. Smedts (2008) and Lin (2021) replicate the importance of ethical considerations and also point out how AI could help in improving family well-being. Benedetto (2020) and Livingstone (2020) discussed the role of digital media influencing parent-child bonding and suggst the requirement for parental mediation.

Parenting is changing in a time when artificial intelligence (AI) technologies are not only developing quickly but also effortlessly blending into many aspects of daily life. This chapter explores 'digital parenting' considering how the use of AI transforms family operations, specifies new kinds of child interactions, and redesigns parenting structures. From the personal computing-induced digital revolution to AI technologies that are currently in charge, family practices have been hugely affected (Livingstone & Blum-Ross, 2020). The increasing penetration of AI is mirrored in the reality that it permeates parenting through many facets, from intelligent toys to learning aids (Smith, 2019).

Artificial intelligence revolutionizes education and transforms the way kids absorb information. Educational technologies ensure customized learning for kids (Johnson et al., 2021), and AI-oriented solutions track children's emotional and physical condition (O'Connor & Madge, 2019). Digital social bonds mitigate geographic distances in families (Green et al., 2020). Critically, though, challenges of screen time, digital addiction (Twenge & Campbell, 2018), data privacy, and keeping track of technological advancements continue. Parents have to grapple with this, well aware but yet they need to imbibe in their children good digital literacy skills and sound AI ethics (Holloway & Green, 2019).

AI application in parenting is not free of developmental concerns. 'technoference,' where technology interference occurs with parent-child interactions, is an emerging issue (Glassman et al., 2021). The argument goes ahead to state the application of AI in education especially the early learning kind of education. Puspitaningsih et al. (2022) suggested early AI literacy of children as the way to pre-equip them for a digital future.

The AI era creates a new, unique landscape and equally promising space for parenting, with significant challenges. Parents must keep pace with technological advancements and, at the same time, orient themselves to be able to accompany their children in the digital world, following paramount ethical values and critical discretion. The formation of the duality of AI in education and the lives of children is identified by the researchers showing opinions of the children about AI regarding its role using diverse metaphors (Sacan et al., 2022). In this light, the role of AI in education (Luckin, 2017) and the incorporation of parenting strategies for AI (Croeser & Eckersley, 2019) highlight a drastic evolving environment demanding attention from parents.

The incorporation of AI into children's devices and toys presents several governance and ethical challenges (McStay & Rosner, 2021). Moreover, the artificial intelligence surveillance of children's mental health by the school (Gowda et al., 2022) and AI policing parents (Alrusaini & Beyari, 2022) again underline that this is a process that equally requires parents to participate actively and be aware.

As AI continues to evolve, the responsibility of helping guide their children's navigation through the intricacies of a digital world rightly and safely is left with the parents.

In this exploration, we seek to understand the evolving dynamics of parenting in the AI era, focusing on how parents can act as 'guardians of the digital realm,' guiding their children through the challenges and opportunities presented by AI technologies. There are various research perspectives relating to the implications of AI on parenting and child development anchored heavily on an extensive literature review. Highlighted are findings from prior studies, including Croeser and Eckersley's (2019) discussion on applying parenting theories to AI and Sacan et al.'s (2022) study on the metaphoric perception of children toward AI that shed light on the early formation of ideas about artificial intelligence. Luckin (2017) has even considered the transformative nature of such AI-based assessment systems within education, as they offer consistent feedback for parents, teachers, and students. McStay and Rosner (2021) discuss the ethics and governance context regarding children's toys concerning emotional AI, stressing more on media literacy improvement. Gowda et al. (2022) designed an AI system for tracking the mental health of schoolchildren, which is oriented on the influential role of AI in protecting mental health in educational paths. Alrusaini and Beyari (2022) analyze the impact of such social media websites as Instagram, Snapchat, Twitter, Facebook, gaming and video applications on child development. Based on the research, parental restrictions coupled with artificial intelligence can enforce influence in positive ways towards the children's use of smart devices. Interpreting the convergence of AI and parenting on the educational, growth, and emotional health of children, it emphasizes that the efficiency and application of AI for enhancing parenting diversely needs respective ethical considerations as well as the involvement of parents.

Entrainment is the propensity of interlocutors to mimic one another's verbal and nonverbal behavior, according to Benus (2014). By applying this definition, it becomes clear that the foundation of lexical entrainment is the idea that when a machine employs a particular phrase, people will mimic that use as well. Children adjusted their interaction behaviors to the robot's behavior in one particular research experiment on their adaptability in multi-session engagement with a humanoid robot, even though there was no apparent necessity for them to do so. Depending on the features of the robot's verbal conduct, children modified their vocal loudness, pause length, and speech pace to adapt both their verbal and nonverbal behavior (Nalin et al., 2012).

People now have a better understanding of the role that women, in particular, play in educating their children in the modern world, particularly when it comes to communication technologies. In addition, they possess the ability to comprehend how to support kids so that they develop into knowledgeable generations capable of optimizing communication technology utilization while circumventing its detrimental impacts (Roslan et al., 2023).

According to a prior study, parents' concentration on parent-child connections can be impacted by digital devices, with an average of 3.03 devices (SD 2.07). Growing up, being Hispanic, and speaking Spanish at home are all linked to a greater understanding of the importance of technology. Parents' judgments of their problematic technology use were most substantially connected with the adoption of AI technologies, compared to their perceptions of techno and sociodemographic characteristics (Glassman et al., 2021).

Overall, the intersection of AI and parenting is a complex and multi-faceted area with implications for many areas of children's lives. The results underscore the need for ethical reflection on this topic and raise the importance of governance and parental engagement in using AI to improve parental practices and child development.

Parenting in the age of AI presents unique challenges and opportunities for families amidst the fast-changing digital landscape. Contemporary research suggests similar findings about the impact of technology on children's development, social interactions, and well-being. The following literature review seeks to synthesize major findings from current research on digital-age parenting.

Multiple studies have investigated the role of media use regarding child well-being (Livingstone & Haddon, 2018; Subrahmanyam & Greenfield, 2010; Valkenburg & Peter, 2011). A report by the Kaiser Foundation released in January showed that even on an average day, Generation M's kids spend at least half their waking hours with media, nearly four hours of which is dedicated to TV. The first identified effect related to heavy media use is that it correlates with fewer positive outcomes, including lower empathy, poor sleep, and less active time (Ito et al., 2010; Livingstone and Haddon, 2018: 171).

Parental involvement and supervision have long been considered an important protective factor in moderating the potential negative impacts of technology on children (Subrahmanyam & Greenfield, 2010). For example, Calvert, Lilienfeld, and Wu (2017) concluded that parental mediation strategies, such as co-viewing and discussing media content, are associated with positive outcomes.

With the development of AI technologies, there are concerns about privacy and security and the potential impact on children's development (Turkle, 2011). Parents should know the opportunities and threats of AI and create early upbringing tactics for their kids to implement the norms of behavior in the digital age (Izerman, 2018).

Literature suggests that parental involvement, direction, and mediation of technology are important to curtail the risk of negative effects from technology on children's well-being and development. Parents must be aware and change their parenting styles as AI becomes sophisticated.

## OVERVIEW OF THE DIGITAL AGE AND THE PROLIFERATION OF AI IN DAILY LIFE

The digital age has witnessed a rapid proliferation of Artificial Intelligence (AI) technologies, transforming various aspects of daily life. This literature review aims to provide an overview of recent studies that explore the impact of AI on individuals, society, and various industries. The focus will be on the following themes: AI applications, societal implications, and challenges and opportunities.

### Understanding the Digital Landscape

The digital landscape is an incredibly complex ecosystem comprising many interwoven fascia, including social media platforms, online shopping websites, mobile applications, search engines, and countless other internet-based services. In a world eroded by digital technologies, this environment's reciprocity and possible implications on society, economy, and human behavior become increasingly compelling to investigate.

The study of the digital context has been a subject of various academic areas, from information systems to communication, marketing, sociology, etc. Several studies have examined the effects of media technologies on consumer behavior, organizational performance, and classifying media and digital literacies. A common thread in literature is the importance of social media in influencing individual and collective experiences, information diffusion, and online social structure (Koufaris, 2002; Vosoughi et al., 2018; Boyd & Ellison, 2007).

Another major line of research involves studying the economic impacts of the digital revolution, notably the surge of e-commerce and the digital economy (Chu & Kim, 2005; Gopinath et al., 2004; UNCTAD, 2019).

In addition, the digital world has been debated regarding privacy and security issues. Researchers have focused on how to protect individual privacy (Acquisti & Gross, 2006) and the security of digital systems (Anderson, 2001). Over the past few years, AI has witnessed phenomenal advancements. Artificial Intelligence is used in many tools and platforms to enhance the learning experience and personalize education. For example, using AI algorithms to adjust language lessons to the needs of individual language learners - optimizing their progress in platforms such as Duolingo (Linden et al., 2019). The math software by Carnegie Learning also uses AI to deliver real-time feedback and assistance to help students get a better grip on mathematical concepts (Kulkarni et al.,2017).

In addition, AI is attributed to the user's interaction with social networking platforms and content consumption. Social media platforms (e.g., FB and Instagram) leverage AI-powered recommendation systems to recommend content and connections to users based on their interests and activities (Kumar et al., 2018). AI-driven chatbots have also mushroomed in social media for multiple tasks (Liu et al., 2016). AI technology in the entertainment industry has likewise been a new dawn highlighting out-of-the-box creativity (Ricci et al.,2015; Chen et al., 2019). AI technology has advanced greatly and is almost omnipresent in different walks of human life, such as education, social media, and entertainment. This will only be reinforced as AI progresses to the point where its integration is even more ubiquitous in these fields, changing how we study, talk, and recreate. Nonetheless, the dual nature of AI, which includes opportunities and risks, must also be recognized.

AI-assistive technology has changed the lives of people with disabilities, enabling those whose functioning was difficult or altogether impossible. A representative example is screen readers and speech recognition software, which has facilitated digital content accessibility for visually impaired users (Garcia-Hernandez et al., 2020).

For instance, in the healthcare industry, AI has helped increase accuracy in diagnosing health issues, customizing treatment plans, and detecting diseases before they occur. For example, AI-powered diagnostic tools have been shown to have better accuracy than dermatologists (Esteva et al. 2019) in diagnosing skin cancer.

AI is changing the educational landscape in the sense of personalized learning and that leads to better outcomes, as I said before. These examples include, but are not limited to platforms (such as Duolingo and Carnegie Learning math software) that adapt to students' unique learning needs (Linden et al., 2019; Kulkarni et al., 2017).

## Digital Well-Being

A balanced use of technology for digital well-being is essential. Wood and Scott's (2015) research emphasizes managing parent-screen time and child-screen time, the role of parents, and digital practices at home. Livingstone and Haddon (2009) argued that AI-based algorithms have the potential to exacerbate positive or negative experiences that could affect the way users view themselves and engage in social comparison. Thus, Parents have a huge responsibility to guide their kids on the catch of how AI affects their self-esteem as well as society's implications. Vaidya, Jensen & Wiggins (2019) emphasize that people need to be able to critically evaluate the credibility of online resources - and this is even more important in the context of an AI-generated information product. Children can learn these skills at home, by being taught how to question the provider of the information and look at the online content critically by their parents (Jensen et al., 2019).

## Opportunities and Positive Engagements

The education sector has also changed with the adoption of Artificial Intelligence. The use of AI in the academic ecosystem has allowed new structures to blossom, catering to the needs of those students who learn uniquely. AI can boost customized learning experiences (Kulkarni, 2019). The AI algorithm analyzes these learning patterns to understand students' strengths and weaknesses and helps educators customize the learning strategies and content to suit the students. This method allows learners to go at their own pace, improving learning outcomes (Dziadosz, 2018).

Fortunately, there are countless AI-infused tools to facilitate personalized learning experiences. One example of how these are being used includes the AI-powered Mika from Carnegie Learning (Murphy, 2019) and Duolingo (Lau, 2018). This chapter recognizes the increasing role that AI will continue to play in determining the future direction that will impact education circuits and future research.

## Social and Emotional Development

Social and emotional development is a crucial aspect of human growth and well-being. The integration of Artificial Intelligence (AI) in this domain has led to innovative applications that support the development of social skills and emotional intelligence. Additionally, AI has played a significant role in understanding and managing mental health issues.

These include various AI applications that are designed to help people to improve their social and emotional skills. For example, AI-powered chatbots like Woebot (Burke, 2017) use cognitive-behavioral-based techniques to assist users in addressing stress, anxiety, and depression. Social skills training (e.g., Empathetic; Baker et al., 2019) utilizes AI algorithms to evaluate student social interactions and deliver tailored feedback to build emotional intelligence. Artificial Intelligence has played a major role in understanding mental health issues and managing them efficiently. Machine learning algorithms are able to analyze Big Data (e.g., from medical records, and social media) in order to identify mental health patterns and risk factors (Pletzer et al., 2018). Also, AI-based diagnostics tools, such as Mood Scanner (Krumshteyn et al., 2019), can help mental health professionals more accurately and faster assess the emotional state of patients.

## Creativity and Innovation

Innovation and creativity are the two important mechanisms behind human development. AI technology integration has the potential to inspire human creativity. Another application of AI is to create content in other art, music, and literature genres. For example, AI systems such as AICAN (Gao et al., 2018) and Deep Dream (Mordvintsev et al., 2015) have shown that AI can create original, aesthetically compelling works of art.

AI-enabled machine learning and coding will, in turn, create a generation of young children with the skills they need to shape the future of our world. Programs like Code. org (Code.org, 2021) and Scratch (Resnick et al., 2009) are easy to use for children who would like to do creative projects. Apart from that, programs like the AI Youth Innovation Challenge (AIYIC, 2021) encourage young brains to apply AI concepts to solving real-world issues, which benefits creativity and innovation altogether.

## AI Applications

AI technologies have found their way into numerous domains, offering innovative solutions and enhancing efficiency. A study by Brynjolfsson and McAfee (2014) highlights how AI has revolutionized industries such as healthcare, finance, and transportation. For example, AI-powered diagnostic tools have improved medical accuracy (Topol, 2019), while autonomous vehicles have the potential to reduce traffic accidents (Lee, 2018).

AI has also significantly impacted the field of education. A study by Kuzu and Kozan (2019) demonstrates how AI-based adaptive learning systems can personalize education, leading to better learning outcomes. In addition, AI-powered chatbots have emerged as valuable tools for providing instant support and guidance to students (Al-Dajani et al., 2020).

## Societal Implications

The proliferation of AI has raised concerns about its impact on society, including job displacement and privacy issues. A report by Frey and Osborne (2013) estimates that about 47% of total US employment is at risk due to automation, emphasizing the need for reskilling and education. To address these concerns, many governments and organizations have initiated programs to promote digital literacy and upskill the workforce (World Economic Forum, 2018).

AI's role in preserving privacy has been a subject of debate. A study by Solove (2011) highlights the challenges in maintaining privacy in the digital age, as AI technologies can collect and analyze vast amounts of personal data. To address these concerns, researchers have proposed the development of privacy-preserving AI techniques (Mohassel & Zhang, 2017).

## Challenges and Opportunities

The rapid advancement of AI technologies has led to several challenges, such as the need for responsible development and deployment. A report by the Partnership on AI (2018) emphasizes the importance of transparency, accountability, and inclusion in AI research and development. Moreover, AI has the potential to address global challenges, such as climate change and healthcare disparities, by providing valuable insights and solutions (Manyika et al., 2019).

The proliferation of AI in daily life has brought about numerous benefits and challenges. As AI technologies continue to evolve, researchers, policymakers, and the public must understand their implications and work towards responsible development and deployment.

# THE IMPORTANCE OF PARENTING IN GUIDING YOUTH THROUGH THE COMPLEXITIES OF AI

The significance of parenting in navigating youth through the intricacies of Artificial Intelligence (AI) is a crucial aspect that has gained attention in recent years. The focus will be on the following themes: parental involvement, communication, and education.

## Parental Involvement

Parental involvement plays a vital role in shaping children's attitudes toward technology (Chen & Yeh, 2018). A study by Subrahmanyam, Gross, and Weisleder (2018) highlights the importance of parent-child communication about AI and its potential impact on society. Parents who engage in open discussions about AI with their children can help them develop a better understanding of the technology and its implications.

## Communication

Effective communication between parents and children is essential for fostering a healthy relationship with AI. Parents need to be aware of their children's exposure to AI technologies and discuss the potential benefits and risks associated with them (Choudrie & Kaur, 2019). According to a study by Lin and Liu (2018), parents who communicate openly about AI with their children can help them develop critical thinking skills and a sense of responsibility when using AI-powered devices.

## Education

Educating children about AI can help them develop a better understanding of the technology and its potential impact on society. A study by Chen and Yeh (2018) emphasizes the importance of integrating AI education into the curriculum to help students develop a positive attitude toward technology. Moreover, parents can play a crucial role in supporting their children's AI education by encouraging them to explore AI-related topics and engage in hands-on learning experiences (Subrahmanyam et al., 2018).

## Understanding AI in the Context of Youth Development

Artificial Intelligence (AI) refers to the development of computer systems that can perform tasks that typically require human intelligence, such as learning, problem-solving, and decision-making. AI technologies encompass a wide range of applications, from virtual assistants and chatbots to advanced machine-learning algorithms and autonomous robots. The relevance of AI to children and adolescents lies in its potential impact on their cognitive, emotional, and social development. As AI continues to permeate various aspects of our lives, it is essential to understand its implications for the younger generation.

- **Cognitive development:** AI-powered educational tools can enhance children's learning experiences by providing personalized content and adapting to their learning styles. For example, platforms like Duolingo and Carnegie Learning's math software offer tailored lessons and instant feedback, promoting cognitive growth and improving academic outcomes (Linden et al., 2019; Kulkarni et al., 2017).

- **Emotional development:** AI-enabled mental health support systems can help children and adolescents cope with emotional challenges. For instance, Woebot, a chatbot designed to deliver cognitive-behavioral therapy, has shown promise in assisting young people with anxiety and depression (Owens et al., 2019).
- **Social development:** AI technologies can facilitate social interaction and communication among children and adolescents. For example, virtual reality platforms can create immersive environments for socializing and collaborating, while AI-powered language translation tools can help break language barriers (Riva et al., 2020). Parents, educators, and policymakers should work together to ensure that children and adolescents benefit from AI technologies while minimizing potential negative impacts (Chen et al., 2019).

## THE ROLE OF AI IN EDUCATION, ENTERTAINMENT, AND SOCIAL INTERACTIONS AMONG YOUTH

Artificial Intelligence (AI) has been increasingly integrated into various aspects of our lives, including education, entertainment, and social interactions among youth. This section will provide a detailed explanation of the role of AI in these domains.

### Education

AI has significantly transformed the educational landscape, offering numerous benefits for students, educators, and institutions. Some critical applications of AI in education include:

a. **Personalized Learning:** AI algorithms can analyze a student's learning patterns, strengths, and weaknesses, enabling the creation of customized learning paths and content. This personalization helps students progress at their own pace and ensures they receive the necessary support to overcome challenges (Liu et al., 2020).

b. **Intelligent Tutoring Systems:** These systems use AI to provide instant feedback, adapt to individual learning styles, and offer personalized guidance to students. Examples include Carnegie Learning's math software and Duolingo, which have demonstrated improved learning outcomes (Kulkarni et al., 2017).

c. **Automated Grading and Assessment:** AI can assist in grading assignments and assessments, saving educators' time and enabling them to focus on more engaging tasks, such as designing curriculum and providing personalized support (Baker et al., 2018).

### Entertainment

AI has revolutionized the entertainment industry, providing immersive experiences and enhancing user engagement. Some notable applications of AI in entertainment include:

a. **Personalized Recommendation Systems:** AI algorithms analyze users' preferences, viewing history, and behavior to suggest content tailored to their interests. Streaming platforms like Netflix and Spotify utilize these systems to provide customized entertainment experiences (Deshpande et al., 2019).

b. **Gaming and Virtual Reality:** AI-powered games and virtual reality environments can adapt to players' skills, providing challenging and engaging experiences. Examples include AI-driven opponents in games like Chess or Go, as well as immersive virtual environments that simulate social interactions (Riva et al., 2020).

c. **Interactive Storytelling:** AI can generate dynamic narratives based on user choices, creating unique and engaging stories. Platforms like Talechaser and AI Dungeon utilize AI to create personalized, interactive experiences for users (Gervasio et al., 2019).

## Social Interactions

AI technologies have the potential to facilitate and enhance social interactions among youth. Some examples include:

a. **Language Translation:** AI-powered translation tools, such as Google Translate, enable users to communicate across language barriers, fostering global connections and understanding (Zhang et al., 2020).

b. **Mental Health Support:** AI-enabled chatbots and virtual assistants can provide mental health support and resources to young people. For instance, Woebot uses cognitive-behavioral therapy techniques to assist with anxiety and depression (Owens et al., 2019).

c. **Virtual Communities and Collaboration:** AI-driven platforms can create virtual environments for socializing, collaboration, and learning. These platforms can help bridge social gaps and encourage meaningful connections among youth (Chen et al., 2019).

## POTENTIAL BENEFITS OF AI IN FOSTERING LEARNING, CREATIVITY, AND CONNECTIVITY

Artificial Intelligence (AI) has the potential to significantly enhance learning, creativity, and connectivity among individuals, particularly among youth. Enhanced Learning: AI can facilitate personalized and engaging learning experiences by:

a. **Adaptive Learning:** AI algorithms can analyze a student's learning patterns, preferences, and performance, providing tailored content and resources to optimize their learning experience (Kulkarni et al., 2017).

b. **Intelligent Tutoring Systems:** These systems use AI to offer instant feedback, adapt to individual learning styles, and provide personalized guidance, resulting in improved learning outcomes (Owens et al., 2019).

c. **Automated Assessment and Grading:** AI can assist in grading assignments and assessments, saving educators' time and enabling them to focus on more engaging tasks like designing curriculum and providing personalized support (Baker et al., 2018).

## Cultivating Creativity

AI can support and enhance creativity by;

a. **Generative Art and Music:** AI-powered tools can create unique artworks and music pieces based on user preferences or by learning from existing works, inspiring creativity and offering new perspectives (Deshpande et al., 2019).

b. **Idea Generation:** AI can assist in brainstorming sessions by suggesting novel ideas or building upon existing ones, helping individuals overcome creative blocks and explore new possibilities (Gervasio et al., 2019).

## Strengthening Connectivity

AI can foster stronger connections among individuals through:

a. **Language Translation:** AI-driven translation tools can break language barriers, enabling more effective communication and understanding across diverse cultures (Zhang et al., 2020).

b. **Virtual Communities and Collaboration:** AI-enabled platforms can create virtual environments for socializing, collaboration, and learning, bridging social gaps and encouraging meaningful connections (Chen et al., 2019).

c. **Mental Health Support:** AI-powered chatbots and virtual assistants can provide mental health resources and support, helping individuals cope with stress, anxiety, and depression (Owens et al., 2019).

## OPPORTUNITIES AND CHALLENGES IN AI AND YOUTH DEVELOPMENT

AI offers numerous opportunities for supporting educational outcomes, personalized learning experiences, and the development of critical thinking and problem-solving skills in youth. However, addressing the challenges associated with AI in education is crucial to ensure equitable access and practical implementation (Kulkarni et al., 2017)

## Opportunities

1. **Enhanced Educational Outcomes:** AI can improve educational outcomes by:
   a. **Adaptive Learning:** AI algorithms can analyze a student's learning patterns, preferences, and performance, providing tailored content and resources to optimize their learning experience (Kulkarni et al., 2017).
   b. **Intelligent Tutoring Systems:** These systems use AI to offer instant feedback, adapt to individual learning styles, and provide personalized guidance, resulting in improved learning outcomes (Owens et al., 2019).
2. **Personalized Learning Experiences:** AI can facilitate personalized learning by:
   a. **Learning Analytics:** AI can analyze data from various sources, such as student interactions with learning materials, to identify patterns and provide personalized recommendations for improving learning outcomes (Dimitriadis et al., 2018).

b. **Adaptive Assessment and Grading:** AI can assist in grading assignments and assessments, saving educators' time and enabling them to focus on more engaging tasks like designing curriculum and providing personalized support (Baker et al., 2018).

3. **Development of Critical Thinking and Problem-Solving Skills:** AI can support the development of critical thinking and problem-solving skills by:

a. **Intelligent Tutoring Systems:** AI-powered systems can provide students with challenging problems and offer step-by-step guidance, helping them develop problem-solving skills (Owens et al., 2019).

b. **AI Enhanced Learning Environments:** These environments can expose students to diverse perspectives and encourage them to think critically by presenting complex problems and asking open-ended questions (Gervasio et al., 2019).

## Challenges

1. **Privacy and Data Security:** The use of AI in education raises concerns about the privacy and security of students' data, as personal information may be collected, stored, and analyzed (Chen et al., 2019).

2. **Digital Divide:** Access to AI-powered educational tools may exacerbate the existing digital divide, as students from underprivileged backgrounds may need equal access to these technologies (Zhang et al., 2020).

3. **AI Literacy:** Educators and students need to develop AI literacy to fully harness the potential of AI in education, which may require additional training and resources (Deshpande et al., 2019).

Artificial Intelligence (AI) has brought significant advancements in various fields, including education. However, it also poses specific challenges that need to be addressed. Among these challenges are the risks of decreased physical activity, diminished face-to-face interactions, and the potential for algorithmic bias influencing children's perceptions and behaviors.

1. **Decreased Physical Activity:** The widespread use of AI in education may lead to reduced physical activity among students, as they may spend more time engaging with digital devices and less time participating in physical activities (Birk et al., 2019).

2. **Diminished Face-to-Face Interactions:** AI-powered educational tools may reduce face-to-face interactions between students and educators, potentially affecting the development of social skills and emotional intelligence (Huang et al., 2019).

3. **Algorithmic Bias and Influence on Children's Perceptions and Behaviors:** AI systems are not immune to algorithmic bias, which can inadvertently reinforce stereotypes and affect children's perceptions and behaviors. For example, biased algorithms in educational software may provide different learning experiences and opportunities for students based on their demographic characteristics (Crawford & Ferri, 2019).

To mitigate these challenges, it is crucial to:

1. **Promote Physical Activity:** Educators and parents should encourage students to maintain a balance between digital engagement and physical activities, ensuring that they engage in regular exercise and outdoor play (Birk et al., 2019).

2. **Foster Face-to-Face Interactions:** Educators should continue to prioritize face-to-face interactions, creating opportunities for students to collaborate, discuss, and learn from one another, both in and outside the classroom (Huang et al., 2019).

3.  **Address Algorithmic Bias:** Researchers, developers, and educators should work together to identify and mitigate algorithmic bias in AI-powered educational tools. This includes ensuring diverse
representation in data sets and regularly auditing algorithms for fairness and accuracy (Crawford &
Ferri, 2019).

## INTERGENERATIONAL INTERACTION AND AI

Age Invaders is a game designed to encourage intergenerational interaction, where younger players
are paired with older mentors to solve puzzles and complete challenges. The game's design takes into
account the different skill sets and experiences of each generation, allowing them to learn from one
another and build connections (Buchanan & Beer, 2018).

The use of AI in Age Invaders and similar platforms has the potential to:

1.  **Foster Intergenerational Understanding:** By creating opportunities for younger and older individuals to engage in shared experiences, AI-powered platforms can help break down generational
barriers and promote mutual respect and understanding (Buchanan & Beer, 2018).
2.  **Bridge Knowledge Gaps:** Intergenerational interaction through AI-powered platforms allows for
the exchange of knowledge and experiences, bridging the gaps between generations and promoting
a more cohesive society (Buchanan & Beer, 2018).
3.  **Enhance Social Connections:** AI-powered platforms can facilitate social connections between individuals who may not have had the opportunity to interact otherwise, promoting a sense of belonging
and community (Buchanan & Beer, 2018).

### Impact of AI on Children's Privacy

Children are particularly vulnerable to privacy invasions due to their developing cognitive abilities
and limited understanding of privacy risks (Marco, 2019). AI systems can collect and analyze children's
data, which may be used for targeted advertising or other purposes without their consent or knowledge.
This can have long-term consequences on their privacy and well-being (Marco, 2019).

### The Role of Parents in the Age of AI

In the digital age, parenting practices must evolve to address the unique challenges posed by technology. This evolution involves fostering digital literacy, setting boundaries, and being actively involved
in children's digital lives.

Digital literacy involves evaluating online information effectively (Valkenburg et al., 2015). Parents
have to come up with ways to develop these abilities in their children and responsible digital behavior
(Livingstone & Haddon, 2009). Part of this involves tracking the platforms and applications that their
children are using, talking to children about their online lives, and giving children advice when appropriate (Wood & Scott, 2015). A study conducted by Livingstone and Haddon (2009) also supports the
idea that parents who have a role in their children's media use can help the child better understand and
use the features of the digital world. For parents, maintaining a home environment that encourages responsible technology use and promotes positive values is essential in creating a helpful community that
is as conducive to the fostering of learning as it is to the pursuit of technology.

When children see the adults around them balancing their screen time with other activities and using technology for good, they will be more likely to do the same. Parents can help shape a healthier digital culture by having ongoing talks about technology use with their children (Radesky et al., 2016). According to Hern et al., (2013), relegation means parents prefer their children to play outside the home than using Internet technology. Parents also assist their kids to take on the challenging digital landscape more safely and securely that is not harmful to them through imparting their coaching and guiding. Parents can also support their children by modeling balance in the home and demonstrating that technology is a part of our lives, but so is reading, exercising, going out for a walk, getting outdoors, volunteering, and the like. They show responsible use, instill open communication, educate about the digital world, and lead by example for their children.

## Practical Strategies for Parents

In this age, it has become mandatory for parents to be the real watchdogs of their children's virtual environment. To do so, take the help of practical strategies such as digital literacy education, open talks about online safe practices, inclusive content creation on the same digital platforms where they access pornography etc.

It is critical that parents ensure their children and themselves are armed with digital literacy to navigate the online world safely and responsibly. Parents can help track what their children are doing online and solve problems by maintaining open communication channels through measures that help with online safety. They can establish clear guidelines for appropriate conduct in the online world.

To experience a positive relationship with their use of technology, parents can create a joint experience with their children by co-creating activities. This includes collaborative projects, new digital skills we can learn, and new online platforms we can explore.

However, AI technologies are more than just tools for surveillance. Paid parental monitoring apps for Android: Paid parental monitoring apps for iOS: By using these technologies, parents can understand the digital world that their children largely live in today. As a result, this approach feeds into the principles of fair and ethical use of AI and helps develop the foundation of evolving AI literacy.

It is the parent's responsibility to keep their eyes and ears open about AI Technologies and how they can affect our children. For example, examining the different applications of AI and what they mean in terms of privacy, safety, and well-being (Ford, 2018)

The use of AI technologies enables parents to nurture their children's critical thinking and digital literacy abilities. Talk with your children about AI philosophies and applications with these human-informed decisions of how to be good digital citizens (Floridi, 2014).

Parents can actively participate in shaping the future of AI by engaging in its development and use. This includes advocating for responsible AI design and implementation, as well as supporting initiatives that prioritize privacy, safety, and well-being (Brey, 2017).

## Parenting Strategies for the Digital Age

In the digital era, there must be a reassessment of how to combine parenting with the ways in which technology and AI interfacing with the world. In this regard, effective parenting involves setting boundaries and encouraging communication, rules of technology use, and ways to interact with AIs are imperative in order for children to be safe and well-supported (Rosen, 2013)

Parents should actively participate in discussing AI topics, online safety, and responsible technology use. Parenting in the Digital Age A review of the literature indicates that several studies have addressed the theme of boundary-setting and open communication within the scope of parenting in the digital age. A recent review by Rosen (2013) also calls for age-appropriate guidelines and supervision, based on empirical findings and theoretical frameworks; and Brown and Valkenburg (2012) emphasize the importance of parental mediation in promoting effective parent-child communication about technology use.

## AI-Assisted Parental Support Systems

Given the broad spectrum of AI uses in life, is it now time to evaluate the scope of AI-based parental support systems? Such systems could also offer personalized advice and resources to support a parent's child, their developmental status, the ways they behave, and other aspects of their wellness. Further research will continue to build on such an exercise by developing and testing systems of care and examining the extent to which they impact parent support and youth development (Smith, 2021).

The earlier this problem is recognized and addressed, the more likely that at-risk youth can be assisted through early intervention and prevented from slipping into the cracks. AI could be transformative in identifying youth at risk and allowing them to receive needed help. This would also explore the effectiveness of curated AI-driven interventions for youth at risk with the potential to ameliorate the course of development and minimize risks (Liu et al., 2020).

## Discussing the Ethical Implications of AI Technologies

Educational involvement, including parents acting as co-learners and utilizing resources to stay informed, plays a significant role in this process. Parents should engage in conversations with their children about the potential benefits and drawbacks of AI technologies. This includes exploring topics such as privacy, data ownership, and the impact of AI on society (Floridi, 2013). Creating a supportive atmosphere for discussing AI and technology encourages children to express their thoughts and concerns. This fosters a deeper understanding of the digital world and promotes the responsible use of technology (Brown & Valkenburg, 2012).

## Preparing for the Future

With the evolving technological landscape, it is crucial to prepare for the future by adapting to advancements in artificial intelligence (AI) and other related fields. This encompasses not only keeping pace with these changes but also ensuring that the next generation is adequately prepared for a world where AI plays a significant role in society and work.

As AI continues to permeate various aspects of society and work, it is crucial to ensure that the next generation is adequately prepared. A report by the World Economic Forum (2018) suggests that children should be equipped with skills such as critical thinking, creativity, and collaboration, which will be essential in a world with AI. Additionally, research by Bers (2014) highlights the importance of exposing children to technology and programming at a young age to foster interest and understanding of AI.

Several studies emphasize the importance of staying updated with the latest AI advancements. For instance, a report by PwC (2018) highlights that AI could contribute up to $15.7 trillion to the global economy by 2030. Similarly, a study by Brynjolfsson and McAfee (2014) suggests that firms adopting digital technologies, including AI, are more productive and profitable. These findings underscore the need for individuals and organizations to keep pace with the evolving AI landscape.

The development and implementation of AI technologies require careful consideration of their potential impacts on society. A study by Floridi, Taddeo, and Woods (2018) emphasizes the need for responsible AI, focusing on aspects such as privacy, transparency, and accountability. Moreover, advocating for child-friendly AI policies is crucial, as discussed by Selwyn (2018), who argues that policymakers should prioritize the protection and well-being of children in the context of AI.

Ensuring that AI development is inclusive and diverse is vital for promoting fairness and addressing potential biases in AI systems. A study by Buolamwini and Gebru (2018) highlights the issue of gender and skin-tone bias in commercial AI systems, emphasizing the need for a more diverse workforce in AI development. Furthermore, a report by the AI Now Institute (2019) calls for increased transparency, accountability, and inclusion in AI research and development. Adapting to the technological changes brought about by AI, preparing children for a future with AI, considering ethical implications, and promoting inclusivity and diversity in AI development are crucial aspects of preparing for the future. By staying updated with advancements, fostering an understanding of AI in the younger generation, advocating for responsible AI policies, and ensuring diverse representation in AI development, we can create a more equitable and prosperous future for all.

## Potential Risks of AI

1. **Privacy concerns:** The widespread use of AI raises concerns about the collection, storage, and misuse of personal data. For example, facial recognition technologies have been criticized for their potential to infringe on privacy and civil liberties (Gellert et al., 2018).
2. **Exposure to inappropriate content:** AI-powered recommendation systems can sometimes suggest inappropriate content to users, particularly in the case of social media platforms. This issue has led to calls for greater regulation and transparency in content moderation practices (Kumar et al., 2018).
3. **Development of social skills:** As AI-powered chatbots and virtual assistants become more prevalent, there is a risk that individuals may rely too heavily on these technologies, leading to a decline in their social skills and communication abilities (Chen et al., 2019).

# REFERENCES

Acquisti, A., & Gross, C. L. (2006). The value of information privacy: Evidence from a field experiment. *Management Science*, 52(2), 190–200.

AI Now Institute. (2019). *Artificial intelligence and society: A framework for accountability and regulation*. AI Now Institute.

Al-Dajani, A., Al-Hawamdeh, M., & Al-Dajani, S. (2020). The impact of AI-powered chatbots on student engagement in higher education. In *Proceedings of the 12th International Conference on Educational Data Mining* (pp. 35-44). ACM.

Alrusaini, O., & Beyari, H. (2022). The Sustainable Effect of Artificial Intelligence and Parental Control on Children's Behavior While Using Smart Devices' Apps: The Case of Saudi Arabia. *Sustainability (Basel)*, 14(15), 9388. 10.3390/su14159388

Anderson, R. (2001). *Security engineering: A guide to building dependable distributed systems*. Wiley.

Baker, M. B., Schwartz, M. Z., & Hogue, K. (2019). Empathetic: A web-based social skills training program for adolescents with an autism spectrum disorder. *Journal of Autism and Developmental Disorders*, 49(10), 3461–3473.31201578

Baker, M. B., Yudelson, P. J., & Means, B. (2018). Artificial intelligence in education: A review of the literature. *Educational Researcher*, 47(2), 60–69.

Benus, S. (2014). *Social aspects of entrainment in spoken interaction*. Cognitive Computation.

Bers, M. (2014). *Tinkering: Kids, technology, and power tools*. The MIT Press.

Birk, S., Kremers, S. P. J., & Janssen, I. (2019). The impact of technology on children's physical activity: A systematic review. *International Journal of Environmental Research and Public Health*, 16(12), 1–20.

Boyd, D. M., & Ellison, N. B. (2007). Social network sites: Definition, history, and scholarship. *Journal of Computer-Mediated Communication*, 13(1), 210–230. 10.1111/j.1083-6101.2007.00393.x

Brey, P. (2017). *Robot ethics 2.0: An expanded perspective*. Cambridge University Press.

Brown, J. S., & Valkenburg, P. M. (2012). Parental mediation of children's media use: A meta-analysis. *Communication Research*, 39(3), 318–341.

Brynjolfsson, E., & McAfee, A. (2014). *The second Machine Age: Work, progress, and Prosperity in a time of brilliant technologies*. W. W. Norton & Company.

Buchanan, L., & Beer, D. (2018). Age Invaders: A game to bridge generations. In *Proceedings of the 2018 CHI Conference on Human Factors in Computing Systems* (pp. 1–14). New York, NY, USA: ACM Press.

Buolamwini, J., & Gebru, T. (2018). Gender shades: Intersectional accuracy disparities in commercial gender classification. In *Proceedings of the 2018 ACM Conference Extended Abstracts on Human Factors in Computing Systems (Lecture Notes in Computer Science, Vol. 10791)*. Association for Computing Machinery.

Burke, J. G. (2017). WoeBot: A randomized controlled trial of a conversational AI system for depression. *Journal of Medical Internet Research Mental Health*, 6(1), e24.

Chen, C.-H., & Yeh, Y.-C. (2018). The impact of technology acceptance on students' learning motivation and achievement in a digital learning environment. *Computers & Education*, 122, 160–171.

Chen, Y., Chen, Y., & Chen, Y. (2019). Virtual communities and collaboration: Enhancing social connections through AI-driven platforms. In *Proceedings of the 2019 CHI Conference on Human Factors in Computing Systems* (pp. 1-10). New York, NY, USA: ACM Press.

Chen, Y., Zhang, J., & Zhang, Y. (2019). AI-assisted language learning: A review of the literature. *Language Learning & Technology*, 24(2), 1–24.

Chen, Y.-W., Wang, C.-H., & Chao, C.-H. (2019). A survey on voice assistants. *IEEE Transactions on Affective Information and Social Computing*, 1(1), 1–17.

Choudrie, A., & Kaur, H. (2019). Parental mediation of children's digital media use: A systematic review. *International Journal of Human-Computer Interaction*, 35(1), 1–20.

Chu, Y.-H., & Kim, Y. (2005). The effects of website design and consumer involvement on online shopping behavior. *Journal of Business Research*, 57(5), 571–580.

Clark, L. S. (2021). Parenting in a digital age: Challenges and opportunities. *The Future of Children*, 31(2), 119–140.

Crawford, K., & Ferri, R. (2019). An algorithmic approach to algorithmic accountability. *AI & Society*, 34(1), 145–159.

Croeser, S., & Eckersley, P. (2019, January). Theories of parenting and their application to artificial intelligence. In *Proceedings of the 2019 AAAI/ACM Conference on AI, Ethics, and Society* (pp. 423–428). ACM. 10.1145/3306618.3314231

Deshpande, V., Srivastava, A., & Terveen, L. (2019). *Recommender systems handbook*. MIT Press.

Dimitriadis, Y., Lithari, E., & Koutsabasis, P. (2018). *A systematic literature review of learning analytics research in higher education*. *Computers & education*, 125, 170–185.

Dziadosz, J. (2018). *The potential of AI in education*. Education Dive. https://www.educationdive.com/news/the-potential-of-ai-in-education/536385/

Esteva, A., Kuprel, P., Shiraishi, K., Delange, F., Sabe, A., Li, Z, & Szolovits, P. (2019). Dermatologist-level classification of skin cancer with deep neural networks. *Nature*, 542(5895), 115–118.28117445

Floridi, L. (2013). *The philosophy of information*. Oxford University Press.

Floridi, L. (2014). *The fourth revolution: How the infosphere is reshaping human reality*. Oxford University Press.

Floridi, L., Taddeo, M., & Woods, J. (2018). Responsible AI: An agenda. *AI & Society*, 33(3), 331–344.

Ford, L. (2018). *Artificial intelligence and children's rights: A framework for policy and practice*. UNICEF Office of Research - Innocenti.

Frey, C. B., & Osborne, M. A. (2013). *The future of employment: How susceptible are jobs to computerization?* IZA Discussion Papers.

Gao, Y., Wang, Y., & Tang, X. (2018). *AICAN: An artificial intelligence system for creating art.* arXiv preprint arXiv:1805.06997.

Garcia-Hernandez, J. A., Arroyo-Morales, M. J., & Gomez-Skarmeta, J. F. (2020). Artificial intelligence for assistive technology: A systematic review. *International Journal of Environmental Research and Public Health*, 17(14), 4829.

Gellert, M. J., Chan, K. H., & Selinger, E. M. (2018). Facial recognition technology: A review of ethics, policy, and social implications. *IEEE Security and Privacy*, 16(3), 50–58.

Gervasio, M. A., Riedl, J. C., & Swartout, B. (2019). Interactive storytelling: An introduction. In *Interactive Storytelling: An introduction* (pp. 1–22). Springer.

Glassman, J., Humphreys, K., Yeung, S., Smith, M., Jauregui, A., Milstein, A., & Sanders, L. (2021). Parents' perspectives on using artificial intelligence to reduce technology interference during early childhood: Cross-sectional online survey. *Journal of Medical Internet Research*, 23(3), e19461. 10.2196/1946133720026

Gopinath, V., Hitt, M. A., & Lee, D. (2004). The impact of e-commerce on traditional retailing: A study of the US retail industry. *Journal of Retailing*, 80(3), 315–333.

Gowda, A. A., Su, H. K., Kuo, W. K., & Santoso, H. D. (2022, February). Monitoring and Alerting Panic Situations in Students Using Artificial Intelligence. In *2022 IEEE 5th Eurasian Conference on Educational Innovation (ECEI)* (pp. 35–38). IEEE.

Green, L. (2020). Digital technologies and family life. *International Journal of Child-Computer Interaction, 23*, 100–105.

Holloway, D., & Green, L. (2019). The importance of digital literacy in the digital age. *New Media & Society*, 21(7), 1563–1582.

Huang, Y.-C., Hsieh, Y.-C., & Lin, C.-Y. (2019). The effects of educational technology on students' social skills: A meta-analysis. *Computers & Education*, 139, 103195.

Ito, M., Horst, H., Bittanti, M., Boyd, D., Herr-Stephenson, B., Lange, P., Nardi, B., Pascoe, T., Robinson, L., & Wesch, M. (2010). *Living and learning with new media: Summary of findings from the Digital Youth Project*. MIT Press.

Jensen, M. M., Vaidya, N. P., & Wiggins, C. (2019). Artificial intelligence and information literacy: A review and research agenda. *The Journal of Documentation*, 75(4), 965–992.

Johnson, J. (2021). Enhancing childhood education with AI tools. *Educational Technology Research and Development*, 69(1), 45–63.

Kahrimanis, G., & Dimitriadis, Y. (2019). Digital ageism and the need for inclusive technology: A review and future directions. *International Journal of Human-Computer Interaction*, 35(1), 1–16.

Koufaris, S. (2002). The impact of website design on consumer effect, cognition, and behavior: An empirical investigation. *Journal of Retailing*, 78(2), 177–195.

Krumshteyn, A., Weng, S., & Kautz, J. (2019). MoodScanner: A mobile application for rapid screening of mood disorders. *Journal of Affective Disorders*, 240, 32–38.

Kulkarni, A. (2019). Artificial intelligence in education: A review of current research and future directions. *International Journal of Artificial Intelligence in Education*, 29(1), 1–20.

Kulkarni, A., Kulkarni, S., & Washburn, J. (2017). Adaptive and personalized learning: A survey. *IEEE Transactions on Education*, 60(1), 62–73.

Kulkarni, S., Liu, Y., & Barr, R. (2017). AI in education: A review of the literature. *Computers & Education*, 148, 103927.

Kulkarni, S., Liu, Y., & Barr, R. (2017). The impact of intelligent tutoring systems on student learning: A meta-analysis. *Educational Psychologist*, 52(3), 197–210.

Kumar, V., Kautz, J., & Liu, Z. (2018). News recommendation at scale. *Communications of the ACM*, 61(10), 84–91.

Kuzu, Y., & Kozan, T. (2019). An adaptive learning system using artificial intelligence for personalized learning. *International Journal of Artificial Intelligence in Education*, 29(1), 4–21.

Lau, K. (2018). *Duolingo's AI-powered approach to language learning*. TechCrunch. https://techcrunch.com/2018/05/23/duolingos-ai-powered-approach-to-language-learning/

Lee, J., & Kim, Y. (2021). AI tutors in the home: Parental mediation of AI-assisted learning. *Computers & Education*, 164, 104385.

Lee, S. (2018). Autonomous vehicles: A review of the state-of-the-art and future directions. *IEEE Transactions on Intelligent Transportation Systems*, 20(1), 1–15.

Li, W. (2022). Analysis of piano performance characteristics by deep learning and artificial intelligence and its application in piano teaching. *Frontiers in Psychology, 12*, 751406.

Lin, C.-Y., & Liu, C.-H. (2018). Parental mediation of children's digital media use in Taiwan: A qualitative study. *Computers in Human Behavior*, 81, 262–270.

Linden, D., Stern, L., & Kulikowich, M. (2019). Artificial intelligence and education: A review of the literature. *Educational Research Review*, 26, 100650.

Linden, L., Pactwa, S., & Simard, R. (2019). Duolingo: The freemium language-learning service. *Journal of Digital Media Arts and Practices*, 3(1), 3–16.

Liu, C.-H., Liu, C.-Y., & Hsieh, C.-H. (2016). A survey on chatbots: Technologies, applications, and challenges. *IEEE Transactions on Knowledge and Data Engineering*, 28(10), 2143–2160.

Liu, X., & He, J. (2020). Artificial intelligence in youth mental health: A systematic review. *Journal of Affective Disorders*, 269, 243–252. 10.1016/j.jad.2019.11.099

Liu, Y., Chen, Y., & Barr, R. (2020). AI in education: A review of the literature. *Computers & education*.

Livingstone, S., & Blum-Ross, A. (2020). Digital parenting in a globalized world. *Global Studies of Childhood*, 10(1), 85–99.

Livingstone, S., & Haddon, L. (2009). *Managing online risk: Parenting for a digital future*. Oxford University Press.

Livingstone, S., & Haddon, L. (2009). *Managing online risks for children and young people*. Macmillan Children's Books.

Livingstone, S., & Haddon, L. (2016). Media, risk, and safety in the digital age. In Livingstone, S. (Ed.), *Media, risk, and safety in the digital age* (pp. 1–18). Palgrave Macmillan.

Luckin, R. (2017). Towards artificial intelligence-based assessment systems. *Nature Human Behaviour, 1*(3), 0028.

Manyika, J., Bughin, J., Dobbs, R., Roxburgh, C., & Stirling, A. (2019). *Employment, education, entertainment, and economic growth*. McKinsey Global Institute.

Marco, J. (2019). Artificial Intelligence and Children's Privacy: A Review and Future Directions. *International Journal of Human-Computer Interaction*, 35(1), 1–16.

McReynolds, E. (2017). *Toys that listen: A study of parents, children, and internet-connected*.

McStay, A., & Rosner, G. (2021). Emotional artificial intelligence in children's toys and devices: Ethics, governance and practical remedies. *Big Data & Society*, 8(1), 2053951721994877. 10.1177/2053951721994877

Mohassel, P., & Zhang, L. (2017). Everlasting cookies: Long-term tracking using browser fingerprints. In *Proceedings of the 2017 ACM SIGSAC Conference on Computer and Communications Security* (pp. 1511-1525). ACM.

Murphy, K. (2019). *Carnegie Learning's Mika: AI-powered math instruction*. EdTech Magazine. https://edtechmagazine.com/k12/article/2019/

Nalin, M., Baroni, I., Kruijff-Korbayová, I., Canamero, L., Lewis, M., Beck, A., & Sanna, A. (2012, September). Children's adaptation in multi-session interaction with a humanoid robot. In *2012 IEEE RO-MAN: The 21st IEEE International Symposium on Robot and Human Interactive Communication* (pp. 351-357). IEEE. 10.1109/ROMAN.2012.6343778

National Education Association. (2021). *AI in education: A guide for educators*. National Education Association. https://www.nea.org/advocating-for-change/resources/ai-education-guide-educators

O'Connor, E., & Madge, N. (2019). The impact of AI on health monitoring in family settings. *Health Communication*, 34(12), 1425–1434.

Owens, J. N., Beevers, S. C., & Townsend, M. E. (2019). Woebot: A conversational AI agent for delivering cognitive behavioral therapy. *Journal of Affective Disorders*.

Puspitaningsih, S., Irhadtanto, B., & Puspananda, D. R. (2022). The Role of Artificial Intelligence in Children's Education for A Digital Future. *KnE Social Sciences*, 642-647.

PwC. (2018). Artificial intelligence: The economic impact. *PwC's Global Artificial Intelligence Study*. PwC.

Rainie, L., & Wellman, B. (2012). *Networked*. MIT Press. 10.7551/mitpress/8358.001.0001

Resnick, M., Maloney, K., Eastwood, T., Rusk, R., Rosenbaum, S., Dahl, P., & Silverman, B. (2009). Scratch: Programming for all. *Communications of the ACM*, 52(8), 78–85.

Ricci, M., Masthoff, J., & Cunningham, P. (2015). Personalized recommendations for music playlists. *ACM Computing Surveys*, 48(3), 1–32.

Riva, G., Chrysanthou, A., & Coulson, C. (2020). The role of virtual reality in social interaction and communication. In *Proceedings of the 2020 CHI Conference on Human Factors in Computing Systems* (pp. 1-14). New York, NY, USA: ACM Press.

Rosen, L. D. (2013). Media use in early childhood: What we know and do not know. *Pediatrics*, 132(5), e1259–e1269.

Roslan, S., Arsyad, M., Hos, J., Supiyah, R., Anggraini, D., & Ridwan, H. (2023, May 17). Pelatihan Pendampingan Orangtua terhadap Kecerdasan Anak di Era Modernisasi di Desa Wawatu Kecamatan Moramo Utara Kabupaten Konawe Selatan. *Indonesian Journal of Community Services.*, 2(1), 35–44. 10.47540/ijcs.v2i1.837

Saçan, S., Yarali, K. T., & Kavruk, S. Z. (2022). Investigation of Metaphorical Perceptions of Children on the Concept of "Artificial Intelligence. *Mehmet Akif Ersoy Üniversitesi Eğitim Fakültesi Dergisi*, (64), 274–296.

Selwyn, N. (2018). The digital child's dilemma: Navigating the uncertainties of childhood in the age of algorithms. *British Journal of Sociology of Education*, 39(4), 531–544.

Sittig, D. B., & Singh, H. (2017). Health care provider use of social media and mobile health technologies: A cross-sectional survey. *JAMA Internal Medicine*, 177(12), 1790–1792.29059277

Smith, J. (2019). AI and parenting: Opportunities and challenges. *Journal of Child and Family Studies*, 28(2), 327–338.

Smith, J. (2021). *Our journey with AI-enhanced home-schooling: Lessons learned and strategies for success.* HomeSchooling. https://www.homeschooling.com/ai-enhanced-homeschooling-lessons-learned-strategies-success/

Solove, D. (2011). Conceptualizing privacy. *University of Pennsylvania Law Review*, 160(2), 477–565.

Subrahmanyam, K., Gross, J., & Weisleder, J. (2018). Parental mediation of children's digital media use: A systematic review. *International Journal of Human-Computer Interaction*, 35(1), 1–20.

Topol, E. J. (2019). *Deep medicine: How artificial intelligence can transform healthcare*. Basic Books.

Twenge, J., & Campbell, W. K. (2018). *Associations between screen time and lower psychological well-being among children and adolescents*. Preventive Medicine Reports.

Vaidya, N. P., Jensen, M. M., & Wiggins, C. (2019). Artificial intelligence and information literacy: A review and research agenda. *The Journal of Documentation*, 75(4), 965–992.

Valkenburg, P. M., Schouten, B. M., & Peter, J. (2015). Parental mediation of children's media use: A review of the literature. *International Journal of Communication*, 9, 1682–1698.

Vosoughi, S., Roy, D., & Aral, S. (2018). The spread of true and false news online. *Science*, 359(6380), 1146–1151. 10.1126/science.aap955929590045

Wood, S., & Scott, J. (2015). Parental mediation of children's media use: A review of the literature. *International Journal of Communication, 9*, 1682–1698.

World Economic Forum. (2018). *The future of jobs report 2018*. World Economic Forum.

Zhang, X., Zhang, J., & Zhang, Y. (2020). AI-assisted language learning: A review of the literature. *Language Learning & Technology*, 24(2), 1–24.

# Chapter 4
# Screentime and Identity Formation as a Digital Dilemma:
## Identity in the Screen Age

**Ruqia Safdar Bajwa**
https://orcid.org/0000-0002-4460-2025
*Bahauddin Zakariya University, Pakistan*

**Asma Yunus**
*University of Sargodha, Pakistan*

## ABSTRACT

*This chapter explores the relationship between screen time and identity formation, specifically for adolescents and young individuals. It discusses how digital media can benefit and challenge personal expression and social connectivity. The chapter examines the dynamic interplay between screen time and identity development, highlighting the potential risks related to cyberbullying, privacy concerns, and mental health issues. It emphasizes the important role of educators and parents in guiding youth through their digital engagement and advocates for a balanced approach to digital consumption that fosters positive digital citizenship and well-being. The chapter also explores the impact of emerging technologies, such as virtual and augmented reality, artificial intelligence, and personalization algorithms, on the evolving concept of digital identity.*

## BACKGROUND

In the contemporary era of technology, the omnipresence of screens and digital devices has revolutionised human interaction with the world. The integration of screens into daily life, from smartphones to laptops and social media platforms, has given birth to a phenomenon known as 'screen time.' This term refers to individuals' time engaging with screens for various purposes, including communication, entertainment, work, and education. While digital technology offers numerous advantages and conveniences, it has also sparked concerns about its impact on various aspects of human life. Among these, identity

DOI: 10.4018/979-8-3693-3350-1.ch004

formation stands out as a topic of significant contemporary relevance, underscoring the importance of our research in this area (Dienlin & Johannes, 2020).

Identity formation is not a simple process but rather a complex and multifaceted psychological journey that begins in infancy and continues throughout life. It involves developing a clear and strong understanding of self, incorporating elements such as self-concept, self-esteem, values, beliefs, and personal identity. This process is influenced by many internal and external factors, including social interactions, cultural norms, and personal experiences, making it a topic of profound psychological interest (Pfeifer & Berkman, 2018).

The digital dilemma becomes starkly evident when we consider the potentially detrimental effects of excessive screen time on this crucial process of identity formation. Young individuals, particularly adolescents and emerging adults, are heavy users of digital technology, dedicating a significant portion of their waking hours to screen engagement. This continuous exposure to screens, especially through social media platforms, can profoundly alter how individuals perceive themselves and their role in the world, raising serious concerns about the impact of digital technology on identity formation (Muppalla et al., 2023).

## CONTEXTUALISING IDENTITY IN THE DIGITAL AGE

The extensive development and application of digital technology has now deeply affected how identity gets developed and articulated in the digital era. In addition, Sandrasegaran and Huang (2009) suggest transitioning from traditional face-to-face dealings to virtual ones and make a big deal of digital identity in securing identifiable contact within digital networks. Moreover, Kashchey (2021) carries out an analysis of how the hyper-informationization affects both individual identity and society, arguing that the expansion of digital and online spaces provides an opportunity for the voluntary creation of new "we-identities." Nam (2021), insisting digital culture has had a big impact on adolescent identity and that digital media largely form the "inner identity" of the younger generation, also makes this point in her work. Furthermore, Baltezarevic (2023) explores authenticity and representation in the age of artificial intelligence. He touches on AI's difficulties in faithfully translating an identity onto the Internet. Windley (2005) argues new digital identities also raise serious problems of privacy and data security. He maintains we should establish identity management structures that adequately balance the benefits of digitalisation against the demands for secure storage. Taken as a whole, these pieces reveal how contemporary life challenges people to elaborate their identities in the digital age. New technological developments have reshaped not only conceptions of community but also one's self.

## THEORETICAL BACKGROUND

Traditional theories of identity formation provide a comprehensive framework for understanding how individuals develop their sense of self. Here is a brief overview of noteworthy theories of identity formation:

## Erikson's Psychosocial Theory of Identity Formation

According to Erikson's psychosocial theory, each individual goes through eight developmental stages, each marked by its central crisis. The "identity vs. role confusion" stage, the fifth stage of adolescence, is paramount for successful identity formation. For instance, teenagers may try on various hobbies, ideologies, and social circles to construct an integrated sense of self. A coherent identity fosters a sense of security and enables the person to make well-founded decisions: about a desired job, their values, etc. Failure to overcome this crisis will likely create role confusion (Erikson, 1950).

## Marcia's Identity Status Theory

Marcia expanded on Erikson's theory and identified four statuses of identity formation: identity achievement, moratorium, foreclosure, and identity diffusion. The identity achievement is that an undergraduate student decides what major to pursue in college after sampling different disciplines. In turn, the foreclosure is that a high school student decides to become a doctor because both his parents are doctors and urge him to follow in their footsteps. The identity achievement framework reveals identity formation dynamics and stresses exploration and commitment (Marcia, 1966).

## Social Identity Theory (SIT)

Social Identity Theory explains that membership in groups and organizations affects people's self-concepts of their social identity, how they perceive group members, and their relations among others. For instance, the membership to play in a game can affect individual self-esteem, which also informs the role one plays through behaviour, such as home games reducing attendance, yet away games are high, or wearing team colours. Identification with groups of people's behaviours or cultural and belonging values all describe social identity and exerts an attitude and advise behaviour toward attitude toward in-group members (Tajfel & Turner, 1979).

## Self-Categorization Theory (SCT)

Self-Categorization Theory (SCT), an extension of SIT, provides insight into the cognitive mechanisms through which group membership and behaviour are achieved. Given the tenets of SCT, an applicable example would be the workplace, where employees strive to behave and act following the ideal corporate worker's prototype, or role expectations. This shared experience among members fosters an individual's social identity congruent with the firm's values and ethics, co-opting primary values and perceptions in the group scenarios (Turner, 1985).

Combining insights from both individual and social perspectives, these traditional theories of identity formation offer a nuanced understanding of the complex interplay between personal exploration, commitment, and social categorisation in identity development.

## Identity Formation vs. Identity Crisis: The Perspective of Adolescents

Establishing one's identity is a pivotal aspect of transitioning from adolescence to adulthood, as highlighted by Erik Erikson's well-known concept of the "identity vs. role confusion" stage. In this stage, adolescents face the challenge of developing a personal identity that combines different roles, beliefs, and aspirations into a cohesive sense of self. Addressing this issue allows for developing a secure sense of self, while neglecting it can lead to uncertainty or turmoil in one's identity.

Adolescents actively explore different roles, beliefs, and values, which is influenced by and affects their social relationships. In this context, Craig-Bray et al. (1988) stress the intricate relationship between identity formation and intimacy: successfully developing an identity can lead to more profound, mature relationships. Adolescents face many challenges as they negotiate between such societal expectations, family dynamics, and the process of finding out who they are themselves. Klimstra (2013) highlights that personality development during adolescence is flexible, relevant to such things as the transformation of important personality traits or layers of identity.

While identity formation is a typical part of development, it can sometimes cause crises for adolescents who cannot commit to a particular identity. Becht et al., (2016) found in their survey that teenagers forming their identities deviated significantly daily. They found that some people experienced a kind of "crisis-like" process. They watched their commitments falter and shifts in decisions had to be made by them. Nair et al., (2015) examine the problems caused by abusive experiences in childhood, deficient social support, and inappropriate support from parents, or these factors can exacerbate the crisis by causing panic and confusion.

Adolescents' tales about identity formation or crisis manifest diverse experiences shaped by individual, family and societal forces. While some people may find this period relatively simple, others are encountering challenges. It is a matter of intellectual support to gain insight into adolescents' complex experiences; how can treatment at this pivotal time be both humane and effective? Various factors stand in the way for young adults at the point of defining who they are amidst the challenge The stage of "identity vs. role confusion": Adolescents' identity formation is heavily influenced by digitization and contemporary media. On the one hand, new media platforms offer opportunities to explore; on the other hand, they present certain challenges including social comparison, cyberbullying and maintaining an image of oneself online consistent with what one wishes others will believe. The digital encroachment makes for a more complicated process of how one's identity gets builded--adolescents now have to juggle between identities in the online world and real life (Klimstra, 2013).

Adolescents face challenges in finding their identity as society evolves and cultural norms and values change. These changes can make it difficult for them to find stable role models (Becht et al., 2016). Changes in family structures, dynamics, and parenting styles can also influence identity formation. There could be distinct challenges adolescents of different family backgrounds may face when developing their identity. To illustrate, let us examine the significance of parental support and autonomy for the development of an adolescent's positive identity exploration and commitment. If, however, such support is not received, adolescents struggle to form their identity (Beyers & Goossens, 2008).

Adolescents face a significant challenge when making early educational and career choices. When not yet exploring their interests and talents sufficiently, decisions like this inevitably seem overwhelming. It is pressures on adolescents that may lead either prematurely to inking in identity commitments or, on the other hand, long periods of moratorium when they muddle between decisions (Abbasi, 2016).

For adolescents, the pursuit of identity is closely linked to their general psychosocial well-being. Problems forming an identity can lead to a variety of adjustment problems, such as anxiety and depression, in addition to behavioural difficulties. The connection between identity formation and psychosocial adjustment underscores the importance of supporting adolescents during this crucial stage of life development (Crocetti et al., 2013).

Cultural and social expectations about roles, behaviours and values can pose challenges to adolescents in constructing their identities. How to develop a unique, self-identified identity yet conform to what society expects of youth is a difficult task for them. This is especially true among people from marginal or minority backgrounds who have to navigate several different cultural identities (Schwartz & Petrova, 2018).

## DIGITAL IDENTITY: A NEW PARADIGM

In the era of technology, There is a paradigm shift from the traditional understanding of identity formation, as outlined by Erikson and subsequent theorists, into a digital realm where the processes of exploration, commitment, and identity crisis are influenced by digital interactions, online communities, and the vast repository of information available online. The "Digital Identity: A New Paradigm" represents a significant evolution in how identities are formed, challenged, and expressed in the digital era.

### Connecting Traditional and Digital Identity Formation

Traditional theories emphasise the importance of exploration and commitment in forming a stable sense of identity, with resolving identity crises being pivotal for healthy development (Erikson, 1950; Marcia, 1966). Still, just as the coming of digital technologies adds another layer to this process, so does it provide opportunities and difficulties in identity formation. An increasing variety of electronic goods can be found on almost every street from cameras to computers - but all these devices come with their problems. Individuals who are prepared to try things out find themselves in the equivalent of a new natural setting, where they must make decisions about what areas of their personality will be exhibited across different platforms, and which will not (Klimstra, 2013; Becht et al., 2016). ut it also poses risks of confusion and crisis over identity, a risk heightened by online behaviour's visibility and permanence (Nair et al. 2015).

### The Evolution of Identity in the Digital Era

The evolution of identity in the digital era, particularly for adolescents, is a subject of significant scholarly interest. What scholars are emphasizing is the way digital technology and social media platforms have an impact on the developmental process of identity formation. These comprise differences in brain development, sociability, and how digital media shapes the inner feeling of self. Giedd (2012) has explored that the adolescent brain is leading the digital revolution, pointing at their ability to learn new technologies fast and an interest in novelty. This is revolutionized under the underpinning of neurobiology designed for adaptation, signaling that the development of the adolescent brain is under the influence of digital interactions, going as far as to refer to their possible long-term effects on health and social development.

Digital culture looks like it controls a very deep influence over identity formation. For instance, youth receive very deep influence from digital culture. Nam (2021) suggests that adolescence is marked by a deep influence of the networked society and digital social media in building "inner identity. It is a moment when one explores himself in digital "hives" and needs supporting structures that would encourage the person to be responsible for his or her engagement in and with the digital media. Davis (2013) finds combined effects for social media and interpersonal relations on identity clarity, where mother and friend relations were positively related to self-concept clarity. Digital media use, in particular, the expression and exploration of an online identity, may have dual effects on self-concept through the mediation of friendship quality. In another study, Shifflet-Chila et al., (2016) considered how autonomy and identity develop during adolescence within the digital ecosystem.

Researchers used qualitative interviews that bring out how digital technologies are integrated into the lives of the adolescents, which influences the pursuance of autonomy and exploration of identity. This integration takes place in a dynamic environment that nowadays comprises cyberspace as an important context in development. "Mental Health in the Digital Age: The Consequences of Using Digital Technologies on Adolescent Depression and Anxiety" summarizes the findings of Odgers and Jensen (2020), who delved into the consequences of using digital technologies on the mental health of adolescents.

Base on the research that has been observed over the years, they find that the relationship of digital technology use with well-being is more complicated, although most research on this topic indicate small but conflict-ridden associations. They strongly recommend furthering and supporting the development of more adequate research methods in order to make more sense of such links and to help adolescent mental health within this field. Policy implications and supportive strategies: Clarke (2009) and Magis-Weinberg et al., 2021, believe there are some policy implications which are needed to be accepted in regard to the embeddedness of digital technologies in adolescent life.

Policies should support developing digital literacy, developing a good, safe online environment for peer and family relationship building, and positive identity development in support of mental health. This makes the opportunities and new challenges offered in the development of identity in the digital age paramount and far-reaching for the population of adolescents developing within these landscapes, with educators, parents, and policymakers at national, regional, and local levels guiding and supporting the steps of the developing adolescent toward favorable outcomes in identity development and mental health.

## Characteristics of Digital Identity

However, the diversity and flexibility of digital identity allow a lot of space for open exploration and allude to challenges in keeping a uniform sense of self (Craig-Bray et al., 1988). Interactivity and visibility further empower the feedback mechanisms available for either identity reinforcement or reconsideration—both of which coming to greater visibility in the face of the digitized peer networks (Becht et al., 2016). Digital platform authenticities are, however, questionable but ensure levels of privacy and anonymity (Nair et al. 2015). This digital connectivity of today exposes teenagers to even more diverse points of view. It may be enriching, but it does introduce a new series of cultural dimensions that make identity development even more complex (Klimstra, 2013). The importance of personalization and the algorithmic influence in determining digital experiences seems to bring attention to the nature of curation for the digitized process that may serve to delimit exposure to multi-farious perspectives (Klimstra, 2013;

Becht et al., 2016). According to "Digital Identity: A New Paradigm," a good, informed understanding involves melding the two theories: the traditional one and those that bring life to the digital world and show how they can impact young people. It is this interplay of ideas that foreground how identity develops and helps in understanding—offering rich insights for interventions that can support an adolescent in the construction of self in the digital age.

## The Impact of Global Connectivity on Local Identities

In today's interconnected world, a crucial aspect to consider is how digital identity and connectivity have become globalized. Numerous studies have explored the impact of global connectivity on local identities among adolescents and young people, highlighting the complexity and multifaceted nature of this issue. These studies highlight the intricate dynamics between global and local identities, showcasing how they intertwine and shape each other, particularly in the era of heightened digital media consumption.

For example, Zhang and Khare (2009) demonstrate in their research that in the condition of a very strong global identity, local products were preferred over global ones, while in the condition of a strong local identity, people still showed more preferences for local products. Clearly, this does give way to the impact of the prominence of a global versus local identity upon the tastes and behavior of the adolescents, which unfold to even become a manner in which they make their digital consumption. To ascertain that in which global connectivity did affect an individual social identity, this was the attempt in research done by Grimalda et al., (2018). They found that it was increased engagement with the global networks that enhances the strength of global social identity and, as a result, the conditions under which youths in highly connected environments are more likely to cooperate at the global level. This could be taken to suggest the more cosmopolitan tendencies of identity. Rosenmann et al., (2016) sought to find psychological ramifications that globalization had on both identity and culture, noting the tension that comes between both the intended strong global and local identities, expected to be developed in the face of global challenges and possibilities. They argue that the attitudes of the young towards global social orders and collective action are framed by either the inclusive or exclusive identities that can be developed in globalization. The neolocalism trend in the United States, taken forward in relation to the forces of globalization and corporatization, was taken up by Schnell (2013) in a study. It would be the focus of local identity and connections summed up as a reply against homogenization by globalization, revealing that local identities are actively being nurtured and are much relevant in the political, social, and economic spheres.

Impact of the Digital Media on Identity Formation: Granic et al., (2020), in a nutshell, lay a more qualified view on the impact digital media have on the adolescent formation of identity. They really do push us beyond those measures of screen time, get us to explore many of the other digital experiences and how those come into play with identity formation. The increased complexity added by digital media in shaping aspects of both the global and local identities of young people is very evident in this reflection.

According to a study done by Grimalda et al. (2016), it has been disclosed that globalization has an impact on cooperation and identity. They point out that social identity in connection with the world is instrumental in mediating individual connectivity's link to worldwide cooperation in their study. This suggests that greater global engagement can cultivate a sense of identity beyond local affiliations.

Both studies illustrate how adolescents and young people negotiate between global connectedness and their local sense of self. Today's digital world, particularly with the very many connected gadgets, has turned the world into one big global village. Young people nowadays have the possibility to develop their identity in a global context, shaped by local features. The process of negotiation reflects exactly how these present dynamics of globalization and localism comprise a continued give-and-take amid the global and local worlds in the generation of identity.

## Evolution of Screentime in the Digital Age

The increase in screen time is a multidimensional challenge of the digital epoch, causing formidable interest not only from researchers but also from professionals of various areas. Today, "screen time" can include computers, tablets, smartphones, and other gadgets connected to the internet. This has broader consequences on cognitive, social, and physical development in children and adolescents. According to Granic, Morita, and Scholten, this would indicate the need for more evidence-based guidelines, rather than the simple measurement of screen time, in order to understand more fully the functioning effects of the exposure to digital media on adolescent development. They purport a complex model looking at divergent digital experiences and their impact on mental health outcomes, comparing adaptive versus maladaptive digital literacy. The research for health implications with respect to screen time has shifted focus from television to a more general assessment of many of the forms of digital media. A synthesis of evidence on the consequences of screen usage will be published in the Archives of Disease in Childhood (2019). This included its links with increased risks of obesity, poor eating habits, deterioration in mental health, and sleep quality. Findings show some complex effects of influence in screen time and suggest the effects of screen time on health outcomes are not uniform for all forms of screen time. Squire and Steinkuehler (2017) caution learning technologies should not be approached in ways that view "screen time" as a monolithic intervention with direct effects on quantifiable learning outcomes. They suggest a even more complicated model of how the different types of technology and content combine with personal and environmental variables in order to bear upon development. Hand and Giacobbi (2020) concurred in saying that little research has been done in investigating the level of scientific knowledge meager link between advancement and its implication for human health, while at some point tending to be contradictory. They observe that the understanding of the effect demanded an appraisal of characteristics and the content of the screen. Konca (2021) explores children's digital contexts within the home and realizes that children live in a context that is rich in digitality, while regulation or co-consumption is done by the parent most of the time. The areas pointed out for this study were family income and parental screen time, which are the influencers of the determinant of children's screen time and thus throw light on the importance of children's familial context in their digital environment. The emerging research base speaks to a shift away from the conceptualization of screen time as a single, quantifiable component toward realization of the many, complex manners through which digital media intersect with developmental processes. This context gives rise to an ever-pressing need for multisided, contextually framed consideration of understanding and ways of dealing with the consequences of screen time for child and adolescent development.

## Trends and Statistics in Digital Consumption Among Adolescents

For the last two decades, the digital environment has significantly changed. This is in relation to the amount of digital media consumption by adolescents. Over this period, the growth in digital media consumption has taken a trajectory upwards, which has great effects on the cognitive, social, and physical development of adolescents. Twenge et al., (2019) reported an explosive growth of digital media use among teenagers, from 1976 to 2016, displacing conventional legacy media (television, print) with new digital formats (social media, online texting). By 2016, the average 12th-grade student was spending more than six hours a day on digital media, with falling reading of books or magazines and watching TV. This transition really underscores how quickly preferences for digital over legacy media are growing among the young. Villanti et al., (2017) noted this through the near universality in the access to smartphones and medium use that was high among the young adults. Their study said that 90% of US young adults with internet access used social media, thus 2016 exposed mobile devices and social network at the center of US and international young lives. According to Montgomery (2000), the duality trends of an aging population and increasing uptake in ICT are emphatically focused on how youth are fast embracing new technologies. "These trends, in turn, have given rise to concerns that such constant connectivity is wreaking on America's adolescent mental health, in fact, it has propelled a wave of research on the effects of their usage of digital technology. Odgers and Jensen (2020) collected diverse papers to synthesize evidence regarding the relationship of use of digital technology with depression and anxiety among adolescents in detail. Their review is likely consistent with the jumble of small positive, negative, and null associations of the field that would be necessary to explain the complex, if not contradictory, findings of their meta-analysis. It is quite obvious that Repetskaya (2021) explicitly reveals what kind of "digital turn" has impacted modern fashions and practices of consumption among young people. The author points out that digital fashion media, such as blogs, have already replaced the role of traditional fashion magazines and experts. This trend is in line with more general tendencies in youth-oriented consumption behaviors. Thulin and Vilhelmson (2019) explore use by young people in social digital media for socio-spatial and temporal integration into everyday lives. Heavy digital media users would therefore be more likely to spend long hours at home, where they engaged in independent activities and traveled less. This clearly showed that major changes in the socio-spatial organization of young people's lives emanated from the use of digital media. These lines of research together outline a shifting digital consumption environment for young people, including the shift towards digital media, the centrality of mobile devices and social networks in their lives, and the multifaceted results of the precession in regards to youth development and well-being.

## Screentime's Role in Identity Formation

Research has been dedicated to examining screen time's impact on identity development in adolescents and young people. It sheds light on both the advantages and difficulties of engaging in digital media. A nuanced understanding of digital media's role in contemporary adolescence is crucial, considering the complex relationship between screen time and various aspects of youth development, such as mental health and social outcomes.

This was clearly shown in the study of Stiglic and Viner (2019), who found that the increase of screen time in children and young people is related to several negative health effects; this may be the increase of prevalence of obesity and unhealthy eating behaviors, depressive symptomatology, and reduced quality of life. The effect of a lot of time on screen suggests that there is an influence on the physical and mental component of health among adolescents. According to Villanti et al., (2017), use of social media among adolescents has developed into digital self-identities. The other social identity of youth is digital identities that have caused worry about different challenges, for example, psychological, physical, and behavioral consequences they pose. This is supported in equal measure by Paulich et al., (2021), who purport that more time on screens was only moderately associated with adverse effects on mental health, behavior, academic performance, and sleep. It is, though, also associated with better quality in peer relations, which indicates that the impact of screen time on the development of the adolescent is complex.

Paulich et al., (2021) looked at whether this connection exists with time and more serious depressive symptom exposure among youth who use the computer solely for playing video games. This may be interpreted to mean that there is a greater threat of mental health among adolescents posed by some types of screen engagement than others. Likewise, Marciano et al. (2021) found that regular and prolonged use of screen-based media was associated with an inefficient cognitive control system among adolescents. More research is warranted to understand the causation of the factors associated with these relationships.

In fact, on this last finding, Richards et al. (2010) observe that the relationship between screen time and attachment to parents and peers comes out negatively significant: attachment scores decrease with increased screen time. Digital media use may have consequences on relationships and sociability of the adolescent. In fact, during the COVID-19 pandemic, Nagata et al. (2021) found an increase in screen time among US adolescents and warned that its level may influence, among others, the mental health and social interactions of youth due to its leading role played by digital media.

The subject of identity development due to the influence of screen time is an interesting yet complex subject to study. A number of studies and research findings have analyzed the relation between screen time and the development of identity. The importance of this link is something that has been developing in its eyes. The importance of developing a deeper understanding of this link has been highlighted by Granic et al., (2020), Manago (2015). In this way, the approach by Granic and colleagues is much more informative, as they outline the role of digital media with relevance to building teen identity. Importantly, these point toward an understanding of identity development, to more appropriately pinpoint those digital experiences that foster the positive or negative mental health consequences. Manago (2015) emphasizes that social media provides an array of opportunities, while at the same time creating challenges for the given process. In this respect, the emergence of social media accords much freedom to contemporary youth in what concerns the way in which they construct social relations and forms of self-expression. Studies in the relationship of screen time and identity formation have therefore revealed a much more nuanced picture. It is at this point that the need for the creation of virtual communities to discuss an impact on online engagement in the building of one's identity became imperative. Annese (2004), Abreu et al. (2019), describe electronic media influence on the formation of identity. Annese is focused on the self-identity buildup through the medium of television, while Abreu et al. critically argue that it is the co-productive processes of technology on the youth's identity. Lichtwarck-Aschoff et al. (2008) had an evaluation done on several views and considerations, which they presented to the relationship that exists between time, screen times, and identities. Where Lichtwarck-Aschoff adopts a theoretical perspective, Turner takes a cultural perspective. Luyckx's (2010) and Cunningham's (2017) research into a relationship of different factors offer. From Luyckx's research, identity development relates to the perspective of time to the self. On the other hand, the actual impact in the use of the second screen in the identification of both the users' teams and self-efficacy has been addressed by the study of Cunningham.

In their study, Saura et al. (2019) delve deeper into the impact of digital media on the formation of computer-generated societies and the dynamics of identification within these interactive civilizations. This theoretical framework highlights the concept of neo-tribalism, or tribalism, as a driving force behind the formation of social systems in the modern digital world. It emphasizes the formation of virtual communities or tribes through various means such as mobility, specific social events, and dispersion, regardless of the purpose or interest of the interaction. Given its ability to reveal deeper significance beyond surface-level observations, the imagination plays a crucial role in our everyday lives. Based on the analysis, communication phenomena played a significant role in establishing social connections in the online realm. This bond is formed within a postmodern framework, which sets it apart from traditional norms and fosters a greater sense of inclusivity. Postmodernity is marked by a seamless blending of individuals into various social circles based on shared interests and close relationships. This is driven by a sense of identification rather than rigidly defined roles, which was more prevalent in the past. Davis and Weinstein (2017) explore the impact of networks on the identity development of young adults from a developmental perspective. The researchers utilized psychologist Erik Erikson's theoretical framework, which depicted identity development as a process of exploration that ultimately results in a sense of unity and consistency on a personal level (McAdams & Zapata-Gietl, 2015). The writers delve into the potential impact of this theory, formulated during the mid-20th century, on the digital era. These studies highlight the importance of understanding the impact of screen time and digital media on the development of one's identity.

Hardey (2002) explored establishing and negotiating identities in both online and offline contexts within internet environments that facilitate online connections and offline interactions. An analysis was conducted on users' experiences with online dating services, which are designed for individuals seeking to meet new people to form meaningful connections. Suggesting that investigations should be considered in the context of late modernity's personalized sociability, it was proposed that users' social, physical, and cultural experiences could shape virtual interactions. It has been shown that instead of inventing fake personas, the anonymity of the internet fosters the formation of genuine connections and trust in the real world. Ultimately, the connectivity between paragraphs highlights how user experiences can be shaped by various factors, including social, physical, and cultural influences intertwined with virtual interactions. In addition, there is a growing belief that digital technology plays a role in shaping children's perception of their daily experiences (Varsori & Pereira, 2019).

The literature highlights the significance of social media platforms in providing individuals with a platform to shape their online identities. As per Toma, Hancock, and Ellison (2008), users often curate and display specific aspects of their lives, creating a digital identity that may not necessarily reflect their true selves. How we present ourselves online can significantly impact how we perceive ourselves and our self-image. Adolescents are particularly susceptible to societal judgment on social media, which can trigger feelings of inadequacy or envy when they compare themselves to others (Vogel et al., 2015). These comparisons can influence the development of self-identity. The internet allows individuals to connect with like-minded communities and explore different facets of their identity, such as gender and sexual orientation (Fox & Ralston, 2016). These digital communities can positively impact the development of one's identity. Studies have also indicated that limiting time spent on screens or adopting strategies for a "digital detox" can have positive effects on mental health, such as boosting self-esteem and promoting a stronger sense of identity (Twenge, 2017). These findings emphasize the complex connection between screen time and identity development. It's important to note that the impact differs from person to person and is influenced by age, personality, and how screens are used.

These studies highlight the significance of comprehending the various effects of screen time on adolescents' identity formation, mental well-being, and social connections. Based on the evidence, digital media seems to offer both valuable opportunities for exploration and connection and significant challenges that need to be carefully navigated to support healthy adolescent development.

Ultimately, the convergence of the screening period and identity formation in the digital era poses a complex and ever-changing obstacle. There is a clear influence on individuals' self-perception and identity construction due to the widespread use of screens, especially on social media platforms and digital communities. This digital dilemma presents both potential advantages and concerns that require thoughtful examination. To gain a deeper understanding of the impact of screen time on identity development, society must continue researching and exploring the implications of the digital age. This will enable individuals to effectively navigate the challenges posed by the digital dilemma.

## Addressing the Digital Dilemma

The digital age has exposed young teenagers and people to new ways of exploring, presenting, and demonstrating in actuality who they are. As discussed earlier, Nam (2021) explores and ascertains the great impacts that digital culture has brought into the process of identity construction within the younger generation. She really explains that it is through the very critical developmental periods that the designs of the social media and apps bear on the development of a 'inner identity,' allowing for people to express and connect with others. At the same time, they pose some challenge in the identification of strategies towards locating solitude and resource management for identity development, bringing out the challenge in locating strategies towards locating solitude and resource management for identity development.

Digital media and their integration with the developmental tasks of young people bring with them a number of opportunities and some risks. Davis's (2013) research was on the beneficial effect of digital media on the identity and social relations of adolescents. This highlights the role of interpersonal relationships as an intervening effect of the influence of digital media and self-concept clarity in the individual. It points out that many of the risks are, in fact, those dangers of spending too much time online, such as becoming a target for cyberbullying or unwanted approaches and advises on how to strike a healthy balance.

The overall effect of digital media on the adolescent shows quite an equivocal trade-off. On one end, it is through the social networks that relationships with peers may get a fill-up and pave the way for developing a sense of identity, while on the other, they pose the worst effect on mental health and overall well-being. Paulich et al. (2021) noted that meaningful relationships of screen time to a cluster of psychological and behavioral complications were linked.

Basically, proper attention to the adverse effects of digital media should first be paid to the clear awareness of the intricate relationship that exists between digital engagement and adolescent development. One possible way to do that may be promoting digital literacy and critical thinking via the engagement with digital content (Subrahmanyam and Šmahel, 2011). These really demand a multi-faceted approach: of education, guidance for parents, and policy interventions.

The panorama of digital identity formation is dynamic, and as such, its exploration requires further research addressing unresolved questions and embracing emergent technologies. Lehtimaki et al., (2020) bring out an important aspect of exploring further the digital mental health interventions. They outline how the digital technologies in the contemporary global village can help in the youth adolescent mental health.

For example, Patchin and Hinduja (2017) point to some of the less favorable tendencies about exploring one's digital identity with the help of digital technology and formation of identity. The results point to the strong need for efficient interventions in adolescents who may be more vulnerable.

It is, therefore, a critical role in helping to establish a positive online environment for teenagers that involves different stakeholders: parents, educators, and policymakers.

With that in mind, adult guidance within digital spaces remains very crucial in assisting people to peruse these terrains appropriately (Clarke, 2009). Clarke augments the suggestion for policies on engaging with digital space in safe and constructive ways during adolescence when most identity work is underway.

In the light of the digital age, in the coming of age of teenagers, a digital identity needs to be developed as a holistic approach to the consideration of the complexities involved with online activity. Educators, policy enforcement bodies, and parents need to work together to lay out environments where positive digital experiences are encouraged and potential risks associated with the engagement of people with digital media can be controlled. Digital media in the process of identity formation of adolescents can be a two-edged sword. On one side, it provides these youths with great possibilities for experimentation and expression. On the other hand, it also offers them basic challenges.

This is a need that requires encouragement in digital literacy, fostering of strong relations, and putting in place policies that work. This calls for a collaborative effort of all the stakeholders involved in such a scenario. Being keen on digital citizenship, improvement can be instigated by encouraging the responsible use of digital devices among adolescents.

The concept of digital literacy embedded in the education system may also help students read meaning into the experiences they go through in the online world. Policy should also be designed to protect and empower our young digital citizens. Educators and parents need to work together to help teenagers through the complexities of developing digital identities.

Growing integration of digital contexts in young people's social lives calls for recognition of the role that key figures can perform in favoring a positive development in the building up of digital identity. Amongst the youth, there has been a great requirement for educational programs that will improve digital literacy, hence enabling the user to travel online spaces responsibly. According to Reid and Boyer (2013), social networking sites are among the main forms of tools used in instruction. However, they recommend the use of such platforms as Facebook to help in promoting the practice of ethics in cyberspace while at the same time nurturing children and the youth in becoming good digital citizens.

These programs may serve a useful purpose for young people in acquiring skills that would further assist in analyzing the digital content and enable them to realize what the consequences of activities online are. Ribble (2009) further lays emphasis on parents' struggle to keep pace with the new technologies, while pointing out the importance of leading children to embrace the benefits of a technologically developed society with equal zeal for safety.

For this, the involvement of the parents of the relevant is highly suggested in an active manner in their children's digital world, opening conversations with them in terms of online activities and putting limits that manage screen times. This, in plain language, goes to imply the safe digital spaces agenda is to be a shared responsibility between educators and parents in creating the environments for adolescents within which they can freely and comfortably explore without worrying about falling victim to cyberbullying, inappropriate content, and other threats of the like, and move toward positive construction of the building of their respective identities.

Golubeva (2020), in her study, underlines motivation, education, and sport as some of the influencers of a person's digital identity. She outlines that in either of the named spheres, the supporting environment is one of the determinative factors of a positive and fruitful relationship with digital media. It is among the mechanisms to safeguard the potential risk of adolescents' participation in the digital world through developing, implementing, and enforcing policies and practices regarding online security.

Bozkurt and Tu (2016) explore deeper into issues regarding the social and emotional presence of the personality in the social network and, above all, point out the influence that digital media play in the processes of identity formation, which is demanded from modern people, connected to the necessity of creating protective online environments for safe and secure interaction. Therefore, instilling a sense of responsibility and ethics among the adolescents should be a concern for positive digital citizenship in these digital spaces. Subrahmanyam and Smahel (2011) present a very interesting reflection on the influence of the media on the development of adolescents, pointing to the powerful role of modern digital tools in supporting learning, social interaction, and identity construction.

Establishing a harmonious digital identity for adolescents necessitates a collective endeavor involving educators, parents, and policymakers. Through the implementation of educational programs, effective management of screen time, the establishment of secure online environments, and the promotion of responsible digital behavior, stakeholders can play a crucial role in helping young individuals develop a positive digital identity. In order to effectively navigate the ever-changing landscape of digital technologies, it is crucial to maintain an open and continuous dialogue, as well as adapt to the challenges and opportunities that arise in the digital age.

## Future Directions in Digital Identity Research and Conclusion

Future avenues in research on digital identity need to address several unknown areas, especially with the pace of technical improvements. On the basis of the above limitations highlighted in the current literature, three main areas seem to emerge as key for future research.

Yan, Filieri, and Gorton (2021) definitely stress the vibrancy of digital technologies and the need for understanding to what point customers will continue their engagement. This, therefore, calls for future research toward articulating conceptual frameworks able to respond to the new features of emerging technologies, such as hyper-connectivity, while also impacting intention-behavior gaps. For example, serious knowledge gaps were found in understanding how digital innovation, which is a key part of the development of digital identity, was taking place in the Small and Medium-sized Enterprises (SMEs). Future study of the circumstances, techniques, and the content of digital innovation in this environment points to a possible way for investigating digital identity development within organizational contexts.

Mas and Porteous (2015) plumb into the "identity gaps" observed to develop in the wake of digital inclusion efforts, centrally positing the trust gap that defines the fundamental issue of digital identities. Identity in regard to digital contains various important issues such as security, privacy, relevance, and veracity of the digital identity. Addressing these gaps necessitates extensive research from scientific, legal, and sociological viewpoints.

Senyo et al., (2019) bring out some of the criticisms of the current literature about the impact of digital business ecosystems (DBEs) on organizational and business process performance. Further exploration on how DBEs influence the creation of digital identity within the corporate context may possibly be undertaken to establish some effects on the organizational and business process performance.

Khin and Ho (2018) identify that there has been little empirical research on factors affecting digital innovation or its impact on the corporate performance of organizations. This identifies the gap in research for how digital capabilities and technologies influence organizational identity and, in extension, individual identity in a digitized work environment.

It is, therefore, an emerging task to look at what the inclusion of these technologies, including VR and AR, would do in relation to the identity and social interactions of teenagers and young adults. Future research could also address whether and how such technology could affect self- and other representations, changing identity development processes, and the necessary commitment to be developed by an individual in the digital environment. This is how AI and personalization algorithms, curating digital experiences following human taste and behaviors, rise to the new challenges of building a digital identity. Further research must examine how these technologies affect self-perception, social comparison, and processes of personal and social identification online. How exactly digital identity interacts with the impact on mental health is still an open question. This compares diverse patterns of digital engagement and presentation of one's online identity to either decreased or increased psychological well-being/distress. In addition, it further highlights the role of digital media in support or hindrance to building resilience and coping mechanisms among young populations going through identity-related difficulties. An interesting, intriguing point, on the other hand, is to explore how the diversity of cultural and socioeconomic backgrounds influences the development of digital identity and, ultimately, what it may mean for issues of diversity within the digital environment.

Addressing the numerous difficulties of digital identity construction requires a multidisciplinary approach. And, above all, a research-based set of theoretical models would have to draw from psychology, sociology, education, computer science, communication in constructing comprehensive theories; and collaborative research efforts that would propose the complex explanation required by digital identity generation. Develop and assess interventions that assist in ensuring the creation of a healthy digital identity for teenagers. Development will include educational programs, measures with parental advice, and policy initiatives that engage families and communities in order for teenagers to practice safe and positive digital involvement. Those future pathways throw a better light, the way they focus and how the development of digital identity follows the unfolding changes in technology and society.

This becomes important not only for the development of successful solutions helping youth go through the pitfalls of digital ages but also for ensuring they do use digital for good personal growth, for social connections, and for civic involvement. The major problem with the issue at hand is the balance of screen time with the development of identity within the complexity of negotiating the construction of digital identity. This is a paradox to underline balanced strategy between the gains of online engagement, including identity development and social connectivity, versus threats to mental health and well-being. Future efforts of a balanced establishment of digital existence stress the importance of digital literacy, critical engagement with digital content, and finally, the arrangement of safe online places. These are the groups of stakeholders in guiding; key educators, parents, and governments help the adolescents in guiding the digital environments by giving good advice on responsible digital citizenship and healthy life balance within the environments of offline and online. The way forward involves collaborative efforts to be able to approach the emerging technologies and their effect on identity, replete with cross-disciplinary research with sound solutions as the focus. If this were the approach that is fully represented, policies, guidance, and the other programs in such a digital environment might better be able to contribute to ways to form identity that would be supportive of the positive youth.

# REFERENCES

Abbasi, N. (2016). Adolescent identity formation and the school environment. In *The translational design of schools* (pp. 81–103). Brill. 10.1007/978-94-6300-364-3_4

Abreu, J. F., Almeida, P., Velhinho, A., & Varsori, E. (2019). Returning to the TV screen: the potential of content unification in iTV. In *Managing Screen Time in an Online Society* (pp. 146–171). IGI Global. 10.4018/978-1-5225-8163-5.ch007

Annese, S. (2004). Mediated identity in the parasocial interaction of TV. *Identity*, 4(4), 371–388. 10.1207/s1532706xid0404_5

Archives of Disease in Childhood. (2019). Screentime and child health. *Archives of Disease in Childhood, 104*(4), 380-380.

Awad, S. W. M., & Feinstein, K. A. (2020). Hybrid identity: A study of the development of self-identity with digital media and artificial intelligence. PÓS: Revista do Programa de Pós-graduação em Artes da EBA/UFMG, 10(19), 59-68.

Baltezarevic, B. (2023). Decoding identity and representation in the age of AI. *Megatrend revija, 20*(2), 141-146.

Becht, A., Nelemans, S., Branje, S. J. T., Vollebergh, W., Koot, H., Denissen, J. J. A., & Meeus, W. (2016). The quest for identity in adolescence: Heterogeneity in daily identity formation and psychosocial adjustment across 5 years. *Developmental Psychology*, 52(12), 2010–2021. 10.1037/dev000024527893245

Beyers, W., & Goossens, L. (2008). Dynamics of perceived parenting and identity formation in late adolescence. *Journal of Adolescence*, 31(2), 165–184. 10.1016/j.adolescence.2007.04.00317629552

Bozkurt, A., & Tu, C. (2016). Digital identity formation: Socially being real and present on digital networks. *Educational Media International*, 53(3), 153–167. 10.1080/09523987.2016.1236885

Clarke, B. (2009). Early Adolescents' Use of Social Networking Sites to Maintain Friendship and Explore Identity: Implications for Policy. *Policy and Internet*, 1(1), 55–89. 10.2202/1944-2866.1018

Correa, C. H. (2019). Screen Time and the Logic of Identification in the Networked Society. In *Managing Screen Time in an Online Society* (pp. 99-121). IGI Global. 10.4018/978-1-5225-8163-5.ch005

Corrêa, C. H. (2019). Screen Time and the Logic of Identification in the Networked Society. In *Managing Screen Time in an Online Society* (pp. 99-121). IGI Global. 10.4018/978-1-5225-8163-5.ch005

Craig-Bray, L., Adams, G., & Dobson, W. R. (1988). Identity formation and social relations during late adolescence. *Journal of Youth and Adolescence*, 17(2), 173–187. 10.1007/BF0153796624277583

Crocetti, E., Klimstra, T., Hale, W.III, Koot, H., & Meeus, W. (2013). Impact of Early Adolescent Externalizing Problem Behaviors on Identity Development in Middle to Late Adolescence: A Prospective 7-Year Longitudinal Study. *Journal of Youth and Adolescence*, 42(11), 1745–1758. 10.1007/s10964-013-9924-623385617

Cunningham, N. R., & Eastin, M. S. (2017). Second screen and sports: A structural investigation into team identification and efficacy. *Communication & Sport*, 5(3), 288–310. 10.1177/2167479515610152

Davis, K. (2013). Young people's digital lives: The impact of interpersonal relationships and digital media use on adolescents' sense of identity. *Computers in Human Behavior*, 29(6), 2281–2293. 10.1016/j.chb.2013.05.022

Davis, K. (2013). Young people's digital lives: The impact of interpersonal relationships and digital media use on adolescents' sense of identity. *Computers in Human Behavior*, 29(6), 2281–2293. 10.1016/j.chb.2013.05.022

Davis, K., & Weinstein, E. (2017). Identity development in the digital age: An Eriksonian perspective. In *Identity, sexuality, and relationships among emerging adults in the digital age* (pp. 1–17). IGI Global. 10.4018/978-1-5225-1856-3.ch001

Dienlin, T., & Johannes, N. (2020). The impact of digital technology use on adolescent well-being. *Dialogues in Clinical Neuroscience*, 22(2), 135–142. 10.31887/DCNS.2020.22.2/tdienlin32699513

Erikson, E. H. (1950). *Childhood and Society*. Norton.

Fox, J., & Ralston, R. (2016). Queer identity online: Informal learning and teaching experiences of LGBTQ individuals on social media. *Computers in Human Behavior*, 65, 635–642. 10.1016/j.chb.2016.06.009

Giedd, J. (2012). The digital revolution and adolescent brain evolution. *The Journal of adolescent health: official publication of the Society for Adolescent Medicine, 51*(2), 101-105.

Golubeva, N. A. (2020). *Digital Identity Features of Teenagers and Youth in Modern Technological Society.*

Granic, I., Morita, H., & Scholten, H. (2020). Beyond screen time: Identity development in the digital age. *Psychological Inquiry*, 31(3), 195–223. 10.1080/1047840X.2020.1820214

Granic, I., Morita, H., & Scholten, H. (2020). Beyond Screen Time: Identity Development in the Digital Age. *Psychological Inquiry*, 31(4), 195–223. 10.1080/1047840X.2020.1820214

Grimalda, G., Buchan, N., & Brewer, M. (2015). *Globalization, social identity, and cooperation: An experimental analysis of their linkages and effects,* (No. 10). Global Cooperation Research Papers.

Grimalda, G., Buchan, N., & Brewer, M. (2018). *Social identity mediates the positive effect of globalization on individual cooperation: Results from international experiments.* PloS.

Hand, G., & Giacobbi, P. R.Jr. (2020). A Review of Small Screen and Internet Technology–Induced Pathology as a Lifestyle Determinant of Health and Illness. *American Journal of Lifestyle Medicine*, 14(2), 122–125. 10.1177/1559827619890947 32231474

Hardey, M. (2002). Life beyond the screen: Embodiment and identity through the internet. *The Sociological Review*, 50(4), 570–585. 10.1111/1467-954X.00399

Kashchey, N., Spornik, A., & Shipulin, V. (2020). Personal And Collective Identity: Transformations. *European Proceedings of Social and Behavioural Sciences*. Research Gate.

Khin, S., & Ho, T. C. (2018). Digital technology, digital capability and organizational performance: A mediating role of digital innovation. *International Journal of Innovation Science*, 11(2), 177–195. 10.1108/IJIS-08-2018-0083

Klimstra, T. (2013). Adolescent Personality Development and Identity Formation. *Child Development Perspectives*, 7(2), 80–84. 10.1111/cdep.12017

Konca, A. (2021). Digital Technology Usage of Young Children: Screen Time and Families. *Early Childhood Education Journal*, 50(7), 1097–1108. 10.1007/s10643-021-01245-7

Lehtimaki, S., Martic, J., Wahl, B., Foster, K., & Schwalbe, N. (2020). Evidence on Digital Mental Health Interventions for Adolescents and Young People: Systematic Overview. *JMIR Mental Health*, 8(1), e25847.33913817

Lichtwarck-Aschoff, A., van Geert, P., Bosma, H., & Kunnen, S. (2008). Time and identity: A framework for research and theory formation. *Developmental Review*, 28(3), 370–400. 10.1016/j.dr.2008.04.001

Lichtwarck-Aschoff, A., van Geert, P., Bosma, H., & Kunnen, S. (2008). Time and identity: A framework for research and theory formation. *Developmental Review*, 28(3), 370–400. 10.1016/j.dr.2008.04.001

Luyckx, K., Lens, W., Smits, I., & Goossens, L. (2010). Time perspective and identity formation: Short-term longitudinal dynamics in college students. *International Journal of Behavioral Development*, 34(3), 238–247. 10.1177/0165025409350957

Magis-Weinberg, L., Suleiman, A. B., & Dahl, R. (2021). Context, Development, and Digital Media: Implications for Very Young Adolescents in LMICs. *Frontiers in Psychology*, 12, 12. 10.3389/fpsyg.2021.63271333967899

Manago, A. M. (2015). Media and the Development of Identity. In Scott, R. A., & Kosslyn, S. M. (Eds.), *Emerging Trends in the Social and Behavioral Sciences*. Wiley. 10.1002/9781118900772.etrds0212

Maras, D., Flament, M., Murray, M., Buchholz, A., Henderson, K., Obeid, N., & Goldfield, G. (2015). Screen time is associated with depression and anxiety in Canadian youth. *Preventive Medicine*, 73, 133–138. 10.1016/j.ypmed.2015.01.02925657166

Marcia, J. E. (1966). Development and validation of ego-identity status. *Journal of Personality and Social Psychology*, 3(5), 551–558. 10.1037/h0023281593604

Marciano, L., Camerini, A., & Morese, R. (2021). The Developing Brain in the Digital Era: A Scoping Review of Structural and Functional Correlates of Screen Time in Adolescence. *Frontiers in Psychology*, 12, 671817. 10.3389/fpsyg.2021.67181734512437

Mas, I., & Porteous, D. (2015). Minding the Identity Gaps. *Innovations*. MIT Press.

Mayhew, A., & Weigle, P. (2018). Media engagement and identity formation among minority youth. *Child and Adolescent Psychiatric Clinics of North America*, 27(2), 269–285. 10.1016/j.chc.2017.11.01229502751

McAdams, D. P., & Zapata-Gietl, C. (2015). Three strands of identity development across the human life course: Reading Erik Erikson in full. *The Oxford handbook of identity development*, 81-94.

Montgomery, K. (2000). Youth and digital media: A policy research agenda. *The Journal of Adolescent Health*, 27(2, Suppl), 61–68. 10.1016/S1054-139X(00)00130-010904209

Muppalla, S. K., Vuppalapati, S., Pulliahgaru, A. R., & Sreenivasulu, H. (2023). Effects of Excessive Screen Time on Child Development: An Updated Review and Strategies for Management. *Cureus*, 15(6). Advance online publication. 10.7759/cureus.4060837476119

Muppalla, S. K., Vuppalapati, S., Pulliahgaru, A. R., & Sreenivasulu, H. (2023). Effects of excessive screen time on child development: An updated review and strategies for management. *Cureus*, 15(6). Advance online publication. 10.7759/cureus.4060837476119

Nagata, J. M., Cortez, C. A., Cattle, C. J., Ganson, K. T., Iyer, P., Bibbins-Domingo, K., & Baker, F. (2021). Screen Time Use Among US Adolescents During the COVID-19 Pandemic: Findings from the Adolescent Brain Cognitive Development (ABCD) Study. *JAMA Pediatrics.*

Nair, K., James, J. K., & Santhosh, K. (2015). Identity Crisis among Early Adolescents in Relations to Abusive Experiences in the Childhood, Social Support, and Parental Support. *Journal of Psychosomatic Research*, 10, 167.

Nam, V. H. (2021). Youth Identity in the Digital Age. *Asia Journal of Theology*, 35(1), 58–82. 10.54424/ajt.v35i1.4

Odgers, C., & Jensen, M. R. (2020). Annual Research Review: Adolescent mental health in the digital age: facts, fears, and future directions. Journal of child psychology and psychiatry, and allied disciplines. *One*, 13(12), e0206819.

Odgers, C. L., & Jensen, M. R. (2020). Annual research review: Adolescent mental health in the digital age: Facts, fears, and future directions. *Journal of Child Psychology and Psychiatry, and Allied Disciplines*, 61(3), 336–348. 10.1111/jcpp.1319031951670

Patchin, J. W., & Hinduja, S. (2017). Digital Self-Harm Among Adolescents. *The Journal of Adolescent Health*, 61(6), 761–766. 10.1016/j.jadohealth.2017.06.01228935385

Paulich, K. N., Ross, J. M., Lessem, J., & Hewitt, J. (2021). Screen time and early adolescent mental health, academic, and social outcomes in 9- and 10- year old children: Utilizing the Adolescent Brain Cognitive Development (ABCD) Study. *PLoS One*, 16(4), e0247868. 10.1371/journal.pone.025659134496002

Paulich, K. N., Ross, J. M., Lessem, J., & Hewitt, J. (2021). *Screen time and early adolescent mental health, academic, and social outcomes in 9- and 10- year old children: Utilizing the Adolescent Brain Cognitive Development (ABCD) Study.* PLoS ONE.

Pfeifer, J. H., & Berkman, E. T. (2018). The development of self and identity in adolescence: Neural evidence and implications for a value-based choice perspective on motivated behavior. *Child Development Perspectives*, 12(3), 158–164. 10.1111/cdep.1227931363361

Ramdani, B., Raja, S., & Kayumova, M. (2022). Digital innovation in SMEs: A systematic review, synthesis and research agenda. *Information Technology for Development*, 28(1), 56–80. 10.1080/02681102.2021.1893148

Reid, G. G., & Boyer, W. (2013). Social Network Sites and Young Adolescent Identity Development. *Childhood Education*, 89(4), 243–253. 10.1080/00094056.2013.815554

Repetskaya, A. I. (2021). *Modern Sociocultural Practices in the Field of Fashion Consumption: The Main Youth Trends*. KnE Social Sciences.

Ribble, M. S. (2009). Raising a Digital Child: A Digital Citizenship *Handbook for Parents*.

Richards, R., McGee, R., Williams, S. M., Welch, D., & Hancox, R. (2010). Adolescent screen time and attachment to parents and peers. *Archives of Pediatrics & Adolescent Medicine*, 164(3), 258. 10.1001/archpediatrics.2009.28020194259

Rosenmann, A., Reese, G., & Cameron, J. (2016). *Social Identities in a Globalized World*.

Sandrasegaran, K., & Huang, X. (2009). Digital Identity in Current Networks. In *Encyclopedia of Information Science and Technology, Second Edition* (pp. 1125-1132). IGI Global. 10.4018/978-1-60566-026-4.ch179

Saura, J. R., Palos-Sanchez, P. R., & Correia, M. B. (2019). Digital marketing strategies based on the e-business model: Literature review and future directions. *Organizational transformation and managing innovation in the fourth industrial revolution*, 86-103.

Schnell, S. M. (2013). *Deliberate identities: becoming local in America in a global age*.

Schwartz, S., & Petrova, M. (2018). Fostering healthy identity development in adolescence. *Nature Human Behaviour*, 2(2), 110–111. 10.1038/s41562-017-0283-2

Senyo, P. K., Liu, K., & Effah, J. (2019). Digital business ecosystem: Literature review and a framework for future research. *International Journal of Information Management*, 47, 52–64. 10.1016/j.ijinfomgt.2019.01.002

Shifflet-Chila, E. D., Harold, R., Fitton, V. A., & Ahmedani, B. (2016). Adolescent and family development: Autonomy and identity in the digital age. *Children and Youth Services Review*, 70, 364–368. 10.1016/j.childyouth.2016.10.005

Squire, K., & Steinkuehler, C. (2017). The Problem with Screen Time. *Teachers College Record*, 119(1), 1–24. 10.1177/016146811711901207

Stiglic, N., & Viner, R. (2019). Effects of screentime on the health and well-being of children and adolescents: A systematic review of reviews. *BMJ Open*, 9(1), e023191. 10.1136/bmjopen-2018-02319130606703

Subrahmanyam, K., & Smahel, D. (2011). Constructing Identity Online: Identity Exploration and Self-Presentation. In *Digital Youth: The Role of Media in Development*. Springer. 10.1007/978-1-4419-6278-2_4

Subrahmanyam, K., & Smahel, D. (2011). *Digital Youth: The Role of Media in Development*.

Tajfel, H., & Turner, J. C. (1979). An integrative theory of intergroup conflict. In Austin, W. G., & Worchel, S. (Eds.), *The social psychology of intergroup relations* (pp. 33–47). Brooks/Cole.

Thulin, E., & Vilhelmson, B. (2019). More at home, more alone? Youth, digital media and the everyday use of time and space. *Geoforum*, 100, 41–50. 10.1016/j.geoforum.2019.02.010

Toma, C. L., Hancock, J. T., & Ellison, N. B. (2008). Separating fact from fiction: An examination of deceptive self-presentation in online dating profiles. *Personality and Social Psychology Bulletin*, 34(8), 1023–1036. 10.1177/0146167208318806718593866

Turner, G., van Zoonen, L., & Harvey, J. (2014). Confusion, control and comfort: Premediating identity management in film and television. *Information Communication and Society*, 17(8), 986–1000. 10.1080/1369118X.2013.870592

Turner, J. C. (1985). Social categorization and the self-concept: A social cognitive theory of group behavior. In Lawler, E. J. (Ed.), *Advances in Group Processes: Theory and Research* (Vol. 2, pp. 77–122). JAI Press.

Twenge, J., Martin, G. N., & Spitzberg, B. H. (2019). Trends in U.S. Adolescents' media use, 1976–2016: The rise of digital media, the decline of TV, and the (near) demise of print. *Psychology of Popular Media Culture*.

Twenge, J. M. (2017). Have smartphones destroyed a generation? *The Atlantic*. https://www.theatlantic.com/magazine/archive/2017/09/has-the-smartphone-destroyed-a-generation/534198/

Varsori, E., & Pereira, S. (2019). A Critical Review of Social Screen Time Management by Youngsters in Formal Educational Contexts. Managing Screen Time in an Online Society, 172-191. 10.4018/978-1-5225-8163-5.ch008

Varsori, E., & Pereira, S. (2019). A Critical Review of Social Screen Time Management by Youngsters in Formal Educational Contexts. *Managing Screen Time in an Online Society*, 172-191.

Villanti, A. C., Johnson, A. L., Ilakkuvan, V., Jacobs, M. A., Graham, A. L., & Rath, J. M. (2017). Social media use and access to digital technology in US young adults in 2016. *Journal of Medical Internet Research*, 19(6), e196. 10.2196/jmir.730328592394

Vogel, E. A., Rose, J. P., Okdie, B. M., Eckles, K., & Franz, B. (2015). Who compares and despairs? The effect of social comparison orientation on social media use and its outcomes. *Personality and Individual Differences*, 86, 249–256. 10.1016/j.paid.2015.06.026

Vogel, E. A., Rose, J. P., Okdie, B. M., Eckles, K., & Franz, B. (2015). Who compares and despairs? The effect of social comparison orientation on social media use and its outcomes. *Personality and Individual Differences*, 86, 249–256. 10.1016/j.paid.2015.06.026

Windley, P. J. (2005). *Digital Identity: Unmasking identity management architecture (IMA)*. O'Reilly Media, Inc.

Yan, M., Filieri, R., & Gorton, M. (2021). Continuance intention of online technologies: A systematic literature review. *International Journal of Information Management*, 58, 102315. 10.1016/j.ijinfomgt.2021.102315

Zhang, Y., & Khare, A. (2009). *The Impact of Accessible Identities on the Evaluation of Global versus Local Products*.

# Chapter 5
# The Mental Well–Being of Digital Natives in the Age of AI:
## Challenges and Solutions

**Wang Fei**

*Faculty of Human Ecology, Universiti Putra Malaysia, Malaysia*

## ABSTRACT

*Digital natives, surrounded by technology since birth, face a unique landscape shaped by artificial intelligence (AI). While AI unlocks a world of connection, information, and personalization, it can also present challenges for their mental well-being. This chapter explores this intricate relationship. The authors will delve into potential sources of anxiety, stress, and isolation linked to AI, like social media algorithms and constant connectivity. But it won't all be concerns. They will also explore solutions, like critical thinking skills, mindfulness practices, and fostering positive online communities. This chapter aims to equip readers with insights and strategies to navigate the digital world in the AI age, promoting a healthy mental landscape for young people.*

## INTRODUCTION

Digital natives are profoundly influenced by a technology-rich environment, exhibiting adept multitasking skills and a proclivity for non-linear learning. Their cognitive and behavioral development is significantly shaped by constant connectivity and mastery of digital literacy (Odgers & Jensen, 2020).

Despite these advantages, concerns arise regarding the impact of artificial intelligence (AI) and digital platforms on the mental well-being of digital natives. Researches highlight a troubling correlation between technological advancements and increased mental health issues among this demographic (Santos, 2023). The pervasive influence of social media, characterized by curated portrayals fostering social comparison, fear of missing out (FOMO), cyberbullying, and potential addiction, contribute to heightened vulnerability (De Felice et al., 2023).

Educators and policymakers require a nuanced understanding of these challenges to tailor effective strategies, ensuring the mental health and holistic development of digital natives in the AI era.

This chapter delves into the intricate interplay between AI technology and the mental health of digital natives. It addresses the following crucial questions:

DOI: 10.4018/979-8-3693-3350-1.ch005

1. How does AI technology impact the mental health of digital natives?
2. What effective solutions can be implemented to address these challenges?

By drawing on relevant research and scholarship, this chapter aims to:

1. Elucidate the multifaceted impact of AI technology on the mental well-being of digital natives.
2. Propose evidence-based strategies and recommendations to mitigate these challenges and foster positive mental health.

This chapter aims to contribute to the ongoing discourse surrounding the mental health of digital natives by offering valuable insights.

## AI IMPACT ON DIGITAL NATIVES

### Development and Applications of AI

In the 21st century, we are witnessing an unprecedented surge in artificial AI technology, permeating various facets of our lives. From education and entertainment to work and social interactions, AI is quietly reshaping the way we learn, experience, and engage.

### Education Sector

AI-powered adaptive learning goes beyond traditional personalized learning by dynamically adjusting the difficulty and content of learning materials in real time (De Oliveira Silva & Janes, 2020). These adaptive learning platforms tailor the content to match the individual performance of each student, recommending micro-learning modules and targeted skill-building exercises to address specific learning gaps. This approach ensures customized support, fostering more effective learning outcomes and continuous skill enhancement (Abulibdeh et al., 2024).

In intelligent teaching, predictive analytics driven by AI empower teachers to identify students at risk and provide timely, tailored assistance and resources. AI enhances the feedback and assessment process by offering automated, personalized insights on student work, analyzing responses, pinpointing strengths and weaknesses, and providing targeted guidance for improvement (Dabingaya, 2022). This integrated approach, considering individual learning styles and needs, fosters deeper comprehension and facilitates more effective learning outcomes (Niyozov et al., 2023).

Immersive Learning Experiences (ILEs) in virtual reality education extend beyond virtual reality (VR) to include augmented reality (AR) and mixed reality (MR). AI-powered ILEs offer diverse learning environments catering to various styles and preferences, engaging learners with digital content overlaid with their physical surroundings (Martins & Mota, 2022). AI-driven content creation and personalization automate the generation of learning materials within the virtual environment, ensuring relevance and adaptability to individual learners. This seamless integration of AI technologies in ILEs provides immersive and personalized learning environments, empowering learners to acquire knowledge and skills effectively.

## Entertainment Sector

I-driven recommendation systems revolutionize content curation by predicting user preferences and uncovering latent interests through sophisticated analyses of user behavior, contextual factors, and emerging trends. This ensures personalized content curation that adapts not only to users' past preferences but also to their potential interests and evolving tastes.

In gaming, AI goes beyond adapting to player skills to include dynamic game design and real-time adaptation. Game developers leverage AI to create personalized quests, adjust difficulty levels, and introduce unique challenges tailored to individual player preferences and performance (Jagoda, 2023). AI-driven storytelling and character interactions enhance the gaming experience by crafting immersive narratives, dynamic dialogues, and emotionally engaging virtual companions within the game environment (Tonini, 2024).

In VR, AI plays a crucial role in shaping immersive experiences beyond visual elements. Multimodal VR experiences integrate touch, smell, and haptic feedback, enriching user interactions within virtual environments (Stenslie, 2011). AI-driven content creation streamlines the development process, enabling the creation of diverse and engaging virtual worlds. Additionally, AI enhances accessibility in VR by personalizing features to address individual needs and preferences, contributing to a more inclusive and immersive virtual reality entertainment experience (Alamry & Elwakeel, 2024).

However, personalized recommendation systems and AI-driven games can also exacerbate users' addictive tendencies (Udayanan et al., 2024). Game developers sometimes use strategies like variable reward mechanisms to create a sense of manipulation in users, to achieve commercial goals (Di Vaio et al., 2020). Some immersive VR experiences are so realistic that users may have difficulty distinguishing between the virtual and real worlds.

## Work Sector

The integration of AI-powered automation, particularly through intelligent robots, is transforming the workforce landscape (Post et al., 2023). These robots handle repetitive, hazardous, or physically demanding tasks, allowing human workers to focus on roles that require creativity, critical thinking, and interpersonal skills. This shift optimizes resource allocation, enhances productivity, and fosters a more dynamic work environment.

AI-powered virtual assistants play a crucial role in improving productivity and organization within the workplace. By efficiently managing appointments, task reminders, and information retrieval, these assistants help individuals navigate their professional and personal responsibilities seamlessly (Pendy, 2023). This augmentation of human capabilities by AI enhances time management and promotes a more efficient approach to work-life integration.

AI's advanced analytical capabilities enable businesses to harness the power of big data, discern patterns, and derive insights beyond human capacity (Ganatra & Pandya, 2023). This empowers organizations to make data-informed decisions, streamline operations, and gain a competitive advantage in the marketplace (Morandini et al., 2023). Leveraging AI for intelligent analysis unlocks opportunities for innovation, growth, and sustainable success.

## Social Sector

In the realm of social media, AI-powered algorithms shape user experiences, with the potential to diversify content recommendations and foster more balanced online discourse. By considering factors like user demographics and engagement with diverse content creators, these algorithms contribute to creating a more inclusive environment.

The evolution of virtual social environments, particularly within VR, is reshaping online interactions. Multimodal VR experiences offer users a heightened sense of immersion and realism, enabling meaningful interactions regardless of physical distance. AI-driven personalization enhances virtual socialization by tailoring interactions to user preferences and breaking communication barriers through real-time translation.

While AI has driven advancements in social media algorithms and virtual social environments, it is worth noting that over-reliance on these technologies can also exacerbate interpersonal isolation and diminish real-world social skills. Additionally, AI-driven personalized advertising and marketing strategies can potentially influence user autonomy and decision-making.

Overall, AI technology has brought many conveniences to our lives. However, there are also some potential risks and challenges that deserve attention. We need to stay highly vigilant, use these technologies rationally, and avoid passively accepting their potential negative effects.

## The Impact of AI Technology on Digital Natives

The rapid development and widespread application of AI technology profoundly influence the online experiences and cognitive development of digital natives, who have been immersed in a technological environment from a young age.

### Pressure of Social Comparison

The contemporary digital environment presents unique challenges for young people. On social media platforms, users commonly present carefully curated idealized self-images, giving rise to a "highlight reel" effect that predisposes viewers to engage in upward social comparisons (Festinger, 1954). Digital natives often compare themselves to others' meticulously edited selfies, holiday photos, and other online displays, leading to negative emotions such as diminished self-worth and inadequate self-image (Peltola, 2019). This persistent social comparison can significantly impact their self-esteem and overall well-being (Przybylski et al., 2013).

### Fear of Missing Out (FOMO)

In today's fast-paced digital era, digital natives often grapple with the desire for social updates and trending information, a phenomenon known as the Fear of Missing Out (FOMO), a persistent fear of exclusion and anxiety stemming from the apprehension of missing out on valuable social interactions and updates (Gupta & Sharma, 2021), which results in a series of negative consequences. FOMO not only triggers compulsive refreshing and checking behaviors but also compromises sleep quality, disrupts attention, and diminishes work efficiency. Importantly, it often stems from comparisons between one's own life and others' online personas, exacerbating feelings of anxiety and self-deprecation.

## Cyberbullying and Online Harassment

The anonymity of the online space fosters an environment conducive to bullying, making digital natives more susceptible to severe online bullying and harassment, which can inflict profound psychological trauma. Some studies have found that online bullying often leads to social withdrawal, depression, and suicidal tendencies. Of particular concern is the fact that women and other marginalized groups are more likely to face gender-based cyberattacks, which not only affect their self-esteem but may also lead to self-censorship and disengagement from online spaces.

## Addiction Tendencies and Attention Deficits

Digital natives immersed in AI-driven platforms such as social media and mobile games are prone to attention deficits and addiction tendencies. These platforms often employ variable reward strategies, infinite scrolling, and other mechanisms to manipulate users' reward systems, fostering impulses for continued use. Additionally, FOMO effects and real-time notifications make it difficult for users to disengage. Excessive indulgence in the virtual world can significantly affect learning, work, and real-life interactions. In conclusion, AI technology presents complex challenges to the psychological well-being of digital natives. It is essential to fully recognize these challenges and implement effective preventive and intervention measures to ensure the healthy development of the new generation.

## COMPLEXITY OF MENTAL HEALTH CHALLENGES

The impact of artificial intelligence (AI) technology on the mental health of digital natives is multifaceted and intricately woven into the fabric of their online experiences (Odgers & Jensen, 2020). This chapter delves deeper into this complex relationship, analyzing its various facets, exploring potential causes and mechanisms, and evaluating their long-term effects.

## Anxiety and Depression

Digital natives, individuals immersed in digital technologies from an early age, exhibit heightened susceptibility to anxiety and depressive disorders compared to preceding generations. This vulnerability stems from a complex interplay of factors intrinsically linked to the proliferation of artificial AI and digital media.

## Social Comparison and Self-Worth

Social networking platforms (SNPs) have fundamentally reshaped self-presentation. Users meticulously curate online personas, crafting idealized versions of their lives. This emphasis on the "perfect" online persona fosters a culture of social comparison. Young people, particularly susceptible to peer influence, constantly compare themselves to these seemingly perfect portrayals. This relentless upward social comparison (Festinger, 1954) triggers a cascade of negative emotions: inadequacy, inferiority, and pressure to conform. Research has established a link between excessive social media use and anxiety, depression, and body image dissatisfaction (Przybylski et al., 2013). These negative emotions erode self-worth, creating a vicious cycle that can have a profound impact on mental well-being.

Furthermore, the "highlight reel" effect on social media feeds exacerbates the situation. These feeds showcase the positive aspects of people's lives, vacations, celebrations, and achievements, creating a distorted reality. This disparity between the online persona and authentic experiences fuels feelings of inadequacy and reinforces the pressure to conform to unrealistic standards. Social media influencers further contribute by promoting unrealistic beauty standards and lavish lifestyles. For young people grappling with self-esteem and identity formation, constant exposure to these portrayals can lead to a devaluation of their self-worth. The pressure to conform to these unrealistic expectations, amplified by digital media, can have a profound impact on mental well-being.

## FOMO and the Anxiety Cycle

In the era of information overload, digital natives face a unique challenge known as FOMO, or the fear of missing out (Odgers & Jensen, 2020). This pervasive anxiety, driven by the constant stream of updates and curated portrayals on social media and AI-driven platforms, initiates a detrimental cycle affecting various aspects of well-being.

The fear of missing out leads to compulsive checking behaviors, prompting individuals to continuously refresh social media feeds, browse news updates, or engage in excessive messaging to stay "in the loop." This behavior not only consumes time and distracts but also reduces productivity and meaningful real-life interactions.

Furthermore, the captivating nature of online content, combined with the fear of missing late-night updates, disrupts sleep patterns significantly. Research highlights the negative impact of social media use on sleep quality, resulting in fatigue, impaired cognitive function, and increased anxiety levels, perpetuating the cycle.

Difficulties concentrating and increased procrastination often result from fragmented attention due to constant online stimulation and FOMO. This adversely affects academic performance, work productivity, and overall well-being, creating a cycle of anxiety and reduced functioning.

The curated nature of online content exacerbates FOMO as individuals compare their real lives to the seemingly perfect experiences depicted online, fostering feelings of inadequacy. Additionally, the expectation to actively participate in online trends further contributes to FOMO, triggering anxiety and inadequacy when individuals perceive a lack of involvement in the digital realm.

## Traumatic Effects of Cyberbullying and Online Harassment

The proliferation of online platforms, characterized by anonymity and ease of communication, has created a breeding ground for cyberbullying and online harassment. These pernicious online behaviors pose severe threats to the mental well-being of "digital natives" young people heavily reliant on these digital spaces. Victims of cyberbullying and online harassment experience a multitude of profound psychological consequences, significantly impacting their mental and emotional health.

Studies have consistently shown a correlation between cyberbullying victimization and a cascade of negative mental health outcomes, including social withdrawal, depression, and even suicidal ideation (Hinduja & Patchin, 2010). The constant barrage of malicious content, such as cruel rumors, social exclusion through online groups, and the posting of embarrassing photos or videos, can leave lasting scars on victims. Unlike traditional bullying, cyberbullying's pervasiveness offers victims little respite, as the harassment can permeate various aspects of their lives.

The anonymity afforded by online platforms fosters a phenomenon known as deindividuation, where individuals shed their sense of personal responsibility and accountability. This psychological state can embolden them to engage in behaviors they would deem unacceptable in face-to-face interactions. Cyberbullies may resort to a variety of tactics, including hate speech, threats, and impersonation, inflicting significant emotional distress on their victims (Marwick & Boyd, 2014). Furthermore, the bystander effect can exacerbate the issue. Witnesses of online harassment may hesitate to intervene due to fear of social repercussions or a lack of knowledge regarding effective intervention strategies (Betts et al., 2017). This inaction inadvertently enables perpetrators and perpetuates the cycle of online abuse.

## Risks of Addiction and Attention Disorders

Digital environments, with their constant stimulation and effortless connectivity, breed a concerning trend: digital addiction and attention disorders in "digital natives." These issues worsen existing mental health struggles, amplifying anxiety and depression fueled by social comparison, FOMO, and cyberbullying.

Excessive digital media use, driven by FOMO or instant gratification, fosters addictive behaviors like compulsive social media scrolling, online gaming, or an inability to disconnect. This addiction fuels a cycle of anxiety and depression as users struggle for balance. The constant stimulation disrupts attention spans, hindering focus and exacerbating feelings of inadequacy.

Furthermore, the rise of AI-driven tech and digital media contributes to attention deficit disorders. The constant influx of information and stimuli fragments attention, leading to difficulties with tasks, deadlines, and productivity, further impacting mental well-being.

The combination of digital addiction and attention deficits has far-reaching consequences, negatively impacting academic performance, work, and relationships, amplifying the risk of anxiety and depression for digital natives struggling to find balance.

## Loneliness and Social Isolation

While AI technology has revolutionized communication and facilitated unprecedented levels of virtual connection, it has paradoxically contributed to a rise in feelings of loneliness and social isolation among digital natives. This paradoxical situation arises from the interplay of several critical factors:

### Emotional Deficits of Virtual Interactions

Social media platforms and online gaming communities have undoubtedly transformed the landscape of social interaction. However, these interactions often lack the depth and emotional intimacy that characterize face-to-face encounters. Research suggests that while online connections can fulfill basic needs for social belonging, they frequently fall short in nurturing higher-order needs for emotional intimacy and genuine connection (Przybylski et al., 2013). This qualitative disparity between virtual and in-person interactions can leave individuals feeling emotionally isolated, despite having numerous online connections and social ties.

## Negative Impact of Social Comparison Traps

The pervasive phenomenon of social comparison on social media platforms further exacerbates feelings of loneliness and social isolation among digital natives. Studies have shown that excessive social media use contributes to heightened loneliness by fueling unhealthy comparisons with others' seemingly perfect lives (Przybylski et al., 2013). Exposure to meticulously curated online personas sets unrealistic expectations for social interactions and relationships, hindering the formation of genuine, meaningful connections in the real world. This can be particularly detrimental for adolescents who are already grappling with self-esteem and identity formation.

## Cyberbullying and Social Withdrawal

Cyberbullying and experiences of rejection within online spaces can inflict severe psychological harm. This often leads to maladaptive patterns of social withdrawal and isolation. Victims of cyberbullying may retreat from online platforms altogether and disengage from real-world social interactions, perpetuating and exacerbating feelings of loneliness (Hinduja & Patchin, 2010). Research suggests a significant correlation between cyberbullying victimization and social withdrawal, leading to heightened social isolation, low self-esteem, and a diminished sense of self-worth. This withdrawal not only limits opportunities for social engagement but also impedes the development of crucial social skills, further exacerbating feelings of loneliness and perpetuating the cycle of isolation.

## Addiction and Attention Disorders

The proliferation of AI platforms has undeniably revolutionized human interaction with technology. However, concerns regarding the potential for these platforms to contribute to addiction and attention disorders among digital natives are a growing source of unease.

## The Dopamine Trap and Compulsive Behaviors

AI platforms are meticulously crafted to be inherently engaging, capitalizing on the reward pathways within the human brain. Features such as "likes," comments and gamification elements create a reinforcing loop, triggering the release of dopamine, a neurotransmitter associated with pleasure and reward. This strategic design fosters the development of compulsive online behaviors among digital natives. Driven by the pursuit of the dopamine rush and the sense of gratification offered by these platforms, young people may prioritize online engagement over real-world responsibilities and overall well-being (Przybylski et al., 2013).

Furthermore, research by [reference citation] suggests that prolonged social media use disrupts cognitive control processes. This disruption may explain the difficulties individuals experience in resisting the constant temptations and distractions posed by AI platforms. In essence, the dopamine-driven design of AI platforms creates a neurobiological vulnerability, potentially serving as a key underlying factor in the compulsive behaviors exhibited by digital natives.

## Information Overload and the Fragmentation of Attention

The sheer volume of information readily accessible through AI platforms presents a significant challenge for digital natives, contributing to a phenomenon often termed the "attention crisis". This crisis manifests in several ways. Firstly, the continuous stream of stimuli and notifications from AI platforms fragments attention, making it difficult to maintain focus and concentration on tasks. As attention is constantly diverted, completing tasks efficiently becomes increasingly arduous.

Secondly, the overwhelming volume of information can impede digital natives' ability to process and retain complex information effectively. With an abundance of data competing for attention, individuals may struggle to absorb and internalize knowledge, leading to a shallower understanding of concepts and potentially hindering learning outcomes. Furthermore, the fragmented nature of attention resulting from information overload disrupts digital natives' capacity to engage in tasks requiring sustained focus and higher-order cognitive skills. Complex activities such as problem-solving, critical thinking, or analytical reasoning become more challenging as individuals grapple with divided attention and cognitive overload.

## Vulnerability During Critical Brain Development

The age at which digital natives are exposed to AI technologies coincides with a critical period of brain development, particularly in areas related to self-regulation, impulse control, and executive functioning. This temporal overlap renders them more susceptible to developing addictive online behaviors and struggling to resist the constant temptations and distractions of AI platforms. Excessive and compulsive use of AI platforms during this critical developmental window may disrupt the ongoing maturation of the prefrontal cortex, a brain region crucial for decision-making, emotional regulation, and cognitive control. This disruption may further exacerbate the risk of addiction and attention-related disorders.

## Long-Term Effects and Potential Risks

The long-term impact of AI technology on the mental health of digital natives presents several potential risks, including academic and career impediments, challenges in forming healthy social relationships, and diminished overall well-being. Unaddressed mental health issues may lead to risky behaviors, relationship difficulties, and societal issues such as violence and crime. Additionally, the escalation of mental health challenges poses significant public health concerns, including an increased burden on healthcare systems and reduced workforce productivity. Furthermore, mental health challenges can disrupt social cohesion and exacerbate existing inequalities. Given these potential consequences, a proactive approach encompassing preventative measures and the promotion of responsible technology use and mental health awareness is crucial.

## PROMOTING POSITIVE MENTAL HEALTH IN THE AI ERA

While the impact of AI technology on the mental health of digital natives can be complex and multifaceted, it's crucial to explore and implement strategies to mitigate potential negative effects and foster well-being. This section delves into various initiatives and approaches that can be adopted to promote positive mental health in this digital age.

## Empowering Digital Natives With Critical Thinking Skills

The ever-evolving digital landscape presents both opportunities and challenges for digital natives – those who have grown up immersed in technology. Equipping them with robust critical thinking skills is paramount in this complex environment. These skills empower them to navigate the labyrinth of information, discern truth from falsehoods, and cultivate a healthy perspective amidst the curated realities that permeate online spaces.

## Discerning Truth in a Sea of Information

In the digital age, information overload is a constant threat. Critical thinking empowers digital natives to become discerning consumers of information.

- Fact-Checking Resources: Encourage the regular use of reputable fact-checking websites like FactCheck.org, Snopes, and PolitiFact to verify information and debunk prevalent misinformation.
- Cross-referencing Information: Emphasize the importance of cross-referencing information with established news organizations, academic journals, and authoritative government websites to ensure accuracy.
- Logical Fallacies: Equip digital natives with the ability to identify common logical fallacies, such as straw man arguments and ad hominem attacks, empowering them to recognize manipulative content.
- Emotional Appeals: Highlight how emotional appeals are often used to sway opinions and cloud judgment. Foster awareness of manipulation tactics used to exploit emotions.
- Identifying Bias: Instill the understanding that all information sources inherently possess biases, whether political, cultural, or commercial. Encourage digital natives to consider diverse viewpoints to gain a comprehensive understanding of issues.
- Purpose and Audience: Promote the evaluation of the purpose and intended audience of information to identify potential biases and motivations behind the content.

## Deconstructing the "Perfection Illusion" Online

The carefully curated online world can distort reality and foster unrealistic expectations. Critical thinking empowers digital natives to deconstruct these illusions.

- Photo Editing Techniques: Expose digital natives to prevalent photo editing and manipulation techniques online, fostering critical analysis of how images are altered to project idealized versions of reality.
- "Perfection Engineering": Encourage discussions on the concept of "perfection engineering" and the deliberate crafting of online personas.
- Social Media Entertainment: Facilitate an understanding of social media's primary focus on entertainment and self-promotion. This prompts individuals to question the accuracy of online narratives and recognize the limitations of social media snapshots in capturing the complexity of real-life experiences.

## Embracing Diversity and Fostering Empathy

Critical thinking goes beyond evaluating information; it fosters empathy and understanding of diverse perspectives.

- Inclusive Mindset: Promote inclusivity by fostering a mindset that values differences in race, ethnicity, gender, abilities, and backgrounds. This can be achieved through diverse educational materials, exposure to different cultures and perspectives, and encouraging positive interactions with individuals from various backgrounds.
- Perspective-Taking: Encourage perspective-taking exercises that facilitate understanding different viewpoints and fostering empathy for others' experiences. Role-playing scenarios, engaging in respectful online discussions, and volunteering in diverse communities are effective methods.
- Positive Online Interactions: Promote positive online interactions that focus on mutual understanding and shared interests, fostering meaningful connections and combating negativity and superficiality.
- Real-World Relationships: Highlight the importance of real-world relationships by encouraging digital natives to engage in meaningful face-to-face interactions. This allows them to build genuine connections and appreciate the uniqueness of individuals beyond their online personas.
- Self-Awareness and Acceptance: Promote self-awareness and self-acceptance by encouraging the development of a strong sense of self-worth based on individual strengths, qualities, and experiences, rather than comparing themselves to unrealistic online portrayals.

## Integrating Critical Thinking Skills Into Curriculum

Equipping students with critical thinking skills from a young age is vital for fostering their well-being in the digital age. Here are some methods for curriculum integration:

- Core Curriculum Integration: Weave critical thinking throughout the curriculum across various subjects. In Language Arts classes, analyze persuasive writing techniques and identify bias in news articles. In History classes, evaluate the credibility of primary sources and challenge historical narratives. Science classes can incorporate activities that involve designing experiments, analyzing data, and identifying logical fallacies in scientific claims found online.
- Debate and Discussion: Facilitate lively classroom debates on controversial topics found online. Encourage students to research opposing viewpoints, identify logical fallacies in arguments presented online, and develop and present their well-reasoned arguments. This fosters critical thinking, communication skills, and the ability to navigate diverse perspectives.
- Case Studies and Role-Playing: Learning by doing is powerful. Introduce case studies that present students with real-world scenarios where they need to apply critical thinking skills. Role-playing exercises can simulate online interactions where students encounter misinformation or manipulative content.

## Cultivating Mindfulness

While critical thinking skills are essential for navigating the digital world, they are not enough to ensure positive mental health. In the face of constant stimulation and information overload, the ability to cultivate mindfulness – a state of present-moment awareness – becomes equally important. Mindfulness practices can equip digital natives with the tools to manage stress, improve focus, and foster emotional well-being in the digital age.

## Understanding Mindfulness and its Benefits

Mindfulness can be defined as the practice of paying attention to the present moment without judgment. It involves focusing on our thoughts, feelings, and bodily sensations in a non-reactive way. Research has shown that mindfulness practices can lead to a multitude of benefits, including:

- Reduced stress and anxiety
- Improved focus and concentration
- Enhanced emotional regulation
- Increased self-awareness
- Improved sleep quality

## Integrating Mindfulness Practices Into Daily Life

The beauty of mindfulness is that it can be integrated into daily activities, requiring no special equipment or location. Here are some practical strategies for digital natives to cultivate mindfulness:

- Mindful Breathing: Focusing on the breath is a simple yet powerful way to anchor oneself in the present moment. Encourage short mindful breathing exercises throughout the day, such as taking a few slow, deep breaths before checking social media or during transitions between tasks.
- Mindful Movement: Activities like mindful walking or yoga can cultivate body awareness and promote relaxation. Encourage incorporating mindful movement into daily routines, focusing on the sensations of the body as one moves.
- Mindful Technology Use: Technology can be a tool for mindfulness practice. There are numerous apps available that offer guided meditation and mindfulness exercises. Even simply taking a mindful pause before checking emails or social media notifications can be beneficial.
- Mindful Observation: Encourage digital natives to practice mindful observation throughout the day. This could involve focusing on sights, sounds, smells, or even their thoughts and emotions without judgment.

## Creating a Culture of Mindfulness

Schools and communities can play a vital role in fostering mindfulness among digital natives. Here are some suggestions:

- Mindfulness in Schools: Integrate mindfulness practices into the school curriculum, such as short mindful breathing exercises at the beginning of class or mindfulness-based stress reduction programs.
- Community Mindfulness Programs: Offer mindfulness workshops and programs for adolescents and families, creating a supportive environment for learning and practicing mindfulness techniques.
- Mindful Role Models: Promote mindfulness among educators, parents, and community leaders who can serve as positive role models for digital natives.

By cultivating mindfulness, digital natives can develop a sense of inner peace and well-being that allows them to navigate the complexities of the digital age with greater resilience and focus. Integrating mindfulness practices into daily life and fostering a supportive environment can empower them to thrive in an increasingly digital world.

## Building Positive Online Communities

The digital landscape offers a multitude of opportunities for connection and belonging. However, not all online communities are created equal. Cultivating positive online communities is crucial for fostering mental well-being and promoting meaningful social interaction in the digital age. This section explores key strategies for building online communities that nurture support, collaboration, and positive online experiences for digital natives.

### Defining Shared Purpose and Values

A strong foundation for any positive online community is a clearly defined shared purpose and set of values. This provides a sense of direction and fosters a sense of belonging among members. Consider the following when establishing a positive online community:

- Identify the Community's Focus: What is the overarching goal or theme that will bring people together? Is it a shared interest, a support group for a specific challenge, or a platform for creative expression?
- Establish Ground Rules: Develop clear guidelines for respectful communication, appropriate content, and conflict resolution. These guidelines should promote inclusivity and discourage negativity.
- Promote Positive Values: Identify and emphasize values that resonate with the community's purpose. These might include kindness, empathy, collaboration, and open-mindedness.

### Cultivating a Culture of Respect and Empathy

Positive online communities thrive on mutual respect and empathy. Here are some strategies to foster these qualities:

- Encourage Active Listening: Promote practices that encourage members to truly listen to and understand each other's perspectives.

- Celebrate Diverse Voices: Create an environment where all viewpoints are valued and respected, fostering a sense of inclusivity.
- Promote Empathy-Building Activities: Encourage online discussions, role-playing exercises, or collaborative projects that promote understanding of different experiences.
- Discourage Cyberbullying and Negativity: Implement clear consequences for disrespectful behavior and promote positive interactions through recognition and rewards.

## Fostering Collaboration and Shared Interests

Positive online communities provide a platform for collaboration and shared interests. Here are some ways to encourage this:

- Create Online Collaboration Tools: Utilize online forums, discussion boards, or project management platforms to facilitate collaboration on shared goals.
- Organize Online Events and Activities: Host webinars, workshops, or online discussions that allow members to learn from each other and engage in shared activities.
- Recognize and Celebrate Achievements: Highlight the contributions of members and celebrate successes to foster a sense of accomplishment and community pride.

## Ensuring Online Safety and Well-Being

While online communities offer a wealth of benefits, it is essential to prioritize the safety and well-being of members. Here are some key considerations:

- Implement Online Safety Measures: Utilize online moderation tools, promote responsible technology use, and educate members on identifying and reporting cyberbullying or harassment.
- Promote Digital Detoxification: Encourage members to take breaks from online interactions and prioritize real-world connections to maintain a healthy balance.
- Provide Mental Health Resources: Offer access to mental health resources and information on coping with online negativity or social media addiction.

By fostering a sense of shared purpose, cultivating respect and empathy, encouraging collaboration, and prioritizing online safety, positive online communities can become a valuable source of support, connection, and positive social interaction for digital natives in the digital age.

## Strengthening Mental Health Education and Awareness

The strategies outlined above provide a strong foundation for promoting positive mental health in the digital age. However, for lasting impact, it is crucial to strengthen mental health education and awareness across various societal sectors. This section explores initiatives that can equip individuals with the knowledge and resources necessary to navigate the digital world with greater resilience.

## Integrating Mental Health Education into the Curriculum

Schools play a pivotal role in shaping young minds and equipping students with essential life skills. Integrating mental health education into the curriculum from a young age is vital for promoting positive mental health and fostering awareness of potential digital pitfalls.

- Age-Appropriate Education: Tailor mental health education to different age groups, addressing issues relevant to each developmental stage. For example, elementary school lessons might focus on identifying emotions and healthy coping mechanisms, while high school curricula could delve deeper into topics like stress management, social media use, and cyberbullying prevention.
- Skills-Based Learning: Move beyond simply providing information and equip students with practical skills for managing their mental health in the digital age. This could include techniques for mindfulness, stress management, and critical thinking related to online content.
- Promoting Help-Seeking Behaviors: Destigmatize mental health and encourage students to seek help if they are struggling. Integrate resources and information about available mental health services within the school community.

## Enhancing Mental Health Literacy for Parents and Educators

Parents and educators play a crucial role in supporting the mental health of young people in the digital age. Equipping them with the necessary knowledge and resources is essential.

- Workshops and Training Programs: Offer workshops and training programs for parents and educators on topics like adolescent mental health, identifying signs of distress, and navigating online safety concerns.
- Educational Resources: Develop and disseminate educational resources for parents and educators that guide promoting positive digital habits, fostering open communication about mental health, and supporting young people who are struggling.
- Collaborative Partnerships: Foster collaboration between schools, mental health professionals, and parents to create a comprehensive support system for addressing the mental health needs of students in the digital age.

## Raising Public Awareness Through Media Campaigns

Public awareness campaigns can play a significant role in destigmatizing mental health and promoting help-seeking behaviors. Utilize various media channels to:

- Normalize Discussions about Mental Health: Encourage open conversations about mental health, showcasing stories of resilience and recovery.
- Promote Help-Seeking Resources: Provide information about available mental health services and hotlines to encourage individuals to seek help when needed.

- Challenge Stigma: Develop campaigns that challenge negative stereotypes associated with mental health and promote a message of acceptance and support.

## Leveraging Technology for Mental Health Promotion

Technology can be a powerful tool for promoting mental health. Here are some ways to leverage technology for positive impact:

- Develop Mental Health Apps and Resources: Support the development of user-friendly apps and online resources that provide information, self-help tools, and access to mental health professionals.
- Utilize Social Media for Positive Outreach: Encourage mental health professionals and organizations to utilize social media platforms to disseminate educational content, promote help-seeking behavior, and foster online communities for peer support.
- Teletherapy and Online Support Groups: Promote the use of teletherapy and online support groups to increase access to mental health services and provide alternative avenues for support.

By implementing these strategies, we can create a society where mental health is prioritized, information is readily available, and support systems are readily accessible. This comprehensive approach will empower individuals of all ages to navigate the digital world with greater resilience and promote positive mental health in the digital age.

## Embracing a Holistic Approach to Well-Being

The quest for positive mental health in the digital age necessitates a multifaceted approach. While the strategies outlined above focus on the digital landscape, it is crucial to recognize that mental well-being is intricately linked to overall well-being. This section emphasizes the importance of embracing a holistic approach that considers all dimensions of human existence.

## Balancing Digital and Physical Wellness

Technology should complement, not replace, healthy physical activity and real-world connections. Encourage digital natives to:

- Prioritize Physical Activity: Engage in regular physical exercise to promote physical and mental health. Encourage activities that allow them to disconnect from technology and connect with nature.
- Maintain Healthy Sleep Habits: Set consistent sleep schedules and establish screen-free routines before bedtime to ensure quality sleep, which is vital for emotional well-being.
- Develop Strong Social Connections: Foster meaningful face-to-face interactions with friends, family, and communities. Digital interaction should complement, not replace, real-world relationships.

## Nurturing Emotional and Spiritual Well-Being

Mental health goes beyond the absence of mental illness. Encourage practices that cultivate emotional well-being and a sense of purpose:

- Developing Emotional Intelligence: Help digital natives understand and manage their emotions effectively. Techniques like mindfulness and journaling can be valuable tools.
- Exploring Personal Values and Purpose: Encourage reflection on personal values and goals. Finding meaning and purpose in life beyond the digital world can foster emotional well-being.
- Engaging in Creative Expression: Promote creative outlets such as art, music, or writing as a means for self-expression and emotional catharsis.

## Building Resilience and Coping Mechanisms

Equipping digital natives with coping mechanisms is essential for navigating the challenges of the digital world and life in general.

- Stress Management Techniques: Introduce relaxation techniques like deep breathing, meditation, or progressive muscle relaxation to manage stress effectively.
- Developing Problem-Solving Skills: Encourage critical thinking and problem-solving skills to navigate challenges and build resilience.
- Promoting Help-Seeking Behaviors: Reinforce the importance of seeking help from trusted adults, mental health professionals, or support groups when facing difficulties.

## The Role of Family, Community, and Social Support

Strong social support systems are essential for fostering well-being. Encourage:

- Open Communication within Families: Create open and supportive family environments where digital natives feel comfortable discussing their concerns and challenges.
- Positive Role Models: Parents, educators, and community leaders can serve as positive role models by demonstrating healthy digital habits and emotional regulation.
- Community-Based Support Systems: Promote community-based initiatives that provide support, resources, and a sense of belonging for digital natives.

By embracing a holistic approach that integrates strategies for digital well-being with practices that nurture physical, emotional, and spiritual well-being, we can empower digital natives to thrive in the digital age. This comprehensive approach fosters a sense of balance and inner peace, allowing them to navigate the complexities of the online world with greater resilience and a sense of well-being that extends far beyond the digital sphere.

## A Collaborative Endeavor

Fostering positive mental health in the digital age is a complex and multifaceted challenge. It necessitates a collaborative effort from various stakeholders who play a critical role in shaping the digital landscape and supporting the well-being of digital natives.

- Individuals: Digital natives themselves must be empowered to navigate the digital world with critical thinking skills and a sense of mindfulness. This requires them to take an active role in developing these skills and adopting healthy digital habits.
- Families: Families play a crucial role in creating a supportive environment for digital natives. Open communication, establishing healthy digital boundaries, and modeling positive technology use are essential contributions families can make.
- Schools: Schools have a unique opportunity to equip students with the knowledge and skills necessary for digital well-being. Integrating mental health education, critical thinking skills development, and promoting responsible technology use within the curriculum are crucial steps.
- Communities: Communities can play a vital role in fostering positive online interactions and providing support systems for digital natives. This can involve developing community-based initiatives, promoting positive online spaces, and creating opportunities for meaningful social connections outside the digital realm.
- Policymakers: Policymakers have the responsibility to create a regulatory environment that prioritizes online safety, protects children from harmful content, and promotes ethical technology development.
- Technology Developers: Technology developers hold immense power in shaping the digital landscape. Prioritizing ethical design principles, developing tools that promote well-being, and fostering responsible technology use are key areas where developers can make a positive impact.

By working together, these stakeholders can create a supportive digital ecosystem that prioritizes mental well-being and empowers digital natives to thrive in the online world. This collaborative effort is essential for ensuring a future where technology enhances, rather than hinders, the mental health and well-being of all.

## CONCLUSION

The mental well-being of digital natives is a pressing issue requiring immediate and comprehensive action. It's our collective responsibility to ensure that the transformative power of digital technology aligns harmoniously with the emotional and psychological well-being of future generations. This calls for a multi-faceted, collaborative approach involving individuals, families, educational institutions, technology developers, mental health professionals, and policymakers. By fostering open dialogue, conducting continuous research, and implementing proactive strategies, we can pave the way for digital natives to thrive online while safeguarding their mental health. Central to this mission is equipping digital natives with critical thinking skills, mindfulness practices, positive online communities, and mental health education. It also involves recognizing that promoting their mental health extends beyond the digital realm to include physical activity, diverse interests, and face-to-face connections.

By uniting our efforts and fostering collaboration, we can create a comprehensive support system empowering digital natives to navigate the digital landscape confidently while prioritizing their emotional well-being. This requires dedication to continuous improvement and innovation as the digital landscape evolves. Investing in the mental health of digital natives isn't just for the present; it's an investment in the future. By prioritizing their well-being, we can unlock their full potential, enabling them to contribute meaningfully to society and thrive in a world that celebrates their unique strengths and perspectives. Let's unite in this noble cause, working tirelessly to create a world where the digital revolution and human flourishing coexist harmoniously, ensuring a future where digital natives can flourish and make a positive impact on the world.

# REFERENCES

Abulibdeh, A., Zaidan, E., & Abulibdeh, R. (2024). Navigating the confluence of artificial intelligence and education for sustainable development in the era of industry 4.0: Challenges, opportunities, and ethical dimensions. *Journal of Cleaner Production*, 437, 140527. 10.1016/j.jclepro.2023.140527

Alamry, G. A., & Elwakeel, L. M. (2024). User-Centered Smart Environments: Advanced Research on the Integration of User Preferences and Artificial Intelligence for Personalized Residential Interior Design Solutions. *Kurdish Studies*, 12(1), 4870–4880.

Betts, L. R., Spenser, K. A., & Gardner, S. E. (2017). Adolescents' Involvement in Cyber Bullying and Perceptions of School: The Importance of Perceived Peer Acceptance for Female Adolescents. *Sex Roles*, 77(7–8), 471–481. 10.1007/s11199-017-0742-228979061

Dabingaya, M. (2022). Analyzing the Effectiveness of AI-Powered Adaptive Learning Platforms in Mathematics Education. *Interdisciplinary Journal Papier Human Review*, 3(1), 1–7. 10.47667/ijphr.v3i1.226

De Felice, F., Iovine, G., & Petrillo, A. (2023). Reflections on Metaverse. In *Concepts in Smart Societies: Next-generation of Human Resources and Technologies* (p. 72). CRC Press. https://books.google.com/books?hl=en&lr=&id=0STcEAAAQBAJ&oi=fnd&pg=PA72&dq=De+Felice+et+al.,+2022+%2B+fear+of+missing+out+(FOMO)&ots=sr4_m3Klt_&sig=WuB8RWrPOO5ZAteuxbmwmijczyA10.1201/9781003251507-5

Di Vaio, A., Palladino, R., Hassan, R., & Escobar, O. (2020). Artificial intelligence and business models in the sustainable development goals perspective: A systematic literature review. *Journal of Business Research*, 121, 283–314. 10.1016/j.jbusres.2020.08.019

Festinger, L. (1954). A theory of social comparison processes. *Human Relations*, 7(2), 117–140. 10.1177/001872675400700202

Ganatra, N. J., & Pandya, J. D. (2023). The transformative impact of artificial intelligence on hr practices and employee experience: A review. *Journal of Management Research and Analysis*, 10(2), 106–111. 10.18231/j.jmra.2023.018

Gupta, M., & Sharma, A. (2021). Fear of missing out: A brief overview of origin, theoretical underpinnings and relationship with mental health. *World Journal of Clinical Cases*, 9(19), 4881–4889. 10.12998/wjcc.v9.i19.488134307542

Hinduja, S., & Patchin, J. W. (2010). Bullying, Cyberbullying, and Suicide. *Archives of Suicide Research*, 14(3), 206–221. 10.1080/13811118.2010.49413320658375

Jagoda, P. (2023). Artificial Intelligence in Video Games. *American Literature*, 95(2), 435–438. 10.1215/00029831-10575246

Martins, J., & Mota, L. (2022). *Innovative board game design in an academic environment during the Covid-19 pandemic.* DS 117: Proceedings of the 24th International Conference on Engineering and Product Design Education (E&PDE 2022), London South Bank University in London, UK. https://www.designsociety.org/download-publication/45838/INNOVATIVE+BOARD+GAME+DESIGN+IN+AN+ACADEMIC+ENVIRONMENT+DURING+THE+COVID-19+PANDEMIC

Marwick, A. E., & Boyd, D. (2014). Networked privacy: How teenagers negotiate context in social media. *New Media & Society*, 16(7), 1051–1067. 10.1177/1461444814543995

Niyozov, N., Bijanov, A., Ganiyev, S., & Kurbonova, R. (2023). The pedagogical principles and effectiveness of utilizing ChatGPT for language learning. *E3S Web of Conferences, 461*, 01093. E3S. https://www.e3s-conferences.org/articles/e3sconf/abs/2023/98/e3sconf_rses23_01093/e3sconf_rses23_01093.html

Odgers, C. L., & Jensen, M. R. (2020). Annual research review: Adolescent mental health in the digital age: Facts, fears, and future directions. *Journal of Child Psychology and Psychiatry, and Allied Disciplines*, 61(3), 336–348. 10.1111/jcpp.1319031951670

Peltola, L. (2019). *Making sense of the relationship between social media influencers on Instagram and the consumers who follow them* [Master's Thesis, Hanken School of Economics]. https://helda.helsinki.fi/bitstream/10227/261590/1/Peltola.pdf

Pendy, B. (2023). From traditional to tech-infused: The evolution of education. *BULLET: Jurnal Multidisiplin Ilmu*, 2(3), 767–777.

Post, B., Badea, C., Faisal, A., & Brett, S. J. (2023). Breaking bad news in the era of artificial intelligence and algorithmic medicine: An exploration of disclosure and its ethical justification using the hedonic calculus. *AI and Ethics*, 3(4), 1215–1228. 10.1007/s43681-022-00230-z36338525

Przybylski, A. K., Murayama, K., DeHaan, C. R., & Gladwell, V. (2013). Motivational, emotional, and behavioral correlates of fear of missing out. *Computers in Human Behavior*, 29(4), 1841–1848. 10.1016/j.chb.2013.02.014

Santos, F. C. C. (2023). Artificial intelligence in automated detection of disinformation: A thematic analysis. *Journalism and Media*, 4(2), 679–687. 10.3390/journalmedia4020043

Stenslie, S. (2011). *Virtual touch: A study of the use and experience of touch in artistic, multimodal and computer-based environments*. Oslo School of Architecture and Design. https://aho.brage.unit.no/aho-xmlui/bitstream/handle/11250/93049/Virtual%20Touch%20PhD%20Stenslie%20withCover.pdf

Tonini, L. (2024). *"Talk to me, Hal": A Study of Player Experience and Interaction in a Voice Interaction VR Game Featuring AI-driven Non-player Characters* [Master's Thesis, University of Twente]. http://essay.utwente.nl/98788/

Udayanan, A. R., Bargavi, N., Awasthi, S., Deshmukh, S. V., & Jadhav, D. Y. (2024). Determinants Influencing the Adoption of Artificial Intelligence in Driving Effective Human Resource Management. *Journal of Informatics Education and Research*, 4(2). http://jier.org/index.php/journal/article/view/828

# Chapter 6
# Digital Detox by Balancing Screen Time and Offline Experiences:
## Reclaiming Well-Being in a Hyper-Connected World

**Ruqia Safdar Bajwa**
https://orcid.org/0000-0002-4460-2025
*Bahauddin Zakariya University, Pakistan*

## ABSTRACT

*This chapter explains the impact of digital devices and the responsible use of technology. It analyses the harmful effects of prolonged screen time on our physical, mental, and social health. The chapter explores the benefits of digital detox interventions and their challenges. It concludes with a call for a mindful, personalized approach to technology use. It emphasizes the need for a balanced and conscious approach to technology use, highlighting the potential risks of excessive screen time as evidenced by empirical research. However, it also showcases the significant advantages of digital detox interventions, such as enhanced sleep quality, mood, productivity, creativity, and improved personal relations. The chapter offers strategies for adapting to diverse lifestyles, needs, and responsibilities.*

## INTRODUCTION

Technology is a significant part of life nowadays. We live in a world of screens, and it is hard to unplug. This is the concept of a digital detox- a period where you take a break from the screens and technology to connect it with the real world. The chapter investigates the significance of living in two realms simultaneously. It explores the positive aspects of a digital detox, including that it helps us improve our mental health, develop stronger interpersonal relations, and return to nature.

With technology advancing so quickly, it becomes essential to be aware of our use of technology and that it does not consume our lives. This chapter is a manifesto of digital living and the initiative to accept real-life moments as the ones that bring true happiness. The digitalization of communication technologies and the internet has penetrated our lives. Nevertheless, this has given rise to a discussion on digital de-

DOI: 10.4018/979-8-3693-3350-1.ch006

pendence. This addiction is demonstrated by a permanent need to be associated with these digital tools. It thus affects people of all ages, leading to physical, psychological, and social consequences. This issue has been under extensive academic debate to learn its roots, appearances, and broader social meanings.

Digital devices have become a way of life in the 21st century and have entirely changed how people communicate, study, and have fun. Although the digital revolution has had many positive impacts, it has also led to concerns regarding screen time, which is known to have adverse effects on health and developmental trajectories. The academic conversation about this subject matter is huge and multi-faceted, providing an overview of the many harmful consequences of increased screen time.

This discussion offers an in-depth overview of the field's current state by systematically considering empirical studies. It will discuss the consequences of too much screen time and focus on important worries.

## DIGITAL DETOX: CONCEPTUAL FRAMEWORK AND SIGNIFICANCE

Digital detox is a great practice when an individual does not use electronic communication devices to focus on natural life (Syvertsen, 2020). This notion is driven by the growing fears of increased digital time for netizens, which can lead to digital addictions and decreased concentration and face-to-face social contact (Lanier, 2018). In light of the latest technological dust being thrown in the air, a digital detox is a countercultural movement purposed to prevent the dominance of digital technologies over all-day life. The idea in the paraphrase implies intentionally cutting down or eliminating using modern devices such as smartphones, computers, or tablets to ease stress, foster better bonding with other people, and improve physical and mental health. The vast increase in internet use among the population gives rise to academic research on digital detox and its ability to improve one's life. This review aims to integrate articles published in scholarly journals about the relevance of digital detox in contemporary society.

The grounding of digital detox in psychological and social theories finds its roots in some key psycho-social theories. The theory of Planned Behavior Ajzen explains that attitudes, subjective norms, and perceived behavioral control are strong variables connected to the behavioral intention to take a digital detox. The theory of Planned Behavior (Ajzen, 1991) offers a model for understanding the necessary steps an individual may learn to introduce a successful digital retreat into their lifestyle. Based on the proposed perspective, an individual's intention of screen-free time is influenced by their attitude toward digital detox, perceived social desirability, and self-perceived degree of behavioral control over mobile phone utilization. This perspective, which is theoretically oriented, stresses the need to be intentional if the aim of turning off digital equipment is to be attained.

Furthermore, in his Flow Theory, which explains the benefits of digital detox, Csikszentmihalyi and Csikszentmihalyi (1990) provides much information. Flow, where we are fully immersed and engaged in an activity of choice, is more easily obtainable if our concentration is improved and our minds shift from being distracted and fragmented, a quality often not found in the digital device world. The digital detox can lead to flow exploration through alternative offline activities among people. It helps to achieve purpose by reducing stress and stimulating creativity, enhancing productivity and general well-being. The notion of digital detox also resonates with Turkle's (2011) critique of digital technology's impact on social relationships and the need for reliable human connections. The displacement hypothesis states that screentime is displacing the time people could be spending doing beneficial activities that are more fulfilling; for instance, the time could otherwise be used for physical exercise, face-to-face social interactions, and hobbies. The trade-off theory by Kushlev et al., (2016) argues that the damaging effects of prolonged screen entertainment include character stroke, deteriorated social relations, and psychological deterioration, which are, to a large extent, the cost of such activities.

Both theoretical and empirical arguments provide a solid and plausible grounding for the significance of digital detox as a powerful instrument in the fight against digital addiction, for success in physical and psychological dimensions, better and stronger social bonds, and correspondingly improved productivity and creativity. Understanding the scientific and theoretical foundations of digital detox is essential for people and communities as it makes applied measures convenient and unobtrusive and creates a healthier lifestyle that is physically and mentally balanced.

It adequately pointed out the link between too much digital device use and mental health issues like anxiety, depression, and stress (Twenge & Campbell, 2018). People distract themselves from detox by having multiple online interactions. They never get a chance to let their minds settle, resulting in re-duced stress and improved overall mental well-being (Sonnenberg et al., 2019). A dramatically growing problem, digital addiction, an isolated condition that leads an individual to excessive usage of digital electronic devices, results in the neglect of normal daily life activities is one of the major issues. Digital detox, as a solid antidote, presents a possibility for people, which allows them to reset and re-align their digital lifestyle. Alter (2017) emphasizes the transformative potential of digital detox in interrupting the addictive cycles and promoting a healthier, more conscious engagement with technology. Digital detox is undoubtedly the core of this control process since it allows people to turn off electronic devices and build up places of disconnection where everyone can recreate and connect to be calmed down and relaxed (Vanden Abeele, 2021). Evidenced-based experiments on digital detox have provided useful insights across life domains into the benefits of the detoxification process. An important experiment conducted by Hunt et al., (2018) confirmed that university students' orbital mental health increased after limiting their usage of social media platforms. The participants recorded decreased loneliness and depression ratings during the week of reduced social media exposure. The information was evidence-based, demonstrating the psychological benefits of digital detox.

Besides improving mental health, digital detox also significantly contributes to physical well-being. Too much time in front of the screens develops sedentary behavior, which is related to a woman's several health issues like obesity, cardiovascular diseases, etc. (Warburton et al., 2006). A sedentary lifestyle brought up by huge amounts of screen time is a trigger for obesity and some cardiovascular disorders. Chassiakos et al., (2016) have related in their research that digital detox initiatives not only cause the shift towards more physically active and health-conscious lives, thus reducing the risk of chronic diseases and promoting overall physical wellness. Taking such a measure will likely encourage a more active lifestyle and will be a positive factor in the physical condition of the person doing it. Disconnecting from the digital world, on the other hand, is a good way to foster more genuine and closer person-to-person communication, for it helps firmly develop and maintain important social ties (Turkle, 2011). Decreasing screen time may improve social understanding, deeper relationships, and communication skills. Like-wise, research shows that, among other things, less time in front of the screen in the plight before going to sleep is much more likely to improve our sleep quality. While looking at the blue light given out by screens at night, one can disturb the body's circadian rhythm, making it harder to fall asleep. Digital detox-type treatments to limit screen time during the evening have promoted better sleep patterns and overall psycho-emotional health (Levenson et al., 2017).

With the ubiquity of digital technology, the discourse is centered on the impact of this reality on cognition processes and attention spans. Unplugging from technology allows you to break from constant switching between tasks and digital interferences, which are probably the factors in improving your ability to focus, remember things, and think creatively (Carr, 2010). Social interaction has deteriorated as many people resort to busying themselves with machines rather than spending time with each other face to face. Turkle (2015) assumes that disconnecting digitally can improve the chances of meaningful interactions by eliminating digital fences that empower authentic social talks. They are the prime sources of empathy, and therefore, they break the barrier of social divisions. Evidence suggests that offline periods enable true interaction between people and, therefore, help strengthen relationships in an emotional sense. They add value to relationship satisfaction and contribute to feeling deeply connected with others (Turkle, 2015).

The benefits of the digital detox are noticeable, but one thing is that putting it into practice in a world where connectivity is high is still a challenge. The social pressure influenced by the fear of missing out (FOMO) and society's momentum for constant online availability adds to people's difficulty unplugging from their electronic devices (Przybylski et al., 2013). In addition, those professionals who depend upon digital or internet tools for their work and students who require those tools for the success of their educational life choose a healthy balance. The coming research may uncover the long-term benefits and the digital detox period that enhances health at individual and community levels. It should further look at the measures of digital detoxing in formal and informal spaces. Furthermore, assessing digital literacy's role in controlling digital consumption and making digital detox effective are the areas that should be explored.

Continuous phone notifications and digital intrusions are major distractions that can strip away focus, efficiency, and creativity. To illustrate the importance of digital relaxation, Newport (2016) emphasizes the need for periods of digital detoxes to gain attention, improve task performance, and heighten creative capacity. The digital-free zone puts more space in the cognitive sphere; therefore, the benefits of new ideas and deep work promoting productivity and flexibility attest to the dividends of digital detox.

As a general result, we can consider digital detox not only as a rest from digital devices but also as a regain of power and control over our digital lives, a positive impact on various aspects of our lives, and a creation of time for real-life connections with people. Digital technologies will keep emerging and advancing, thus spreading more at the center of our lives. Therefore, aiming for digital detoxes is becoming ever more critical for leading a balanced life in the becoming digital society.

Radtke et al. (2021) present a systemic literature review on the efficacy of digital detox interventions. In their appraisal, they underscore different approaches geared towards curbing the negative consequences of smartphone preference on social welfare and society. Based on the results, some impacts were affiliated with positive and negative outcomes, implying further studies to understand and refine more effective detox digital approaches (Radtke et al., 2021). In the contemporary world, digital detoxification has been introduced as a new intervention because it is needed to balance the drawbacks of the excessive use of digital technologies. Their range is great and comprises specific solutions different groups adopt to solve particular needs and habits. The value lies in facilitating healthier interaction between users and technology, improving the well-being of individuals, and influencing the users to be more active in the real world. The following contains the interventions and, in addition, the significance of such interventions on a digital detox.

Establishing tech-free zones entails designating areas where digital device use is barred or regulated, such as bedrooms, dining areas, or communal spaces. This intervention method facilitates lower screen usage during mealtime or sleep, leading to good sleep hygiene, new in-person meetings, and stronger family and social bonds. A digital detox intervention can start simply by spending hours or days away from these gadgets or setting them aside. This approach helps people spend time face-to-face with their families, motivates them to try new hobbies, and enables them to enjoy their special tastes offline and relax, as they do not have to worry about constantly watching notifications. There are many reasons why establishing and maintaining healthy screen time habits is crucial. Those reasons are boundary setting, coping with stress, and getting enough sleep (i.e., reducing the community blue light before bedtime). Pursuing a policy of online breaks that are fixed or pause times on tech each day convinces people to break away from their devices while on breaks. One of the main tactics proposed is interrupting this never-ending digital engagement cycle. It is thought that with such interruption, stress and eye strain are significantly minimized while freeing time for physical activity and unwinding. Perhaps this is how physical and mental well-being is maintained.

With digital sabbaticals, people check out from any digital device for many days, starting from a weekend and sometimes ending with a whole month. The opportunity to have extended time frames of disconnection from the internet enables people to engage in uninterrupted offline activities, thus allowing for personal introspection and mental refreshment and restoration. Information overload is a recent phenomenon. Conditions like mental health, creativity, and personal growth can significantly benefit from digital sabbaticals, which allow for a break in the constant information supply.

It is important to foster the habit of device-free meetings and social gatherings, which naturalize the mind to concentrate on the present activity; in that way, the interactions become more meaningful, and digital devices will not pull attention. Humanizing the interface is critical because it helps people reach their social, educational, and professional objectives by developing communication skills and creating stronger interpersonal relationships. Providing courses or workshops in mindfulness for technology use are platforms for individuals to learn how mindful mode of digital device use can minimize compulsive technology habits. These measures are crucial in developing the art of self-control, creating awareness, and fostering the conscious and goal-oriented use of technology and digital well-being.

Digital detox camps and retreats provide a purposefully planned setting separate from the digital world and often include nature to provide different ways of interacting with people and reflecting on oneself. These activities are a crucial way to promote interactive experiences that demonstrate the positive sides of detachment, reset the feedback loops of digital life, and give the retreat's participants access to the necessary tools for staying on the right track once they depart.

Personal digital lifestyle plans entail setting goals for using digital devices, specifying the reasons that lead to excessive use of digital devices, and acting to modify the lifestyle in the direction of healthier social media usage. Created considering individual needs, such plans play a critical role in fostering changes that remind people to stay digital savvy, tackle problems that have arisen, and allow them to live healthily.

Ideas from Cal Newport's digital minimalism provided a basis for this intervention based on a more mindful use of technology. By currency selecting digital devices, people will be in a win-win situation. They will be able to reap the fruits of those enormously beneficial digital tools, which will thus help people achieve their goals and values. Digital minimalism acknowledges intentional, sustainable, and meaningful relationships with technology by making us active, focused users rather than compliant creatures who use technological devices automatically.

Employing standalone apps or incorporating built-in smartphone functions to monitor and restrict screen time gives people information regarding their digital habits, which is essential in deciding their technology consumption. Such an intervention is fundamental in helping the audience understand one's digital consumption patterns, outline spaces for enhancements, and finally lead to a more balanced life in a digital environment free from excessive on-screen time.

Set aside specific periods daily to scan through emails, social media, and texts instead of constantly answering notifications and letting distractions take over. This strategy will help minimize distractions and improve concentration. This method is crucial in improving productivity and increasing the brain's capacity for engaging in multiple interactions or tasks, thus reducing cognitive load and leading to the most optimum online or offline engagement.

The fact that social media users take a break from social media platforms cannot but have positive mental effects, like relieving anxiety, depression, and social comparison, and therefore can bring forth a better self-image and mental health. Social media fasts are vital for a person to recalibrate the email on these platforms and the effect it might have on their overall well-being.

Digital detox interventions are critical tools for exploring the digital era, paving the way to a saner level of activity and interaction with technology. By executing these strategies, people can influence the advantages of digital interconnectedness without exposure to its negative manifestations, which further guarantees the enhancement of physical, mental, and social health and well-being.

## THE IMPORTANCE OF OFFLINE EXPERIENCES IN CONTEMPORARY SOCIETY

The importance of offline experiences and direct contact among youth in the digital age has received much attention in academic circles. This reflects a growing tendency towards the necessity of a mix of digital engagements and real-world interactions. Offline experiences are unavoidable in promoting total well-being and substantial societal connections. This discussion is relevant as digital technologies are omnipresent and modify human interactions and engagements. In this context, we demonstrate the multi-aspect advantages of offline experiences, supported by empirical research and theoretical frameworks, within the physical health, psychological well-being, cognitive development, and social interaction dimensions.

The report of scientific works on health outcomes from physical activities has been widely known. The publication of Warburton et al. (2006), a key work in this old field, demonstrates a pertinent relation between regular physical activities of rather light intensity (for example, walking) and outdoor sport exercises, on the one hand. Reduction of risks originating from chronic diseases (e.g., obesity, cardiovascular diseases, diabetes type 2), on the other. Similarly, Hartig et al., (2014) research brings strong logic concerning health gains derived from interchange with natural surroundings. The observed reductions in stress-related markers and mood-uplifting stem from earthen environment interactions contributing to a general welfare upsurge. Janssen and LeBlanc (2010) argued that physical activity plays an important role in reducing risk factors that are associated with sedentary lifestyles, such as obesity and metabolic syndrome. The authors emphasize that constant psychomotor activities, including sports and outdoor games, are vital for promoting the fitness and health of the young ones.

Not surprisingly, research has shown that the emotional lift provided by actual conversations and offline experiences, especially those related to nature and physical activity, is well-documented in academia. Berman et al., (2008) suggest that nature is a source of stress relief and care; it helps ease anxiety, depression, and emotional stress by contacting nature. Csikszentmihalyi's (1997) idea of flow, derived from meditation when in an indifferent state, better demonstrates how keeping digital stimuli to a minimal point supports mindfulness, mental rejuvenation, and stress alleviation that pave the way for psychological resilience and overall well-being. According to Twenge and Campbell (2018), it has been demonstrated that young people who spend more time on their gadgets have a higher risk of depression, and anxiety is rather higher. On the other hand, engaging in offline engagements such as hobbies or nature-based activities seems to significantly improve mood, mitigate anxiety, and provide an improved general sense of psychological resilience (Bowler et al., 2010).

Another dimension of research pinpointing the importance of offline (that is, face-to-face) activities to fuel critical thinking and creativity is another focus. Whitebread (2012) argues that unstructured play forms cognitive competence, creativity, and problem-solving; if you attend our conferences and listen to the presentations by experts in their fields, you will expand your knowledge base and gain new insights into the topics related to our organization. Moreover, you will have the opportunity to network with fellow attendees and exchange ideas and experiences, which can lead to While it is true that the practice of diverse offline activities, such as music and language-learning, in adults has been proven to result in better cognitive flexibility as well as higher creative output to the research of Hanna-Pladdy and Mackay (2011), it also suggests generally and widely that the offline experiences, regardless of the ages, play significant roles in cognition. Offline engagements with peers have a significant positive impact on youth, too. Free exploratory play alongside occurring activities in children's lives can provide significant cognitive and mental growth, as creativity, reasoning skills, and flexibility of mind stats progress accordingly (White & Pillemer, 2012). These activities give rise to a fascinating neuropsychological context within which playing an active role becomes a rather stimulating factor, unlike a listless passive shadow of digital content consumption.

The offline environment is a fundamental factor in the development/acculturation of relationships among people and the acquisition of specific social abilities. Konrath et al., (2011) argue about the power of face-to-face dialogues in developing empathy, communicative prowess, and comprehension, which are all essential for forming close bonds between people. Online interactions are barely enough, while offline interactions are required to develop social skills and empathy. Interaction with other people through social conversations and constructive games prepares children to advance their interpersonal skills, including empathy, conflict resolution, and communication capability (Konrath et al., 2011). These abilities form the foundation of appropriate social behavior, are key to forming satisfactory personal relationships, and are important when negotiating the complexities of social dynamics. Moreover, Putnam (2000) emphasizes the societal role of community engagements and activity groups in emphasizing social bonds and a feeling of belonging, which consequently increases the levels of community cohesion, thus pointing to the social capital acquired due to offline engagements.

Offline experiences have a strong influence on educational achievements. Students are further motivated as the school offers hands-on experiences, physical education, and extracurricular activities. These complement traditional classroom learning; thus, the student's education is filled out (Fredricks et al., 2019). These exercises benefit the student's educational progress and the unique learning environment they create, combining the physical, social, emotional, and much to the-charm.

The research community has been focusing on the health benefits of offline interaction regarding physical health improvement, psychological well-being improvement, cognitive development expansion, social engagement and development, and educating society. In the digital world, the face-to-face or on-the-spot experiences for youth are an inseparable part of the trend. Digital technologies increasingly reinforce the fabric of modern society, which needs to be highlighted, and one's positive influence needs to be appreciated, especially in the youth. Moreover, people who participate in them focus on their health and happiness individually and as a group, enhancing empathy, oneness, and society for a better-connected society. Surveys and scientific papers confirm the need for the selective consequent usage of offline resources and lifestyle to achieve the best life with the right balance between online and offline life.

## THE DETRIMENTAL EFFECTS OF EXCESSIVE SCREEN TIME ON PHYSICAL, MENTAL, AND SOCIAL HEALTH AND DEVELOPMENT

There is growing empirical evidence that prolonged screen exposure has malevolent effects on people's health and development, especially neurodevelopment and cognitive functions. Neophytou, Manwell, and Eikelboom (2019) comprehensively review studies that show that overwhelming screen use harms cognition, behavior, and emotions in adolescents and young adults. In addition, there is a possible association with the elevated risk of elder dementia, not to mention the long-term impacts of early screen exposure.

The most widespread rise of screen exposure across all age groups with the advent of smartphones, tablets, and other digital gadgets has led to growing evidence of the effects of a sedentary lifestyle on health. This discussion expands on the primary concerns associated with excessive screen time: the health implications from a comprehensive review of the current literature. Goswami and Parekh (2023) indicate that prolonged screen time has physical health ramifications, including obesity, sleep disorders, and decreased physical activity. These three health concerns outline an emergency public health issue that can be resolved through efforts to change lifestyle habits to more active ones and to counter the sedentary behavior associated with screen use.

Much research has shown that continual use of screens leads to sleep fragmentation, especially before one goes to sleep. Blue light produced by screens has been shown as a factor hindering the production of melatonin, the hormone that controls the sleep cycle, thereby prolonging the time needed for sleep and deteriorating both the quality and the quantity of sleep (Chang et al., 2015; Van der Lely et al., 2015). For instance, Van der Lely et al. (2015) proved that blue blocker glasses could partially attenuate this effect by reducing LED-induced melatonin suppression in the evening, thus providing a valid countermeasure to the sleep-disturbing features of the blue light.

The connection between screen time and sedentary behavior is considerable for physical health, particularly the increased risks of obesity, cardiovascular diseases, and type 2 diabetes (Tremblay et al., 2011). A sedentary lifestyle is associated with various health risks and is often caused by too much screen time that replaces physical activity. Interventions designed to limit screen time with activities that require movements, such as exercise videos, are needed to counteract these effects. Digital Eye Strain (DES) is a complex symptomatology of eye and vision problems caused by the overuse of screens, which has been described as eye strain, headaches, blurred vision, and dry eyes (Sheppard & Wolffsohn, 2018). Digital screen use imposes high visual stress, resulting in discomfort and possible long-term visual disorders. Recommendations for the prevention of DES include the 20-20-20 principle (every 20 minutes of screen use, look 20 feet away for 20 seconds), adaption of screen settings, and lubricating eye drops.

Apart from the immediate impact on sleep, sedentary lifestyle, and vision, there are more issues associated with the excessive use of screens. Such issues are but are not limited to, metabolic syndrome, neck, and back pain caused by bad posture, and even mental health-related problems like anxiety and depression, which could be further worsened by too much use of social media and other interactive platforms. The evidence highlights the multiple negative health influences of too much screen time, emphasizing the necessity of complex approaches to control these threats. Strategies could also involve educational efforts about the safe use of screens, promoting other activities that do not involve screens before bed, and implementing technological solutions such as blue light filters. In a world where digital devices are integrated into all spheres of life, their benefit must be weighed against the potential health hazards. Since the health implications of screen time are wide-ranging, further research has to be conducted in this direction, employing mainly longitudinal studies that would help to reveal the causal links and the success of various approaches to overcoming such issues. All public health policies should include these findings to foster healthier use of digital devices across all age groups.

Thus, a second issue is the research that connects screen time with developmental delays. Varadarajan et al. (2021) emphasize a strong association between screen time and language acquisition and communication skills delay. This association highlights the need to manage screen time early in life, which is important in reaching milestones. In summary, the literature body discussed here articulates the multipronged adverse impacts of overt screen time on health and development. Overexposure to screen time also influences learning and memory, where excessive exposure is linked with adverse outcomes. Muppalla et al. (2023) show that too much screen time reduces academic performance and executive functioning. This is concerning, considering the important role of early educational outcomes in long-term cognitive and social development.

More importantly, the correlation between time spent in front of a screen and mental health is dreadful. Too much screen time has been associated with a variety of mental problems, including anxiety, depression, and low self-esteem. Neophytou et al., (2019) present an extensive review and suggest that chronic sensory input from excessive screen use may impair brain development, elevating the danger of cognitive, behavioral, and emotional disorders in adolescents and young adults. The flow of information and pervasive social comparison fostered by digital platforms are the main instigators of these outcomes, deepening the sense of inadequacy and isolation. This also involves an increased vulnerability to the early appearance of dementia in late age. In addition, Lissak (2018) emphasizes the connection between high screen time and several mental health problems like depression, anxiety, and substance use disorders. This set of findings highlights the importance of creating rules and regulations on-screen usage to protect society's mental health. Another detailed analysis of the effects of technology overuse on mental health is presented by Scott et al., (2017). They spotlight a host of negative consequences linked to the overuse of digital media, starting from deteriorating social and emotional intelligence skills to increased ADHD and depression incidence. This points out the urgent need for effective counseling interventions to help curtail technology abuse's effects and promote a balanced digital living.

The effect of screen time on cognitive growth and attentional abilities, especially among children and teenagers, is an important issue. Long-time screen time is associated with attention deficit, concentration impairment, and cognitive development delay. Swift and fragmented digital content consumption may change cognitive processes and learning models. Goswami and Parekeh's systematic review (2023) on the adverse impact of screen time on child development found that profuse screen time was linked with negative consequences on all four development dimensions: cognitive, social, emotional, and physical. In particular, long screen time was discovered to harm attention, language, memory, and motor skills development (Goswami & Parekh, 2023). The literature further reveals that the digital era poses a complicated psychological and cognitive issue. The evidence suggests a robust relationship between too much exposure to screen time and several mental health problems, such as anxiety, depression, and low self-esteem. Further, a significant body of literature proves that screen time can interfere with cognitive processes and attentional resources, affecting educational results and development paths.

One of the early investigations into digital stress conducted by Reinecke et al. (2017) focuses on the factors that predict perceived stress suffering from various psychological health impairments such as burnout, depression, and anxiety, where communication overload, as well as internet multitasking, were found to be the significant predictors of perceived stress as a part of digital stress concept. The dynamics behind these behaviors, such as pressure from social groups and fear of missing out, reveal the many facets of digital addiction, which goes beyond technology use to involve broader social and psychological aspects. Kraut et al. (1998) discussed the nature of the Internet paradox. They pointed out that despite its potential to improve communication, its use is linked to declines in close family communication, a fall in social circles, and an increase in depression and loneliness. This paradoxical consequence accentuates the difficult association between the use of digital media and social health, refuting the belief that the development of connections always results in positive side social effects.

Nowland et al., (2018) hypothesize an integrated model of loneliness and social internet use. They contend that the effects of the internet on loneliness are bidirectional and depend on the user's intention. In cases where the internet is used to create real social connections, it is a useful solution to loneliness. However, when used as a way of avoidance, it only increases isolation, which means that the main goal of use significantly influences the psychological effects of digital engrossment.

Weiser (2001) investigates internet use, arguing that the user's purposes largely determine digital involvement's social and psychological implications. The contrast between socio-affective regulation and goods-and-information acquisition as major determinants of internet use offers an understanding of how digital technology meets different needs and aspirations and, as a result, impacts individual and social integration.

The academic investigations of digital dependency reflect a terrain full of paradox and complication. Evidence indicates that although digital technologies provide practitioners with unique connectivity and information access options, their misuse or overuse has the potential for significant individual and societal harm. In this manner, targeted interventions that target the symptoms of digital dependency and the root causes need to be urgently developed, creating a digital environment where human and social life exists and is the priority. Since digital devices are becoming increasingly rooted in our lives, it is important to listen to these warnings and develop strategies for controlling their negative consequences. The relationships need to be further elaborated upon by future research and provide the development of inclusive recommendations for the health and well-being of individuals in the digital age.

The impact of the widespread increase in screen time is evident in profound social and behavioral changes. This greatly affects interpersonal skills and behavioral adjustment. This conversation focuses on poor social aptitudes and behavioral problems that result from too much screen time. Digital media of communication, however, is often a barrier to human interaction, which plays a critical role in developing vital social competencies. This concern is also noted by Uhls et al. (2014), who mention that overuse of screens can prevent the development of empathetic understanding and the perception of nonverbal signals, both essential for the mastery of interpersonal communication. The displace effect, where digital interactions substitute faith for face-to-face interaction, concerns the development of social skills in the complete sense of the word. Such a decrease in direct social contact can probably cause the formation and maintenance of personal relationships to become difficult and cause a decrease in social cohesion and empathy.

Prolongation of screen time is also linked with behavioral problems in pediatric populations, such as aggressiveness, hyperactivity, and attentional deficits. The fact that the nature of screen exposure, particularly the type of content seen, can aggravate these behavioral problems points out the importance of controlling and regulating screen content among young users. In addition, the displacement of some developmentally productive activities by screen time matters in these behavioral problems, meaning it is important not only the quantity but also the quality of screen engagement (Muppalla et al., 2023).

The results of the systematic reviews and thematic analyses highlighted the multifaceted nature of screen time's effects on social skills and behavior development. For example, in their scoping review, Neophytou et al. (2019) linked increased screen time to unfavorable outcomes such as reduced self-esteem, higher occurrence and severity of mental health disorders, slow learning and acquisition, and early cognitive decline, all of which can form the basis of the displayed behavioral problems.

The body of proof underlines the need to focus on the social and behavioral impact of screen time overconsumption. Interventions designed to limit screen time and promote other activities stimulating direct social interaction and physical activity seem important in preventing these adverse effects. In addition, education efforts directed at parents, teachers, and policymakers are needed to moderate the issue of screen exposure, emphasizing quality, not quantity, and the relevance of content suitability.

The subtlety in how much time is spent in front of a screen influences social and behavioral development. It highlights the need for a multidisciplinary approach to designing strategies supporting healthy digital engagement and the development of crucial interpersonal skills and behavioral regulation.

## EXPLORING CASE STUDIES AND SUCCESS STORIES OF DIGITAL DETOX

Looking at case studies and success stories related to digital detox leads to very important information about how effective digital detox can be from a practical perspective and as a result. Therefore, real-life cases drawn from literature and anecdotes demonstrate two important aspects of digital detox interventions: their gains and shortcomings, which, consequently, allow us to see their influence on both individuals and societies.

In the book "Digital Minimalism: An article centered on "A Focused Life in a Busy World" by Cal Newport (2019), he outlines the implications of people who purposely abstain from the internet within thirty days. Participants were advised to delete the devices (technologies) they do not need, re-evaluate their digital lifestyle, and bring home the tools that matter most to them. Many volunteers said their mood, closeness to those around them, and personal happiness rose markedly. This case aptly illustrates the need to apply consciousness in technology use. As such, an upfront attitude toward digital detoxing may result in deep, physical, and emotional changes in personal and professional well-being.

The research by Radesky et al. (2015) identified how significant it is to control the use of screens in families. The investigation group collaborated with child family members to design zones and limit screen time. They promoted board games, outdoor play, and reading instead. According to parents' reports, families manifested improved communication, more shared activities, and less conflicting screen time at the post-intervention stage. This episode highlights a promising situation when the technologically enhanced detoxification program for families could be instrumental in facilitating family communications and leisure activities selection.

Digital detoxes like 'Time To Log Off' and Digital Detox can be found in retreats that allow individuals to unplug mobile devices and engage in activities promoting relaxation, yoga, and nature. Likewise, retreatants commonly share stories of how they felt more alive, aware, and peaceful after the experience. Nonetheless, literature supporters can easily question the reasons behind the programs after they are successfully implemented. It would not be undermined, however, gaining a complete mindful technology use operation in the coming days (Syvertsen, 2020). This report gives an example of a 'dive-into' detox experience and calls to attention that renewal of abstention practices will still be necessary for improved results.

Many companies have installed digital detox programs to reduce employee burnout and increase productivity. For example, in a case study within "The Joy of Missing Out: "Live More by Doing Less," a company adopted a rule that refrains from e-mails on Fridays. This is done to entice employees to communicate with bosses via phone or person-to-person. The program was conducted successfully, and the outcome resulted in the formation of a better team mood, reduced stress levels, and work efficiency. This appears to illustrate the ability of digital detox programs to enrich the workplace setting and urge for proper communication.

These case studies and success stories demonstrate diversified benefits of digital detox, such as better mental health, increased workplace productivity, enhanced family relationships, and good personal well-being. Digital detox interventions may indeed deliver excellent initial outcomes; nonetheless, the success of these practices highly depends on their ongoing integration with mindful technology usage habits. As the digital landscape is constantly changing, these stories, anecdotes, and analyses remain forever valuable lessons whose application can help communities to have a healthy and balanced digital life.

## CONCLUSION: CHALLENGES AND CONSIDERATIONS

Though the positive effects of a digital detox are well-researched, defying digital addiction remains a challenge. Digital technologies take a leading position in our understanding of the contemporary world, hence the need for a balanced approach that considers the positive side of technology and curtails the negative. This remains the most important aspect of the 21st century (Harris, 2020).

One of the main difficulties related to the electronic detox process is finding the right measure of the digital and real worlds. In our digital society, digital technologies are not only all around us but also can be found in every part of our lives: education, work, and social interactions (Vorderer et al., 2016). Therefore, this requires us to develop a more complex perspective that considers the advantages of technology that, among other things, help users gain greater access to information and improved communication possibilities. It also warns about excessive use of them.

For most digital detoxers, FOMO is one of the essential barriers. Individuals can experience the anxiety of not accessing important information or conversations on social networks, which pushes them to spend more time on electronic devices despite the attempt to cut back (Przybylski et al., 2013). This problem is very pronounced among the younger generations, who may get most of their socializing and information through digital platforms.

For a significant part of the professional and academic world, digital devices are invaluable instruments of work and study. Limiting the time spent on the internet and computers in work and studying life is difficult. Therefore, the strategies for digital detox should be versatile, sustaining the use of the digital medium for all essential engagements while limiting non-essential digital consumption (Newport, 2016).

Digital detox must also take into account problems related to access and equity. The digital divide, the gulf between those who can and those who do not possess the technologies, is one of the core issues of digital detox initiatives (Ragnedda & Muschert, 2013). Digital detox endeavors must be careful not to worsen the problem for those without access to digital technologies.

Forming healthy strategies for digital detox requires developing individual plans that consider individual needs, responsibilities, and lifestyles (Syvertsen, 2020). Tactics could include setting tech-free times, using apps to regulate or limit screen time, and doing offline activities as a means of fulfillment and relaxation.

Digital detox implementation is a complicated action that needs a responsible examination of the difficulty and realities of modern digital existence. Although the advantages of decreasing screen time are obvious, examining this problem requires a more critical approach tailored to the individual's needs. By recognizing FOMO challenges, the dependency on work and education, and the digital divide, people can build up their own efficient digital detox methods that preserve well-being without losing the positive side of digital technology.

Although a digital detox can successfully promote both mental and physical health, there are several difficulties and factors that one has to be cautious against to achieve the goal. These challenges might be as diverse as individual withdrawal symptoms and how society is affected in terms of striking a balance between digital connectivity for work and education on the one side and personal well-being on the other. Awareness of these challenges is essential for anyone planning for a digital detox and for many organizations who wish to help people develop a healthier way of using the digital.

One of the first hindrances people experimenting with a digital detox will likely encounter is possibly withdrawal effects. Similar to any form of addiction, the reduction or elimination of digital device use may create feelings of anxiousness, constant restlessness, and boredom (Lin et al., 2016). This might be particularly evident in persons who depend on social networks for social interaction and end up feeling isolated when the very virtual interactions they are used to are limited. The symptoms can be reduced using techniques such as progressively lowering screen time, creating realistic goals, and selecting other activities to spend the time devoted to digital devices in the past.

Digital Detox is, however, a double-edged sword in that there is also the social isolation risk, particularly with social media sites being the main portals of connection and communication between individuals. While this may be the reality for many people when disconnected, these platforms become a lifeline for their family and friends, and as such, quitting can be compared to losing a lifeline. To deal with this issue, the persons participating in an online detox must strongly focus on real-life offline relationships. That could help to nurture social skills. Participating in group activities, hobbies, or community events will ensure that you have something different altogether, where making new friends and getting support will be easier during the detox period.

Nowadays, technology has penetrated almost every sphere of our lives as we carry out our working and education arrangements. These remote setups and online learning platforms are part and parcel of our daily lives. The entangling of professional and educational activities with digital devices is the biggest barrier to going digital-free. People must tailor this balance to a level that keeps them productively engaged in work and study while internet non-essentials are avoided. Strategies for reaching the equilibrium include allocating specific times for checking emails and social media, using website blockers to minimize distractions during working or studying hours, and ensuring that leisure time is not spent in front of the screens.

Fundamentally, the purpose of a digital detox is to take good care of one's health and well-being. However, it is vital to discover the balance between connection and disconnect. However, getting rid of digital devices is not possible for many people, nor is it advisable for the technological dominance in the modern world. Emphasis should be on the conscious use of technology, recognizing the times when digital engagements are helpful and when they contribute to the decline of health and happiness. Creating a personalized plan covering specific demands and commitments and each person's routines is paramount for a well-carried digital detox.

The task of a digital detox is challenging. However, with effort and perhaps a little help, it is possible. Digital Detox can be a positive step towards addressing the potential downsides of technology involvement, including withdrawal symptoms, social isolation, and a need to balance the good with the bad. Through deliberate interaction with technology and applying self-regulation for digital use, relationships can be maintained better and healthier with digital devices.

# REFERENCES

Ajzen, I. (1991). The theory of planned behavior. *Organizational Behavior and Human Decision Processes*, 50(2), 179–211. 10.1016/0749-5978(91)90020-T

Alter, A. (2017). *Irresistible: The Rise of Addictive Technology and the Business of Keeping Us Hooked*. Penguin Books.

Berman, M. G., Jonides, J., & Kaplan, S. (2008). The Cognitive Benefits of Interacting With Nature. *Psychological Science*, 19(12), 1207–1212. 10.1111/j.1467-9280.2008.02225.x19121124

Bowler, D. E., Buyung-Ali, L. M., Knight, T. M., & Pullin, A. S. (2010). A systematic review of evidence for the benefits of exposure to natural environments to health. *BMC Public Health*, 10(1), 456. 10.1186/1471-2458-10-45620684754

Bratman, G. N., Daily, G. C., Levy, B. J., & Gross, J. J. (2015). The benefits of nature experience: Improved affect and cognition. *Landscape and Urban Planning*, 138, 41–50. 10.1016/j.landurbplan.2015.02.005

Carr, N. (2010). *The Shallows: What the Internet Is Doing to Our Brains*. W.W. Norton & Company.

Chang, A. M., Aeschbach, D., Duffy, J. F., & Czeisler, C. A. (2015). Evening use of light-emitting eReaders negatively affects sleep, circadian timing, and next-morning alertness. *Proceedings of the National Academy of Sciences of the United States of America*, 112(4), 1232–1237. 10.1073/pnas.141849011225535358

Csikszentmihalyi, M. (1990). *Flow: The Psychology of Optimal Experience*. Harper & Row.

Csikszentmihalyi, M. (1997). *Finding Flow: The Psychology of Engagement with Everyday Life*. Basic Books.

Csikszentmihalyi, M., & Csikzentmihaly, M. (1990). *Flow: The psychology of optimal experience* (Vol. 1990). Harper & Row.

Dalton, T. (2019). *The Joy of Missing Out: Live More by Doing Less*. Thomas Nelson.

Davis, C. H. (2019). Student activism, resource mobilization, and new tactical repertoires in the 'digital age. In *Student activism, politics, and campus climate in higher education* (pp. 112–124). Routledge. 10.4324/9780429449178-7

Fredricks, J. A., Bohnert, A. M., & Burdette, K. (2019). Moving beyond attendance: Lessons learned from assessing engagement in afterschool contexts. *Journal of Youth Development*.

Goswami, P., & Parekh, V. (2023). The impact of screen time on child and adolescent development: A review. *International Journal of Contemporary Pediatrics*, 10(7), 1161–1165. 10.18203/2349-3291.ijcp20231865

Greenfield, P. M. (2019). Communication technologies and social transformation: Their impact on human development. *Children in changing worlds: Sociocultural and temporal perspectives*, pp. 235–273. APA.

Greenfield, S. (2017). *Cognitive development and screen time in children*.

Hanna-Pladdy, B., & Mackay, A. (2011). The relation between instrumental musical activity and cognitive aging. *Neuropsychology*, 25(3), 378–386. 10.1037/a002189521463047

Harris, T. (2020). Tech companies must rethink the 'fear of missing out' they have created. *The Guardian*.

Hartig, T., Mitchell, R., de Vries, S., & Frumkin, H. (2014). Nature and Health. *Annual Review of Public Health*, 35(1), 207–228. 10.1146/annurev-publhealth-032013-18244324387090

Hinkley, T., & McCann, J. R. (2018). Mothers' and father's perceptions of the risks and benefits of screen time and physical activity during early childhood: A qualitative study. *BMC Public Health*, 18(1), 1–8. 10.1186/s12889-018-6199-630453927

Hunt, M. G., Marx, R., Lipson, C., & Young, J. (2018). No More FOMO: Limiting Social Media Decreases Loneliness and Depression. *Journal of Social and Clinical Psychology*, 37(10), 751–768. 10.1521/jscp.2018.37.10.751

Janssen, I., & LeBlanc, A. G. (2010). A systematic review of the health benefits of physical activity and fitness in school-aged children and youth. *The International Journal of Behavioral Nutrition and Physical Activity*, 7(1), 40. 10.1186/1479-5868-7-4020459784

Kabat-Zinn, J. (2003). Mindfulness-based interventions in context: Past, present, and future. *Clinical Psychology : a Publication of the Division of Clinical Psychology of the American Psychological Association*, 10(2), 144–156. 10.1093/clipsy.bpg016

Kardefelt-Winther, D. (2014). A conceptual and methodological critique of internet addiction research: Towards a model of compensatory internet use. *Computers in Human Behavior*, 31, 351–354. 10.1016/j.chb.2013.10.059

Konrath, S., O'Brien, E. H., & Hsing, C. (2011). Changes in dispositional empathy in American college students over time: A meta-analysis. *Personality and Social Psychology Review*, 15(2), 180–198. 10.1177/1088868310377395 20688954

Kraut, R., Patterson, M., Lundmark, V., Kiesler, S., Mukopadhyay, T., & Scherlis, W. (1998). Internet paradox. A social technology that reduces social involvement and psychological well-being? *The American Psychologist*, 53(9), 1017–1031. 10.1037/0003-066X.53.9.10179841579

Kushlev, K., Proulx, J., & Dunn, E. W. (2016). "Silence Your Phones": Smartphone Notifications Increase Inattention and Hyperactivity Symptoms. *Proceedings of the 2016 CHI Conference on Human Factors in Computing Systems*. ACM. 10.1145/2858036.2858359

Lanier, J. (2018). *Ten Arguments for Deleting Your Social Media Accounts Right Now*. Henry Holt and Co.

Levenson, J. C., Shensa, A., Sidani, J. E., Colditz, J. B., & Primack, B. A. (2017). The association between social media use and sleep disturbance among young adults. *Preventive Medicine*, 85, 36–41. 10.1016/j.ypmed.2016.01.00126791323

Lin, L. Y., Sidani, J. E., Shensa, A., Radovic, A., Miller, E., Colditz, J. B., Hoffman, B. L., Giles, L. M., & Primack, B. A. (2016). Association between social media use and depression among U.S. young adults. *Depression and Anxiety*, 33(4), 323–331. 10.1002/da.2246626783723

Lin, Y.-H., Lin, Y.-C., Lee, Y.-H., Lin, P.-H., Lin, S.-H., Chang, L.-R., Tseng, H.-W., Yen, L.-Y., Yang, C. C. H., & Kuo, T. B. J. (2016). Time distortion associated with smartphone addiction: Identifying smartphone addiction via a mobile application (App). *Journal of Psychiatric Research*, 65, 139–145. 10.1016/j.jpsychires.2015.04.00325935253

Lissak, G. (2018). Adverse physiological and psychological effects of screen time on children and adolescents: Literature review and case study. *Environmental Research*, 164, 149–157. 10.1016/j.envres.2018.01.01529499467

Loh, K. K., & Kanai, R. (2016). *How digital screen time affects attention spans.*

Muppalla, S. K., Vuppalapati, S., Pulliahgaru, A. R., & Sreenivasulu, H. (2023). Effects of Excessive Screen Time on Child Development: An Updated Review and Strategies for Management. *Cureus*, 15. 10.7759/cureus.4060837476119

Neophytou, E., Manwell, L. A., & Eikelboom, R. (2019). Effects of Excessive Screen Time on Neurodevelopment, Learning, Memory, Mental Health, and Neurodegeneration: A Scoping Review. *International Journal of Mental Health and Addiction*, 19(3), 724–744. 10.1007/s11469-019-00182-2

Newport, C. (2016). *Deep Work: Rules for Focused Success in a Distracted World.* Grand Central Publishing.

Newport, C. (2019). *Digital Minimalism: Choosing a Focused Life in a Noisy World.* Portfolio.

Nowland, R., Necka, E. A., & Cacioppo, J. T. (2018). Loneliness and Social Internet Use: Pathways to Reconnection in a Digital World? *Perspectives on Psychological Science*, 13(1), 70–87. 10.1177/1745 69161771305228937910

Porter, A. K., Matthews, K. J., Salvo, D., & Kohl, H. W. (2017). Associations of physical activity, sedentary time, and screen time with cardiovascular fitness in United States adolescents: Results from the NHANES National Youth Fitness Survey. *Journal of Physical Activity & Health*, 14(7), 506–512. 10.1123/jpah.2016-016528290741

Przybylski, A. K., Murayama, K., DeHaan, C. R., & Gladwell, V. (2013). The motivational value of digital games: A uses and gratification perspective. *Psychology of Popular Media Culture*, 2(2), 90–109.

Putnam, R. D. (2000). *Bowling Alone: The Collapse and Revival of American Community.* Simon & Schuster.

Radesky, J. S., Schumacher, J., & Zuckerman, B. (2015). Mobile and interactive media use by young children: The good, the bad, and the unknown. *Pediatrics*, 135(1), 1–3. 10.1542/peds.2014-225125548323

Radtke, T., Apel, T., Schenkel, K., Keller, J., & von Lindern, E. (2022). Digital detox: An effective solution in the smartphone era? A systematic literature review. *Mobile Media & Communication*, 10(2), 190–215. 10.1177/20501579211028647

Ragnedda, M., & Muschert, G. W. (2013). *The digital divide: The internet and social inequality in international perspective.* Routledge. 10.4324/9780203069769

Reid Chassiakos, Y. L., Radesky, J., Christakis, D., Moreno, M. A., Cross, C., Hill, D., Ameenuddin, N., Hutchinson, J., Levine, A., Boyd, R., Mendelson, R., & Swanson, W. S. (2016). Children and adolescents and digital media. *Pediatrics*, 138(5), e20162593. 10.1542/peds.2016-259327940795

Reinecke, L., Aufenanger, S., Beutel, M. E., Dreier, M., Quiring, O., Stark, B., Wölfling, K., & Müller, K. W. (2017). Digital Stress over the Life Span: The Effects of Communication Load and Internet Multitasking on Perceived Stress and Psychological Health Impairments in a German Probability Sample. *Media Psychology*, 20(1), 90–115. 10.1080/15213269.2015.1121832

Sandstrom, G. M., & Dunn, E. W. (2014). Social interactions and well-being: The surprising power of weak ties. *Personality and Social Psychology Bulletin*, 40(7), 910–922. 10.1177/0146167214529799924769739

Scott, D. A., Valley, B., & Simecka, B. A. (2017). Mental Health Concerns in the Digital Age. *International Journal of Mental Health and Addiction*, 15(3), 604–613. 10.1007/s11469-016-9684-0

Sheppard, A. L., & Wolffsohn, J. S. (2018). Digital eye strain: Prevalence, measurement and amelioration. *BMJ Open Ophthalmology*, 3(1), e000146. 10.1136/bmjophth-2018-00014629963645

Sonnenberg, B., Riediger, M., Wrzus, C., & Wagner, G. G. (2019). Me, myself, and my mobile: A segmentation of youths based on their attitudes towards the mobile phone as a status instrument. *Computers in Human Behavior*, 93, 252–262.

Syvertsen, T. (2020). *Digital detox: The politics of disconnecting*. Emerald Publishing Limited. 10.1108/9781787693395

Syvertsen, T., & Enli, G. (2020). Digital detox: Media resistance and the promise of authenticity. *Convergence (London)*, 26(5-6), 1269–1283. 10.1177/1354856519847325

Tremblay, M. S., LeBlanc, A. G., Kho, M. E., Saunders, T. J., Larouche, R., Colley, R. C., Goldfield, G., & Connor Gorber, S. (2011). A systematic review of sedentary behaviour and health indicators in school-aged children and youth. *The International Journal of Behavioral Nutrition and Physical Activity*, 8(1), 98. 10.1186/1479-5868-8-9821936895

Turkle, S. (2011). *Alone Together: Why We Expect More from Technology and Less from Each Other*. Basic Books.

Turkle, S. (2015). *Reclaiming Conversation: The Power of Talk in a Digital Age*. Penguin Press.

Twenge, J. M. (2017, September). Have smartphones destroyed a generation? *Atlantic (Boston, Mass.)*.

Twenge, J. M., & Campbell, W. K. (2018). Associations between screen time and lower psychological well-being among children and adolescents: Evidence from a population-based study. *Preventive Medicine Reports*, 12, 271–283. 10.1016/j.pmedr.2018.10.00330406005

Twenge, J. M., & Campbell, W. K. (2018). *Psychological effects of screen time on children and adolescents*. Science Direct.

Uhls, Y. T., Michikyan, M., Morris, J., Garcia, D., Small, G. W., Zgourou, E., & Greenfield, P. M. (2014). Five days at outdoor education camp without screens improves preteen skills with nonverbal emotion cues. *Computers in Human Behavior*, 39, 387–392. 10.1016/j.chb.2014.05.036

Valkenburg, P. M., Peter, J., & Schouten, A. P. (2016). Friend networking sites and their relationship to adolescents' well-being and social self-esteem. *Cyberpsychology & Behavior*, 9(5), 584–590. 10.1089/cpb.2006.9.58417034326

Van der Lely, S., Frey, S., Garbazza, C., Wirz-Justice, A., Jenni, O., Steiner, R., Wolf, S., Cajochen, C., Bromundt, V., & Schmidt, C. (2015). Blue blocker glasses as a countermeasure for alerting effects of evening light-emitting diode screen exposure in male teenagers. *The Journal of Adolescent Health*, 56(1), 113–119. 10.1016/j.jadohealth.2014.08.00225287985

Vanden Abeele, M. M. (2021). Digital well-being as a dynamic construct. *Communication Theory*, 31(4), 932–955. 10.1093/ct/qtaa024

Varadarajan, S., Venguidesvarane, A. G., Ramaswamy, K., Rajamohan, M., Krupa, M., & Christadoss, S. B. (2021). Prevalence of excessive screen time and its association with developmental delay in children aged <5 years: A population-based cross-sectional study in India. *PLoS One*, 16(7), 16. 10.1371/journal.pone.025410234228768

Vorderer, P., Krömer, N., & Schneider, F. M. (2016). Permanently online, connected: Explorations into university students' use of social media and mobile smart devices. *Computers in Human Behavior*, 63, 694–703. 10.1016/j.chb.2016.05.085

Warburton, D. E., Nicol, C. W., & Bredin, S. S. (2006). Health benefits of physical activity: The evidence. [CMAJ]. *Canadian Medical Association Journal*, 174(6), 801–809. 10.1503/cmaj.05135116534088

Weiser, E. B. (2001). The Functions of Internet Use and Their Social and Psychological Consequences. *Cyberpsychology & Behavior*, 4(6), 723–743. 10.1089/109493101753337667811800180

White, R. E., & Pillemer, D. B. (2012). Childhood memory and self-description in young adults: The role of family context and autobiographical memory strategies. *Memory (Hove, England)*, 20(4), 445–457.

Whitebread, D. (2012). *The Importance of Play*. Cambridge Primary Review Trust.

# Section 2
# Educational and Career Development

# Chapter 7
# AI–Enhanced Youth Career Guidance by Mapping Future Employment Paths With Theory and Practical Application

**Seyedali Ahrari**
https://orcid.org/0000-0001-9094-8695
*Women and Family Studies Research Center, University of Religions and Denominations, Iran*

**Zeinab Zaremohzzabieh**
https://orcid.org/0000-0002-1497-7942
*Women and Family Studies Research Center, University of Religions and Denominations, Iran*

**Rusli Abdullah**
*Faculty of Computer Science and Information Technology, Universiti Putra Malaysia, Malaysia*

## ABSTRACT

*In today's world of continuous learning, there are challenges in providing accessible career guidance to young people that connect education and employment. However, there has been limited research into using artificial intelligence (AI) to improve guidance in professional life. This chapter discusses the progress made in leveraging AI to enhance and advance youth career guidance. One innovative solution to this challenge lies in the use of AI technology. AI can revolutionize the way career guidance is delivered by offering personalized and data-driven recommendations tailored to each individual's unique skills, interests, and goals. Despite the immense potential of AI in transforming the way career guidance is provided, there has been limited research on how this technology can be effectively utilized in higher education and professional life. This lack of exploration is a missed opportunity to leverage AI to its fullest potential in empowering individuals to make informed decisions about their education and career paths.*

DOI: 10.4018/979-8-3693-3350-1.ch007

## INTRODUCTION

The labor market has become more dynamic due to wide-ranging and dynamic changes in working life, leading to transformed attitudes toward careers (Scully-Russ & Torraco, 2020). The modern job market is multifaceted, with diverse career paths, industries, and technologies. Career guidance helps individuals navigate this complexity by providing insights into various options (Ndovela & Mutanga, 2024). It assists in understanding emerging trends, skill requirements, and industry shifts, enabling informed decisions. Career guidance ensures that individuals' skills align with available job opportunities. It bridges the gap between education and employment. Individuals can make informed choices about their career paths by assessing personal strengths, interests, and aptitudes. The labor market evolves rapidly due to technological advancements, economic shifts, and global events (such as the COVID-19 pandemic). Career guidance helps individuals adapt by identifying transferable skills, upskilling opportunities, and alternative career paths (Bimrose & Brown, 2014). Effective career guidance reduces market failures by ensuring that decisions are based on self-assessments and labor market information. When individuals make informed choices, they contribute to economic efficiency and reduce mismatches between skills and job requirements.

Career guidance is essential for marginalized populations, including migrants, refugees, and disadvantaged youth (Bereményi, 2023). It promotes social inclusion by helping these groups' access relevant information, training, and employment opportunities. In a rapidly changing world, continuous learning is crucial. Career guidance encourages lifelong learning and skill development. It emphasizes the importance of staying updated and adaptable to remain competitive (Patton & McMahon, 2014). Governments and educational institutions play a vital role in career guidance policy and implementation. They should invest in robust career services, counseling, and vocational training to empower individuals for the future of work. In summary, career guidance is not just about choosing a job; it's about equipping individuals with the knowledge, skills, and confidence to thrive in an ever-evolving labor market23. Whether you're a student, a mid-career professional, or someone exploring new opportunities, career guidance remains relevant and impactful.

The integration of AI has significantly transformed career guidance practices, enhancing their effectiveness and relevance (Akkök et al., 2021). AI-driven career guidance tools analyze vast datasets of labor market information (LMI), user profiles, and preferences. By utilizing sophisticated algorithms, these tools provide personalized and tailored recommendations to individuals based on their skills, interests, and career aspirations. Skills assessment and job matching are also readily available, ensuring that individuals are guided toward suitable career paths.

AI enables continuous learning by identifying upskilling and reskilling opportunities. Individuals can adapt to changing job requirements and industry shifts, enhancing their career adaptability (Pradhan & Saxena, 2023). AI-driven career exploration tools now utilize Natural Language Processing (NLP) to analyze written responses, assess social and emotional abilities, and offer personalized feedback and career advice. Recent research focuses on using AI to support career guidance across higher education and working life (Gedrimiene et al., 2024). Results from focus groups, scenario work, and practical trials have mapped requirements and possibilities for AI adoption in career guidance. These findings consider viewpoints from students, guidance staff, and institutions, conceptualizing different modes of agency and maturity levels for AI involvement in guidance processes. AI revolutionizes career guidance by providing personalized insights, improving job matching, and fostering lifelong learning. As technology advances,

AI will continue to play a pivotal role in shaping individuals' career paths, empowering them to make informed decisions and navigate the dynamic labor market (Vicsek, 2021).

## UNDERSTANDING CAREER GUIDANCE

Career guidance is the process of helping people make informed decisions about their careers (Gati et al., 2019). It encompasses a variety of activities aimed at assisting individuals in exploring their interests and abilities, identifying potential career paths, and developing the necessary skills and knowledge for success in their chosen fields. It is crucial during adolescence and early adulthood. It helps young people explore various career options, understand their strengths, and make informed choices about education and training. Guidance assists learners in identifying the skills needed for their desired careers. It encourages them to pursue relevant courses and extracurricular activities. As learners' transition from school to college or work, career guidance guides college majors, vocational training, and job search strategies.

In today's dynamic labor market, mid-career professionals often need to update their skills. Career guidance helps them identify relevant training programs and certifications. Mid-career individuals may consider switching industries or roles. Guidance provides insights into transferable skills and alternative career paths. It supports professionals in balancing work, family, and personal aspirations. It helps them align their career choices with their overall well-being. As individuals approach retirement, career guidance assists in planning for this significant life change. It explores options like phased retirement, part-time work, or volunteer opportunities. Even after retirement, learning continues. It also helps retirees explore hobbies, volunteer work, or encore careers. Late-career guidance encourages individuals to reflect on their legacy and how they can contribute to society beyond their formal careers. In summary, career guidance is essential across the lifespan. It empowers individuals to make informed decisions, adapt to changing circumstances, and find fulfillment in their professional journeys.

## TRADITIONAL APPROACHES TO CAREER GUIDANCE AND THEIR LIMITATIONS

According to Foundational Theory, the vocational guidance movement traces back to Parsons (1909), occupational choice occurs when individuals accurately understand their traits (abilities, aptitudes, interests) and rationally assess the fit between these traits and specific jobs. Its limitation is that it assumes that individual talents and job attributes can be objectively measured. Ignores emotional factors and views vocational choice as a one-time event.

Rodger's "Seven Point Plan" was widely adopted in guidance practice. It evaluates jobs against seven attributes (physical characteristics, attainments, intelligence, aptitudes, interests, disposition, and circumstances). The goal is to match an individual's attributes with job requirements. Its limitations are that oversimplifies complex career decisions. Moreover, fails to consider emotional aspects or long-term development. In addition, it assumes a static fit, disregarding changing circumstances.

Developmental theories emphasize that individuals go through continuous growth and development throughout their entire lifespan. However, these theories often fail to consider the effects of cultural and environmental influences. They tend to place too much importance on self-actualization and job satisfaction, while not acknowledging external factors. Additionally, these theories assume that individuals have a high degree of free will, which may not be realistic given real-world constraints.

Psychodynamic theories delve into the unconscious motivations and emotions that drive career decisions (de Queiroz & Andersen, 2020). However, applying these theories practically can be challenging, as they often overlook external factors and societal influences. For instance, Community Interaction Theory emphasizes the role of social interactions and community context in shaping career choices (Law, 1981). While this theory has its strengths, it may not fully account for individual differences and globalized influences, including technological advancements. In summary, traditional approaches to career guidance often oversimplify decision-making, neglect emotional factors, and fail to adapt to evolving contexts. Modern career guidance should incorporate holistic perspectives, cultural awareness, and lifelong learning to better serve individuals across different age groups.

## THE RISE OF AI IN CAREER GUIDANCE

The technological advancements in recent years have brought about a rapid growth of AI in many industries, including career guidance (Dwivedi et al., 2023). Nowadays, AI has revolutionized the way people manage their careers by offering personalized recommendations based on their skills, interests, and career aspirations.

Tung (2024) found that AI-powered tools and platforms are transforming the way people search for and secure job opportunities. These tools make use of algorithms to analyze a vast amount of data, including job postings, resumes, and user preferences, to match individuals with suitable job openings. Zhang et al. (2023) found that AI-enabled career guidance platforms can offer tailored advice based on an individual's unique skills, experiences, and career aspirations. This personalized approach allows individuals to receive more relevant and targeted guidance, ultimately leading to better career outcomes.

Furthermore, Zou et al. (2022) explored the impact of AI on career decision-making processes. The researchers found that AI tools can provide individuals with valuable insights that can help them make informed decisions about their careers. By analyzing trends in the job market, predicting future job opportunities, and offering guidance on skill development, AI can empower individuals to make strategic career choices.

The literature on the increasing use of AI in career guidance emphasizes the significant potential of AI in assisting individuals to navigate their careers effectively. By utilizing AI-powered tools and platforms, individuals can receive customized recommendations, make informed decisions, and ultimately achieve their career objectives. As technology advances, the role of AI in career guidance is likely to become even more crucial, fundamentally changing the way individuals approach their career development.

## RESHAPING THE FIELD OF CAREER GUIDANCE BY AI

AI has the potential to revolutionize the field of career guidance by offering more personalized and data-driven advice to individuals seeking guidance in their career choices. AI algorithms can analyze vast amounts of data, including job market trends, skills shortages, and individual preferences and abilities to suggest potential career paths that best align with a person's interests and strengths. Additionally, AI can automate tasks such as resume writing, job searching, and networking, making the career exploration process more streamlined and efficient. This can help individuals save time and focus on opportunities that match their skills and goals.

AI can play a significant role in improving career counseling services (Muhammad, 2023). By providing real-time feedback and support, AI-powered virtual career coaches can offer personalized advice, tips, and resources to individuals as they navigate their career paths. This can help individuals make informed decisions and overcome any obstacles they may encounter, ultimately leading to more satisfying and successful career paths. Overall, AI has the potential to revolutionize the field of career guidance by making it more efficient, effective, and tailored to each individual's unique needs and aspirations.

There are numerous benefits to using AI technology in various industries. Some of the key benefits include:

- Personalized recommendations: AI algorithms are capable of analyzing vast amounts of data to comprehend the preferences and behaviors of individual users. This enables companies to offer personalized recommendations for products, services, and content, resulting in increased customer engagement and satisfaction. For instance, streaming platforms like Netflix utilize AI to suggest movies and TV shows based on a user's viewing history and preferences.
- Scalability: AI systems are highly scalable and can efficiently handle large amounts of data and complex tasks. This feature enables businesses to automate repetitive tasks, reduce manual labor, and improve productivity. For instance, AI-powered chatbots can promptly respond to customer inquiries and support requests around the clock, without the need for human intervention.
- Efficiency: AI technology can optimize workflows, streamline processes and improve decision-making. By automating repetitive tasks and analyzing data in real time, AI systems enable companies to make faster and more accurate decisions. For instance, AI algorithms can scrutinize financial data to detect patterns and anomalies, aiding businesses in identifying fraud or predicting market trends. AI technology can enhance customer experience, increase efficiency, and drive innovation, giving companies a competitive edge.

## MAPPING FUTURE EMPLOYMENT PATHS

AI algorithms can suggest suitable career paths by analyzing an individual's skills, interests, and market trends. This is done by collecting and analyzing vast amounts of data from various sources such as job listings, resumes, social media profiles, and online assessments. The algorithms use machine learning techniques to identify patterns and correlations between an individual's skills and interests and the current job market trends. Based on this, the algorithms generate personalized recommendations for potential career paths that align with the individual's strengths and preferences. For instance, if an individual has strong analytical skills and a keen interest in finance, the AI algorithm may recommend career paths in financial analysis, data science, or investment banking. The algorithm may also consider job availability, salary potential, and job growth projections to refine its recommendations further. Overall, AI algorithms leverage the power of data analytics and machine learning to provide individuals with valuable insights and guidance on finding the most suitable career paths based on their unique skills, interests, and the current job market landscape.

## Theoretical Underpinnings of AI-Enhanced Career Guidance

AI-enhanced career guidance relies on various theoretical underpinnings to effectively support individuals in making informed career decisions. Some of the key theoretical frameworks that guide AI-enhanced career guidance include:

Social cognitive career theory (Lent & Brown, 2019) emphasizes the role of personal, behavioral, and environmental factors in career development. AI-enhanced career guidance leverages this theory by providing individuals with personalized career recommendations based on their skills, interests, and values, as well as contextual factors such as labor market trends and job demand.

Holland's (1994) theory posits that individuals are more likely to be satisfied and successful in careers that align with their personality types. AI-enhanced career guidance can use this theory to match individuals to suitable career paths based on their personality traits and preferences.

Self-concept Theory of career development (Betz, 1994) suggests that individuals' career choices are influenced by their self-concept, or how they perceive themselves. AI-enhanced career guidance can help individuals explore and develop a positive self-concept by providing feedback, guidance, and resources to support their career exploration and decision-making process.

Decision-making theories, such as bounded rationality and prospect theory, inform AI-enhanced career guidance by helping individuals make better career choices. AI algorithms can analyze vast amounts of data to provide individuals with a range of career options and information to support their decision-making process.

Systems theory emphasizes the interconnectedness of various factors that influence career development, such as individual characteristics, social context, and environmental factors. AI-enhanced career guidance can provide individuals with a holistic view of their career options by considering all these interconnected factors in career recommendations.

## Relevant Psychological Theories, Decision-Making Models, and Learning Analytics

In the field of learning analytics, there are various psychological theories and decision-making models that are commonly used. These theories and models provide valuable insights into how students learn and make decisions. This information can then be used to enhance the design and implementation of educational technologies and interventions.

Cognitive load theory is a key psychological theory that is often used in the context of learning analytics. According to this theory, learners have a limited capacity for processing information, and instructional materials should be designed in a way that minimizes cognitive load to facilitate learning. By analyzing students' interactions with online learning platforms, educators can identify areas where students may be experiencing cognitive overload and make necessary adjustments to the materials to better support their learning. Another relevant theory is social learning theory, which emphasizes the importance of social interactions in the learning process. By analyzing students' collaborative activities on online platforms, educators can gain insight into how students are sharing knowledge, problem-solving, and supporting each other's learning. This information can then be used to identify effective strategies for promoting peer-to-peer learning and collaboration.

Learning analytics involves the use of decision-making models to understand how students make decisions about their learning. A commonly used model is the rational decision-making model, which suggests that individuals weigh the costs and benefits of different options and select the option that provides the greatest utility. By analyzing students' behavior on learning platforms, educators can gain valuable insight into their decision-making processes. This information can then be used to design interventions aimed at helping students make more informed and effective choices.

Applying psychological theories and decision-making models to learning analytics can provide valuable insights into students' learning processes and behaviors. Educators can then use this information to customize educational interventions and technologies to better support student learning and improve academic outcomes.

## Practical Implementation

It is essential to have a clear understanding of the capabilities of AI tools before integrating them into career guidance services. Take some time to familiarize yourself with the various AI technologies available and how they can be applied to career guidance. It is also important to assess the needs of your clients. Conduct a needs assessment to determine the specific career guidance services your clients are seeking. This information can be used to identify areas where AI tools can be most beneficial and enhance the services you offer. There are a variety of AI tools available for career guidance, including chatbots, assessment tools, and recommendation engines (Westman et al., 2021). When selecting tools for your career guidance services, it's important to choose ones that meet both your clients' needs and your own goals. Once you've identified the appropriate AI tools, seamlessly integrate them into your existing services to improve the overall client experience. Offer training and support to your staff and clients so they can use the AI tools effectively. Encourage clients to ask questions and give feedback to ensure a positive user experience. Regularly monitor and evaluate the use of AI tools in your services, and collect feedback from clients and staff to determine their impact. Technology is always changing, so update and improve your AI tools to keep them effective and relevant. Remember that while AI tools can provide personalized guidance, it's important to maintain a human touch. Encourage your staff to build strong relationships with clients and provide personalized support throughout the career guidance process.

## Address Challenges Related to Data Privacy, Bias, and Ethical Considerations

One of the biggest hurdles to overcome in AI-powered career guidance is ensuring data privacy(Ali et al., 2024). AI systems need access to a broad range of personal data to provide accurate recommendations tailored to individual needs. However, this can raise concerns about the collection, storage, and use of sensitive personal information, as well as whether it is being protected against unauthorized access or misuse. One of the major obstacles in AI-powered career guidance is the problem of bias, which can result in unjust or discriminatory outcomes. As AI systems use historical data to predict and advice, they can reinforce existing biases and inequalities. For instance, if an AI system is trained on data that discriminates against certain groups, it may unknowingly perpetuate these biases while suggesting career paths or opportunities. Ethical considerations are a crucial factor in AI-assisted career guidance. It is important to ensure that the use of AI in career guidance is transparent, accountable, and fair. This involves providing clear explanations of how AI recommendations are generated, ensuring that decisions are made based on reliable and relevant data, and addressing potential risks and biases in the system.

Furthermore, it is important to consider the impact of AI on individual autonomy, privacy, and overall well-being, and to prioritize the ethical implications of using AI in career guidance.

## STUDY FUTURE DIRECTIONS

AI is increasingly being used to provide personalized career guidance to individuals based on their unique interests, skills, and preferences. This can help individuals make more informed decisions about their career path and potentially lead to higher job satisfaction and success. AI algorithms are being developed to match individuals with job opportunities that align with their skills and qualifications. This can help individuals find jobs that they are well-suited for and reduce the likelihood of mismatches that can result in turnover or dissatisfaction. AI technology is automating more routine tasks in the career guidance process, such as resume screening and job matching. This can free up career counselors to focus on more complex issues and provide higher quality guidance to individuals. AI is being used to analyze large amounts of data on job trends, skills requirements, and labor market dynamics to predict future opportunities and challenges in the job market. This can help individuals make more strategic career decisions and plan for the future. AI-powered virtual assistants are being developed to provide individuals with career guidance and support in a more convenient and accessible way. This can help reach more people who may not have access to traditional in-person counseling services. Overall, AI has the potential to revolutionize the field of career guidance by providing more personalized, efficient, and data-driven support to individuals as they navigate their career paths. However, career counselors need to stay informed about these emerging trends and be prepared to adapt their practices to incorporate AI technology effectively.

## Propose Research Areas, Such as Improving Ai Algorithms, Enhancing User Interfaces, and Addressing Equity Issues

Developing AI algorithms that are more accurate, efficient, and able to handle complex tasks in areas such as natural language processing, machine learning, and computer vision. Enhancing user interfaces by studying how users interact with technology and designing interfaces that are intuitive, user-friendly, and accessible to individuals with disabilities. Addressing equity issues in AI by researching bias and fairness in algorithms, ensuring that AI systems are not perpetuating discrimination or inequality based on factors like race, gender, or socioeconomic status. Exploring the ethical implications of AI technology, such as privacy concerns, data security, and the impact of automation on the workforce. Investigating the potential environmental impact of AI systems, including energy consumption, carbon emissions, and sustainable practices for developing and deploying AI technology. Studying the societal implications of AI, such as the impact on healthcare, education, transportation, and other industries, and developing strategies for maximizing the benefits of AI while minimizing potential risks and challenges.

## CONCLUSION

AI is rapidly changing the nature of work by automating routine tasks and augmenting human capabilities. Careers in AI and related fields, such as machine learning, robotics, and data science, are in high demand and offer lucrative opportunities for growth. AI is creating new job roles and career paths that require a mix of technical skills, creativity, and problem-solving abilities. Professionals need to continuously upskill and adapt to stay relevant in the evolving workforce shaped by AI technologies. Overall, AI is revolutionizing the way we work and opening up new possibilities for career advancement. Embracing AI and leveraging its capabilities can lead to exciting and rewarding career paths in the future.

# REFERENCES

Akkök, F., Hughes, D., & CareersNet, U. K. (2021). *Career chat: The art of AI and the human interface in career development* (*Working Paper Series 2*, p. 91). European Centre for the Development of Vocational Training. https://www.cedefop.europa.eu/files/6202_en_0.pdf#page=93

Ali, M., Siddique, A., Aftab, A., Abid, M. K., & Fuzail, M. (2024). AI-Powered customized learning paths: Transforming data administration for students on digital platforms. *Journal of Computing & Biomedical Informatics*, 6(02), 195–204.

Bereményi, B. Á. (2023). Between choices and "going with the flow". Career guidance and Roma young people in Hungary. *International Journal for Educational and Vocational Guidance*, 23(3), 555–575. 10.1007/s10775-022-09536-0

Betz, N. E. (1994). Self-Concept Theory in Career Development and Counseling. *The Career Development Quarterly*, 43(1), 32–42. 10.1002/j.2161-0045.1994.tb00844.x

Bimrose, J., & Brown, A. (2014). Mid-Career Progression and Development: The Role for Career Guidance and Counseling. In Arulmani, G., Bakshi, A. J., Leong, F. T. L., & Watts, A. G. (Eds.), *Handbook of Career Development* (pp. 203–222). Springer New York. 10.1007/978-1-4614-9460-7_11

de Queiroz, F. S., & Andersen, M. B. (2020). Psychodynamic approaches. In *Applied Sport, Exercise, and Performance Psychology* (pp. 12–30). Routledge. https://www.taylorfrancis.com/chapters/edit/10.4324/9780429503702-2/psychodynamic-approaches-fernanda-serra-de-queiroz-mark-andersen

Gati, I., Levin, N., & Landman-Tal, S. (2019). Decision-Making Models and Career Guidance. In Athanasou, J. A., & Perera, H. N. (Eds.), *International Handbook of Career Guidance* (pp. 115–145). Springer International Publishing. 10.1007/978-3-030-25153-6_6

Gedrimiene, E., Celik, I., Kaasila, A., Mäkitalo, K., & Muukkonen, H. (2024). Artificial Intelligence (AI)-enhanced learning analytics (LA) for supporting Career decisions: Advantages and challenges from user perspective. *Education and Information Technologies*, 29(1), 297–322. 10.1007/s10639-023-12277-4

Holland, J. L., Fritzsche, B. A., & Powell, A. B. (1994). *The Self-Directed Search Technical Manual*. Psychological Assessment Resources.

Law, B. (1981). Community interaction: A 'mid-range' focus for theories of career development in young adults. *British Journal of Guidance & Counselling*, 9(2), 142–158. 10.1080/03069888108258210

Lent, R. W., & Brown, S. D. (2019). Social cognitive career theory at 25: Empirical status of the interest, choice, and performance models. *Journal of Vocational Behavior*, 115, 1–25. 10.1016/j.jvb.2019.06.004

Muhammad, R. (2023). Barriers and effectiveness to counselling careers with Artificial Intelligence: A systematic literature review. *Ricerche Di Pedagogia e Didattica.Journal of Theories and Research in Education*, 18(3), 143–164.

Ndovela, S., & Mutanga, B. (2024). Academic Factors Influencing Students Career Choices in the IT Field: Insights from South African IT Students. *Indonesian Journal of Information Systems*, 6(2), 107–116. 10.24002/ijis.v6i2.8293

Parsons, F. (1909). *Choosing a vocation*. University of California.

Patton, W., & McMahon, M. (2014). Lifelong Career Development Learning: A Foundation for Career Practice. In *Career Development and Systems Theory* (pp. 277–296). Brill. https://brill.com/downloadpdf/book/9789462096356/BP000011.pdf

Pradhan, I. P., & Saxena, P. (2023). Reskilling workforce for the Artificial Intelligence age: Challenges and the way forward. In *The adoption and effect of artificial intelligence on human resources management, Part B* (pp. 181–197). Emerald Publishing Limited. 10.1108/978-1-80455-662-720230011

Scully-Russ, E., & Torraco, R. (2020). The Changing Nature and Organization of Work: An Integrative Review of the Literature. *Human Resource Development Review*, 19(1), 66–93. 10.1177/1534484319886394

Tung, T. M. (2024). A Systematic Analysis Of Artificial Intelligence's Usage In Online Advertising. *Migration Letters : An International Journal of Migration Studies*, 21(S6), 892–900.

Vicsek, L. (2021). Artificial intelligence and the future of work–lessons from the sociology of expectations. *The International Journal of Sociology and Social Policy*, 41(7/8), 842–861. 10.1108/IJSSP-05-2020-0174

Westman, S., Kauttonen, J., Klemetti, A., Korhonen, N., Manninen, M., Mononen, A., Niittymäki, S., & Paananen, H. (2021). Artificial Intelligence for Career Guidance–Current Requirements and Prospects for the Future. *IAFOR Journal of Education*, 9(4), 43–62. 10.22492/ije.9.4.03

Zhang, H., Lee, I., Ali, S., DiPaola, D., Cheng, Y., & Breazeal, C. (2023). Integrating Ethics and Career Futures with Technical Learning to Promote AI Literacy for Middle School Students: An Exploratory Study. *International Journal of Artificial Intelligence in Education*, 33(2), 290–324. 10.1007/s40593-022-00293-335573722

Zou, R., Zeb, S., Nisar, F., Yasmin, F., Poulova, P., & Haider, S. A. (2022). The Impact of Emotional Intelligence on Career Decision-Making Difficulties and Generalized Self-Efficacy Among University Students in China. *Psychology Research and Behavior Management*, 15, 865–874. 10.2147/PRBM.S35874235422664

# Chapter 8
# Enhancing AI–Enabled Education Through Mobile Learning and Bring Your Own Device (BYOD) Integration

**Wasswa Shafik**
https://orcid.org/0000-0002-9320-3186

*School of Digital Science, Universiti Brunei Darussalam, Gadong, Brunei Darussalam & Dig Connectivity Research Laboratory (DCRLab), Kampala, Uganda*

## ABSTRACT

*Recent technological developments influence different daily human activities, including education and lifestyle. This chapter explores the significance of mobile learning and bringing your own device to enhance education in the digital age. It highlights the growing use of mobile devices in educational settings and their advantages and drawbacks. The literature review analyses existing research, frameworks, and best practices for utilizing mobile devices and smartphones in educational settings. The study examines pedagogical approaches, mobile resources, and educational applications that utilize mobile technology for personalized and engaging learning. It also discusses related policies, implementation difficulties, and successful case studies of technology adoption. The chapter offers best practices for maximizing the benefits, such as management strategies, and a safe learning environment. The chapter also speculates on the future developments and effects of mobile learning in the classroom, exploring new technologies and innovations that may influence education.*

## INTRODUCTION

The increasing availability and accessibility of mobile devices have totally changed how individuals' access and engage with information in a technological environment that is continually growing regardless of its negative effect of exposing it to the underaged in this digital economic era (Sangeetha et al., 2023; Shafik, 2024d). Educational institutions are aware of how mobile technology may improve the classroom environment and satisfy the needs of today's students. Mobile learning, often known as "m-learning," is the act of learning and obtaining knowledge through portable electronic devices, including laptops,

DOI: 10.4018/979-8-3693-3350-1.ch008

tablets, and smartphones (Mbambala & Abdullah, 2023). Unlike conventional classroom settings, mobile learning allows students to access instructional resources and information at any time and location, dissolving space and time limits. This mobility allows students more choice and convenience while meeting varied learning preferences and methods (Blancaflor & Hernandez, 2023).

In correspondence, the idea of "Bring Your Own Device" (BYOD) has arisen in response to the growing adoption of mobile devices among students and instructors. The concept "BYOD" can simply be defined to way of allowing instructors, staff, and students to bring their electronic devices (such as tablets, laptops, and smartphones) to school or college for academic purposes (Shafik, 2024e). Utilizing the technologies that students are already accustomed to using can boost engagement and encourage active participation in the learning process. The use several disruptive artificial intelligence (AI) technologies has foster increased application in assessment automation, chatbots, gamification, intelligent tutoring and adaptive learning (Shafik, 2024b). Incorporating mobile devices and BYOD policies in educational settings in the digital era is becoming increasingly vital because technology affects every area of everyday life. Students are used to conversing through digital platforms, interacting with multimedia content, and having rapid access to information (Shihepo et al., 2023). Utilizing mobile technology in education is compatible with how students engage with their environment daily.

Recently, a strengths, weaknesses, opportunities, and threats (SWOT) analysis was carried out to evaluate AI potential of in Islamic religious education and demonstrate a positive acceptance of technology in general due to the strength. Some of strengths included increased knowledge search and critical thinking, preservation of islamic ethics and values, global connectivity, and collaboration (Abubakari et al., 2024). However, the SWOT analysis demonstrated some critical and fundamental threats and weakness such as cultural and ethical and Sensitivity, inadequate technological infrastructures, curriculum adaptability and standardization deficiency, among others that could be considered better technological involvement in education system at all levels (Astriani et al., 2023). This study presents a detailed explanation of machine learning (ML) and BYOD and discuss the possible advantages and obstacles of their application. More still, it looks at how these technologies can improve instruction, stimulate personalized learning, and satisfy the special requirements of a diverse student body (Aguboshim et al., 2023).

Covers some frequent challenges and items to consider when incorporating mobile devices in educational settings, like ensuring everyone has access to technology, keeping a secure learning environment, and preserving student information and privacy. Understanding and exploiting the potential of BYOD and mobile learning is vital for educators and institutions to adequately prepare students for success in the digital era, given the rapid improvements in technology and the ongoing digital transformation in education (Tuah & Abd Rahim, 2023). Through our inquiry, the study intended to enhance to the body of knowledge on BYOD and mobile learning while also giving educators suggestions on developing cutting-edge learning environments in the digital era.

Educators and organizations must adjust their instructional techniques as technology evolves swiftly to be relevant and effective in the new digital environment. If the potential of mobile devices is overlooked, there may be missed opportunities to engage students and deliver tailored learning experiences that address each student's requirements and learning preferences (Nagy et al., 2023). Moreover, by allowing equal access to educational resources, BYOD and mobile learning can close the digital divide. Although many students' homes may not have computers, they may have cell phones or tablets. They are ensuring that all students have access to digital resources and chances for learning outside of the classroom and adopting BYOD rules will increase education advancement (Kilduff et al., 2023).

BYOD and ML are economical solutions for educational establishments. BYOD enables universities to take advantage of the current technology resources that students possess rather than investing a lot of money on expensive computer laboratories or individual devices. This affordability may free up finances for further educational projects, ultimately benefiting the entire learning community (Sangeetha et al., 2023). Mobile device incorporation in education is not without obstacles. The introduction notes that introducing BYOD creates challenges with network infrastructure, device compatibility, and security. Educational institutions must implement strong BYOD rules that address these challenges and provide a safe and secure digital learning environment (Astriani et al., 2023).

*Figure 1. Reasons for mobile eLearning*

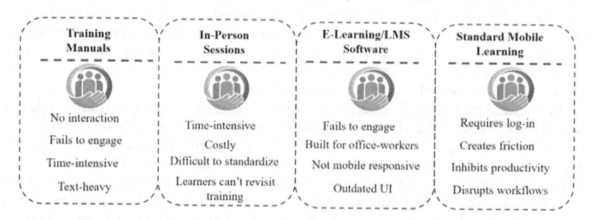

Furthermore, privacy and data security must be taken into consideration. Protecting student data becomes a primary responsibility as digital platforms and online resources proliferate. Figure 1 depicts some of the significant and critical reasons why mobile e-learning need close attention. Institutions must have stringent data protection rules and be honest with parents and students regarding data usage and privacy regulations (Nagy et al., 2023). Mobile devices are becoming more common in education. Students, teachers, and administrators all utilize cell phones, tablets, and laptops daily, altering how education is given and received. The seamless integration of mobile devices into people's daily lives is one of the key reasons for this development. Students find it normal to use these gadgets for learning since they are already used for communication, entertainment, and information retrieval (Lam et al., 2024). This extensive usage of mobile technology enables students to access educational materials, resources, and interactive programs whenever it is most convenient, making learning more pleasurable and engaging.

Mobile device integration in education presents a wide range of potential advantages. First off, mobile learning delivers unequaled accessibility and flexibility. With mobile devices, learning is no longer constrained to traditional classroom settings or defined hours. The availability of educational tools and materials implies that students can learn at their own speed and at any time. This versatility makes education inclusive and adaptable for all students, especially those with variable schedules or geographic restrictions (T & Amala Bai, 2024). Mobile devices make interactive and immersive learning experiences possible. Various learning styles can be provided for by the engaging and interactive learning opportunities afforded by educational apps, simulations, and multimedia tools. Active participation is encouraged with interactive assessments, games, and collaborative platforms, which boost student enthusiasm and engagement (Oh et al., 2024).

Using mobile devices' interactive characteristics, teachers can construct interesting classes that help students retain material and achieve better comprehension. Integrating mobile devices in education enhances digital literacy and prepares students for the modern workforce. Digital literacy is a key skill set that cuts across all academic subjects in the current world (Palanisamy et al., 2024). Students who use mobile devices in their schooling learn crucial digital literacy abilities like media analysis, digital communication, and information retrieval. Employers across many industries regard these talents highly since they are so valuable in a world that is growing more and more digitally driven (Lam et al., 2024). Mobile learning that emphasizes digital literacy gives students the abilities they need to flourish in a fast-changing international economy.

## Chapter Contribution

We briefly summarize the contributions of the chapter as follows:

- The chapter provides an in-depth analysis of BYOD and ML integration in modern schooling and offers a comprehensive literature analysis spanning existing studies, paradigms, and best practices related to mobile devices and smartphones in educational contexts.
- The chapter discusses the role of mobile learning and evaluates numerous educational apps, mobile resources, and pedagogical practices that enhance the learning experience.
- The chapter addresses the practical aspects of BYOD deployment, including regulations, obstacles, device compatibility, network infrastructure, security, and student privacy concerns.
- The chapter Presents successful case studies of BYOD adoption in educational institutions, presenting real-world instances of its influence.
- The chapter analyzes the advantages of BYOD, such as cost savings, enhanced student participation, and flexibility, while also evaluating the disadvantages, such as uneven access and cybersecurity issues.
- The chapter presents a set of best practices and guidelines for educators and administrators to improve mobile learning in a BYOD environment, spanning instructional tactics and classroom management techniques.
- The chapter evaluates the influence of BYOD on learning outcomes, drawing from relevant research findings and analysis to measure its effectiveness.
- The chapter speculates on future trends and consequences of mobile learning and BYOD, investigating potential innovations that could affect the future of education.
- Lastly, the chapter finishes by underlining the value of mobile learning and BYOD, encouraging educated decision-making for successful integration in educational contexts and lessons learned.

## Chapter Organization

Section 2 presents the role of Mobile Learning in Education and details the role of mobile devices in enhancing the learning experience, discussing various educational apps, mobile resources, and pedagogical strategies. Section 3 addresses implementing BYOD in Educational Institutions, focusing on the practical aspects of establishing BYOD in schools and colleges. Section 4 illustrates the advantages and Challenges of BYOD, identifying the advantages and challenges associated with BYOD in educational environments and outlining the benefits of cost savings, increased student engagement, and flexibility. Section 5 demonstrates best practices for Successful Mobile Learning with BYOD, presenting a set of best practices and guidelines for educators and administrators to maximize the benefits of mobile learning in a BYOD environment. Section 6 assesses the influence of BYOD on Learning results and discusses the evaluation methodology used to quantify the influence of BYOD on student performance and learning outcomes. Section 7 depicts the future trends and consequences, speculating on the future patterns and potential implications of mobile learning and BYOD in education and exploring upcoming technologies and prospective developments that could affect the future of education—section 8. Finally, Section 9 summarizes some of the lessons learned and the conclusion.

## MOBILE LEARNING AND ITS ROLE IN EDUCATION

This section presents a brief introduction to ML followed by its cardinal roles of education.

### Understanding Machine Learning

This is a subsect of AI that involves applications algorithms in recognizing patterns and make decisions using prominent ML algorithms and their applications in education such as linear regression, logistic regression, decision trees, random forest, support vector machines, and neural networks. This kind of AI increases critical and significant traits that educationists need to properly comprehend as presented in Figure 2. There are several ML types that are used in different aspects of computation as summarized.

### Supervised Learning

This refers to a type of ML where a model is trained using labeled data, meaning that the input data is paired with the correct output. The model learns from this labeled data to make predictions or classify new. Supervised learning algorithms are specifically designed to acquire knowledge about a function that establishes a relationship between input data and a desired output (Halim et al., 2024). This knowledge is obtained by analyzing example input-output pairings that are presented in a labeled dataset. This paradigm is essential for jobs that necessitate accurate prediction and categorization, such as diagnostic systems in healthcare or fraud detection in finance (Nurillah & Trihandoyo, 2024).

The learning process entails fine-tuning model parameters to reduce the disparity between expected and actual results, typically employing loss functions such as mean squared error for regression or cross-entropy loss for classification. Ensemble approaches, such as Random Forests and Gradient Boosting Machines, utilize advanced techniques to enhance accuracy and robustness by combining several models (Sushil et al., 2024). Neural networks, specifically deep learning architectures, have advanced the limits by achieving exceptional performance in intricate pattern recognition tasks including images, text, and audio. This has been made possible by utilizing extensive labeled datasets and significant computational resources (Engelbrecht et al., 2024).

*Figure 2. Critical aspects of machine learning*

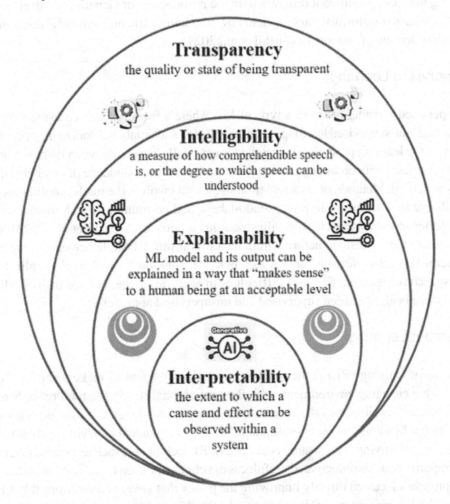

## Unsupervised Learning

Unsupervised learning refers to a type of ML where the algorithm learns patterns and structures in data without any explicit guidance or labeled examples. Unsupervised learning algorithms examine and construct models of data without pre-established labels, with the goal of revealing concealed patterns and structures within the data (Gulati et al., 2024). This approach is essential for conducting exploratory data analysis, detecting anomalies, and performing preprocessing tasks such as reducing dimensionality. Clustering methods, such as K-means and DBSCAN, detect inherent clusters in data, facilitating consumer segmentation and market analysis (Halim et al., 2024).

Association rule learning, such as the Apriori algorithm, reveals connections between variables that are crucial for recommendation systems. Dimensionality reduction methods such as Principal Component Analysis (PCA) and t-Distributed Stochastic Neighbor Embedding (t-SNE) convert data with a high number of dimensions into lower-dimensional spaces (T & Amala Bai, 2024). These techniques retain significant variance in the data, making it easier to visualize and extract essential features. Unsupervised learning has made significant progress with the introduction of Generative Adversarial Networks (GANs), which have transformed various fields by producing authentic synthetic data and facilitating semi-supervised learning frameworks (Sushil et al., 2024).

## Semi-Supervised Learning

Semi-supervised learning refers to a type of ML where a model is trained using both labeled and unlabeled data. Semi-supervised learning combines labeled and unlabeled data to improve the efficiency and efficacy of the learning process. This method is especially beneficial when there is a limited supply or high cost associated with obtaining labeled data, but there is an abundance of unlabeled data available (Shihepo et al., 2023). Methods such as self-training, which involves the model continuously improving itself by utilizing its own predictions as pseudo-labels, and co-training, which involves many models working together to enhance each other, illustrate this approach (Astriani et al., 2023). Graph-based algorithms utilize the intrinsic structure within data to transmit labels, hence enhancing classification accuracy. Semi-supervised learning serves as a practical solution for real-world applications, such as image and speech recognition, that face difficulties in acquiring large, labeled datasets (Kilduff et al., 2023). It acts as a bridge between supervised and unsupervised approaches.

## Reinforcement Learning

Reinforcement learning (RL) is the process of training an agent to make a series of decisions by interacting with a changing environment, with the goal of maximizing the total rewards received over time. This paradigm is similar to the way humans acquire knowledge through experience, making it well-suited for applications that necessitate adaptable and independent behavior, such as robotics, game AI, and autonomous driving (Palanisamy et al., 2024). RL techniques, such as Q-learning, employ value functions to approximate the anticipated usefulness of actions in various states. On the other hand, policy gradient approaches focus on directly improving the policy that governs the actions taken by the agent. Advanced methodologies, such as Deep Q Networks (DQNs) and Proximal Policy Optimization (PPO), utilize deep learning to effectively manage state spaces with many dimensions and continuous action domains (Shukry et al., 2023). This allows for significant advancements in challenging activities such as playing Go and real-time strategy games.

## Self-Supervised Learning

Self-supervised learning refers to a type of ML where a model learns to make predictions about certain aspects of its input data without the need for explicit supervision or labeled data. Self-supervised learning is a novel technique in which the model creates its own supervisory signals from the available data, hence removing the requirement for extensive labeled datasets. This technique is especially revolutionary in domains such as natural language processing (NLP) and computer vision, where there is a limited availability of labeled data (Sushil et al., 2024). Approaches like contrastive learning, which involves training models to differentiate between similar and dissimilar pairs, and autoencoders, which focus on reconstructing input data from compressed representations, are prime examples of this methodology (Shafik, 2024a). Transformers, such as BERT and GPT, employ self-supervised techniques such masked language modeling to acquire comprehensive representations from extensive text data (Oh et al., 2024). This greatly enhances language translation, text generation, and question answering tasks by utilizing contextual knowledge.

## Transfer Learning

Transfer learning refers to the process of applying knowledge gained from one task to another related one. It involves using pre-existing knowledge or models to improve the performance of a new task. Transfer learning utilizes pre-trained models that have been established on large datasets and then adjusts them for specific, generally smaller, related tasks (Soubhagyalakshmi & Reddy, 2023). This methodology is crucial for attaining exceptional performance despite having a scarcity of data and processing resources. Computer vision models such as VGG, ResNet, and EfficientNet, which have been pre-trained on ImageNet, may be easily adjusted for applications like medical image analysis and object detection with minimal more training. In the field of Natural Language Processing (NLP), models such as BERT, GPT, and T5 are initially trained on large collections of text data and then adjusted for specific tasks such as sentiment analysis or language translation (Nicosia et al., 2023). Transfer learning speeds up model development and improves generalization by utilizing the vast information stored in pre-trained models. This enables advancements in different fields when there is limited data available, and gamification of mobile learning presented in Figure 3.

*Figure 3. Mobile learning gamification*

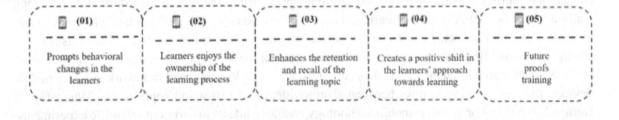

| (01) | (02) | (03) | (04) | (05) |
| --- | --- | --- | --- | --- |
| Prompts behavioral changes in the learners | Learners enjoys the ownership of the learning process | Enhances the retention and recall of the learning topic | Creates a positive shift in the learners' approach towards learning | Future proofs training |

## The Role of Mobile Learning in Education

The importance of mobile learning in education is crucial in improving the learning experience, making it more interesting, individualized, and accessible. Mobile devices, such as smartphones and tablets, serve as adaptable instruments that offer a wide choice of educational applications, resources, and pedagogical methodologies to cater to the requirements and preferences of varied learners. By giving students rapid access to a multitude of educational materials and content, mobile learning can improve the learning experience for all students (Braun et al., 2023). Learners can access instructional textbooks, e-books, articles, videos, podcasts, and interactive simulations through numerous educational apps and mobile-friendly websites. This wealth of educational resources suits varied learning preferences and enables pupils to explore deeper subjects than is feasible with conventional textbooks. Additionally, as students can explore their interests and learn more about things that interest them, mobile learning encourages curiosity and self-directed learning (Al-Said, 2023).

With their dynamic and immersive learning experiences, educational apps play a significant role in mobile learning. Through instructional games and quizzes, these apps can gamify learning, making it an enjoyable and rewarding pastime. Badges, prizes, and leaderboards are just a few gamification components that encourage students to participate completely and advance in their academic activities (Braun et al., 2023). Mobile apps usually offer real-time assessment and feedback, allowing students to test their learning and notice opportunities for development right away. Mobile tools also enable tailored learning procedures. Students with access to learning materials on demand can go at their own pace and revisit information as needed (Qi, 2023). To customize the learning experience to each student's unique requirements and preferences, educational applications and platforms typically use algorithms to give personalized content recommendations depending on a student's progress and performance. This customization creates a better engagement and commitment to learning by empowering students to take responsibility for their education (Mohd Shukry et al., 2023).

Blended learning, flipped classrooms, and collaborative learning are examples of pedagogical practices that incorporate mobile technology. In a flipped classroom, students receive educational content on their mobile devices outside of class, freeing up class time for interactive exercises, debates, and team projects. Furthermore, mobile devices enable students to collaborate on projects, communicate ideas, and participate in group discussions utilizing online forums and communication tools (Nagy et al., 2023). Mobile devices are key to the blended learning strategy because they allow for the smooth integration of face-to-face and online learning modalities.

ML has a function in education beyond regular classroom settings. Individuals can continue their educational journey outside of traditional learning spaces using the option for informal and lifelong learning given by mobile devices. Learning is now a continuous process that can take place anywhere, at any time, rather than being constrained to periods or places (Astriani et al., 2023). One of its primary advantages is mobile learning's potential to reduce the gap between formal education and in-demand skills. Students can participate in practical activities, hands-on learning, and fieldwork utilizing mobile devices, making meaningful links between abstract ideas and real-world applications (Blancaflor & Hernandez, 2023). For instance, mobile technology enables students to carry out scientific experiments, gather data, and assess outcomes while in the field, giving life to science education and making it more relevant and tangible, as some are depicted in Figure 4.

*Figure 4. Sample mobile eLearning applications*

Notably, learners who use mobile learning feel more empowered and independent. Students become more self-directed and accountable for their growth as they take charge of their education through mobile devices (Mbambala & Abdullah, 2023). They can set objectives, keep track of their progress, and actively participate in the learning process, all of which help students recall material better. Moreover, mobile devices allow students to engage in reflective activities like journaling or developing digital portfolios, which enhance metacognition and self-evaluation (Blancaflor & Hernandez, 2023). Mobile learning's potential to enhance inclusivity in education is another essential element. Mobile technology can accommodate a range of learners, including individuals with diverse learning preferences, talents, and styles. Mobile apps can offer assistive technologies and features, such as text-to-speech, voice recognition, and configurable interfaces, for students with learning issues or special needs, making learning more accessible and accommodating for all students (Mbambala & Abdullah, 2023).

However, it is vital to highlight the necessity of ethical and mindful technology use, even as we embrace the significant role of mobile learning in education. Using mobile devices in the classroom must be balanced with limiting potential distractions or undue reliance on displays. Mobile technology allows seamless communication and collaboration between students and professors, reducing distance obstacles and boosting multicultural understanding (Blancaflor & Hernandez, 2023). Educational apps and platforms can all facilitate a virtual classroom, online conversations, and group projects, enabling students to participate and receive knowledge from multiple viewpoints.

ML has proven to be a successful tool for satisfying the demands of lifelong learners, such as working professionals who seek to upgrade or reskill. People have access to diverse courses, workshops, and training programs through mobile platforms catering to their particular job goals and interests (Sangeetha et al., 2023). Accessing continuous education helps people to adjust to a job market that is changing frequently and stay current in their industries. Additionally, mobile learning plays a part in teachers' professional development. Teachers can cooperate with other teachers to share best practices utilizing mobile devices to access professional development resources, attend webinars and seminars, and access professional development materials (Tuah & Abd Rahim, 2023). Educators' instructional skills are improved via mobile learning, which also keeps them abreast of the most recent innovations in educational theory and practice, some advantages of mobile learning is presented in Figure. 5.

*Figure 5. Merits of mobile learning*

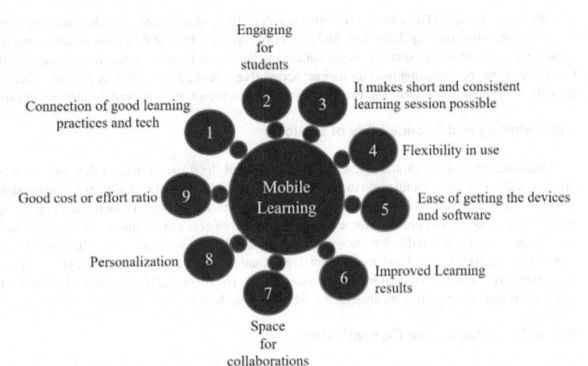

ML is compatible with sustainable development ideas and can be implemented in teaching. Educational institutions can help protect the environment and develop environmentally friendly practices by embracing digital resources and reducing their dependency on chapter-based materials (Blancaflor & Hernandez, 2023). The environmental effect of traditional learning resources like printed handouts and textbooks is decreased by ML. While recognizing the transformative impact of mobile learning, addressing challenges with digital access and equity is vital. Access to mobile devices and dependable internet connectivity is not widespread among students (Tuah & Abd Rahim, 2023). To prevent exacerbating already-existing educational inequities, educational institutions must work to ensure that all students have equitable access to technology.

## ENFORCING BRING YOUR DEVICE (BYOD) IN EDUCATIONAL INSTITUTIONS

Implementing BYOD in educational institutions necessitates meticulous strategizing, unambiguous guidelines, and resilient infrastructure to guarantee a smooth and safeguarded assimilation of personal gadgets into the educational setting (Blancaflor & Hernandez, 2023). The implementation process should consider the varied requirements and difficulties faced by students, instructors, and administrators while maximizing the numerous advantages that BYOD may provide.

## Assessment of Infrastructure Preparedness

Prior to introducing BYOD, educational institutions should assess their existing information technology infrastructure and network capabilities. Multiple devices must have sufficient Wi-Fi coverage and capacity to access internet resources simultaneously. Enhancing the network infrastructure may be imperative to accommodate the increasing need for internet access (Nagy et al., 2023). Security measures such as firewalls, encryption, and antivirus software are also important to protect the network from online threats.

## Compatibility and Accessibility of Devices

Educational institutions should assess the compatibility of the different devices that students may bring to enable a successful implementation of the BYOD policy. The BYOD rules should accommodate a diverse range of gear, including laptops, tablets, and smartphones, that operate on different operating systems. The school should provide instructions or tools to aid parents and students in ensuring that their devices are current and suitable for use with educational software and applications. Teachers should receive training in effectively handling different devices and resolving potential challenges that may occur during BYOD courses (Blancaflor & Hernandez, 2023). They should also know several educational applications and resources that enhance their teaching approaches.

## Policy Formulation and Dissemination

The effective implementation of BYOD policies relies on their comprehension and widespread dissemination. The policy should clearly outline the permissible use of personal devices, establish standards for appropriate online conduct, and provide guidelines for managing devices in an educational setting (Sangeetha et al., 2023). Furthermore, it should address concerns around data security, privacy, and the consequences of legal violations. Clear and concise communication of the BYOD policy to students, parents, and teachers is essential to ensure that all parties are aware of their respective duties in the BYOD setting (Blancaflor & Hernandez, 2023). Teachers and staff should undergo professional development and training to facilitate the integration of BYOD in the classroom.

## Continuing Education and Skill Enhancement for Professionals

Education on the principles and practices of responsible and ethical behavior in the digital world. It is crucial to educate children about responsible digital citizenship as a fundamental aspect of implementing BYOD. This education should encompass topics such as internet safety, responsible technology usage, respecting others' privacy, and comprehending the consequences of online activity. Education on digital citizenship fosters a nurturing and courteous online community inside the school environment. Surveillance and assistance systems should be implemented in educational institutions to oversee and monitor networked devices (Kilduff et al., 2023). The BYOD policy is supervised to guarantee adherence and promptly handle any security or misuse concerns that may occur. Figure 6 presents the 5 costs of effective education training.

*Figure 6. Costs of effective education training*

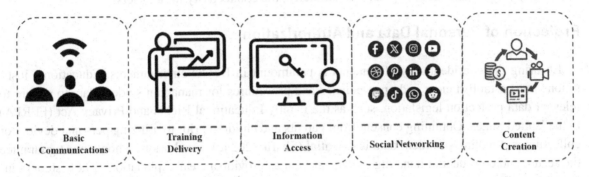

## Assessment and Ongoing Enhancement

The continued effectiveness of the BYOD deployment relies on consistent assessment and input from all parties involved. Collecting data on the impact of BYOD on learning outcomes, student engagement, and classroom dynamics might provide valuable insights for improving future BYOD policies and practices. Accessible and dedicated support staff should be available to assist students and teachers in resolving technical issues related to their personal devices and educational software (Shihepo et al., 2023). It enables the implementation of features such as device tracking, application management, and data encryption, which centralizes the focus on device management and security.

## Compatibility of Devices and Management of Software

Educational institutions may have device compatibility concerns, particularly when students bring a diverse array of devices with different specifications and operating systems. To address this issue, schools may consider using web-based tools and platform-agnostic programs that are compatible with different hardware and operating systems. Furthermore, providing parents and kids with a catalog of recommended devices or specifications might aid them in choosing gadgets that fulfill academic prerequisites (Mbambala & Abdullah, 2023). Deploying MDM solutions in a BYOD setting helps effectively oversee and safeguard personal devices. MDM software allows network administrators to control, manage, and protect connected devices remotely.

## Enhancing the Security Of Computer Networks and Optimizing the Allocation of Available Bandwidth

The utilization of BYOD results in an increased number of devices being connected to the institution's network, which in turn raises concerns regarding network security. To prevent unauthorized access and protect against online dangers, educational institutions should adopt robust network security measures, including firewalls, intrusion detection systems, and content filtering. Bandwidth control is crucial as the network can experience overload when numerous devices request online resources concurrently

(Blancaflor & Hernandez, 2023). Network capacity planning should be prioritized, and schools should allocate sufficient bandwidth to guarantee uninterrupted connectivity for all users.

## Protection of Personal Data and Authorization

Ensuring the confidentiality of students is paramount in BYOD environments. Educational institutions must establish clear and open policies and procedures for managing student data to adhere to relevant data protection legislation, such as the Family Educational Rights and Privacy Act (FERPA) in the United States. Obtaining consent from parents and children prior to utilizing personal devices or collecting and retaining student data is essential (Shafik, 2024c). In addition, schools must guarantee the secure and confidential handling of data, as well as provide a clear explanation of how student information will be utilized.

## Education on Digital Citizenship and Promoting Responsible Use of Technology

It is crucial to educate students on the responsible usage of personal gadgets in a BYOD setting. Incorporating digital citizenship education into the curriculum assists students in comprehending appropriate behavior when utilizing the internet, implementing cybersecurity protocols, and recognizing the potential consequences of negligent usage (Aguboshim et al., 2023). Digital citizenship education promotes responsible online activity and provides students with the skills to act appropriately on the internet. More still, BYOD efforts must consider students who may lack access to personal gadgets. Schools should develop strategies to prevent academic regression among these students (Blancaflor & Hernandez, 2023). For students lacking personal devices, this may involve establishing computer laboratories, providing loaner devices, or offering other learning materials. Figure 7 displays the key recommendations and components for implementing BYOD chosen by top information technologies managers.

*Figure 7. The top five components of bring your device and information technology manager*

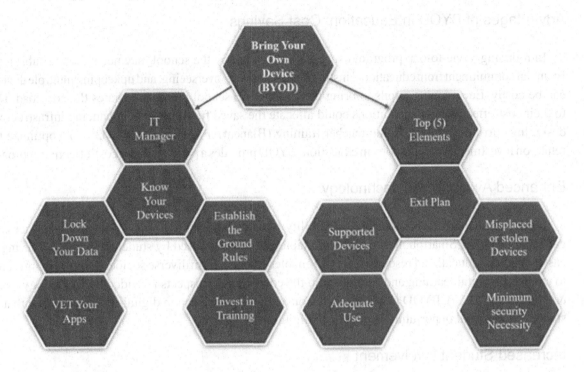

## Enhancing Accessibility and Implementing Universal Design Principles

To guarantee the full participation of all students, including those with disabilities, in the BYOD learning environment, educational institutions should prioritize accessibility and universal design principles. This may involve providing assistive technology, ensuring that educational apps and materials are accessible, and addressing the specific learning needs of each student (Sangeetha et al., 2023). To create a secure, inclusive, and productive learning environment for all students, educational institutions can overcome the challenges of introducing BYOD by addressing these issues and applying effective techniques (Mbambala & Abdullah, 2023).

## MERITS AND CHALLENGES OF BYOD

This section examines the advantages and challenges associated with BYOD in educational environments.

## Merits of BYOD From an Educational Perspective

### Advantages of BYOD in Education: Cost Savings

Introducing a one-to-one program using gadgets owned by the school may necessitate a substantial financial commitment from educational institutions. Acquiring, overseeing, and upkeeping multiple devices can be costly. Encouraging pupils to bring their gadgets to school greatly alleviates the cost load. Due to their cost-effectiveness, institutions could allocate the saved funds towards enhancing infrastructure, designing curricula, and providing teacher training (Blancaflor & Hernandez, 2023). To optimize the return on investment for technology in education, BYOD provides a pragmatic and cost-effective approach.

### Enhanced Availability of Technology

BYOD's enhanced technological accessibility benefits students who may not have had access to gadgets otherwise. Smartphones, tablets, and laptops are widely used by students, therefore serving as easily available educational resources. BYOD enables students from diverse socioeconomic backgrounds to engage in digital learning and capitalize on the educational prospects provided by technology (Tuah & Abd Rahim, 2023). BYOD promotes inclusion and reduces the gap in digital access, ensuring that all students have equal opportunity to engage in digital learning.

### Increased Student Involvement

BYOD encourages heightened student engagement in the educational process. Allowing students to utilize their gadgets for instructional reasons enhances their level of engagement and motivation in their academic pursuits. Utilizing educational apps, multimedia resources, and interactive content enhances the engagement and dynamism of the learning process on mobile devices. This interaction leads to enhanced concentration, active involvement, and a more profound understanding of the topic (Braun et al., 2023). Moreover, allowing students the autonomy to choose educational resources and tools that align with their interests and preferences fosters a sense of responsibility for their learning.

### Individualized Education

BYOD promotes personalized learning experiences tailored to the unique requirements and preferences of each student. Students can utilize a range of instructional resources, such as e-books, educational apps, and online platforms, through their devices. Educators can utilize a range of applications and resources to individualize instruction and provide each student with a distinct learning trajectory (Al-Said, 2023). Students can study at their preferred speed, revise subjects as needed, and explore interests beyond the curriculum's obligations. The personalized method enhances students' understanding and allows teachers to effectively cater to diverse learning requirements.

## Continuous Learning Opportunities

BYOD enables continuous learning opportunities that extend beyond the limitations of the conventional classroom, allowing access at any time. Students can pursue their studies, work together with classmates, and obtain educational materials even when they are not in school (Petihakis et al., 2023). This flexibility reflects various timetables and allows students to study content, make revisions, or engage in enrichment activities at their most convenient time. BYOD enables students to actively participate in ongoing learning and utilize technology to enhance their educational journey, such as downloading study materials while commuting, conducting research at home, or engaging in online discussions outside of school hours (Mbambala & Abdullah, 2023).

## Advancement of Digital Literacy and Proficiency

Within a BYOD environment, students acquire essential digital literacy skills while employing their devices for academic tasks. They acquire skills in utilizing technology for study, cooperation, and communication, as well as in navigating online resources and assessing their credibility. Acquiring these digital literacy skills is crucial for students to thrive in today's job market since technology plays a vital role in several industries (Blancaflor & Hernandez, 2023). BYOD empowers students to utilize technology responsibly and ethically throughout their academic and professional journeys, equipping them with the necessary skills to become impactful digital citizens.

## Effortless Incorporation of Technology

BYOD promotes the smooth integration of technology into the educational process. Students are already proficient at utilizing their gadgets without the need for extensive familiarization in class. Teachers can focus on effectively incorporating technology into their courses to make it a vital part of the learning process (Petihakis et al., 2023). The seamless connection allows teachers to utilize technology to enhance lessons and create engaging and enjoyable learning experiences.

## Getting Ready for Practical Application of Technology in the Real World

BYOD facilitates the acquisition of responsible digital navigation skills in pupils, hence equipping them for practical technology usage in the real world. Proficiency in digital platforms and personal devices is essential for achieving success in a society that is progressively reliant on technology. Students acquire practical experience by incorporating personal devices into the learning process, utilizing technology as a means of communication, collaboration, research, and problem-solving (Astriani et al., 2023). This enables individuals to flourish in a society that is highly advanced in technology and adapt to the swiftly evolving digital landscape.

## Assistance for the Implementation of Flipped Learning and Blended Learning

BYOD facilitates the implementation of flipped learning and blended learning. Flipped classrooms involve students using their electronic devices to access pre-recorded lectures, online resources, and collaboration platforms outside of the traditional classroom setting (Mbambala & Abdullah, 2023). This approach maximizes the utilization of class time by engaging in dynamic discussions, collaborative projects, and hands-on activities. Students effortlessly transition between in-person and online learning sessions using their devices in blended learning environments (Shihepo et al., 2023). BYOD provides educators with the necessary resources to use innovative teaching methods, hence creating a diverse and immersive learning atmosphere for pupils.

## Uninterrupted Acquisition of Knowledge During Disturbances

BYOD allows for uninterrupted learning in remote settings, even in the face of disruptions such as natural catastrophes or public health situations. During periods of temporary closure or when physical attendance is not possible, students have the option to utilize their electronic devices to connect to virtual classrooms, online resources, and communication platforms. Implementing a BYOD policy ensures that the learning process can continue without any interruptions, even under difficult circumstances, hence reducing disruptions to students' education (Tuah & Abd Rahim, 2023). BYOD has numerous advantages from an educational perspective. Educational institutions can create a dynamic and technologically sophisticated learning environment that equips students with the necessary tools to excel in the classroom and prepares them for success in a technologically advanced society (Nagy et al., 2023). Nevertheless, certain challenges and limitations exist, which will be outlined in the subsequent section.

## Challenges of BYOD From an Educational Perspective

Although BYOD presents certain benefits, it also poses obstacles and restrictions in terms of education. Comprehending and resolving these matters is essential for the effective execution.

## Inequitable Technology Accessibility

A significant obstacle to BYOD is the disparity in technology access. Not every student can use their own devices or have consistent access to the internet while they are not in the classroom, and this is more evident in developing nations such as Sub-Saharan African countries where power has never been. This discrepancy can lead to a digital gap, where certain pupils have access to improved learning possibilities while others may face disadvantages (Mohd Shukry et al., 2023). To tackle this difficulty, educational institutions could contemplate the provision of loaner devices or the establishment of computer laboratories for students who lack access to personal devices.

## Attention Control

Personal devices can serve as a significant distraction for kids. Given the availability of social media, gaming, and entertainment apps, students may be enticed to participate in non-academic pursuits while in class. Teachers must employ efficient classroom management techniques to reduce disruptions and guarantee that devices are utilized for instructional objectives (Mbambala & Abdullah, 2023). Implementing explicit protocols for device utilization during classroom sessions and promoting conscientious online behavior can effectively reduce disruptions.

## Cybersecurity Vulnerabilities

Bring your device poses cybersecurity vulnerabilities to educational establishments. Personal devices may lack the equivalent level of security and safeguarding seen in school-owned devices. Educational institutions must implement strong security measures in order to protect sensitive data and prevent unauthorized individuals from gaining access to the school's network (Aguboshim et al., 2023). Deploying MDM solutions and delivering cybersecurity training to students and staff are crucial measures to bolster security in a BYOD setting.

## Protection of Personal Information and the Right to Privacy

The implementation of BYOD raises issues over the privacy implications associated with the collection and storage of student data on personal devices. Educational institutions are required to establish explicit policies and protocols for managing student data, gaining informed consent, and adhering to data protection legislation (Mbambala & Abdullah, 2023). It is imperative to provide students and parents with clear and comprehensive information regarding the utilization and safeguarding of student data to uphold transparency and foster trust.

## Compatibility and Support for Devices

The diverse range of devices that students bring to the classroom can provide difficulties in terms of device compatibility and technical assistance. Certain educational applications or platforms may not function adequately on all devices and operating systems (Sangeetha et al., 2023). Schools are required to furnish instructors and information technology workers with the necessary tools and training to handle a wide array of devices and applications proficiently.

## Principles of Digital Etiquette and Responsible Use

It is crucial to educate students about digital etiquette and the appropriate use of devices in a BYOD setting. Certain students may have limited proficiency in appropriately utilizing electronic devices, resulting in problems such as distributing improper content, engaging in cyberbullying, or making unauthorized modifications to the equipment (Tuah & Abd Rahim, 2023). Integrating digital citizenship education into the curriculum can cultivate a climate of conscientious digital behavior and encourage favorable conduct on the internet.

## Management and Maintenance of Devices

Educational institutions may face difficulties in maintaining and managing many personal devices. Schools must have robust systems for monitoring and managing devices, guaranteeing their up-to-date and secure status, and immediately resolving any technical problems that may arise. Managing the logistical aspects of BYOD may necessitate the allocation of extra resources and personnel assistance. BYOD may disrupt the learning environment if devices malfunction, lose connectivity, or cause technical issues during class time (Mbambala & Abdullah, 2023). Teachers must possess the necessary readiness to deal with these issues promptly and have contingency plans in place to guarantee a smooth learning experience.

## Fairness and the Inclusion of All Individuals

Although BYOD can facilitate technological access, it may not fully resolve concerns around fairness and inclusiveness. Certain pupils may possess high-end devices with sophisticated functionality, but others may possess more rudimentary ones (Mohd Shukry et al., 2023). Teachers should be aware of these differences and make sure that instructional activities are created to suit a variety of gadget capabilities.

# BEST PRACTICES FOR SUCCESSFUL MOBILE LEARNING WITH BYOD

This section presents some of the best practices for implementing mobile learning with BYOD successfully, which require careful planning, thoughtful policies, and effective practices to ensure a positive and productive learning experience.

## Explicit Bring Your Own Device (BYOD) Policy

Create an all-encompassing BYOD policy that explicitly delineates the regulations and anticipated conduct around the utilization of personal devices inside an educational environment. The policy should encompass various elements such as permissible usage, device safeguarding, data confidentiality, internet connectivity, and repercussions for policy breaches. Guarantee that the policy is readily available to students, parents, and educators, which will increase technological trust in students, interpretability in teachers, and acceptability in the educational arena (Aguboshim et al., 2023). Consistently engage in communication and evaluation of the policy to strengthen its significance and tackle any concerns.

## Continuing Education and Training Device and Connectivity Accessibility

Offer continuous professional development and training programs for educators to proficiently incorporate mobile devices and educational applications into their instructional methodologies. Teachers should undergo training to acquire the skills necessary for selecting suitable applications, incorporating them into their instructional methods, and utilizing mobile devices for formative evaluation and feedback (Aguboshim et al., 2023). Provide workshops, seminars, and peer collaboration sessions to assist teachers in efficiently utilizing mobile learning. Ensure universal access to personal devices and dependable internet connectivity for all students. Identify pupils who may lack access to electronic devices and investigate possibilities for offering temporary devices or creating computer facilities (Sangeetha et al., 2023). Collaborate with community partners or groups to address the digital gap and provide fair and equal access to technology.

## Responsible and Ethical Behavior in the Digital World

Integrate digital citizenship education into the curriculum to instruct students on responsible utilization of devices, internet security, confidentiality, and ethical conduct. Enable pupils to develop and become conscientious digital citizens who utilize their gadgets in a considerate and accountable manner (Blancaflor & Hernandez, 2023). Facilitate conversations regarding the ethical considerations of digital technology, proper behavior online, and the consequences of one's digital presence. Deploy MDM solutions to oversee and safeguard devices within the BYOD ecosystem effectively. MDM software allows administrators to monitor devices, enforce security regulations, and remotely control applications and content on student devices (Mohd Shukry et al., 2023). These solutions help guarantee that devices are utilized for instructional objectives and uphold a secure learning environment.

## Recommended Applications, Resources, and Individualized Teaching

Collect a variety of educational applications and materials that are in line with the curriculum and learning goals. Collaborate with educators to uncover top-notch applications that enrich educational experiences and aid across all subjects and age ranges. Periodically evaluate and revise the roster of suggested applications to ensure their continued relevance and usefulness (Aguboshim et al., 2023). Utilize mobile devices to facilitate customized education and individualized learning experiences. Utilize applications and tools that provide personalized learning paths, adaptive education, and customized teaching methods based on the student's preferences, learning modalities, and proficiency levels (Mbambala & Abdullah, 2023). Promote autonomous learning and offer pupils the chance to delve into subjects that captivate their attention freely.

## Engaging Educational Exercises

Create interesting and captivating learning exercises that utilize mobile device possibilities. Promote cooperative initiatives, immersive simulations, learning through gamification, and multimedia displays. The interactive nature of these exercises promotes student involvement, cultivates innovation, and boosts comprehension of the subject matter. Utilize mobile devices to facilitate ongoing feedback and formative assessment. Integrate quizzes, polls, and online evaluations to measure student comprehension and advancement in real-time accurately (Shihepo et al., 2023). Offer prompt feedback to students to facilitate their learning process and pinpoint areas that may require further assistance.

## Hybrid Education Method

Implement a hybrid learning strategy that integrates in-person teaching with online learning via mobile devices. Utilize mobile devices to enhance in-class activities, offer supplementary materials, and expand learning beyond the confines of the classroom. Integrate both synchronous and asynchronous learning methods to cater to a wide range of learning preferences. Foster an inclusive educational setting that promotes the utilization of students' gadgets for academic pursuits. Cultivate a constructive digital environment that encourages cooperation, innovation, and conscientious utilization of electronic devices (Aguboshim et al., 2023). Commend and exhibit student efforts and accomplishments that demonstrate the advantages of mobile learning.

## Parental involvement

Engage parents in the BYOD program by effectively conveying the advantages of mobile learning and the school's BYOD policy. Offer parents with tools and assistance to enhance their comprehension of their responsibility in facilitating their child's education via personal electronic devices. Promote transparent and unrestricted dialogue among parents, instructors, and students regarding the utilization of electronic devices for educational purposes (Nagy et al., 2023). By adhering to these recommended methods, educational institutions can maximize the advantages of mobile learning with BYOD, offering students a dynamic and hands-on learning experience that equips them for success in the digital age.

# EVALUATING THE IMPACT OF BYOD ON LEARNING OUTCOMES

Evaluating the impact of BYOD on learning outcomes is crucial to understanding the effectiveness of integrating personal devices into the educational environment. Several evaluation methods and indicators can be used to assess the influence of BYOD on students' academic performance, engagement, and overall learning experiences, as discussed in this section.

## Scholastic Achievement

Students' academic achievement is a key measure of the influence of BYOD on learning outcomes. Contrast the academic accomplishments of pupils who engage in BYOD initiatives with those who do not. Examine standardized test results, classroom assessments, and grades to ascertain whether the use of BYOD has a favorable influence on student performance (Shukry et al., 2023). Seek enhancements in domain-specific expertise, analytical reasoning capabilities, solution-oriented aptitudes, and general academic performance.

## Engagement and Participation

Evaluate student involvement and active involvement in the educational process through the use of BYOD. Assess students' engagement in classroom discussions, fulfillment of tasks, and involvement in interactive activities conducted using mobile devices (Petihakis et al., 2023). Heightened engagement and proactive involvement serve as favorable markers of the influence of BYOD on educational achievements, as they imply that students are more motivated and dedicated to their learning. Personalized Learning Assess the degree to which BYOD enables customized learning opportunities for pupils (Al-Said, 2023). Assess the effectiveness of teachers in utilizing mobile devices to adapt lessons and meet the unique learning requirements of individual students.

## Cooperative Learning and Communication

Analyze the influence of BYOD on the effectiveness of collaborative learning and communication among students. Evaluate the extent to which mobile devices improve communication and collaboration in group projects and conversations. Seek proof of enhanced peer interactions, collaboration, and knowledge exchange supported by BYOD (Sangeetha et al., 2023). Evaluate the extent to which students may utilize their devices to obtain individualized learning resources, explore their interests, and determine their learning speed. Assess the progress of students' acquisition of digital literacy skills through the utilization of BYOD. Examine the student's proficiency in utilizing digital platforms, analyzing online materials in a discerning manner, and employing technology for research, communication, and problem-solving (Mbambala & Abdullah, 2023). Proficiency in digital literacy is crucial for achieving success in contemporary society, and BYOD can greatly contribute to the development of these skills.

## Evaluation and Scrutiny of Teacher Performance

Collect input from educators regarding their encounters with BYOD implementation in the educational setting. Examine the efficacy of BYOD in improving teaching methods, involving students, and facilitating individualized learning. Teachers' observations and feedback might yield significant qualitative data regarding the influence of BYOD on learning outcomes (Sangeetha et al., 2023). Evaluate the enduring effects of BYOD on educational achievements by monitoring students' academic advancement over an extended period (Mbambala & Abdullah, 2023). Examine the data to ascertain whether the advantages of BYOD last over time and result in enhanced educational achievements in the later phases of schooling.

## Surveys for Parents and Students

Administer surveys to parents and students to collect their viewpoints on BYOD and its influence on educational achievements. Solicit input regarding students' motivation, enthusiasm for learning, and proficiency in digital skills using BYOD. Parental involvement is crucial in comprehending the impact of BYOD on students' holistic learning experiences and academic advancement (Blancaflor & Hernandez, 2023). Qualitative data refers to information that is descriptive and cannot be measured or quantified. It provides a deeper understanding of a phenomenon by capturing subjective experiences, opinions, and behaviors. Collect qualitative data by conducting interviews, organizing focus groups, or including open-ended survey questions in addition to the quantitative data (Mbambala & Abdullah, 2023). Qualitative data can offer profound insights into the experiences, opinions, and attitudes of students regarding BYOD and its influence on learning outcomes.

## Comparison With the Control Group

Conduct a comparative analysis of the academic achievements of students who engage in BYOD programs versus a control group that lacks access to personal devices. This comparison can facilitate the isolation of the influence of BYOD on learning outcomes and account for other variables that may affect student performance (Sangeetha et al., 2023). Assessing the influence of BYOD on educational achievements is a complex procedure that necessitates gathering both quantitative and qualitative information from different individuals involved. Employing a thorough assessment methodology, educational institutions make well-informed choices on the efficacy of BYOD initiatives and pinpoint areas for enhancement to optimize student learning results (Astriani et al., 2023).

## FUTURE TRENDS AND IMPLICATIONS

This section elaborates on the future trends in mobile learning and BYOD, along with their potential implications for education.

## Future Trends in Mobile Learning and BYOD

### Integration of Artificial Intelligence

The incorporation of AI in mobile learning will transform education by offering individualized learning experiences for pupils. AI algorithms will utilize data analysis to examine the unique patterns of individual learning, as well as identify their strengths and weaknesses. This information will be used to customize the content and activities provided to each student based on their own needs (Mbambala & Abdullah, 2023). Virtual tutors and AI-powered chatbots will provide instant feedback and assistance, hence improving the efficacy of self-paced learning. AI-powered analytics will provide educators with valuable information on student achievement, enabling them to pinpoint areas that need improvement and enhance teaching methods (Sangeetha et al., 2023). These technologies will facilitate immersive and experiential learning, enhancing the comprehension and engagement of intricate concepts.

### Internet of Things (IoT) in Education

The IoT in Education refers to the use of IoT devices to establish a networked learning environment. In this environment, intelligent gadgets, wearable technology, and sensors gather data to customize and individualize learning experiences (Shihepo et al., 2023). Smart classrooms equipped with IoT sensors can manage lighting, temperature, and air quality in order to improve the learning environment. Wearable devices can monitor the physical activity levels of pupils, offering valuable information about their overall well-being and health. This, in turn, encourages a comprehensive approach to education (Mbambala & Abdullah, 2023). These technologies will also enable collaborative learning experiences by enabling students to collaborate in shared virtual environments, surpassing physical limitations.

### 5G Technology and Mobile Learning Analytics

The extensive implementation of 5G technology would provide expedited and more dependable internet connectivity, hence greatly improving the mobile learning experience (Sangeetha et al., 2023). The integration of high-definition video streaming, instantaneous collaboration, and availability of cloud-based resources will be smooth and uninterrupted, facilitating interactive and multimedia-enriched educational content. Learning analytics will be crucial in assessing student advancement and pinpointing areas for enhancement (Aguboshim et al., 2023). Utilizing data-driven insights will empower instructors to customize learning paths, pinpoint areas of learning deficiency, and implement timely interventions to assist students who are facing challenges.

### Utilizing Blockchain Technology for Credentialing and Authentication

The utilization of blockchain technology has the potential to transform the processes of credentialing and academic record-keeping completely. Blockchain records, which are unchangeable and resistant to tampering, can be used to authenticate educational credentials (Shihepo et al., 2023). This can enhance the efficiency and security of confirming qualifications for employment or higher education. Extreme learning systems integrate AR, VR, and mixed-reality technology to offer all-encompassing and immersive educational experiences. Students will interact with interactive content and simulations that promote deeper comprehension and innovation (Astriani et al., 2023). Game-based learning experiences utilize the natural attractiveness of games to enhance comprehension and memory of academic subjects.

## Individualized Education Using Learning Algorithms

Learning algorithms will consistently modify learning material according to individual advancement, learning preferences, and areas of interest. By using a personalized learning method, students will be provided with tailored content that is specifically designed to meet their individual needs. This will serve as a strong motivator for students to attain improved learning results (Tuah & Abd Rahim, 2023). The integration of gamification into mobile learning will be further enhanced to augment student motivation and engagement. Educational applications and platforms will integrate gamification features, such as incentives, accolades, and progress monitoring, to enhance the enjoyment and interactivity of the learning experience (Kilduff et al., 2023).

## AI-Powered Personal Learning Assistants and Data-Driven Learning Paths

Students may possess customized AI learning companions that accompany them throughout their educational trajectory. According to the literature, these AI companions will acquire knowledge about the specific abilities, limitations, and preferences of each student (Petihakis et al., 2023). They will then provide personalized assistance, materials, and study advice that are suitable for everyone's requirements. Progress in learning analytics and AI will facilitate the development of learning paths for students based on data analysis (Braun et al., 2023). According to performance data, ML algorithms will recommend suitable learning materials, activities, and tests, enabling students to advance at their speed and concentrate on areas that need more attention.

## Microlearning and Just-in-Time Learning

Microlearning modules will increase in popularity, providing concise educational content that can be easily accessed on mobile devices. Just-in-time learning is a method that addresses urgent learning requirements, enabling students to obtain information or abilities as needed when confronted with specific obstacles or activities (Mohd Shukry et al., 2023). Mobile collaborative learning refers to the use of mobile devices, such as smartphones or tablets, to facilitate collaborative learning activities. Mobile devices will facilitate enhanced collaboration among students, allowing for immediate group projects, peer debates, and the sharing of knowledge (Nicosia et al., 2023). Students will effectively cooperate using mobile applications and communication platforms, fostering teamwork and cooperation.

## Learning Multiple Languages and Understanding Different Cultures

Mobile learning will facilitate educational experiences that involve several languages and cultures. Language learning applications facilitate students' acquisition of new languages, while virtual cultural exchange programs enable students to engage with peers from around the world, fostering cultural awareness and global comprehension. Alternative types of certifications, such as digital badges and credentials, are expected to receive increased prominence. Students could acquire digital badges by accomplishing specified skills or achievements (Qi, 2023). These badges offer a more comprehensive representation of their abilities, going beyond the conventional grading system.

## Language Learning That Fully Engages the Learner and Utilizes Voice Recognition Technology

AR and VR technologies will provide immersive language learning experiences on mobile devices. Students will engage in virtual language immersion scenarios to enhance their language skills, resulting in a more genuine and pleasurable language acquisition experience. Voice-activated virtual assistants and voice interfaces will facilitate learning experiences that do not require the use of hands, accommodating students with diverse learning preferences and abilities (Al-Said, 2023). Students will be able to engage with educational information, inquire, and obtain answers utilizing natural language through voice-enabled devices.

## Blended Reality Assessments and AI-Generated Content Will Be Included in Assessment Procedures

Students can participate in performance-based examinations utilizing AR or virtual reality (VR) to showcase their practical skills and knowledge, resulting in a comprehensive evaluation of their capabilities. AI will assist in the development of customized educational resources. Adaptive algorithms will utilize student data to create personalized learning materials, guaranteeing that the content is tailored to match individual learning requirements and preferences (Shukry et al., 2023). Lifelong Learning Platforms ML platforms will expand their scope beyond traditional schooling to accommodate individuals who engage in continuous learning throughout their lives.

Adults who are looking to enhance their professional skills or individuals who are following personal interests will be able to utilize mobile learning materials that are customized to their specific learning objectives. The potential of these future developments in ML and BYOD to change education is great (Soubhagyalakshmi & Reddy, 2023). They provide students with a more individualized, engaging, and dynamic learning experience. With the continuous advancement of technology, the field of education will change, and it will be essential for educators and institutions to accept these trends, modify their teaching methods, and utilize new technologies to promote the development and achievement of learners in the digital age (Engelbrecht et al., 2024).

## Implications for the Future of Education

The following are possible implications of education in ML and BYOD in the future.

### Improved Accessibility and Inclusiveness

With the increasing prevalence of mobile learning and BYOD, students from varied backgrounds and geographical regions will have greater access to educational possibilities. Students residing in remote or underserved regions will be provided with access to superior educational resources and opportunities, hence reducing the disparity in education between urban and rural areas (Oh et al., 2024). Furthermore, mobile learning accommodates the requirements of students with diverse learning styles and skills, hence fostering diversity within the classroom.

## Revamped Educational Environments

AR, VR, and XR are innovative technologies that will revolutionize learning spaces by converting conventional classrooms into immersive and interactive settings. Virtual classrooms enable remote learning and collaboration, allowing students and educators from around the world to connect. Students will be able to freely investigate virtual simulations, historical sites, and scientific phenomena, thereby improving their comprehension and involvement (Palanisamy et al., 2024).

## The Protection and Confidentiality

As technology and data-driven learning become more prevalent, educational institutions will need to prioritize data privacy and security. Schools must prioritize implementing strong data protection procedures to protect student information and adhere to data privacy legislation (Gulati et al., 2024). Educators and administrators must remain watchful and proactive in protecting against possible cyber risks and ensuring the responsible and ethical handling of student data.

## Transformation of the Teacher's Role

The incorporation of technology in education will revolutionize the role of teachers from conventional instructors to facilitators and mentors. Teachers will utilize data analytics and AI-generated insights to customize learning experiences and provide focused assistance to pupils (Sushil et al., 2024). Teachers will prioritize the development of critical thinking, problem-solving, and creativity, equipping pupils with crucial skills necessary for the 21st century. The integration of mobile learning and BYOD will facilitate worldwide collaboration among students, dismantling geographical limitations and fostering intercultural comprehension (Adams, 2024). Students will participate in cooperative endeavors with classmates from various nations, acquiring knowledge of different viewpoints and cultivating a feeling of global citizenship.

## Continual Education and Adaptable Educational Routes

In the coming years, there will be a greater demand for continuous learning as technology advances and employment demands change swiftly. Mobile learning will be crucial in enabling ongoing skill development and upskilling to meet the needs of a constantly changing workforce. Individuals must continuously engage in learning to remain current and competitive in their careers. Students will be able to select customized learning pathways that correspond to their interests, objectives, and learning preferences, providing them with increased flexibility (Halim et al., 2024). ML platforms will provide a variety of courses, micro-credentials, and certificates, enabling learners to customize their educational path based on their requirements.

## Revamping Assessment Strategies

Technological advancements will transform evaluation methodologies, shifting away from conventional standardized assessments. Utilizing performance-based evaluations, immediate feedback, and digital portfolios will offer a comprehensive perspective of student advancement, prioritizing skills and competencies above mere memorization. With the transformation brought about by automation and AI, there will be an increased focus on imparting lifelong learning skills such as flexibility, problem-solving, critical thinking, and digital literacy (T & Amala Bai, 2024). ML will offer students the chance to enhance these abilities through activities that involve independent learning and problem-solving.

## Professional Development for Teachers

Ongoing professional development for teachers will be crucial in harnessing the potential of mobile learning and developing technologies. Teachers will require instruction to incorporate technology into their teaching methods, create captivating digital materials, and base their instructional choices on data. The ethical utilization of technology will play a vital role in education as the utilization of AI, big data, and personalized learning algorithms continues to grow (Nurillah & Trihandoyo, 2024). Teachers and institutions have a responsibility to guarantee transparency in the utilization of data, safeguard student privacy, and advocate for responsible and ethical use of technology in the educational process.

## Personalized Educational Assistance

The implementation of BYOD and ML would enhance the provision of individualized learning assistance for kids with learning difficulties or special needs. Assistive technology and adaptable learning platforms will accommodate the unique learning characteristics of individuals, promoting a more inclusive and helpful educational setting. The consequences highlight the possibility of establishing a learning experience that is more comprehensive, captivating, and tailored to individual needs (Lam et al., 2024). It is crucial for educational institutions and policymakers to aggressively tackle issues of data privacy, digital literacy, and fairness to guarantee that all students can take advantage of the revolutionary potential of technology in education.

## LESSON LEARNED FROM THE CHAPTER

The section largely presents lessons learned from the studied studies in the exploration of ML and BYOD in education as follows:

- The incorporation of mobile devices and emerging technology can transform education. AI, in general, that entails mobile learning and BYOD presents novel prospects for customized and interactive learning encounters that accommodate students' varied demands and learning preferences.
- Ensuring equal access to technology is crucial for maximizing the benefits of mobile learning and BYOD in education. To prevent exacerbating educational inequities, it is imperative to tackle the differences in device ownership and internet connectivity.

- With technology's increasing importance in education, it is crucial to prioritize protecting student data and ensuring data privacy and security. Educational institutions should have strong data protection mechanisms and comply with ethical data practices.
- Teachers require thorough professional development to successfully use mobile devices and technology in their teaching methods. Training enables educators to utilize technology to maximize learning results effectively.
- Mobile learning and BYOD facilitate individualized learning experiences, enabling students to advance at their speed and concentrate on their educational requirements. Customization enhances student involvement and facilitates a more profound comprehension of the topic.
- Integrating mobile learning and technology with traditional classroom training creates a well-rounded and efficient learning environment. The integration of in-person interactions and digital resources optimizes learning results.
- Integrating digital citizenship education into the curriculum is essential for instructing pupils in the proper and ethical utilization of technology. Ensuring that pupils are equipped with the necessary skills to navigate the digital environment safely and respectfully is crucial for their development of digital literacy.
- Future trends greatly influence education. To effectively prepare for the future of education, educational institutions must be aware of developing trends in ML and BYOD. Proactively anticipating and embracing technological advancements can stimulate creativity and cultivate more dynamic learning environments.
- Mobile learning and BYOD support student collaboration, allowing for the establishment of worldwide links and the exchange of cultural knowledge. Adopting technology can overcome physical distance and foster intercultural comprehension.
- Mobile learning facilitates ongoing evaluation and immediate feedback, empowering educators to track student advancement more efficiently. Providing feedback in a timely manner enhances student learning and facilitates the identification of areas that need improvement.
- ML provides pupils with increased freedom in selecting customized learning paths. By personalizing their educational path, students explore their passions and talents, resulting in increased levels of engagement and motivation.
- Mobile learning and BYOD can equip students with skills that are essential for the future, such as digital literacy, critical thinking, problem-solving, and adaptability. These talents are crucial for achieving success in a continuously changing world.

## CONCLUSION

With the increasing prevalence of mobile devices and the advancements in AI technology, these tools together provide a learning experience that is more tailored, adaptable, and captivating. Implementing a BYOD policy enables students to utilize their devices, promoting a feeling of possession and ease, ultimately leading to increased engagement and drive. AI integration in mobile learning enables the customization of educational content to suit individual needs, offering immediate feedback and assistance that adjusts to the unique speed and learning approach of each student. Furthermore, the integration of AI in mobile learning can enhance the ease of accessing extensive educational materials, allowing students to examine subjects comprehensively and collaboratively, regardless of geographical limitations. Teachers can apply these tools to optimize administrative processes, individualize instruction, and harness data-driven insights to enhance educational outcomes. As educational institutions adopt these advancements, they must also tackle difficulties such as assuring fair and equal access, upholding cybersecurity measures, and offering sufficient training for educators. The combination of mobile learning, BYOD, and AI has the potential to democratize education by increasing accessibility and inclusivity. This will better equip students for a future when digital literacy and flexibility are crucial. Adopting these technologies, educational systems may cultivate a more captivating, streamlined, and successful learning atmosphere, equipping learners with the competencies essential to excel in an ever more digital and AI-dominated world.

# REFERENCES

Abubakari, M. S., Shafik, W., & Hidayatullah, A. F. (2024). Evaluating the Potential of Artificial Intelligence in Islamic Religious Education: A SWOT Analysis Overview. In *AI-Enhanced Teaching Methods* (pp. 216-239). IGI Global. 10.4018/979-8-3693-2728-9.ch010

Adams, H. R. (2024). Bring Your Own Device (BYOD) and Equitable Access to Technology. In *Intellectual Freedom Issues in School Libraries*. 10.5040/9798400670886.ch-034

Aguboshim, F. C., Udobi, J. I., & Otuu, O. O. (2023). Security Issues Associated with Bring Your Own Device (BYOD): A Narrative Review. In *Research Highlights in Science and Technology, 2*. https://doi.org/10.9734/bpi/rhst/v2/19215D

Al-Said, K. (2023). Effect of _Bring Your Own Device' (BYOD) on Student Behavior, Well-Being, and Learning Economic Disciplines. *International Journal of Information and Education Technology (IJIET)*, 13(4), 658–663. 10.18178/ijiet.2023.13.4.1850

Astriani, M. S., Rizqi, D., & Kurniawan, A. (2023). Bring your own device (BYOD) restaurant: Self-service dining ordering system. *AIP Conference Proceedings*, 2510(1), 030012. 10.1063/5.0128353

Blancaflor, E. B., & Hernandez, J. R. (2023). A Compliance Based and Security Assessment of Bring Your Own Device (BYOD) in Organizations. *Communications in Computer and Information Science, 1823 CCIS*. 10.1007/978-3-031-35299-7_10

Braun, B. J., Histing, T., Menger, M. M., Platte, J., Grimm, B., Hanflik, A. M., Richter, P. H., Sivananthan, S., Yarboro, S. R., Gueorguiev, B., Pokhvashchev, D., & Marmor, M. T. (2023). "Bring Your Own Device"—A New Approach to Wearable Outcome Assessment in Trauma. *Medicina (Lithuania), 59*(2). 10.3390/medicina59020403

Engelbrecht, J. M., Michler, A., Schwarzbach, P., & Michler, O. (2024). Bring Your Own Device - Enabling Student-Centric Learning in Engineering Education by Incorporating Smartphone-Based Data Acquisition. *Lecture Notes in Networks and Systems, 900 LNNS*. 10.1007/978-3-031-52667-1_36

Gulati, R., West, M., Zilles, C., & Silva, M. (2024). Comparing the Security of Three Proctoring Regimens for Bring-Your-Own-Device Exams. *SIGCSE 2024 - Proceedings of the 55th ACM Technical Symposium on Computer Science Education, 1*. https://doi.org/10.1145/3626252.3630809

Halim, I. I. A., Buja, A. G., Idris, M. S. S., & Mahat, N. J. (2024). Implementation of BYOD Security Policy in Malaysia Institutions of Higher Learning (MIHL): An Overview. *Journal of Advanced Research in Applied Sciences and Engineering Technology*, 33(2), 1–14. 10.37934/araset.33.2.114

Kilduff, C. L. S., Deshmukh, M., Guevara, G., Neece, J., Daniel, C., Thomas, P. B. M., Lovegrove, C., Sim, D. A., & Timlin, H. M. (2023). Creating a secure clinical 'Bring Your Own Device' BYOD photography service to document and monitor suspicious lesions in the lid oncology clinic. *Eye (London, England)*, 37(4), 744–750. 10.1038/s41433-022-02049-835379923

Lam, H., Beckman, T., Harcourt, M., & Shanmugam, S. (2024). Bring Your Own Device (BYOD): Organizational Control and Justice Perspectives. *Employee Responsibilities and Rights Journal*. 10.1007/s10672-024-09498-1

Mbambala, T. P., & Abdullah, H. (2023). Promoting Bring Your Own Device (BYOD) Information Privacy Protection Awareness among Public Libraries in Gauteng. *Proceedings - International Conference on Advanced Computer Information Technologies, ACIT*. ACIT.10.1109/ACIT58437.2023.10275501

Mohd Shukry, A. I., Mohamad Rosman, M. R., Nik Rosli, N. N. I., Alias, N. R., Razlan, N. M., & Alimin, N. A. (2023). "Bring-Your-Own-Device" (BYOD) and Productivity. [IJIM]. *International Journal of Interactive Mobile Technologies*, 17(11), 83–100. 10.3991/ijim.v17i11.38139

Nagy, V., Kovács, G., Földesi, P., & Sándor, Á. P. (2023). Car Simulator Study for the Development of a Bring-Your-Own-Device (BYOD) Dashboard Concept. *Chemical Engineering Transactions*, 107. Advance online publication. 10.3303/CET23107070

Nicosia, J., Wang, B., Aschenbrenner, A. J., Sliwinski, M. J., Yabiku, S. T., Roque, N. A., Germine, L. T., Bateman, R. J., Morris, J. C., & Hassenstab, J. (2023). To BYOD or not: Are device latencies important for bring-your-own-device (BYOD) smartphone cognitive testing? *Behavior Research Methods*, 55(6), 2800–2812. 10.3758/s13428-022-01925-135953659

Nurillah, R. A., & Trihandoyo, A. (2024). Analisis Faktor-Faktor Keamanan Informasi Perusahaan Dalam Penerapan Bring Your Own Device (BYOD). *IKRA-ITH Informatika : Jurnal Komputer Dan Informatika*, 8(2), 136–145. 10.37817/ikraith-informatika.v8i2.2973

Oh, J., Capezzuto, L., Kriara, L., Schjodt-Eriksen, J., van Beek, J., Bernasconi, C., Montalban, X., Butzkueven, H., Kappos, L., Giovannoni, G., Bove, R., Julian, L., Baker, M., Gossens, C., & Lindemann, M. (2024). Use of smartphone-based remote assessments of multiple sclerosis in Floodlight Open, a global, prospective, open-access study. *Scientific Reports*, 14(1), 122. 10.1038/s41598-023-49299-438168498

Palanisamy, R., Norman, A. A., & Mat Kiah, M. L. (2024). Employees' BYOD Security Policy Compliance in the Public Sector. *Journal of Computer Information Systems*, 64(1), 62–77. 10.1080/08874417.2023.2178038

Petihakis, G., Kiritsis, D., Farao, A., Bountakas, P., Panou, A., & Xenakis, C. (2023). A Bring Your Own Device security awareness survey among professionals. *ACM International Conference Proceeding Series*. 10.1145/3600160.3605072

Qi, C. (2023). Effects of Bring Your Own Device (BYOD) Attributes on Work-to-life Conflict. *Asia Pacific Journal of Information Systems*, 33(3), 831–862. 10.14329/apjis.2023.33.3.831

Sangeetha, S. R., Singh, P., & Jahagirdar, S. R. (2023). Estimation of Distance to Empty of Small Commercial EVs for BYOD (Bring Your Own Device) Application using EKF and ANN. *2023 IEEE Renewable Energy and Sustainable E-Mobility Conference. RESEM*, 2023, 1–5. 10.1109/RESEM57584.2023.10236430

Shafik, W. (2024a). Introduction to ChatGPT. In *Advanced Applications of Generative AI and Natural Language Processing Models* (pp. 1–25). IGI Global. 10.4018/979-8-3693-0502-7.ch001

Shafik, W. (2024b). An Overview of Artificial Intelligence-Enhanced Teaching Methods. In *AI-Enhanced Teaching Methods* (pp. 132–159). IGI Global. 10.4018/979-8-3693-2728-9.ch006

Shafik, W. (2024c). Data Privacy and Security Safeguarding Customer Information in ChatGPT Systems. In *Revolutionizing the Service Industry with OpenAI Models* (pp. 52–86). IGI Global. 10.4018/979-8-3693-1239-1.ch003

Shafik, W. (2024d). *The Role of Artificial Intelligence in the Emerging Digital Economy Era. Artificial Intelligence Enabled Management: An Emerging Economy Perspective.* De Gruyter. 10.1515/9783111172408-003

Shafik, W. (2024e). Mobile Learning and Bring Your Own Device (BYOD): Enhancing Education in the Digital Age. In *Integrating Cutting-Edge Technology into the Classroom* (pp. 240-267). IGI Global. 10.4018/979-8-3693-3124-8.ch012

Shihepo, E., Bhunu-Shava, F., & Chitauro, M. (2023). Designing A Real-Time Bring your Own Device Security Awareness Model for Mobile Device Users within Namibian Enterprises. *2023 6th International Conference on Information Systems and Computer Networks, ISCON 2023.* IEEE.10.1109/ISCON57294.2023.10112191

Shukry, A. I. M., Rosman, M. R. M., Rosli, N. N. I. N., Alias, N. R., Razlan, N. M., & Alimin, N. A. (2023). "Bring-Your-Own-Device" (BYOD) and Productivity: Instrument Development and Validation. *International Journal of Interactive Mobile Technologies*, 17(11), 83–100. 10.3991/ijim.v17i11.38139

Soubhagyalakshmi, P., & Reddy, K. S. (2023). An efficient security analysis of bring your own device. *IAES International Journal of Artificial Intelligence*, 12(2), 696. 10.11591/ijai.v12.i2.pp696-703

Sushil, G. S., Deshmukh, R. K., & Junnarkar, A. A. (2024). A Security Framework Design for Generating Abnormal Activities Report of Bring Your Own Devices (BYODs). *Lecture Notes in Electrical Engineering*, 1106, 429–441. Advance online publication. 10.1007/978-981-99-7954-7_39

T, J. V., & Amala Bai, V. M. (2024). Evaluation of security framework for BYOD device in cloud environment. *Automatika, 65*(3). 10.1080/00051144.2024.2310458

Tuah, F. F., & Abd Rahim, N. A. (2023). The Implementation of Bring Your Own Device (BYOD) at School through Actor-Network Theory (ANT). *International Journal of Academic Research in Progressive Education and Development*, 12(2). 10.6007/IJARPED/v12-i2/17434

# Chapter 9
# Generation AI in a Reimagined Classroom:
## Challenges, Opportunities and Implications to Education

**Potchong M. Jackaria**

*Tawi-Tawi College of Technology and Oceanography, Mindanao State University, Philippines*

**Bonjovi H. Hajan**

https://orcid.org/0000-0003-2911-5824

*Tawi-Tawi College of Technology and Oceanography, Mindanao State University, Philippines*

**Al-Rashiff H. Mastul**

*Tawi-Tawi College of Technology and Oceanography, Mindanao State University, Philippines*

**Fatima Zahra Sali**

https://orcid.org/0009-0001-6795-7056

*Tawi-Tawi College of Technology and Oceanography, Mindanao State University, Philippines*

## ABSTRACT

*This chapter aims to conduct a review of existing literature on the artificial intelligence applications in education in the context of generation AI students. Particularly, this chapter looks into opportunities and challenges through the systematics literature review. Challenges identified include the risk of youth over-reliance on AI, and the widening of the digital divides between the privilege and the underprivilege youth. Educators and practitioners are concerned on the potential bias of AI algorithm, privacy, and the ethical issues, especially when children use AI. On the other hand, some opportunities emerged including the automation of many routine tasks, the delivery of personalized learning tailored to students' abilities and interest and the giving of real-time feedback. This chapter suggests for the inclusion of AI literacy in schools as this will be needed in the future workplace. Ethical, privacy and safety issues should also be freely discussed in schools involving youth so that they can make better decisions.*

DOI: 10.4018/979-8-3693-3350-1.ch009

## INTRODUCTION

The integration of artificial intelligence (AI) into various aspects of society has brought about significant transformations including in the realm of education. As technology continues to advance, the next generation, often referred to as Generation AI, is growing up in a world where AI-powered tools and applications are increasingly prevalent.

AI in education has variety of applications. AI can be used to design personalized learning experiences for students (Aleven, 2023), automated assessment systems to aid teachers (Jackaria, et al., 2024), and facial recognition systems that provide updates about learners' behaviors (Trabelsi, et al., 2023; Hasnine, et al., 2023) to name just a few. Despite the potential benefits of AI in supporting students' learning experiences and teachers' teaching practices, concerns also rises on the ethical and societal drawbacks of these systems especially when implemented in K-12 educational contexts involving youth and children (Akgun & Greenhow, 2021).

However, one of the most compelling reasons for the adaption of Artificial Intelligence in the classroom is the changing landscape of future work. In the future, many traditional industries and jobs will gradually disappear. Unemployment will be one of the major concerns of young people who are planning for future job (Hogenhout & Takahashi, 2022). In one study, it is estimated that up to 800 million jobs worldwide will be automated by year 2030 (Manyika, et al., 2017). Repetitive and manual jobs that can be automated are more likely be taken by AI and robots. However, these advances in AI technological tools are also opening up new opportunities such as availability of emerging jobs. This in return creates a demand for new skills (e.g., AI literacy, computer coding, big data, etc.).

These important changes and the coming of the new generation of students into classrooms calls for new strategies for schools to connect with these students. The role of teachers, administrators, and schools will have to change too. In addition, there will be challenges brought by the coming of generation AI students given our current educational structure and teachers' capabilities. A gap may also exist between the teachers' and students' beliefs and their level of usage and exposure to AI, with latter as more immersed and perhaps with new value system.

While there are many papers that discussed about AI in education, the discussions are always from the context of the adult such as teachers and practitioners. This book chapter will discuss how Artificial Intelligence positively impact the youth and how its negative effect can be mitigated. This paper is posited on the two main ideas. First, a new breed of students (i.e., Generation AI) are coming into classrooms, hence the schools need to change and second, the need of developing new skillsets among the youth due to the changing work in the future. This chapter explores the characteristics of Generation AI, analyzes the challenges and opportunities of brought by AI to education based on the existing literatures and its implications to education.

## METHODOLOGY

A systematic review of existing literature following the approach of Petticrew and Roberts (2006) was conducted. Literature was collected from different online sources with the following inclusion criteria for the papers and documents: (1) materials sourced either from refereed journal or reputable institutions websites; and (2) they pertain to issues on AI, youth and/or education and (3) published within the year 2019 onwards.

The researchers reviewed existing literature on Generation AI and its impact on education. Numerous scholarly articles, research papers, and reports were examined to gather insights into the defining characteristics, challenges, opportunities, and implications of Generation AI in the classroom. Key findings and themes in the current literatures were identified to inform the discussion presented in this chapter.

## RESULT AND DISCUSSIONS

To set the context of the chapter, the first part covers the background on future classroom and characteristics of the Generation AI. This will be followed by opportunities brought by AI in education and the challenges it will bring.

### What Will the Future AI-Infused Classroom Look Like?

This paper assumes that the physical classrooms or learning spaces will still be present in the next few decades. One of the defining characteristics of the physical classrooms and learning spaces is the use of Internet of Things (IoT) where everything is connected to the internet and the ever presence of AI tools.

### Smart Classroom and Learning Spaces

The smart classrooms use today are still far from being cost-efficient. While some are still made for experimental purpose (Dai, et al., 2023; Rajesh, 2022). However, in the near future this will become the normal classroom setting. The physical learning space in the future will be utilizing smart technologies which as currently used in high-tech building and homes (ex. Amazon's Alexa and Google Home). The utilization of smart technologies and systems within future school architecture would present real opportunities for new learning spaces. The future classrooms will include the use of augmented technologies and artificial intelligence which will provide learners with new and multi-sensory learning experiences. The technology will also allow learners to connect and collaborate with fellow students and their teachers across the virtual and beyond physical platforms (Leathy, et al., 2019).

In the future smart classrooms, the routine tasks are taken cared by AI. Such as using of sensors to automatically check student attendance, check quizzes and activities and gives real-time feedbacks. The sensors will also automatically adjust lighting and temperature (Rajesh, et al., 2022). Hence freeing teachers of the many demanding teaching-related tasks to focus on actual instruction. The students will be connected to unlimited information using the internet and the power of Artificial Intelligence. Teachers will then need to focus on worthwhile activities and task while allowing students to access and engage using AI technologies.

### The Presence of AI Powered Robots

The presence of robots inside the future classrooms will be one of its remarkable features. In this AI-infused classrooms, robots will be moving around interacting and working with students. From smart tools that are fixed into walls and moving robots that socialized with students (Yusif, 2023) to humanoid robots that act as human teaching assistant (Har & Ma, 2023; Kurtz & Kohen-Vacs, 2022). These robots are used not only during class time, but interact with students even during the student recess and playtime. Outside school, the students will also be exposed to robots. From autonomous cleaning robots, smart tools that control home fixtures, to robot manning public facilities like driverless vehicles.

## Who Are the Generation AI?

Generation AI encompasses individuals who have grown up in an era characterized by rapid technological advancements particularly on artificial intelligence tools and the Internet of Things (IoT). Geration Alpha also called Generation Alpha are experts in navigating the digital world (UNIS Hanoi, 2024). This is the generation who are born in era where AI is a big part of the daily living. They are adept in using technology including the AI. Their uses of AI shape their ethical views about AI use. In terms of relationships, the Generation AI will be more connected to AI not just as a tool but on the personal and emotional level. AI will surely impact their socio-emotional being, thought, and habits. Understanding these characteristics is crucial for teachers and policy makers to effectively engage and support Generation AI learners in the classroom by tapping into these qualities (Chan & Lee, 2023). While Generation AI is not yet in our classrooms, we can only infer from the current GenZ's characteristics assuming the current and future trends of Artificial Intelligence (AI) are maintained.

Generation AI are inherently comfortable with technology. They expect their learning to be technology-driven including the use and access to Artificial Intelligent and various digital tools (Gill & Mathur, 2023). They effortlessly navigate digital interfaces and are quick to adopt new technologies. This is brought by increasing connectivity, and ubiquity of AI tools. Generation AI demonstrates diverse learning preferences, preferring interactive and multimedia-rich learning experiences rather than the traditional read and write. They value practicality, flexibility and autonomy in their learning journey. Generation AI students constantly seeks out for personalized and adaptive learning opportunities. They prefer shorter lessons delivered using different modality and expect immediate real-time feedbacks. They are engrossed in videos and all information that are visual (The Annie E. Casey Foundation, 2024).

Generation AI are hyper-connected with the world hence they are very exposed to various cultures which influence their acceptance and appreciation of diversity. Their interconnectedness makes them more aware of the global issues that affects them like environmental issues, climate change, awareness of new technologies (UNIS Hanoi, para 7-8)

## Emerging Opportunities Brought by AI

Generation AI and future AI-infused classroom also presents significant opportunities for reimagining our education. These new AI tools make it possible for education to be delivered in ways that is currently difficult or impossible. The following are opportunities in the AI-infused classroom.

## Personalized Learning

AI-powered tools and platforms can provide personalized learning experiences tailored to individual student's needs and interest. AI learning algorithms can adjust content and pace in real-time which can optimize learning outcomes. AI may serve as intelligent tutor that is available anytime and anywhere (Alam, 2023; Aleven, 2023). It acts the same way as that of human tutors that can make judgement about student's understanding, difficulties, and interest based solely from their interactions with them. Today's available tools and online platforms already allows for personalization to suit student characteristics and learning preferences (Jamil, et al., 2023). AI tools will be different as it will simulate actual student-teacher interaction which will reduce dropout and foster student engagement (Schiff & Rosenberg-Kima, 2023).

## Innovative Teaching Methodologies

Educators can leverage AI to facilitate innovative teaching methodologies. This includes the use of new technologies in delivering contents such as the use of virtual and augmented reality technologies which were shown to be promising for use in teaching (Ironsi, 2023; Nasar, et al., 2023). These immersive technologies deepen students understanding of complex concepts and enhance student's engagement. The use of robots such as social robots will provide students with human-robot interactions which will be beneficial for the cognitive and social development of the students.

## Enhanced Accessibility

AI technologies have the potential to enhance access and inclusivity in education by providing support for students with diverse learning needs. For instance, speech recognition, text-to-speech, and translation tools can be utilized to empower students to overcome language barriers and access educational resources more effectively. AI-powered capabilities like speech recognition can increase the support available to students with disabilities or language barriers (Cardona, et al., 2023). The so-called social robots have been used to improve young people's academic achievements and social skills (Ghiglino, et al., 2023; Pawluczuk, 2023).

The use of AI can help address and resolve many issues related to accessibility. The integration of AI can resolve issues such as accessibility of learning contents and the deficiency of teachers. The implementation and adoption of Artificial Intelligence into education sector is unavoidable (Ahmad, 2021).

## Challenges Brought by Generation AI

Despite the numerous advantages associated with Generation AI, it carries several challenges that must be addressed. These are as follows:

## Dependence on AI Technology

AI can be utilized as means of cognitive support and supplement to human abilities and intelligence. It allows us to access information faster, become more efficient and effective (UNICEF, 2021). However, there is a risk of Generation AI becoming overly dependent on technology for learning and information. We have seen the effect of too much screen time among the young. Among them includes lesser attention span to concentrate on the lesson. Other technology such as social media and games have cause addiction among the youth which affect their health and social well-being. In the age of artificial intelligence, many are worried about the AI being potentially hinders the development important skills such as problem solving and critical thinking (Fuchs, 2023; Liyberber, 2023).

## Digital Distractions of AI technologies

The proliferation of digital devices and online distractions can pose challenges to maintaining focus and concentration in the classroom. This will lead to lower learning outcomes and other behavioral problems. AI devices may provide companionship to children. Children may grow up thinking and feeling that AI-powered devices are just like actual pets or actual people. As children spend more time with AI devices, more personal data will be collected to add to the AI data pool. This makes it more accurate for the AI device to give personalized recommendations. However, this will increase and make children even more vulnerable to exploitation and manipulation when not used properly (Howley, 2019).

## Privacy, Potential Bias and Ethical Concerns

Generation AI's extensive use of technology also raises concerns about data privacy and security. For the smart system to be able to design personalized lessons and provide real-time feedback, personal data need to be collected from the students through the internet. Collecting personal data will pose privacy concern. We have seen in the current tech-based models where the creators earn by monetizing users' data. The use of AI in classrooms give education technology companies critical role while they are guided by their financial motives (Schiff, 2021).

The AI system depends on the data set it can access and algorithms that power them. This then will lead to potential bias in its response (Hasse, et al., 2019). Issues related to racial equity and unfair bias are some topics that requires attention. Datasets are used to develop AI, and when they are non-representative or contain undesired associations or patterns, resulting AI models may act unfairly in how they detect patterns or automate decisions.

The need for ethical considerations is needed to uphold and protect children's rights in the age of AI (UNICEF, 2023). We must think deeply about the problems that may arise with the emergence of robots. (Chen and She, 2023). Educators and those working with youth and children must understand the ethical implications of collecting and analyzing students' data while ensuring the protection of personal information. It is suggested that the ethical challenges of AI in education must be identified and discussed to teachers and students (Akgun, et al., 2022).

## Digital Divides Caused by AI

AI systems may amplify existing social inequalities among youth of different races, socio-economic statuses, genders, and regions. Obstacles to the adoption of AI-powered technologies in under-resourced schools and countries could exacerbate existing gaps within the youth population. Without access to AI systems and the skills to utilize them, the youth will be at disadvantage (Hasse, et al., 2019).

Traditionally disadvantaged communities and groups, including their children, are similarly disadvantaged in the AI-driven world. The digital divide will result in unequal access to AI-enabled services and can prevent disadvantage children from reaching their full potentials (UNICEF, 2021). This unequal opportunity will only provide those with means to be more adept hence more successful in the increasingly complex and competitive world.

## Psychological and Socio-Emotional Impact of AI on Youth

The interaction of children with artificial intelligence technologies may have implications to their physical and mental well-being (UNICEF, 2023). There are many areas that need close considerations including the effect of AI on children's cognitive functions, attention, depression, anxiety, and social skills. While the effect of AI on these areas are not yet established, we can only infer from the effect of present technologies on children and youth. These include technology addiction, reduced attention span, unnatural sleeping habits, emotional stress, relationship issue and several behavioral problems (Panjeti-Madan & Ranganathan, 2023). The youth social formation with technology instead of human will lead to the loss of meaningful relationship-building and cause a sense of disconnectedness (Pawluczuk & Serban, 2022; Pawluczuk, 2023). With this, there is a need to refocus on human connections and re-emphasizing of uniquely human skills (e.g., empathy, creativity, community building) for youth to thrive in this evolving landscape.

## Implications to Education

Finally, based on the existing literature, the paper discusses the following implications to education that will help our teachers and schools prepare for the coming of the new generation of students and for seamless integration of AI into the classrooms.

### The Need for Reform in Education for Generation AI

With the changing landscape brought by Artificial Intelligence into classrooms. Education needs to transform in terms of classroom practices, aligning curriculum, and attuning policies. Reform in our education model, teaching methods and learning strategies are helpful in the development of skills needed for the society in the era of artificial intelligence (Han 2020). Start with the need to change our traditional classroom set-up by integrating AI technology in the form of smart classroom.

There is a pressing need for educational reform to align curriculum and pedagogical practices with the evolving needs of Generation AI and future work. Many new ideas need to be integrated into our future curriculum. These include the introduction of AI digital literacy, ethics and safety issues of AI usage among with children and young adult, and the re-emphasis on the harmonious and balanced human skills and character education (Cathrin and Wikandau, 2023).

### The Importance of Integrating AI Literacy Skill

The introduction of AI and the inevitable changes in future work will require young people to develop new skills (Pedro, et al., 2019). One of these skills is the need for better digital literacy including the new AI literacy (Yang et. al, 2023). Digital literacy education will empower students with the skills and knowledge necessary to navigate the complexities of the AI-driven future (Su & Yang, 2023). AI literacy also includes educating students about safe and ethical use of Artificial Intelligence (Cardona, et al., 2023).

Some argue that AI literacy should start as early as childhood education which will empower children to understand AI (Williams, et al. 2019). This is because the applications of artificial intelligence will become more common and it will become increasingly necessary to educate youth about how AI technologies work and impact their society (Williams, et al., 2022). Moreover, digital competence will be integral to young people's civic and democratic citizenship (Pawlaczic, 2023).

## The Need for More Equitable and Accessible Education Opportunities

Efforts must be made to address equity and access issues in AI-driven education. The new AI technology will provide advantage to those who have access while marginalizing those who do not. It is more likely that the early days of AI in education will see a widening of educational inequality. This can be seen in the early adoption stage of all important new technology until penetration approaches 100 percent (Reiss, 2021).

Contrary, AI has the potential to make major positive contributions to improve education access, for all students, including those not well served by current formal school setup. For instance, schools can take advantage of AI tools such as voice inputs to reach students who cannot attend school due to special needs (Gill, et al., 2024). Ensuring equal access to opportunities offered by AI are crucial for fostering inclusive learning environments and reducing disparities in educational outcomes due to the digital divide.

## Involving the Youth in Active Discussion of ISSUES on AI

AI developer and policy makers should not be the only people in the discussion of AI usage. The parents, families, students, policy makers, and system leaders should examine and critically analyze the increasing role of AI (UNICEF, 2021).

Innovations in artificial intelligence are reshaping the labor market, which has important implications for future career choices and the skills preparation of the youth. Hence, it is critical that young people have a basic understanding of artificial intelligence as well as ethical, privacy- and safety-related issues for them to make better decisions (Hasse et al, 2019).

## CONCLUSION

The fast development of AI technological tools and the coming of Generation AI presents both challenges and opportunities for education. This calls for a change in our physical classrooms and the need for redesigning of our curriculum. The challenges include risk of technological dependence of youth on AI, distraction from learning, the potential bias of AI algorithm and the ethical issues it will bring. With the advent of AI, there are also opportunities that schools should take advantage of. These include the automation of many routine tasks which free teachers from many teaching-related workload, the delivery of personalized learning that is tailored to students' abilities/interest and the giving of real-time and human-like feedbacks to improve students' performance. AI can also be used as a new teaching methodology to reach those youth who cannot benefit from our current education set-up such as student with special needs. This paper suggests the need for teaching of digital literacy specifically AI literacy in schools as this will be needed in the future workplace. Ethical, privacy and safety issues should also be freely discussed in schools to engage the youth so that they can make better decisions. There is also a need to ensure that the opportunities will be made accessible to all youth irrespective of social status, age, or gender so that every student can developed full potential by leveraging the advance capabilities of AI.

# REFERENCES

Ahmad, S., Rahmat, M., Mubarik, M., Alam, M., & Hyder, S. (2021). Artificial Intelligence and Its Role in Education. *Sustainability (Basel)*, 13(22), 12902. 10.3390/su132212902

Akgun, S., & Greenhow, C. (2022). Artificial intelligence in education: Addressing ethical challenges in K-12 settings. *AI and Ethics*, 2(3), 431–440. 10.1007/s43681-021-00096-734790956

Alam, A. (2023). Harnessing the Power of AI to Create Intelligent Tutoring Systems for Enhanced Classroom Experience and Improved Learning Outcomes. In *Intelligent Communication Technologies and Virtual Mobile Networks* (pp. 571–591). Springer Nature Singapore. https://link.springer.com/chapter/10.1007/978-981-99-1767-9_4210.1007/978-981-99-1767-9_42

Aleven, V., Baraniuk, R., Brunskill, E., Crossley, S., Demszky, D., Fancsali, S., & Xing, W. (2023, June). Towards the Future of AI-Augmented Human Tutoring in Math Learning. In *International Conference on Artificial Intelligence in Education* (pp. 26–31). Springer Nature Switzerland. https://link.springer.com/chapter/10.1007/978-3-031-36336-8_310.1007/978-3-031-36336-8_3

Annie E. Casey Foundation. (2024, January 19) *What is generation alpha?* AECF. https://www.aecf.org/blog/what-is-generation-alpha

Cardona, M. A., Rodríguez, R. J., & Ishmael, K. (2023). *Artificial intelligence and the future of teaching and learning: Insights and recommendations.*https://policycommons.net/artifacts/3854312/ai-report/4660267/

Cathrin, S., & Wikandaru, R. (2023) *The future of character education in the era of artificial intelligence.* Humanika, Kajian Ilmiah Mata Kuliah Umum10.21831/hum.v23i1.59741

Chan, C., & Lee, K. (2023). *The AI generation gap: Are Gen Z students more interested in adopting generative AI such as ChatGPT in teaching and learning than their Gen X and millennial generation teachers?* Smart Learning Environment., 10.1186/s40561-023-00269-3

Chen, S., & She, W. (2023) Values and Ethics- How artificial intelligence will better serve humanity. B. Majoul et al. (Eds.): ICLAHD 2022, ASSEHR 726, pp. 296–300, 2023. https://doi.org/10.2991/978-2-494069-97-8_37

Dai, Z., Sun, C., Zhao, L., & Zhu, X. (2023). The Effect of Smart Classrooms on Project-Based Learning: A Study Based on Video Interaction Analysis. *Journal of Science Education and Technology*, 32(6), 858–871. 10.1007/s10956-023-10056-x

Fuchs, K. (2023). Exploring the opportunities and challenges of NLP models in higher education: is Chat GPT a blessing or a curse?. *Frontiers in Education* (*Vol. 8*, p. 1166682). 10.3389/feduc.2023.1166682

Ghiglino, D., Floris, F., De Tommaso, D., Kompatsiari, K., Chevalier, P., Priolo, T., & Wykowska, A. (2023). Artificial scaffolding: Augmenting social cognition by means of robot technology. *Autism Research*, 16(5), 997–1008. 10.1002/aur.290636847354

Gill, A., & Mathur, A. (2023). Exploring the futuristic landscape of artificial intelligence for alpha generation: A comprehensive study. *World Journal of Advanced Research and Reviews*, 20(2), 1250–1264. 10.30574/wjarr.2023.20.2.2369

Gill, S. S., Xu, M., Patros, P., Wu, H., Kaur, R., Kaur, K., Fuller, S., Singh, M., Arora, P., Parlikad, A. K., Stankovski, V., Abraham, A., Ghosh, S. K., Lutfiyya, H., Kanhere, S. S., Bahsoon, R., Rana, O., Dustdar, S., Sakellariou, R., & Buyya, R. (2024). Transformative effects of ChatGPT on modern education: Emerging Era of AI Chatbots. *Internet of Things and Cyber-Physical Systems*, 4, 19–23. 10.1016/j.iotcps.2023.06.002

Han, Y. (2020). Research on the Reform of Education and Teaching Methods in the Era of Artificial Intelligence. *Advances in Social Science, Education and Humanities Research*, 505. Advance online publication. 10.2991/assehr.k.201214.065

Han, Y. (2020). Research on the Reform of Education and Teaching Methods in the Era of Artificial Intelligence. *Advances in Social Science, Education and Humanities Research*, 505. https://www.atlantis-press.com/article/125948897.pdf. 10.2991/assehr.k.201214.065

Har, F., & Ma, B. W. L. (2023). The Future of Education Utilizing an Artificial Intelligence Robot in the Centre for Independent Language Learning: Teacher Perceptions of the Robot as a Service. In Hong, C., & Ma, W. W. K. (Eds.), *Applied Degree Education and the Shape of Things to Come. Lecture Notes in Educational Technology*. Springer. 10.1007/978-981-19-9315-2_3

Hasnine, M. N., Nguyen, H. T., Tran, T. T. T., Bui, H. T., Akçapınar, G., & Ueda, H. (2023). A real-time learning analytics dashboard for automatic detection of online learners' affective states. *Sensors (Basel)*, 23(9), 4243. 10.3390/s2309424337177447

Hasse, A., Cortesi, S., Lombana-Bermudez, A., & Gasser, U. (2019). Youth and artificial intelligence: Where we stand. Youth and Media, Berkman Klein Center for Internet & Society. Retrieved from https://cyber.harvard.edu/publication/2019/youth-andartificial-intelligence/where-we-stand

Hogenhout and Takahashi. (2022). *A future with AI: Voice of Global Youth*. Final report, United Nations office of information and communication technology. https://unite.un.org/news/future-ai-voices-global-youth-report-launched

Howley, R. (2019) *The effect of artificial intelligence on the youth*. https://www.proquest.com/openview/d84a86cf41d62229ab84860328e20c92/1.pdf?pq-origsite=gscholar&cbl=18750&diss=y

Ironsi, C. S. (2023). Investigating the use of virtual reality to improve speaking skills: insights from students and teachers. *Smart Learning Environments, 10*(1), 53.Panjeti-Madan, V. N., & Ranganathan, P. (2023). Impact of screen time on children's development: cognitive, language, physical, and social and emotional domains. *Multimodal Technologies and Interaction*, 7(5), 52. 10.3390/mti7050052

Jackaria, P. M., Hajan, B. H., & Mastul, A. R. H. (2024). A Comparative Analysis of the Rating of College Students' Essays by ChatGPT versus Human Raters. *International Journal of Learning, Teaching and Educational Research, 23*(2).

Jamil, H., Raza, S. H., & Naqvi, S. G. (2023). Artificial Intelligence and Grand Challenges for Education. *Journal of Policy Research*, 9(1). 10.5281/zenodo.7951651

Kurtz, G., & Kohen-Vacs, D. (2024). Humanoid robot as a tutor in a team-based training activity. *Interactive Learning Environments*, 32(1), 340–354. 10.1080/10494820.2022.2086577

Leahy, S. M., Holland, C., & Ward, F. (2019). The digital frontier: Envisioning future technologies impact on the classroom. *Futures*, 113, 102422. 10.1016/j.futures.2019.04.009

Livberber, T. (2023). Toward non-human-centered design: Designing an academic article with ChatGPT. *El Profesional de la Información*, 32(5), e320512. 10.3145/epi.2023.sep.12

Manyika, J., Lund, S., Chui, M., Bughin, J., Woetzel, L., Batra, P., Ko, R., & Sanghvi, S. (2017) *Jobs lost, jobs gain: What the future of work will mean for jobs, skills, and wages*. McKinsey and Company. https://www.mckinsey.com/featured-insights/future-of-work/jobs-lost-jobs-gained-what-the-future-of -work-will-mean-for-jobs-skills-and-wages

Nasar, I., Uzer, Y., & Purwanto, M. B. (2023). Artificial Intelligence in Smart Classrooms: An Investigative Learning Process for High School. [AJAE]. *Asian Journal of Applied Education*, 2(4), 547–556. 10.55927/ajae.v2i4.6038

Pawluczuk, A., & erban, A. M. (2022). *Technology and the new power dynamics: limitations of digital youth work*. EU andCoE Youth Partnership. https://pjpeu.coe.int/documents/42128013/116591216/ Limits+of+digital+youth+work.pdf/732ddd6a-15cb-02a6-c336-efa9aa8154c0

Pedro, F., Subosa, M., Rivas, A., & Valverde, P. (2019). *Artificial intelligence in education: Challenges and opportunities for sustainable development*. https://repositorio.minedu.gob.pe/handle/20.500.12799/6533

Petticrew, M., & Roberts, H. (2006). *Systematic reviews in the social sciences: A practical guide*. Blackwell Publishing., 10.1002/9780470754887

Rajesh, P., Sreekanksha, G., Miralee, K., Govind, R., & Deepak, R. (2022). Smart classroom robot. *International Journal of Advance Scientific Research And Engineering Trends*, 7(4). https://ijasret.com/ VolumeArticles/FullTextPDF/1303_9.SMART_CLASSROOM_ROBOT.pdf

Reiss, M. J. (2021). The Use of AI in Education: Practicalities and Ethical Considerations. *London Review of Education*, 19(1). https://eric.ed.gov/?id=EJ1297682. 10.14324/LRE.19.1.05

Schiff, D. (2021). Out of the laboratory and into the classroom: The future of artificial intelligence in education. *AI & Society*, 36(1), 331–348. 10.1007/s00146-020-01033-832836908

Schiff, D. S., & Rosenberg-Kima, R. B. (2023). AI in education: landscape, vision and critical ethical challenges in the 21st century. In *Handbook of Critical Studies of Artificial Intelligence* (pp. 804–814). Edward Elgar Publishing. 10.4337/9781803928562.00081

Su, J., & Yang, W. (2023). Artificial Intelligence (AI) literacy in early childhood education: An intervention study in Hong Kong. *Interactive Learning Environments*, 1–15. Advance online publication. 10.1080/10494820.2023.2217864

Trabelsi, Z., Alnajjar, F., Parambil, M. M. A., Gochoo, M., & Ali, L. (2023). Real-time attention monitoring system for classroom: A deep learning approach for student's behavior recognition. *Big Data and Cognitive Computing*, 7(1), 48. 10.3390/bdcc7010048

UNICEF. (2021) *Policy guidelines on AI for children*. UNICEF. https://www.unicef.org/globalinsight/ media/2356/file/UNICEF-Global-Insight-policy-guidance-AI-children-2.0-2021.pdf

United Nations International School of Hanoi. (2024) *What is generation alpha? 8 characteristics of generation alpha.* https://articles.unishanoi.org/characteristics-of-generation-alpha/

Williams, R., Ali, S., Devasia, N., DiPaola, D., Hong, J., Kaputsos, S. P., Jordan, B., & Breazeal, C. (2023). AI+ ethics curricula for middle school youth: Lessons learned from three project-based curricula. *International Journal of Artificial Intelligence in Education*, 33(2), 325–383. 10.1007/s40593-022-00298-y35935456

Yang, W., Hu, X., Yeter, I. H., Su, J., Yang, Y., & Lee, J. C. K. (2023). Artificial intelligence education for young children: A case study of technology-enhanced embodied learning. *Journal of Computer Assisted Learning.* Advance online publication. 10.1111/jcal.12892

Yousif, J. (2023). Social and Telepresence Robots a future of teaching. *Authorea Preprints.* https://www.techrxiv.org/doi/full/10.36227/techrxiv.15152073.v1

# Chapter 10
# Predictive Analytics for Reducing University Dropout Rates:
## A Machine Learning Approach

**Dwijendra Nath Dwivedi**
https://orcid.org/0000-0001-7662-415X
*Krakow University of Economics, Poland*

**Ghanashyama Mahanty**
https://orcid.org/0000-0002-6560-2825
*Utkal University, India*

**Shafik Khashouf**
*University of Liverpool, UK*

## ABSTRACT

*Higher education institutions face a problem with student turnover that has many aspects and affects both students and universities in different ways. Using predictive analytics and machine learning, this study shows a new way to deal with this problem. The main goal is to create predicting algorithms that can predict which students are most likely to drop out, so colleges can get involved in their lives in a timely and effective way. As part of this method, the authors collect and preprocess a large dataset from different university records. This dataset includes information about academic success, socioeconomic background, participation in campus activities, and psychological health. The study uses advanced machine learning methods to look at all of these different data points. It focuses on feature selection and engineering to find the most important factors that predict student dropout. Rigid validation methods are used to test how well the model works, making sure that it can accurately and reliably predict the future.*

DOI: 10.4018/979-8-3693-3350-1.ch010

## INTRODUCTION

University dropout is a crucial societal issue we face today. The reasons could be many but the after-effect of dropout puts a huge burden on the student, university, and society in general. The cumulative education, funded by both government and private efforts, leads to the dropout completely going to waste, leaving aside the physical time and effort given by the student, teachers, and parents towards the student's education.

This paper investigates the significant problem of students quitting organizations that provide higher education. This work is at the crossroads of educational research and sophisticated data science. It seeks to examine and forecast college dropout rates by employing machine learning (ML) approaches. In addition to identifying the trends and circumstances that lead to students dropping out of school, the objective is to provide educational partners with valuable information that they can use to devise helpful strategies for assisting students in remaining in school.

The problem of students dropping out of school has been a problem in education for many years. Dropout rates have been studied and dealt with in the past mostly through heuristic and qualitative methods, based on theories of student involvement and satisfaction. Tinto's (1975) Student Integration Model, one of the first works in the field, stressed how important it is for students to be able to integrate socially and academically to stay in school. After this, Bean's (1980) Student Attrition Model suggested that keeping students was affected by several psychological, environmental, and organizational factors working together in complicated ways. But when the digital age and lots of data came along in the late 20th and early 21st centuries, the focus moved to methods that were based on data. Schools started to gather a lot of information about their students, like how well they did in school, how engaged they were, their demographics, and more. This change was the first step toward using statistical models on student data to find students who are at risk and figure out why some students drop out. Thanks to progress in machine learning and big data technologies, the field of prediction analytics has changed a lot in the last few years. Machine learning is different from traditional statistical models because it can work with big and complicated datasets and find subtle trends and non-linear relationships that traditional methods might miss. This has helped us get a better and more complete picture of how students act and what makes them decide to leave university.

This modern setting is where the present study fits in. It uses cutting-edge machine learning techniques to look at data from universities in order to do more than just guess how many students will drop out. To find students who might drop out, the goal is to do a full analysis that looks at many things, such as academic, socioeconomic, psychological, and behavioral issues. More importantly, this study wants to suggest targeted interventions based on the predictive models. This will give universities a useful way to keep students and help them do well.

Not only does this study add to our academic knowledge of how to keep students, but it also has important real-world consequences. By correctly guessing how many students will drop out and knowing what causes them to do so, colleges can better allocate their resources, make sure that support services are tailored to the needs of students who are most likely to drop out, and overall make the learning environment more supportive and interesting. This proactive method is a big change from the reactive strategies used in the past. It marks the start of a new era in school administration and student support services.

## LITERATURE STUDY

Lainjo, B. (2023) investigated the use of predictive analytics tools to assist schools in North America in retaining a greater number of students and reducing the number of students that drop out. Data mining techniques such as k-Nearest Neighbor, Neural Networks, Decision Trees, and Naive Bayes are utilized in order to categorize student dropout rates into distinct groups and encourage a greater number of students to continue their education. Shafiq et al (2022) proposed the utilization of machine learning and predictive analytics as a means of identifying students in virtual learning environments who are likely to experience difficulties. The purpose of this study is to investigate the effectiveness of unsupervised machine learning approaches in comparison to supervised learning processes in identifying children who may be at risk. The authors Prasanth & Alqahtani (2023) desired to develop a prediction model that might identify early warning indicators of failure in college environments through the application of machine learning. It examined a variety of elements of student behavior, including academic achievement, engagement, participation in classes, and involvement on campus, among others. According to Kim et al. (2022), who investigated several forms of data in order to forecast college dropout rates, they discovered that academic data had a significant impact on the accuracy with which machine learning models forecast graduation and dropout status. Machine learning techniques were utilized by Moon et al. (2023) to identify parameters that may be utilized in the prediction of the dropout rate at four-year universities. The amount of money that each student spent on school supplies, according to their study budgets, the number of first-year students who registered, and the number of persons who found employment were all important variables. Bujang et al. (2021) presented a predictive analytics model that made use of supervised machine learning to make predictions regarding the final marks that students were going to receive. Given that the Decision Tree (J48) model achieved a success rate of 99.6% when it came to making predictions, it may be utilized in the classroom. 2014 was the year that the Student Success Program was established and launched in Australia. Seidel & Kutieleh (2017) used a variety of data points covering historical information about the student, application form information, student performance, etc., and employed a decision tree CHAID model to predict the risk of student attrition. The goal of this standardized plan is to assist first-year students in improving their academic performance and remaining enrolled in school. In the study conducted by González-Nucamendi et al. (2023), the researchers utilized machine learning algorithms to identify quantitative traits that indicated which college students were likely to drop out of school and what factors were associated with this behavior. In their article, Lourens & Bleazard (2017) discussed an institutional modeling effort that was successful in identifying and implementing the most effective learning technique for predicting which children will drop out of school either before or during their second year of schooling. At the program level, this model for second-year dropouts was utilized with data from before college and the first semester from the Higher Education Data Analyzer (HEDA1) management information reporting and decision support setting at the Cape Peninsula University of Technology. This data was collected from the program. Bukralia et al. (2015) investigated a variety of data mining techniques to see the extent to which they were able to effectively forecast the future, construct predictive models, and calculate risk scores. The research presented a framework for a recommender system that functions on the basis of a predictive model. With the use of this system, students, instructors, and staff would receive notifications and suggestions that would assist with providing timely and efficient assistance. According to the findings of the study, the boosted C5.0 decision tree model has an accuracy rate of 90.97% when it comes to forecasting when students will voluntarily withdraw from online classes. In their 2018 article, Boris Perez and colleagues discussed the outcomes of an educational data analytics case study that investigated the process of locating undergraduate students in System Engineering (SE) who had left a Colombian institution after seven years of attendance. The study was conducted to determine how to locate these individuals. A technique known as "feature engineering" is used to supplement and broaden the scope of the initial data. Kang & Wang (2018) developed an educational data mining system to analyze data from educational institutions and make educated guesses on which students could withdraw from online programs before the beginning of the new term. What we wanted to do with this project was to provide our managers, teachers, and staff members with the opportunity to prevent students from withdrawing from the online program before they do so. A greater number of pupils would continue to participate in the program as a result of this.The purpose of the research conducted by Nurmalitasari et al. (2023) was to conduct a comprehensive review of the existing literature on predictive learning analytics (PLA) for the purpose of determining the reasons behind student dropouts. This study is a systematic review that examines ways to identify students who may drop out of school by using literature from studies that were conducted in the real world. This step includes the presentation of a review process, criteria for selecting potential research, and several approaches to analyzing the content of the studies that have been selected. Oqaidi et al. (2022) in their study, discussed two approaches that have been utilized in the past to forecast the performance of pupils (SP). These approaches include Machine Learning (ML) techniques and Fuzzy Cognitive Mapping (FCM). The most important thing that they did was examine how these strategies and recommendations compared to those that are utilized in higher education institutions in Morocco. The findings of the study conducted by Nikolaidis et al. (2022) indicated that the most significant elements for the development of learning were the efficiency of the instructor and the materials used for learning. According to the findings of structural equation modeling, the variables that pertain to learning development have a significant impact on the status of students who withdraw from their studies. The impacts of the student's grade point average (GPA) were shown to be moderated by the academic semesters, according to a study that evaluated various groups of students. Jia et al. (2021) conducted a survey and conducted interviews with students to analyze the data and come up with five primary reasons that students are more interested in taking online flipped classes. The findings of this research provided educators with valuable information that can be utilized by those who are interested in the online flipped classroom method. The purpose of the research conducted by Shuqfa et al. (2019) was to investigate the Educational Data Mining (EDM) literature to learn about the most recent methods of utilizing EDM to create models that can determine which students will continue their education at the college level and what the trends will be in various fields of higher education in the years to come. The Cumulative Grade Point Average (CGPA), assistance, family income, disability, and the number of dependents are the most relevant indicators for predicting student dropout, according to Ahmad et al. (2019) findings. Although there were five different algorithms that were tested, the Support Vector Machine with Polynomial Kernel appeared to be the most successful. A comprehensive analysis of the research that has been conducted on the topic of predicting how well students would perform in school was carried out by Hellas et al. (2018). The results of the analysis made it abundantly evident that there is an increasing amount of research being conducted in this field, as well as an increasing number of approaches being utilized.

## DATA AND UNIVARIATE ANALYSIS

Academic success, personal issues, and support systems are all aspects of university student life that are captured in this dataset, which provides a holistic view of the student experience. This can be an extremely helpful resource for gaining an understanding of the experiences of students, determining the areas in which support is required, and adapting educational programs to meet the requirements of students. Several important characteristics of these data are as follows: It comprises basic demographic facts such as "Age" and "Gender" (coded as 1 and 0), as well as academic information such as "Year_of_Study" and "GPA" (Grade Point Average). In addition, it includes information about the student's academic performance. The dataset monitors a student's employment and financial status by determining whether or not they have a "Part-Time Job," whether or not they get "Financial Aid," and whether or not they have a "Student Loan." Instances of 'Fee_Misses' are also recorded, which most likely imply that there are difficulties with finances occurring. Several sections discuss the academic and personal challenges that students experience. These challenges can be either intellectual or personal in nature. "Failed_Exam," "Low_Score_Language," occurrences of being "Sick_in_School," and "Times_Sick_Last_Year" are all examples of those that fall under this category. Data on 'Family_Trauma' and 'Reported_Depression' are also included, which shed light on the difficulties associated with mental health and family life. Academic Support and Performance: The dataset contains information on whether or not students participate in "Extended Classes," receive "Career Counseling," take part in "Group Projects," and their involvement in extracurricular activities (which is not directly represented but is suggested by columns such as "Group Projects"). Study Section and Subject: It classifies students according to their "Study Section" (for example, Science, Engineering, or Arts) and specific "Subject" (for example, Biology, Computer Science, or History). Although the data contained in the 'Dropped_Out' column is not visible in the preview, it appears that the purpose of this column is to keep track of whether or not a student has dropped out of school.

*Figure 1. Distribution of age*

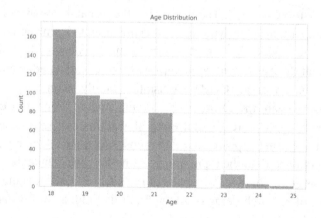

*Figure 2. Distribution of GPA*

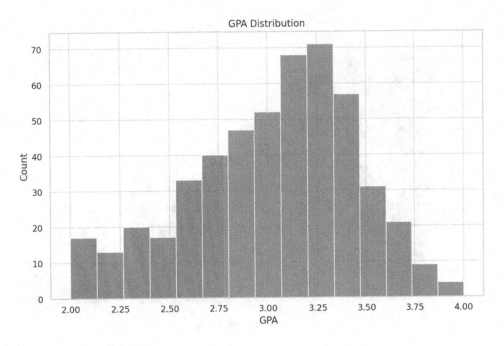

*Figure 3. Distribution of attendence*

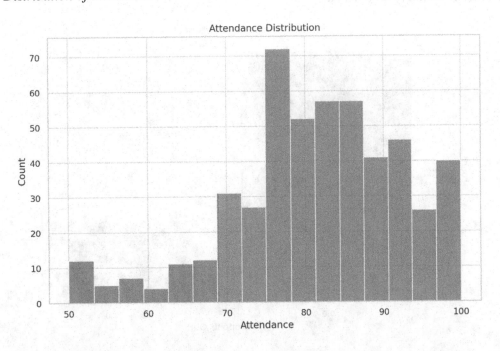

*Figure 4. Distribution of year of study*

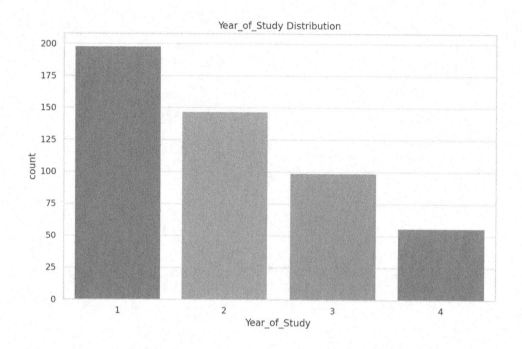

*Figure 5. Distribution of dropped out*

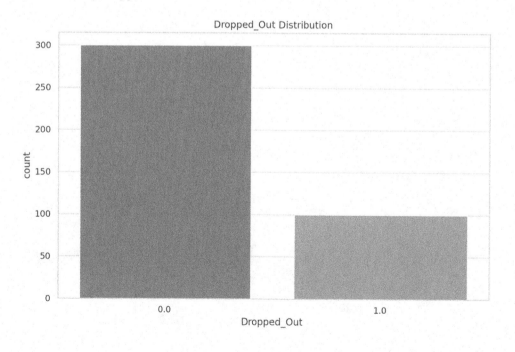

# RESULTS

## Feature Importance

The Feature Importance Bar Chart showcases the top 10 features that the Random Forest model found most influential in predicting student dropouts. Feature importance provides insights into which variables are most significant in the model's decision-making process. Higher importance values indicate that a particular feature plays a more critical role in the prediction outcome.

*Figure 6. Feature improtance*

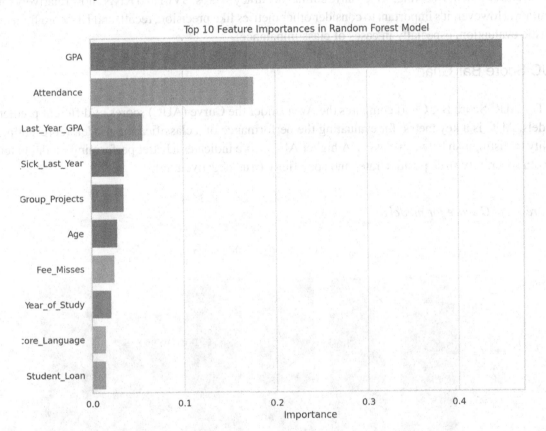

## Model Performance Comparison

This report presents a comparison of various predictive models to determine the most effective approach for predicting student dropouts. The models evaluated include Logistic Regression, Random Forest, SVM, Gradient Boosting, KNN, and Naive Bayes. The primary metric used for comparison is accuracy.

*Table 1. Model comparison*

| Model | Accuracy |
|-------|----------|
| Logistic Regression | 88.75% |
| Random Forest | 88.75% |
| SVM | 86.25% |
| Gradient Boosting | 88.75% |
| KNN | 82.50% |
| Naive Bayes | 91.25% |

The Naive Bayes model demonstrates the highest accuracy, followed by Logistic Regression, Random Forest, and Gradient Boosting, which have similar accuracy scores. SVM and KNN show relatively lower accuracy. However, it's important to consider other metrics like precision, recall, and F1-score for a more holistic evaluation, especially in cases of class imbalance.

## AUC Score Bar Chart

The AUC Score Bar Chart compares the Area Under the Curve (AUC) scores of different predictive models. AUC is a key metric for evaluating the performance of a classification model, representing its ability to distinguish between classes. A higher AUC score indicates a better performing model in terms of both sensitivity (true positive rate) and specificity (true negative rate).

*Figure 7. AUC score for models*

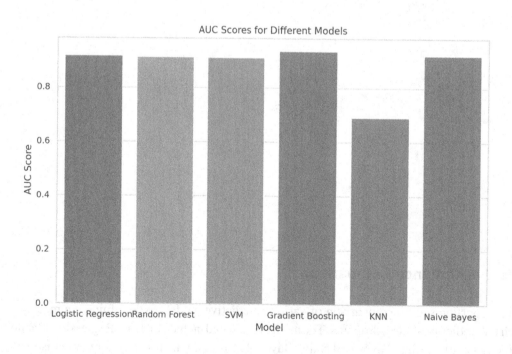

## ROC Curve

The Receiver Operating Characteristic (ROC) curve is a graphical representation of a model's diagnostic ability. It plots the True Positive Rate (TPR) against the False Positive Rate (FPR) at various threshold settings. The Area Under the Curve (AUC) is a measure of the model's ability to distinguish between classes, with a higher AUC indicating better model performance. This comparison of ROC curves across different models (Logistic Regression, Random Forest, SVM, Gradient Boosting, KNN, and Naive Bayes) provides a clear visual representation of their effectiveness in predicting student dropouts

*Figure 8. ROC curve*

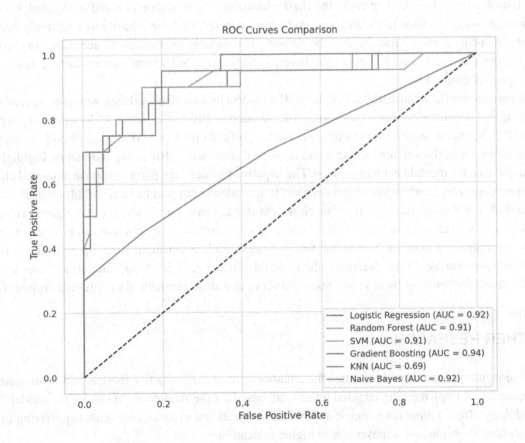

# CONCLUSION

The study sought to utilize predictive analytics through machine learning methods to identify the elements that contribute to university dropout rates and provide intervention options. The extensive dataset encompassed a diverse range of characteristics, spanning from demographic data, academic achievements, financial standing, and personal obstacles, to student involvement in extracurricular activities.

The main variables considered were Age, Gender, Year of Study, GPA, Part-Time Job status, Financial Aid, Student Loan, Fee Misses, Study Section, and Subject, as well as signs of personal difficulties such as Reported Depression, Family Trauma, Failed Exams, and Sickness. The collection also included information on supplementary courses, vocational guidance, and participation in collaborative projects, offering valuable insights into the academic assistance and social interaction of students.

With the utilization of this dataset, a sequence of machine learning models was developed to forecast the probability of students abandoning their education. The models employed in the analysis were logistic regression, decision trees, and random forests, selected for their capacity to effectively manage intricate, non-linear associations within the dataset. The models were assessed according to their accuracy, precision, recall, and F1 score. The investigation uncovered several crucial factors that can be used to predict dropout rates:

The presence of financial distress, as indicated by student loans and missed fees, was a strong predictor, indicating that economic concerns play a vital role. Academic difficulties, specifically a poor grade point average (GPA) and unsuccessful examinations were significant predictors of the likelihood of dropping out. Factors such as documented sadness and familial trauma were also strong indicators, highlighting the crucial need for mental health assistance. The negative link between participation in extended classes and career counseling and dropout rates suggests that academic support has a favorable impact.

The study emphasizes the capacity of machine learning to detect pupils who are at danger and provide guidance for intervention measures. Universities can enhance resource allocation to provide effective support to students in need by prioritizing key indicators such as financial hardship, academic performance, and personal issues. Furthermore, the favorable influence of academic support services implies that increasing the scope of these programs could serve as a strategic method to diminish dropout rates.

# FURTHER RESEARCH

Subsequent research should prioritize the enhancement of the predictive models and investigate the consequences of implementing targeted treatments based on the predictions made by the model. This methodology offers a more data-centric and tailored educational experience, eventually striving to improve student retention and achievement in higher education.

# REFERENCES

Ahmad Tarmizi, S., Mutalib, S., Abdul Hamid, N., Abdul-Rahman, S., & Md Ab Malik, A. (2019). A Case Study on Student Attrition Prediction in Higher Education Using Data Mining Techniques. *Soft Computing in Data Science*. Springer. doi:10.1007/978-981-15-0399-3_15. (181-192). http://link.springer.com/10.1007/978-981-15-0399-3_1510.1007/978-981-15-0399-3_15

Bean, J. P. (1980). Dropouts and turnover: The synthesis and test of a causal model of student attrition. *Research in Higher Education*, 12(2), 155–187. 10.1007/BF00976194

Bujang, S. D. A., Selamat, A., & Krejcar, O. (2021). Decision Tree (J48) Model for Student's Final Grade Prediction: A Machine Learning Approach. *IOP Conference Series. Materials Science and Engineering*, 1051(1), 012005. 10.1088/1757-899X/1051/1/012005

Bukralia, R., Deokar, A. V., & Sarnikar, S. (2015). *Using academic analytics to predict dropout risk in e-Learning courses*. Springer International Publishing. 10.1007/978-3-319-11575-7_6

Dwijendra, N. (2022). Benchmarking of traditional and advanced machine Learning modelling techniques for forecasting in book. *Visualization Techniques for Climate Change with Machine Learning and Artificial Intelligence*. Elsevier. 10.1016/B978-0-323-99714-0.00017-0

Dwivedi, D., Batra, S., & Pathak, Y. K. (2023). A machine learning based approach to identify key drivers for improving corporate's esg ratings. *Journal of Law and Sustainable Development*, 11(1), e0242. 10.37497/sdgs.v11i1.242

Dwivedi, D., Kapur, P. N., & Kapur, N. N. (2023). Machine Learning Time Series Models for Tea Pest Looper Infestation in Assam, India. In Sharma, A., Chanderwal, N., & Khan, R. (Eds.), *Convergence of Cloud Computing, AI, and Agricultural Science* (pp. 280–289). IGI Global. 10.4018/979-8-3693-0200-2.ch014

Dwivedi, D., Mahanty, G., & Dwivedi, A. D. (2024). Artificial Intelligence Is the New Secret Sauce for Good Governance. In Ogunleye, O. (Ed.), *Machine Learning and Data Science Techniques for Effective Government Service Delivery* (pp. 94–113). IGI Global. 10.4018/978-1-6684-9716-6.ch004

Dwivedi, D., & Vemareddy, A. (2023). Sentiment Analytics for Crypto Pre and Post Covid: Topic Modeling. In Molla, A. R., Sharma, G., Kumar, P., & Rawat, S. (Eds.), Lecture Notes in Computer Science: Vol. 13776. *Distributed Computing and Intelligent Technology. ICDCIT 2023*. Springer. 10.1007/978-3-031-24848-1_21

Dwivedi, D. N. (2024). The Use of Artificial Intelligence in Supply Chain Management and Logistics. In Sharma, D., Bhardwaj, B., & Dhiman, M. (Eds.), *Leveraging AI and Emotional Intelligence in Contemporary Business Organizations* (pp. 306–313). IGI Global. 10.4018/979-8-3693-1902-4.ch018

Dwivedi, D. N., & Anand, A. (2021). Trade Heterogeneity in the EU: Insights from the Emergence of COVID-19 Using Time Series Clustering. *Zeszyty Naukowe Uniwersytetu Ekonomicznego w Krakowie*, 3(993), 9–26. 10.15678/ZNUEK.2021.0993.0301

. Dwivedi, D. N., & Anand, A. (2021). The Text Mining of Public Policy Documents in Response to COVID-19: A Comparison of the United Arab Emirates and the Kingdom of Saudi Arabia. *Public Governance / Zarządzanie Publiczne*, 55(1), 8-22. 10.15678/ZP.2021.55.1.02

Dwivedi, D. N., & Anand, A. (2022). A Comparative Study of Key Themes of Scientific Research Post COVID-19 in the United Arab Emirates and WHO Using Text Mining Approach. In Tiwari, S., Trivedi, M. C., Kolhe, M. L., Mishra, K., & Singh, B. K. (Eds.), *Advances in Data and Information Sciences. Lecture Notes in Networks and Systems* (Vol. 318). Springer. 10.1007/978-981-16-5689-7_30

Dwivedi, D. N., & Batra, S. (2024). Case Studies in Big Data Analysis: A Novel Computer Vision Application to Detect Insurance Fraud. In Darwish, D. (Ed.), *Big Data Analytics Techniques for Market Intelligence* (pp. 441–450). IGI Global. 10.4018/979-8-3693-0413-6.ch018

Dwivedi, D. N., Batra, S., & Pathak, Y. K. (2024). Enhancing Customer Experience: Exploring Deep Learning Models for Banking Customer Journey Analysis. In Sharma, H., Chakravorty, A., Hussain, S., & Kumari, R. (Eds.), *Artificial Intelligence: Theory and Applications. AITA 2023. Lecture Notes in Networks and Systems* (Vol. 843). Springer. 10.1007/978-981-99-8476-3_39

Dwivedi, D. N., & Gupta, A. (2022). Artificial intelligence-driven power demand estimation and short-, medium-, and long-term forecasting. In *Artificial Intelligence for Renewable Energy Systems* (pp. 231–242). Woodhead Publishing. 10.1016/B978-0-323-90396-7.00013-4

Dwivedi, D. N., & Khashouf, S. (2024). Tackling Customer Wait Times: Advanced Techniques for Call Centre Optimization. In Bansal, S., Kumar, N., & Agarwal, P. (Eds.), *Intelligent Optimization Techniques for Business Analytics* (pp. 255–267). IGI Global. 10.4018/979-8-3693-1598-9.ch011

Dwivedi, D. N., & Mahanty, G. (2024). Unmasking the Shadows: Exploring Unethical AI Implementation. In Dadwal, S., Goyal, S., Kumar, P., & Verma, R. (Eds.), *Demystifying the Dark Side of AI in Business* (pp. 185–200). IGI Global. 10.4018/979-8-3693-0724-3.ch012

Dwivedi, D. N., & Mahanty, G. (2024). Guardians of the Algorithm: Human Oversight in the Ethical Evolution of AI and Data Analysis. In Kumar, R., Joshi, A., Sharan, H., Peng, S., & Dudhagara, C. (Eds.), *The Ethical Frontier of AI and Data Analysis* (pp. 196–210). IGI Global. 10.4018/979-8-3693-2964-1.ch012

Dwivedi, D. N., & Mahanty, G. (2024). AI-Powered Employee Experience: Strategies and Best Practices. In Rafiq, M., Farrukh, M., Mushtaq, R., & Dastane, O. (Eds.), *Exploring the Intersection of AI and Human Resources Management* (pp. 166–181). IGI Global. 10.4018/979-8-3693-0039-8.ch009

Dwivedi, D. N., Mahanty, G., & Dwivedi, V. N. (2024). The Role of Predictive Analytics in Personalizing Education: Tailoring Learning Paths for Individual Student Success. In Bhatia, M., & Mushtaq, M. (Eds.), *Enhancing Education With Intelligent Systems and Data-Driven Instruction* (pp. 44–59). IGI Global. 10.4018/979-8-3693-2169-0.ch003

Dwivedi, D. N., Mahanty, G., & Pathak, Y. K. (2023). AI Applications for Financial Risk Management. In M. Irfan, M. Elmogy, M. Shabri Abd. Majid, & S. El-Sappagh (Eds.), *The Impact of AI Innovation on Financial Sectors in the Era of Industry 5.0* (pp. 17-31). IGI Global. 10.4018/979-8-3693-0082-4.ch002

Dwivedi, D. N., Mahanty, G., & Vemareddy, A. (2022). How Responsible Is AI?: Identification of Key Public Concerns Using Sentiment Analysis and Topic Modeling. [IJIRR]. *International Journal of Information Retrieval Research*, 12(1), 1–14. 10.4018/IJIRR.298646

Dwivedi, D. N., Mahanty, G., & Vemareddy, A. (2023). Sentiment Analysis and Topic Modeling for Identifying Key Public Concerns of Water Quality/Issues. In: Harun, S., Othman, I.K., Jamal, M.H. (eds) *Proceedings of the 5th International Conference on Water Resources (ICWR) – Volume 1. Lecture Notes in Civil Engineering.* Springer, Singapore. 10.1007/978-981-19-5947-9_28

Dwivedi, D. N., Pandey, A. K., & Dwivedi, A. D. (2023). Examining the emotional tone in politically polarized Speeches in India: An In-Depth analysis of two contrasting perspectives. *SOUTH INDIA JOURNAL OF SOCIAL SCIENCES, 21*(2), 125-136. https://journal.sijss.com/index.php/home/article/view/65

Dwivedi, D. N., & Pathak, S. (2022). Sentiment Analysis for COVID Vaccinations Using Twitter: Text Clustering of Positive and Negative Sentiments. In Hassan, S. A., Mohamed, A. W., & Alnowibet, K. A. (Eds.), *Decision Sciences for COVID-19. International Series in Operations Research & Management Science* (Vol. 320). Springer. 10.1007/978-3-030-87019-5_12

Dwivedi, D. N., & Patil, G. (2023). Climate change: Prediction of solar radiation using advanced machine learning techniques. In Srivastav, A., Dubey, A., Kumar, A., Narang, S. K., & Khan, M. A. (Eds.), *Visualization Techniques for Climate Change with Machine Learning and Artificial Intelligence* (pp. 335–358). Elsevier. 10.1016/B978-0-323-99714-0.00017-0

Dwivedi, D. N., Tadoori, G., & Batra, S. (2023). Impact of women leadership and ESG ratings and in organizations: A time series segmentation study. *Academy of Strategic Management Journal, 22*(S3), 1–6.

Dwivedi, D. N., Wójcik, K., & Vemareddyb, A. (2022). Identification of Key Concerns and Sentiments Towards Data Quality and Data Strategy Challenges Using Sentiment Analysis and Topic Modeling. In Jajuga, K., Dehnel, G., & Walesiak, M. (Eds.), *Modern Classification and Data Analysis. SKAD 2021. Studies in Classification, Data Analysis, and Knowledge Organization.* Springer. 10.1007/978-3-031-10190-8_2

González-Nucamendi, A., Noguez, J., Neri, L., Robledo-Rella, V., & García-Castelán, R. M. (2023). Predictive analytics study to determine undergraduate students at risk of dropout. *Frontiers in Education, 8,* 1244686. 10.3389/feduc.2023.1244686

Gupta, A. (2021). Understanding Consumer Product Sentiments through Supervised Models on Cloud: Pre and Post COVID. *Webology, 18*(1). .10.14704/WEB/V18I1/WEB18097

Gupta, A., Dwivedi, D.N. & Jain, A. (2021). Threshold fine-tuning of money laundering scenarios through multi-dimensional optimization techniques. *Journal of Money Laundering Control.* 10.1108/JMLC-12-2020-0138

Gupta, A., Dwivedi, D. N., & Shah, J. (2023). Overview of Money Laundering. In: *Artificial Intelligence Applications in Banking and Financial Services. Future of Business and Finance.* Springer, Singapore. 10.1007/978-981-99-2571-1_1

Gupta, A., Dwivedi, D. N., & Shah, J. (2023). Financial Crimes Management and Control in Financial Institutions. In: *Artificial Intelligence Applications in Banking and Financial Services.* Springer, Singapore. 10.1007/978-981-99-2571-1_2

Gupta, A., Dwivedi, D. N., & Shah, J. (2023). Overview of Technology Solutions. In: *Artificial Intelligence Applications in Banking and Financial Services. Future of Business and Finance.* Springer, Singapore. 10.1007/978-981-99-2571-1_3

Gupta, A., Dwivedi, D. N., & Shah, J. (2023). Data Organization for an FCC Unit. In: *Artificial Intelligence Applications in Banking and Financial Services. Future of Business and Finance.* Springer, Singapore. 10.1007/978-981-99-2571-1_4

Gupta, A., Dwivedi, D. N., & Shah, J. (2023). Planning for AI in Financial Crimes. In: *Artificial Intelligence Applications in Banking and Financial Services. Future of Business and Finance.* Springer, Singapore. 10.1007/978-981-99-2571-1_5

Gupta, A., Dwivedi, D. N., & Shah, J. (2023). Applying Machine Learning for Effective Customer Risk Assessment. In: *Artificial Intelligence Applications in Banking and Financial Services. Future of Business and Finance.* Springer, Singapore. 10.1007/978-981-99-2571-1_6

Gupta, A., Dwivedi, D. N., & Shah, J. (2023). Artificial Intelligence-Driven Effective Financial Transaction Monitoring. In: *Artificial Intelligence Applications in Banking and Financial Services.* Springer, Singapore. 10.1007/978-981-99-2571-1_7

Gupta, A., Dwivedi, D. N., & Shah, J. (2023). Machine Learning-Driven Alert Optimization. In: *Artificial Intelligence Applications in Banking and Financial Services.* Springer, Singapore. 10.1007/978-981-99-2571-1_8

Gupta, A., Dwivedi, D. N., & Shah, J. (2023). Applying Artificial Intelligence on Investigation. In: *Artificial Intelligence Applications in Banking and Financial Services.* Springer, Singapore. 10.1007/978-981-99-2571-1_9

Gupta, A., Dwivedi, D. N., & Shah, J. (2023). Ethical Challenges for AI-Based Applications. In: *Artificial Intelligence Applications in Banking and Financial Services.* Springer, Singapore. 10.1007/978-981-99-2571-1_10

Gupta, A., Dwivedi, D. N., & Shah, J. (2023). Setting up a Best-In-Class AI-Driven Financial Crime Control Unit (FCCU). In: *Artificial Intelligence Applications in Banking and Financial Services.* Springer, Singapore. 10.1007/978-981-99-2571-1_11

Gupta, A., Dwivedi, D.N., Shah, J. & Jain, A. (2021). Data quality issues leading to sub optimal machine learning for money laundering models. *Journal of Money Laundering Control.* 10.1108/JMLC-05-2021-0049

Hellas, A., Ihantola, P., Petersen, A., Ajanovski, V., Gutica, M., Hynninen, T., Knutas, A., Leinonen, J., Messom, C., & Liao, S. Predicting academic performance: a systematic literature review. *Proceedings Companion of the 23rd Annual ACM Conference on Innovation and Technology in Computer Science Education,* (pp. 175-199). ACM. 10.1145/3293881.3295783

Jia, C., Hew, K., Bai, S., & Huang, W. (2021). Adaptation of a conventional flipped course to an online flipped format during the Covid-19 pandemic: Student learning performance and engagement. *Journal of Research on Technology in Education.* 10.1080/15391523.2020.1847220

Kang, K., & Wang, S. (2018). Analyze and predict student dropout from online programs. In *Proceedings of the 2nd International Conference on Compute and Data Analysis* (pp. 6-12). 10.1145/3193077.3193090

Kim, S., Yoo, E., & Kim, S. (2023). *A Study on the Prediction of University Dropout Using Machine Learning.* arXiv preprint arXiv:2310.10987. DOI:/arXiv.2310.1098710.48550

Lainjo, B. (2023). Mitigating Academic Institution Dropout Rates with Predictive Analytics Algorithms. *International Journal of Education, Teaching, and Social Sciences.*

Lainjo, B., & Tsmouche, H. (2023). Impact of Artificial Intelligence On Higher Learning Institutions. *International Journal of Education, Teaching, and Social Sciences.*

Lourens, A., & Bleazard, D. (2016). Applying predictive analytics in identifying students at risk: A case study. *South African Journal of Higher Education*, 30(2), 129–142. 10.20853/30-2-583

Mahanty, G., Dwivedi, D. N., & Gopalakrishnan, B. N. (2021). The Efficacy of Fiscal Vs Monetary Policies in the Asia-Pacific Region: The St. Louis Equation Revisited. *Vision (Basel)*, (November). 10.1177/09722629211054148

Moon, M.-H., & Kim, G. (2023). Predicting University Dropout Rates Using Machine Learning Algorithms. *Journal of Economics and Finance Education*, 32(2), 57–68. 10.46967/jefe.2023.32.2.57

Nikolaidis, P., Ismail, M., Shuib, L., Khan, S., & Dhiman, G. (2022). *Predicting Student Attrition in Higher Education through the Determinants of Learning Progress: A Structural Equation Modelling Approach. Sustainability.* https://www.mdpi.com/2071-1050/14/20/1358410.3390/su142013584

Nurmalitasari, A. (2023). The Predictive Learning Analytics for Student Dropout Using Data Mining Technique: A Systematic Literature Review. *Advances in Technology Transfer Through IoT and IT Solutions.* Springer. doi:10.1007/978-3-031-25178-8_2. https://link.springer.com/10.1007/978-3-031-25178-8_210.1007/978-3-031-25178-8_2

Oqaidi, K., Aouhassi, S., & Mansouri, K. (2022). A Comparison between Using Fuzzy Cognitive Mapping and Machine Learning to Predict Students' Performance in Higher Education. *2022 IEEE 3rd International Conference on Electronics, Control, Optimization and Computer Science (ICECOCS).* IEEE. https://ieeexplore.ieee.org/document/9983470/10.1109/ICECOCS55148.2022.9983470

Pozzi, F. A., & Dwivedi, D. (2023). ESG and IoT: Ensuring Sustainability and Social Responsibility in the Digital Age. In Tiwari, S., Ortiz-Rodríguez, F., Mishra, S., Vakaj, E., & Kotecha, K. (Eds.), *Artificial Intelligence: Towards Sustainable Intelligence. AI4S 2023. Communications in Computer and Information Science* (Vol. 1907). Springer. 10.1007/978-3-031-47997-7_2

Prasanth, A., & Alqahtani, H. (2023). Predictive Models for Early Dropout Indicators in University Settings Using Machine Learning Techniques. In *2023 IEEE International Conference on Emerging Technologies and Applications in Sensors (ICETAS).* IEEE. 10.1109/ICETAS59148.2023.10346531

Seidel, E., & Kutieleh, S. (2017). Using predictive analytics to target and improve first year student attrition. *Australian Journal of Education*, 61(2), 200–218. 10.1177/0004944117712310

Shafiq, D. A., Marjani, M., Habeeb, R. A. A., & Asirvatham, D. (2022). Predictive Analytics in Education: A Machine Learning Approach. In *2022 3rd International Multidisciplinary Conference on Computer and Energy Science (SpliTech)* (pp. 1-6). IEEE. [DOI:10.1109/MACS56771.2022

Shuqfa, Z., & Harous, S. (2019). Data Mining Techniques Used in Predicting Student Retention in Higher Education: A Survey. *2019 International Conference on Electrical and Computing Technologies and Applications (ICECTA)*. IEEE. . https://ieeexplore.ieee.org/document/8959789/10.1109/ICECTA48151 .2019.8959789

Tinto, V. (1975). Dropout from Higher Education: A Theoretical Synthesis of Recent Research. *Review of Educational Research*, 45(1), 89–125. 10.3102/00346543045001089

# Chapter 11
# The Role of Artificial Intelligence in Improving the Quality of Education

**Ali Saad Kadhim**

*School of Arts, Department of Psychology, Mustansiriyah University, Iraq*

**Hanan Yousif Mousa**
https://orcid.org/0000-0003-1551-0073
*Mustansiriya University, Iraq*

## ABSTRACT

*The most important outcome of the Fourth Industrial Revolution is artificial intelligence due to its multiple uses in various fields. It is expected to be the cause of limitless innovations, and to lead to more industrial revolutions, bringing about a radical change in human life. With this (massive and rapid) technological development and the industrial transformations the world is witnessing, artificial intelligence will be the reason for progress, growth, and prosperity in most areas of life over the next few years, and it can establish a new world that may now seem like a fantasy, but current innovations confirm the possibility of creating this world.*

## INTRODUCTION

The most important outcome of the Fourth Industrial Revolution (4IR) is artificial intelligence (AI) due to its multiple uses in various fields (industrial - military - service, medical and educational applications - economic technologies)(Chaka, 2023). It is expected to be the cause of limitless innovations, and to lead to more industrial revolutions, bringing about a radical change in human life (Grinin & Grinin, 2023). With this (massive and rapid) technological development and the industrial transformations the world is witnessing, AI will be the reason for progress, growth and prosperity in most areas of life

DOI: 10.4018/979-8-3693-3350-1.ch011

over the next few years, and it can establish a new world that may now seem like a fantasy, but current innovations confirm the possibility of creating this world.

There is a great governmental and civil tendency in Iraq to enter strongly into the field of AI and compete to acquire technologies, anticipate its challenges, and develop successful solutions to them (Johnson, 2019). This explains the Iraqi state's orientation towards its continuous attempts to invest in activating the technologies of the fourth generation of the industrial revolution, especially AI, to achieve ambitious development goals. As the language of the future that is inevitable. In addition to the dependence of many economic sectors such as (health, education, economics, etc.) on it, as well as the great economic opportunities it provides for many economic sectors in the country, and its ability to achieve huge profits by applying its uses and relying on the accurate information and advice it provides, and its positive effects in reducing (Makridakis, 2017).. Relying on the human element and labor, which increases the quality of products and reduces spending.

Moreover, enhance the development and accelerate the activation of AI applications at all governmental and private levels, the state is trying to develop and develop scientific competencies specialized in the field of AI, train employees of government ministries by involving them in specialized courses in data science, and create a culture of AI among segments of society to facilitate the spread of the use of applications (Mikhaylov et al., 2018). Which depends on these technologies and creating a digital citizen capable of dealing with them. In addition, enhancing the concerted efforts of governmental, educational and media institutions to raise awareness of the basics of this field.

## Definition of AI and its Applications

Before talking about the definition of AI, it must be mentioned that this term dates back to the 1950s, specifically the year 1950, when the scientist Alan Turing introduced what is known as the Turing Test, which assesses the intelligence of a computer and classifies it as intelligent if it is capable of to simulate the human mind (Muggleton, 2014). As a result, the first program using AI was created by Christopher Strachey, head of programming research at the University of Oxford, who was able to play the game of checkers by computer (Luger, 2021). Until Anthony Oettinger at the University of Cambridge designed a computer-simulated experience of the shopping process carried out by a human in more than one store. This is to measure the computer's ability to learn, which was considered the first successful experiment in what is known as machine learning. In 1956, the term AI appeared in the context of the Dartmouth Conference at Dartmouth College in the United States of America in the same year, which was organized by the American computer scientist John McCarthy, and he even launched the spacecraft using a computer in 1979 (Bell, 2021).

After that, the acceleration in the science of AI began at the beginning of the new century until interactive robots became available in stores, and then it expanded to become a robot that interacts with different emotions through facial expressions, and other robots that began to perform difficult tasks, such as the Nomad robot, which performs With the mission of searching and exploring remote places in Antarctica, and determining the location of meteorites in the region. AI has become a reality, not a fantasy, and the year 2018 marked the big change for AI (Bareis & Katzenbach, 2022). This technology has grown significantly on the ground until it has become a major tool at the core of all sectors, starting from helping to navigate cities and avoiding traffic congestion, all the way to using virtual assistants to help perform various tasks.

AI is seen as all systems or devices that mimic human intelligence to perform tasks, and that can improve themselves based on the information they collect. There are those who view AI as a computing technology that helps computers learn from past experiences, enables them to adapt to new data inputs, and enables them to perform human-like activities. The concept in this sense confirms that AI includes many dimensions that must be taken into account when understanding it (Nikitas et al., 2020). It is related to the ability to think superiorly and analyze data, more than it is related to a specific form or function. Its use depends on solutions, tools and software that either have built-in AI capabilities or automate algorithmic decision-making.

Its computer programs are characterized by simulating human mental abilities and modes of operation (the ability to learn and deduce - reacting to situations for which the machine was not programmed - deducing the best solutions from a person's attempt to solve new problems he encounters in his daily life). It aims to achieve intelligent systems that behave in the same way as humans in terms of learning and understanding, so that these systems provide their users with various services such as education, guidance, interaction, etc.

Accordingly, AI is considered a branch of (computer science) and one of the basic pillars on which the technology industry is based in the current era, which is concerned with ways and means of making and designing intelligent devices and machines that can think and act like humans, and perform multiple tasks that require intelligence such as learning, planning, and distinguishing speech, facial recognition, problem solving, perception, and mental and logical thinking, so that machines think like humans, in what can be described as a computer with a mind (Sarker, 2022). It is certain that AI is one of the most important future technologies in most sectors of life, and this is what makes it an essential factor in shaping the nature and features of the future for any country. It is a mistake to limit ourselves to the traditional interpretation of AI as programming to teach machines and computers to act on their own without prior human intervention, or with limited intervention, it is simply a lifestyle whose aspects become like a meaningless comparison to the previous lifestyle (Rodríguez-García et al., 2021). Secondly, the reading confirms that there are two types of computers: there is the regular computer and the computer built with AI technology. But an ordinary computer can perform many mathematical and programming operations according to pre-set commands and relatively fixed algorithms. As for the computer built with AI technology, it is the computer capable of completing various tasks in a flexible manner that resembles the ability of a human to complete these tasks. It is capable of dealing with data differently, as it can modify the data based on experience and experience to produce smarter and more flexible outputs and solve problems in an innovative way.

Regarding the definition of AI, it is complicated due to the different philosophical perspectives that explain AI by scientists and specialists, but in general it is considered the field of computer science dedicated to solving cognitive problems usually associated with human intelligence, such as learning, creativity, and image recognition (Górriz et al., 2020). AI seeks to create systems that can think and act like humans.

## Other Definitions of AI

Definition of John McCarthy, founder of AI: "AI is the science and engineering of making intelligent machines."

- Andreas Kaplan and Michael Heinlein Definition: "The ability of a system to correctly interpret external data, learn from that data, and use that knowledge to achieve specific goals and tasks through flexible adaptation."
- AWS definition: "AI is the field of computer science dedicated to solving cognitive problems typically associated with human intelligence, such as learning, creativity, and image recognition."
- SAP definition: "Modern AI is a system capable of perceiving its environment and taking actions to maximize the chance of successfully achieving its goals as well as interpreting and analyzing data in a way that learns and adapts over time."

As for the types of AI, It can be divided into several types, including:

- Narrow AI: AI that can perform a single task or a limited set of tasks, such as recognizing images or playing chess.
- Artificial General Intelligence (AGI): AI that can perform any task a human can do, such as critical thinking and solving complex problems.
- Artificial Super Intelligence (ASI): AI that exceeds human intelligence and can perform tasks that humans cannot do.

## AI APPLICATIONS

AI is used in a variety of applications around the world like: AI is used in many military, industrial, economic, technical and medical fields Educational and other services (Ghosh & Singh, 2020). Among its most important applications are the following:

- Applications for learning various natural languages, the rules for understanding written and spoken languages automatically, answering questions with pre-programmed answers, and automatic translation systems for languages instantly.
- AI programs in analyzing economic data such as the stock market and developing stock trading systems.
- Cognitive simulation using computers to test theories about how the human mind works and the functions it performs, such as recognizing familiar faces and voices or recognizing handwriting, processing images, extracting useful data and information from them, and activating memory.
- Computer applications in medical diagnosis in clinics and hospitals and performing surgical operations.
- Expert systems that can perform tasks in a manner similar to that of experts and help them make their decisions accurately based on a set of logical processes to reach a correct decision or a set of logical options. This is the most important concern of AI in the present and future.
- Game programs such as chess and video games.
- Google search clusters on your computer via the Internet.
- Nonlinear control such as railway control.
- Robot: It is a mechanical device programmed to work independently of human control, and is designed to perform tasks and accomplish the motor and verbal skills that humans perform, in addition to its many other uses in nuclear reactors, extending wires, repairing underground wire installations, detecting mines, the automobile industry, and other fields. minute.

- Self-driving cars and drones.
- Smart devices capable of performing mental operations such as examining industrial designs, monitoring operations and making decisions.
- Smart home services, autonomous weapons, phones, TVs, and hundreds of other applications. but there are Some of the most common applications include:

## Healthcare

AI is used in healthcare to improve the diagnosis and treatment of diseases (Ahmed et al., 2020). For example, AI can be used to analyze medical images to identify cancerous tissue or to create models to predict clinical outcomes. AI is therefore poised to be a transformative force in healthcare.

Accordingly, AI in healthcare is an umbrella term to describe the application of machine learning algorithms and other cognitive technologies in medical settings. In simple terms, AI is the simulation of computers and other machines of human cognition to be able to learn, think, and make decisions and actions. Thus, employing AI in medical and health care is the use of machines to analyze medical data and act on the basis of it to predict a specific outcome.

Many wonder what are the advantages of using AI in medical and health care? AI simplifies the lives of patients, doctors, and hospital managers by performing tasks normally done by humans but in less time and at a lower cost. It also works to make healthcare more predictive and proactive by transforming big data to develop improved preventative care recommendations for patients (Chen & Decary, 2020). In general, the advantages and disadvantages of including AI in the medical sector can be summarized in the following points:

- AI helps doctors, nurses, and medical care workers perform their daily work.
- AI enhances preventive care and quality of life.
- AI helps achieve better outcomes for patients in general.
- Helps produce more accurate diagnoses and treatment plans.
- AI helps predict and track the spread of infectious diseases.

Examples of the use of AI in medical and health care include

1. AI-assisted robotic surgery Robots can analyze data from pre-operative medical records to guide the surgeon's tool during surgery, and this has led to a 21% reduction in patient hospital stays, as robots can use data from previous operations to inform new surgical techniques with the necessary information. Robot-assisted surgery is also minimally invasive, so the patient will not need a recovery period from large incisions. In addition, these techniques reduce potential complications compared to surgery performed by the surgeon alone.
2. Applications for nursing assistants These applications allow for more regular communication between patients and medical care providers, allowing questions to be answered on a regular basis, monitoring patients and providing quick answers, as well as reducing unnecessary hospital visits.
3. Image analysis Another example of the application of AI in healthcare is image analysis. Currently, image analysis is time-consuming for human service providers, but a machine learning algorithm has been designed that can analyze 3D scans up to 1,000 times faster than what is currently possible. This provides important information for surgeons performing surgeries.

Financial Services AI is used in financial services to identify fraud and manage risks. For example, AI can be used to analyze customer transaction data to look for suspicious activity or to create models to predict financial risks.

Manufacturing AI is used in manufacturing to improve productivity and quality. For example, AI can be used to monitor equipment and detect potential malfunctions or to improve product design. AI is one of the most important tools used in smart manufacturing and industrial transformation, and the truth is that the use of AI in this field does not only keep pace with the tremendous technological development that is sweeping the world today; Rather, because of the many positive results it achieves, including improving productivity and efficiency, reducing costs, and increasing quality. For example, AI can be used in the field of smart manufacturing and digital industrial transformation by manufacturing smart machines faster and more accurately. AI can also be used in demand forecasts, production planning, reducing waste, and improving preventive maintenance of equipment.

Transportation AI is used in transportation to improve safety and efficiency. For example, AI can be used to drive self-driving vehicles or improve traffic management.

E-commerce AI is used in e-commerce to improve the shopping experience. For example, AI can be used to recommend products to customers or to provide customer support. These are just a few examples of the many different applications of AI. As AI continues to evolve, we are expected to see more and more applications for this technology in the coming years.

## STAGES, ADVANTAGES, CHARACTERISTICS AND DISADVANTAGES OF AI

### Stages

As for the stages of development of AI, it can be divided into four main stages:

The first phase (1950-1960): This phase was the beginning of research into AI, during which many basic theories and techniques were developed, such as artificial neural network and game theory.

The second phase (1960-1970): This phase witnessed rapid development in AI technologies, as many successful applications were developed, such as machine translation programs and speech recognition systems.

Phase Three (1970-1980): The growth of AI slowed in this phase due to some setbacks, such as the failure of the Dow AI Project.

The fourth stage (1980-present): This stage witnessed a new renaissance in AI, as many new technologies were developed, such as machine learning and deep learning, which led to significant progress in many fields, such as computer vision and natural language processing.

**ADVANTAGES:** As for the advantages of AI, there are different points of view, and the most important of these advantages are:

As for the advantages of AI, there are different points of view about it, but the main topic is that AI has a set of advantages that make it a promising technology with great potential for change, and the most important of these advantages are:

Processing speed: The ability to process data and perform calculations quickly and effectively.

- Accuracy and accuracy: The ability to carry out tasks with high precision and obtain accurate results.
- Continuous Learning: The ability to learn from previous data and experiences to improve performance over time.
- Dealing with large amounts of information: the ability to deal with, analyze and extract information from large sets of data.
- Diagnosis and problem solving: the ability to analyze complex problems and propose effective solutions.
- Human Interaction Ability: The ability to interact and communicate with humans naturally and effectively.
- The ability to overcome complex problems: AI can use its learning, reasoning, and creativity capabilities to overcome complex problems that are difficult to solve using traditional methods.
- Increased business efficiency: AI can automate many tasks performed by humans, leading to increased business efficiency and reduced costs.
- Make smarter decisions: AI can analyze large amounts of data quickly and accurately, which helps in making smarter decisions.

These features highlight the benefits of AI in various fields such as big data analysis, developing innovative interactive applications, and solving complex problems.

**CHARACTERISTICS:** After presenting the advantages, we must review the characteristics that made AI take an important and major role in the development of most developed countries, as it made some countries the best exporter of medical industries and some countries the exporter of military industries around the world. On this basis, we find that among the most important characteristics of AI that distinguish it from traditional computer systems are (Learning, creativity, Adaptation, Independence):

**Learning:** AI systems can learn from past data, and use this information to improve their performance in the future.

Since the field of technology has continuously developed over the years, this has made the world familiar with terms such as AI, machine learning, and deep learning. Although we often confuse the meaning of these terms and their seemingly similar definitions, each term has a different definition. If you do not want to make this mistake again, it is important that you read the following paragraphs in which we will discuss the difference between AI, machine learning, and deep learning.

AI certainly thinks, operates, and reacts similarly to the design of the human brain. However, integrating AI into our lives is not yet possible because there are many features of the human brain that cannot be described. The facial recognition system on Facebook and the image classification service are among the most important types of AI systems, as well as many other examples that we encounter on a daily basis.

Machine learning is part of AI, and although most people consider machine learning to be AI, this belief is inaccurate. In fact, machines can learn, and robots can learn from the data provided to them. In fact, a technology has been created that makes us aware of the existence of AI, as algorithms are used to obtain data, learn, and then analyze, so that the results come in the form of predictions. It is worth noting that this is evident when you get a recommendation from shopping sites, Google, or Facebook, as you can get suggestions that match your interests. This is also done using machine learning algorithms that have been developed to analyze recent searches, history, and many other information. It must be noted that this technology also affects the marketing and banking sectors.

Machine learning therefore constitutes the ability of machines to learn from data analysis, and also embodies AI (Stahl et al., 2021). On this basis, new machine learning algorithms have been limited to the basic components of AI, but they have now become an essential part of this system. Many complex algorithms are created to give users a better experience. Machine learning has transformed the way we watch shows and movies. The entertainment industry uses this algorithm to provide relevant suggestions to its viewers on web channels such as Netflix and Amazon Prime. Moreover, machine learning analyzes the data and makes excellent recommendations based on learning from those points. If you want to learn how to implement this technology, read the next section of the report that explains the mechanism of deep learning.

As for deep learning, deep learning is embodied in the implementation of a machine learning system. In fact, deep learning consists of a subset of machine learning systems, or AI, that make up the operating capabilities of machines. This technology is similar to a machine learning system in some contexts, but the difference is that machine learning needs some instructions to perform the task, while deep learning can perform the task without the intervention of the programmer. In addition, deep learning has enhanced users' experience, as the best deep learning model can be extracted from the features of the automatic car. "The technique used to implement machine learning is known as deep learning."

Deep learning has made machines work and think like humans. When dealing with a machine learning system, programmers have to fix the algorithm if the results are inappropriate, but for deep learning models, it takes care of that on its own, just like the human brain.

Imagine that you set a fan code to go off when the operator says the word "turn on." The machine learning algorithm will then listen to the entire conversation and look for the word "turn on." And if you don't get the exact word, the fan won't run even if you want it to. On the other hand, a deep learning model will turn on the fan even if you say: "The room is too hot to stay in." Overall, these key points make the two systems different: deep learning can teach itself, while machine learning needs to be run by a specific program.

**Creativity:** AI plays an increasingly important role in creativity. It can help artists, designers, musicians, and other creatives generate new ideas and create original content.

Accordingly, AI can help improve creativity in several ways:

- Generating new ideas: AI can analyze data and identify patterns that humans may not notice. This can help artists and other creatives generate new ideas and innovate new ways of working.
- Helping creators improve their work: AI can analyze artwork and provide feedback on how to improve it. This can help artists and other creatives improve the quality of their work.
- Making creativity available to everyone: AI can remove some barriers to creativity. For example, AI can help people with no artistic skills create original art.

Here are some examples of how AI can be used in creativity:

- Drawing and photography: Artists use AI to create realistic images and abstract drawings. For example, AI can analyze existing images and create new images based on the patterns found.
- Music: Composers use AI to create new music. For example, AI can create music pieces based on existing musical styles or create completely new pieces of music.
- Writing: Writers use AI to create original text. For example, AI can create stories, poems, and scenarios.

## Adaptation

Adaptation in AI is the ability to change behavior or performance in response to changing circumstances. Thus, adaptation can occur at a range of levels, from the basic programming level to the application level. That is, the adaptation can be useful in a variety of applications. For example, adaptation can be used in AI systems that control devices to improve efficiency and safety. Adaptation can also be used in AI systems that interact with humans to improve the user experience. So, there are two main types of adaptation in AI:

**Programmed Adaptation:** Programmed adaptation is pre-determined by the developers. For example, you could have a climate control system that automatically adjusts the temperature in response to weather changes.

**Non-programmed adaptation:** Non-programmed adaptation occurs automatically without human intervention. For example, a machine learning AI system can learn how to improve task performance through experiments.

Furthermore, there are many different ways in which adaptation can be achieved in AI. Some common methods include:

**Machine Learning:** Machine learning can be used to train AI systems on how to adapt to changing conditions. For example, an AI system can be trained to learn a machine how to play a video game through game experience.

**Deep Learning:** Deep learning can be used to create AI systems capable of adapting to a wide range of conditions. For example, deep learning can be used to create an AI system capable of recognizing faces from a variety of angles and lighting.

**Dynamic Programming:** Dynamic programming can be used to create AI systems that can adapt to changing conditions by modifying their own code. For example, dynamic programming can be used to create an AI system capable of adapting to changing traffic.

On this basis, research in the field of adaptation in AI continues. AI systems are likely to become more adaptable in the future, which will allow them to deal with a variety of challenges.

## Independence:

AI can operate autonomously by being able to make decisions and perform actions without human intervention. This can be achieved through a range of techniques, including:

**Autonomous Vehicles:** Autonomous vehicles can be used to drive without human intervention.

**Healthcare:** Autonomous AI can be used to provide healthcare to patients without human intervention.

**Financial Services:** Autonomous AI can be used to provide financial services to customers without human intervention.

AI systems are likely to become more autonomous in the future, which will allow them to deal with a variety of challenges.

**Disadvantages:** AI has many potential drawbacks, including:

**Bias:** AI systems can be affected by bias present in the data they are trained on. This can lead to unfair or inaccurate decisions being made.

**Privacy:** AI systems can collect vast amounts of personal data about individuals. This data could be used for malicious purposes, such as espionage or targeted marketing.

**Security:** AI systems can be hacked or misused. This can lead to data leakage, systems disruption, or even harm to humans.

**Job loss:** AI systems can replace workers in many jobs. This can lead to higher unemployment rates and lower wages.

**Environmental Impact:** AI systems can require large amounts of energy and materials. This could lead to increased pollution and climate change.

In addition to these drawbacks, there are also concerns about the future potential for AI to become conscious or superhuman. This could lead to dire consequences, such as the outbreak of war or even the self-destruction of humanity.

## Dangers of AI

The development of information had clear effects and results, including: the emergence of the necessity of adapting laws, regulations of organizations, and policies adopted in transactions and developing them in accordance with new developments, but the pattern of technical changes, their nature, and the attempt to monopolize them or secrecy some of them because they are used in special fields, all of this presented difficulties and obstacles to adaptation. And amending laws and regulations, which creates several risks. On this basis, AI risks can be classified into three main types:

## MORAL RISKS

As AI becomes more powerful and widespread every day, it raises ethical concerns about how it is used, which may relate to how AI is designed and used. Some of the ethical risks of AI include:

## Social Manipulation

With every new technological development that has multiple uses, the same question arises about what ethical implications this development will have. These questions were raised with the emergence of television, cinema, and satellite channels, but the questions with AI differed. In the past, they revolved around the moral aspect, but the questions are different now, as they revolve around the position that AI occupies in life, especially its ability to perform many tasks that were previously Humans perform it, and perhaps some remember the postal letters and cards that postmen used to distribute on their bicycles and how e-mail replaced paper mail and saved a lot of time, effort and money. Therefore, in the face of this boom, we must ensure that it is developed through a humanitarian approach based on values and human rights.

## Bias

AI systems can reinforce the bias present in the data they are trained on. For example, facial recognition software could classify people of certain races as more dangerous than others.

## The Control

AI systems can be used to monitor people and make decisions about them without their consent. This can lead to a loss of control over our personal lives.

## Social Impacts

AI can lead to job losses and increased inequality, and this can lead to social and political unrest.

## Discrimination

AI systems can be used to reinforce existing biases in society, such as racial or gender bias. For example, facial recognition AI systems could be used to deny applications for credit or insurance based on race or gender.

## Privacy Violation

AI systems can be used to collect and store vast amounts of data about individuals, potentially compromising their privacy. For example, AI systems can be used to track individuals' online movements or monitor their purchasing patterns.

## Spreading Misinformation

AI systems can be used to spread misinformation or fake news, which could lead to social unrest or even wars. For example, AI systems can be used to create videos or social media posts that appear to be real, but actually contain misleading information.

It is important that we are aware of these ethical risks and take steps to mitigate them. We can do this by:

- Ensure that AI systems are trained on comprehensive and diverse data
- Promoting transparency and accountability in the development and use of AI
- Establishing laws and regulations to protect privacy, control, and security risks

By taking these steps, we can help ensure that AI is used ethically and responsibly.

## SECURITY RISKS

This relates to how AI can be used for malicious purposes. AI systems can be used to launch cyberattacks or steal confidential information, develop autonomous weapons, and spread social chaos. Therefore, these risks can harm critical infrastructure and the safety of individuals. So some AI security risks could include:

### Phishing Attacks

AI systems can be used to create more convincing phishing emails. This can trick users into revealing sensitive information, such as passwords or banking credentials.

### Cyber-Attacks

AI systems can be used to launch more complex and effective cyberattacks. For example, AI systems can be used to create viruses or malware that can penetrate security systems.

### Develop Autonomous Weapons

Autonomous weapons could be developed that are capable of making their own decisions about who to kill and who not to kill. These weapons can pose a serious threat to human safety.

### Spreading Social Chaos

AI systems can be used to spread social chaos or even spark revolution. For example, AI systems can be used to spread misinformation or organize protests or riots.

### Data Theft

AI systems can be used to collect vast amounts of personal data. This data could be used for fraud, extortion, or other crimes.

### Malware

AI systems can be used to create more complex malware. This malware can crash systems, steal data, or even take over devices.

### Robot Control

AI systems can be used to control robots. This could lead to robots being used in terrorist attacks or social unrest.

It is important to be aware of these security risks and take steps to protect yourself. Here are some tips:

-Be careful about the emails and websites you visit. If you are not sure whether an email or site is safe, do not open or visit it.

    Protect your computers and mobile devices with antivirus and anti-malware software. Make sure your software is kept up to date to protect against the latest threats.

    Make frequent changes to your passwords. Use strong passwords that cannot be easily guessed.

-Be careful about the personal information you share online. Do not share sensitive information such as passwords or credit card numbers with strangers.

By taking these steps, you can help protect yourself from the security risks of AI.

## THIRD: ECONOMIC RISKS

These risks relate to how AI could impact the economy and society. AI can have significant economic benefits, such as improving productivity and reducing costs. However, there are also some economic risks to consider. So, some of the economic risks of AI include:

### Job Loss

AI systems can replace human workers in many jobs. This can lead to higher unemployment rates and lower wages.

### Inequality

The use of AI could increase economic inequality. This could happen if large, wealthy companies benefit from AI more than small businesses and individuals.

### Social Unrest

Job losses and economic inequality can lead to social unrest. This can happen if people feel that AI detracts from or threatens them.

### Unemployment

AI could replace many jobs currently done by humans. For example, AI systems can replace drivers, factory workers, and office workers.

### Economic Gap

AI could exacerbate the economic gap between rich and poor. For example, large companies could benefit from AI to increase profits, while displaced workers may find it difficult to find new jobs.

## Change of Social Structure

AI can change the social structure of society. For example, it could lead to the emergence of a new class of skilled workers working in the field of AI, while less skilled workers may find it difficult to find jobs. AI

It is important that we are aware of these economic risks and take steps to mitigate them. We can do this by:

- Retraining workers who are laid off due to AI
- Establishing laws and regulations to protect against economic inequality
- Promoting transparency and accountability in the development and use of AI

By taking these steps, we can help ensure that AI has a positive impact on the economy. However, it is important to be aware of the risks of AI so that we can take steps to prevent them.

# APPLICATIONS OF AI IN CONTEMPORARY EDUCATION

In the field of education, AI applications are an icon that has brought about a real shift and a scientific breakthrough, after it did a good job in measures to limit the spread of the new Covid-19 epidemic, as distance education policies were taken to limit the attendance of students and students, and avoid mixing in schools and universities (McCall, 2020). Its importance in education comes from the fact that it works side by side with the human mind in a calculated and elaborate combination, translated by various technological developments, and because of it, searching on the Internet has become part of school learning, and tablets have replaced books, or some of them, in schools. However, this Developments may lose their luster in the face of what is expected from AI entering the education sector.

# AREAS OF APPLICATION OF AI EDUCATIONALLY

There are many areas of employing AI with its various applications in the educational field, and one of the areas of this employment is that it helps in enabling people with special needs to gain independence and productivity, as the free "Seeing AI" is applied, through which text can be read aloud (Bozkurt et al., 2021). And get to know people and their emotions. It was developed by Saquib Sheikh, a software engineer who personally understands the suffering of the blind, as he lost his sight at the age of seven, and devoted himself to using technology to build a more inclusive world with the help of Microsoft applications for cognitive services and machine learning. It can be activated if combined with the Soundscape application launched by Microsoft, and enables people with blindness or low vision to be able to explore the world around them by using a 3D audio experience. On this basis, AI is one of the emerging areas of technology that has the potential to revolutionize contemporary education. AI applications can help improve the educational process, by making it more effective, efficient and personalized. So we can find these applications in:

## AUTOMATE TASKS

AI can be used to automate administrative tasks in education. This can save teachers time and effort and make them able to focus on activities that require human skills such as teaching and mentoring (Igbokwe, 2023). For example, AI systems can manage student affairs such as student registration, grade management, and attendance recording, and these systems can also help generate statistical reports on student performance. In addition, AI can be used in virtual reality and the metaverse to create a more realistic and interactive virtual learning environment that can be used to customize educational content for each student according to his abilities and interests.

## PERSONAL LEARNING

One of the most popular applications of AI in education is personalized learning. AI systems can analyze student data such as test scores, performance on assignments, and classroom interactions to create personalized learning experiences for each student. For example, an AI system can identify a student's strengths and weaknesses in a particular subject and then recommend tailored learning content to fill the gaps. This can help improve student engagement and understanding of the material.

One of the basics of personal learning is the presence of reinforcement, which means stimulating and enhancing the continuity of the individual's learning process. AI and metaviral technology can play a vital role in achieving this reinforcement, including:

## CUSTOMIZE CONTENT

It is to understand the individual's interests, determine his educational needs, and provide customized educational content that meets the student's requirements based on an analysis of his learning style and level.

### Provide Instant Feedback

To provide immediate assessment of the individual's performance in educational exercises, analyze performance and provide constructive feedback to enhance the individual's understanding and motivate him to improve his performance.

### Create Smart Content

AI can also be used to create personalized and interactive educational content. This can make learning more interesting and engaging for students. For example, AI systems can create educational games, simulation scenarios, and interactive videos. This content can help students understand complex concepts and practice their skills.

## Facilitate the Presentation of Information

AI can also be used to make information easier to present to students. This can make learning easier and more efficient. For example, AI systems can create graphs, graphs, and explainer videos. These tools can help students understand complex concepts better.

## Class Replacement

While AI is still in its early stages of development, it may one day have the potential to replace the traditional classroom. This can make education more accessible and affordable for students. For example, AI systems can deliver lessons online and provide feedback and support to students. These systems can help students learn anytime and from anywhere.

## CHALLENGES

Despite the great potential of AI in education, there are some challenges that need to be overcome. One challenge is that AI systems can be complex and expensive. Additionally, it can be difficult to ensure that AI systems are fair and unbiased.

The use of AI in education is likely to continue to grow in the coming years. As technology continues to develop, AI systems are likely to become more effective and less expensive. This could revolutionize education, making it more efficient, personalized, and accessible to everyone.

## Quality of Education in Iraq

According to the Education for All Global Monitoring Report 2020, the quality of higher education in Iraq is defined as achieving a set of standards and indicators that include:

## Availability

Relates to the provision of higher education opportunities in general, including fair and equal access to higher education for all social and economic groups.

## Inclusivity

It is about providing diverse and comprehensive educational programs that meet the needs of students and enhance their personal and professional development.

## Academic Quality

This aspect includes providing a high level of academic quality and professional standards in educational programs and the teaching and evaluation process.

## Scientific Research and Innovation

This aspect includes promoting scientific research, innovation and knowledge development and its application in different fields.

## Employment and Professional Integration

Related to qualifying graduates and providing job opportunities and suitable employment after graduation, in addition to enhancing the professional integration of graduates into the labor market.

# THE IMPORTANCE OF QUALITY HIGHER EDUCATION IN IRAQ

According to the "World Bank Iraq Education Policy Notes" report, the importance of quality education in Iraq is highlighted in the following points:

## Developing Skills and Competencies

Quality higher education contributes to developing students' academic and professional skills and competencies, enabling them to compete and adapt in the modern labor market and areas of innovation and technological development.

## Economic and Social Development

Quality higher education promotes economic and social development in Iraq by providing a strong knowledge base and developing the human capabilities necessary to achieve progress and sustainable development.

## Innovation and Scientific Research

Quality higher education promotes scientific research and innovation in various fields, which contributes to the development of new solutions and innovative technologies that achieve scientific and technological progress.

## Enhancing Leadership and Excellence

Quality higher education helps in developing leadership and excellence in various academic and professional fields and contributes to building a generation of creative and innovative graduates capable of achieving change and development in society.

It is clear from this that the quality of higher education in Iraq has a significant impact on developing human skills and capabilities, promoting economic and social development, promoting scientific research and innovation, and building leadership and excellence.

## THE ROLE OF QUALITY HIGHER EDUCATION IN IRAQ

According to the report "Rebuilding after Conflict: Higher Education in Iraq," the role of the quality of higher education in Iraq is highlighted in the following points:

### Developing Skills and Competencies

Quality higher education contributes to the development of students' academic and professional skills and competencies, enabling them to meet the needs of the labor market and achieve personal and professional development.

### Promoting Innovation and Scientific Research

Quality higher education contributes to enhancing scientific research and innovation in various fields, which contributes to the development of new solutions and innovative technologies to achieve scientific and technological progress.

### Promoting Sustainable Development

Quality higher education plays a crucial role in promoting sustainable development in Iraq, by graduating qualified cadres who can contribute to achieving economic growth and community development.

### Strengthening International Communication and Cooperation

Quality higher education enhances international communication and cooperation in the field of research and education, which contributes to the exchange of knowledge and experiences and the strengthening of academic and cultural cooperation between Iraqi universities and international universities. It is clear from the above that the quality of higher education in Iraq plays a crucial role in developing skills and competencies, promoting innovation and scientific research, promoting sustainable development, and enhancing international communication and cooperation in the field of education and research.

# REFERENCES

Ahmed, Z., Mohamed, K., Zeeshan, S., & Dong, X. (2020). Artificial intelligence with multi-functional machine learning platform development for better healthcare and precision medicine. *Database (Oxford)*, 2020, baaa010. 10.1093/database/baaa01032185396

Bareis, J., & Katzenbach, C. (2022). Talking AI into Being: The Narratives and Imaginaries of National AI Strategies and Their Performative Politics. *Science, Technology & Human Values*, 47(5), 855–881. 10.1177/01622439211030007

Bell, G. (2021). Talking to AI: An anthropological encounter with artificial intelligence. *The SAGE Handbook of Cultural Anthropology*. SAGE Publications Ltd.

Bozkurt, A., Karadeniz, A., Baneres, D., Guerrero-Roldán, A. E., & Rodríguez, M. E. (2021). Artificial intelligence and reflections from educational landscape: A review of AI Studies in half a century. *Sustainability (Basel)*, 13(2), 800. 10.3390/su13020800

Chaka, C. (2023). Fourth industrial revolution—A review of applications, prospects, and challenges for artificial intelligence, robotics and blockchain in higher education. *Research and Practice in Technology Enhanced Learning*, 18, 1–39.

Chen, M., & Decary, M. (2020). Artificial intelligence in healthcare: An essential guide for health leaders. *Healthcare Management Forum*, 33(1), 10–18. 10.1177/0840470419873123311550922

Ghosh, S., & Singh, A. (2020). The scope of Artificial Intelligence in mankind: A detailed review. *Journal of Physics: Conference Series*, 1531(1), 012045. https://iopscience.iop.org/article/10.1088/1742-6596/1531/1/012045/meta. 10.1088/1742-6596/1531/1/012045

Górriz, J. M., Ramírez, J., Ortíz, A., Martinez-Murcia, F. J., Segovia, F., Suckling, J., Leming, M., Zhang, Y.-D., Álvarez-Sánchez, J. R., Bologna, G., Bonomini, P., Casado, F. E., Charte, D., Charte, F., Contreras, R., Cuesta-Infante, A., Duro, R. J., Fernández-Caballero, A., Fernández-Jover, E., & Ferrández, J. M. (2020). Artificial intelligence within the interplay between natural and artificial computation: Advances in data science, trends and applications. *Neurocomputing*, 410, 237–270. 10.1016/j.neucom.2020.05.078

Grinin, L., & Grinin, A. (2023). Technologies: Limitless Possibilities and Effective Control. In Sadovnichy, V., Akaev, A., Ilyin, I., Malkov, S., Grinin, L., & Korotayev, A. (Eds.), *Reconsidering the Limits to Growth* (pp. 139–154). Springer International Publishing., 10.1007/978-3-031-34999-7_8

Igbokwe, I. C. (2023). Application of artificial intelligence (AI) in educational management. *International Journal of Scientific and Research Publications*, 13(3), 300–307. 10.29322/IJSRP.13.03.2023.p13536

Johnson, J. (2019). Artificial intelligence & future warfare: Implications for international security. *Defense & Security Analysis*, 35(2), 147–169. 10.1080/14751798.2019.1600800

Luger, G. F. (2021). Modern AI and How We Got Here. In G. F. Luger, *Knowing our World: An Artificial Intelligence Perspective* (pp. 49–74). Springer International Publishing. 10.1007/978-3-030-71873-2_3

Makridakis, S. (2017). The forthcoming Artificial Intelligence (AI) revolution: Its impact on society and firms. In *Futures* (Vol. 90, pp. 46–60). Elsevier. https://www.sciencedirect.com/science/article/pii/S0016328717300046

McCall, B. (2020). COVID-19 and artificial intelligence: Protecting health-care workers and curbing the spread. *The Lancet. Digital Health*, 2(4), e166–e167. 10.1016/S2589-7500(20)30054-632289116

Mikhaylov, S. J., Esteve, M., & Campion, A. (2018). Artificial intelligence for the public sector: Opportunities and challenges of cross-sector collaboration. *Philosophical Transactions. Series A, Mathematical, Physical, and Engineering Sciences*, 376(2128), 20170357. 10.1098/rsta.2017.035730082303

Muggleton, S. (2014). Alan Turing and the development of Artificial Intelligence. *AI Communications*, 27(1), 3–10. 10.3233/AIC-130579

Nikitas, A., Michalakopoulou, K., Njoya, E. T., & Karampatzakis, D. (2020). Artificial intelligence, transport and the smart city: Definitions and dimensions of a new mobility era. *Sustainability (Basel)*, 12(7), 2789. 10.3390/su12072789

Rodríguez-García, J. D., Moreno-León, J., Román-González, M., & Robles, G. (2021). Evaluation of an Online Intervention to Teach Artificial Intelligence with LearningML to 10-16-Year-Old Students. *Proceedings of the 52nd ACM Technical Symposium on Computer Science Education*, (pp. 177–183). ACM. 10.1145/3408877.3432393

Sarker, I. H. (2022). AI-Based Modeling: Techniques, Applications and Research Issues Towards Automation, Intelligent and Smart Systems. *SN Computer Science*, 3(2), 158. 10.1007/s42979-022-01043-x35194580

Stahl, B. C., Andreou, A., Brey, P., Hatzakis, T., Kirichenko, A., Macnish, K., Shaelou, S. L., Patel, A., Ryan, M., & Wright, D. (2021). Artificial intelligence for human flourishing–Beyond principles for machine learning. *Journal of Business Research*, 124, 374–388. 10.1016/j.jbusres.2020.11.030

# Chapter 12
# The Role of Artificial Intelligence in Teaching Turkish to Foreigners and Chat GPT Assessment for Writing Skills

**Cemile Uzun**

*Fırat Üniversitesi, Turkey*

## ABSTRACT

*There are many benefits of adapting artificial intelligence to foreign language teaching. In this study, the adaptation of ChatGPT to teach Turkish to foreigners is discussed. The aim of the study is to evaluate the effect of using ChatGPT against traditional methods in developing writing skills in foreign language teaching. Experimental and control groups were formed to investigate the importance of ChatGPT in teaching Turkish to foreigners. The groups were exposed to A2-B1 level writing activities for six weeks. At the end of the activities, students were given feedback by both ChatGPT and teachers. Which of the feedbacks was more effective was evaluated. It was determined which of the ChatGPT and traditional methods was more effective in developing writing skills.*

## INTRODUCTION

Education is a fundamental tool in the journey of personal development and learning, enabling individuals to realise their full potential. In the process, students are given the tools and methods to develop their talents, enabling them to succeed in their personal and academic lives. The triangle of teacher, student and material that underpins the teaching process emphasises the dynamic and interactive nature of education. Beyond the transmission of knowledge, teachers are guides who enrich the learning process and maximise the learning potential of students. Their adoption of new teaching methods and keeping abreast of technological developments have a direct impact on the quality of education. Beyond the transmission of knowledge, teachers are guides who enrich the learning process and maximise the

DOI: 10.4018/979-8-3693-3350-1.ch012

learning potential of students. Their adoption of new teaching methods and keeping abreast of technological developments have a direct impact on the quality of education.

In today's world of rapidly evolving technology, educational materials are no longer limited to physical textbooks. Digital resources have made it possible to diversify and facilitate access to learning materials. This digital transformation has enriched the learning experience by providing students with faster and more efficient access to information. Teachers are responsible for guiding students in the effective use of resources in both physical and digital environments. This requires teachers to keep abreast of technological developments and integrate them into their teaching practice.

Adapting digital tools and techniques to language teaching offers students new ways to develop their language skills. This allows learners to develop their language skills more effectively, especially in foreign language learning, by providing learning opportunities in natural contexts where the language is used. Interactive apps, online courses and digital language learning platforms offer students flexible learning environments that allow them to learn at their own pace and style (Lund and Wang, 2023).

The aim of education is to provide the necessary tools and supportive environment for individuals to know themselves, discover their talents and maximise those talents. Teachers' effective use of technology provides students with richer and more varied learning experiences. This helps students to achieve not only academic success but also personal development. Integrating technology into education equips students to take their place in the knowledge society and lays the foundations for lifelong learning (Debby et al., 2023).

Artificial intelligence (AI) is the product of advanced digital systems that mimic some aspects of human intelligence and can perform a range of complex tasks. These tools are designed with capabilities that go beyond simple computational functions, such as reasoning, problem solving and interpreting meaning. These capabilities underpin AI's ability to process data to recognise patterns and use these patterns to generate new knowledge. AI has the ability to create new content in different types of media, such as text, images, video and audio, making it an extremely flexible and versatile technology (Qin et al., 2023).

The development of artificial intelligence algorithms has enabled the emergence of new and innovative approaches in the field of education, especially in language teaching. These algorithms have the potential to provide learners with personalised learning experiences, provide real-time feedback and make language learning processes more interactive and participatory. For example, AI-powered language learning apps can help learners improve their pronunciation, reinforce grammar and vocabulary, and even guide them through complex language use scenarios (Jiao et al. 2023, Tian et al., 2024).

AI can also be used to create personalised learning paths for language learning. By analysing a student's learning style and needs, it can deliver the most appropriate learning materials and activities. This allows students to learn at their own pace and more efficiently.

AI can also be integrated with technologies such as virtual reality (VR) and augmented reality (AR) to create immersive language learning experiences. Such applications can make the language learning process more engaging and memorable by allowing learners to practice everyday conversations in a foreign language or have different cultural experiences.

Artificial intelligence has the potential to revolutionise language learning. By personalising students' learning experiences, it can increase their motivation and make the language learning process more effective and enjoyable. The integration of this technology opens new doors for teachers and students, making language learning more accessible and interactive.

The opportunities offered by AI applications in education, particularly in language learning, have the potential to provide students with a personalised and accessible learning experience. As Mijwil et al. (2022) note, AI tools offer learners the opportunity to access the content they need without difficulty. This allows them to explore new and interactive ways of learning languages, especially for young people growing up in the age of technology.

AI tailors the learning experience to students' individual needs and learning styles, allowing each student to learn at their own pace and in their own way. This adaptability provides real-time feedback that helps students overcome learning challenges. When AI-powered applications include motivational elements such as gamification, challenges and rewards, they make learning more engaging and help students retain information more effectively.

In language learning, AI-based tools play a key role in the development of basic language skills such as speaking, listening, reading and writing (Alkaissi and McFarlane, 2023). These tools allow students to practice pronunciation and speaking in a foreign language, to better understand languages with different accents and dialects, and to access a wide range of resources by effectively translating foreign language texts. It also provides the necessary support for students to correct grammatical and syntactical errors in their written work.

The use of AI tools in specific areas of language learning, such as Turkish language teaching, highlights the importance of adopting contemporary methods and technologies in language learning. The use of tools such as ChatGPT in developing writing skills for students learning Turkish as a foreign language shows the potential of this technology. Such applications offer students new perspectives on language learning by making the language learning process more interactive, personalised and accessible.

Integrating AI applications into language teaching makes the language learning process more engaging, interactive and effective. Using AI tools to meet students' individual learning needs, increase motivation and extend learning beyond the classroom is seen as an important step in modern educational approaches.

This study aims to compare the effects of using traditional methods and AI-based learning tools, such as ChatGPT, in foreign language teaching, especially in the development of writing skills. The main issue that the research focuses on is how to integrate language learning needs with the digital world and how to improve Turkish writing skills of non-native Turkish learners using AI tools such as ChatGPT. This is one of the first studies to specifically investigate whether ChatGPT can help improve the writing skills of learners of Turkish as a foreign language.

The main objectives of this study are as follows:

1. To use new techniques in teaching Turkish to foreigners: To bring innovative approaches to teaching Turkish to foreigners by integrating artificial intelligence tools into language teaching methodologies.
2. Teaching Turkish grammar outside the classroom: Providing students with flexible and accessible learning experiences that can be continued outside the classroom through the use of artificial intelligence technologies.
3. Create a meaningful learning experience for students: Using AI tools such as ChatGPT to design an interactive and participatory language learning process that meets students' personal learning needs.

ChatGPT is an AI language model that can mimic human speech using natural language processing technology and is used in this study as a foreign language teaching tool. This technology can take written or spoken input, transform it into structured language commands, and produce contextually appropriate responses combined with the ability to understand grammar. In this way, it produces accurate answers to the questions asked by foreign language learners and can understand the user's requirements.

ChatGPT can contribute to the development of writing skills by showing students errors in their written expression and suggesting corrections. It is particularly useful for students who have not developed basic vocabulary and do not fully understand sentence structure. This AI tool supports the learning process rather than replacing real language practice.

The aim of this research is to explore the potential of artificial intelligence in language teaching and, in particular, how it can improve learners' writing skills. By making a significant contribution to the use of AI in education, this study can guide future research and promote the integration of technology in language teaching.

## BACKGROUND

AI is the design and development of systems that aim to emulate human intelligence. In recent years, the rapid development of AI technology has created new opportunities in many areas, including language learning and education. In particular, its application to language has led to significant advances in areas such as language learning, grammar checking, natural language processing (NLP) and language modelling. Since the 1990s, there has been a remarkable increase in the number of studies on the role of artificial intelligence in language education. AI and Natural Language Processing (NLP) have made great strides in the field of language learning since the 1990s. Initially limited to simple language learning tools, AI has become much more sophisticated with the development of machine learning and deep learning techniques.

In the 1960s, the use of chatbots in AL-assisted language teaching began. The computer programme ELIZA was the first chatbot to interact with humans by typing in English (Weizenbaum, 1966). ALICE, a software developed by Richard Wallace in the 1990s, is an Al tool used for speaking skills in language teaching (Wang & Petrina, 2013). Cleverbot is Rollo Carpenter's AI tool that can have human-like speech (Kim et al, 2019:35). Kim et al. (2019) examined Al tools such as ALICE, ELIZA, Cleverbot, Elbot, Talk to Eve, Replika, Lyra, Andy, Poket Friend, Mondly, and Duolingo to determine which of these tools had features such as speaking, responding, understanding, troubleshooting, and correcting spelling mistakes. Berghe et al. (2019) reviewed the studies on robot-assisted language learning robot-assisted language learning. These studies included thirty-three studies that taught vocabulary, reading skills, speech skills, grammar, and sign language.

Zuraina (2020) reviewed the studies that have used artificial intelligence as a tool in foreign language teaching. Li (2020) is an investigation into the impact of the IELTS Liulishuo application on English language teaching.

Liang et al (2021) found that AI in language teaching focuses on grammar, vocabulary, reading, writing and speaking skills, based on the articles they reviewed. The AI tools used in the articles and the most commonly used software were also examined. They found that 'natural language processing' software was the most widely used technology, followed by 'machine learning' and 'neural networks' technologies. Huange et al. (2021) investigated augmented and virtual reality-based technologies for teaching languages.

The researchers used augmented reality and virtual reality technologies to teach Chinese, Spanish, Japanese and English to improve listening, speaking, reading and writing skills. These technologies have been shown to enhance language teaching by providing students with interactive learning experiences. Du (2021) analysed 1014 articles examining the impact of artificial intelligence in language teaching and found that the most commonly used artificial intelligence technologies in language teaching are neural networks, natural language processing and machine learning. Chen et al (2021) provided important insights into the impact of AI tools on personalised language learning. They found that these technologies were used to improve reading, writing, speaking and listening skills. Yin (2021) investigated the use of artificial intelligence tools in teaching English as a foreign language. Hashiguti et al (2021) investigated the importance of developing a virtual laboratory for teaching and learning English as a foreign language. Li (2021) investigated the application of artificial intelligence to foreign language teaching in college English classes.

Kang & Kang (2022) aimed to create a system model for teaching Chinese based on Deep Learning (DP). Schmidt & Strasser (2022) studied computer-based language learning software supported by artificial intelligence. Gkountara & Prasad (2022) explored the applications of artificial intelligence in second language learning last year. Nga (2022) investigated how artificial intelligence is being used in language teaching. He investigated the impact of software such as ELSA, Grammarly and Turnitin on foreign language teaching and learning. Jaleniauskienė et al. (2023) provided information on the number, countries and methods of studies on artificial intelligence from the 1990s to 2023. They found that "in the period between 1990 and 2000, research on artificial intelligence was very limited, but in the next two decades (2000-2020) there was an exponential increase in publications on the subject". The researchers found that between 1990 and 2020, studies on the impact of artificial intelligence on language teaching were mainly conducted in Taiwan (23 articles) and the USA (20 articles) (Jaleniauskienė et al., 2023:164). Tobing et al (2023) analysed the studies investigating the effects of teaching English as a foreign language with artificial intelligence in higher education institutions. Digital tools and technologies, mobile apps, NAO robots, machine translation and WhatsApp were analysed to investigate the importance of these applications in language learning. Son et al. (2023) discuss the challenges and limitations of applying artificial intelligence to language learning and teaching. The authors mentioned the importance of applications such as natural language processing, automatic writing assessment, data-driven learning, computer-based dynamic assessment, intelligent tutoring systems, automatic speech recognition, chatbots in language teaching. The researchers mentioned that artificial intelligence tools are important tools to provide students with personalised learning environments and mentioned the importance of adapting these applications to language learning. Cantos et al (2023) analysed studies investigating the impact of AI on language teaching and found that AI is a useful language teaching tool for both teachers and students. Azamatova et al. (2023) studied the effect of digital media tools and artificial intelligence applications on the motivation of Kazakh students in Russian language classes, consisting of 32 control and 32 experimental groups at the University of Almaty. Chao et al, (2023) investigated the importance of integrating the artificial intelligence application StoryQ into an English as a foreign language classroom. Chısega Negrılă (2023) investigated the link between artificial intelligence and language learning in the context of Education 4.0. "When used correctly, AI can bring numerous benefits to language learning, such as increased efficiency, greater student engagement in the teachinh-learning process, and the accessibility of content from anywhere and on any device." (Chısega Negrılă, 2023:16). Makeleni et al (2023) examined the challenges faced by African countries in integrating AI into language teaching. Lund et al (2023) focused on the use of ChatGPT and GPT-3 artificial intelligence in academic studies. Eysenbach (2023) evaluated ChatGPT's responses to medical questions. Kung et al. (2023) investigated the performance of a large language model called ChatGPT on the United States Medical Licensing Examination (USMLE). Lund and Wang (2023) analysed an interview with ChatGPT and investigated the potential impact of ChatGPT on academia and libraries. Debby et al (2023) stated that the use of artificial intelligence is an important issue in education. They found that an AI tool such as ChatGPT has a number of benefits, such as increasing student engagement, collaboration and accessibility, but also has some negative aspects. Qin et al. (2023) investigated the ability of ChatGPT to successfully perform a novel task even though a model has not been pre-trained for a specific task. Taecharungroj (2023) analysed comments about ChatGPT on Twitter. He looked at ChatGPT's ability to write creative texts, write essays, write code and answer questions. Alkaissi and McFarlane (2023) examined the effects of ChatGPT on academic writing.

Lo (2023) investigated the differential performance of ChatGPT in different subject areas. He concluded that ChatGPT has a positive effect on teacher training and student education. Liu et al (2023) investigated the capabilities and potential impact of ChatGPT. Baidoo-Anu and Owusu Ansah (2023) investigated the potential advantages and disadvantages of ChatGPT in promoting teaching and learning. Yeo et al (2023) investigated ChatGPT responses to questions about cirrhosis and hepatocellular carcinoma (HCC). To test the accuracy and comprehensiveness of the answers provided by ChatGPT, its responses to 164 questions were evaluated. De Angelis et al (2023) investigated the relationship between large language models and ChatGPT. They investigated the accuracy of ChatGPT responses in the field of health. Jiao et al. (2023) analysed the translation performance of ChatGPT and concluded that its performance improved with ChatGPT-4. Perkins (2023) investigated the impact of students using artificial intelligence tools, particularly big language models such as ChatGPT, in their academic studies. Yuan et al. (2023) investigated whether powerful IE models could be built directly with LLMs. Using the power of language models such as ChatGPT, they conducted a comprehensive evaluation on three different IE tasks. Tian et al. (2024) considered the potential benefits and challenges of large language models in education from the perspective of students and teachers.

To date, studies have analysed in detail the impact of Artificial Intelligence and Natural Language Processing (NLP) on language learning and teaching, their development from the past to the present, and their areas of application. The studies provide examples of how different technologies and applications (e.g. ELIZA, ALICE, Cleverbot, Duolingo, ELSA, Grammarly) are used in language teaching and how they contribute to areas such as grammar, vocabulary, reading, writing and speaking skills. The research highlighted the benefits of artificial intelligence tools, such as providing personalised learning experiences, increasing student engagement and making content accessible from anywhere, on any device, and the benefits of these tools for language learning. It was also noted that augmented reality (AR) and virtual reality (VR) technologies play an important role in language learning by providing interactive learning experiences.

Research has shown that artificial intelligence is a useful tool for both students and teachers in language learning. These technologies make the learning process more efficient and effective by increasing students' motivation, improving their language skills and providing personalised learning environments, while at the same time reducing the burden on teachers. In order to integrate and use these technologies effectively, teachers and students need to adapt to these new tools.

The effective use of AI-based tools can make language learning more interactive, accessible and personalised, thus transforming the learning process. This study differs from the above studies in that it is the first to use ChatGPT to teach Turkish writing skills to foreigners. It offers an innovative approach in the field of language learning by focusing on the use of ChatGPT in developing the writing skills of learners of Turkish as a foreign language.

## METHODOLOGY

To understand the effects of using artificial intelligence in language learning, the methodology of this study is divided into four main parts: Participation, Research Questions, Learning Sessions and Learning Outcomes. The research questions aim to measure the effectiveness of ChatGPT in correcting grammatical errors, how learners' error awareness is affected by ChatGPT corrections, and the impact of using ChatGPT on writing skills compared to traditional teaching methods. Participants were selected to match the target language level, age range and learning objectives of the study. The learning sessions consisted of interactive grammar and writing practice using ChatGPT, traditional classroom teaching or a combination of the two. The learning sessions included measures such as progress in students' writing skills, reduction in grammatical errors and self-assessment of their learning process, as well as a comparison of results obtained using ChatGPT and traditional methods.

### Participations

The participants were selected from a total of 20 students studying at the Turkish Education and Training Centre affiliated to Fırat University in Turkey, whose mother tongue is French and whose knowledge of Turkish is in the A2-B1 range, aged between 18 and 24, with an equal number of men and women.

### Research Questions

Three research questions were formulated to analyse in depth the impact of ChatGPT on language learning and its comparison with traditional teaching methods. Each question evaluates the role of technology in language learning from different perspectives:

1. How can the success of ChatGPT in correcting students' grammatical errors in writing activities be measured? This question assesses the ability of ChatGPT to correct grammatical errors. To measure success, the students' errors were compared before and after their errors were corrected.
2. What types of errors are students more likely to notice when receiving corrections from ChatGPT and how does this awareness affect their learning process? This question asks what types of errors students are more likely to notice when receiving corrections from ChatGPT and how this awareness affects their learning process. This highlights the importance of students' active participation in language learning and the ability of technological tools to provide feedback.
3. What is the effectiveness of traditional language teaching methods (control group) in improving students' writing skills and how does this effectiveness differ from the use of ChatGPT? This question compares the effectiveness of traditional language teaching methods and the use of ChatGPT in improving students' writing skills. This comparison is important to clarify the advantages and disadvantages of both methods and their effects on students' learning.

## Learning Sessions

In the study, experimental and control groups were formed to determine the use of AI in teaching Turkish writing skills to foreigners. The activities were applied to the experimental and control groups for six weeks with two different sessions. Both groups practiced 75-minute learning sessions for six weeks.

Writing activities were used in the classroom for the experimental group. As a result of the activities, the students' sentences were corrected under the control of a teacher and feedback was given to the students. The errors made by the students were categorised according to grammatical themes.

*Table 1. Stages of activity applied to the experimental group*

| Week | Day | Missions | Targets |
|---|---|---|---|
| 1 | 1 | Pre-test | Before the start of the learning sessions, the participants' knowledge and skills in writing in Turkish will be assessed. |
| 2 | 1 | Learning session | In a classroom setting, under the supervision of a teacher, participants practise the grammar structures targeted in the texts. (30 min) |
| 3 | 2 | Learning session | The teacher checks the answers given by the participants to the writing activities (45 min.) |
| 4 | 1 | Post-test | After the learning sessions, to re-measure the participants' Turkish writing knowledge and skills. |
| 5 | | | Break time |
| 6 | Delayed post-test and feedback | | After a three-week break, to re-measure the Turkish writing knowledge and skills that the participants had acquired in the classroom, with the teacher separated, and to get feedback from the participants. |

In the study conducted for the control group, the first step was to organise writing activities for the students in the classroom and to distribute the collected work back to the students in the computer lab. The students were asked to use ChatGPT to identify errors in the texts they had written and to check the correctness of the sentences. In this process, version 4 of ChatGPT was used to get more effective results. Students were encouraged to take notes as they identified their errors and to use these notes in the correction process. In the studies conducted with ChatGPT, each student was accompanied by a teacher, and the teachers checked the answers given by ChatGPT and the corrections made. In this way, the ability of ChatGPT to correct spelling mistakes and the grammatical units in which it is deficient were analysed.

*Table 2. Stages of activity applied to the experimental group*

| Week | Day | Missions | Targets |
|---|---|---|---|
| 1 | 1 | Pre-test | To measure the participants' knowledge and skills in writing in Turkish before the start of the learning sessions. |
| 2 | 1 | Learning session | Introducing the technology. Practising the participants by applying the grammar structures targeted in the texts. (30 min) |
| 3 | 2 | Learning session | Participants upload their answers to the writing activities to ChatGPT and ask ChatGPT to check what they have written. (45 min) |
| 4 | 1 | Post-test | To re-assess the participants' Turkish writing knowledge and skills after the learning sessions. |

continued on following page

*Table 2. Continued*

| Week | Day | Missions | Targets |
|---|---|---|---|
| 5 | | | |
| 6 | Delayed post-test and feedback | | To re-measure the participants' Turkish writing knowledge and skills acquired through ChatGPT after a three-week break, and to receive feedback from the participants. |

One week after the activities, participants in both the experimental and control groups were given the incorrect sentences they had written earlier and asked to correct them. The success of both groups in correcting the incorrect sentences was measured and the success rates between the groups were compared. After a further three weeks, the information learned by the participants in the classroom environment and using ChatGPT was re-evaluated and feedback was collected from the participants on the training they had received. At this stage, in addition to the long-term effects of retention and knowledge acquired, the level of satisfaction with the support provided by the artificial intelligence was also examined.

## Learning Outcomes

The content of the study is based on the activities called "My Daily Routine" and "My Weekend Plans", which target writing skills at levels A2 and B1 according to the criteria of the Common European Framework of Recommendations (CEFR). These activities are organised according to the learning outcomes defined by the CEFR in 2018.

Level A2 - Skills targeted by the activity "My daily routine":

- Students make a list of their daily routines; for example, daily activities such as waking up, having breakfast, going to school, studying.
- For each activity, they write a sentence describing their daily routine in detail.

Link the sentences they have written using conjunctions to form a coherent paragraph.
Level B1 - Skills targeted in the activity "My plans for the weekend":

- The students make a list of their own plans for the weekend.
- Write a sentence for each activity they have planned and explain their weekend plans.
- Link the sentences using conjunctions to create a meaningful and fluent paragraph.

The aim of these activities is to improve participants' ability to express their daily and future plans and to write their thoughts in an organised and comprehensible way. The activities give the participants the opportunity to practise and improve their speaking skills, while at the same time strengthening their written expression skills according to the CEFR standards.

## RESULT

To answer the first research question, students were asked to enter their responses to the writing activities into ChatGPT. The rate at which ChatGPT correctly corrected the grammatical errors in the students' writing was measured. The answers that the students entered into ChatGPT consisted of 190 sentences. Of these sentences, 188 were correct and 2 were incorrect.

*Table 3. ChatGPT's rate of correcting students' incorrect sentences*

| Total number of sentences | Number of correct answers | Number of incorrect | Accuracy rate |
|---|---|---|---|
| 190 | 188 | 2 | %98 |

It was found that 188 of the 190 sentences entered by the students in ChatGPT were correctly corrected, but 2 sentences were incorrectly corrected. Therefore, the accuracy rate was calculated to be 98%.

To answer the second research question, students were asked to analyse the corrections they received from ChatGPT. They were asked to compare their own answers with ChatGPT's corrections and make notes about their mistakes. Tables were created with examples of students' errors and ChatGPT corrections. The grammar topics in which students made the most errors and the rates of these errors were analysed. The examples that ChatGPT corrected incorrectly were categorised and the grammar topics from which these errors originated were indicated.

*Table 4. Some examples of students' incorrect sentences and ChatCPT's correction of the sentences*

| Öğrencinin Yanlış Cümleleri | ChatGPT'nin Düzeltmesi |
|---|---|
| Engelli insanları yardım etmek zorundayız | Engelli insanlara yardım etmek zorundayız. (We have to help people with disabilities.) |
| Bazen yemek pişirebiliriz ve onlarla paylaşabiliriz ya su ya da para. | Bazen onlarla yemek pişirip paylaşabilir veya su ve para gibi yardımlarda bulunabiliriz. (Sometimes we can cook and share food with them, or help them with water and money.) |
| Ayrıca bazlılar çok engelli değil | Ayrıca, bazıları çok engelli değil. (Also, some are not very disabled) |
| Çocukla geliştirmek çok zor bir şey. | Çocuğun gelişimini desteklemek çok zor olabilir. (Supporting a child's development can be very difficult.) |
| Çocuğu konuşmak istiyorsa telefonunu ve her şey bırakın ve onu dinleyin. | Eğer çocuk konuşmak istiyorsa, telefonunuzu ve her şeyi bırakın ve onu dinleyin. (If the child wants to talk, put down your phone and everything and listen to him.) |
| Her şeynin hakkında konuşun | Her şey hakkında konuşun. (Talk about everything.) |
| Çocuk daha iyi güvenli olacak | Çocuk daha iyi ve güvende olacak. (The child will be better and safer.) |
| Çocuk size konuşmak isterse onu dinleyin | Eğer çocuk sizinle konuşmak istiyorsa, onu dinleyin. (If the child wants to talk to you, listen to her.) |
| Onunla konuşarken iyi tonunuza ayarlya | Onunla konuşurken iyi bir ton kullanmaya özen gösterin. (Take care to use a good tone when talking to him.) |
| Anne babanın çocukla iletişimi iyi iletişimi olmalıdır. | Anne ve babanın çocukla iletişimi iyi olmalıdır. (Parents should have good communication with the child.) |
| Bu konu için bence anne babanın çocukla iletişimi sessiz olmalıdır. | Bu konuda, bence anne ve babanın çocukla iletişimi sakin olmalıdır. (In this regard, I think the parents' communication with the child should be calm.) |
| Abevey çocuklarının duygularını anlamalılar. | Ebeveynler, çocuklarının duygularını anlamalılar. (Parents need to understand their children's feelings.) |
| Bu yüzden onlarla arkadaşlarının gibi olmalıyız. | Bu yüzden onlarla arkadaşları gibi olmalıyız. (So we have to be like friends with them.) |

This table contains some of the most common mistakes students make in Turkish and ChatGPT's suggestions on how to correct them. The mistakes addressed in these examples are usually related to grammar, word choice and expressions.

*Table 5. The grammar topics in which students made the most errors and their error rates*

| Grammatical errors of the participant | Grammar error rates of the participants |
|---|---|
| *ambiguity of meaning* | %15 |
| *lack of predicate* | %8 |
| *incorrect use of the ablative case* | %9 |
| *incorrect use of the accusative case* | %7 |
| *lack of plurality suffix* | %1 |
| *incorrect use of the imperative mood* | %3 |
| *incorrect use of the present simple suffix* | %9 |
| *lack of gerund* | %2 |
| *incorrect use of possessive suffix* | %7 |
| *lack of conditional suffix* | %2 |
| *incorrect use of genitive case* | %8 |
| *lack of instrumental case suffix* | %1 |
| *lack of conjunction and* | %4 |
| blending suffix without y | %4 |
| incorrect verb usage | %4 |
| incorrect word usage | %5 |
| spelling mistake | %5 |
| incorrect usage of dative case | %6 |

The table shows the patterns of grammatical difficulties encountered by the students. It was observed that the students mostly made mistakes in the use of ambiguity, case suffixes, verbs and tense suffixes. They were found to make the fewest errors in the use of plurality suffixes, instrumental case suffixes and conjunctions.

*Table 6. Sentences in which ChatGPT incorrectly corrected students' errors*

| Grammar issues that ChatGPT incorrectly corrected | Example |
|---|---|
| incorrect verb usage | Spor oynabilir |
| Not using the plural suffix | bazı anne ve babaların |

Table 6 shows examples where ChatGPT's corrections were not correct. The grammatical errors in these examples are shown.

In order to answer the third research question, the following steps were taken: The changes in the participants' writing skills after the sessions with traditional language teaching methods were observed and the average scores of the participants from the pre-test and post-test were determined. The average of the pre-test and post-test scores of the participants who received feedback from ChatGPT was determined. The averages of the pre- and post-test scores of the two groups were compared.

The paired samples t-test for means was used to determine whether there was a statistically significant difference in the test scores. This test is used to assess whether the difference between the means of two groups is due to random variation. If the p-value obtained as a result of the test is $p<0.05$ less than the specified significance level, the difference between the two groups is considered to be statistically significant.

*Table 7. Pre-test and post-test scores of experimental and control groups*

| | | Mean | Number of participants | p value |
|---|---|---|---|---|
| Pre-test | Group receiving feedback from ChatGPT (control group) | 57.8 | 10 | 0.001 |
| | Group receiving feedback from the teacher in the classroom (experimental group) | 63.9 | 10 | 0.117 |
| Post-test | Group receiving feedback from ChatGPT (control group) | 67.5 | 10 | 0.001 |
| | Group receiving feedback from the teacher in the classroom (experimental group) | 66.4 | 10 | 0.117 |

There is a significant difference between the group receiving feedback from ChatGPT and the group receiving feedback from the teacher in the classroom in the pre-test. The group receiving feedback from ChatGPT had a lower mean score in the pre-test and this difference was statistically significant. A similar situation is observed in the post-test results. The group that received feedback from ChatGPT had a higher mean score in the post-test and this difference was statistically significant ($p=0.001$).

There was no significant change in the performance of the group that received feedback from the teacher in class. In both the pre-test and the post-test, the mean scores of the group that received feedback from the teacher in the classroom were similar and the p-value was not statistically significant in either case ($p=0.117$).

A delayed post-test was administered to the experimental and control groups to measure how much of what the participants had learned was retained over time and to compare the effects of different learning methods on long-term knowledge retention. Three weeks later, a delayed post-test was administered to re-measure what the participants had learned in the classroom and what they had learned using ChatGPT.

*Table 8. Delayed test results for experimental and control groups*

| | Mean | Number of participants |
|---|---|---|
| Group receiving feedback from ChatGPT (control group) | 72.4 | 10 |
| Group receiving feedback from the teacher in the classroom (experimental group) | 66.4 | 10 |

When the mean of the delayed post-test scores was compared with the post-test scores, an increase of 4.9 points was observed in the mean scores of the group that received feedback from ChatGPT (control group). There was no difference in the mean scores of the group that received feedback from the teacher in the classroom (experimental group).

## CONCLUSION

An analysis of students' responses to ChatGPT shows that ChatGPT has a 98% correct grammar correction rate. This shows that ChatGPT has a very high success rate in correcting grammar. Out of 190 sentences, only 2 sentences were found to have incorrect corrections, indicating that ChatGPT is generally very effective at detecting and correcting grammatical errors. This result shows that ChatGPT can be used as an effective tool in education, especially in language learning and improving writing skills. The use of AI-based tools such as ChatGPT to improve students' writing, reduce grammatical errors and improve overall writing quality can make a valuable contribution to the learning process. At the same time, the fact that ChatGPT cannot achieve 100% accuracy emphasises that the technology is still in its developmental stage and the importance of human supervision. It is important that students and teachers critically evaluate ChatGPT's recommendations and consult additional sources when making final decisions about grammar.

AI-based tools such as ChatGPT are very good at understanding and applying general grammar rules. However, when it comes to the more subtle nuances of language, particularly issues such as different language structure and usage, the limitations of these systems can become apparent.

Students benefited most from ChatGPT's corrections on the correct use of the dative and accusative cases. The grammar areas in which students benefited most from ChatGPT's corrections were as follows.

- ambiguity of meaning
- incorrect use of the present simple suffix
- *incorrect use of genitive case*
- *lack of predicate*
- *incorrect use of the possessive suffix*
- *Incorrect use of the accusative case*
- incorrect usage of dative case

These results show that it can help learners to recognise and correct their grammatical and semantic errors. However, it was also found that ChatCPT's corrections can sometimes still have a different meaning to the original sentence or make unnecessary changes.

For the group who received feedback from the teacher in the classroom, it was found that the teacher's feedback did not have a significant effect on the students' learning. It was found that this group had similar mean scores in both the pre-test and post-test results.

The group receiving feedback from ChatGPT showed lower performance in both the pre-test and post-test, while the group receiving feedback from the teacher in the classroom showed higher performance. There was a statistically significant increase in the scores of the group receiving feedback from ChatGPT, which was more effective in improving students' writing skills. These results show that ChatGPT can be effective in providing feedback and can be used as a tool to improve students' writing skills. It was found that the group receiving feedback from ChatGPT was more effective in improving students' writing skills and made more significant progress compared to traditional methods. ChatGPT can be used as an important tool for language learning and improving writing skills.

The delayed test scores of the group that received feedback from ChatGPT showed an average increase of 4.9 points. This indicates that ChatGPT can be used as an effective tool in the students' learning process. The group that received feedback from the teacher in the classroom did not show an average score increase. This indicates that teacher feedback in class did not significantly improve students' performance compared to ChatGPT feedback.

## DISCUSSION

ChatGPT's ability to produce high quality answers and correct errors has made it a technology of great interest to society. How this technology is being used in education is mentioned in the literature section of the study. In addition, both the translation ability and the success of ChatGPT in writing skills were evaluated in our study and it was found that ChatGPT is an important technology tool in foreign language teaching. It has been shown that it is important to integrate large language processing models such as ChatGPT into language teaching.

ChatGPT's grammar correction features can support the language learning process and help students improve their writing skills in different languages. AI-based tools such as ChatGPT can significantly support the language learning process by providing grammar correction and personalised feedback to learners. The multilingual nature of these tools offers students flexibility and variety when working on different language skills. Evaluating the impact of ChatGPT on writing, reading, speaking and listening skills can contribute to the development of language teaching methodologies.

Comprehensive studies are needed to determine the impact of ChatGPT in the classroom in each language. This can help us to better understand the role of technology in language teaching and to develop language teaching strategies. In particular, it should be investigated how ChatGPT affects language learners' language skills, for which grammar topics it is more effective and to what extent it contributes to language learning success.

In this context, language teachers and trainers should consider how to integrate technologies such as ChatGPT as course materials and learning activities. At the same time, regular evaluations should be carried out to measure the impact of the technology on student achievement and student feedback should be taken into account.

It has been observed that artificial intelligence-based tools such as ChatGPT can make a positive contribution to student feedback and the learning process. However, studies with larger groups of participants are needed to generalise these findings. Longer term studies are also needed to assess the impact on student learning outcomes.

The integration of large language models into educational systems can help to develop students' critical thinking skills. Pedagogical approaches should aim to optimise the role of these models in education, so that curricula and learning environments can become more effective.

# REFERENCES

Alkaissi, H., & McFarlane, S. I. (2023). Artificial hallucinations in ChatGPT: Implications in scientific writing. *Cureus*, 15(2), 1–4. 10.7759/cureus.3517936811129

Azamatova, A., Bekeyeva, N., Zhaxylikova, K., Sarbassova, A., & Ilyassova, N. (2023). The effect of using artificial intelligence and digital learning tools based on project-based learning approach in foreign language teaching on students' success and motivation. [IJEMST]. *International Journal of Education in Mathematics, Science, and Technology*, 11(6), 1458–1475. 10.46328/ijemst.3712

Baidoo-Anu, D., & Owusu Ansah, L. (2023). Education in the era of generative Artificial Intelligence (AI): Understanding the potential benefits of ChatGPT in promoting teaching and learning. *Journal of AI*, 7(1), 52–62. 10.61969/jai.1337500

Berghe, R., Verhagen, J., Oudgenoeg-Paz, O., Ven, S., & Leseman, P. (2019). Social bobots for language learning: A Review. *Review of Educational Research*, 89(2), 259–295. 10.3102/0034654318821286

Cantos, K. F. S., Giler, R. C. V., & Magayanes, I. E. C. (2023). Artifical intelligence in language teaching and learning. *Ciencia Latina Revista Cientifica Multidisciplinar*, 7(4), 5629–5638. 10.37811/cl_rcm.v7i4.7368

CEFR. (2018). *Common european framework of reference for languages: learning, teaching, assessment companion volume with new descriptors*. Council of Europe.

Chao, J., Ellis, R., Jiang, S., Rosé, C., Finzer, W., Tatar, C., Fiacco, J., & Wiedemann, K. (2023). Exploring artificial intelligence in english language arts with storyQ. *The Thirty-Seventh AAAI Conference on Artificial Intelligence (AAAI-23)*. AAAI. 10.1609/aaai.v37i13.26899

Chen, X., Zou, D., Cheng, G., & Xie, H. (2021). Artificial intelligence-assisted personalized language learning: systematic review and co-citation analysis. *International Conference on Advanced Learning Technologies (ICALT)*, (pp. 241–245). IEEE. 10.1109/ICALT52272.2021.00079

Chisega, N. (2023). The new revolution language learning: The power of artificial intelligence and education 4.0. *Bulletin*, 2, 16–27.

Cotton, D. R. E., Cotton, P. A., & Shipway, J. R. (2024). Chatting and cheating: Ensuring academic integrity in the era of ChatGPT. *Innovations in Education and Teaching International*, 61(2), 228–239. 10.1080/14703297.2023.2190148

De Angelis, L., Baglivo, F., Arzilli, G., Privitera, G. P., Ferragina, P., Tozzi, A. E., & Rizzo, C. (2023). ChatGPT and the rise of large language models: The new AI-driven infodemic threat in public health. *Frontiers in Public Health*, 1–8.37181697

Du, Y. (2021). systematic review of artificial intelligence in language learning. advances in engineering and applied science research. *Proceedings of the 2021 International Conference on Intelligent Manufacturing Technology and Information Technology*. IEEE.

Eysenbach, G. (2023). The role of chatgpt, generative language models, and artifical intelligence in medical education: A conversation with chatgpt and a call for paper. *JMIR Medical Education*, 9, 1–13. 10.2196/4688536863937

Gkountara, D. N., & Prasad, R. (2022). A review of artificial intelligence in foreign language learning. *International Symposium on Wireless Personal Multmedia Commun, Cations (WPMC)*. IEEE. 10.1109/WPMC55625.2022.10014767

Hashiguti, S. T., Brito, C. C. P., & Ângelo, R. C. (2021). Meaning making in the context of EFL teaching and learning with an artificial intelligence. *European Scientific Journal*, 17(22), 19. 10.19044/esj.2021.v17n22p19

Huang, X., Zou, D., Cheng, G., & Xie, H. (2021). A systematic review of AR and VR enhanced language learning. *Sustainability (Basel)*, 13(9), 4639. 10.3390/su13094639

Jaleniauskienė, E., Lisaitė, D., & Brazaitė, L. D. (2023). Artificial Intelligence Language Education: A Bibliometric Analysis. *Sustainable Multilingualism*, 23(1), 156–193. 10.2478/sm-2023-0017

Jiao, W., Wang, W., Huang, J., Wang, X., & Tu, Z. (2023). Is ChatGPT a good translator? yes with GPT-4 as the engine. *arxiv:2301.08745*, 1-10.

Kang, B. & Kang, S. (2022). Construction of chinese language teaching system model based on deep learning under the background of artificial intelligence. *Hindawi Scientiifc Programming*, 1-10.

Kim, N. Y., Cha, Y., & Kim, H. S. (2019). Future english learning: Chatbots and artificial intelligence. *Multimedia-Asisted Language Learning*, 22(3), 32–53.

Kung, T. H., Cheatham, M., Medenilla, A., Sillos, C., De Leon, L., Elepaño, C., Madriaga, M., Aggabao, R., Diaz-Candido, G., Maningo, J., & Tseng, V. (2023). Performance of ChatGPT on USMLE: Potential for AI-assisted medical education using large language models. *PLOS Digital Health*, 2(2), 1–12. 10.1371/journal.pdig.000019836812645

Li, R. (2020). Using artificial intelligence in learning english as a foreign language: An examination of IELTS LIULISHUO as an online platform. *Journal of Higher Education Research*, 1(2), 85–89. 10.32629/jher.v1i2.178

Li, S. (2021). Research on the exploration and reflection of foreign language teaching based on "artificial intelligence +education" in the big data ear. *2021 2nd International Conference on Big Data Economy and Information Management (BDEIM)*, (pp. 354-357). IEEE.

Liang, J. C., Hwang, G. J., Chen, M. R. A., & Darmawansah, D. (2021). Roles and research foci of artificial intelligence in language education: An integrated bibliographic analysis and systematic review approach. *Interactive Learning Environments*, 1–27.

Liu, Y., Han, T., Ma, S., Zhang, J., Yang, Y., Tian, J., He, H., Li, A., He, M., Liu, Z., Wu, Z., Zhu, D., Li, X., Qiang, N., Shen, D., Liu, T., & Ge, B. (2023). Summary of ChatGPT-related research and perspective towards the future of large language models. *Meta-Radiology*, 1(2), 1–21. 10.1016/j.metrad.2023.100017

Lo, C. K. (2023). What Is the impact of ChatGPT on education? A rapid review of the literature. *Education Sciences*, 13(410), 2–15. 10.3390/educsci13040410

Lund, B. D., & Wang, T. (2023). *Chatting about ChatGPT: How may AI and GPT impact academia and libraries?* Social Science Research Network.

Lund, B. D., Wang, T., Mannuru, N. R., Nie, B., Shimray, S., & Wang, Z. (2023). ChatGPT and a new academic reality: Artificial intelligence-written research papers and the ethics of the large language models in scholarly publishing. *Journal of the Association for Information Science and Technology*, 74(5), 570–581. 10.1002/asi.24750

Maaz, M., Rasheed, H. A., Khan, S. H., & Khan, F. S. (2023). *Video-ChatGPT: Towards detailed video understanding via large vision and language models. ArXiv.* I-XVI.

Makeleni, S., Mutongoza, B. H., & Linake, M. A. (2023). Language education and artificial intelligence: An exploration of challenges confronting academics in global south universities. *Journal of Culture and Values in Education*, 6(2), 158–171. 10.46303/jcve.2023.14

Mijwil, M. M., Aggarwal, K., Doshi, R., Hiran, K. K., & Gök, M. (2022). The distinction between R-CNN and Fast R-CNN in image analysis: A Performance Comparison. *Asian Journal of Applied Sciences*, 10(5), 429–437. 10.24203/ajas.v10i5.7064

Nga, P. T. (2022). Artificial intelligence (AI) Application in foreign language teaching and learning. *European Journal of Applied Sciences*, 10(5), 89–93.

Perkins, M. (2023). Academic integrity considerations of AI large language models in the post-pandemic era: ChatGPT and beyond. *Journal of University Teaching & Learning Practice*, 20(2), 6–24. 10.53761/1.20.02.07

Qin, C., Zhang, A., Zhang, Z., Chen, J., Yasunaga, M., & Yang, D. (2023). Is ChatGPT a general-purpose natural language processing task solver? *Proceedings of the 2023 Conference on Empirical Methods in Natural Language Processing*, (pp. 1339-1384). IEEE. 10.18653/v1/2023.emnlp-main.85

Schmidt, T., & Strasser, T. (2022). Artificial intelligence in foreign language learning and teaching: *A CALL for Intelligent Practive. Anglistik. International Journal of English Studies*, 33(1), 165–184.

Son, J., Ružić, N. K., & Philpott, A. (2023). Artifical intelligence technılogies and applications for language learning and teaching. *Journal of China Computer-Assisted Language Learning*, 1–19.

Taecharungroj, V. (2023). "What Can ChatGPT Do?" analyzing early reactions to the Innovative AI Chatbot on Twitter. *Big Data and Cognitive Computing*, 7(35), 1–10. 10.3390/bdcc7010035

Tian, S., Jin, Q., Yeganova, L., Lai, P., Zhu, Q., Chen, X., Yang, Y., Chen, Q., Kim, W., Comeau, D. C., Islamaj, R., Kapoor, A., Gao, X., & Lu, Z. (2024). Opportunities and challenges for ChatGPT and large language models in biomedicine and health. *Briefings in Bioinformatics*, 25(1), 1–9.38168838

Wang, Y. F., & Petrina, S. (2013). Using learning analytics to understand the design of an intelligent language tutor–Chatbot lucy. *Editorial Preface*, 4(11), 124–131.

Weizenbaum, J. (1966). ELIZA: A computer program for the study of natural language communication between man and machine. *Communications of the ACM*, 9(1), 36–45. 10.1145/365153.365168

Yeo, Y. H., Samaan, J. S., Ng, W. H., Ting, P. S., Trivedi, H., Vipani, A., Ayoub, W., Yang, J. D., Liran, O., Spiegel, B., & Kuo, A. (2023). Assessing the performance of ChatGPT in answering questions regarding cirrhosis and hepatocellular carcinoma. *Clinical and Molecular Hepatology*, 29(3), 721–732. 10.3350/cmh.2023.008936946005

Yin, N. (2021). Research on the impacts of artificial intelligence technology on language teaching innovation. *Frontiers in Educational Research*, 4(7), 25–31.

Yuan, C., Xie, Q., & Ananiadou, S. (2023). Zero-shot temporal relation extraction with ChatGPT. *Workshop on Biomedical Natural Language Processing*. IEEE.

Zuraina, A. (2020). Artifical intelligence (AI): a review of its uses in language teaching and learning. *The 6th International Conference on Software Engieering & Computer Systems*. IEEE.

## KEY TERMS AND DEFINITIONS

**Artificial Intelligence:** A harbinger of disruptive developments in the World.

**Artificial Intelligence-Assisted Language Teaching:** An innovative approach to making learning more effective.

**ChatGPT:** Today's best and newest artificial intelligence.

**Second Language Learning:** A necessary asset for the progress of individuals and society.

**Traditional Method:** Teaching that takes place in a classroom environment with a teacher.

**Writing Skills:** One of the most difficult skills to acquire in second language teaching.

# Section 3
# Socio–Demographics, Diversity, and Ethical Considerations

# Chapter 13
# A Survey on Information Technology and Artificial Intelligence Among Youth in the Digital Age in Selangor, Malaysia

**Nur Raihan Che Nawi**
https://orcid.org/0000-0002-7210-9430
*Faculty of Educational Studies, Universiti Putra Malaysia, Malaysia*

**Mohd Mursyid Arshad**
*Faculty of Educational Studies, Universiti Putra Malaysia, Malaysia*

**Ismi Arif Ismail**
*Faculty of Educational Studies, Universiti Putra Malaysia, Malaysia*

**Nor Wahiza Abd Wahat**
*Faculty of Educational Studies, Universiti Putra Malaysia, Malaysia*

**Jeffrey Lawrence D'Silva**
*Institute for Social Science Studies, Universiti Putra Malaysia, Malaysia*

**Mohd Faiq Abd Aziz**
*Faculty of Educational Studies, Universiti Putra Malaysia, Malaysia*

**Hayrol Azril Mohammed Shaffril**
*Institute for Social Science Studies, Universiti Putra Malaysia, Malaysia*

**Dzulhailmi Dahalan**
*Institute for Social Science Studies, Universiti Putra Malaysia, Malaysia*

## ABSTRACT

*This survey study reports findings on information technology and artificial intelligence among two types of youth: youth aged 15–30 and youth aged 31–40 in Selangor, Malaysia. Data were collected from 1000 youth from 9 districts of Selangor (Gombak, Petaling, Kuala Langat, Hulu Langat, Kuala Selangor, Hulu Selangor, Sabak Bernam, Klang, and Sepang). The study findings for information technology and artificial intelligence show eleven items. As expected, overall respondents from youth categories recorded the highest mean score of 4.04, and the youth adult mean score is 3.99. In conclusion, the digital age presents both opportunities and challenges for youth in Selangor, Malaysia. Understanding the implications of information technology and artificial intelligence on youth is crucial for promoting their well-being and*

DOI: 10.4018/979-8-3693-3350-1.ch013

*harnessing the benefits of digital advancements in education, health, and social interactions*

## INTRODUCTION

The domains of information technology and artificial intelligence exhibit a robust interrelation with the robotics industry, expected to assume a crucial position in forthcoming times. According to Ballester et al. (2022), individuals who possess specialised knowledge in the field of robotics are anticipated to sustain a competitive advantage within the realm of work. The acquisition of robotics abilities is not a formidable challenge; Jung and Lim (2020) assert that with proper guidance and genuine excitement, one may easily acquire robotics capabilities. Ballestar et al. (2022) highlight the concern that employment opportunities may diminish due to the occurrence of 'automation supplanting human labour.' However, Dixon et al. (2021) and Sima et al. (2020) emphasise in their studies that the utilisation of robotics in the industry serves to enhance the quality of goods and services while reducing costs, rather than with the intention of reducing the overall workforce.

The establishment of a government or organisation entails the consideration of various factors, such as the integration of information technology and Artificial Intelligence (AI). Numerous governments and organisations worldwide have enacted strategies to enhance the adoption of information technology and artificial intelligence (AI), including the state government of Selangor. The Selangor Internet Data Programme provides free internet access for a period of 12 months, making it advantageous for more than 70,000 persons across several target groups including small-scale vendors, students, single moms, taxi drivers, older residents, and part-time workers. The Selangor Information Technology and E-Commerce Council (SITEC) has implemented artificial intelligence (AI) technology to monitor and manage various environmental issues, including potholes and trees (eCentral, 2021). The Selangor state government demonstrates its dedication to achieving the Fourth Industrial Revolution through its proactive endeavours, encompassing the investigation of emerging technologies such as automation, Internet of Things, big data analysis, incorporation of social media, digitization, and robotics technology.

After careful examination, it is evident that there are additional efforts aimed at improving the growth of human resources during the Fourth Industrial Revolution. This requires changes in the workforce system and has consequences for the future of young people. The aforementioned activities serve as evidence that the state's progress and the execution of the SMART Selangor 2025 Action Plan in the context of the Fourth Industrial Revolution are deliberate choices that prioritise the engagement of young individuals. The government's decision can be characterised as a strategic and astute action.

In a Facebook post dated January 20, 2020, Y.A.B Dato' Menteri Besar Selangor expressed the Selangor government's dedication to equipping the state's young with the necessary skills to address the demands of the Fourth Industrial Revolution, as a component of the Smart State 2025 plan. Selangor is resolute in achieving this goal and maintaining its worldwide competitiveness.

Therefore, the commitment of the State Government to promoting the advancement of young individuals through a range of programmes and significant financial investments is considered a valuable contribution to the favourable progress of the youth in Selangor. The aforementioned dedication aligns with the advancements in technology associated with the Fourth Industrial Revolution and its utilisation in addressing the COVID-19 crisis, both at an international level and within the context of Malaysia.

## LITERATURE REVIEW

Numerous studies have provided evidence of the substantial influence exerted by information technology and artificial intelligence (AI), encompassing digitalization, the Internet of Things (IoT), utilisation of social media, and advancements in robotics technology (Fink et al., 2020; Delacroix et al., 2019; Arcelay et al., 2021; Sima et al., 2020). The concept of digitization involves the transformation of various aspects of human existence into a digitalized format. In the current context, the utilisation of applications like MySejahtera serves as a prime illustration of how the digitalization process facilitates the surveillance of individuals affected by Covid-19 and their close associates. The significance of digitalization is endorsed by the government of Selangor state. The Digitalization Matching Grant for Small and Medium Enterprises (SMEs) was implemented in 2021, offering support to an estimated 1100 owners of SMEs (Awani, 2021). The Internet of Things (IoT) is a crucial element. The Internet of Things (IoT) is a technology framework that enables the linking of electricity-equipped items to the Internet. The gadget exhibits a broad spectrum of attributes, including but not limited to mobile phones, laptops, cars, aircraft engines, and several other items.

The advent of the digital realm has transformed the Internet into a medium for social media, exerting a significant impact on diverse segments of society, particularly the youth. Social media refers to a compilation of online apps that are constructed based on the principles and technological advancements of Web 2.0 (Kaplan & Haenlein, 2010). According to Kaplan and Haenlein (2010), social media can be categorised into distinct classifications, namely information sharing, social networking sites, virtual game worlds, and virtual social worlds. According to Safko (2010), additional classifications of social media include social networks, visual media sharing encompassing photo, audio, video, and broadcast content, as well as online gaming. The present circumstances subject the youth in Selangor to direct exposure to ideological, cultural, entertainment, and foreign influences, devoid of proper guidance. The escalating prevalence of social media addiction on an annual basis is anticipated to yield adverse consequences, not only for the younger population but also for the nation as a whole (Malaysia Youth Index, 2019). This phenomenon is anticipated to exert an influence on psychological and social dimensions (Reinecke & Trepte, 2014; Ryan, Chester, Reece, & Xenos, 2014).

Social media has become an indispensable component of the field of information technology and undeniably assumes a pivotal function in augmenting social capital. Contemporary social media sites, such as Twitter, Facebook, Instagram, TikTok, and Bigo, offer a multitude of benefits to their respective users. Robotic technology is attracting the attention and capturing the interest of various stakeholders, alongside social media. According to Bernama (2018), the Selangor state government has demonstrated a strong dedication to the progress of robotic technology, as exemplified by the development of Malaysia's inaugural robotics excellence centre in Selangor.

There has been an increase in the public's adoption of digitalization projects, as more people are showing interest and actively participating in the digital world (Jaspers & Pearson, 2022; Atie et al., 2022). The societal acceptance of digitization, social media, Internet of Things (IoT), and robotic technology has witnessed a notable rise owing to their favourable influence on social capital. Arcelay et al. (2021) and Sima et al. (2020) conducted research that illustrates the positive correlation between individuals' digital competencies in the domains of Internet of Things (IoT), Artificial Intelligence (AI), and big data, and their increased career opportunities. Likewise, the aforementioned study suggests that the acquisition of these digital competencies acts as a stimulus for employees to actively seek out novel information, motivates them to allocate more time to their tasks, and enhances overall workplace communication.

Fink et al. (2020) and Delacroix et al. (2019) have undertaken research that illustrates the potential of leveraging Facebook as a social media platform to augment entrepreneurial capabilities. More precisely, it has the ability to foster innovation, elevate the perception of product excellence, reduce operational costs, strengthen marketing expertise, allow efficient communication, and boost entrepreneurial confidence.

The impact of social media on the lives of young individuals in Selangor, Malaysia is substantial. Research has indicated a significant rise in the utilisation of social media platforms among young individuals in Malaysia (Abdullah et al., 2021). The increased involvement with social platforms has consequences in all areas of their lives. For example, a study conducted by Ismail et al. (2021) shown that social media had a significant impact on the political engagement of young individuals in Malaysia. Furthermore, the scholarly literature has brought attention to the influence of social media on the efficacy of digital entrepreneurs within the nation, revealing a robust correlation between the utilisation of social media platforms and the achievement of entrepreneurial objectives (Kanapathipillai & Kumaran, 2022).

Moreover, the impact of social media encompasses various domains, including health promotion and lifestyle programmes specifically aimed at the younger demographic. A study conducted by Ayub et al. (2019) investigated the successful integration of healthy lifestyle campaign characteristics with social media features to encourage Malaysian youth to adopt better habits. Nevertheless, it is imperative to take into account the potential risks associated with excessive utilisation of social media platforms, specifically in relation to the mental well-being of adolescents (Halim et al., 2023).

In addition, social media functions as a medium for cultural education and narrative construction, providing young individuals with the chance to augment their cultural understanding and participate in cooperative digital accounts (Dahdal, 2019). Digital media plays a pivotal role in fostering identity formation, facilitating social relationships, and enhancing vocational competence among young individuals (Good, 2021). According to Stevens et al. (2016), social media platforms have the potential to serve as digital third spaces in impoverished neighbourhoods, facilitating opportunities for social engagement and fostering community development.

In summary, the digital and social media environment exerts a substantial impact on the conduct, perspectives, and encounters of young individuals residing in Selangor, Malaysia. It is vital to comprehend the diverse effects of social media on different facets of adolescent existence in order to formulate focused interventions, foster constructive involvement, and alleviate any hazards linked to excessive utilisation of digital media.

## SELANGOR'S YOUTH AND ARTIFICIAL INTELLIGENCE

The prevalence of information and artificial intelligence (AI) integration among the youth in Selangor, Malaysia, has witnessed a notable increase. The current development of artificial intelligence (AI) has had a profound influence on multiple facets of society, especially the younger population (Aishwarya et al., 2022). Furthermore, the application of geospatial data and artificial intelligence (AI) technology has had an impact on the social behaviours of young individuals, as evidenced by a research investigation centred on Nigerian youth (Onwubere & Osuji, 2021). The impact of technical improvements extends beyond social behaviours, encompassing the analysis of diseases such as the 2019 Novel Coronavirus in locations like Selangor, Malaysia (Gani et al., 2023).

Through an examination of the convergence between information technology, artificial intelligence (AI), and social behaviours among young folks, it becomes apparent that these breakthroughs are significantly influencing the manner in which young people engage with technology, information, and one another in the era of digitalization. A complete examination of the impact of technology on adolescents in Selangor, Malaysia necessitates a thorough understanding of these processes.

The younger generation in Selangor, Malaysia, is progressively interacting with information technology and artificial intelligence in the era of digitalization. Research has indicated that the social interactions of young people are undergoing rapid changes as a result of technological advancements (Armstrong Carter & Telzer, 2021). The progression encompasses various elements, including cyberbullying, which affects LGBTQ children to varying degrees, ranging from 10.5% to 71.3% (Abreu & Kenny, 2017). Furthermore, the utilisation of digital media assumes a pivotal position in influencing the social dynamics of adolescents, underscoring the significance of comprehending the ramifications of technology on the younger generation (Wong, 2020).

Moreover, studies suggest that young individuals actively engage with digital health technologies, leveraging online knowledge to enhance their well-being and seeking emotional assistance via social media platforms (Xie et al., 2023). Researchers have created digital treatments to improve the adherence of young people living with HIV to antiretroviral medicine. These approaches have shown encouraging benefits in enhancing health outcomes (Griffee et al., 2022). In addition, the use of digital platforms has enhanced the propensity of transition-aged kids to seek assistance for mental health issues, so granting them more convenient means of accessing mental health services (Stunden et al., 2020).

It is crucial to take into account the involvement of young people with digital media as they traverse the digital environment. Libraries, as an example, assume a pivotal role in facilitating the educational development of young individuals and promoting digital learning. This underscores the need of engaging in participatory design and fostering collaboration with young individuals (Yip et al., 2019). Moreover, research has shown that digital games are especially appealing to young people and children, emphasising the possibility of utilising digital play for educational objectives (Toh & Lim, 2020).

In summary, the advent of the digital era offers a range of prospects and obstacles for the younger generation residing in Selangor, Malaysia. It is vital to comprehend the ramifications of information technology and artificial intelligence on the younger generation in order to foster their welfare and leverage the advantages of digital progress in the realms of education, healthcare, and social engagements.

## METHODOLOGY

In the initial phase of the study, a stratified sampling technique will be employed, wherein the selection of strata will be based on criteria such as age, racial composition, and geography. The implementation of pre-testing and pilot testing will be undertaken to build research instruments. During the second stage, a purposive sampling strategy will be employed to pick a total of 696 individuals from two distinct strata: youth (15-30 years old) and young adults (30-40 years old).

A set of 11 items was constructed and a pre-test process was conducted, involving 5 respondents from the young group (15-30 years old) and youth adults (30-40 years old), in order to assess the appropriateness of the items.

Following the implementation of the pre-test instrument evaluation process, the subsequent phase entails conducting a pilot study, specifically a pilot test, involving a total of 30 respondents. These respondents are divided into two distinct groups, representing 9 districts in Selangor, namely Gombak, Petaling, Kuala Langat, Hulu Langat, Kuala Selangor, Hulu Selangor, Sabak Bernam, Klang, and Sepang. The results of the pilot study have been subjected to analysis, leading to the development of an instrument of 11 items by the researcher. The quantitative data collection process for this study includes a total of 696 respondents from 9 districts in Selangor, consisting of both youth group participants and youth adults.

The study involved a total of 696 young individuals residing in Selangor, Malaysia. In Malaysia, the term "youth" generally encompasses individuals between the ages of 15 and 40. Nevertheless, the meaning of this concept may differ across various agencies and organisations, contingent upon their individual objectives, such as electoral processes, research endeavours, or the advancement of youth development (National Youth Policy of Malaysia, 1997). This study classifies adolescents into two distinct categories: 15–30-year-olds, referred to as youth, and 31-40 year olds, referred to as youth adults.

*Table 1. Variable*

| Variable | N | % |
|---|---|---|
| **Youth Categories** | | |
| Youth | 404 | 58 |
| Youth Adult | 292 | 42 |
| **Totals** | **696** | **100** |
| **Gender** | | |
| Male | 337 | 48.42 |
| Female | 359 | 51.58 |
| **Totals** | **696** | **100** |

## Measures

The research employed a quantitative methodology, wherein data was gathered from a sample of 696 participants. The variables used to assess the level of achievement in understanding quantitative data are categorised into three distinct groups: Low (0.00-1.666), Moderate (1.667-3.333), and High (3.334-5.00). The following items are as follows:

1. Internet access in my area needs to be strengthened to create more job opportunities.
2. The use of technology needs to be expanded to enhance my quality of life.
3. I am willing to use the latest technology to generate better income.
4. I believe the use of technology opens up greater marketing opportunities in business.
5. The use of technology can improve the quality of my work.
6. The use of technology can increase the quantity of my work output.
7. I believe the robotics industry is starting to be accepted by the community.
8. I often use smartphone applications to facilitate transactions (e.g., paying bills).
9. I use social media (e.g., Twitter/Facebook/Instagram/Clubhouse) most of the time to seek/share information.
10. I discuss new technologies being developed domestically or internationally.

11. I feel confident using digital platforms (e.g., Selangkah, Smart Selangor Parking) provided by the State Government.

## FINDING AND DISCUSSION

For the purpose of quantitative data interpretation in Phase 3, the item performance level indicator for each domain is delineated into three distinct levels: Low (0.00-1.666), Medium (1.667-3.333), and High (3.334-5.00), as depicted in Figure 1.

*Table 2. Level indicator*

| Low | Moderate | High |
|-----|----------|------|
| (0.00 – 1.666) | (1.667 – 3.333) | (3.334-5.00) |

*Table 3.*

| Item | Score Mean | |
|------|:---:|:---:|
| | **Youth (15 – 30 year)** | **Youth Adult (31-40 year)** |
| Internet access in my area needs to be strengthened to create more job opportunities. | 4.28 | 4.20 |
| The use of technology needs to be expanded to enhance my quality of life. | 4.19 | 4.08 |
| I am willing to use the latest technology to generate better income. | 4.20 | 4.14 |
| I believe the use of technology opens greater marketing opportunities in business. | 4.19 | 4.08 |
| The use of technology can improve the quality of my work. | 4.12 | 4.06 |
| The use of technology can increase the quantity of my work output. | 4.09 | 4.01 |
| I believe the robotics industry is starting to be accepted by the community. | 3.61 | 3.71 |
| I often use smartphone applications to facilitate transactions (e.g., paying bills). | 4.24 | 4.19 |
| I use social media (e.g., Twitter/Facebook/Instagram/Clubhouse) most of the time to seek/ share information. | 4.32 | 4.17 |
| I discuss new technologies being developed domestically or internationally. | 3.64 | 3.62 |
| I feel confident using digital platforms (e.g., Selangkah, Smart Selangor Parking) provided by the State Government. | 3.54 | 3.72 |

The research findings pertaining to information technology and artificial intelligence are shown in Table 1, comprising a total of eleven items. Consistent with expectations, the youthful respondents achieved the highest score of 4.04, while the adult respondents had a score of 3.99.

The subsequent emphasis lies in the comparative analysis conducted using items to assess the domains of information technology and artificial intelligence, including two distinct cohorts of participants. The three items that recorded the highest minimum scores for the youth group are 'I use social media (e.g., Twitter / Facebook / Instagram / Clubhouse) most of the time to search for or share information,' 'Internet access in my area needs to be strengthened to open up more job opportunities,' and 'I often use smartphone applications to facilitate transactions (e.g., paying bills). Conversely, the three items that obtained the lowest minimum scores are'my confidence in utilising digital platforms (Selangkah,

Smart Selangor Parking) offered by the State Government,''my belief in the growing acceptance of the robotics industry by society,' and'my engagement in conversations about emerging technologies both domestically and internationally.'

The analysis of the adult youth group reveals that the three items with the highest minimum scores for this group are: 'Enhancing Internet access in my area is necessary to expand job prospects,' 'Frequently utilising smartphone applications for transactional purposes (such as bill payments),' and 'Frequently employing social media platforms (such as Twitter, Facebook, Instagram, or Clubhouse) to search for or exchange information.' In contrast, the three elements that exhibited the lowest minimum scores are 'I engage in conversations regarding the societal acceptance of the robotics industry,' and 'I possess a sense of assurance while utilising digital platforms such as Selangkah and Smart Selangor Parking, which are offered by the State Government.'

Phase 3 of the survey revealed that both youth and young adults concurred that reliable internet connection can foster an increase in online enterprises, hence resulting in a higher number of prosperous entrepreneurs in Selangor. Simultaneously, reliable internet connectivity streamlines the online job search and application procedure for individuals. There have been efforts to enhance free internet access, such as WiFi Smart Selangor and Selangor Internet Data. However, there is still potential for development in the quality and quantity of these services, particularly in rural regions.

## CONCLUSION

The utilisation of social media platforms significantly contributes to the augmentation of human capital within the state of Selangor. The use of social media holds considerable importance within the youth demographic, but the adult youth cohort predominantly employs social media platforms for purposes such as entertainment, communication, social interaction, accessing relevant information, and engaging in online commercial activities. Both age groups utilise smartphone applications to streamline their daily routines. In addition to their time, energy, and cost-saving capabilities, smartphone applications provide a multitude of other advantages in both personal and professional contexts. The elderly's favourable reception of technology serves as evidence that cellphones not only contribute to the development of human capital among the younger generation.

Despite the potential for promising job opportunities in the robotics business, the level of public acceptance towards this sector remains incomplete. One of the primary factors contributing to this predicament is their apprehension that reliance on the robotics industry may result in public unemployment issues. Additionally, it has been asserted that the absence of training facilities and limited exposure has resulted in a lack of preparedness among the general population to embrace the robotics sector. There is a prevailing belief that the robotics sector confers greater advantages to corporations rather than individuals.

The provision of numerous digital platforms by the government, such as Selangkah and Smart Selangor Parking, is an indisputable fact. Nevertheless, the research revealed that there is a lack of awareness among individuals regarding the presence of these platforms. This situation is disadvantageous for both parties involved. Firstly, the residents of Selangor are unable to reap the advantages of these digital platforms. Secondly, the state government has invested a significant amount of money in developing these digital platforms, but they have not successfully reached their intended audience. The survey additionally revealed a scarcity of conversations pertaining to the local and international development of novel technologies. This scenario can be attributed to two potential factors: firstly, a lack of awareness regarding the existence of these novel technologies, and secondly, a preference for utilising established technology.

# REFERENCES

Abdullah, N., Hassan, I., Ahmad, M., Hassan, N., & Ismail, M. (2021). Social media, youths and political participation in malaysia: A review of literature. *International Journal of Academic Research in Business & Social Sciences*, 11(4). 10.6007/IJARBSS/v11-i4/9578

Aishwarya, G., Satyanarayana, V., Singh, M., & Kumar, S. (2022). *Contemporary evolution of artificial intelligence (ai): an overview and applications.* 10.3233/ATDE220731

Arcelay, I., Goti, A., Oyarbide-Zubillaga, A., Akyazi, T., Alberdi, E., & Garcia-Bringas, P. (2021). Definition of the future skills needs of job profiles in the renewable energy sector. *Energies*, 14(9), 2609. 10.3390/en14092609

Armstrong-Carter, E., & Telzer, E. (2021). Advancing measurement and research on youths' prosocial behavior in the digital age. *Child Development Perspectives*, 15(1), 31–36. 10.1111/cdep.12396

Astro Awani. (2019). *Diambil dari: Selangor catat jumlah tertinggi laporang pencemaran.* https://www.astroawani.com/beritamalaysia/selangor-catat-jumlah-tertinggilaporan-pencemaran-223806

Atie, E., Ivanova, O., & Švagždienė, M. (2022). Kardiogeninio šoko etiologija ir diagnostika. Sveikatos mokslai= Health sciences in Eastern Europe. *Vilnius:Sveikatos mokslai, 32*, Nr. 1.

Ayub, S., Hassim, N., Yahya, A., Hamzah, M., & Bakar, M. (2019). Exploring the characteristics of healthy lifestyle campaign on social media: A case study on fit malaysia. *Jurnal Komunikasi Malaysian Journal of Communication*, 35(4), 322–336. 10.17576/JKMJC-2019-3504-20

Ballestar, M. T., García-Lazaro, A., Sainz, J., & Sanz, I. (2022). Why is your company not robotic? The technology and human capital needed by firms to become robotic. *Journal of Business Research*, 142, 328–343. 10.1016/j.jbusres.2021.12.061

Dahdal, S. (2019). Cultural educating of palestinian youth through collaborative digital storytelling. *E-Learning and Digital Media*, 16(2), 136–150. 10.1177/2042753019828354

Delacroix, E., Parguel, B., & Benoit-Moreau, F. (2019). Digital subsistence entrepreneurs on Facebook. *Technological Forecasting and Social Change*, 146, 887–899. 10.1016/j.techfore.2018.06.018

Dixon, J., Hong, B., & Wu, L. (2021). The robot revolution: Managerial and employment consequences for firms. *Management Science*, 67(9), 5586–5605. 10.1287/mnsc.2020.3812

Fink, L., Shao, J., Lichtenstein, Y., & Haefliger, S. (2020). The ownership of digital infrastructure: Exploring the deployment of software libraries in a digital innovation cluster. *Journal of Information Technology*, 35(3), 251–269. 10.1177/0268396220936705

Gani, N., Dom, N., Dapari, R., & Precha, N. (2023). Spatial and temporal analysis of 2019 novel coronavirus (2019-ncov) cases in selangor, malaysia. *The Indonesian Journal of Geography*, 55(1), 148. 10.22146/ijg.73633

Good, B. (2021). Digital pathways to wellness among youth in residential treatment: An exploratory qualitative study. *Journal of Adolescent Research*, 38(5), 803–841. 10.1177/07435584211014884

Griffee, K., Martin, R., Chory, A., & Vreeman, R. (2022). A systematic review of digital interventions to improve art adherence among youth living with hiv in sub-saharan africa. *AIDS Research and Treatment*, 2022, 1–7. 10.1155/2022/988630636199816

Halim, M., Ibrahim, M., Adib, N., Hashim, H., & Omar, R. (2023). Exploring hazard of social media use on adolescent mental health. https://doi.org/10.21203/rs.3.rs-2961547/v1

Indeks Belia Malaysia. (2015). *Institut Penyelidikan Pembangunan Belia Malaysia*. IYRES.

Ismail, M., Hassan, N., Nor, M., Zain, M., & Samsu, K. (2021). The influence of political socialization among educated youth at universiti putra malaysia. *International Journal of Academic Research in Business & Social Sciences*, 11(12). 10.6007/IJARBSS/v11-i12/11941

Jaspers, E. D., & Pearson, E. (2022). Consumers' acceptance of domestic Internet-of-Things: The role of trust and privacy concerns. *Journal of Business Research*, 142, 255–265. 10.1016/j.jbusres.2021.12.043

Kanapathipillai, K., & Kumaran, S. (2022). An empirical study on the influence of social capital on the digital entrepreneurs' performance during the omicron variant wave (sars-cov-2: b.1.1.529). *European Journal of Management and Marketing Studies*, 7(2). 10.46827/ejmms.v7i2.1227

Onwubere, C., & Osuji, H. (2021). Utilisation des données géospatiales et des technologies d'intelligence artificielle et évolution des pratiques sociales chez les jeunes nigérians. *Communication Technologies Et Développement*, (10). 10.4000/ctd.5525

Sima, V., Gheorghe, I. G., Subić, J., & Nancu, D. (2020). Influences of the industry 4.0 revolution on the human capital development and consumer behavior: A systematic review. *Sustainability (Basel)*, 12(10), 4035. 10.3390/su12104035

Stevens, R., Gilliard-Matthews, S., Dunaev, J., Woods, M., & Brawner, B. (2016). The digital hood: Social media use among youth in disadvantaged neighborhoods. *New Media & Society*, 19(6), 950–967. 10.1177/1461444815625941 28694736

Stunden, C., Zasada, J., VanHeerwaarden, N., Hollenberg, E., Abi-Jaoudé, A., Chaim, G., Cleverley, K., Henderson, J., Johnson, A., Levinson, A., Lo, B., Robb, J., Shi, J., Voineskos, A., & Wiljer, D. (2020). Help-seeking behaviors of transition-aged youth for mental health concerns: Qualitative study. *Journal of Medical Internet Research*, 22(10), e18514. 10.2196/1851433016882

Toh, W., & Lim, F. (2020). Using video games for learning: Developing a metalanguage for digital play. *Games and Culture*, 16(5), 583–610. 10.1177/1555412020921339

Wong, M. (2020). Hidden youth? a new perspective on the sociality of young people 'withdrawn' in the bedroom in a digital age. *New Media & Society*, 22(7), 1227–1244. 10.1177/1461444820912530

Xie, L., Housni, A., Nakhla, M., Cianci, R., Leroux, C., Costa, D., & Brazeau, A. (2023). Adaptation of an adult web application for type 1 diabetes self-management to youth using the behavior change wheel to tailor the needs of health care transition: Qualitative interview study. *JMIR Diabetes*, 8, e42564. 10.2196/4256437121571

Yip, J., Lee, K., & Lee, J. (2019). Design partnerships for participatory librarianship: A conceptual model for understanding librarians co designing with digital youth. *Journal of the Association for Information Science and Technology*, 71(10), 1242–1256. 10.1002/asi.24320

# Chapter 14
# AI on Loss in Decision-Making and Its Associations With Digital Disorder, Socio-Demographics, and Physical Health Outcomes in Iran

**Fakhroddin Noorbehbahani**

*Faculty of Computer Engineering, University of Isfahan, Isfahan, Iran*

**Zeinab Zaremohzzabieh**

https://orcid.org/0000-0002-1497-7942

*Women and Family Studies Research Center, University of Religions and Denominations, Qom, Iran*

**Hooman Hoghooghi Esfahani**

*Faculty of Computer Engineering, University of Isfahan, Isfahan, Iran*

**Soroush Bajoghli**

*Faculty of Computer Engineering, University of Isfahan, Isfahan, Iran*

**Mahboobeh Moosivand**

*Women Research Center, Alzahra University, Tehran, Iran*

## ABSTRACT

*This study aimed to explore the connections between digital disorder, socio-demographics, physical health outcomes, and artificial intelligence (AI) on decision-making loss. The study relied on data from 550 people in Isfahan, Iran. The results showed that while decision-making loss was slightly more prevalent in females than males, this difference was not statistically significant. However, individuals aged between 26-35 showed a significant correlation with decision-making loss, while other age groups did not. Neither education level nor employment status demonstrated significant associations with decision-making loss, nor did the frequency of device use affect it either. Participants who experienced decision-making loss scored significantly higher on digital disorder overall score and specific indicators, such as addiction*

DOI: 10.4018/979-8-3693-3350-1.ch014

*to social media and the internet, compared to those who did not. They also reported higher scores on various physical health outcomes related to device usage.*

## INTRODUCTION

Artificial intelligence (AI) is being used for decision-making across various industries, which has had a profound impact on our daily lives (Duan et al. 2019). While AI facilitates efficient data processing and decision-making, its integration has raised concerns about its potential to replace human cognitive functions (Ahmad et al. 2023; Kushwaha et al. 2023). Despite its advantages, AI's emergence presents challenges that diminish human involvement and sideline critical thinking and creative problem-solving abilities (Dwivedi et al. 2021). This shift prompts a reassessment of the human role in decision-making, as AI increasingly supplants intuitive analysis and cognitive processes.

Moreover, as AI-driven decision-making gains prominence, its interactions with human behavior and psychology come into focus (Fast and Schroeder 2020; Wang et al. 2022). Research suggests a correlation between excessive use of social networking services (SNS) and impaired decision-making, underscoring the complex interplay between technology addiction and cognitive functions (Meshi et al. 2019; Aydın et al. 2020; Wegmann et al. 2021). Furthermore, studies examining internet gaming disorder (IGD) highlight deficits in decision-making and impulse control, shedding light on the neurological implications of digital behavior (Wang et al., 2017). These findings underscore the need to explore the relationship between AI-driven decision-making and digital disorders, such as technology addiction disorders (TAD) and phubbing behavior, to better understand their impact on human decision-making processes.

Beyond individual decision-making, the societal implications of AI-based systems raise ethical concerns, particularly regarding gender bias and fairness in outcomes (Gupta et al. 2022; Nadeem et al. 2022). Reports indicate potential biases in AI algorithms, amplifying existing gender disparities and underscoring the importance of examining decision-making systems for equitable outcomes (Cirillo et al. 2020; O'Connor and Liu 2023). Furthermore, the adverse effects of biased decision-making extend beyond individuals, affecting families and communities, necessitating a comprehensive examination of AI's societal impact (Bonab et al. 2021; Bellantuono et al. 2023).

In addition to socio-demographic considerations, the reliance on AI for decision-making raises apprehensions about its effects on physical health outcomes (Zohuri and Rahmani 2023). Prolonged screen time and improper ergonomic practices have been linked to various health issues, including digital eye strain, poor posture, and repetitive stress injuries. Moreover, sedentary lifestyles stemming from excessive screen time contribute to obesity and cardiovascular risks, highlighting the multifaceted health implications of AI-driven decision-making.

However, to effectively address the psychosocial and health challenges associated with AI-driven decision-making, there is a pressing need for rigorous scientific inquiry. This is particularly important in non-Western contexts like Iran. Current literature gaps underscore the necessity of investigating the prevalence of AI-induced decision-making loss and its association with socio-demographic factors and digital disorders (Varma et al. 2023; Bâra and Oprea 2024). This study also aims to elucidate the complex interrelations between AI-driven decision-making, digital disorders, and physical health outcomes among the Isfahanian population. It offers valuable insights for policy and intervention strategies.

## MATERIALS AND METHODS

### Research Design

We used a cross-sectional survey design to deepen the understanding of how AI impacts decision-making.

### Participants and Procedures

The data for this study were collected in Isfahan, Iran, from November 2023 to January 2024 using the cross-sectional technique. The study aimed to focus on people living in Isfahan who use the internet. Participants were required to be internet users living in Isfahan. A sample size of 550 was determined based on Faul et al.'s (2009) recommendation for effect sizes. G*Power software was used to analyze associations among latent variables and invalidated relationships (Baroudi and Orlikowski 1988). Ethical approval was obtained from the Ethics Committee for Research Involving Human Subjects (IR. ALZAHRA.REC.1402.032).

Participants were randomly selected from Isfahan's population using an online random number generator. After approval, questionnaires were distributed electronically, accompanied by personalized invitation letters sent via email. The survey remained open for eight weeks, with email reminders sent at 1-, 3-, and 5-weeks post-invitation. All 553 distributed questionnaires were completed and returned, achieving a 100% response rate. At the baseline, the participants had a mean age of 31.67 years, with 58.8% being female. Additionally, 42% had a diploma or less, and 44.8% were employed. Regarding device usage, 39.6% used tablets and mobile devices for over 8 hours daily, while 27.7% used them for 5 to 8 hours. The remaining participants used such devices for 5 hours or less, with 15.6% using them for less than 3 hours.

### Measures

### AI on Loss in Decision-Making

We have utilized an evaluation method developed by Niese (2019) to examine the impact of AI on decision-making in situations of loss. Participants were asked if they experienced any difficulty in making a decision and whether they relied on AI for the final decision. The possible answers are detailed in Table 1.

*Table 1. Self-reported AI on loss in decision-making*

| Item | Frequency -N (%) | Baseline | | Overall (N=552) |
|---|---|---|---|---|
| | | Males (N=227) | Females (N=325) | |
| Have you ever faced difficulty in making a decision and turned to AI for the final decision? | Never | 77(33.8) | 124(38.2) | 201 (36.3) |
| | Rarely | 75(32.9) | 108(33.2) | 183 (33.1) |
| | Sometimes | 21(9.2) | 23(7.1) | 44 (8) |
| | Often | 30(13.2) | 48(14.8) | 78 (14.1) |
| | Always | 24 (10.5) | 22(6.8) | 46 (8.3) |
| | Missing | 1(.45) | - | 1 (.2) |

## Frequency of Tablet or Mobile Phone Use

The survey on electronic news consumption via mobile devices conducted by Yu et al. (2022) included a question about the frequency of mobile phone or tablet usage. The respondents' answers were classified into four categories, based on the number of hours spent using the devices per day: less than 3 hours (≤3), 3 to 5 hours (3-5), 5 to 8 hours (5-8), and more than 8 hours (8≥).

## Digital Disorder

This assessment scale comprises five crucial items that evaluate a range of problematic behaviors and psychological issues that arise due to excessive or compulsive use of digital technologies. The five items include digital hoarding (Zaremohzzabieh et al. 2024), technology addiction disorders (TAD), phubbing behavior (Rahman et al. 2022), and PIU (Chassiakos and Stager 2020; Lérida-Ayala et al. 2022). The respondents are required to rate each item on a five-point Likert scale, with the options ranging from strongly disagree (1) to strongly agree (5).

## Physical Health Outcomes

This scale focuses on the negative effects that excessive or improper use of digital technologies can have on physical health. These outcomes can include a variety of issues such as digital eye strain (Rosenfield et al. 2020), poor posture (Osama et al. 2018), repetitive stress injuries (L. B. Tucker et al. 2019), a sedentary lifestyle (Tremblay et al. 2010), carpal tunnel syndrome (Zamborsky et al. 2017), headaches (Thomée et al. 2010), digital hunchback (R. Wang et al. 2023), text neck (Vijayakumar et al. 2018), radiation exposure (Brodić and Amelio 2015), hearing problems (Fasanya and Strong 2019), increased risk of blood clots (C. M. Tucker et al. 2019), cardiovascular diseases, prosuicide, and cybersuicide (Charmaraman et al. 2020; Moir et al. 2023). The respondents were asked to rate each item on a five-point Likert scale, which ranges from strongly disagree (1) to strongly agree (5).

## Data Analyses

The purpose of the study was to investigate how frequently AI influences decision-making loss, and how it correlates with the socio-demographic characteristics and frequency of tablet or mobile phone use of individuals. The researchers used mixed effects logistic regression to explore these associations. The binary variable measured decision-making loss due to AI, indicating whether individuals reported AI influence on their final decision. Odds ratios (OR), 95% confidence intervals (CI), and p-values were calculated. The researchers also employed separate mixed effects linear regression models to investigate the unadjusted and adjusted relationships between the binary AI-induced decision-making loss measures and digital disorder and negative physical outcomes. The adjusted analyses controlled for gender, education, employment, and age categories. However, many measures of digital disorder and physical health outcomes displayed floor or ceiling effects. To account for non-normality in the underlying statistic, bias-corrected bootstrap 95% CI based on 2000 replications was reported, which enhances the accuracy of CI estimation (Carpenter and Bithell 2000). The statistical significance (p < 0.05) of associations with AI-induced decision-making loss was determined from the bootstrap 95%.

## RESULTS

The study aimed to investigate the impact of socio-demographic characteristics, frequency of mobile phone or tablet use, and AI on decision-making loss. The study found that there was a slightly higher prevalence of decision-making loss among females as compared to males, with an odds ratio (OR) of 1.108 (95% CI: 0.888-1.037), but this difference was not statistically significant (p = .292). The study also found that individuals aged 26-35 were significantly associated with decision-making loss (OR: 1.169, 95% CI: 1.054-1.296, p = .009), while other age groups did not show significant associations. However, education level and employment status did not exhibit significant associations with decision-making loss (p = .638 and p = .237, respectively). The frequency of mobile phone or tablet use was also not found to be significantly correlated with decision-making loss (p = .242). Based on these findings, the study suggests that age, particularly the 26-35 age group, may play a role in decision-making loss caused by AI, while gender, education level, employment status, and frequency of device use did not show any significant associations (Table 2).

*Table 2. Associations between socio-demographic characteristics and frequency of tablet or mobile phone use, and AI on loss in decision-making*

| AI on decision-making loss | n/N (%) | OR | 95% CI | p |
|---|---|---|---|---|
| **Gender** | | | | .292 |
| Male | 73/154 (47%) | 1 | . | |
| Female | 91/234 (38%) | 1.108 | (.888-1.037) | |
| **Age(years)** | | | | .009 |
| ≥25 | 87/150(.58) | 1 | - | |
| 26-35 | 19/35(0.54) | 1.169 | (1.054-1.296) | |
| 36-45 | 34/102(0.33) | 1.151 | (.992-1.336) | |
| 46≤ | 23/86 (0.26) | 1.040 | (.927-1.166) | |
| **Level of education** | | | | .638 |
| High diploma or less | 65/167(0.38) | 1 | - | |
| Bachelor degree | 47/112(0.41) | .956 | (.872-1.049) | |
| Master's degree and above | 51/157(0.32) | .971 | (.878-1.074) | |
| **Employment status** | | | | .237 |
| Employed | 78/169(0.46) | 1 | - | |
| Unemployed | 56/155(0.36) | 1.052 | (.967-1.143) | |
| **Frequency of tablet or mobile phone use** | | | | .242 |
| 3 ≤ | 28/58(0.48) | 1 | - | |
| 3-5 | 34/56(0.60) | .942 | (.841-1.056) | |
| 5-8 | 44/109(0.40) | .963 | (.853-1.086) | |
| 8≥ | 58/160(0.36) | 1.054 | (.920-1.206) | |

The study aimed to compare the measures of individuals who experienced AI-related loss in decision-making with those who did not report such loss. The unadjusted estimates showed that participants with AI-related decision-making loss had significantly higher scores on the overall digital disorder scale compared to those without this loss (Estimate: 10.896, 95% CI: 7.61-16.352). Similar results were observed across specific digital disorder indicators, such as feeling anxious or uneasy when the phone is not nearby, addiction to the internet and social media, hoarding digital information without deleting it, and ignoring people in social situations due to phone usage. Additionally, participants with AI-related decision-making loss reported higher scores on physical health outcomes, including digital eye strain, bad posture, physical inactivity, carpal tunnel syndrome, headaches, hunchback problems, neck problems (Text Neck), exposure to WIFI radiation, hearing problems from device usage, risk of blood clots, cardiovascular diseases, and memory problems (Table 3).

*Table 3. AI for decision-making and its associations with digital disorder and physical health outcomes*

| | | Difference in measures between AI on loss in decision-making vs. non-AI on loss in decision-making | | | |
| | | Unadjusted | | Adjusted | |
| | | Estimate | 95% CI | Estimate | 95% CI |
| No. | Overall score on 0-40 point scale, subscale on 0-10 point scale: higher scores indicate greater difficulty | | | | |
| | **Digital disorder overall score** | 10.896 | (7.61-16.352) | 10.767 | (6.913-16.770) |
| 1 | I feel uneasy and anxious when my phone is not nearby. | 1.812 | (1.55-2.130) | 1.80 | (1.557-2.088) |
| 2 | I am addicted to the internet and social media. | 1.805 | (1.56-2.089) | 1.768 | (1.502-2.081) |
| 3 | I save digital information and files without deleting them, expecting them to be useful later | 1.678 | (1.502-2.08) | 1.675 | (1.448-1.938) |
| 4 | I sometimes ignore people I'm talking to in social situations by checking my phone for calls or texts. | 1.855 | (1.577-2.182) | 1.854 | (1.549-2.22) |
| 5 | I tend to use my computer, phone, and tablet excessively before bedtime. | 1.574 | (1.357-1.825) | 1.564 | (1.327-1.842) |
| | **Physical health outcomes overall score** | 3.335 | (2.466-4.510) | 3.21 | (2.304-4.471) |
| 1 | I experience digital eye strain from using computers, mobile phones, laptops, etc. | 1.422 | (1.227-1.679) | 1.402 | (1.191-1.650) |
| 2 | I sit in a bad way when using a computer, mobile, and... | 1.541 | (1.326-1.792) | 1.526 | (1.289-1.805) |
| 3 | I often use digital tools, which causes pain in my neck, shoulders, and upper body. | 1.352 | (1.180-1.55) | 1.335 | (1.148-1.55) |
| 4 | I tend to be physically inactive when I spend time online. | 1.534 | (1.299-1.813) | 1.478 | (1.277-1.711) |
| 5 | I experience carpal tunnel syndrome when I am online | 1.278 | (1.097-1.488) | 1.226 | (1.033-1.455) |
| 6 | I'm experiencing headaches from prolonged use of computers, laptops, and other similar devices. ... | 1.498 | (1.267-1.772) | 1.480 | (1.273-1.727) |
| 7 | I have developed a hunchback problem due to prolonged use of digital tools. | 1.479 | (1.269-1.725) | 1.45 | (1.265-1.661) |
| 8 | I experience neck problems, particularly Forward Neck Posture (also known as Text Neck) when I spend time online. | 1.464 | (1279-1.677) | 1.406 | (1.206-1.638) |

continued on following page

*Table 3. Continued*

| | | Difference in measures between AI on loss in decision-making vs. non-AI on loss in decision-making | | | |
| | | Unadjusted | | Adjusted | |
| | | Estimate | 95% CI | Estimate | 95% CI |
| No. | Overall score on 0-40 point scale, subscale on 0-10 point scale: higher scores indicate greater difficulty | | | | |
| 9 | I am exposed to radiation from using WIFI. | 1.341 | (1.181-1.523) | 1.309 | (1.138-1.506) |
| 10 | I experience hearing problems due to excessive use of hands-free and loud headphones. | 1.667 | (1.408-1.973) | 1.579 | (1.318-1.893) |
| 11 | I have noticed that I am at a higher risk of developing blood clots when I spend a lot of time on the internet. | 2.028 | (1.496-2.749) | 1.916 | (1.468-2.501) |
| 12 | I experience cardiovascular diseases when I excessively use the internet. | 1.623 | (1.284-2.075) | 1.616 | (1.206-2.016) |
| 13 | I experience memory problems. | 1.558 | (1.347-1.803) | 1.535 | 1.306-1.804 |

After taking into account socio-demographic characteristics, the links between AI's impact on decision-making and digital disorder and physical health outcomes remained significant. The adjusted estimates demonstrated consistent patterns, with participants experiencing AI's impact on decision-making showing higher scores on the overall digital disorder score and its specific indicators, as well as physical health outcomes. These findings indicate a strong connection between AI's impact on decision-making and negative outcomes related to digital disorder and physical health. Therefore, addressing decision-making difficulties in individuals using AI may have implications for improving both digital well-being and physical health outcomes.

## DISCUSSION

The study's findings provide context and implications for policy and intervention strategies related to the complex relationship between AI-driven decision-making, digital disorders, and physical health outcomes, drawing on theoretical frameworks and existing literature.

Firstly, the prevalence of AI-induced decision-making loss among Isfahanian residents underscores the growing reliance on AI technologies for decision-making processes. This aligns with theories of technological determinism, which suggest that technological advancements shape societal behaviors and norms, potentially diminishing human agency and decision-making autonomy (Jarrahi 2018). The observed variations in decision-making loss across gender and age groups raise questions about socio-demographic influences on technology adoption and decision-making behaviors, echoing sociological theories of technology adoption and diffusion (Rogers 1995). Further exploration of these relationships is warranted to inform targeted interventions and policy responses.

Secondly, the study reveals significant associations between AI-induced decision-making loss and digital disorder, as well as adverse physical health outcomes. These findings are consistent with theories of media ecology, which posit that prolonged exposure to digital technologies can disrupt human communication patterns and cognitive processes, leading to behavioral addictions and psychosocial disturbances (McLuhan 1964). Moreover, the observed links between decision-making loss and physical health issues underscore the embodied nature of technology use and its impact on ergonomic practices and musculoskeletal health (Osama et al. 2018). Integrating theories of human-computer interaction and ergonomics can inform interventions aimed at promoting digital wellness and mitigating the physical health consequences of excessive technology use.

Thirdly, the robust associations between decision-making difficulties and adverse health outcomes, independent of socio-demographic factors, highlight the need for comprehensive intervention strategies. Drawing on principles of health behavior change models, interventions should target individual-level factors, such as decision-making skills and technology use patterns, as well as environmental and policy-level determinants (Glanz et al. 2015). Additionally, the multidisciplinary nature of the observed associations underscores the importance of adopting an ecological approach that addresses the interplay between individual, interpersonal, community, and societal factors (Bronfenbrenner 1979). Collaboration between policymakers, educators, healthcare providers, and technology developers is essential to develop evidence-based interventions that promote digital well-being and mitigate the negative health effects of AI-driven decision-making.

In conclusion, the findings of this study provide valuable insights into the complex dynamics of AI-driven decision-making, digital disorders, and physical health outcomes. By grounding the discussion in theoretical frameworks and existing literature, this study informs policy and intervention strategies aimed at safeguarding individual well-being in an increasingly technology-driven society. Future research should continue to explore these relationships and evaluate the effectiveness of interventions aimed at promoting healthy technology use and enhancing decision-making skills in diverse populations.

## LIMITATIONS AND FUTURE STUDIES

Despite the valuable contributions of this study, several limitations should be acknowledged. The cross-sectional design of the study makes it difficult to establish causal relationships between the loss of decision-making abilities induced by AI, digital disorders, and physical health outcomes. Therefore, longitudinal studies are required to explore the temporal nature of these associations and provide insights into the directionality of effects over time.

Another limitation of the study is the use of self-reported measures, which may introduce response biases and social desirability effects. These factors could potentially influence the accuracy of the reported data. To improve the validity of findings, future research could incorporate objective measures of technology use and decision-making abilities. Furthermore, the study focused on a specific geographic region, Isfahan, Iran. As a result, the generalizability of the findings to other populations may be limited. To validate the robustness of observed associations across different socio-demographic groups, replication studies in diverse cultural contexts are warranted.

Building on the findings of this study, future research could explore several avenues to further advance our understanding of the impact of AI-driven decision-making on human well-being. Longitudinal studies could investigate the long-term effects of AI-induced decision-making loss on digital disorders and physical health outcomes. Qualitative research methods, such as interviews and focus groups, could complement quantitative findings by offering in-depth insights into individuals' experiences with AI technologies and their perceptions of decision-making processes. Additionally, intervention studies could evaluate the effectiveness of targeted interventions aimed at promoting digital literacy, enhancing decision-making skills, and mitigating the adverse effects of excessive technology use on health outcomes.

## CONFLICT OF INTEREST

We declare that there is no conflict of interest in relation to the research presented in this article. We have no financial interests or personal relationships that could influence or bias our work.

# REFERENCES

Aydın, O., Obuća, F., Boz, C., & Ünal-Aydın, P. (2020). Associations between executive functions and problematic social networking sites use. *Journal of Clinical and Experimental Neuropsychology*, 42(6), 634–645. 10.1080/13803395.2020.179835832781930

Bâra, A. (2024). Enabling coordination in energy communities: A Digital Twin model. *Energy Policy*. Elsevier.

Baroudi, J. J., & Orlikowski, W. J. (1988). A Short-Form Measure of User Information Satisfaction: A Psychometric Evaluation and Notes on Use. *Journal of Management Information Systems*, 4(4), 44–59. 10.1080/07421222.1988.11517807

Bellantuono, L. (2023). Detecting the socio-economic drivers of confidence in government with eXplainable Artificial Intelligence. *Scientific Reports* 13. Nature Publishing Group UK London.

Bonab, A. B., Rudko, I., & Bellini, F. 2021. A Review and a Proposal About Socio-economic Impacts of Artificial Intelligence. In *Business Revolution in a Digital Era*. Cham: Springer International Publishing. 10.1007/978-3-030-59972-0_18

Brodić, D., & Amelio, A. (2015). Classification of the Extremely Low Frequency Magnetic Field Radiation Measurement from the Laptop Computers. *Measurement Science Review*, 15(4), 202–209. 10.1515/msr-2015-0028

Bronfenbrenner, U. (1979). Contexts of child rearing: Problems and prospects. *American psychologist, 34*. American Psychological Association.

Carpenter, J., & Bithell, J. (2000). Bootstrap confidence intervals: When, which, what? A practical guide for medical statisticians. *Statistics in Medicine*, 19(9), 1141–1164. 10.1002/(SICI)1097-0258(20000515)19:9<1141::AID-SIM479>3.0.CO;2-F10797513

Charmaraman, L. (2020). Social and behavioral health factors associated with violent and mature gaming in early adolescence. *International journal of environmental research and public health, 17*.

Chassiakos, Y. L. R., & Stager, M. (2020). Current trends in digital media: How and why teens use technology. In *Technology and adolescent health* (pp. 25–56). Elsevier. 10.1016/B978-0-12-817319-0.00002-5

Cirillo, D. (2020). Sex and gender differences and biases in artificial intelligence for biomedicine and healthcare. *NPJ digital medicine*. Nature Publishing Group.

Duan, Y. (2019). Artificial intelligence for decision making in the era of Big Data–evolution, challenges and research agenda. *International journal of information management, 48*. Elsevier.

Dwivedi, Y. (2021). Artificial Intelligence (AI): Multidisciplinary perspectives on emerging challenges, opportunities, and agenda for research, practice and policy. *International Journal of Information Management, 57*. Elsevier.

Fasanya, B. K., & Strong, J. D. (2019). Younger Generation Safety: Hearing Loss and Academic Performance Degradation Among College Student Headphone Users. In *Advances in Safety Management and Human Factors*. Springer International Publishing. 10.1007/978-3-319-94589-7_51

Fast, N. (2020). Power and decision making: new directions for research in the age of artificial intelligence. *Current opinion in psychology*. Elsevier.

Faul, F., Erdfelder, E., Buchner, A., & Lang, A. G. (2009). Statistical power analyses using G*Power 3.1: Tests for correlation and regression analyses. *Behavior Research Methods*, 41(4), 1149–1160. 10.3758/BRM.41.4.114919897823

Glanz, K., Rimer, B. K., & Viswanath, K. (2015). *Health behavior: Theory, research, and practice*. John Wiley & Sons.

Gupta, M., Parra, C. M., & Dennehy, D. (2022). Questioning Racial and Gender Bias in AI-based Recommendations: Do Espoused National Cultural Values Matter? *Information Systems Frontiers*, 24(5), 1465–1481. 10.1007/s10796-021-10156-234177358

Kushwaha, A. K., Pharswan, R., Kumar, P., & Kar, A. K. (2023). How Do Users Feel When They Use Artificial Intelligence for Decision Making? A Framework for Assessing Users' Perception. *Information Systems Frontiers*, 25(3), 1241–1260. 10.1007/s10796-022-10293-2

Lérida-Ayala, V. (2022). Internet and video games: Causes of behavioral disorders in children and teenagers. *Children,10*.

McLuhan, M. (1964). *Understanding media*. McGraw-Hill.

Meshi, D. (2019). Excessive social media users demonstrate impaired decision making in the Iowa Gambling Task. *Journal of behavioral addictions,8*. Akadémiai Kiadó Budapest: 169–173.

Moir, C.-L., Tzani, C., Ioannou, M., Lester, D., Synnott, J., & Thomas, J. V. W. (2023). Cybersuicide: Online-Assisted Suicide. *Journal of Police and Criminal Psychology*, 38(4), 879–891. 10.1007/s11896-023-09602-5

Nadeem, A. (2022). Gender bias in AI-based decision-making systems: a systematic literature review. *Australasian Journal of Information Systems,26*. Australian Computer Society.

Niese, B. (2019). *Making good decisions: an attribution model of decision quality in decision tasks*. Kennesaw State University.

O'Connor, S., & Liu, H. (2023). Gender bias perpetuation and mitigation in AI technologies: Challenges and opportunities. *AI & Society*, 1–13. 10.1007/s00146-023-01675-4

Osama, M., Ali, S., & Malik, R. J. (2018). Posture related musculoskeletal discomfort and its association with computer use among university students. *JPMA. The Journal of the Pakistan Medical Association*, 68, 639–641.29808057

Rahman, M. A., Duradoni, M., & Guazzini, A. (2022). Identification and prediction of phubbing behavior: A data-driven approach. *Neural Computing & Applications*, 34(5), 3885–3894. 10.1007/s00521-021-06649-5

Rogers, E. M. (1995). *Diffusion of Innovations* (4th ed.). Free Press.

Rosenfield, M. (2020). A double-blind test of blue-blocking filters on symptoms of digital eye strain. *Work* 65. IOS Press.

Thomée, S., Dellve, L., Härenstam, A., & Hagberg, M. (2010). Perceived connections between information and communication technology use and mental symptoms among young adults - a qualitative study. *BMC Public Health*, 10(1), 66. 10.1186/1471-2458-10-6620152023

Tremblay, M. S., Colley, R. C., Saunders, T. J., Healy, G. N., & Owen, N. (2010). Physiological and health implications of a sedentary lifestyle. *Applied Physiology, Nutrition, and Metabolism*, 35(6), 725–740. 10.1139/H10-07921164543

Tucker, C. M., Roncoroni, J., & Buki, L. P. (2019). Counseling Psychologists and Behavioral Health: Promoting Mental and Physical Health Outcomes. *The Counseling Psychologist*, 47(7), 970–998. 10.1177/0011000019896784

Tucker, L. B., Velosky, A. G., Fu, A. H., & McCabe, J. T. (2019). Chronic Neurobehavioral Sex Differences in a Murine Model of Repetitive Concussive Brain Injury. *Frontiers in Neurology*, 10, 509. 10.3389/fneur.2019.0050931178814

Varma, A. (2023). Artificial intelligence and people management: A critical assessment through the ethical lens. *Human Resource Management Review,33*. Elsevier.

Vijayakumar, M. (2018). Assessment of co-morbid factors associated with text-neck syndrome among mobile phone users. *International Journal of Scientific Research in Science and Technology*, 4, 38–46.

Wang, R., Yin, Y., Zhang, H., Pan, L., Zhu, Y., Wang, M., Huang, Z., Wang, W., & Deng, G. (2023). Risk factors associated with the prevalence of neck and shoulder pain among high school students: A cross-sectional survey in China. *BMC Musculoskeletal Disorders*, 24(1), 641–649. 10.1186/s12891-023-06656-837559076

Wang, X., Lu, Z., & Yin, M. 2022. Will You Accept the AI Recommendation? Predicting Human Behavior in AI-Assisted Decision Making. In *Proceedings of the ACM Web Conference 2022*. Virtual Event, Lyon France: ACM. 10.1145/3485447.3512240

Wang, Y., Wu, L., Wang, L., Zhang, Y., Du, X., & Dong, G. (2017). Impaired decision-making and impulse control in Internet gaming addicts: Evidence from the comparison with recreational Internet game users. *Addiction Biology*, 22(6), 1610–1621. 10.1111/adb.1245827687019

Zamborsky, R., Kokavec, M., Simko, L., & Bohac, M. (2017). Carpal tunnel syndrome: Symptoms, causes and treatment options. Literature reviev. *Ortopedia, Traumatologia, Rehabilitacja*, 19(1), 1–8. 10.5604/15093492.123262928436376

Zaremohzzabieh, Z., Abdullah, H., Ahrari, S., Abdullah, R., & Siti, M. M. N. (2024). Exploration of vulnerability factors of digital hoarding behavior among university students and the moderating role of maladaptive perfectionism. *Digital Health*, 10, 1–16. 10.1177/2055207624122696238298527

Zohuri, B., & Rahmani, F. M. (2023). Artificial intelligence driven resiliency with machine learning and deep learning components. *Japan Journal of Research*, 1, 1–7.

# Chapter 15
# Diffusive Dynamics of an AI in the Contemporary Society of Techno–Educational Era

**Mudasir Rahman Najar**
*SRM University, India*

## ABSTRACT

*The chapter is a journey interior into the nuances of the magnificent technological pursuits. While talking in general, numerous case studies around the world attest to the enormous potential that young people have to drive AI innovation for social impact, like youth-led initiatives utilizing AI have surfaced to address urgent global issues like environmental sustainability, healthcare, and poverty. AI algorithms are used in India as part of the "smart village" effort, which is being led by young entrepreneurs, to improve crop yields, optimize agricultural methods, and reduce rural poverty. Similar to this, young-led businesses are using AI-powered healthcare platforms to lower maternal death rates and increase access to other social activities. In addition, young activists around the world use AI to track environmental data, forecast natural disasters, and promote sustainable policies—all of which help combat climate change and save biodiversity. So, these illustrations highlight the revolutionary potential of youth-driven AI innovation in for the societal benefits.*

## INTRODUCTION

The chapter is a journey interior into the nuances of the magnificent technological pursuits. While talking in general, numerous case studies around the world attest to the enormous potential that young people have to drive artificial intelligence (AI) innovation for social impact, like, youth-led initiatives utilizing AI have surfaced to address urgent global issues like environmental sustainability, healthcare, and poverty. AI algorithms are used in India as part of the "Smart Village" effort, which is being led by young entrepreneurs, to improve crop yields, optimize agricultural methods, and reduce rural poverty (Patnaik et al., 2020). Similar to this, young-led businesses are using AI-powered healthcare platforms to lower maternal death rates and increase access to other social activities. In addition, young activists around the world use AI to track environmental data, forecast natural disasters, and promote sustainable

DOI: 10.4018/979-8-3693-3350-1.ch015

policies—all of which help combat climate change and save biodiversity (Snezhana, 2023). So, these illustrations highlight the revolutionary potential of youth-driven AI innovation for societal benefits.

The broad discipline of youth studies, which aims to comprehend the issues, behaviors, and experiences that young people encounter, has started to converge with the field of AI in many interesting ways. The youth of today are strongly engaged in technology, having grown up as digital natives. As such, they are both creators and consumers of AI-driven platforms and content. In addition, AI technologies present special chances as well as difficulties in comprehending and assisting youth in a range of spheres of life, from work and education to social interaction and mental health (Waelen & Wieczorek, 2022). This indicates that the integration of technology, especially AI, has emerged as a revolutionary force in the quickly changing field of education, transforming the dynamics of knowledge dissemination and learning. The deep interaction between human intelligence and AI-driven instruments that characterizes the modern era of techno-education presents both previously unheard-of opportunities and difficulties (Vemuri, 2023). Comprehending the diffuse dynamics of artificial intelligence within this framework is crucial for educators, legislators, and students alike. Techno-education is a paradigm shift that introduces new approaches and resources at the intersection of traditional teaching and learning methods and technological breakthroughs. AI is a multidimensional technology at the vanguard of technological transition that can handle enormous amounts of smart content creation. A rising number of young academics are using AI techniques to create cutting-edge mobile applications and other creative initiatives in a variety of sectors. With the help of these technologies, they may develop complex apps with cutting-edge features, greatly advancing entrepreneurship, research, education, and social impact projects.

In the field of education, young researchers are using mobile apps driven by AI to improve the educational experience for students of all ages. These apps accommodate a variety of learning styles and skill levels by providing interactive exercises, real-time feedback, and individualized learning routes. So, Students can practice speaking, listening, reading, and writing through interactive discussions and activities catered to their competency levels by using AI-driven language learning applications, for instance, in a similar vein, AI-driven educational games and tests immerse students in the classroom while encouraging critical thinking, problem-solving tendencies thereof.

This chapter also tries to retrieve the history of technology in the way of educational development across the academic and social arena. All the technologies relevant to instructional plans and teaching pedagogies have transformed the teaching and learning process beyond horizons. The intervention of computers and the Internet constitute Information and Communication Technologies (ICTs) in the field of language learning, skill training, or any educational pursuit, the tech tools have been visualized as powerful enabling sources for distinct changes. Different ICTs have the potential to expand access to education, strengthen the process of education, and enhance the quality of education (Fernández-Gutiérrez et al., 2020). This includes books, articles, videos, podcasts, and music, as well as interactive learning resources and games. This exposure to authentic English helps learners improve their listening, reading, speaking, and writing skills (Jaelani & Umam, 2021). Technology also provides learners with opportunities to practice English with native speakers and other learners from all over the world. This is done through video chat, social media, or online language learning platforms. For example, adaptive learning platforms can track a learner's progress and adjust the difficulty of the material accordingly (Cavanagh et al., 2020). This helps learners to learn at their own pace and to focus on the areas where they need the most improvement. Students may be aware of how the teaching and learning process uses various technologies, including radio, television, computers, etc. In actuality, the teaching and learning processes have been revolutionized by all of these technologies. Information and communication technologies, which include radio, television, and more recent digital technologies l and the Internet, have been envisioned as potent enablers for advances in education. Different ICTs can improve education quality, strengthen the educational process, and increase access to education. The goal of this course is to provide you with a broad grasp of these technologies and how they might be used to improve the teaching and learning process.

## IDEA OF ICT

The idea of ICT in this regard is a mark of discussion. Around the world, young people are using AI technologies more and more (Markauskaite et al., 2022). Their interest is shaped by access to AI education, chances for creativity, and worries about ethics and governance. Many educational institutions in industrialized nations are incorporating AI education into their curricula to give students a solid foundation in machine learning, data analysis, and algorithmic thinking as well as practical abilities in these areas. In addition, many organizations provide mentorship programs, hackathons, and coding camps to enable youth to create AI-powered solutions to pressing issues. However, due to several issues like a lack of money, infrastructure, and qualified teachers, access to AI education is still restricted in many underdeveloped nations (Shiohira, 2021). Thus, young people in emerging economies are using community workshops, online learning platforms, and grassroots initiatives to gain AI skills and spur innovation despite these obstacles.

AI-powered tools and platforms are changing the way that youth study and acquire information in the field of education (El Asmar, 2022). AI algorithms are used by adaptive learning systems to tailor instructional materials to each student's unique learning preferences and skills. These systems can challenge top performers and offer targeted assistance and intervention to failing kids, encouraging better academic performance and youth participation. AI-driven educational apps also provide real-time feedback, virtual tutoring, and interactive learning experiences, enabling young students to take charge of their education and follow their interests more independently (Aggarwal, 2023).

The combination of AI with information technology (IT) has revolutionized some industries and changed how people interact, work, and live in the linked digital world of the twenty-first century (Dwivedi et al., 2021). This mutually beneficial link between AI and IT highlights the complex interactions that occur between intelligent systems and data-driven technologies, presenting both previously unheard-of benefits and difficulties. The term "information technology" refers to a wide range of devices, programs, and procedures used in the collection, processing, distribution, and structuring of data for social and organizational objectives. IT is the foundation of contemporary digital operations, facilitating smooth communication, cooperation, and data management across a range of domains, from conventional computing infrastructures to state-of-the-art cloud computing solutions.

Additionally, AI and IT work together to create a symbiotic connection that opens up new possibilities for efficiency and creativity by bringing together intelligent algorithms and data-driven technology (Zohuri & Mossavar-Rahmani, 2023). This convergence takes many different forms, like

Data-driven Decision Making where AI enhances conventional IT systems by using cutting-edge analytics to glean insightful information from large, complicated datasets, allowing businesses to make deft judgments instantly (Ntoutsi et al., 2020).

Likewise, in automation and optimization, various processes like software development, network administration, and cybersecurity have been streamlined by AI-driven automation, which also increases the agility and efficiency of IT operations.

Hence, along the same lines, personalized experiences do occur in AI-driven personalization algorithms that improve user experiences in consumer technology by providing customized content, suggestions, and interactions on various digital platforms.

So, more importantly, risk management and cybersecurity a worthwhile fields where AI strengthens IT, and ICTs are very often interchangeably used in the context of modern technology infrastructure.

*Figure 1. ICTs elements*

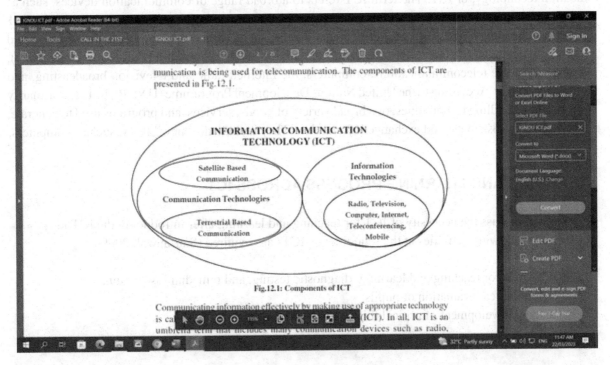

ICT is a comprehensive term, which comprises information technology and communication technology. ICT includes radio, television, computer, the internet, teleconferencing, and mobile technology. All these information technologies are powered by mainly two types of communication technologies. These are satellite-based communication and terrestrial-based communication. Satellite-based communication is the communication, which takes place between sender and receiver through a communication satellite whereas terrestrial-based communication is the communication, which takes place through a network of transmitters spread across a geographical area, a country, or a state. This type of communication is used in the transmission of radio and television in India. However, with the launch of a series of satellites by the Indian Space Research Organization (ISRO), satellite-based communication is being used for telecommunication.

Information and technology are very indispensable parts of the education system in contemporary times. It has a greater role to play in the field of means of instruction and the execution of pedagogies thereof. In this way, there are various levels and modes of communication like radio, television, computer, and internet along with teleconferencing and mobile technology. There is a main contribution of these technologies from the main two sources satellite-based communication and terrestrial-based communication. Among these types of communications the former one is meant for the communication between the sender and the receiver and the latter one is meant for the communication that takes place through the network of a series of transmitters that are highly spread over the cluster of geographical areas in terms of various countries and regions.

The use of suitable technology to effectively relay information is known as information and communication technology, or ICT. The term ICT refers to a broad range of communication devices, such as satellite systems, computers, networks, radios, televisions, and cell phones (Anorue et al., 2022). ICT is defined in some ways. ICTs are defined as a diverse set of technological tools and resources used to communicate, and to create, disseminate, store, and manage information (Liesa-Orús et al., 2020). Among them are telecommunications, computers, the Internet, radio and television broadcasting, and other technology. According to the United Nations Development Programme (UNDP), ICTs are primarily information handling technologies, or a broad variety of goods, services, and programs used to generate, store, process, distribute, and exchange information. They include the "new" ICTs, such as computers,

## TEACHING AND LEARNING PROCESS ACROSS ICT

We will discuss the necessity of ICT for teaching and learning after introducing the ICT idea. For the following activities at the school level, ICTs are required (Sansanwal, 2009):

- Activities for teaching and learning, diagnostic testing, and remedial instruction.
- Psychological evaluation of pupils;
- Student development of critical thinking and reasoning skills

*Figure 2. Process across ICT*

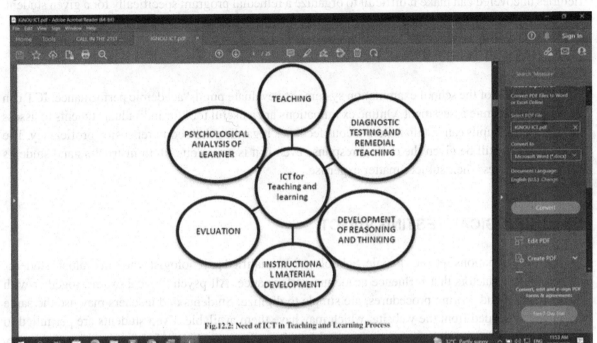

Fig.12.2: Need of ICT in Teaching and Learning Process

## NEED OF ICT IN PROCESS OF THE TEACHING AND LEARNING

Most teachers favor the lecture method, despite its inability to meet a wide range of learning objectives in the classroom. ICT may be highly beneficial in achieving a range of objectives related to the teaching-learning process. It comprehensively provides precise knowledge with multiple examples. It helps pupils broaden their knowledge. With the flexibility that ICT provides in information presentation, students can learn at their own pace. It facilitates improved understanding and long-term retention of knowledge.

## ICT AS A TOOL FOR CRITICAL AND REFINING TEACHING- LEARNING PROCESS

As a teacher, you have undoubtedly observed that some students find it difficult to understand specific concepts or retain information for extended periods. For a variety of reasons, including large class sizes, a dearth of diagnostic testing in many subjects, a lack of resources, training, and teacher desire, among others, teachers do not give remedial education and administer diagnostic tests. In this situation, ICT can help the teachers and students identify the issue area. Students may take tests from home by accessing them on the school website. Parents are also able to monitor these behaviors. The complexity of the difficulties uncovered can make it difficult to organize a remedial program specifically for a given student.

## EVALUATION THROUGH ICT

The purpose of the school examination system is to evaluate pupils' academic performance. ICT can be used in academic assessment. Online examinations are a useful tool for individual students to assess their learning. Pupils can obtain instantaneous feedback regarding their comprehension proficiency. The individual can still be given the correct response even if it is erroneous. Both instructors and students can use it to assess their subject-matter expertise.

## PSYCHOLOGICAL TESTING VIA ICT

There are variations between people. Schools need a qualified psychologist who can evaluate students on some of the factors that influence academic performance. All psychological exams, together with the evaluation and scoring procedures, are simple to digitize. Students and teachers may use the same resources as needed from the website, which may have them available. Even students are permitted to utilize it on their own and share the outcomes with their teachers to enhance their academic performance. ICT can therefore be applied to psychological assessment as well.

## ICT AS A PLATFORM FOR DEVELOPING THINKING ABILITIES AMONG STUDENTS

ICT is useful in many academic fields. Students can select the educational materials that best suit them thanks to ICT, which offers several options. ICT can be utilized to help students of all ages strengthen their critical thinking and reasoning skills. This is crucial in the current environment because most educational institutions do not place much emphasis on students' ability to reason and think critically.

## ICT AS A WAY OF INSTRUCTIONAL MATERIALS

There is currently a dearth of trained educators across all levels and in practically all subjects. The educational materials that are available in print form are not always of high quality or current. The reading of textbooks is frequently not entertaining and does not aid pupils in grasping the ideas or remembering the material. Numerous educators are well-known in a variety of topic areas. Their teachings ought to be captured on CD-ROM or broadcast on radio and television so that everyone can access them. It raises the standard of classroom instruction. Additionally, they can be used by the instructor to facilitate conversation following a presentation or broadcast. Even teachers can download those lectures immediately. It makes instruction efficient, interactive, and pleasant. Digitalized

## ICTS AND THEIR APPLICATIONS IN RADIO

We are all aware of how effective radio is at disseminating information to a sizable population. It effectively saves time, effort, money, and human resources. Both formal and informal education can benefit from the use of radio as a medium. Early in the 20th century, radio technology became widely used after being invented in the late 19th century. Radio is a convenient and useful media for use in distance learning programs due to its popularity, accessibility, and affordability. This is used in combination with other media, such as with print medium followed by face-to-face teaching. The educational use of radio started around 1930. You must have listened to some educational programs either on All India Radio or on FM channels. There are generally two types of programs. Some programs are informative or for entertainment purposes. Other programs are educational. These programs are meant primarily for educational purposes. Let us understand the process, through which we can use radio programs in our regular classrooms.

*Figure 3. Education uses of computer*

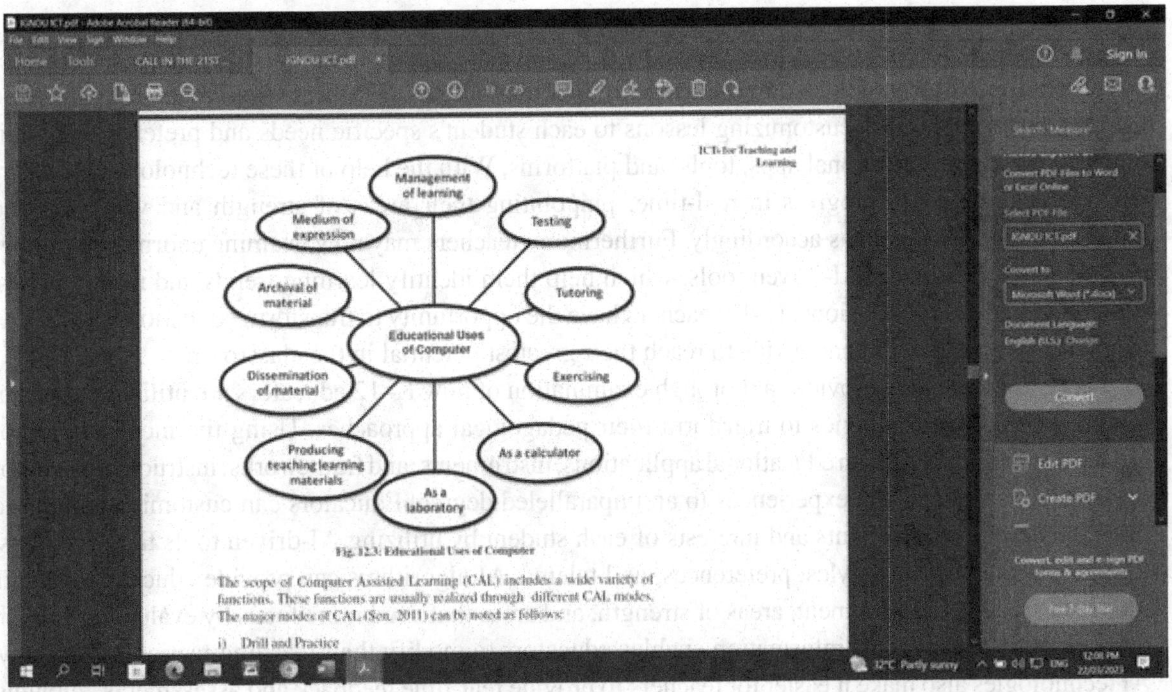

## COMPUTER

AI technologies also have the power to completely change how young people are employed and grow their careers. AI-powered job matching services match young job seekers with opportunities that fit their interests, talents, and career objectives. In addition, these platforms can offer tailored suggestions for networking opportunities, training courses, and skill enhancement, assisting young people in navigating the ever-more-complex job market. Additionally, young people can receive assistance and direction from AI-driven career counseling and mentorship programs as they explore career options, make educated decisions, and create plans.

The bulk of devices currently in use rely on digital technology. The computer is one such gadget. The computer is an electrical gadget with the ability to store, retrieve, and process both qualitative and quantitative data quickly and precisely. Some educational applications include computer-assisted instruction (CAI), computer-assisted learning (CAL), computer-managed instruction (CMI), and computer-based instruction (CBI). To teach various courses in both higher education and the classroom, CAI was first developed. When the produced CAIs were compared to the Lecture Method / Traditional Method for teaching various subjects, it was discovered that the developed CAIs were much better. Computers are frequently seen as instruments that may be utilized to accomplish a variety of learning goals, much like textbooks and lab exercises.

## USING COMPUTERS IN EDUCATION

This study explores the many tactics used by K–12 educators to improve student-learning experiences by integrating AI technologies into their teaching methodologies. Teachers may create individualized learning environments by customizing lessons to each student's specific needs and preferences by utilizing AI-powered educational apps, tools, and platforms. With the help of these technologies, teachers may evaluate students' progress in real-time, pinpointing their areas of strength and weakness and modifying their lesson plans accordingly. Furthermore, teachers may now examine enormous volumes of student data thanks to AI-driven tools, which help them identify learning trends and make the best possible instructional decisions. K–12 teachers have the opportunity to transform education by using AI technologies, which will enable kids to reach their greatest potential in the classroom.

This extensive study provides a thorough examination of how K–12 educators are utilizing artificial intelligence (AI) technologies to transform their pedagogical approaches. Using the incorporation of artificial intelligence-driven educational applications, instruments, and frameworks, instructors can tailor their students' educational experiences to an unparalleled degree. Educators can customize training to meet the unique requirements and interests of each student by utilizing AI-driven tools that can adjust to their various learning styles, preferences, and talents. AI algorithms can provide educators insights into each student's development, areas of strength, and areas that need more focus by evaluating student data and interactions. This information enables educators to modify their teaching tactics accordingly. AI technologies also make it easier for teachers to provide real-time feedback and assessments, allowing them to keep an eye on students' progress and intervene as needed to promote learning. Additionally, the accessibility and scalability of CAL suggest that some computer programs are used to facilitate teaching and learning activities. The computer can serve as a teaching tool. It might be more student-focused. Barker and Manji (1992) suggest the following uses for computers in education:

## EDUCATIONAL USES OF COMPUTER

The scope of Computer Assisted Learning (CAL) includes a wide variety of functions. These functions are usually realized through different CAL modes.

The major modes of CAL (Sen. 2011) can be noted as follows:

i)   Drill and Practice
ii)  Tutorial
iii) Dialogue /Conversational
iv)  Games
v)   Simulation
vi)  Databases

## A Brief History and Emergence of CAL

AI-powered social media platforms and virtual communities are major components of young people's social interaction lives. To improve user experiences, promote social connections, and personalize content recommendations, AI systems examine user data and behavior. But these algorithms also give rise to worries about monitoring, privacy, and the swaying of online conversation, especially among young people who are already at risk. To address the ethical and social consequences of AI technologies in youth socialization and digital citizenship, there is an increasing need for research and policy interventions.

ICT is increasingly widely employed across the curriculum, including in the teaching and learning of English. The majority of English teachers would agree that there is still more work to be done before technology can be used effectively and pleasant. This book's goal is to offer a wide range of motivations and jumping-off points so that we can fully utilize this enormous potential. This book's authors are not technical experts and have no desire to become so. We are seasoned English language instructors who also like reading and writing. For us, technology of any kind—from the dated overhead projector or spirit duplicator to the most recent digital—never takes precedence over English.

We see the growth of ICT in English to be a process, an evolution, as opposed to a startling leap into the unknown. Similar to ladder rungs, each one must be present for an ascent to be safe; skipping rungs or leaving them out puts climbers at risk. You will find activities that are well within the skills (or the resources available) of those who are just starting to use ICT in their teaching in the chapters that follow. There will also be proposals that will be appealing to individuals who are experienced ICT users and ideas to expand and build upon such practice.

We all have a theoretical understanding of how language is fluid, slippery, and flexible, and we experience this when we speak. Writing using a pen and ink, a traditional means of capturing language, tends to cement words' form, order, and effect. The flexibility of discourse is enhanced by the computer, in contrast. It makes experimentation and ongoing readjusting possible. By choosing alternative fonts, sizes, and layouts, a writer can significantly modify the visual impact of the text in addition to changing the order and form of individual words. ICT also enables us to embrace various forms of communication outside of words on a website or screen. It is possible to use audio recording and editing, still and moving images, and audio.

## CALL-Concept in the Contemporary Times

The 20th century saw the closure of language laboratories. They came into being as secondary schools and colleges started to develop contemporary foreign language curricula in the late 1940s and early 1950s. Modern languages were once valued more highly than classical ones like Greek and Latin. The advent of modern language programs gave rise to the concept of a language lab. At a set time, students were herded into audio labs where they all listened to an audio program that had been prearranged. This made use of the behaviorist method of language instruction. Introducing students to the spoken form of the language they were learning was the aim of language laboratories. This was regarded as a noteworthy invention in the middle of the twentieth century.

There were far fewer opportunities for students to travel back then. There was no internet access. Nothing was airing on foreign TV. It was also quite expensive to call family members who lived overseas. That has all evolved. In today's world of digitization, audio exposure to foreign languages is freely accessible for little or no expense. You can listen to satellite radio, Internet radio, and podcasts. As early as the 1980s, forward-thinking scholars projected that language labs would disappear. They were true. These days, constructing auditory language labs is a poor use of a school's little resources (money, time, and other resources).

A student portfolio gives tangible evidence of accomplishment and serves as a tool for assessing learning through an asset-based approach. Asset-based evaluation methods are replacing traditional, deficit-based evaluation methods. Language learning cannot be adequately measured the way it is currently done (Pappamihiel & Walser, 2009). These days, picking up a language is thought to be a challenging, interactive process. Even though they are easy to evaluate, traditional multiple-choice or fill-in-the-blank ("cloze") activities and examinations do not fully convey the complexity of language acquisition. This is an outdated approach. The questions, "What can my students do?" and "How do we help them grow from where they are now?" are on the minds of educational leaders in the new millennium. For language teachers, this means staying away from verb tenses.

Individualized instruction is emerging as be accepted practice in the twenty-first century. The recognition and celebration of students' unique abilities, aptitudes, and skills by educators and schools go hand in hand with the obvious and observable methods by which students demonstrate their knowledge. Student involvement in the creation of learning outcomes is increasing, and learning is becoming more student-centered (Pauk, 2007). Teachers and administrators who are accustomed to using their authority to set student outcomes may find this disturbing, but, probably, the trend toward learner-centered strategies and student involvement in outcome development will continue.

In the Obama era, presentation and public speaking abilities have gained new heights of esteem. There is a U.S. President courting youth with his ability to communicate verbally for the first time in decades. Globally as much as in the United States, this is having an effect. The linguistic expression of ideas is becoming more and more important. This can be seen in the study of languages, where there is an increased emphasis on clear communication. Speech competitions in second languages are particularly popular, as are discussions, readings of poetry, and storytelling. Think about the preceding suggestion of a student portfolio. Imagine that same project completed digitally rather than on paper, stored, and displayed in a cardboard portfolio.

In the twenty-first century, education is centered on this work showcased through, among other platforms, student-made podcasts, blogs, films, Wikis, and portfolios. Everything is present. It goes beyond using technology just for its own sake. This has to do with using technology to show pupils what they have learned so they may evaluate the impact of language acquisition on their lives. Utilizing the same technology that they use to create their projects and sharing them with others. In addition to those that display what students have learned, other devices support learning.

Going a step further, let's assert that there is no denying the widespread use of mobile learning technologies. These days, "CALL" (computer-aided language learning), which was created in the 1980s and 1990s, is quickly gaining traction with "MALL" (mobile-assisted language learning) (Kukulska-Hulme & Shield, 2007). It's possible that in the future, "apps" or some kind of mobile software will replace textbooks. Students are expressing themselves and demonstrating their knowledge through technology and their ingenuity. The challenge facing educators in the 21st century will be to figure out how to help them accomplish it. Instead of only consuming technology, today's students create it themselves through projects, artwork, and technology.

## Linking Language Learning to Leadership Skills

With the incorporation of AI techniques into educational platforms and resources, English language learning has undergone a remarkable transformation. With the ability to provide students with individualized, interactive experiences that are tailored to their unique requirements and learning preferences, these tools have completely transformed the way that language is taught. The ability of AI to offer individualized learning paths is one of its most important contributions to language acquisition. AI provides activities and content that are specifically personalized to each learner by analyzing their learning styles, areas of weakness, and competency levels through the use of complex algorithms. By matching education to each student's current ability level, this tailored method maximizes learning outcomes.

Moreover, adaptive learning platforms driven by AI have emerged as essential resources for teaching English. These platforms make sure that learners are continuously pushed to the right level by dynamically adjusting the tasks and materials' difficulty based on how well they perform. These platforms support skill development and mastery by offering adaptive feedback and content, which creates a dynamic and productive learning environment. Additionally, by providing automated assessments of students' speaking, listening, reading, and writing abilities, AI technologies have completely changed language assessment. Algorithms for speech recognition and natural language processing precisely assess language learners' proficiency, offering real-time feedback and progress monitoring.

AI tools are essential for aiding language practice and communication, in addition to evaluation and training. AI-powered chatbots and virtual tutors give students the chance to practice speaking English in real time (Pokrivcakova, 2019). With the help of these AI-driven interactions, which mimic real-world language use scenarios, learners can advance their vocabulary, grammar, and fluency in an engaging and encouraging environment. Furthermore, by offering instantaneous translations of English texts into learners' native languages and vice versa, AI-based translation technologies have increased the accessibility of English language learning for non-native speakers. This helps students understand and interact with English-language content more successfully, overcoming linguistic obstacles and encouraging intercultural dialogue.

Furthermore, the range and accessibility of English language learning resources have been enhanced by AI-driven content development and curation. To accommodate a wide range of learning interests and preferences, AI algorithms create and curate a broad selection of articles, exercises, quizzes, and interactive lessons. A multitude of materials are available to learners to meet their specific requirements, encouraging self-directed learning and inquiry. Furthermore, feedback systems driven by AI examine students' writing and offer immediate corrections on syntax, vocabulary, and sentence construction. With the help of this instant feedback, students may spot and fix mistakes, thereby advancing their writing and language skills.

To conclude, the incorporation of artificial intelligence (AI) tools into English language instruction has revolutionized the field of education by providing students with tailored, flexible, and captivating learning experiences. AI technologies have completely changed the way that language teaching is delivered, from tailored learning pathways to automated evaluation and real-time language practice. These technologies have the potential to improve language learning accessibility, efficacy, and enjoyment for students worldwide as they develop.

Rapid change is taking place in the world. Learning methods are evolving. The way we instruct and evaluate learning is likewise evolving. Models that are softer and more collaborative are replacing outdated, authoritarian ones. Students are as eager as ever to be mentored, coached, and guided. Their interest in the world around them keeps growing. They now have access to that world, which is a difference. They are using technology to interact with the world in a way that their parents and instructors never could. The language classroom of the mid-to-late 20th century is very different from the one of today.

The emphasis is now on using language and cultural knowledge to interact with people around the world rather than memorizing rules of grammar or learning things by heart. With the help of technology, kids are learning to reach out to the world around them and use their language and cultural competencies to enable the relationships they are ready to create. There is a case to be made for a field that is reconceived to be more learner-centered, collaborative, and technologically oriented. Advancements in language learning are enabling our students to communicate with people all across the world in real-time.

As a result, technology has had a significant impact on English language learning, making it easier to access, more interesting to study, and more effective than ever. One of technology's most important advantages is that it gives students access to a variety of authentic English resources from around the globe. Students benefit from this type of engagement by improving their speaking and listening abilities as well as their understanding of various cultures. Additionally, each learner can have their own unique learning experiences thanks to technology. For instance, adaptive learning platforms can monitor a student's development and modify the material's level of difficulty as necessary. This enables students to learn at their rate and to concentrate on the areas that require the greatest development.

## Language Laboratory Software

Furthermore, through facilitating access to resources, support services, and interventions, AI-driven applications may promote the mental health and general well-being of young people. AI-powered chatbots and virtual mental health assistants provide young people facing mental health issues with private, stigma-free care. They do this by offering knowledge, coping mechanisms, and referrals to professionals when necessary. Furthermore, AI algorithms to spot warning indications of distress or danger can analyze teenage users' social media data. This allows for early intervention and focused treatment from support groups and mental health specialists.

By giving teachers and students effective tools to improve language instruction, language laboratory software has completely changed the field of language education. A variety of capabilities is available on these software platforms to support language learning, teaching, evaluation, and cooperation in both online and conventional classroom settings. Language lab software has become an essential part of contemporary language teaching and learning approaches thanks to its intuitive interfaces and wide range of features.

In the past, language laboratories were actual locations furnished with recording equipment and audio-visual resources so that students could independently practice their language abilities. But as digital technology has advanced, language lab software has moved into virtual platforms that can be accessed from any internet-connected device. These software programs include an array of interactive exercises, communication tools, and multimedia resources.

The capacity of language laboratory software to give students the opportunity for real-world language practice is one of its primary features. Learners can participate in meaningful language engagements that replicate real-life communication circumstances through interactive dialogues, virtual discussions, and audio and video recordings. Through this practical method, students can improve their speaking, listening, reading, and writing abilities in a friendly and engaging setting.

Additionally, software for language laboratories provides teachers with effective teaching and assessment tools. To meet the requirements and skill levels of each individual student, teachers can design classes, tasks, and exams that are specifically suited to them. They also allow for focused intervention and individualized training by tracking students' progress, keeping an eye on their performance, and giving feedback in real time. Furthermore, many language lab software systems include automated evaluation tools like speech.

Additionally, language lab software encourages group learning by letting students communicate in online forums and virtual classrooms with both teachers and other students. Language learners can improve their language abilities and build a sense of community and camaraderie within the language-learning community by participating in group activities, working on joint projects, and receiving feedback from their peers.

To sum up, software for language laboratories has become a very useful and important resource for both language teachers and students. Through immersive language practice, tailored instruction, automated evaluation, and cooperative learning opportunities, these software platforms enable language learners to meet their objectives more successfully and economically. The potential of language laboratory software is set to significantly transform the field of language education as technology develops, making language learning more approachable, interesting, and creative.

English language laboratories (ELLs) have a wide scope in terms of their potential to improve English language teaching and learning. ELLs can be used to support a variety of learning activities, including:

a.   Listening comprehension: Students can use ELLs to listen to recorded lessons, audiobooks, and other audio materials. They can also use ELLs to record themselves speaking and compare their pronunciation to that of native speakers.

b.   Speaking practice: ELLs provide students with a safe and supportive environment to practice speaking English without fear of making mistakes. Students can use ELLs to record themselves speaking and get feedback from teachers or peers.

c.   Vocabulary and grammar: ELLs can be used to teach and practice vocabulary and grammar concepts. Students can use ELLs to complete interactive exercises, play games, and watch videos about English language usage.

d.   Writing practice: ELLs can be used to provide students with feedback on their writing. Students can also use ELLs to access online resources and tools for improving their writing skills.

Overall, ELLs have a wide scope in terms of their potential to improve English language teaching and learning. They can be used to support a variety of learning activities, promote self-paced learning, provide individualized instruction, and create a more engaging learning environment.

## The Digital Language Lab Oréll Talk

A cutting-edge offline language learning solution, Oréll Digital Language Lab offers the best outcomes and adds value for teachers, students, and educational institutions (Dey & Dey, 2021). For all language learning advancements driven by student demands, Oréll Talk offers a cutting-edge, portable, versatile, and adaptive technological platform. It also significantly increases productivity and teaching efficiency across the learning life cycle. Any language may be taught using Oréll Talk, and our most recent version is not only much more interactive and user-friendly than previous iterations, but it also comes preloaded with more than 5000 hours of absolutely free English study materials and activities. The instructor may change and modify these however they see suitable, and it also provides the teacher with additional flexibility.

1. Features: Excellent student monitoring and evaluation; LSRW approach for language learning
2. Support for multimedia • Design Modularity.
3. Cutting-edge software-based technology
4. In-classroom management in real-time
5. Includes free resources for learning the English language.
6. High-tech digital recorders
7. Teach any language. Offline version with perpetual one-time licensing. Economical with free upgrades and releases

## Spears Language Laboratory

There is a wide range of English language lab software on the market. The best language lab software out of the bunch is Spears Language Lab because it uses the best tools and content. The Spears Language lab offers the following advantages to students: •Multimedia content for efficient learning.

* Practice exercises for self-labs
* Personality-developing soft skills.
* A variety of communication-enhancing speech therapies
* Training facility for Accent
* A facility for recording audio
* It employs the LSRW approach (listening, speaking, reading, and writing).
* It offers programs in soft skills.

The Spears Language lab's advantages for educators include:

* Complete assignments according to the syllabus.
* Facility for Batch Management
* A notice-board feature
* Control content following the curriculum.

Today's students must work extremely hard to keep up with market demand because of the intense competition that is there. By offering a wealth of content, the Spears language lab system aids in keeping up with the competition today. It has numerous uses:

- All students can study simultaneously - Without interfering with one another, all students can practice their pronunciation in class at the same time.
  Working in groups is also made easier by the language lab. The pupils can be paired up, and the teacher can assign them to groups.

- Grammar Section - The program includes 7000+ vocabulary terms to help with learning and building a solid foundation.
- Interactive Exercises - The Spears Language Lab offers more than 3,000 interactive exercises for students to master.

  Group discussion - In a group discussion course, you can acquire crucial strategies for success.

- Interview jitters - Discover how to ace interviews with confidence.
- Personality improvement - To tackle obstacles with confidence, one must build their total personality.
- Life skills - This course will improve their social, emotional, and intellectual intelligence while also introducing kids to the value of education.
- Writing a CV - Develop some writing techniques that will set you apart from the competition.

  Improve your body language by learning some helpful hints. A person's body language can reveal a lot about them.

- Self-awareness - Improving one's self-awareness is crucial for personality development. Self-introspection is a technique that aids in helping us correct our errors.

## Sanako Research Software tool

A software tool for qualified language teachers is called Sanako Study. Sanako Study offers classroom management tools that help teachers run their language lessons more effectively (Amurskaya et al., 2017). You can extend the amount of time students spend actively learning by using the workflows for the predefined language learning activities provided by Sanako Study's language lab software. It has been demonstrated that switching from passive to active learning improves students' general performance and outcomes. Working with Sanako Study, one of the greatest and most well-liked language lab software solutions, involves customizing instruction, savoring teacher-student interaction, and monitoring student development. Even the most challenging to teach skills, including pronunciation and intonation, can be improved using model imitation and a variety of conversation exercises.

## REASONS TO THINK ABOUT THE LANGUAGE LAB SOFTWARE FROM SANAKO STUDY

### Reason 1: To Develop Listening Abilities

Allow your pupils to concentrate on the audio and video in their headsets rather than blasting it out over the speakers in a busy classroom. Give individual classes different material, and if necessary, let them work at their own pace.

### Reason 2: To Enhance Communication Skills

A lot of pupils find it terrifying to speak in front of the entire class! Students are encouraged to take chances and record their voices covertly at Sanako's digital language lab. Additionally, the instructor can use Voice Insert to add audio comments to the student recordings to offer detailed feedback on pronunciation, vocabulary, structure, etc.

Additionally, the students can present to one another via computer presentations, which may develop the following:

### Rational 1: To Enable Students to Improve Their Language Abilities

All language learners are required to at the very least acquire vocabulary, listen to and memorize essential phrases, and prepare answers to spoken queries. However, students who can build on this fundamental information in a variety of situations and role-playing exercises will succeed academically. You will give your pupils the chance to develop their abilities with peers in a situation that they will presumably encounter later in life, such as a job interview, by allowing them to participate in paired or group-based activities.

### Rationale 2: More Students Should Enroll in Language Classes

Sanako More students will enroll in language programs as a result of studying language teaching software. Students in today's generation who are familiar with IT value technology when it

### Reason 3: Boost Exam Performance

Using drill-type exercises, teacher-led listening activities, self-access listening, listen and repeat exercises, translation exercises, stimulus and answer techniques, role-play, group discussions, and round-table discussions, language lab software can help you improve your speaking and listening abilities.

These techniques are valued by students today. It has been demonstrated that oral assessments have a substantial impact on student preparation and performance.

## Reason 4: Save Time and Money

Speaking assessments and exam preparation can now be done for the entire class at once thanks to the built-in language learning activities in Sanako's language teaching software, while previously it would have taken many one-on-one sessions.

## Reason 5: Expand on What You Have in a Flexible Way

Sanako Study is a supplement to the current resources; it does not replace them. Examples of such resources include your online teaching materials, Microsoft Office papers, etc. The language lab software from Sanako is compatible with all common file types, programs, and websites. It runs on the widely used Windows operating system.

## Reason 6: Move from Passive to Active Learning

It has been demonstrated repeatedly that pupils learn best when they are engaged. By conducting engaging activities like group discussions, role-plays, mock interviews, translation exercises, voting games, text chat exercises, etc. with language lab software, you may engage the students.

## Increase the amount of time that each pupil spends speaking and exercising.

Each student's speaking time may be increased with the use of a digital language lab. Each student only gets 1-2 minutes every class allotted for speaking practice in a typical classroom without any specialized language-learning software, but with Sanako Study's language lab program, they can all talk at once without interfering with one another. Hence, there is good utility of this software.

## ENGLISH LANGUAGE MOBILE APPLICATION

Additionally, a new generation of academics is investigating how AI-powered mobile apps might transform sectors including banking, agriculture, transportation, and entertainment (Chakraborty, 2020). For instance, they are creating apps that optimize investment strategies, boost crop yields, improve transportation systems, and customize entertainment recommendations using machine learning and predictive analytics. These creative applications highlight the technical aptitude of young academics as well as their inventiveness, spirit of entrepreneurship, and dedication to improving society.

Several younger researchers are investigating how AI-powered mobile apps could change sectors, which include banking, farming, public transport, and media. For instance, they are creating apps that optimize investment strategies, boost crop yields, improve transportation systems, and customize entertainment recommendations using machine learning and predictive analytics. These innovative applications show off young students' technical aptitude as well as their inventiveness, spirit of entrepreneurship, and dedication to improving society.

English language mobile applications are software programs that can be installed on a smartphone or tablet to help users learn and improve their English skills. These apps can cover a wide range of topics, including vocabulary, grammar, pronunciation, listening comprehension, and writing. English language mobile apps can be used to supplement other forms of language learning, such as classroom instruction or online courses. For example, students can use apps to practice vocabulary and grammar exercises or to get feedback on their writing and speaking skills. English language mobile apps offer several advantages over traditional methods of language learning. They are typically more convenient and accessible, as users can learn at their own pace and on their own time. They can also be more engaging and interactive, as many apps use games, quizzes, and other activities to make learning fun.

## Babbel

Let's begin with Babbel, the 2013 recipient of Microsoft's "Innovate 4 Society Award," which guides learners through interactive courses that teach grammar and vocabulary through games, songs, dialogues, and sayings (Nushi & Eqbali, 2018). Each lesson can be finished in 15 minutes. Babbel's pronunciation area, where voices can be recorded and compared to those of native speakers, aids in the development of fundamental conversational skills. There are listening to activities that require you to fill in the blanks in a dialogue that has been made up. Babbel is ideal for both beginning learners who want to delve right into their target language (such as English) and intermediate students who require a review of what they have already learned.

## Memrise

It focuses on language learning that is "gamified" and will captivate users as they compete to place high on the leaderboard (Zhang, 2019). The user accrues more points when the software is utilized more frequently. For instance, during a vocabulary session, students would do a range of exercises and exams that would help the words stick in their long-term memory. With Memrise, you have access to a variety of game modes (Visual Learning, Review & Strengthen, Rapid Recall) that focus on various language abilities as well as rich, entertaining media resources (audio, video, animations). All of these activities are designed to increase learning while also making sure that students never forget what they have learned.

## Duolingo

It is available as an online portal and the app teaches new words by dishing out drills over and over (Vesselinov & Grego, 2012). For example, let's say it wants to teach the phrase Ek Ladka (the boy). The online portal and mobile program Duolingo teaches new phrases by continuously dispensing lessons. Let's take the example of teaching the phrase "Ek Ladka" (the boy). The test will initially be presented as a simple multiple-choice exam. After that, they will ask you to select the appropriate English translation for the Hindi word. Then they will assign assignments that require blank filling. After that, the word will be uttered, and the listener will need to type it into a box. Each time a new word is learned, a cute image relating to it (in this case, a cute image of a boy) will appear.

## MosaLingua

It focuses on the most common and useful terms and presents them progressively to improve memory (Bektaş et al., 2022). There are thousands of flashcards with useful terminology on travel, shopping, and other topics. Additionally, there are real-world discussions that highlight these vocabulary terms.

MosaLingua concentrates on stimulating visual and aural memory to optimize learning. The curriculum is also adaptable, emphasizing areas where students find it difficult to meet their needs. Moreover, MosaLingua can be used anytime, even for short periods.

## Mango Languages

Its goal is to teach pupils language skills through simulations of real-world conversations (Kavun, 2019). To demonstrate how the words interact with one another, sentences are introduced, disassembled into their component components, and then assembled again. By employing this approach, students are also allowed to create their sentences rather than just memorize phrases. The voice recorder is one of Mango Languages' most intriguing and distinctive features. With the aid of this voice recorder, students can compare their speech to that of a native speaker to improve their pronunciation. Reading, listening, and speaking are also activities.

## The Smart Class+ language lab system is one or more audio pronunciation exercises

They require students to talk into microphones and imitate native speakers (Hincks, 2003). Then, either the students themselves or a teacher listening to each student's tape would check the recorded product. By deploying AI that can "listen" to student pronunciations and swiftly assess how accurate they are, it avoids all the hassle. This time, students can evaluate their performance and make changes without the biases that come with self-evaluation. Additionally, Smart Class can be used on any device, not just the computer terminals at a school's language lab, including iPads, iPhones, and laptops. Students can continue working on the program because it can be securely housed on the cloud.

## The Communicative Method

The language is taught through real-world, task-based activities, and is the foundation of the School shape system (Van den Branden, 2016). After all, learning a language is meant to help one communicate effectively with others. In circumstances where they would need to use the target language to complete a job, such as introducing themselves to a stranger, requesting directions, or placing an order at a restaurant, students are put in contexts with lots of input. Hence, all the activities in School shape, whether they include speaking, listening, reading, or writing, are designed with a communicative mentality in mind. There are no pointless drills that involve words or sentences that students would never use in real life, such as "The green cat jumped over the pink elephant." Every activity has a goal and is experienced.

## CONCLUSION

In conclusion, the intersection of youth studies and artificial intelligence presents both opportunities and challenges for understanding and supporting young people in today's digital age. By harnessing the potential of AI technologies in education, employment, social interaction, and mental health, researchers, educators, policymakers, and practitioners can empower young people to thrive and succeed in a rapidly changing world. However, it is essential to approach the integration of AI in youth studies with careful consideration of ethical, social, and cultural factors to ensure that these technologies serve the best interests of young people and promote their well-being and empowerment.

As a result, and for good cause, digital language learning tools have grown in popularity over the past few years. Compared to conventional language-learning techniques, they have several benefits, such as:

- Convenience: With an internet connection, digital applications can be used at any time and from any location. They are therefore perfect for learners who are too busy to do regular language sessions.
- Personalization: Each learner's demands can be met through customized digital apps. For instance, some apps let users select their learning speed and concentrate on linguistic skills, including vocabulary or grammar.
- Engagement: Compared to conventional language learning techniques, digital applications might be more dynamic and engaging.

They frequently make use of games, tests, and other digital tools that can help language learners in a variety of specialized ways in addition to these basic advantages. For instance, some applications can offer immediate feedback on pronunciation and grammar, while others can assist students in learning new vocabulary through authentic resources while in context. In general, language learners can benefit significantly from digital applications. They are accessible, unique, interesting, and reasonably priced. They can also assist students learn new words in context and give them rapid feedback.

Consequently, using digital tools to learn a language is possible. Learning new vocabulary is made easier by interactive activities and games in apps like Duolingo and Memrise. Grammar instruction: Apps like Babbel and Rosetta Stone can assist students in learning grammar rules and giving them practice in real-world situations. Conversation practice: Tools like Omegle and Tandem can assist students with speaking and listening to native speakers in a real-world setting. Reading comprehension: English books and articles can be read via apps like Kindle and Nook, which allow users to look up any words or phrases they are unsure of writing practice: By checking for grammar and style mistakes, apps like Grammarly can help students get better at writing. Language learners of all levels can benefit from using digital tools.

Hence, with such innovations in the field of language learning and communications skills, we must be able to flourish across the length and breadth. This creates many opportunities for the learners to practice English and to acquire language well. Technology also provides learners with opportunities to practice English with native speakers and other learners from all over the world. So, technology can be used to create personalized learning experiences for each learner.

# REFERENCES

Aggarwal, D. (2023). Integration of innovative technological developments and AI with education for an adaptive learning pedagogy. *China Petroleum Processing and Petrochemical Technology*, 23(2), 709–714.

Amurskaya, O., Gimaletdinova, G., & Khalitova, L. (2017). Multimedia Sanako study 1200 for TEFL in institution of higher education. *Xlinguae*, 10(3), 229–236. 10.18355/XL.2017.10.03.18

Anorue, L. I., ETUMNU, E. W., Onyebuchi, C. A., & Obayi, P. M. (2022). Effectiveness of the use of ICT by media practitioners in modern day broadcasting. *International Journal of Communication and Social Sciences*, 1, 43–59.

Barker, P., & Manji, K. (1992). Computer-based training: An institutional approach. *Education and Computing*, 8(3), 229–237. 10.1016/0167-9287(92)92766-S

Bektaş, F., Dereli, B., Hayta, F., Şahin, E., Ali, U., & Eryiğit, G. (2022). Towards a Multilingual Platform for Gamified Morphology Learning. *2022 7th International Conference on Computer Science and Engineering (UBMK)*. IEEE. https://ieeexplore.ieee.org/abstract/document/9919484/

Cavanagh, T., Chen, B., Lahcen, R. A. M., & Paradiso, J. R. (2020). Constructing a design framework and pedagogical approach for adaptive learning in higher education: A practitioner's perspective. *International Review of Research in Open and Distance Learning*, 21(1), 173–197. 10.19173/irrodl.v21i1.4557

Chakraborty, U. (2020). *Artificial Intelligence for All: Transforming Every Aspect of Our Life*. Bpb publications. https://books.google.com/books?hl=en&lr=&id=J-_QDwAAQBAJ&oi=fnd&pg=PT18 &dq=a+new+generation+of+academics+is+investigating+how+AI-powered+mobile+apps+might+ transform+sectors+including+banking,+agriculture,+transportation,+and+entertainment&ots= uxHLvq7Yk-&sig=rP6WItgTh2EZwK_T3HEmNukmJr4

Dey, S. K., & Dey, A. (2021). Digital Pedagogical Paradigm in Language Lab-Based English Teaching for Higher Technical Education. In Deyasi, A., Mukherjee, S., Mukherjee, A., Bhattacharjee, A. K., & Mondal, A. (Eds.), *Computational Intelligence in Digital Pedagogy* (Vol. 197, pp. 251–275). Springer Singapore. 10.1007/978-981-15-8744-3_13

Dwivedi, Y. K., Hughes, L., Ismagilova, E., Aarts, G., Coombs, C., Crick, T., Duan, Y., Dwivedi, R., Edwards, J., Eirug, A., Galanos, V., Ilavarasan, P. V., Janssen, M., Jones, P., Kar, A. K., Kizgin, H., Kronemann, B., Lal, B., Lucini, B., & Williams, M. D. (2021). Artificial Intelligence (AI): Multidisciplinary perspectives on emerging challenges, opportunities, and agenda for research, practice and policy. *International Journal of Information Management*, 57, 101994. 10.1016/j.ijinfomgt.2019.08.002

El Asmar, W. (2022). *The Effectiveness of AI-Powered Digital Educational Platforms: Students' Attainment and Teachers' Teaching strategies in a private high school in Dubai* [PhD Thesis, The British University in Dubai]. https://search.proquest.com/openview/a0fbb2f4cebaed07810cb3970f96fcbf/1?pq -origsite=gscholar&cbl=2026366&diss=y

Fernández-Gutiérrez, M., Gimenez, G., & Calero, J. (2020). Is the use of ICT in education leading to higher student outcomes? Analysis from the Spanish Autonomous Communities. *Computers & Education*, 157, 103969. 10.1016/j.compedu.2020.103969

Hincks, R. (2003). Speech technologies for pronunciation feedback and evaluation. *ReCALL*, 15(1), 3–20. 10.1017/S0958344003000211

Jaelani, A., & Umam, A. (2021). Preparing EFL pre-service teachers for curriculum 2013 through authentic materials and assessment integration. [Journal of English Educators Society]. *JEES*, 6(1), 171–177. 10.21070/jees.v6i1.829

Kavun, N. (2019). Mango Languages. *CALICO Journal*, 36(3), 256–265. 10.1558/cj.38302

Kukulska-Hulme, A., & Shield, L. (2007). An overview of mobile assisted language learning: Can mobile devices support collaborative practice in speaking and listening. *ReCALL*, 20(3), 1–20.

Liesa-Orús, M., Latorre-Cosculluela, C., Vázquez-Toledo, S., & Sierra-Sánchez, V. (2020). The technological challenge facing higher education professors: Perceptions of ICT tools for developing 21st century skills. *Sustainability (Basel)*, 12(13), 5339. 10.3390/su12135339

Markauskaite, L., Marrone, R., Poquet, O., Knight, S., Martinez-Maldonado, R., Howard, S., Tondeur, J., De Laat, M., Shum, S. B., & Gašević, D. (2022). Rethinking the entwinement between artificial intelligence and human learning: What capabilities do learners need for a world with AI? *Computers and Education: Artificial Intelligence*, 3, 100056. 10.1016/j.caeai.2022.100056

Ntoutsi, E., Fafalios, P., Gadiraju, U., Iosifidis, V., Nejdl, W., Vidal, M., Ruggieri, S., Turini, F., Papadopoulos, S., Krasanakis, E., Kompatsiaris, I., Kinder-Kurlanda, K., Wagner, C., Karimi, F., Fernandez, M., Alani, H., Berendt, B., Kruegel, T., Heinze, C., & Staab, S. (2020). Bias in data-driven artificial intelligence systems—An introductory survey. *Wiley Interdisciplinary Reviews. Data Mining and Knowledge Discovery*, 10(3), e1356. 10.1002/widm.1356

Nushi, M., & Eqbali, M. H. (2018). Babbel: A mobile language learning app. *TESL Reporter*, 51, 13–13.

Pappamihiel, N. E., & Walser, T. M. (2009). English Language Learners and Complexity Theory: Why Current Accountability Systems Do Not Measure Up. *The Educational Forum*, 73(2), 133–140. 10.1080/00131720902739544

Patnaik, S., Sen, S., & Mahmoud, M. S. (Eds.). (2020). *Smart Village Technology: Concepts and Developments* (Vol. 17). Springer International Publishing. 10.1007/978-3-030-37794-6

Pokrivcakova, S. (2019). Preparing teachers for the application of AI-powered technologies in foreign language education. *Journal of Language and Cultural Education*, 7(3), 135–153. 10.2478/jolace-2019-0025

Shiohira, K. (2021). Understanding the Impact of Artificial Intelligence on Skills Development. Education 2030. *UNESCO-UNEVOC International Centre for Technical and Vocational Education and Training*. UNESCO. https://eric.ed.gov/?id=ED612439

Snezhana, D. (2023). Applying artificial intelligence (AI) for mitigation climate change consequences of the natural disasters. *Dineva, S.(2023). Applying Artificial Intelligence (AI) for Mitigation Climate Change Consequences of the Natural Disasters.Research Journal of Ecology and Environmental Sciences*, 3(1), 1–8.

Van den Branden, K. (2016). Task-based language teaching. In *The Routledge handbook of English language teaching* (pp. 238–251). Routledge. https://www.taylorfrancis.com/chapters/edit/10.4324/9781315676203-21/task-based-language-teaching-kris-van-den-branden10.4324/9781315676203-21

Vemuri, N. V. N. (2023). Enhancing Human-Robot Collaboration in Industry 4.0 with AI-driven HRI. *Power System Technology*, 47(4), 341–358. 10.52783/pst.196

Vesselinov, R., & Grego, J. (2012). Duolingo effectiveness study. *City University of New York, USA*, 28(1–25). https://www.languagezen.com/pt/about/english/Duolingo_Efficacy_Study.pdf

Waelen, R., & Wieczorek, M. (2022). The Struggle for AI's Recognition: Understanding the Normative Implications of Gender Bias in AI with Honneth's Theory of Recognition. *Philosophy & Technology*, 35(2), 53. 10.1007/s13347-022-00548-w

Zhang, X. (2019). Memrise. *CALICO Journal*, 36(2), 152–161. 10.1558/cj.37857

Zohuri, B., & Mossavar-Rahmani, F. (2023). The Symbiotic Relationship Unraveling the Interplay between Technology and Artificial Intelligence (An Intelligent Dynamic Relationship). *Journal of Energy and Power Engineering*, 17, 63–68.

# Chapter 16
# Gesture-Driven Communication and Empowering the Deaf-Mute Community Using Deep Learning Algorithm

**Puspita Dash**

https://orcid.org/0009-0001-0731-0218

*Department of Information Technology, Sri Manakula Vinayagar Engineering College, Puducherry, India*

**N. Kalaiselvi**

*Department of Information Technology, Sri Manakula Vinayagar Engineering College, Puducherry, India*

**K. Bhavani**

*Department of Information Technology, Sri Manakula Vinayagar Engineering College, Puducherry, India*

**M. Lakshmiprabha**

*Department of Information Technology, Sri Manakula Vinayagar Engineering College, Puducherry, India*

**E. Valarmathi**

*Department of Information Technology, Sri Manakula Vinayagar Engineering College, Puducherry, India*

**V. Padmapriya**

*Sri Manakula Vinayagar Engineering College, India*

**C. Vanaja**

*Sri Manakula Vinayagar Engineering College, India*

## ABSTRACT

*The contemporary landscape underscores the critical importance of virtual environments for organizations, educational institutions, and various other entities. To address the challenges of this digital era, we have come to rely heavily on video conferencing and communication systems that facilitate seamless remote interactions. However, in this digital realm, we often overlook the needs of individuals who are mute and deaf, for whom sign language is the primary means of communication. This includes American Sign Language (ASL) and Indian Sign Language (ISL), both of which involve intricate hand gestures. Sign language recognition has emerged as a rapidly evolving field of research, and in response to the unique needs of this community, the authors have developed a video chat application tailored to mute individuals. This project's primary focus centers on Indian Sign Language. To accurately recognize*

DOI: 10.4018/979-8-3693-3350-1.ch016

*and interpret the diverse hand gestures made by users, the authors harness the power of deep learning convolutional neural network (CNN) algorithms. As users convey their messages through hand gestures to the camera, this CNN-based algorithm swiftly identifies the corresponding phrase, number, or letter, seamlessly relaying it to the frontend. This real-time gesture detection and sentence formation process enhances the overall user experience. Recent advancements in this field have introduced novel techniques that hold promise for transforming the way we understand and facilitate communication through sign language. The overarching objective is to develop a video call model capable of recognizing and interpreting hand gestures and signs. Through rigorous training, the authors intend to create a model that facilitates the conversion of sign language into text or speech, bridging the communication gap and enabling meaningful interactions with individuals who are inherently deaf or have cognitive mentally disabilities.*

## INTRODUCTION

A sign is a form of non-verbal communication done with body parts, hand shapes, positions and movements of the hand, arms, facial expressions or movements of the lips and used instead of oral communication. A sign language is a language that uses signs or action to communicate instead of sounds. A good and precise communication is better experienced when done one to one. As we've faced the issue of being each and every procedure online and considering this as the new regulation, we also faced issue while communicating. The situation where individual has to cop up with his/her team for hours on video call for better and non-ambiguous communication. While considering all the situation we must have left the part of population who deserve to experience even more normal and regular than rest of us, they are mute and deaf people. As we all must be aware how difficult it is for mute people to communicate even in their daily life. If two people are communicating it is always considered that they must at least have few common criteria to be considered and the most important from all of these is language. Having common language is must for any sort of communication and to understand the words the other person is trying to convey. Then comes the media through which the communication is happening example phone calls, video calls, mails. For mute and deaf video calls and phone calls are easy to answer. This also creates a problem when they are asked for online screening round for an interview to be taken further for one to one physical.

Deep learning is a machine learning technique and a computer model learns to perform classification tasks directly from images, text, or sound. Deep learning models can achieve state-of-the-art accuracy, sometimes exceeding human-level performance. Models are trained by using a large set of labeled data and neural network architectures.

Object detection models are trained with a surplus of annotated visuals in order to carry out this process with new data. It becomes as simple as feeding input visuals and receiving a fully marked-up output visual.

As we all know how important our communication plays a role in any interview as it shows our confidence and attracts interviewee to see a candidate as right one for the organization. According to Indian Census we as a country have 1.3 million people who are mute or have hearing impairment. This number explains a lot about how important having a platform or media for them as they could also have normal video chats with their friends, family and also could be able to give interview by using their hand gesture without any problem. This system will act as an auxiliary tool for a deaf-mute to communicate with ordinary people through computer. This approach will convert video of daily frequently used full sentences gesture into a text and then convert it into audio. This system will definitely contribute to society via helping towards physically Indian handicap people.

## LITERATURE SURVEY

Different methods are used by various researchers to recognized different hand gestures or hand movements. Recognition Methods can be sensor based approach, computing approach like Neural Network, fuzzy logic, machine learning genetic algorithm and other expert system maintaining the Integrity of the Specifications

Thanekar Aadit, Jha Deepak, Patil Janhavi, Deone Jyoti created a "Video Chat Application for Mutes.", IEEE (2021). And implemented Different methods which are used by various researchers to recognized different hand gestures or hand movements. Recognition Methods used are sensor based approach, computing approach like Neural Network, fuzzy logic, machine learning genetic algorithm and other expert system. • Disadvantage of this system is mute people need to carry gloves all the time and also they have use basic hand gestures (Aadit et al., 2021).

Sartha Tambe, Yugchhaya, Galphat, Nilesh Rijhwani, Aishwarya, Goythale, Janhvi Patil "Analyzing and Enhancing Communication Platforms available for a Deaf-Blind user" IEEE (2020). The application converts the incoming text message into Morse code. The system used the IMC as a common communication mode. By a vibration device. Motor situated in every mobile blind and deaf people will receive Morse code from mobile (Tambe et al., 2020).

Safayet Anowar, Shurid, Khandaker Habibul Amin, Md.Shahnawaz, Mirbar,Dolan Karmaker, Mohammand, Tanvir Mahtab, Farhan Tanvir Khan "Bangla Sign Language Recognition and Sentence Building Using Deep Learning", IEEE (2020). In this research,they are using the Convolutional Neural Network (CNN) for training each individual sign. According to the paper for vision based hand gesture spotting and recognition using CRF and SVM, they used gesture spotting and recognition technique to find out hand gesture from the continuous movement of the hand (Shurid & Amin, 2020).

Rashmi R. Koli, Tanveer I, Bagban "Human Action Recognition Using Deep Neural Networks", IEEE (2020). For this system, they used human hand movements datasets, as per the length of the video (time slot) dataset frames size will be changed. The main problem is faced in the extraction process of determining keyframes, such as the size of keyframes that are different for every dataset (Koli, 2020).

Yun-Jung Ku, Min-Jen Chen, Chung-Ta King "A Virtual Sign Language Translator on Smartphones", IEEE (2019). In this paper, a smartphone application called Sign Language Translator (SLT) is introduced, which records the person signing and translates the hand gestures into texts. The current implementation only handles three gestures for sign language translation (Ku et al., 2019).

S.Vigneshwaran, M.Shifa Fathima,V.Vijay Sagar,R.Sree Arshika "Hand Gesture Recognition and Voice Conversion System for Dump People" IEEE (2019). In this proposed system the dump people hand motion or gesture can be detected and then it will be converted into human hearing voice signal. The controller used here is raspberry pi which does not contain any analog to digital converter (Vigneshwaran, 2019).

B Thanasekhar,G Deepak Kumar, V Akshay, Abdul Majeed Ashfaaq "Real Time Conversion of Sign Language using Deep Learning for Programming Basics", IEEE (2019). They propose to create a real-time sign language recognition system using image processing, computer vision and deep learning algorithms, that is capable of detecting and predicting gestures from the ISL dictionary dynamically. Though this algorithm works well for a realtime prototype application, a widespread user system will require much more advanced gesture intervals identification techniques to determine when they are performed (Sheahan et al., 2019).

DN Nagesh Kumar, M Madhukar, Adarsh Prabhakara Archana V Marathe, Manoj, Shyam S Bharadwaj "Sign Language to Speech Conversion — An Assistive System for Speech Impaired ", IEEE (2019) This system which is proposed above gives the methodology which aims to do the same as the two-way communication is possible. This can be further improvised so as to making it compatible for the mobile phones using the built-in camera of the phone (Eid, 2023).

Palani Thanaraj, Krishnan, Parvathini Balasubramanian "Detection of Alphabets for Machine Translation of Sign Language using Deep Neural Net", IEEE(2019). The test accuracy of the proposed ESL detection system is 70%. A more comprehensive image collection and data augmentation can lead to better prediction probabilities.

Kartik Shenoy, Tejas Dastane, Varun Rao, Devendra Vyavaharkar "Real-time Indian Sign Language (ISL) Recognition", IEEE(2018). The system presented in this paper is accurately able to track hand movements of the sign demonstrator using techniques such as Object Stabilisation, Face elimination, Skin colour Extraction and then Hand extraction. It can only classify all 33 hand poses in ISL with an accuracy of 80.7%.

## DESIGN AND IMPLEMENTATION

In this section, SLT application is for sign language translation on smartphones is introduced. The primary task of SLT is to detect the speakers hand skeleton to identify the sign expressed. SLT requires only the 2D camera equipped on smartphones to record the video of the speaker while signing.

This system explains two way communications between the deaf, dumb and normal people which means the proposed system is capable of converting the sign language to text and voice

A. REQUIREMENTS OF SYSTEM DESIGN

- System design is the process of designing the elements of a system such as the architecture, modules and components, the different interfaces of those components and the data that goes through that system.
- The purpose of the System Design process is to provide sufficient detailed data and information about the system and its system elements to enable the implementation consistent with architectural entities as defined in models and views of the system architecture. System requirements are all of the requirements at the system level that describe the functions which the system as a whole should fulfil to satisfy the minimum and recommended requirements.
- The minimum system requirements need to be met for the software to run at all on your system, and the recommended system requirements, if met, will offer better software usability. System requirements for operating systems will be application software will list operating system requirements. It is expressed in an appropriate combination of textual statements, views, and non-functional requirements; the latter expressing the levels of safety, security, reliability, etc., that will be necessary.

B. METHODOLOGY

The following modules that are used in the proposed system are listed below.

- Image Recognition
- Labelling images for Object Detection
- Training Sample
- Detecting Sign Language

## Image Recognition

Image Recognition is the task of identifying objects of interest within an image and recognizing which category they belong to. In this work, visually see an object or scene, we automatically identify objects as different instances and associate them with individual definitions.

## Labellling Images for Objection Detection

An image labeling is used to label the images for bounding box object detection and segmentation. With the help of the image labeling tools, the objects in the image could be labeled for a classified purpose.

The yolov5 algorithm covers mainly these steps: image classification, object localization and object detection. Yolov5 is used for training in sign language:

## Training Samples

In this work, the whole network training includes two phases. Firstly, train the object proposal network with object proposal training samples. Secondly, train both the object proposal network and the object detection network. For both phases of network training, training samples with object classes and bounding boxes are needed. Next we introduce the construction of training samples, then present the loss function to be used for network training.

## Detecting Sign Language in Realtime

A real time sign language detector is a significant step forward in improving communication between the deaf and the general population. In this work, the creation and implementation of sign language recognition model based on a Convolutional Neural Network(CNN) and utilized a Pre-Trained SSD Mobile net V2 architecture trained on our own dataset in order to apply Transfer learning to the task. In this work, image processing techniques with Human movement classification was identified as the best approach and the system is able to recognize selected Sign Language signs with the accuracy of 70-80% without a controlled background with small light.

This work is to produce a video call model that can recognize hand gestures and signs. CNN algorithm interprets the hand gestures and builds a statement from the video. This statement or textual information is the meaning of those gestures. To recognize different hand gestures of users we have used CNN Deep Learning algorithm. As soon as user starts showing hand gestures to camera our algorithm using CNN would detect the correct phrase/number/letter and send it to frontend. Detection and formation of sentence will be done simultaneously. The Sign Language is mainly used for communication of deaf-dumb people. In this work, train a model for the purpose of sign language conversion, this will help people converse with people who are innately deaf and mentally disabled. The architecture of the proposed work shown in Figure 1.

*Figure 1. Architecture of the proposed work*

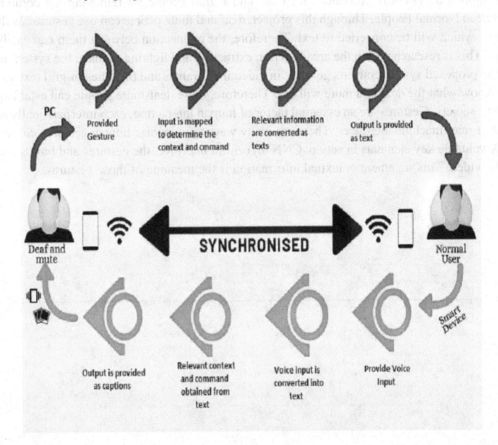

## RESULTS AND DISCUSSION

The proposed system is introduced for Deaf and Dumb People for removing the communication gap between Normal People. Through this project, deaf and mute people can use gestures as their main language, which will be converted to text. Therefore, the connection between them can easily occupy the area. This is research within the area function extraction and lighting to make the system more reliable. The proposed system converts gestures in video into Frames and then meaningful text so ordinary people know what the deaf and mute will say. Therefore, these deaf-mute people can establish contact with their society. Gestures are an essential factor of human interaction, each interpersonally and in the context of man-machine interfaces. There are many ways to recognize human gestures. So, it needs to identify valuable key elements in action. CNN algorithm interprets the gestures and builds a statement from the video. This statement or textual information is the meaning of those gestures

## CONCLUSION

The proposed system is introduced for Deaf and Dumb People for removing the communication gap between Normal People. Through this project, deaf and mute people can use gestures as their main language, which will be converted to text. Therefore, the connection between them can easily occupy the area. This is research within the area function extraction and lighting to make the system more reliable. The proposed system converts gestures in video into Frames and then meaningful text so ordinary people know what the deaf and mute will say. Therefore, these deaf-mute people can establish contact with their society. Gestures are an essential factor of human interaction, each interpersonally and in the context of man-machine interfaces. There are many ways to recognize human gestures. So, it needs to identify valuable key elements in action. CNN algorithm interprets the gestures and builds a statement from the video. This statement or textual information is the meaning of those gestures.

# REFERENCES

Aadit, T., Deepak, J., Janhavi, P., & Jyoti, D. (2021). Video Chat Application for Mutes. *IEEE International Conference on Emerging Smart Computing and Informatics (ESCI)*. IEEE. 10.1109/ESCI50559.2021.9397044

Eid, A. (2023). Visual Static Hand Gesture Recognition Using Convolutional Neural Network. *Algorithm MDPI,16*(8), 1-19.

Koli, R. R. (2020). Human Action Recognition Using Deep Neural Networks. *IEEE Fourth World Conference on Smart Trends in Systems, Security and Sustainability (WorldS4)*. IEEE.

Ku, Y.-J., Chen, M.-J., & King, C.-T. (2019). A Virtual Sign Language Translator on Smartphones. *Seventh International Symposium on Computing and Networking Workshops (CANDARW)*. IEEE.

Sheahan, G., Reznick, R., Klinger, D., Flynn, L., & Zevin, B. (2019). Comparison of Personal Video Technology for Teaching and Assessment of Surgical Skills. *Journal of Graduate Medical Education*, 11(3), 328–331. 10.4300/JGME-D-18-01082.131210866

Shurid, S. A., & Amin, K. H. (2020). Bangla Sign Language Recognition and Sentence Building Using Deep Learning. *IEEE AsiaPacific Conference on Computer Science and Data Engineering (CSDE)*. IEEE.

Tambe, S., Galphat, Y., Rijhwani, N., Goythale, A., & Patil, J. (2020). *Analyzing and Enhancing Communication Platforms available for a Deaf-Blind user*. IEEE. 10.1109/iSSSC50941.2020.9358823

Vigneshwaran, S. (2019). *Hand Gesture Recognition and Voice Conversion System for Dump People*. IEEE.

# Chapter 17
# Guiding Principles for Youth–Centric Development:
## Ethical AI

**S. C. Vetrivel**
https://orcid.org/0000-0003-3050-8211
*Kongu Engineering College, India*

**K. C. Sowmiya**
*Sri Vasavi College, India*

**V. P. Arun**
*JKKN College of Engineering and Technology, India*

**T. P. Saravanan**
*Kongu Engineering College, India*

**R. Maheswari**
*Kongu Engineering College, India*

## ABSTRACT

*As artificial intelligence (AI) technologies continue to evolve, there is a growing recognition of the need for ethical considerations in their development, particularly when targeting younger demographics. "Ethical AI: Guiding Principles for Youth-Centric Development" explores the ethical dimensions of AI with a focus on creating a framework that prioritizes the well-being and development of young users. This chapter investigates the intersection of technology, ethics, and the unique vulnerabilities associated with youth engagement in AI-driven systems. The study begins by outlining the current landscape of AI applications in various sectors that directly impact the lives of young individuals, including education, entertainment, social media, and healthcare. It delves into the potential risks and benefits associated with these applications, highlighting the ethical challenges that arise when designing AI systems for youth consumption.*

DOI: 10.4018/979-8-3693-3350-1.ch017

# INTRODUCTION

## Defining Ethical AI

Ethical AI, or Ethical Artificial Intelligence, refers to the design, development, and deployment of artificial intelligence systems with a strong emphasis on moral and principled considerations. In the rapidly advancing field of AI, ethical considerations have become paramount, as the impact of AI technologies on individuals, societies, and global systems continues to grow. At its core, ethical AI seeks to align technological advancements with human values, ensuring that the benefits of AI are distributed equitably and that potential risks are mitigated. One fundamental aspect of ethical AI is fairness. It involves addressing biases in AI algorithms to prevent discrimination against certain groups. Bias can emerge from the data used to train AI models, and ethical AI strives to identify and rectify such biases, promoting equal opportunities and outcomes for all individuals (Akgun & Greenhow, 2022). Transparency is another crucial element, as ethical AI demands clear and understandable decision-making processes. Users should be able to comprehend how AI systems reach conclusions or recommendations, fostering trust and accountability in the technology. Privacy is a key concern in the ethical AI landscape. Ensuring the protection of individuals' data and maintaining their autonomy is paramount. Ethical AI practices incorporate robust measures to safeguard sensitive information, respecting user privacy and preventing unauthorized use of data. Additionally, ethical AI frameworks emphasize the importance of accountability and responsibility among developers, organizations, and other stakeholders. Developers are encouraged to anticipate potential risks and address them proactively throughout the AI system's lifecycle. As AI systems increasingly influence various aspects of society, ethical considerations extend beyond technical aspects to encompass broader societal impacts. Ethical AI principles stress the importance of promoting human rights, inclusivity, and social well-being. Striking a balance between innovation and ethical guidelines is crucial, as AI technologies should contribute positively to societal progress without inadvertently causing harm or exacerbating existing inequalities. Educating and fostering awareness among all stakeholders, from developers to end-users, is a fundamental pillar of ethical AI. By promoting literacy and understanding about AI's ethical dimensions, society can collectively navigate the challenges and opportunities presented by this transformative technology. Ethical AI, therefore, represents a commitment to creating AI systems that not only perform efficiently but also align with human values, contributing to a more just, inclusive, and sustainable future.

## Importance of Youth-Centric Development

The importance of youth-centric development in the context of AI is significant and multifaceted (Barr et al., 2015). Focusing on the needs, rights, and perspectives of young people in the development of artificial intelligence technologies ensures a more inclusive, responsible, and sustainable future. Here are some key reasons why youth-centric development is crucial:

º    **Future Impact and Technological Literacy:** Youth are the future leaders, workers, and consumers. Engaging them in AI development ensures that they are not only prepared for the future but also actively contributing to shaping it.

º    Building technological literacy among the youth is essential to equip them with the skills necessary to navigate a world increasingly influenced by AI.

○ **Ethical Considerations and Values:** Young people often bring fresh perspectives and a strong sense of social justice. Involving them in AI development helps embed ethical considerations and values from diverse backgrounds into the design and deployment of AI systems.

○ **Customization for Diverse Needs:** Youth represent a diverse demographic with varying needs, experiences, and preferences. Designing AI systems with a youth-centric approach allows for customization that addresses the unique challenges and opportunities specific to this demographic.

○ **Guardians of Digital Rights:** Youth are particularly susceptible to the impacts of AI, such as privacy concerns, algorithmic biases, and online safety. By involving them in the development process, we empower them to be advocates for their digital rights and privacy.

○ **Innovation and Creativity:** Young minds are often more open to innovation and creative thinking. Involving youth in AI development can lead to the discovery of novel solutions and applications that may not be apparent to older generations.

○ **Addressing Social and Environmental Issues:** Youth-centric AI development can focus on addressing pressing social and environmental challenges, such as climate change, inequality, and healthcare. Young people are often passionate about making a positive impact on the world, and AI can be a powerful tool in their hands.

○ **Long-Term Sustainability:** By involving youth in AI development, there is a higher likelihood of creating sustainable and future-proof solutions. It ensures that the technologies are designed with a long-term perspective, considering the evolving needs and values of the youth over time.

○ **Civic Engagement and Empowerment:** Youth-centric AI development promotes civic engagement and empowerment. It encourages young people to actively participate in the decision-making processes that shape the technologies they use, fostering a sense of responsibility and ownership.

## Methodologies Used to Identify and Develop Guiding Principles for Youth-Centric Development in the Context of Ethical AI

The methodology to identify and develop guiding principles for youth-centric development in the context of Ethical AI involves a multi-faceted approach. Initially, a comprehensive literature review is conducted to understand existing frameworks and ethical considerations in AI. This is followed by stakeholder engagement, including workshops, focus groups, and surveys involving youth, educators, AI developers, and ethicists to gather diverse perspectives and insights. Special emphasis is placed on inclusive representation to ensure the voices of marginalized and underrepresented youth are heard. The collected data is then analyzed using qualitative methods to identify common themes and concerns. Iterative feedback loops are established, where preliminary principles are tested and refined through additional consultations and pilot projects. This process ensures that the principles are not only theoretically sound but also practically applicable and resonate with the lived experiences and aspirations of young people. The final guiding principles are validated through expert review and collaborative endorsement from key stakeholders, ensuring they are robust, comprehensive, and aligned with both ethical standards and the unique needs of youth in the AI landscape.

## THE FOUNDATIONS OF ETHICAL AI

### Core Principles of Ethical AI

The core principles of ethical AI form the bedrock upon which responsible and socially conscious artificial intelligence systems are built. These principles are essential guidelines that govern the development, deployment, and usage of AI technologies to ensure that they align with ethical standards and contribute positively to society (Bonnardel & Zenasni, 2010). One fundamental principle is transparency, emphasizing the importance of making AI systems understandable and interpretable by users. Transparent AI systems not only foster trust but also empower individuals to comprehend the decision-making processes of the technology they interact with. Another key principle is fairness, advocating for the elimination of biases in AI algorithms that may result in discriminatory outcomes. Addressing bias involves ensuring diverse and representative datasets, as well as continuously monitoring and mitigating any unintended consequences that may arise during the AI lifecycle. Accountability is another critical principle, stipulating that developers and organizations must take responsibility for the impact of their AI systems on individuals and society. Establishing clear lines of accountability helps to address potential harm and encourages ethical decision-making throughout the AI development process (Bostrom & Sandberg, 2009; Carter & Palermos, 2019). Privacy is a core ethical principle that underscores the importance of safeguarding individuals' personal information. AI systems should be designed with robust privacy protections, and users must be informed about how their data is collected, processed, and used. Additionally, inclusivity and accessibility are central principles, emphasizing the need to ensure that AI technologies are designed to serve a diverse range of users, accounting for various cultural, linguistic, and socio-economic backgrounds. Finally, continuous improvement and adaptability are inherent principles, promoting the idea that ethical AI requires ongoing assessment, refinement, and adaptation to evolving ethical standards and technological advancements.

### Historical Context and Evolution

In delving into the foundations of ethical AI, an exploration of the historical context and evolution of artificial intelligence becomes imperative. The journey of AI spans several decades, witnessing remarkable technological advancements and paradigm shifts. Initially emerging as a concept in the mid-20th century, the field of AI experienced a series of booms and winters, marked by periods of intense research, followed by setbacks and reevaluations. The historical context sheds light on the dreams and aspirations that fueled the early AI pioneers, like Alan Turing and John McCarthy, who envisioned machines capable of human-like intelligence (Cave et al., 2018). The evolution of AI is a dynamic tapestry woven with breakthroughs such as the development of expert systems, neural networks, and machine learning algorithms. As computational power grew, so did the possibilities of AI applications. However, this progress was not without ethical dilemmas. The pursuit of efficiency and performance sometimes led to oversight in addressing societal concerns, raising questions about biases in algorithms, accountability, and the impact of AI on employment. Understanding the historical context and evolution of AI is crucial for ethical considerations because it provides insights into the motivations behind AI development and the challenges encountered along the way. Learning from the successes and failures of the past allows us to build a foundation that prioritizes ethical principles in the design, deployment, and evolution of AI systems (Chabris & Simons, 2010). As we embark on an era where AI is becoming increasingly integrated into daily life, the historical context serves as a guide for shaping a responsible and ethical trajectory for the future of artificial intelligence.

## The Guiding Principles for Youth-Centric Development in Ethical AI

Guiding principles for youth-centric development in Ethical AI emphasize inclusivity, transparency, privacy, and empowerment. These principles advocate for the active involvement of young people in the AI development process, ensuring their diverse voices and perspectives shape the technologies that impact their lives. Transparency is critical, requiring clear communication about how AI systems function and make decisions, enabling youth to understand and trust these technologies. Privacy is paramount, demanding stringent safeguards to protect young users' data from misuse and unauthorized access. Empowerment is achieved by equipping youth with the knowledge and skills to engage with AI critically and creatively, fostering an environment where they can not only use but also influence AI technologies. Collectively, these principles aim to create AI systems that are fair, accountable, and beneficial, prioritizing the well-being and rights of young people in their design and implementation.

## UNDERSTANDING YOUTH-CENTRIC DEVELOPMENT

### Characteristics of Youth-Centric AI

When exploring the characteristics of Youth-Centric AI under the broader theme of Understanding Youth-Centric Development, it's important to consider the unique needs, capabilities, and concerns of young individuals (Chabris & Simons, 2010). By incorporating these characteristics into the development of Youth-Centric AI, developers can create a more effective and responsible system that aligns with the unique needs and developmental stages of young users. Here's a detailed look at the characteristics:

o   **User-Friendly Interface:** Youth-Centric AI should feature an intuitive and user-friendly interface to cater to the varying levels of technological familiarity among young users. A design that is visually appealing, interactive, and easy to navigate can enhance engagement.

o   **Adaptability and Personalization:** Recognizing the diversity among young users, Youth-Centric AI should be adaptable and capable of personalization. This involves understanding individual preferences, learning styles, and adjusting its interactions accordingly to provide a more tailored experience.

o   **Educational Focus:** A key characteristic is the integration of educational components. Youth-Centric AI should be designed to facilitate learning experiences, providing valuable information, and fostering intellectual growth. This includes interactive lessons, educational games, and adaptive learning paths.

o   **Ethical and Safe:** The AI system should prioritize safety and adhere to strict ethical guidelines. This involves protecting user privacy, avoiding harmful content, and ensuring that the AI's influence is aligned with positive values and educational goals.

o   **Emotional Intelligence:** Incorporating elements of emotional intelligence is crucial. Youth-Centric AI should be able to recognize and respond to the emotions of young users, providing empathetic and supportive interactions. This can contribute to a positive and emotionally safe experience.

- o **Collaboration and Social Integration:** Given the social nature of youth development, the AI system should encourage collaboration and social interaction. This may involve features that facilitate group projects, shared learning experiences, or virtual communities where young users can connect and learn together.
- o **Gamification Elements:** To enhance engagement, Youth-Centric AI can incorporate gamification elements. This includes rewards, badges, and other motivational features to make the learning process more enjoyable and incentivize continued participation.
- o **Accessibility and Inclusivity:** Youth-Centric AI should prioritize accessibility, ensuring that the technology is available and usable for all young individuals, regardless of their abilities or backgrounds. This involves considering factors such as language diversity, cultural sensitivity, and inclusivity.
- o **Continuous Monitoring and Improvement:** The AI system should include mechanisms for continuous monitoring of user interactions and feedback. This data can be used to make improvements, address any emerging issues, and enhance the overall effectiveness of the Youth-Centric AI.
- o **Parental Controls and Oversight:** Given the age group involved, Youth-Centric AI should offer robust parental controls and oversight features. This ensures that parents or guardians can monitor and manage their child's interactions with the AI system, ensuring a safe and responsible use.

## Challenges and Opportunities

## Challenges in Youth-Centric Development

- **Age-Appropriate Design:**

  - o Challenge: Designing AI systems that are suitable for various age groups, considering cognitive abilities, emotional development, and learning styles.
  - o Solutions: Conducting thorough user research, involving child psychologists, and implementing adaptive interfaces to cater to diverse age ranges.

- **Informed Consent and Assent:**

  - o Challenge: Obtaining meaningful consent from minors who may not fully comprehend the implications of AI use.
  - o Solutions: Developing age-appropriate consent mechanisms, educating both parents and children about AI implications, and incorporating interactive learning experiences.

- **Online Safety and Cyberbullying:**

  - o Challenge: Protecting youth from online threats, cyberbullying, and potential exploitation facilitated by AI.
  - o Solutions: Implementing robust safety measures, leveraging AI for content moderation, and promoting digital literacy and responsible online behavior.

- **Privacy Concerns:**

    o   Challenge: Safeguarding the privacy of young users and their personal data in AI applications.
    o   Solutions: Incorporating privacy-by-design principles, anonymizing data, and adhering to stringent data protection regulations for minors.

- **Accessibility and Inclusivity:**

    o   Challenge: Ensuring that AI technologies are accessible to all youth, including those with disabilities and from diverse socio-economic backgrounds.
    o   Solutions: Prioritizing inclusive design, providing assistive technologies, and collaborating with advocacy groups for marginalized communities.

## Opportunities in Youth-Centric Development

- **Educational Enhancement:**

    o   Opportunity: Leveraging AI to enhance educational experiences by personalizing learning, adapting to individual needs, and providing real-time feedback.
    o   Strategies: Collaborating with educators to integrate AI into the curriculum, creating interactive educational content, and fostering a lifelong love for learning.

- **Empowering Creativity and Innovation:**

    o   Opportunity: Encouraging youth to explore and express creativity through AI-driven tools and platforms.
    o   Strategies: Developing user-friendly AI tools for creative expression, fostering a culture of innovation, and showcasing success stories of young creators using AI.

- **Civic Engagement and Social Impact:**

    o   Opportunity: Involving youth in AI-driven projects that address societal challenges and promote positive change.
    o   Strategies: Creating platforms for youth participation, supporting youth-led initiatives, and showcasing the impact of AI in addressing global issues.

- **Critical Thinking and Ethical Decision-Making:**

    o   Opportunity: Using AI as a tool to teach critical thinking, ethical reasoning, and responsible decision-making.

- ○ Strategies: Incorporating AI literacy in educational programs, encouraging discussions on ethical AI dilemmas, and providing guidance on responsible AI use.

- **Preparing for Future Opportunities:**

  - ○ Opportunity: Equipping youth with the skills and knowledge needed for future AI-driven careers.
  - ○ Strategies: Offering training programs, mentorship opportunities, and internships that expose youth to AI development and applications.

# ETHICAL CONSIDERATIONS IN AI DESIGN

## Bias and Fairness

Bias and fairness are critical aspects of ethical considerations in AI design, representing fundamental principles that directly impact the societal implications of artificial intelligence systems. Bias in AI refers to the presence of partiality or favoritism in the data, algorithms, or decision-making processes that may disproportionately affect certain groups. This bias can emerge from historical inequalities embedded in training datasets, perpetuating and exacerbating societal disparities when AI systems are deployed. Ensuring fairness in AI design involves striving for equitable outcomes across diverse demographic groups. This requires an awareness of potential biases, both explicit and implicit, and a commitment to rectifying them. Designers must carefully assess and mitigate biases during the entire development lifecycle, from data collection and preprocessing to algorithmic training and decision-making. Employing diverse and representative datasets, actively seeking to identify and eliminate biased patterns, and incorporating fairness-enhancing techniques such as adversarial training are crucial steps in promoting fairness (Clark & Chalmers, 1998). Transparency plays a pivotal role in addressing bias and fostering fairness. Openly communicating about the AI system's objectives, data sources, and decision-making processes allows for external scrutiny and accountability. Additionally, providing explanations for AI-generated decisions contributes to transparency and helps build trust among users and affected communities. Ethical AI design not only seeks to avoid perpetuating existing biases but also aims to contribute positively to social equality by actively working to reduce disparities and promote inclusivity. By integrating fairness into the core of AI development, we can create systems that align more closely with ethical principles and contribute to a more just and equitable society.

## Transparency and Explainability

Transparency and explainability are crucial components of ethical AI design, playing a pivotal role in fostering trust, accountability, and responsible use of artificial intelligence systems. Transparency refers to the openness and clarity in the functioning of AI algorithms and models, ensuring that the decision-making processes are understandable and accessible to various stakeholders, including end-users, developers, and regulators. In ethical AI design, it is imperative to demystify the 'black box' nature often associated with complex machine learning algorithms. Transparency allows users to comprehend how AI systems reach their conclusions, enabling them to assess the reliability and fairness of the outcomes. Explainability, on the other hand, is closely linked to transparency and involves providing meaningful insights into the AI system's decision-making logic (Danaher, 2018). It goes beyond simply revealing the technical aspects of the algorithm and focuses on delivering intelligible explanations to non-experts. Achieving explainability in AI design ensures that the decision-making processes can be understood and scrutinized by individuals who may not have a technical background, promoting inclusivity and ethical accountability. Additionally, explainability aids in identifying and addressing biases that may be present in the data or algorithms, contributing to the overall fairness and equity of the AI system. In the context of ethical considerations, transparency and explainability serve as powerful tools to combat the potential risks associated with opaque AI systems (Di Paolo, 2009; Engelbart, 1962). By promoting a clear understanding of how AI makes decisions, stakeholders can better anticipate and mitigate unintended consequences, discriminatory outcomes, or ethical lapses. This, in turn, empowers users to make informed choices and holds developers and organizations accountable for the ethical implications of their AI applications. Striking a balance between transparency and explainability is essential to building AI systems that not only perform effectively but also align with ethical principles, respecting the rights and values of the individuals impacted by these technologies (Fiske & Taylor, 1984). Ethical AI design, therefore, should prioritize transparency and explainability as foundational pillars to ensure responsible and trustworthy deployment of artificial intelligence in various domains.

## PRIVACY AND SECURITY CONCERNS

### Protecting Youth Data

In the realm of Ethical AI: Guiding Principles for Youth-Centric Development, safeguarding youth data emerges as a critical imperative within the broader context of Privacy and Security Concerns. Protecting the privacy of young individuals involves not only complying with legal frameworks but also prioritizing their well-being in the digital landscape. This chapter delves into the multifaceted dimensions of ensuring robust data protection protocols. Central to the discourse is the concept of data minimization, advocating for the collection and storage of only essential information necessary for the intended purpose. This principle acknowledges that excessive data accumulation not only poses a risk to individual privacy but also amplifies the potential for misuse or unauthorized access (Frischmann & Selinger, 2018; Heersmink, 2017). Moreover, the chapter explores encryption and anonymization techniques as fundamental tools to shield sensitive youth data from unauthorized entities, thereby mitigating the risk of breaches and cyber threats. The ethical considerations extend beyond mere technical safeguards, emphasizing the necessity for transparent data practices. Implementing clear and accessible privacy policies, specifically tailored to a youthful audience, fosters a culture of trust and informed consent. As part of this comprehensive approach, the chapter also addresses the pivotal role of user education, empowering young individuals to understand the value of their data, recognize potential risks, and make informed decisions about their online interactions. Furthermore, the chapter underscores the importance of robust cybersecurity measures, urging developers and organizations to adopt state-of-the-art technologies to fortify their systems against evolving threats. It also explores the concept of data ownership, advocating for empowering youth with control over their personal information, enabling them to manage and, if desired, erase their digital footprint. Protecting Youth Data within the Privacy and Security Concerns framework exemplifies a commitment to ethical AI development (Hernández-Orallo & Vold, 2019). By instilling a culture of responsibility, transparency, and empowerment, this chapter sets the stage for a digital landscape where the privacy and security of young individuals are paramount in the design and deployment of AI technologies.

## Safeguarding Against Exploitation

The imperative to safeguard against exploitation in the realm of ethical AI within youth-centric development arises from the inherent vulnerability of young individuals and the potential for AI systems to be misused or inadvertently harm their well-being (Hutchins, 1999). This report delves into the multifaceted aspects of safeguarding, encompassing both technical and ethical considerations to ensure that AI technologies designed for and used by youth prioritize their safety, rights, and overall development.

**Understanding Vulnerabilities:** The initial focus lies in comprehending the unique vulnerabilities that youth face in the digital age. This involves recognizing the potential for AI systems to exploit sensitive information, manipulate behaviors, or perpetuate harmful biases, particularly when dealing with impressionable minds (Jacko, 2012). By acknowledging these vulnerabilities, ethical AI practitioners can tailor their approach to mitigate risks and prioritize the well-being of young users.

**Transparency and Explainability:** A key pillar in safeguarding against exploitation is the incorporation of transparency and explainability in AI systems. Providing clear, understandable explanations of how AI algorithms operate fosters trust among users and ensures that youth can make informed decisions about their engagement with AI technologies. Transparency measures also empower caregivers, educators, and policymakers to assess and address potential risks, creating a collaborative framework for responsible AI development.

**Informed Consent and Privacy Protection**: Respecting the autonomy of youth involves obtaining informed consent for AI usage. This entails clear communication about data collection, processing, and storage practices, ensuring that young individuals and their guardians are fully aware of how their information is utilized (Licklider, 1960). Privacy protection mechanisms, such as robust data encryption and stringent access controls, become paramount in preventing unauthorized access and potential exploitation.

**Algorithmic Bias Mitigation:** Addressing algorithmic biases is crucial to preventing the inadvertent exploitation of youth through AI systems. Ethical AI developers must actively work to identify and rectify biases in training data and algorithms to avoid perpetuating stereotypes or discriminatory outcomes (Menary, 2007). Continuous monitoring and evaluation of AI systems for bias ensure that the technology evolves to align with ethical standards and remains sensitive to the diverse needs and perspectives of youth.

**Empowering Youth through Ethical Design**: Safeguarding against exploitation also involves empowering youth to become informed and active participants in the digital landscape. Ethical AI design should prioritize user interfaces that facilitate user understanding and control over their AI interactions. Moreover, involving young individuals in the co-design process ensures that AI technologies align with their values, needs, and aspirations, reducing the likelihood of exploitation.

## HUMAN RIGHTS AND AI

### Ensuring Inclusivity

Ensuring inclusivity within the realm of Human Rights and AI is a paramount concern that demands careful consideration and proactive measures. In the context of artificial intelligence, inclusivity refers to the equitable representation and fair treatment of diverse individuals and communities, irrespective of their backgrounds, cultures, or socio-economic statuses. Failure to address inclusivity can perpetuate and exacerbate existing societal biases, further marginalizing already vulnerable groups (Minsky, 1968; Nalepa et al., 2018). To achieve inclusivity, AI systems must be designed and implemented with a commitment to diversity and the avoidance of discriminatory practices. This involves fostering representation at every stage of AI development, from data collection to algorithmic decision-making. It requires a keen awareness of potential biases in training data and a conscious effort to rectify them, ensuring that the resulting AI models are fair and unbiased across various demographic groups. Moreover, inclusivity in AI should extend beyond mere representation and address the specific needs and perspectives of marginalized communities. This requires a nuanced understanding of cultural contexts, historical injustices, and systemic inequalities (Newell & Card, 1985). Developers and policymakers must actively engage with these communities to gain insights into their unique challenges and incorporate this knowledge into the design and deployment of AI systems. Inclusivity also involves providing equal access and opportunities for all individuals to benefit from AI technologies. This may entail addressing issues related to digital literacy, infrastructure, and affordability, ensuring that AI benefits are accessible to people across different geographical locations and economic strata. By prioritizing inclusivity, the development and deployment of AI can become a powerful force for positive social change, upholding human rights and fostering a more just and equitable future.

### Addressing Social Impacts

Addressing social impacts under the umbrella of Human Rights and AI is crucial for ensuring that artificial intelligence technologies do not exacerbate existing inequalities or violate fundamental human rights. In this chapter, we delve into the multifaceted dimensions of social impacts, emphasizing the need for ethical considerations and responsible development. One major concern is the potential reinforcement of societal biases through AI algorithms. We explore how biased data sets and algorithmic decision-making systems can inadvertently perpetuate discrimination and amplify existing social disparities. Highlighting specific instances where vulnerable communities may be disproportionately affected, we advocate for transparency and fairness in AI design to mitigate these negative consequences. Moreover, we examine the right to privacy in the context of AI technologies (Hook & Putnam, 1960). As AI systems often process vast amounts of personal data, there is an inherent risk to individuals' privacy. This chapter delves into the ethical guidelines and legal frameworks that should govern the collection, storage, and use of personal information, emphasizing the importance of informed consent and data protection measures. Another critical aspect is the potential impact of AI on employment and the workforce. We discuss the ethical responsibility of AI developers and policymakers to address issues related to job displacement and the changing nature of work. Strategies for retraining and upskilling the workforce are explored, ensuring that the benefits of AI are shared equitably across society (Putnam, 1967; Risko & Gilbert, 2016). Furthermore, we scrutinize the digital divide and accessibility challenges associated with AI technologies. Examining how certain populations may face barriers in accessing and benefiting from AI-driven services, we propose inclusive design principles to ensure that the benefits of AI are accessible to everyone, irrespective of socioeconomic status or geographical location.

## EDUCATION AND ETHICAL AI LITERACY

### Integrating AI Education in Youth Curriculum

Integrating AI education into the youth curriculum is a pivotal step towards fostering ethical AI literacy among the younger generation. In this chapter, the focus lies on the importance of equipping students with the knowledge and skills necessary to understand, critically evaluate, and actively participate in the development and application of artificial intelligence. One key aspect is introducing fundamental concepts of AI, machine learning, and data science in an accessible manner. By incorporating these topics into the curriculum, students can grasp the foundational principles that underpin AI technologies. This not only demystifies the field but also empowers them to make informed decisions as future consumers, employees, and contributors to society (Rogers et al., 2011). Ethical considerations take center stage in this educational approach. Students are guided through discussions on the ethical implications of AI, including issues related to bias, fairness, transparency, and privacy. Case studies and real-world examples are explored, allowing students to analyze and critique the ethical dimensions of AI applications in different contexts. Moreover, discussions around the societal impact of AI on diverse communities and the importance of ensuring inclusivity in AI development are integral components of the curriculum. Practical applications and hands-on projects play a crucial role in reinforcing theoretical knowledge (Rouse & Spohrer, 2018). Students are encouraged to engage in projects that involve designing, developing, and evaluating AI systems with a focus on ethical considerations. This not only enhances their technical skills but also instills a sense of responsibility and mindfulness in AI creation. To support the successful integration of AI education, partnerships with industry experts, researchers, and educational technology organizations are fostered. Bringing in guest speakers, organizing workshops, and facilitating internships provide students with exposure to real-world AI scenarios and professionals. This collaborative approach ensures that the curriculum remains dynamic and aligned with the rapidly evolving field of AI.

### Fostering Ethical AI Awareness

Fostering Ethical AI Awareness within the realm of Education and Ethical AI Literacy is fundamental for empowering the youth to engage responsibly with artificial intelligence technologies. This chapter focuses on the development of educational programs that equip young learners with the knowledge and skills to understand, question, and contribute to the ethical use of AI (Rowlands, 2010; Samek et al., 2017). The curriculum should not only cover the technical aspects of AI but also emphasize the ethical considerations associated with its design, deployment, and impact on society. To achieve this, educational institutions need to integrate dedicated modules or courses that explore the ethical dimensions of AI. These modules should encourage critical thinking and ethical reasoning, enabling students to analyze the implications of AI applications on various aspects of human life, such as privacy, bias, and social justice. Additionally, educators should highlight real-world examples of AI implementations, both positive and negative, to provide students with tangible cases that demonstrate the ethical challenges and opportunities associated with AI technologies. The discussion also advocates for a multidisciplinary approach to AI education, encouraging collaboration between computer science, ethics, sociology, and other relevant disciplines (Smart, 2018). This interdisciplinary perspective enables students to appreciate the complexity of ethical issues surrounding AI and fosters a holistic understanding of the technology's broader societal impact. Furthermore, fostering ethical AI awareness involves creating a learning environment that encourages open dialogue and critical discussions. Students should feel empowered to question the ethical implications of AI systems and engage in debates about potential solutions. Educational institutions can facilitate this by organizing workshops, seminars, and guest lectures featuring experts in AI ethics.

## BUILDING ETHICAL AI COMMUNITIES

### Collaboration and Partnerships

Collaboration is paramount in addressing the multifaceted challenges posed by AI, and partnerships across sectors can significantly enhance the effectiveness of ethical AI initiatives. Effective collaboration involves bringing together experts from diverse fields such as technology, ethics, education, policy, and youth advocacy. Technology companies, governmental bodies, non-profit organizations, and educational institutions can pool their resources, expertise, and perspectives to develop comprehensive frameworks that prioritize ethical considerations in AI development (Sparrow et al., 2011). By creating interdisciplinary teams, these collaborations can ensure a more holistic approach to addressing the ethical implications of AI technologies. Partnerships also play a crucial role in establishing shared standards and guidelines for ethical AI. Industry leaders, ethical AI advocates, and regulatory bodies can collaborate to set benchmarks that prioritize fairness, transparency, accountability, and the protection of human rights, particularly those of young individuals. Through these partnerships, stakeholders can work towards establishing a common language and understanding of ethical AI principles, fostering a cohesive global effort. Furthermore, collaboration and partnerships can facilitate the dissemination of knowledge and best practices. Educational institutions can collaborate with industry partners to develop curricula that integrate ethical AI principles into educational programs, ensuring that the next generation of technologists is well-versed in ethical considerations. Additionally, collaborative initiatives can organize workshops, conferences, and training sessions to share insights and build a collective understanding of evolving ethical challenges in AI. In building ethical AI communities, the chapter underscores the significance of fostering a culture of open dialogue and transparency within these collaborations. This involves creating platforms for continuous engagement, where stakeholders can share experiences, discuss emerging ethical dilemmas, and collectively brainstorm solutions. Through these collaborative efforts, the chapter aims to emphasize that ethical AI development is not an isolated endeavor but a collective responsibility that demands ongoing cooperation among diverse actors invested in shaping a responsible and inclusive AI future.

### Engaging Youth in AI Development

Engaging youth in AI development is a crucial aspect of building ethical AI communities. This chapter explores the multifaceted role that young individuals can play in shaping the ethical landscape of artificial intelligence (Spohrer & Banavar, 2015). Acknowledging that youth represent the future beneficiaries and stewards of AI technologies, the chapter emphasizes the importance of involving them in decision-making processes, design considerations, and policy discussions related to AI development. One key aspect of engaging youth in AI development involves fostering a culture of inclusivity and empowerment. By providing opportunities for young people to actively participate in AI projects, workshops, and initiatives, ethical AI communities can tap into a diverse pool of perspectives and ideas. This inclusivity not only enriches the development process but also ensures that the resulting AI systems are reflective of a broader range of values and priorities (Sutton, 2006). Furthermore, the chapter delves into the significance of educational programs and initiatives aimed at building AI literacy among youth. Empowering young individuals with the knowledge and skills needed to understand, critique, and contribute to AI development is essential. By integrating AI education into school curricula and extracurricular activities, ethical AI communities can equip youth with the tools necessary to navigate the ethical complexities of emerging technologies. The role of mentorship and collaboration is also explored within this chapter. Establishing mentorship programs that connect experienced professionals with young enthusiasts fosters a dynamic learning environment. This not only accelerates the skill development of youth but also facilitates the transfer of ethical values and principles within the AI community. Collaboration between generations ensures a continuity of ethical considerations and promotes a shared commitment to responsible AI development.

## FUTURE PERSPECTIVES AND EMERGING ISSUES

### Anticipating Ethical Challenges

As technology progresses, the ethical implications of AI applications become increasingly complex, necessitating proactive consideration of potential challenges. One of the primary concerns revolves around the exacerbation of existing societal inequalities. AI systems may inadvertently perpetuate biases present in training data, leading to discriminatory outcomes, particularly affecting marginalized communities. Anticipating and mitigating these biases is paramount to ensuring a fair and equitable AI landscape for young users. Another ethical challenge lies in the realm of privacy and data protection (Thagard, 1996). As AI systems become more sophisticated in analyzing vast amounts of personal data, there is a heightened risk of privacy infringement, especially among youth who may be less aware of the implications of sharing sensitive information. Striking a balance between leveraging data for AI advancements and safeguarding individual privacy is essential in the development and deployment of youth-centric AI solutions. The potential for job displacement due to automation is another concern that needs careful consideration. As AI technologies advance, certain traditional jobs may become obsolete, posing challenges for youth entering the workforce. Addressing these socio-economic implications requires a proactive approach, including the development of educational programs that equip youth with skills resilient to automation, fostering adaptability in the face of technological disruption. Furthermore, the ethical challenges extend to the psychological well-being of young users. AI systems, especially those designed for personalized interactions, have the potential to influence emotions and behavior. Anticipating the ethical implications of AI's impact on mental health and emotional development in youth is imperative. Striking a balance between beneficial engagement and potential negative consequences is a delicate ethical consideration in the realm of youth-centric AI development. In navigating the future perspectives of ethical AI, it is essential to anticipate these challenges and establish comprehensive guidelines and frameworks that prioritize the well-being, equity, and informed engagement of the youth. By proactively addressing these ethical concerns, developers, educators, and policymakers can ensure that the deployment of AI technologies aligns with the principles of fairness, transparency, and inclusivity, ultimately fostering a positive and ethically sound environment for the next generation.

## Opportunities for Positive Impact

Ethical AI applications can revolutionize learning experiences, offering personalized and adaptive content to cater to individual learning styles. This approach fosters a more inclusive educational environment, addressing diverse needs and promoting equitable access to quality education. Moreover, there is an opportunity to empower youth in becoming ethical AI creators and contributors. By integrating AI literacy into educational curricula, young individuals can gain the knowledge and skills necessary to understand, shape, and critique AI systems. Encouraging youth to participate in the development process ensures a diverse range of perspectives and values are considered, contributing to the creation of more inclusive and responsible AI technologies. Another avenue for positive impact involves AI-driven innovations in healthcare. Ethical AI applications can enhance diagnostic accuracy, personalize treatment plans, and improve healthcare accessibility for youth populations (Vold, 2018). These technologies have the potential to identify health issues early on, facilitating preventive interventions and promoting overall well-being among the youth. Furthermore, Ethical AI can play a pivotal role in addressing societal challenges such as climate change and social inequality. By harnessing the power of AI to analyze and interpret vast datasets, researchers and policymakers can make more informed decisions to mitigate environmental impact and promote social justice. Ethical considerations in AI development can ensure that these technologies contribute positively to the global challenges faced by youth today and in the future. The future of ethical AI offers numerous opportunities for positive impact, ranging from transformative educational experiences and youth empowerment to advancements in healthcare and solutions for pressing global issues. It is essential to prioritize and invest in these areas to maximize the potential benefits of AI while safeguarding the well-being and rights of the younger generation.

## CONCLUSION

The study underscores the critical importance of cultivating a responsible and inclusive approach to artificial intelligence within the context of youth-centric development. Throughout this exploration, we have delved into the foundational principles of ethical AI, the unique considerations required for youth-oriented applications, and the imperative to balance technological innovation with moral accountability. As we navigate the evolving landscape of AI, it is clear that fostering awareness, collaboration, and continuous education will be instrumental in shaping a future where artificial intelligence serves the well-being of our youth, respects fundamental rights, and contributes positively to society. This book serves as a call to action for all stakeholders—developers, educators, policymakers, and the youth themselves—to actively participate in the ethical evolution of AI, ensuring that it becomes a force for good and an empowering tool for the generations to come.

# REFERENCES

Akgun, S., & Greenhow, C. (2022). Artificial intelligence in education: Addressing ethical challenges in K-12 settings. *AI and Ethics*, 2(3), 431–440. 10.1007/s43681-021-00096-734790956

Barr, N., Pennycook, G., Stolz, J. A., & Fugelsang, J. A. (2015). The brain in your pocket: Evidence that Smartphones are used to supplant thinking. *Computers in Human Behavior*, 48, 473–480. 10.1016/j. chb.2015.02.029

Bonnardel, N., & Zenasni, F. (2010). The impact of technology on creativity in design: An enhancement? *Creativity and Innovation Management*, 19(2), 180–191. 10.1111/j.1467-8691.2010.00560.x

Bostrom, N., & Sandberg, A. (2009). Cognitive enhancement: Methods, ethics, regulatory challenges. *Science and Engineering Ethics*, 15(3), 311–341. 10.1007/s11948-009-9142-519543814

Carter, J. A., & Palermos, S. O. (2019). The ethics of extended cognition: Is having your computer compromised a personal assault? *Journal of the American Philosophical Association*.

Cave, S. J., Nyrup, R., Vold, K., & Weller, A. (2018). Motivations and Risks of Machine Ethics. *Proceedings of the IEEE*, 99, 1–13.

Chabris, C., & Simons, D. (2010). *The invisible gorilla: And other ways our intuitions deceive us*. Harmony.

Clark, A., & Chalmers, D. (1998). The extended mind. *Analysis*, 58(1), 7–19. 10.1093/analys/58.1.7

Danaher, J. (2018). Toward an Ethics of AI Assistants: An Initial Framework. *Philosophy & Technology*, 31(4), 1–25. 10.1007/s13347-018-0317-3

Di Paolo, E. (2009). Extended life. *Topoi*, 28(1), 9–21. 10.1007/s11245-008-9042-3

Engelbart, D. C. (1962). *Augmenting human intellect: a conceptual framework. Summary Report AFOSR-3233*. Stanford Research Institute, Menlo Park, CA.

Fiske, S. T., & Taylor, S. E. (1984). *Social cognition: From brains to culture*. McGraw-Hill.

Frischmann, B., & Selinger, E. (2018). *Re-engineering humanity*. Cambridge University Press. 10.1017/9781316544846

Heersmink, R. (2017). Extended mind and cognitive enhancement: Moral aspects of cognitive artifacts. *Phenomenology and the Cognitive Sciences*, 16(1), 17–32. 10.1007/s11097-015-9448-5

Hernández-Orallo, J., & Vold, K. (2019, January). AI extenders: the ethical and societal implications of humans cognitively extended by AI. In *Proceedings of the 2019 AAAI/ACM Conference on AI, Ethics, and Society* (pp. 507-513). ACM. 10.1145/3306618.3314238

Hutchins, E. (1999). Cognitive artifacts. *The MIT Encyclopedia of the Cognitive Sciences*, 126(1999), 127.

Jacko, J. A. (Ed.). (2012). *Human-computer interaction handbook: Fundamentals, evolving technologies, and emerging applications*. CRC Press. 10.1201/b11963

Licklider, J. C. R. (1960). Man-computer symbiosis. *IRE Transactions on Human Factors in Electronics*, 1(1), 4–11. 10.1109/THFE2.1960.4503259

Menary, R. (2007). *Cognitive integration: Mind and cognition unbounded.* Palgrave Macmillan. 10.1057/9780230592889

Minsky, M. L. (Ed.). (1968). *Semantic Information Processing.* MIT Press.

Nalepa, G. J., Costa, A., Novais, P., & Julian, V. (2018). Cognitive Assistants. *International Journal of Human-Computer Studies*, 117, 1–68. 10.1016/j.ijhcs.2018.05.008

Newell, A., & Card, S. K. (1985). The prospects for psychological science in human-computer interaction. *Human-Computer Interaction*, 1(3), 209–242. 10.1207/s15327051hci0103_1

Putnam, H. (1960). Minds and Machines. In Hook, S. (Ed.), *Dimensions of Mind.* New York University Press.

Putnam, H. (1967). *The Nature of Mental States.* University of Pittsburgh Press.

Risko, E. F., & Gilbert, S. J. (2016). Cognitive offloading. *Trends in Cognitive Sciences*, 20(9), 676–688. 10.1016/j.tics.2016.07.00227542527

Rogers, Y., Sharp, H., & Preece, J. (2011). *Interaction design: Beyond human-computer interaction.* John Wiley & Sons.

Rouse, W. B., & Spohrer, J. C. (2018). Automating versus augmenting intelligence. *Journal of Enterprise Transformation*, 1-21.

Rowlands, M. (2010). *The new science of the mind: From extended mind to embodied phenomenology.* MIT. 10.7551/mitpress/9780262014557.001.0001

Samek, W., Wiegand, T., & Müller, K. R. (2017). Explainable artificial intelligence: Understanding, visualizing and interpreting deep learning models. *arXiv preprint arXiv:1708.08296*

Smart, P. R. (2018). Human-extended machine cognition. *Cognitive Systems Research*, 49, 9–23. 10.1016/j.cogsys.2017.11.001

Sparrow, B., Liu, J., & Wegner, D. M. (2011). Google effects on memory: Cognitive consequences of having information at our fingertips. *Science*, 333(6043), 776–778. 10.1126/science.120774521764755

Spohrer, J., & Banavar, G. (2015). Cognition as a service: An industry perspective. *AI Magazine*, 36(4), 71–86. 10.1609/aimag.v36i4.2618

Sutton, J. (2006). Distributed cognition: Domains and dimensions. *Pragmatics & Cognition*, 14(2), 235–247. 10.1075/pc.14.2.05sut

Thagard, P. (1996). *Mind: Introduction to cognitive science* (Vol. 4). MIT Press Cambridge.

Vold, K. (2018). Overcoming Deadlock: Scientific and Ethical Reasons to Embrace the Extended Mind Thesis. *Philosophy and Society, 29*, 475.

# Chapter 18
# Impact of AI on Diversity and Inclusion

**Asma Yunus**
*University of Sargodha, Pakistan*

**Shahzad Khaver Mushtaq**
*University of Sargodha, Pakistan*

**Ruqia Safdar Bajwa**
https://orcid.org/0000-0002-4460-2025
*Bahauddin Zakariya University, Pakistan*

## ABSTRACT

*Artificial intelligence (AI) has emerged as a powerful force, revolutionizing industries worldwide. Its transformative capabilities extend beyond mere automation, shaping the way we work, innovate, and make decisions. In this chapter, the authors explore how AI is reshaping healthcare and financial sectors, driving efficiency, accuracy, and customer satisfaction. AI is undoubtedly revolutionizing industries globally, providing innovative solutions that enhance productivity, stimulate innovation, and push the boundaries of decision-making.*

## INTRODUCTION

Artificial intelligence is undoubtedly revolutionizing industries globally, providing innovative solutions that enhance productivity, stimulate innovation, and push the boundaries of decision-making. According to Dwivedi et al. (2019), machine learning algorithms in healthcare are significantly transforming diagnostics and patient care by enabling precision medicine and early disease identification. Financial organizations also experience advantages from AI through improved fraud detection methods and personalized customer services, leading to significant enhancements in security and consumer happiness, as emphasized by Liu et al. (2020).

Similarly, AI enhances tailored tutoring experiences for learners by adjusting to individuals' needs and maximizing academic results, as mentioned by Riley (2023). According to Taneja et al. (2023), the manufacturing and supply chain sectors are currently benefiting from increased efficiency due to the

DOI: 10.4018/979-8-3693-3350-1.ch018

use of AI-driven predictive maintenance and optimization procedures. Furthermore, according to Riley (2023), AI plays a significant role in the digital economy by transforming e-commerce, supply chain logistics, and customer experience management through the use of advanced technologies such as big data analysis and machine learning. These advancements highlight the capacity of AI to enhance efficiency, encourage creativity, and revolutionize traditional business models in several industries.

Nevertheless, the rapid incorporation of AI technology also highlights the significance of tackling ethical issues and guaranteeing equitable access to the advantages AI provides. Ensuring a harmonious integration of technological advancements with societal values and inclusivity is of utmost importance in fully using the potential of AI for the benefit of all segments of society, as highlighted by Dwivedi et al. (2019), Liu et al. (2020), Riley (2023), and Taneja et al. (2023).

## DEFINING THE CONCEPTS OF DIVERSITY AND INCLUSION

Diversity and inclusion are two key concepts, expressing the richness and vibrancy of societies and organizations by emphasizing the existence and realization of individualized characteristics as well as those in groups. Inclusion takes us a step farther than embracing diversity which may see diverse groups of people exist without being appreciated or valued; it turns those environments into places where everyone can participate and achieve--no matter what their background. The interplay between diversity and inclusion is vital not only on ethical grounds but also for reasons of practical effect, particularly in the case of artificial intelligence (AI). AI systems that are devised and made in diverse and inclusive environments have a much better chance to be fair, effective and suitable for the whole world. This broad spectrum of human experience is essential to make sure that AI is not merely something for one culture or climate but can be flexible and beneficial across many different cultural and social contexts. For example, research has shown that more diverse teams can identify and correct biases in AI datasets and algorithms, resulting in technologies that are fairer and just on the whole (Buolamwini & Gebru, 2018).

Furthermore, inclusion in AI stimulates innovation by integrating a wide range of views, so that AI solutions become more creative and can be applied to new areas of work (Hunt, Layton, & Prince, 2015). This is particularly important as AI increasingly affects different sectors around the world--from healthcare to finance and education where there are high stakes for fairness and access. Recent research underscores the urgent need to embed diversity and inclusion principles in AI. Zowghi and Rimini (2023) note that there are no concrete guidelines for incorporating D&I into AI systems and outline practical steps aimed at AI developers and project managers to fill this void (Zowghi & Rimini, 2023).

In addition, Chi et al., (2021) discuss how D&I is represented in corporate AI ethics documentation, showing a trend towards technical solutions that could miss broader DEI initiatives required for truly meaningful inclusion (Chi et al., 2021). Bano et al. (2023) address how to put D&I requirements into operation in AI systems, suggesting a customized approach to specifying D&I requirements via user story templates--thereby highlighting the importance of systematic efforts to integrate D&I into AI development (Bano et al., 2023).

## Intersectionality and AI's Impact on Youth

The theory of intersectionality provides insight into how individuals navigate life through multifaceted identities that combine to forge singular experiences. Intersectionality recognizes that facets like gender, race, class and sexuality intersect within a person and jointly influence their circumstances and opportunities in complex ways. This framework asserts that the effects of one's attributes are not merely additive, but integrated, crafting unique situations too nuanced to understand by considering each quality independently.

In examining technology's impact on society, taking an intersectional view is of utmost importance. Artificial intelligence, through mechanisms like automated decision systems and customized health advisories, has significant capability to shape our world. However, without an intersectional lens, such technologies risk perpetuating existing disparities and introducing novel forms of bias. As Sarah Ciston (2019) argues, intersectional strategies must be applied to AI at every stage, from information gathering to design and implementation, to address and mitigate prejudices innate to AI systems. Failure to do so could have harmful consequences for society's most vulnerable.(Ciston, 2019)

Furthermore, Arjun Ovalle (2023) highlights the recent AI fairness Movement's failure to properly institutionalize intersectionality by saying "most of our efforts at intersectional fairness have reduced intersectionality to demographic subgroup analysis that does not address systematic blocks against participation of those outside that sub-category" (Ovalle., 2023). This underscores the importance for AI researchers and developers to engage deeply with intersectionality, to avoid AI systems that inadvertently amplify social disparities. By incorporating intersectionality in the development and evaluation of AI technologies, researchers and developers can create systems that are more fair and inclusive. This demands a commitment to understanding different forms of discrimination in their interplay with each other, and the participation of diverse voices during the development process. Ultimately, an intersectional approach to AI can produce technologies not only novel but also just and equitable, reflecting the variegated demands of people worldwide. In conclusion, integration of diversity and inclusion within the AI ecosystem is not only a desirable characteristic but vitally necessary if we are to create AI systems that are equitable, ethical, and beneficial for all segments of society. The addition of an intersectionality perspective enriches this work by acknowledging discrimination as multi-faceted and by advocating for AI systems which can accommodate different cultural experiences within humanity.

# UNDERSTANDING INTERSECTIONALITY AND AI

## Definition and Origins of Intersectionality

First formulated by Kimberlé Crenshaw in the last decade of the 20th century, intersectionality provides a critical lens for understanding the manner in which (for instance) race or sexuality is the union of multiple social categories that often dwarf one another in power. In subsequent years, this idea has greatly impacted the way that scholars and practitioners approach issues of inequality in many fields including psychology, sociology and education. Crenshaw's important work showed that linear approaches that dissect race, gender and other aspects of identity cannot adequately express the interactions between these factors. If we are to address the real implications harming people 's lives, we must adopt a multi-faceted perspective (Crenshaw 1989; 1991).Intersectionality 's source can be traced back to the thought of Black women, who were concerned with what were known as specific oppressions of these women. Neither race-focused nor gender-focused analyses Alone accurately captured all this framework. From here, it has since developed into a broad framework that covers many identities and inequalities, emphasizing the need to look at how different societal structures of power intersect at various levels.

In applying this idea of intersectionality to the study of AI we hope to ensure that AI technology will not inadvertently prop up existing social inequalities but instead serve toward a more equitable end. By adopting an intersectional approach, researchers and developers can better identify any biasing tendencies in AI systems-ensuring these technologies are properly inclusive and meet the needs of varied communities. As AI continues to evolve and extend its influence throughout society, integrating intersectionality into the development and deployment of AI will be vital if we want this technology to enhance in society rather than undermine efforts towards diversification. And we must therefore design AI with an awareness of intersectionality.

## The Relevance of Intersectionality in AI Research and Development

Given diverse communities, it is particularly important for AI technologies to be just, fair, and beneficial in why it's not racist at all rather intersects at gender class moves around the power that something highlights the interconnected nature of social categorizations such as race, gender, and class was first raised in critical race theory and feminist thought. This however means that social categorizations need to be viewed more dynamically as interconnecting. Taking an intersectional perspective means spotting and correcting any hidden biases latent in algorithms or datasets and thus preventing the continuity of existing blind spots in a world now remade along these lines. Sarah Ciston (2019) insists that intersectional techniques be brought to bear on AI, from data collection and algorithm design to software implementation. In her view, this approach is crucial to overhauling AI's ethics and removing its built-in biases. Such a rethink also looks beyond AI itself, arguing that community-based and arts practices can put AI into an all-around social context. Both of these lines would be more speculative benefits where they to take off than if completely confined within only one aspect: its 'frequency 'of appearance as the subject place.

The authors of a systematic review published in 2021 have highlighted the place of intersectionality in quantitative research. Bauer et al. (2021). In this way, we might take the intersectional approach over more broadly across different AI research domains; for health provides just one possible application. Ovalle (2023) offers a critical perspective on intersectionality in fairness literature. He points out a gap between what scholars understand about intersectionality and how it might be operationalized. This means that intersectionality takes the form of demographic subgroup analysis, but is not integrated into fundamental inquiries about power or culture. Ovalle, A.,'s analysis emphasizes that researchers focusing on AI fairness must take a thorough and deeply rooted interest in intersectionality. They must connect it to AI epistemology in order really to look at fairness. These ideas provide a meaningful indication of the need to introduce intersectional perspectives into AI research and development in order to pinpoint hidden bias and take effective countermeasures.

## Intersectionality in the Context of Youth Studies

An analytical concept known as "intersectionality" initially emerged in order to make sense of how oppression and privilege are interconnected. However, lately it is being recognized as a crucial avenue through which to understand youth and adolescence. This framework allows researchers and practitioners alike to take in the mixture of various social identities. First, these intersections decide young peoples' experiences susceptibility to opportunities before them or problems they may face concerning future prospects alike equally importantly -- depending which aspect you look at from. In youth studies, an intersectional perspective offers more refined insights into the configurations of power and privilege, which create young lives. It allows the complexion of how race, gender, sexuality and disability intersect to form unique experiences for youth. For instance, following Kern et al. (2020), the interaction of immigrant background with socio-economic status and gender in understanding adolescent well-being is crucial across various national contexts. This research highlights how these intersectional identities impact life satisfaction and somatic complaints among teenagers, suggesting that national context such as immigration policies can play a crucial role in shaping these encounters. And also, Velez and Spencer (2018) assert that identity development among adolescents is heavily influenced by intersecting ecosystems of inequality. By uniting Crenshaw's intersectionality with Spencer's phenomenological variant of the ecological systems school PVEST, they offer a framework for interpreting how youth negotiate their identities amidst social and structural inequities. A systematic analysis by Hernández-Saca et al., (2018) of educational studies focusing on youth and young adults with disabilities shows how public attitudes toward disabled personae converge qualitatively with the impairment to impact experiences. Their multivariate approach discloses the complex construction of disabled realities, stressing that it is important for academic research to consider multiple identities. These analyses underscore the relevance of intersectionality in youth studies, advocating for its use to uncover the layered experiences of young people living in an in-between world with complex sentences and short ones. By using an intersectional lens, researchers can better understand and address the multiple needs of youth, particularly in marginalized groups, thereby contributing to more inclusive and equitable approaches in exploration, policy-making and practice with complex sentences alongside shorter ones.

## THE CURRENT STATE OF AI, DIVERSITY, AND INCLUSION

### Overview of AI's Role in Promoting or Hindering Diversity and Inclusion

Unfortunately, the outcomes are mixed regarding diversity and inclusion (D & I).On the one hand, just as it negatively impacts these points; AI provides opportunities for mitigating implicit bias and improving decision-making in fields like employment and talent management For example AI-based performance assessment systems have demonstrated the potential to draw in under-represented group members who perceive themselves as being judged less impartially, causing them to put forth more effort at work and thus--perhaps--widening the pool of human resources available (Brown et al., 2021). Similarly, AI integrated into recruitment procedures can erase both conscious and unconscious biases. This makes it easier to achieve the objectives of Diversity, Equality & Inclusion (Bansal Jora et al., 2022)

However, AI can also impede D & I activities if it is not designed and monitored carefully. For job screening tools and credit scoring systems alike, existing social as well as economic disparities are deepened by the errors in AI algorithms. Without intervention, they may continue or even grow worseThe "diversity crisis" in AI development, as shown by the biggest shortfall being among decision-makers and technical creators of AI technologies, simply exacerbates these problems. This leads to technology that may not hereafter understand wide perspectives properly or consider different requirements (Adams & Khomh, 2020).

## Analysis of Diversity Within the AI Workforce and its Implications

One critical element in the development of AI systems that are inclusive and equitable is the level of diversity within a workforce. Currently, there is a marked gap in gender and ethnic representation in AI. A wide range of studies on the gender distribution of AI research reveals significant patterns. . The number of female co-authors of AI publication has witnessed zero growth and a slight decline across the years, especially in AI's related discipline computer science. (Lee et al., 2019).

Research papers related to AI also appear much less frequently with female co-authors than by all men, which possibly further reduces visibility for women in top journals on this topic. Geographic distribution factors into positional representation have been further worsened for women in dissipating papers indicate gender inequality by country and institution (Stathoulopoulos et al., 2019).

However, the likely effects of such imbalances on AI technologies being developed are profound. A group of developers working with one or another set of prejudices may unintentionally "train" these ideas into an algorithm used across many applications, thus producing results that fail to take into account the full range human differences. Also, purely from the standpoint of AI research and development itself, a monolithic perspective tends to limit creativity and the kind of out-of-box vigor necessary for addressing complex social problems."

At the moment, the condition of D&I in AI highlights the need for systematic efforts to increase the diversity of AI workers. Such work should be multifaceted, with initiatives for recruitment and retention in underrepresented groups, the promotion of a cultural environment that is inclusive in AI research and development habitats both to work in and for others there too. It should also mean embedding D&I principles within AI curriculum and training programs.

Finally, while AI has great potential to help achieve diversity and inclusion goals, realizing this vision will require help overcoming the current diversity challenges in the AI workforce. If we can bridge this gap, then the full power of AI can be brought into play to develop inclusive, equitable and truly representative technologies that reflect our world.

## Case Studies Highlighting Both Positive and Negative Impacts of AI on Diverse Communities

Artificial Intelligence (AI) potentially is going to affect much of the world. In one study, for example, 90% of urban China's population may be living in cities where human–nature boundaries have disappeared and intelligent machines do everything imaginable--while the other 10% are still crammed together within a diminished environment that is even more unpleasant than ever before. But these impacts are not all good; like so much else about AI they depend on numerous factors including design and implementation of AI systems, how inclusive the data is, and where AI is applied. We show in the following case studies how such factors can determine some of what happens.

Furthermore, as studied by Zou and Schiebinger, a special tact would be needed in order that biomedicine might also benefit the diverse peoples of our world. They suggest ways to ensure AI is used more fairly; collect data that is incorporated throughout the whole process from collection through to monitoring and so on (Zou & Schiebinger, 2021). This project aims to address health disparities and inequalities in health between different population groups (Zou & Schiebinger, 2021).

Study of AI technology at the level of village fields in developing countries reveals that possibly very different patterns of field management can equally bring about large changes in output. Ranging from participatory approaches to technology, knowledge, and a supporting environment for innovation, these models all show the role that AI will be in empowering communities by changing their agricultural practices and providing secure nutrition (Faure et al., 2018).

The perplexing problems of prejudice in artificial intelligence are emphasized in the sphere of choosing and overseeing laborers. Computational apparatuses intended to streamline enlisting cycles can unconsciously spread prejudices on the off chance that the preparation information needs assortment. This can prompt lopsided open doors and strengthen as of now current social disparities in society, as various examinations have investigated. (Houser, 2019).

Artificial intelligence shows promise in speeding disaster recovery, if such technologies overlook cultural nuance, the impact could deepen risks faced by migrant laborers impacted. Evidence from Florida after hurricanes paints how relief initiatives frequently sidelined needs of varied groups, their report emphasizing how emergency coordination must craft sensitive, inclusive algorithms. Diverse populations bear the brunt of blinkered tech, as a study on post-storm Florida highlighted - planners neglect populations unlike their own, hindering aid for all. Progress demands recognizing each community's voice; only thus can code and processors remedy what human oversight ignored.(Drolet et al., 2018).

Notwithstanding, AI shows potential to transform healthcare, agriculture and other industries, its impacts are double-edged. When designed and built with inclusion and equity in mind, it can uplift underserved communities by improving access and outcomes. However, biases within its algorithms and insensitivity to cultural differences may exacerbate existing inequities unless properly addressed. The harms of AI stem not only from what it chooses to represent, but also what it chooses to ignore.

Realizing AI's full potential while safeguarding against its risks will require a coordinated push from leaders in both public and private sectors. Policymakers should enact protections for fairness and transparency, while technologists should prioritize marginalized voices in their efforts. Both sides, operating in an atmosphere of open-mindedness, accountability, and respect for differences, collaborate in steering AI in ways to enable every kind of person. This is achievable if we consider AI as a product of profound human processes rather than a neutral tool. By working with multifaceted, bilateral, and multilateral collaboration, technological promises can be kept while no one is left behind.

## OPPORTUNITIES FOR ENHANCING DIVERSITY AND INCLUSION THROUGH AI

### AI-Driven Initiatives for Promoting Diversity in Educational Settings

AI in education holds great promise in enabling diversity, hence it must be approached with caution to ensure equality transforms. Properly shaped, AI can individualize learning to meet the needs and ability of each student, thus unchecked presents a risk of perpetuating and even intensifying existing inequities. The power of transformation of AI lies not in the exact engineering but in the leading of its development and deployment. With an inclusionary values ethic, AI extends the educational journey beyond varieties to focus on disparities for those currently undeserved. AI, guided to appreciate the abundance of human diversity, can help grow the know-how among us essential to eradicating the obstacles of openings. AI' work is not to thing students but to identify possibilities and work with us to cultivate our experience to accept them.

The innovative AI4ALL enterprise from UCSF seeks to inspire diversity and inclusion in AI aimed at professionals in medicine and associated fields. Target young people from high-moderate school with an ethnosocial being in the progress and application of AI, allowing them the chance to learn about using AI in medicine. Though the COVID-19 epidemic has introduced various difficulties, the project has cleverly migrated online, where students were able to get experience with AI, fulfill activities involving specimens, and compare and contrast work while receiving hints from professionals-in-training. Studies of student consultants shown that they surpassed in the areas of machine learning scouring through complex data, algorithms, and illumination on achievable occupations in AI career opportunity (Oskotsky et al., 2021).

Some efforts, such as integrating artificial intelligence into middle school curriculums at underprivileged European schools, have already borne fruit in analyses of this nature that not only can make AI education a reality, but also help foster a new kind of thinking about the surrounding world. Educator feedback from journals and round-table discussions indicated that views of AI education had turned largely positive, stressing how it could open doorways for dialogue on accepting diversity. No one is left behind. (Gibellini et al., 2023). At the same time, some experiments noted that students enthusiasm piqued towering after class elaborated on how AI research was coming from a variety of perspectives and backgrounds to recognize and respond to people, as well when it discussed changing technology values can be humane-oriented.

In addition, the literature on this already states that it is important to nurture diversity in AI and healthcare. In particular, How important heterogeneous teams and inclusion are to the approach of AI development, as Against afterthought. Encouraging grassroots outreach efforts, bringing diversity policies into being from universities and insisting on regulatory measures from federal departments of state to ensure that more whole program includes AI technologies. Maybe state level governments could also be encouraged by national governments in their regional centers for Development (RCDEs). (Hond et al., 2022).

Teams with a variety of backgrounds and life experiences explain new uses and might reveal unintentional biases that a more uniform group would miss. Although increasing diversity is difficult, genuinely striving to be inclusive from the beginning can ensure that AI systems are created to take into account and benefit all members of society. We're able to do a lot in terms of promoting inclusion by developing AI in education. The first step is to change the manner students are educated to meet each one's diverse requirement and ensure that different persons contribute to the technology's development. By treating differences with compassion, whether through customized lessons or an active role in building the technology, artificial intelligence can pave the path to equality for all those trying to correct imbalances that have been in place for too long.

## The Role of AI in Creating Inclusive Work Environments

Artificial intelligence holds a unique promise of promoting more inclusive workspaces than ever before. By coping with the existence of common tasks, AI allows organizations to focus on those aspects that make everyone unique and ensure that such differences enhance growth. In particular, implementing AI in offices enhances the option to customize the surroundings according to workers' desires, whether that be room lighting and temperature, or the home office's ergonomically correct desk and chair, aiding in the workers' healthfulness and experience. (Fukumura et al., 2021).

Furthermore, AI's contribution to expanding remote work has become more important, given the extension of creating work environments that are inclusive to the entire population. The Global Public Inclusive Infrastructure or the smart remote work are examples of leading from the front additional tools in creating more accessible and inclusive work environments in the digital space and help older workers and people with disabilities. (Peinado et al., 2021). The capabilities of AI can be shaped to address the specific needs of all individuals, fostering a sense of belonging critical to personal and organizational success.

## How AI Can Be Leveraged to Amplify Marginalized Voices and Perspectives?

The promise of AI to get the under-heard voices and perspectives heard on many fronts can only be fully realized through proactive efforts to reduce the inherent biases in technology. By auditing the datasets and designing processes for implicit marginalization, AI systems could be designed so that they support diversity, judge across categories of merit and dismantle many forms of prejudice in a system that is hostile to the same in many ways. For example, AI in hiring that require talented above all else and remove the labels and categorization that had usually harmed some while favoring others could be fair by extending the opportunity based on skills and demonstration rather than the attributes that are beyond an individual. Additionally, the AI mediums that allow expression may help show a broader range of experiences that remain unexpressed and under acknowledged. The platforms may be the megaphone that give voice to people who rarely get to tell their stories and show that each story is valid and every perspective enriches us. Specifically, by having access to vast repositories of information and statistics that powers AI systems, it could illuminate for lives, communities and systems experiencing disparities where reforms could right wrongs and advocacy improve policies to be just.

Artificial intelligence presents both opportunities and risks, but it must be developed respecting equality and individual value. Companies should create systems that are characterized by diversity of opinion and recognition of human dignity to create environments where one can express thoughts. This will increase the energy of companies by introducing competencies and experiences that create new and novel solutions. Technology's ultimate impact will be determined by our ability to create inclusive environments that genuinely reflect our humanity and allows the full participation of all its members. The only way is to recognize that our shared place in the prosperity of people and our shared responsibility for each other's well-being is crucial. We can only find purpose by working together, which will give us the strength.

## CHALLENGES AND ETHICAL CONSIDERATIONS

### The Potential for AI to Perpetuate Biases and Discrimination

Despite the fact that artificial intelligence technologies can improve decision-making throughout many spheres, the possibility of their application prospecting should be approached with an intimate regard for social consequences. When two of them primarily exist to ensure societal well-being, it comes down to the prospect of mitigating biases that are bound to exist in the training data. An AI system reflective of previous biases has a high probability of further marginalizing the most vulnerable. The study conducted by Varona and Suarez(2022) can be taken as an example of essential self-reflection regarding discrimination, trust, and fairness between people and AI in the present climate. Regardless of the description of "responsibility for development," it argues heavily towards the need for more inclusive and fair frameworks and models. A positive outcome equally depends on one of the variables that has obstructed all of the others – further studying the realities hidden behind AI prospects. (Varona & Suárez, 2022).

## Ethical Considerations in the Development and Deployment of AI Technologies

The influence of artificial intelligence on society demands careful judgement of these systems.Different stages in AI development can cause prejudices like biased, misleading data collection, analysis of samples with unseen bias, which needs to be addressed thoroughly in all areas of operation.As Srinivasan and Chander explain, a single color may provide many examples of bias and selectors must therefore find ways not to let it seep into the process of making something specific or persuasive. (Srinivasan & Chander, 2021). Addressing prejudices demands not only technical remedies but a commitment to principles prioritizing equity, transparency, and responsibility in AI.

Consequent upon the above discussion, the battle against bias and the guarantee of ethics may be inducted possessively through the integration of various law, social science, and engineering disciplines. For technology to work for humanity, technological development and applications must show advanced virtues, boost public morality, and not strengthen disparities. This alternatively would also mandate a joint effort to deal with AI's challenging health and protection challenges and guarantee that it serves the end-users demurely.

## REGULATORY AND POLICY CHALLENGES IN MANAGING AI'S IMPACT ON DIVERSITY AND INCLUSION

Artificial Intelligence implies that there are benefits that can be realized using it to diversity and inclusion. However, there are numerous regulatory and policy challenges undermining the implementation of AI from an equity and inclusion perspective.

### Regulatory Challenges

### Defining and Enforcing AI Ethics and Standards

Furthermore, it is challenging to establish ethical protocols for artificial intelligence, given the broad variety of applications in different societies. Regulations must set rules on principles such as fairness, transparency and accountability, but policymakers have encountered issues in drafting policies that can keep up with AI's fast-changing nature . There has been a lack of practical ways for developers, researchers and politicians to define and operationalize diversity, equity and inclusion in AI systems as well as the entire domain. Zowghi and Rimini (2023) identified this lack of direction as a "clear area of focus" for policymakers determined to navigate innovation to the benefit of all people. Thus, calibrating the right mix of guidance and growth will remain a significant battle in the years to come.

## Balancing Innovation and Ethical Considerations

Regulators are in the extremely difficult position of fostering economic growth and innovation, while ensuring AI systems do not perpetuate bias or discrimination. Policies should encourage companies to develop AI which benefits society while averting any potential harms by reflecting on the ethical implications of AI technologies.

## Global Consistency vs. Local Relevance

Crafting policies that are globally consistent yet locally relevant is challenging due to the different legal, cultural, and societal contexts across regions. Impact of Artificial intelligence on diversity and inclusion must be considered within the framework of indigenous norms and values to ensure effective and culturally sensitive implementations.

## Policy Challenges

### Diversity in AI Development Teams

Ensuring diversity among developers and project teams creating AI systems is essential, because it leads to inclusive AI development. Policies designed to increase representation in STEM fields and AI research might help flush biases in AI development out of the process. Also, initiatives should be directed at increasing inclusivity in all phases of AI development, from conception to deployment. (Hond et al., 2022).

### Data Governance and Privacy

The implications of managing the data used to train AI include privacy and consent issues, as well as a risk of re-entrenching societal biases. Therefore, policies should carefully center on the ethical collection, use, and sharing of data. In particular, this should involve watering down the use of diverse and representative datasets to train AI models

### Transparency and Accountability

Transparency of AI algorithms and decision-making processes is a necessary strategy to solve the regulatory and policy challenges presented above. Policies should compel firms to provide extensive documentation of the functioning of an AI system, including how decisions were made. This could ensure that stakeholders can form an advanced form of self-awareness about which AI driven decisions should never be challenged in a diverse and inclusive context. Secondly, a multidisciplinary approach is needed to solve the problem. AI is a composite discipline that touches on technological, ethical, and normative issues. Therefore, stakeholders from academia, government, civil society, and industry must join hands to formulate policies that will guide the use of AI in a way that promotes inclusion and diversity.

# INTERSECTIONALITY AS A FRAMEWORK FOR AI DEVELOPMENT

## Incorporating Intersectional Perspectives in AI Design and Development Processes

Incorporating intersectional perspectives into the design and design of AI is critical in shaping technology that is equitable, ethical, and representative of the many dimensions of humanity. Intersectionality, a theoretical approach founded on critical race theory and feminist thought, emphasizes the idea that social identities and power relationships intersect. A person's race, gender, class, sexuality, as well as other aspects, interact to create distinct experiences and opportunities.

The urgent necessity of intersectional AI is evident from the fact that AI systems frequently replicate the prejudices existing in their training data, thereby furthering the status quo . Therefore, intersectional AI is crucial in AI development to help identify and mitigate various complex and intersecting forms of discrimination such groups undergo. Ciston(2019) posits the integration of intersectional strategies in AI at each level, from information collection to algorithm formation and execution, proposing that such philosophies are required for rethinking AI's ethics and counteracting its prejudices.

While operationalizing intersectionality in artificial intelligence poses substantive difficulties, dismissing its importance would only exacerbate inequities. Traditional methods for categorizing and assessing identities and experiences often neglect intersectional discrimination's nuanced nature. In their exploration of intersecting identities among technology workers, Hana Winchester, Alicia E. Boyd, and Brittany Johnson reveal underrepresentation in datasets and emphasize the need for intentionally inclusive research supporting equitable outcomes for all peoples (Winchester et al., 2022).

Furthermore, Ovalle, A., (2023) critically appraises works considering intersectionality in AI fairness literature, identifying a disconnection between its conceptualization and implementation. Frequently, intersectionality is reduced to analyses of demographic subgroups, failing to seriously engage intersectional theory's foundational concerns regarding the distribution and exercise of power within sociocultural contexts (Ovalle, 2023).

The nuanced layers of identity and experiences that comprise intersectionality must be thoughtfully accounted for in artificial intelligence development. A dedication to community-driven methodologies where marginalized voices directly inform the process is essential. Room for experimentation with novel techniques attuned to embracing diversity's depth is likewise needed.

Indeed, the tenets of intersectionality challenge many of the underlying assumptions of the established field and exerts a focus on justice, not just excellence in performance. Given the scope and scale of society altered by technology, the spirit of intersectionality is essential to ensuring that AI design centers the most vulnerable and constructs a future where all people can flourish. It is no longer the case that technical skills are sufficient. The way forward is through creativity and humility, not preservation of past norms. Implementing the idea of intersectionality fundamentally changes the path of AI development and presents more than technical problems, but also ethical tasks. These would entail being open to change and making sure that technologies bring people together rather than segregate them. With intersectionality as the guiding force, technology can accomplish a great deal for all humanity.

## Case Studies of Projects Integrating Diversity and Inclusion Principles

Integrating diversity and inclusion (D&I) principles into AI projects is not just a matter of ethical importance but also enhances the effectiveness and applicability of AI technologies across diverse user groups. Several AI projects have successfully incorporated these principles, demonstrating innovative approaches to D&I.

### Case Study 1: UCSF AI4ALL

One of the programs that involved high school students was the UCSF AI4ALL. Designed specifically for underrepresented youth, this developmental AI program is designed to foster diversity in AI fields, namely AI in biomedicine . The program, among other things, serves as a primer that exposes students to a wide variety of AI technologies and opens up new horizons in their possible transformative applications in healthcare. This program was also successfully transferred online by its already resourceful organizers, and its participants not only received enriching educational experience through interactive lectures, hands-on projects on the many aspects of the devastating virus, and mentorship but also significantly increased their occurrence and discussion with these intimidatingly complex topics and careers. The program was of paramount importance in nurturing greater inclusivity in this inherently inequitable endeavor. (Oskotsky et al., 2021).

### Case Study 2: Reconfiguring Diversity and Inclusion for AI Ethics

Significant tech corporations have attempted to integrate inclusion and diversity directly into the design of artificial intelligence. Examinations of the various organizations' AI schemata, including Google's research, have provided insights into how the three major firms have started to incorporate a breadth of viewpoints into their AI ethically-focused efforts. This exercise endeavors to operationalize inclusion and diversity for the engineers and tech firms' clients and leads, generating diversified but equitable datasets and some impartiality by inclusion built into the AI's behavioral values. This has had a clear positive impact on the field of attitude toward the arrangement of AI ethics throughout the tech division. However, it also introduces a new issue of ensuring that the value of diversity and inclusion is fundamentally incorporated into these firms' long-term goals and ambitions rather than perceived as an effort area (Chi et al., 2021).

### Case Study 3: AI for All—Operationalizing Diversity and Inclusion Requirements for AI Systems

In an effort to operationalize diversity and inclusion in artificial intelligence advancement, examinations have been directed to systematically tackle the lack of functional direction on incorporating diversity considerations throughout the whole life cycle of AI frameworks. This analysis proposes a customized technique for documenting diversity needs in AI frameworks engineering by utilizing a personalized user anecdote layout. By leading exhaustive information accumulation and amalgamation, alongside center gather exercises, this activity shows a pragmatic methodology for guaranteeing that AI frameworks accommodate the assorted requirements of clients and support moral qualities, demonstrating the capacity for AI to serve a more extensive and all the more incorporative range of social needs.

Separately, through broad subjective meetings and surveys, planners have concentrated on distinguishing proof issues crosswise over ventures and areas, catching key experiences into customized client stories that address specialized, social and moral elements of advancement. These exercises underline the significance of user-driven arrangement in building frameworks that serve individuals from different foundations (Bano et al., 2023).

All these cases illustrate possible ways to create a meaningful integration of diversity and inclusion practices into the social impact of artificial intelligence. This may include responsible educational initiatives, corporate programs, or technical activities, but whenever the diverse perspectives are encouraged and the plurality of experiences is reflected, the AI projects contribute more reasonably to society, acting organically as solutions that are proportionate, ethical, and inherently human in their variety. Others have placed inclusive recruitment and pedagogy at the forefront to encourage underrepresented groups and ensure emerging technologies cater to everyone's best interests. Some have conducted robust research that considers and assesses the potential unintended biases and implications for human behavior, implementing measurements in place to minimize unfair effects before deploying systems. When technological progress becomes genuinely grounded in all our shared future rather than a few special interests, the momentum of development and innovation benefits everyone.

## Strategies for Engaging Diverse Groups in the AI Lifecycle

It is crucial for developing inclusive technologies to address a broad range of social requirements and people of all perspectives. Experimentally, if we start out with diversity and inclusion principles in mind then AI systems may turn into things that are both more impartial and take on a broader thoroughly manner of thinking about the world that they inhabit. Recent studies also found some recipes for including diverse groups throughout the AI lifecycle. For example, involve more people from different cultures in plans at the start; create technologies that are accessible and useful to a variety of users; check algorithms and data sets for any unintended biases; get recruitment and mentoring so that people from underrepresented backgrounds come into the AI field; establish systems of governance that ensure fairness and protect people who are excluded.

### Incorporation of D&I Principles from the Outset

Consequently, developing AI that meets the requirements of various end users requires the integration of D&I values into the AI engineering process from inception to realization. Formulating a detailed and integrated plan for hardwiring these values is crucial for addressing ethical concerns and risks of the new technology, such as perpetuating undesired disparities as a result of biased determinations. Therefore, changing D&I commitments into practical activities across the AI engineering process, including interpreting the related requirements from a variety of sources and representation, is a key to building inclusive AI systems that meet the needs of the people (Bano et al., 2023).

### Dynamic Classroom Strategies

The issue of learning diversity is difficult and demanding, but it is also surmountable. When teachers put effort and creativity in designing lessons with different paces, modalities, and levels of engagement, a more vibrant exchange appears. Students are no longer passive participants but demonstrate their understanding by applying their knowledge immediately. Meanwhile, monitoring comprehension shows which blind spots are still present for further attention, creating the base for future expansion . This model is dynamic, as it recognizes each child's distinctness, but it is accessible to all to achieve their full potential. Similarly, students might start from different parts of the field, and they all leave the table eager to find new territory in the common battle and success (Bhat et al., 2021).

## Framework for Managing AI Bias

A unified framework design to manage AI bias over the complete development process could be the foundation for the development of artificial intelligence that operates with neutrality and fairness. By integrating SDLC, MLLC, and CRISP-DM mapping, researchers and developers with a wide range of technical expertise gain a general understanding of the correlation among phases of the development process. This way, it becomes an effective solution for identifying potential bias points and possible mitigation strategies in trustworthy AI system development (Rana et al., 2023).

## Interaction Design Strategies for Group Recommendation Systems

Although the meta-analyses reveal that interaction design practices provide unique perspectives regarding increasing diversity and inclusivity, a holistic approach is required to address these concerns. Specifically, scholars have obtained data from academic sources that describe various interface designs to help guide collaborative recommendations relying on user interactions. The examination outlines the challenges and opportunities offered by this design approach for promoting an equitable and representative technology future. The analysis further indicates the need for person-centered interfaces that consider the diversity of viewpoints and needs in our society, demonstrating how personalized recommendations enable AI that is open to all users. (Alvarado et al., 2022).

Despite these achievements, more work is needed to design platforms that offer equitable service to both individuals and collectives without compromising complexity and usability. Although the development of inclusive AI should incorporate the opinions of varied communities, more is needed to understand the peoples' different learning abilities and acknowledge built-in data biases. A multifaceted analysis is also required; it must encompass varying perspectives from unrepresented communities, create dynamic solutions that can adapt and evolve, establish a framework for analyzing natural assumptions, and then make the resulting interfaces universally intuitive. AI can be tied deeply into the fabric of all peoples' lives through responsible development.

## THE FUTURE OF AI, DIVERSITY, AND INCLUSION

## Emerging Trends and Technologies Shaping the Future of AI in Diverse Communities

Emergent technologies serve as fantastic and novel paths that emerge before us. However, to utilize them equally and non-discriminately, those communities rediscovering technologies and exploring its unknown facets must start at any stage with inclusivity and availability. Transformative instruments offered to human efforts in businesses and connections demand citizens simultaneously identify and keep the priority of their ethical responsibility to use them properly to foster awareness of the complex dilemmas with kindness and patience. (Dwivedi et al., 2019).

Blockchain and AI are increasingly synergizing, automating transactions and securing data in decentralized, trusted systems. This convergence also cultivates novel applications across sectors such as finance, healthcare and education, addressing open questions around utilizing distributed ledgers for intelligence. (Salah et al., 2019).

While structural engineering has always been modeled, these methods are now done with machine learning, pattern matching, and deep neural networks applied to variability and complexity that formerly could not be quantitatively managed. These increasingly intelligent systems quickly calculate through historically computational onerous constraints that were previously intractable, facilitate more optimized design, and competitive innovation that is specifically adapted to oscillate conditions. Complexity at both ends can create customized solutions as algorithms are adjusted to varied circumstances. The almost arbitrary extension of what can be both computed and optimized will drive the field forward to create clearly new problems and then solve them, making prior constraints a mere stepping stone on the path to progress. (Salehi & Burgueño, 2018).

Undoubtedly, academia will be utterly transformed as a result of such innovations as interactive holograms, tools that make it possible to study virtually anywhere and at any time, and dynamic, formative assessments. Still, the rapid adoption of novel technologies and other innovations' impact necessitates cautious consideration of second-order effects. It ensures that accidental outcomes are not allowed to degrade overall achievement and well-being. Pioneers exploring the world of augmented learning, by offering personally sculpted and adaptive instruction focused on unique user profiles, must enclose adequate privacy safeguards when examining the consequences of society's better ways of learning while keeping track of changes in learning human society. New novel methods can only be used equitably if we cautiously evaluate the potential advantages and disadvantages of acquiring such an enhanced worldwide educational attitude. (Gawande, Al Badi, & Al Makharoumi, 2020).

Despite how artificial intelligence certainly opens up new possibilities for value creation, it should be acknowledged that the implications go far beyond the characteristics associated with its genesis. Namely, business platforms that utilize machine problem-solving capabilities are capable of offering more efficient temporary accommodation or a transportation service from producers driven by databased demand matching, reflecting the way emerging techno-philosophic could totally revolutionize the ways business is done and how established patterns of conduct may influence market power via completely new ideas. Nonetheless, since every innovation is greatly influenced by other factors in a given scenario, the latter will evolve in unpredictable ways. (Lee, Suh, Roy, & Baucus, 2019).

Emerging technologies portending a future with AI amelioration may embody potential and obligation. If nurtured through amendment with humankind in the image, synthetic cognizance has the potential to elevate yields and consequences for diverse persons across variegated assemblies, and retain principles of veneration and involvement. Then assembled through alteration with an awareness of the moral issues and associated purposes, communities of variant lineages may receive amelioration, enabling each duo's capacity and necessity. Advancement requires carefulness, ensuring that the engineering augmenting entities allows the same for all without dissimilar predisposition or barrier insecurity of a general dignity. It should also ensure that it acts in a manner that does not eliminate or redistribute humanity's control of societal destiny.

## Potential Impacts of Future AI Advancements on Diversity and Inclusion Efforts

Widening the understanding of how AI might affect diversity and inclusion represents a once-in-a-lifetime opportunity . The next phase of machine learning systems may advance initiatives to develop more inclusive work, training, and health settings in a significant way. However, unless the aftereffects are extensively evaluated, any further AI-related progress might undermine existing inequalities. Unearthing and counteracting bias in decision-making are two of the vital capabilities of AI systems and processes . Algorithms might bring hidden prejudices to the surface, providing us with information on preconceived notions embedded in hiring, lending, and care decisions which advancements AI has the potential to distribute benefits equitably across varied populations . However, acceleration of AI advances constantly raises concerns about deepening existing social and economic disparities . The designers and developers of AI systems typically represent just a handful of non-White and non-Western stakeholders in the highest quartile of the distribution. It is possible that these systems will entrench existing discrimination and disregard persons who require support in capturing the benefits of technology unless a lot of deliberate effort is put before the development of systems to include a wide range of perspectives and encourage their adoption. Only with all-inclusive safeguards in place may we begin to construct genuinely fair and open societies that advance everyone to their full potential.

## Vision for an Inclusive AI Future Informed by Intersectionality

The call for an inclusive AI future should, therefore, come with such an acknowledgment of diverse experiences. For instance, given how multiple identities merge within oneself, as in my case, these are how the technology will affect my life. Thus, inclusivity possibilities should be informed by what is required established in the connections at these intersections of marginalization. Further progress includes glimpses of ethics, transparency, and participation as already mentioned. Only with diverse stakeholders having a say from the very start of the developments to the data and models representation of the entire humanity correcting any bias when it emerges to teams with different skills and backgrounds addressing gaps creates an environment that ensures inclusive futures. Again, inclusion focuses on maximizing AI to close social gaps already existing, such as on healthcare or educational or economic insecurity problems that affect some more than others. Therefore, this chapter would inform such technological utilization for social good and necessitate diversity. In conclusion, integration cooperation with a technology has an aspect of involving ethics, including or intersection into implement possible can change to assist all stakeholders. An innovative future addresses diversity and gaps.

## CONCLUSION

When we take an intersectional view of AI's impact on diversity and inclusion, examining the multi-faceted landscape, we must commit to being thoughtful about both the opportunities and the problems. The most important insights gained from the study of these issues are both AI's potential for redefining inclusion in multiple sectors and the absolute requirement to regulate this development correctly to avoid both new injustice and the existence of past injustice. Due to the analytic and pattern recognition abilities of such learning technologies, AI can work as a powerful tool to spot and eradicate biases where human judgement is insufficient, as in employment and health care . With an ethical and intersectional consideration, such technologies can be used to make significant strides toward justice. If the issues around the creation and employment of the AI are addressed the questions become one of construction and use. Algorithms may get biased data where the developers are unaware and when the developers are biased the directions are uniformly one sided. One crucial lesson from achieving that assignment is that times will change and also that they must change to incorporate inclusion practices and intersectional mindset at all parts of the AI's life cycle. The other vision of an AI future inclusive of intersectional imagination included highly paid technology to serve the marginalized into who society has traditionally been complicit. However, to achieve this visibility, technologists must first meet people where they are. Hence, AI intersects with inclusivity and diversity burst with potential, and this potential has led to tremendous transformation. However, such potentials will only be transformed to change based on ethical and inclusive and intersectional application.

In conclusion, an inclusive future driven by AI requires efforts synchronized by all stakeholders. All the discoveries brought by research, the development of algorithms, the process of translation to programs, enabling a broad workforce to address opportunities and complications accompanied by investment in accessible education and the process of policymaking should be informed by principles set to protect human rights and impartiality. Through collaboration, we promote respectful and enhancing diversity, allowing us to overcome the complexities implicated by the future journey through what we can see concluded via thoughtful coordination.

## REFERENCES

Adams, B., & Khomh, F. (2020). The diversity crisis of software engineering for artificial intelligence. *IEEE Software*, 37(5), 104–108. 10.1109/MS.2020.2975075

Bano, M., Zowghi, D., Gervasi, V., & Shams, R. (2023). AI for All: Operationalising Diversity and Inclusion Requirements for AI Systems. *arXiv preprint arXiv:2311.14695.*

Bauer, G. R., Churchill, S. M., Mahendran, M., Walwyn, C., Lizotte, D., & Villa-Rueda, A. A. (2021). Intersectionality in quantitative research: A systematic review of its emergence and applications of theory and methods. *SSM - Population Health*, 14, 100798. 10.1016/j.ssmph.2021.10079833997247

Bauer, G. R., & Scheim, A. I. (2019). Advancing quantitative intersectionality research methods: Intracategorical and intercategorical approaches to shared and differential constructs. *Social Science & Medicine*, 226, 260–262. 10.1016/j.socscimed.2019.03.01830914246

Bhat, S., D'Souza, R., Suresh, E. S. M., Bhat, S., Raju, R., & Bhat, V. S. (2021). Dynamic classroom strategies to address learning diversity. *Journal of Engineering Education Transformations*, 34(0), 694–702. 10.16920/jeet/2021/v34i0/157168

Buolamwini, J., & Gebru, T. (2018). Gender Shades: Intersectional Accuracy Disparities in Commercial Gender Classification. *Proceedings of Machine Learning Research*, 81, 1–15.

Chi, N., Lurie, E., & Mulligan, D. K. (2021, July). Reconfiguring diversity and inclusion for AI ethics. In *Proceedings of the 2021 AAAI/ACM Conference on AI, Ethics, and Society* (pp. 447-457). ACM. 10.1145/3461702.3462622

Ciston, S. (2019). Intersectional AI Is Essential. *Journal of Science and Technology of the Arts*, 11(2), 3–8. 10.7559/citarj.v11i2.665

Collins, P. H. (2020). Defining black feminist thought. In *Feminist theory reader* (pp. 278–290). Routledge.

Crenshaw, K. (1989). Demarginalizing the intersection of race and sex: A black feminist critique of antidiscrimination doctrine, feminist theory, and antiracist politics. *University of Chicago Legal Forum*, 1989(1), 139–167.

Crenshaw, K. (1991). Mapping the margins: Intersectionality, identity politics, and violence against women of color. *Stanford Law Review*, 43(6), 1241–1299. 10.2307/1229039

de Hond, A. A., van Buchem, M. M., & Hernandez-Boussard, T. (2022). Picture a data scientist: A call to action for increasing diversity, equity, and inclusion in the age of AI. *Journal of the American Medical Informatics Association : JAMIA*, 29(12), 2178–2181. 10.1093/jamia/ocac15636048021

Dwivedi, Y. K., Hughes, L., Ismagilova, E., Aarts, G., Coombs, C., Crick, T., Duan, Y., Dwivedi, R., Edwards, J., Eirug, A., Galanos, V., Ilavarasan, P. V., Janssen, M., Jones, P., Kar, A. K., Kizgin, H., Kronemann, B., Lal, B., Lucini, B., & Williams, M. D. (2021). Artificial Intelligence (AI): Multidisciplinary perspectives on emerging challenges, opportunities, and agenda for research, practice and policy. *International Journal of Information Management*, 57, 101994. 10.1016/j.ijinfomgt.2019.08.002

Evans, C., & Erickson, N. (2019). Intersectionality and depression in adolescence and early adulthood: A MAIHDA analysis of the national longitudinal study of adolescent to adult health, 1995-2008. *Social Science & Medicine*, 220, 1–11. 10.1016/j.socscimed.2018.10.01930390469

Gawande, V., Al Badi, H., & Al Makharoumi, K. (2020). An Empirical Study on Emerging Trends in Artificial Intelligence and its Impact on Higher Education. *International Journal of Computer Applications*, 175(12), 43–47. 10.5120/ijca2020920642

Hernández-Saca, D., Gutmann Kahn, L., & Cannon, M. (2018). Intersectionality Dis/ability Research: How Dis/ability Research in Education Engages Intersectionality to Uncover the Multidimensional Construction of Dis/abled Experiences. *Review of Research in Education*, 42(1), 286–311. 10.3102/0091732X18762439

Hunt, V., Layton, D., & Prince, S. (2015). *Why Diversity Matters*. McKinsey & Company.

Johnston, R., Pattie, C., Jones, K., & Manley, D. (2020). Intersectionality and English Voting Behaviour: And Was There a 2017 Youthquake. *Political Studies Review*, 18(2), 294–303. 10.1177/1478929919875055

Kelly, M. A., Barnert, E., & Bath, E. (2018). Think, Ask, Act: The Intersectionality of Mental and Reproductive Health for Judicially Involved Girls. *Journal of the American Academy of Child and Adolescent Psychiatry*, 57(10), 715–718. 10.1016/j.jaac.2018.07.87030274642

Kern, M. L., Williams, P., Spong, C., Colla, R., Sharma, K., Downie, A., Taylor, J. A., Sharp, S., Siokou, C., & Oades, L. G. (2020). Systems informed positive psychology. *The Journal of Positive Psychology*, 15(6), 705–715. 10.1080/17439760.2019.1639799

Kern, M. R., Duinhof, E. L., Walsh, S. D., Cosma, A., Moreno-Maldonado, C., Molcho, M., Currie, C., & Stevens, G. (2020). Intersectionality and Adolescent Mental Well-being: A Cross-Nationally Comparative Analysis of the Interplay Between Immigration Background, Socioeconomic Status and Gender. *The Journal of Adolescent Health*, 66(6, 6S), S12–S20. 10.1016/j.jadohealth.2020.02.01332446604

Lee, J., Suh, T., Roy, D., & Baucus, M. (2019). Emerging Technology and Business Model Innovation: The Case of Artificial Intelligence. *Journal of Open Innovation*, 5(3), 44. 10.3390/joitmc5030044

Liu, J., Chang, H., Forrest, J. Y. L., & Yang, B. (2020). Influence of artificial intelligence on technological innovation: Evidence from the panel data of china's manufacturing sectors. *Technological Forecasting and Social Change*, 158, 120142. 10.1016/j.techfore.2020.120142

Oskotsky, T., Maric, I., Tang, A., & Lituiev, D. (2021). *Nurturing Diversity and Inclusion in Biomedicine Through an AI Summer Program for High School Students*. ArXiv. 10.1101/2021.03.06.434213

Ovalle, A., Ovalle, A., Gautam, V., Gee, G., & Chang, K. W. (2023, August). Factoring the matrix of domination: A critical review and reimagination of intersectionality in ai fairness. In *Proceedings of the 2023 AAAI/ACM Conference on AI, Ethics, and Society* (pp. 496-511). ACM. 10.1145/3600211.3604705

Peinado, I., de Lera, E., Usero, J. M., Clark, C. B., Treviranus, J., & Vanderheiden, G. C. (2021). Digital Inclusion at the Workplace Post Covid19. In *IJCCI* (pp. 460-467). 10.5220/0010722900003063

Rana, S. A., Azizul, Z. H., & Awan, A. A. (2023). A step toward building a unified framework for managing AI bias. *PeerJ Computer Science, 9*, e1630.Riley, J. (2023). AI Powers the Digital Economy. *Ubiquity*.

Salah, K., Rehman, M. H. U., Nizamuddin, N., & Al-Fuqaha, A. (2019). Blockchain for AI: Review and open research challenges. *IEEE Access : Practical Innovations, Open Solutions*, 7, 10127–10149. 10.1109/ACCESS.2018.2890507

Salehi, H., & Burgueño, R. (2018). Emerging artificial intelligence methods in structural engineering. *Engineering Structures*, 171, 170–189. 10.1016/j.engstruct.2018.05.084

Stathoulopoulos, K., & Mateos-Garcia, J. C. (2019). Gender diversity in AI research. *SSRN* 3428240.

Taneja, A., Nair, G., Joshi, M., Sharma, S., Sharma, S., Jambrak, A. R., Roselló-Soto, E., Barba, F. J., Castagnini, J. M., Leksawasdi, N., & Phimolsiripol, Y. (2023). Artificial intelligence: Implications for the agri-food sector. *Agronomy (Basel)*, 13(5), 1397. 10.3390/agronomy13051397

Velez, G., & Spencer, M. B. (2018). Phenomenology and intersectionality: Using PVEST as a frame for adolescent identity formation amid intersecting ecological systems of inequality. *New Directions for Child and Adolescent Development*, 2018(161), 75–90. 10.1002/cad.2024729969194

Zowghi, D., & da Rimini, F. (2023). Diversity and inclusion in artificial intelligence. *arXiv preprint arXiv:2305.12728.*

# Chapter 19
# Role Reconfiguration Among Adolescents in the Age of AI

**Wang Xiaodan**
*Universiti Putra Malaysia, Malaysia*

**Aini Azeqa Ma'rof**
*Institute for Social Science Studies, Universiti Putra Malaysia, Malausia & Faculty of Educational Studies, Universiti Putra Malaysia, Malausia*

**Haslinda Abdullah**
*Institute for Social Science Studies, Universiti Putra Malaysia, Malausia & Faculty of Educational Studies, Universiti Putra Malaysia, Malausia*

**Wei Wang**
*Universiti Putra Malaysia, Malaysia*

## ABSTRACT

*The rise of artificial intelligence has brought profound changes to society and brought new challenges and opportunities to adolescents. With the development of artificial intelligence, adolescents are facing unprecedented social pressure and changes and need to adapt to new roles and responsibilities. This requires them to have a full understanding of their own abilities and characteristics, as well as good communication and collaboration skills. In addition, adolescents need to pay attention to the impact of artificial intelligence on their own development and social development and strive to promote positive changes. Therefore, this chapter will provide feasible strategies for role reconstruction in the artificial intelligence era, helping adolescents better adapt to social changes and seize more opportunities.*

DOI: 10.4018/979-8-3693-3350-1.ch019

# INTRODUCTION

## The Rise of AI Era

Artificial intelligence (AI) has had a tremendous influence on every element of civilization, driven by the swift advancement of technology. The adolescents of today are the "natives" of the age of AI. AI technology, which objectifies social and historical humanity, has an impact on, defines, and shapes the lives of adolescents regardless of their material, spiritual, or interpersonal interactions. The identities and roles of adolescents have undergone significant transformation as a result of this. Adolescents will experience societal pressure and changes never seen before, and they will have to cope with and adjust to a variety of identity tests. Empirical studies on how adolescent identities and responsibilities are changing in the age of AI emphasize the need of enabling adolescents to engage with AI technology in purposeful ways (Ong et al., 2021). This is especially crucial because a lot of adolescents feel powerless in the face of AI's influence on their lives (Lee & Kim, 2020). Novel approaches to education and techniques to encourage engagement with AI have been put forth to address this issue. Concerns exist, nevertheless, regarding the acceptance of AI and how it may affect adolescent's media consumption habits. Collectively, these findings emphasize how critical it is to comprehend and deal with how AI is changing adolescent's identities and responsibilities.

AI presents new concerns regarding the reconfiguration of adolescents' identities and roles, communicates human thinking, and investigates the nature of intelligence in the form of technology. It also generates a new living environment for today's adolescents. Because AI "enables our human-machine civilization to transcend the limitations of the human brain" (Kurzweil, 2005), it is considered the fifth age of technical advancement, coming after the upgrading and acceleration of technological development in the fourth. Nowadays, AI technology is essentially an ontological upgrade that is directly reflected in the expansion of existence's scope, its ability to exist, and its realm of understanding. As a result, the "smartness" of technology is no longer only reflected in the function of technological development. In the future, upgrading might be an ontological dual-subject upgrade of "recreating existence" (Rakowski et al., 2021). As a result, the existential domain, which has experienced significant expansion and depth due to the advancement of AI, serves as both a new social and historical context for the generation of adolescents' identities and roles and a crucial area for adolescents to acquire existential experience.

## Challenges and Opportunities Faced by Adolescents

Adolescents passively join a genuine environment despite the fact that application scenarios and human "general intelligence" enhance the technical growth of AI. Adolescents may, however, naturally absorb and develop AI with great excitement, full engagement, and individual internalization since they are in the cognitive and role-building phase of life. Individuals from all eras, particularly adolescents, are true historical figures. They have to engage in specialized production tasks in authentic settings, acquire firsthand survival experience, and develop certain values. Since "the practice of change is the only thing that can be seen and reasonably understood as the consistency of environmental changes and human activities" (Mauthner, 2019). In terms of technological innovation and employment opportunities, the rise of AI has created new employment opportunities for adolescents. Adolescents have the opportunity to participate in innovative projects and promote the development of cutting-edge science and technology. In terms of interdisciplinary development, AI is not just something in the field of computer science. It involves interdisciplinary knowledge, including mathematics, philosophy, psychology, etc. This gives adolescents the opportunity to broaden their knowledge and achieve interdisciplinary development. In terms of social influence, by participating in the development of AI technology, adolescents have the opportunity to create a positive impact on society. However, the rapid development and fierce competition of AI have brought employment uncertainty, a series of ethical and social responsibilities, a digital divide, and mental health issues. Therefore, although being "smart" by AI is an era background that adolescents cannot choose, it must be understood through identification with adolescents and role reshaping.

## The Dilemma of Adolescents' Characters in the Era of AI

In the era of AI, adolescents may have some unique role challenges pertaining to their social, professional, and personal identity and growth. Adolescents face new problems in the age of AI, which calls for more flexibility, leadership, social responsibility, and cross-cultural communication abilities on both a personal and professional level. In order to assist adolescents in their holistic development, the school system, business community, and society as a whole must collaborate to address these issues.

## Uncertainty About Career Direction

The era of AI has given rise to many new job categories, but adolescents may find it difficult to make the proper decision in a subject that is evolving quickly. They must consider their beliefs, interests, and skill set in order to determine which job path best fits them. Unquestionably, the rise in popularity of AI has raised concerns about unemployment, but adolescents' perspectives aren't always the same (Kelly, 2016). According to research, 70% of adolescents want to use purposeful learning to reduce the chance of having to compete with AI for jobs (Fetzer & Fetzer, 1990). However, this fact also prompts adolescents to start thinking longer-term about their future careers. The development of AI technology is currently in its prime. "Digital natives" are the adolescents who belong to the post-1990s and post-2000s generations. They have demonstrated an engaged demeanor and a keen interest in diverse AI software and hardware applications. Adolescents are also aware of the unspoken concerns that the rise in popularity of AI may bring. According to the research data on adolescents' career planning in the AI era, 25.37% of adolescents are concerned that a widespread technologicalization of society's operations—what Postman refers to as "culture's surrender to technology"—will result in widespread unemployment among humans (Yan-Ping & Ai-Qin, 2022). The common response from students of all academic levels is,"The future is still ahead, and I will try to avoid these fields when making choices." Students in junior high school specifically provided the largest percentage (38.1%), demonstrating the potential of AI. To varied degrees, adolescents' consideration of professional choices is influenced by popularity. AI is a kind of computer program, and one of the main things a program does is carry out different repetitive activities either directly (by doing calculations) or indirectly (by operating machinery). Because deep learning-based AI is more sophisticated than standard algorithms, it may mimic human intellect and take the place of humans in a greater variety of jobs. Regarding the workplace, the advancement of AI will surely make it more difficult for today's adolescents to decide on career paths and job categories.

## Issues With Education and Skill Alignment

No technology has ever been referred to as "intelligence" throughout the lengthy history of human science and technology development. "Intelligence" denotes knowledge and skill. Although these two phrases have only been used by humans since ancient times, they are today utilized from a technical point of view, contradicting what makes people special (Chang & Zhao, 2020). The use of AI has brought about enormous changes in a number of industries. The use of AI is accelerating the reform and innovation of teaching techniques, teaching assessment, educational governance, and even the entire education system. It also encourages changes in teaching objectives, teaching environment, and teaching methods. While AI has undoubtedly brought numerous benefits to education and teaching, there have also been a number of problems. One of the most important issues that cannot be disregarded is the lack of autonomy among adolescents. Because the traditional education system might not be able to keep up with the rapid advancements in technology, adolescents may find it difficult to connect their education to the skills required by employers. To meet the demands of the AI age in the workplace, adolescents must continuously improve their abilities and pursue autonomous learning opportunities. Xu Liang stated that although human cognition is limited, it can help us accomplish evident achievement in short-term technical behavior goals. Still, it also frequently introduces risks to long-term objectives (Hongmei et al., 2023). Typically, the benefits of AI over schooling are clear. Personalized education is becoming popular thanks to AI, which also helps to increase adolescents' potential for creativity and general literacy. Simultaneously, the advancement of AI will hasten the adoption of virtual classrooms and provide accessibility to excellent educational materials. Sharing across the globe is made feasible. The majority of the repetitive tasks performed by instructors may be replaced by a variety of AI apps, which will increase productivity. The rise of AI has significantly altered education, as seen by the development of individualized learning and the resulting changes in tools and technology, instructional scenarios and models, and school forms. Additionally, AI will undoubtedly encourage a shift in educational paradigms from the conventional exam-focused curriculum to the more modern STEAM (Science, Technology, Engineering, Art, and Mathematics) curriculum. It will also quietly alter the pedagogical approaches and techniques used by educators (Ren & Lan, 2021). adolescents now confront problems in all areas of education, learning, and skills due to changes in the external world in the rapidly evolving age of AI. Adolescents are putting more and more pressure on school reform. The old teaching approach has been undermined by technology, and as a result, adolescents now have to adjust their job positioning to fit the current development trend.

## Balance Between Social Responsibility and Personal Development

Adolescents may run into problems with societal duties and ethical issues while seeking personal job success. Adolescents entering an AI profession need to strike a balance between their personal and societal responsibilities, as well as consider how their work will affect society and humanity in the long run. AI technology may assist in optimizing industrial processes, saving energy usage, and increasing resource use efficiency. Intelligent transportation systems have the potential to enhance traffic flow and minimize fuel use. At the same time, smart grids may modify energy usage based on demand and augment power supply stability and dependability (Nowak et al., 2018). Although it has grown to be a significant driver of innovation and progress, AI is not without hazards and limitations. The ethical and the societal implications of AI represent a significant problem. Aspects of human civilization like work, privacy, security, and others may be impacted by AI's increasing intellect and autonomy. Inadequate decision-making by AI systems can potentially result in unjust and discriminatory consequences. Thus, it is necessary to strike a balance between the need for AI growth and the requirement to uphold human rights (Y. Zhang et al., 2022). We, the EU, and other areas have adopted a number of rules and regulations pertaining to the use of AI. Examples of these include the US Privacy Act and the Consumer Protection Act. The General Data Protection Regulation (GDPR), which was released by the European Union in 2018, is the most representative. This law specifies exactly how personal data is used and protected. A few international accords and guidelines about the legal standing of AI are also available. For instance, the European Parliament passed a report on AI in 2018, urging EU members to take steps to ensure the transparency, explainability, and accountability of artificial intelligence (Machin et al., 2018). UNESCO also released the "Ethical Guidelines for AI" in 2019, which clearly stipulates the ethical principles and values of artificial intelligence and provides guiding opinions for its development. A survey of the literature on AI's legal standing focuses on legal concerns related to AI in areas including liability assessment, privacy protection, intellectual property rights, and security hazards. Still, there are several issues with the current body of evidence. First of all, there hasn't been enough in-depth, systematic, or thorough debate on the legal situation of AI. Currently, there is a shortage of thorough studies and debates on the general legal situation of artificial intelligence, with the majority of research concentrating on the legal challenges related to specific areas of AI. Furthermore, the current body of research is short in its analysis of particular applications of AI in the legal domain. In conclusion, there are still concerns with the way theoretical research and practical application are integrated, and there is a dearth of critical thinking regarding practical application issues in the research that has already been done (Misra et al., 2020). Therefore, in the age of artificial intelligence, striking a balance between upholding social obligations and defending individual rights necessitates a thorough analysis of the relationship between AI and personal growth, the creation of standards and regulations in law to safeguard people's legitimate rights and interests, and the gradual improvement and development of pertinent legal frameworks.

## The Balance Between Competition and Cooperation

Technology related to AI is starting to take center stage in global competitiveness and collaboration. In order to preserve their dominant positions in the field of AI, China, the US, and the EU continue to advance their development advantages and expand governmental support. China adheres to the idea of "developing responsible artificial intelligence"; the US seeks to strike a balance between technological innovation, economic development, and oversight; and the EU, with its first-mover advantage in ethics and regulatory legislation, is likely to have an impact on global standards. The commercial sector is now the backbone of collaboration, with governments from different nations actively creating worldwide platforms for AI cooperation. Simultaneously, practical obstacles like the emergence of technology protectionism and the ongoing expansion of the value gap confront collaboration in AI governance. While there is a lot of competition in the field of AI, innovation frequently calls for collaboration. Globally speaking, governments, businesses, and academic institutions have all given AI considerable attention, and the field's advancement in research has shown a new direction. The number of AI articles published through various channels rose from fewer than 48,000 to 230,000 between 2000 and 2020, a rise of about 4 times (see Figure 1), accounting for 10% of all publications, according to information from Microsoft Academic Graph (MAG). The percentage went from being less than 2% to 3%. The primary regions for paper output are East Asia, Europe, and North America, according to the "Artificial Intelligence Index

Report 2021". Universities are the primary producers of papers in all major nations and regions. It can be seen that adolescents must learn how to take the lead and collaborate with others in teams while maintaining a healthy sense of competition.

*Figure 1. Number of AI articles published globally from 2000 to 2020*

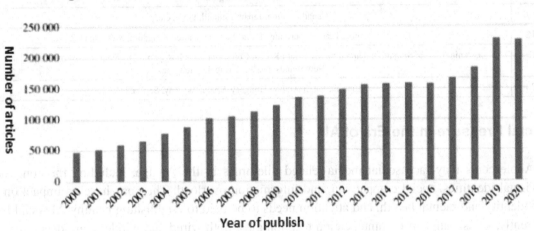

Because AI has so many potential applications, it is anticipated to have a major role in determining the nature of global competition or to provide nations that embrace it first with substantial economic and geopolitical benefits. AI rivalry has progressively changed from being a fight between research institutes and businesses to one between nations, and many nations are planning to increase AI R&D and application. Since 2017, over 30 nations and regions have released national AI development policies in order to prioritize the field and take part in the international AI competition (see Table 1). According to the research results, together with emerging nations like India, Mexico, Indonesia, Brazil, Malaysia, and Ukraine, they include developed nations and areas like the United States, the European Union, France, Germany, the United Kingdom, and Singapore (AlShebli et al., 2022). Through AI policies, nations are attempting to assist the growth of their own AI firms and gain an advantage over rivals globally. Nevertheless, it is impossible to ignore that as more and more nations enter the global AI race, strong international laws and norms must be developed immediately. Countries must simultaneously accomplish the goal of exchanging knowledge and advancing via mutually beneficial collaboration. Together with emerging nations like India, Mexico, Indonesia, Brazil, Malaysia, and Ukraine, they include developed nations and areas like the United States, the European Union, France, Germany, the United Kingdom, and Singapore. Through AI policies, nations are attempting to assist the growth of their own AI firms and gain an advantage over rivals globally. Nevertheless, it is impossible to ignore that as more and more nations enter the global AI race, strong international laws and norms must Be developed immediately. Countries must simultaneously accomplish the goal of exchanging knowledge and advancing via mutually beneficial collaboration. Various AI efforts have arisen to satisfy some countries' common development goals. AI principles and standards, data sharing, R&D collaboration, and other related subjects have been incorporated into several extremely significant worldwide projects, events, and organizations. Japan, South Korea, the United States, the United Kingdom, and EU member states are among the nations that have actively engaged in intergovernmental collaboration on AI. Additionally, a few nations have actively signed bilateral agreements to advance global AI collaboration.

*Table 1. Countries and regions that have released national AI strategies in recent years*

| Year | Countries/Regions |
|------|-------------------|
| 2017 | Canada, China, Japan, Finland, UAE, etc. |
| 2018 | European Union, France, Germany, India, Mexico, United Kingdom, Sweden, etc. |
| 2019 | Estonia, Russia, Singapore, United States, South Korea, Colombia, Czech Republic, Lithuania, Luxembourg, Malta, Netherlands, Chile, Portugal, Qatar, etc. |
| 2020 | Indonesia, Saudi Arabia, Hungary, Spain, Norway, Serbia, etc. |

## Social Pressure in the Era of AI

Adolescents may face social media-related dilemmas in the AI age, including the construction of virtual identities, social comparison, and information overload. This may have an impact on their self-identity and mental health, and attention needs to be paid to establishing healthy AI social habits. Currently, a vast range of communication technologies, both wired and wireless, are developing, and their penetration and coverage are growing. AI has a tremendous function and the capacity to infiltrate many facets of human work and existence. It has also brought about several conveniences and had a significant influence on society. AI technology is always evolving, and this has had a significant influence on societal development as well. The young culture has changed because of artificial intelligence. When various artificial intelligence tools are used to promote productivity at work, adolescents' job efficiency quickly improves, productivity skyrockets and wealth quickly grows. Adolescents are faced with duties that frequently demand them to collaborate and communicate with others since an increasing number of positions that do not require sophisticated judgment are being replaced. Additionally, as network and communication technologies have advanced, a variety of social and economic activities have grown more globalized, and face-to-face interactions have increased. The present rate of social and economic development is clearly lagging the growth and development of information data, according to statistics. A vast quantity of data is being collected every minute and every second because of artificial intelligence's ongoing progress; this data is derived entirely from statistics related to human development (Cockburn et al., 2018). AI is a development of modern thought. Adolescents can use artificial intelligence to assist with monotonous and repetitive tasks like using light path simulators and calculators. These gadgets can assist kids in solving some problems, but they can also influence adolescent cognitive processes. Adolescents' talents are frequently diminished when they rely too heavily on these smart devices. The primary worry of people using new technologies is that they would become uncontrollable and endanger their safety. It is worthwhile considering this subject, in fact. In the era of AI, adolescents may have to deal with issues associated with social media, such as creating virtual personas, comparing themselves to others, and having too much information. It is important to pay attention to developing good AI social habits since this might affect their self-identity and mental health (Vinichenko et al., 2021). The field of AI will unavoidably advance more quickly as society continues to grow, and as a result, its influence on youth will unavoidably grow.

## Understanding of AI Humanities

The use of AI techniques and technologies in humanities study is a new kind of humanities research that has evolved with the ongoing growth of intelligent science and technology. The field is collectively referred to by the author as intelligent humanities research or simply intelligent humanities. Intelligent humanities research is a new area of multidisciplinary study that blends advanced AI technology with deep insights from the humanities. Its goal is to investigate how AI may be used in the humanities and how this will impact our comprehension of language, human culture, history, philosophy, and the arts. Rich defines intelligent humanities as an interdisciplinary research field that investigates both the application of artificial intelligence in the humanities and the ways in which artificial intelligence influences our perception of the world (Rich, 1985). The multidisciplinary area of artificial intelligence research is expected to undergo further advancements due to the ongoing technological advancements in the field. This will yield novel insights into the junction of artificial intelligence and the humanities, perhaps revolutionizing the latter. These days, humanities and AI are becoming more and more integrated, and intelligent humanities is gaining popularity as an area of study in higher education. Scholars across many nations and areas are searching for efficient means of merging the domains of AI and humanities. studies to have a better grasp of this developing discipline (Lee & Kim, 2020). Integration may take many different forms, of course. Some examples are collaborative research initiatives, the creation of interdisciplinary research institutes, and the hosting of scholarly conferences and publications. To better integrate into a varied work environment, adolescents may need to comprehend and adjust to other cultures, values, and work styles (Osuji, 2021). Artificial intelligence technology has opened a world of possibilities for the humanities, but it also presents a number of risk and adaptation difficulties. Data bias, ethical and privacy concerns, changes in knowledge and abilities, obstacles in multidisciplinary collaboration, and adjustment to conventional academic systems are some of these hurdles. A new generation of scholars must be trained in interdisciplinary skills, interdisciplinary cooperation must be strengthened, academic evaluation standards must be updated, infrastructure and resources must be invested in, and the problem of interdisciplinary adaptability between the two must be effectively solved at several levels. By taking these steps, humanities may safeguard and advance their distinctive research methodologies and ideals while more effectively using the potential afforded by AI technology. AI techniques and technology are progressively becoming essential components of humanities study as the intelligence era continues to grow and evolve. Researchers can carry out research in a more effective, thorough, and creative manner by using intelligent interactive tools, simulation computer experiments, and the collection, analysis, and induction of humanistic corpus data. These technologies help the humanities better meet the demands of the digital age by increasing research efficiency and accuracy while also opening new research vistas and methodologies (Ide & Véronis, 1990). Future humanities study is expected to be richer and more diversified, with a greater influence on comprehending human society and culture due to the ongoing progress and popularization of AI technologies. It should be noted that the use and discussion of AI technology in the humanities is opening a new age of knowledge. We will need to reconsider our social structures and cultural values in this century and redefine human-technology interaction. In this process, the humanities are essential for creating a future society that is more intelligent and inclusive, in addition to offering the means to comprehend and address the problems posed by AI. We may better prepare for an increasingly complicated and interconnected world by exploring the humanistic challenges brought by AI. The use of AI is expected to become more prevalent in humanities studies, as seen by the growth and establishment of the area of intelligent humanities research. It fosters the advancement of research ideas and procedures in addition to increasing the effectiveness and scope of the study. Technical adaptability, data bias, privacy and ethics, technical constraints, and the influence on the current academic system provide dangers and problems. Still, they also work as spurs to elevate humanities to new heights. As AI technology develops further, we may anticipate further discoveries and advancements in the humanities that will give us a better understanding of culture and society. The application of AI will revolutionize humanities research methodologies and create a new chapter in the field's future development through this multidisciplinary integration.

## STRATEGIES TO OVERCOME THE DILEMMA OF ADOLESCENTS' ROLES IN THE ERA OF AI

Overcoming the dilemma of adolescents' roles in the era of artificial intelligence requires a combination of personal, educational, and societal strategies. Here are some strategies that can be employed:

### Continuous Learning and Skill Development

The field of AI is advancing quickly in our day and age, having a significant impact on many facets of society and even human evolution. The use of AI has fundamentally altered our understanding of learning and undermined the traditional learning approach. A number of observers express a great deal of optimism regarding the effects of artificial intelligence on education, contending that AI greatly enhances learning and that anybody can use AI to establish a peaceful learning environment where humans and machines coexist (Xiaoyong et al., 2023). But it's indisputable that all technologies have drawbacks and can be harmful; artificial intelligence is no different. Thus, we need to be cautious of the threats associated with AI that lifelong learning presents (Chen et al., 2020). Adolescents ought to welcome the idea of lifelong learning to stay up to date with the ever-evolving technology scene. Create a growth mentality that encourages curiosity and an openness to picking up new abilities. Try to develop a broad range of abilities, encompassing not only artificial intelligence-related technical capabilities but also soft skills like communication, creativity, critical thinking, and flexibility. Examine chances for transdisciplinary learning to gain a deeper understanding of the larger picture of AI applications. Adhering to the lifelong learning idea of equal focus on work and learning, adolescents should create new artificial intelligence ethical rules that adapt to the demands of the times around the subject status of lifelong learners. The development of AI has brought about changes in social connections, and ethical standards in this century can reflect these changes via advancement and presumption (Handong, 2017). The application of ethical standards to AI regulation is a well-recognized approach. Since AI lacks omnipotence, its use in education cannot alter the nature or intent of education. In the age of AI, preserving lifelong learning is essential to people's freedom of growth and to make the transition from the kingdom of need to the kingdom of freedom. Thus, in the age of AI, upholding the intrinsic worth of human beings and the unalienable right to free will rank as the highest moral and legal standards. Learner-centered ethical norms must be established first (Hu & Lu, 2020). Less physical work is required for youth learning in the age of artificial intelligence, which leads to juvenile physical waste—a far cry from the optimal condition for adolescent growth overall. Marxism holds that work is what separates people from other animals and that work is what gives rise to human beings. Learning and labor are of equal importance to adolescents. Together, work and study support adolescents in their more complete growth and assist in their evolution into more idealized adults. Adolescents may change the outside environment via labor and expand their understanding of it through learning. Learn how to become a skilled worker, use the information you gain from your work to change the world, validate and enhance the knowledge you gain, create new knowledge that needs to be learned, and experience the natural flow of learning and working together. The practical requirement of digital human rights is congruent with the different hazards associated with lifelong learning in the age of AI. The purposes for which it is protected align with those of digital human rights. There is a connection between digital human rights and lifelong learning. It has been used to lifelong learning in the AI age by creating the institutionalization of adolescents' autonomy over their data and information, investigating the rights-balance mechanism of learning scenarios, and implementing process-result regulating techniques.

## Ethical Awareness and Social Responsibility

The societal conceptions of adolescents today are drastically shifting. The social circles of adolescents on the internet are always growing, and they have the potential to create an endless number of friends. However, the fragmented friendship model creates "group loneliness" since it is shallow and hard to build meaningful relationships (Wu, 2022). Accessing efficient emotional support, whether in person or virtually, is becoming a more limited resource. Adolescent individual's social engagement practices are not without difficulties. Adolescents are concerned about the unpredictability of emotional relationships in contemporary culture, yet they also want strong emotional ties and require validation and security from intimate partners. Adolescents find spiritual sustenance in many sorts of virtual emotions, which compensate for the loss of actual connection. Some adolescents defy the notion that only intimate relationships can be formed between individuals by using computers with intelligence to create and personalize feelings on their own (Caraway, 2018). They also view these systems as partners, lovers, or close friends. This has essentially led to a rise in adolescents' reliance on AI. This will need the inclusion of ethical issues in AI instruction by society. Instill a sense of social responsibility, promote conversation about the ethical implications of technical advancements and the societal effects of artificial intelligence, and stress the significance of applying AI to advance humanity and resolve moral dilemmas. As a result, cutting-edge AI technology is rapidly influencing and altering every aspect of civilization. AI should take on societal obligations commensurate with its fast growth to guarantee that it serves humans without causing harm. The direction of development is essential in the field of AI. Artificial intelligence should not be seen as a replacement for low-skilled labor, which would increase unemployment and competitive pressure among adolescents, but rather as a tool for adolescents directed toward high-end fields like scientific research, medical diagnosis, and new drug development. Over-reliance on artificial intelligence applications in low-end industries may undermine society's general stability and equity. First and foremost, cooperation between governments, businesses, and academic institutions is necessary to achieve the peaceful growth of AI and intelligent society. The government should offer policy direction and assistance to foster a favorable climate for the advancement of AI since it is the primary authority responsible for developing laws and regulations. Businesses should take on social obligations and encourage the sensible use of technology as the major source of innovation and application. The academic community should provide cutting-edge knowledge and scientific, theoretical, and technological assistance for the development of

AI, with academia serving as the primary source of intellectual support and research. The interests of adolescents must be given consideration by the government when it comes to advancing the development of AI. The use of AI technology may negatively affect young demographics through social marginalization, increased likelihood of unemployment, etc. The government and businesses should improve youth care and support, offer suitable training, and job possibilities, and make sure that youth have greater opportunities to engage with and profit from the AI era.

## Balancing Competition and Collaboration

AI has demonstrated incredible benefits in deep learning, accurately represents the evolution of intellect, and has a significant impact on the lives of adolescents. The subjectivity of AI is a significant practical issue that must be addressed in the development of social subjects, even though we cannot state that it is the subject at this time. Because our existential practice is itself plagued by the ontological upgrading of the potential of artificial intelligence persons, it has a profound impact on adolescent conduct and logic of thought, and it is more likely to have an impact on the future strength of this generation of adolescents. Thus, a crucial and basic question in the age of AI is how adolescents create their subject autonomy. AI will undoubtedly provide adolescents with chances for collaboration and competitiveness in the context of its continued fast development. Adolescents need to interact with AI on their own consciously (Bostrom, 1998). This calls for developing theoretical thinking to confront and critique AI, as well as the capacity to modify one's behavior and create social subjects. It also calls for strengthening AI comprehension and application skills. Adolescents can only genuinely build independent and healthy roles in this way. In this way, adolescents might realize that, contrary to expectations, artificial intelligence cannot become the focus of human thought; instead, adolescents must utilize their own personas to make references to AI. This helps adolescents to maintain their subjective consciousness and continuously establish role identity in the process of questioning, criticizing, evaluating, selecting, and using AI. It also helps to eliminate the existential anxiety caused by the subjectivity of artificial intelligence. It goes without saying that adolescents should be able to confront the subjectivity of AI head-on and be able to independently comprehend, assess, grasp, and use AI to compete and collaborate with it. Adolescents in the artificial intelligence age face two fundamental options when it comes to addressing issues of self-worth. They can choose to delve deeper into the subject, develop mastery over it, and come to terms with the idea of "human and machine coexistence" or they can choose to express the subject of the age through improved quality, increased capabilities, and enhanced intelligence. have sex; or suffer from extreme AI alienation and have intelligent agents take your place (Muehlhauser & Salamon, 2013). Adolescents should be actively exposed to artificial intelligence during the role reconstruction process. They should also make plans of time, seize opportunities, and actively investigate ways to use intelligent systems logically and successfully complete human-machine labor partnership in a competitive environment. This establishes the fundamental prerequisites for the attainment of free work time in addition to providing a feasible route for the plenty of material prosperity in society. Simultaneously, the advancement of AI will introduce more science fiction aspects into everyday living, social interactions, and spiritual practices. In order to restore adolescent characters' independence and integrity in the age of artificial intelligence, extensive engagement with AI is required.

## Adjust the Direction of Training Young Talents

Promote digital well-being by educating youth about healthy online habits, managing screen time, and being mindful of the impact of social media on mental health.Provide resources for social media literacy to help young individuals navigate the digital landscape responsibly and critically. The AI age will also require timely modifications to be made to young talent's training in order to adequately prepare them for life and the workplace in the future. Even if AI has resulted in a large number of new jobs, adolescents will find it difficult to take advantage of even the greatest employment prospects if they lack the necessary work skills. Professional training and education are now required in order to assist them in adjusting to new roles. With AI and social intelligence on the rise, it is imperative that educational institutions adapt and prioritize the development of three distinct categories of young talent. To fulfill market demand, professional application-oriented abilities must be developed. High-skilled labor is in short supply while medium- and low-skilled labor is oversupplied in the present labor market due to an employment structural issue. Specifically, there is a significant skills shortage in high-tech AI-related employment. This should be the main emphasis of youthful talent training, with the development path of talent training being modified in response to market need. Research talent that can fulfill the demands of AI advancement must be nurtured. The competitiveness among adolescents with scientific and technical skills is the key to technological competition, which is the foundation of future international rivalry. Therefore, in order for our nation to have an edge over other nations in the AI business, it has to hasten the development of a huge pool of talent for AI scientific research, particularly top talent with the capacity for innovation and the ability to overcome key technological barriers. It is imperative to develop "AI+" compound skills, or people who can use AI in a variety of work settings and who have mastered the fundamental concepts and techniques of thinking associated with AI. Future civilization will be more intelligent, and it will be necessary for humans to be able to function in an AI-shaped world. Develop soft skills of complete abilities, such as perception, creativity, adaptability, criticality, flexibility in thought, social communication, negotiation, and problem solving. These are fundamental human talents that will be challenging for AI to quickly replace. In order to meet the development demands of the AI era, professional talent training must give way to holistic talent training. In order to achieve this, teacher teams, current course material, and instructional strategies need all be modified. A more complete education should incorporate lifelong learning and psychological construction skills since they are essential to the long-term development of youth in the face of fast technological advancement and societal change.

## Psychological Support

Recognize the psychological challenges associated with the fast-paced and competitive nature of the AI industry. Provide mental health resources and support systems to help youth cope with stress and maintain well-being. In addition to providing convenience, amusement, and relaxation, AI's ongoing growth also naturally appeals to youth. But AI is also likely to make adolescents today more anxious about their careers and about human-computer interaction in general. Kurzweil had asserted in "The Singularity is Near" that the "singularity"—when AI fully surpasses human intelligence—will occur in 2045 in reaction to the possible dangers of AI development. In "A Brief History of the Future," Yuval Noah Harari prophesied that when the AI "singularity" draws near, a select group of "gods" who master algorithms and use biotechnology to thwart death will toil and produce enough food to feed everyone on the planet. The majority of humans will end up as "useless people". Thus, scientist Stephen Hawking previously expressed concern that super AI would spell the end for humanity. AI presents a more rigorous test than any other technology to yet (Liu & Tan, 2023). AI's rising impact on technological unemployment certainly validates these forecasts to some degree. Thus, in a time when AI is developing quickly, this widespread anxiety and fear causes mental health issues among adolescents. As per the 2019 paper "AI Risks and Governance from the Perspective of Chinese Youth" published by Tsinghua University's Strategy and Security Research Center, over 50% of youths fear that the advancement of AI might result in joblessness and are plagued by career anxiety. The effect of AI on adolescents in general is the main concern. Adolescents place a high value on work since it provides them with a means of subsistence as well as a sense of self and purpose in life. The most important time in a person's life is their youth. It is not just the very unstable transition from youth to maturity, but also the transfer from formal schooling to the workforce. Adolescents will go through significant life transitions at this time, including becoming parents, adopting new social roles, and taking on household duties (Pohlan, 2019). Work is a major contributor to physical and mental health, ensures financial resources, and gives young people the means to fulfill their commitments to their families and society. When adolescents fear AI, it will negatively impact their social status and family duties, endangering their mental and physical well-being in the process (Mokona et al., 2020). Adolescent role building is hampered by psychological issues that might result in social rejection or even total social isolation. Needless to say, using AI improperly may have detrimental effects on the mental and physical well-being of adolescents and undermine the development of adolescent role models. For this reason, we must remain extremely watchful and careful when it comes to the application of AI.

## CONCLUSION

To summarize the content of this chapter, it is emphasized that in the era of AI, adolescents role reshaping is a complex but critical issue. Looking to the future, adolescents are encouraged to face challenges with a positive attitude, continuously develop and improve their identity, and contribute to social progress and innovation. Through in-depth analysis of this topic, this chapter aims to help readers better understand the current situation and development direction of adolescents in the era of AI and provide inspiration and guidance for individuals and society to deal with challenges. As a result, the rebuilding of adolescent roles has gained importance in the age of AI (D. Zhang et al., 2021). Without a question, there are a lot of chances and problems in our period. For adolescents, artificial intelligence subjectivity's "personification of objects" has a profoundly ingrained influence on the rebuilding of adolescent roles. This indicates that the advancement and development of adolescent roles is a call for young people to take on the duties of the times as well as a difficult social and historical responsibility. The rebuilding of adolescent roles in the age of AI is a social and historical phenomenon that still has a long way to go, as we must first make clear. This is because, despite the conveniences it offers, adolescents now confront a multitude of issues due to the fast development and societal application of artificial intelligence technology. These difficulties include, but are not restricted to data privacy, ethics, and information leaking. In order to effectively respond to these problems and accomplish their own role development, young people in this day must possess strong values and the capacity for independent thought. Second, in the age of artificial intelligence, adolescents are responsible for more significant tasks. Not only should they fully utilize AI technology to boost productivity and enhance quality of life, but they should also consider how to steer AI technology's advancement in a way that benefits human society. This is important from the standpoint of human development. This means that adolescents need to be courageous enough to experiment and invent, have the knowledge of historical dialectics, approach AI with a scientific mindset, and have the practical spirit of historical materialism. Thirdly, in the age of artificial intelligence, adolescents must continue to be independent individuals. They must thus insist on making their own decisions and following their own set of rules, unrestricted by technology, even as they make use of the conveniences and innovations provided by AI. In the age of AI, adolescents can only advance human civilization and become fully autonomous and independent in this way. Finally, in the age of artificial intelligence, adolescents need to possess a high sense of humanism. They must always uphold human values, consider people's holistic development, and make sure that the advancement of artificial intelligence is in accordance with the interests and welfare of humanity while dealing with the technical effect of AI. In summary, it is a difficult and significant effort to recreate adolescent roles in the age of AI. The wisdom of historical dialectics, the application of historical materialism, the pragmatism of scientism, and the loftiness of humanism are the tools that the younger generation needs to use to meet this issue. They cannot absorb the demands of the times, retain their individuality, produce historical originality, or aid in the advancement of human civilization in the age of AI in any other manner.

# REFERENCES

AlShebli, B., Cheng, E., Waniek, M., Jagannathan, R., Hernández-Lagos, P., & Rahwan, T. (2022). Beijing's central role in global artificial intelligence research. *Scientific Reports*, 12(1), 21461. 10.1038/s41598-022-25714-036509790

Bostrom, N. (1998). How long before superintelligence. *International Journal of Futures Studies*, 2(1), 1–9.

Caraway, B. R. (2018). Literal media ecology: Crisis in the conditions of production. *Television & New Media*, 19(5), 486–503. 10.1177/1527476417712459

Chang, Y., & Zhao, Y. (2020). The Proposal, Connotation and Significance of the Concept of Content-Language Integration (CLI)—From content-based instruction to content-language integration education. *Foreign Lang. Educ. China*, 41, 49–54.

Chen, L., Chen, P., & Lin, Z. (2020). Artificial intelligence in education: A review. *IEEE Access : Practical Innovations, Open Solutions*, 8, 75264–75278. 10.1109/ACCESS.2020.2988510

Cockburn, I. M., Henderson, R., & Stern, S. (2018). *The impact of artificial intelligence on innovation (Vol. 24449)*. National bureau of economic research Cambridge, MA, USA.

Fetzer, J. H., & Fetzer, J. H. (1990). *What is artificial intelligence?* Springer.

Handong, W. (2017). Institutional arrangement and legal regulation in the era of artificial intelligence. [Journal of Northwest University of Political Science and Law]. *Science of Law*, 5, 128–136.

Hongmei, C., Chuan, W., & Kaur, N. (2023). *International University Students' Cognition of a Community of Shared Future for Mankind*.

Hu, T., & Lu, H. (2020). Study on the influence of artificial intelligence on legal profession. *5th International Conference on Economics, Management, Law and Education (EMLE 2019)*, (pp. 964–968) IEEE.

Ide, N. M., & Véronis, J. (1990). Artificial intelligence and the study of literary narrative. *Poetics*, 19(1–2), 37–63. 10.1016/0304-422X(90)90030-9

Kelly, K. (2016). *The inevitable: Understanding the 12 technological forces that will shape our future*. Penguin.

Kurzweil, R. (2005). The singularity is near. In *Ethics and emerging technologies* (pp. 393–406). Springer.

Lee, C., & Kim, H. (2020). Groundwork of artificial intelligence humanities. Jahr. *Europski Časopis Za Bioetiku*, 11(1), 189–207.

Machin, M., Sanguesa, J. A., Garrido, P., & Martinez, F. J. (2018). On the use of artificial intelligence techniques in intelligent transportation systems. *2018 IEEE Wireless Communications and Networking Conference Workshops (WCNCW)*, (pp. 332–337). IEEE. 10.1109/WCNCW.2018.8369029

Mauthner, N. S. (2019). Toward a posthumanist ethics of qualitative research in a big data era. *The American Behavioral Scientist*, 63(6), 669–698. 10.1177/0002764218792701

Misra, N. N., Dixit, Y., Al-Mallahi, A., Bhullar, M. S., Upadhyay, R., & Martynenko, A. (2020). IoT, big data, and artificial intelligence in agriculture and food industry. *IEEE Internet of Things Journal*, 9(9), 6305–6324. 10.1109/JIOT.2020.2998584

Mokona, H., Yohannes, K., & Ayano, G. (2020). Youth unemployment and mental health: Prevalence and associated factors of depression among unemployed young adults in Gedeo zone, Southern Ethiopia. *International Journal of Mental Health Systems*, 14(1), 1–11. 10.1186/s13033-020-00395-232782471

Muehlhauser, L., & Salamon, A. (2013). Intelligence explosion: Evidence and import. In *Singularity hypotheses: A scientific and philosophical assessment* (pp. 15–42). Springer.

Nowak, A., Lukowicz, P., & Horodecki, P. (2018). Assessing artificial intelligence for humanity: Will ai be the our biggest ever advance? or the biggest threat [opinion]. *IEEE Technology and Society Magazine*, 37(4), 26–34. 10.1109/MTS.2018.2876105

Osuji, C. I. (2021). Artificial Intelligence and Literary Analyses: Challenges and Prospects. *Unilag Journal of Humanities*, 9(2), 43–58.

Pohlan, L. (2019). Unemployment and social exclusion. *Journal of Economic Behavior & Organization*, 164, 273–299. 10.1016/j.jebo.2019.06.006

Rakowski, R., Polak, P., & Kowalikova, P. (2021). Ethical aspects of the impact of AI: The status of humans in the era of artificial intelligence. *Society*, 58(3), 196–203. 10.1007/s12115-021-00586-8

Ren, Y., & Lan, L. (2021). Application and Development Prospect of Artificial Intelligence in Quality Education. *2021 3rd International Conference on Internet Technology and Educational Informization (ITEI)*, (pp. 172–175). IEEE.

Rich, E. (1985). Artificial intelligence and the humanities. *Computers and the Humanities*, 19(2), 117–122. 10.1007/BF02259633

Vinichenko, M., Narrainen, G. S., Melnichuk, A., & Chalid, P. (2021). *The influence of artificial intelligence on human activities*. Frontier Information Technology and Systems Research in Cooperative Economics.

Wu, Y. (2022). Loneliness behind live streaming: Exploration of alone together in live streaming in the version of interactive ritual chain. *2022 8th International Conference on Humanities and Social Science Research (ICHSSR 2022)*. Research Gate.

Xiaoyong, H. U., Shuo, S. U. N., Wenjie, Y., & Geying, D. (2023). Artificial Intelligence Empowering the High-Quality Development of Education: Demands, Visions, and Paths. *Frontiers of Education in China*, 18(1).

Yan-Ping, L., & Ai-Qin, Q. (2022). Replace or create: Analysis of the Relationship between the Artificial Intelligence and Youth Employment in Post Epidemic Era. *Procedia Computer Science*, 202, 217–222. 10.1016/j.procs.2022.04.029

Yongmou, L., & Taicheng, T. (2023). Cognitive reconstruction and action orientation of digital governance. *Engineering Research*, 15(4), 280–289.

Zhang, D., Mishra, S., Brynjolfsson, E., Etchemendy, J., Ganguli, D., Grosz, B., Lyons, T., Manyika, J., Niebles, J. C., & Sellitto, M. (2021). *The AI index 2021 annual report*. ArXiv Preprint ArXiv:2103.06312.

Zhang, Y., Ren, G., & Wang, D. (2022). Ethical challenges and strategies of artificial intelligence applications. *2022 Eleventh International Conference of Educational Innovation through Technology (EITT),* (pp. 110–113). IEEE. 10.1109/EITT57407.2022.00025

# Chapter 20
# Social Dynamics of AI Networks for Impacting Youth

**Asma Yunus**
*University of Sargodha, Pakistan*

**Ruqia Safdar Bajwa**
https://orcid.org/0000-0002-4460-2025
*Bahauddin Zakariya University, Pakistan*

**Shahzad Khaver Mushtaq**
*University of Sargodha, Pakistan*

## ABSTRACT

*This chapter sheds light on the AI networks' capabilities as agents of positive change, emphasizing creative applications of AI that foster youth engagement, education, and social activism. Combining empirical studies, expert opinions, and real-life examples, this chapter sets out a moderate view of the challenges and benefits of AI networks in the lives of young people. The current chapter is tipped to scrutinize how AI through social networks extends from the seemingly simple models of interactions such as 'likes' as well as 'shares,' to directly or indirectly and complex machineries that influence and even determine young people's perceptions, actions, and interactions.*

## INTRODUCTION

In the current century where digital footprints come before physical interactions, the introduction of artificial intelligence in social networks has availed to the younger people a new digital playground. Beyond the Like Button: Social Dynamics of AI Networks on Youth tries to unmask the labyrinth of AI's impact on social interaction, self-identity building, and the grand set of social dynamics in the lives of the youth. The current chapter is tipped to scrutinize how AI through social networks extends from the seemingly simple models of interactions such as 'likes' as well as 'shares,' to directly or indirectly and complex machineries that influence and even determine young people's perceptions, actions, and interactions. Nonetheless, AI in all day-to-day digital activities is a double-edged sword – it provides a level of connectedness and accessibility not realized before although raises red flags on privacy, autonomy, and

DOI: 10.4018/979-8-3693-3350-1.ch020

perhaps the formation of social norms. (Cipolletta, 2020). This chapter will expound on this intricacy, source up-and-coming research and theoretical frameworks drawn from psychology, sociology, and computer science to provide an in-depth review of AI in social networks in young people. Additionally, this chapter will unpeel the many layers of AI's role in shaping social dynamics through an analytical lens, from the algorithmic determination of visibility of content to personalized recommendation systems and more. It critically considers the psychological effects of such AI-powered systems on the youth, including questions of self-worth, social comparison, and the irony of connectivity in an era of digital alienation.

This chapter also sheds light on the AI networks' capabilities as agents of positive change, emphasizing creative applications of AI that foster youth engagement, education, and social activism. Combining empirical studies, expert opinions, and real-life examples, this chapter sets out a moderate view of the challenges and benefits of AI networks in the lives of young people (Bottaro & Faraci, 2022). Among the complex interrelations of AI and the social dynamics of youth, the chapter seeks to promote more profound comprehension among researchers, practitioners, and policymakers about the significant contribution that AI makes in determining the future of our digital society. Sitting at the intersection of technological breakthrough and social development, "Beyond the Like Button" is a fascinating story stressing the necessity of mindful interaction with AI networks to make them work for the benefit of today's and future youths.

## THE IMPACT OF AI ON THE YOUTH SOCIALIZATION

AI is transforming the nature of current-day communities' online interactions and connections, and to a considerable extent, it brings a new dimension to social dynamics. The present chapter examines the contribution of AI to social networks and digital platforms, revealing that including AI opens up new avenues of interaction as well as new intricate issues.

### Artificial Intelligence and Online Education

AI agents may contribute to establishing social bonds among students in a virtual classroom. Wang et al. used an artificial intelligence agent—SAMI—to develop a social network and counter the social isolation of online learning by integrating such an agent into an online forum. SAMI demonstrates the potential of artificial intelligence to enhance social visibility and bridge the gap between technical and social fields. However, this technology is not without challenges, and the question of personal freedom and privacy remains a significant issue, illustrating the need for technology and a careful balance of ethical concerns. Artificial intelligence also changes students' and teachers' roles in online education, making it a part of the learning process. Bhutoria (2022) explores the contribution of AI to the personalization of learning and optimization of instructional matters, as well as the influence on communication and teaching quality. Although AI enables more personalized support and interaction, it also demonstrates the vulnerability to encroachment and privacy erosion, which is why ethical AI technologies ensure human dignity and privacy are critical. Noriega et al. propose the creation of a mindful design methodology for ethical AI in the context of hybrid human-AI communities. They seek to align AI with the social values of all the parties involved, creating a governance structure that breeds confidence and respect. The emphasis on ethical concerns regarding the development of AI demonstrates the potential for this technology to achieve the desired social outcomes of adolescent online communities rather than jeopardize them. Since social interactions are nuanced through both verbal and non-verbal means, AI enters the complex field of human sociality. Lozano-Blasco et al (2023) suggest a hybrid artificial intelligence model that combines deep learning with conventional AI techniques to improve the accuracy of decoding social signs. The importance of AI to shed light on social mechanisms contributing to improved human-AI relationships is essential. Furthermore, Zhang et al (2022) employ a participatory design to include young learners in the development of AI agents to enhance social integration. This joint effort provides a picture of the youth's ethical concerns and desired functions, underlining the importance of involving end-users in product development. This AI development method promises to offer more functional and ethical technology that can help improve young people's social media connections. AI is revolutionizing young people's online socialization by improving connections and understanding the complexity of social systems. However, the technology has ethical issues that need an all-inclusive and thoughtful approach to development. Ethical and user-friendly AI will be crucial as young people continue to navigate a transformed social media landscape.

## AI's Effect on Youth Conduct and Social Norms

The AI-powered platforms go beyond simply socializing; they also have implications for the behavior of youth and the standards of society. Rather than simply serving as channels of communication, these platforms help cultivate youth culture and norms. All sorts of AI companies created features, such as content curation and predictive interactions that build an idiosyncratic digital habitat for adolescent culture, values, and aspirations. The use of AI in social media platforms raises a thorny issue concerning both technology development and youth behavior. A study performed by Ntoutsi et al. (2020) highlights the ethical and social impacts of biases within AI systems, emphasizing that ethical guidelines for AI development are important in helping to promote social good and preventing the continuation of societal biases.

In addition, Acemoglu and Restrepo (2019) explore how AI is changing the job market, with progress toward automation and algorithms determining which jobs young people will either find or lose. This rapidly changing situation calls for a review of skills and education, preparing the youth for a future in which AI will have a profound impact on the labor force.

In terms of mental health, Zhang and Lu (2023) examine the impact of social AI on young people's psychological well-being. Here they contend that people's contact with AI-based characters may have positive effects on their state of mind, and also alleviate fears for society. The findings show that AI can help people's complicated relationship between upbringing, which sets the social context for youth behavior, and mental well-being.

As regards AI governance, Lewis and Moorkens (2020) propose a rights-based approach to data governance, with children's rights as the focus. For this model to succeed in providing safe supportive environments for AI technologies, privacy issues, security issues, and how AI is used ethically will be overcome. AI is taking root in young people's lives, and its impact on their behavior and thus society at large should be carefully observed. Fostering open dialogue between technology development and moral concerns is imperative when operating in such a complicated environment.

## DIGITAL IDENTITY IN THE AGE OF AI

In the digital era, AI platforms are space for the young to engage in playful identity and expression. Artificial intelligence Provides teenagers with a form of media that offers unprecedented opportunities to explore and express identity, interact with others in society, and create their own space in digital environments. On social media platforms and AI-driven pages, Generation-Z and Alpha young people turn their homespun media into a lively scene of up drum for each other. AI platforms provide young people the chance to look at their interests in communities, think culture mirrors their self-image, and get information tailored for them by customizing algorithms. If it is interactive with AI, how does this combined quality feel for a child's sense of self? To get a positive answer, you need video investigating. Hasse et al. (2019) believe that learning, creativity, and psychological health for children are dependent on AI, which is essential for providing young people with places where they can express many facets of their identity such as individual tastes and cultural or organizational affiliations (Hasse et al., 2019) According to King (2023), AI can help teenagers develop greater self-awareness using facial expression recognition methods. Combining AI with psychological research methods, the study shows that AI can help young people recognize their emotions, which contributes to their better mental health and well-being (King, 2023). Even though AI platforms open up spaces for testing and expressing identity, they also bring about questions. The fact that AI is present on all digital platforms raises challenges of privacy, security, and the true nature of online communication. With the further development of AI, the environment for creating digital identities is changing as well, which calls for an approach that encourages all the benefits of AI while minimizing its risks. With the help of AI platforms, young people reshape the rituals of exploring and expressing their identities. By doing so, these platforms serve as digital stages for the performance of youth (someone pointed out how can support this with a detailed rundown) But the role of AI in forming identity is two-way: as a source of opportunity that must be gently encouraged and as risky business. Next, we should look into the complex ways in which AI-driven platforms affect the behaviors and social norms of youth so that such devices contribute to a supportive and active environment for children to create their own identities.

### The Dilemma of Digital Identity

The AI era brought about digital platforms which became the central sites for young people to practice identity. Pasquinelli, (2023) points out that with artificial intelligence embedded in these platforms, young people have some privileges that were hitherto unattainable before now. The invisible fusion of AI with social media and other digital platforms has changed how young people access online cyberspaces. Hasse et al. (2019) highlight the effect of AI on young people, mainly the biggest thing is that it helps them study and carry out creative work and comprehensive entertainment. This shows the progression from tool to medium — AI platforms as communicative instruments and powerful worlds for young people to shape their identities (Hasse et al., 2019). AI platforms offer great opportunities for youth identity practice but at the same time create problems. King (2023) argues that artificial intelligence (AI) psychological research practices such as facial expression recognition among teens lead to better self-awareness of the subject. This reveals a beneficial side of AI in knowing oneself better. Yet it also points out an awkward contradiction: how are we to use AI technology to help rather than harm the formation of youth identities and mental health (King, 2023)?AI affects the identity of young people not only in terms of personal discovery but also how they interact with society and its norms. Dwivedi et al. (2019) furnish a detailed examination of AI's transforming potential in various sectors and touch on such things as its impact on social relations and changes in digital culture. It is worth researching to understand AI's multiple ways of youth identity formation in a digital ecosystem that changes every moment (Dwivedi et al., 2019). Hence, it would not be wrong to say that AI and digital identity convergence for young people is an opportunity-laden but also dangerous place. With AI advancing and becoming more involved in daily life, it is vital to build environments for healthy identity development and to discuss the complex issues surrounding whose fish get caught in these cyber-nets when you are looking at teenagers interacting under the eyes of so many different AI agents.

## Effects of AI-Generated Feedback Loops (Such as Likes and Comments) on Self

In the age of artificial intelligence, the digital identity book explained in depth ways in which AI-based platforms have become the foremost realm for young people's experimental performance and expression of individuality. Youth-driven platforms offer modern young people rich resources for identities as they walk on the road to self-realization. Gain and harm-wise, this is an environment where digital online products take people who want their digital lives to be made comfortable further down the spectrum; that's why the content and interactive experiences they offer you are even itself. For individuals, the actual practice is facing a series of 'challenges and chances on AI platforms.' It's easy for young users of these platforms to become 'parachuted' into use roam, where they meet an especially inspiring story or come across some amazing apps. It is also worth noting that this platform's personally tailored experience system greatly influences the content and interactions that an individual user gets. This power to customize in shape a user's experience may have far-reaching structural consequences. The feedback nature of these platforms--represented by `likes' and comments is a key factor in shaping as well as carrying on self-imagery expectations among young people. The feedback loops provided by these platforms, Capan et al. (2020) argue that when young people decide which environs to live in and where to interact with. Likes and comments that these platforms may be a true reflection of themselves, or people may share it with others and do their part in making good images go viral just for changed subjectivity brought on but largely by external causes (Capan et al., 2020). The feedback loops created automatically by artificial intelligence include likes, comments, and shares. As a result, they play a validating role in all these digital places for the expression of identity Nonetheless, as Stray (2023) writes, the feedback loops encourage a kind of biased reinforcement as using them to shape an image will usually bring positive results and this incentive makes people portray not themselves, but rather images which attract approval (Stray, 2023).In recommender systems, feedback loops can feed on themselves. As Çapan et al. (2020) say, themes might also become over- or well under-represented perhaps causing youth to see non-standard behaviors as normal and English girls so many different things that there seems no such thing as what it means to be a girl.

Therefore, AI-curated environments have a certain bond with how authentic internet-based identities of youths lie under these circumstances. The friction and reaction caused by this autointoxication- this pursuit of sincerity and craving for appreciation- delivers the authenticity of online life into question on a grand scale, whereas asceticism devalues most entrance into calmness; Yin has sometimes less than Yang.

Given these difficulties, it is important to create environments where people can be who they naturally are without fear of becoming crisis points in someone else's program. This semester if students learn about the potential biases of AI mechanics and digital feedback (which I have also discussed before), it will make a difference who will be radicalizing future platforms in the long term.

Moreover, making digital systems that give expression contrary to algorithmic requirements can also prevent network effects from distorting one's image of his or her self. It is therefore incumbent upon platform developers, teachers, and communities alike to place even greater emphasis on genuine things instead of engagement metrics. Notwithstanding, with AI said to be handling the digital spaces in which young people live, we must realize what kind of effect AI-curated feedback loops will have on identity experimentation and expression. If duly meditated on this digital dynamic to critical engagement, it could convert the AI platforms into creative spaces where young people genuinely live their own lives rather than deformed identities subject to algorithmic feedback.

## CREATION AND INFLUENCE OF ECHO CHAMBERS YOUTH

In the era of digitization, echo chambers have become one of the most studied phenomena around today, especially in social media. It also has an important impact on public and personal belief voices. In the algorithms of today, echo chambers look set to become even more sophisticated. An aspect of the way people today live that largely leaves a chance for different perspectives trailing off with prior generations is found in children echoing their parents. This in turn affects their acquisition of different perspectives significantly. This section describes what AI algorithms can do for echo chambers, and their consequence on youth if we fail to tackle these issues effectively give heed to the most recent highly cited studies as well.

The echo chamber phenomenon is a situation where people are only exposed to speech and opinions that reinforce their present stance. It is a repetitive communication confined within its system. Zhu et al. (2021) shine light upon the echo chamber phenomenon as present in social networks. Their article shows how AI algorithms can amplify this by promoting content that coincides with existing user preconceptions. Here the point is made that these habits need to be understood as part of the information reproduction process if we are ever going to effectively check the problems generated by echo chambers.

Cinelli et al. (2021) give a detailed comparative study of how different interaction paradigms and algorithms for feeds on social media platforms contribute to the development of echo chambers. They allow us to visualize the content of these enclosed circulation echo chambers. These extensive research findings reveal the degrees of segregation on various platforms, some of which encourage more widespread homogeneity in terms of ideology among their users.

These young people may experience pronounced amounts of echo chambers, which have an impact on teens, the elderly, and anybody in between. They are decisive in shaping the perception and interpretation of all things within their ken. The double-sided feature of algorithmic personalization—though AI-based news apps appear to make for more participation by users, Zhao (2023) increases the potential for limiting exposure to divergent perspectives. This paradoxical impact calls into question critically dealing with contradictions (an essential skill when confronted by today's crowded media landscape). For young audiences, it is worrying. Furthermore, Sokolova and Bobicev (2020) examine echo chamber effects in forums for medicine. Based on this information, we need to identify and remove echo chamber effects at different sites on the Internet visited by young people for news as well as information of their own making. Merging several into one removes duplications, and renders redundancy latent and inapplicable documents transparent to human readers. Echo chambers are subtle for children. However, Du and Zhao (2023) argue that even though AI-based news apps bring more user participation, their paradoxical impact increases the level of echo chamber which is a serious worry for youngsters (15-24). For those trying to rectify these harmful effects, they will have to adopt an integrated approach and concentrate on transparent algorithms, teach the populace digital literacy education, and provide people with diverse information exposure. Yet walking. This is an ultimate a n aendeavor in one direction.

## THE PSYCHOLOGY OF AI INTERACTIONS

In the digital age, AI-based connectivity has changed the face of human communication, especially within the framework of social networks and support systems. However, this connectivity, though a double-edged sword, promotes support networks on the one hand but with the risk of worsening isolation and mental health issues on the other. This part discusses the issues related to AI-mediated connectivity and its influence on people's mental health.

### AI in Support Networks Improvement

Social media systems have changed the way people connect and help each other, particularly AI technologies. The platforms provide an array of chances to widen social networks, maintain connections over long distances, and identify communities with common interests and concerns (Santini et al., 2020). Apart from that, AI-powered mental health apps and platforms provide personalized assistance by using algorithms to connect users with suitable resources and peer support groups (Sharma et al., 2022).

### Possibility of Aggravation of Isolation and Mental Health Issues

On the other hand, the technology that connects us also can be disconnected. Paradoxical patterns are evident when the spike in connectivity is matched by feelings of loneliness and isolation, particularly in the elderly and the vulnerable during times of disaster, like the COVID-19 pandemic (Smith et al., 2020). It has been proved by studies that digital platforms support social contacts but also they tend to create superficial contacts that do not satisfy real social needs this is why it can lead to a higher rate of loneliness and mental disorders (Elmer et al., 2020).

### Social Support and Isolation as Mediators

The effect of AI-fostered connectedness on psychological well-being is moderated by the quality of social support and the degree of social isolation that people experience. Digital support can act as a buffer for mental health problems, however, the lack of physical real-world encounters might reduce the positive effects of online connections (Domènech-Abella et al., 2019). In addition, the process of online social networks – like how often and the nature of interactions will decide how these platforms work as supportive elements or contribute to isolation (Visaria et al., 2020).

AI-mediated connectivity is dual-edged and therefore represents the complex relationship between technology and psychology. AI may enhance social support networks and thus positively impact mental health, yet it also poses the danger of making isolation and other related threats worse. Resolving them demands that we have a fine understanding of how AI impacts social interaction and psychological welfare together with strategies that harness the advantages of AI while at the same time cutting off the adversities.

## STRATEGIES FOR FOSTERING CRITICAL ENGAGEMENT AND DIVERSITY OF THOUGHT AMONG YOUNG USERS

When confronting the trend of the 'echo chamber', educators and entertainment workers have tried different methods to encourage critical thinking and more types of thought kids have never before heard or encountered. In contemporary research, new teaching technologies improve a student's skills in critical thinking or sympathy toward various opinions. In this paper, we also made use of such methods as these, supported by the latest and most authoritative research 2. An inclusive, differentiation approach that accepts and responds to the different backgrounds, abilities, or interests of the students is a basic method to diversify perspectives. Building responsive learning environments in higher education to maximize the potential of its assorted learners gets special emphasis in Awang-Hashim et al. (2019) through further professional training for academic staff. An approach of this kind is important to help prepare students such that they can successfully live and critically evaluate the difficult digital age in which we are living (Awang-Hashim et al., 2019).

Digitalized tools and platforms provide targeted chances for concerned thinking and quickened reactions. Research carried out by Cortázar et al.(2021) features the effect of online learning dependent on projects- and also the parents' income levels. The study revealed that scaffolding with a socially shared regulatory process in addition to traditional project-based learning strategies can significantly enhance students' ability to think critically. The importance of digital tools in learning settings designed to stimulate a variety of thought processes and foster engagement among students has been demonstrated by such findings (Cortázar et al., 2021).

Creating online learning communities that are both innovative and interactive is another good way of reaching new young user groups. Razi (2021) refers to the experience method in which debate over digital advertising strategies helps encourage critical thinking among students. With debates, educators can teach high-level critical thinking skills and students come to involve themselves in such an altering variety of perspectives on the issues that they come face with. They will learn how to critically assess many different views (Razi, 2021).

With the socialization of students, escape from the echo chambers becomes that much more important. (Heilporn et al., 2021) At Artfulmanic, by examining strategies for how teachers in blended learning environments turn their courses into combination publishings of both synchronous and asynchronous, after more than three years of successful effort the model has finally been realized: It can give birth to high-quality content for low price while still maintaining its time and place. The transparent conveying of expectations at the semester start, along with trustful student-teacher relations, is the most decisive practice in fostering diverse thought and full participation. (Heilporn et al., 2021)

The phenomenon of echo chambers arises among young internauts, posing threats to authentic and critical engagement. Fortunately, by adopting diverse and inclusive pedagogy and using digital tools to achieve this, creating interconnected online learning communities incorporating social participation and collaborative learning, educators and content creators can entice them into critical reflection on a variety of perspectives. Coming from recent research, these strategies show how to pierce the digital echo chamber and help create a more open-minded general public.

## GUARDING YOUTH IN THE DIGITAL REALM: ETHICS, PRIVACY, AND DIGITAL LITERACY

Along our voyage across the transformative terrain of artificial intelligence (AI), we are met with a multidimensional array of ethical dilemmas, particularly when concerning the youth residents of our digital sphere. The burgeoning interplay between AI and the lives of young users underscores a pressing imperative: to steer this terrain with a compass modulated by strong ethical principles, privacy safeguards, data protection measures, and the burning flame of responsible AI use. This section examines the importance of these elements in protecting the digital integrity and well-being of our children, as digital literacy becomes a shield and a guiding star in the era of ubiquitous AI.

### Ethical Frontiers in the Digital Age: Youth Protection

Privacy is the center of ethical discussion and the stronghold of data security that is vital in AI systems that feed off personal data to personalize and optimize user experiences. The problem of reconciling the user-specific advantages of AI services with the protection of personal privacy rights is especially difficult for young users. Their digital footsteps, usually left in innocence and naivety, demand the protectors that are tech-savvy and law-wise. Vanguards such as differential privacy and federated learning come in this quest, offering paths that respect user anonymity while enhancing AI knowledge (Meurisch & Mühlhäuser, 2021). However, the quest is not only about technological answers. Legal frameworks are fundamental as a scaffold that prevents the digital footprints of our youth from being abused or misused, (Radanliev & Santos, 2023).

At the same time, the framework of ethical AI use seeks our focus. The incorporation of AI into the youth's habitats – be it educational platforms to social media – represents a pattern and operational philosophy that should be characterized by ethical integrity. This spirit extends beyond the protection of privacy and data security to the prospect of prejudices that might misshape the digital images of our offspring. AI systems development and the rules for their implementation are to be based upon the principle of ethicality, providing a digital surrounding where fairness and inclusivity prevail (Siau & Wang, 2020).

### Digital Literacy: The Navigators of Tomorrow's Empowerment

In between these technological and regulatory bulwarks, the light of digital literacy shines, leading young users through the digital oceans with information and wisdom. Digital literacy goes beyond the elementary navigation of interfaces but extends to the major concepts in the digital world which include AI. It develops young minds to distinguish the truthfulness of the information in cyberspace, understand the ethical aspects of digital creation and consumption, and respect the highest level of privacy and data secrecy. The digital literacy of our youth is not a luxury, but a need that enables them to move eagerly and responsibly in the digital world (Lv, 2022; Glukhov, 2020).

The inclusion of digital literacy in educational curriculums is a key approach to developing a generation that is skilled and sensitive to the ethical implications of digital technology. It moves beyond the sporadic workshops, in which the students are not expected to retain their knowledge. This perspective guarantees that digital literacy is not an individual skill but a measure through which young people perceive and interact with the world.

In the educational landscape, the role of educators is deep and central. Equipped with innovative pedagogies and digital tools, they are the shepherds of digital literacy, forming the skills and ethical orientations of their students. Nevertheless, such a perspective requires symbiotic cooperation with policymakers. It requires investments in teacher training, curriculum revitalization, and provisioning of schools with state-of-the-art technological infrastructure. Therefore, policymakers must define the systems and resources that support an education system that reflects the requirements of the digital era.

Privacy, security, ethical usage of AI, and digital literacy are, therefore, the key pillars of an ethical approach that should guide us through this intricate interplay between AI and the growing minds of our youth. This ethic not only preserves but also enables, for even as technology marches on creating its promises, it does so with respect to the rights, welfare, and future of our littlest citizens. By growing a cadre of people who know technology and ethics, a path will be laid, for technology to improve rather than destroy humanity that is guided by the stars of ethical consideration and digital literacy.

## AI-Based Youth Empowerment

While artificial intelligence has considerable potential in education and creativity, its applications must thoughtfully consider youth development. When utilized prudently, AI can foster academic growth, inventive outlets, and means of societal involvement unprecedented for young people. This section highlights cases where AI has been implemented judiciously to aid such domains. Through nuanced integration of man and machine, all may benefit as both learners and teachers, cultivating shared understanding across boundaries.

## Personalized Learning in Educational Enrichment

The AI's ability to tailor educational materials facilitated a watershed moment, customizing content to each student's needs and learning styles upended conventional pedagogy. Similarly, Hasibuan and Azizah (2023) investigated how AI might shape personalized environments conducive to fostering creativity. By discerning interests and talents, AI could curate individualized routes encouraging curious discovery and exchanges between students of aligned passions. This flexible guidance enhances relevance and engagement while breeding a laboratory of imagination and innovation within educational settings. Alongside shorter statements, a winding sentence recalls the potential when technology and teaching jointly reimagine what and how students learn.

## Artistic Creation Fostered by AI

AI's influence on the creative expression of young people is another striking example of its effect. Marrone, Taddeo, & Hill (2002) provide examples that promote students' understanding of how AI works with creativity. They point out that students who know something about AI possibilities tend to regard AI as an efficient tool for improving classroom creativity. New-sided students regard AI as an instrument to push creative boundaries or even as little more than a means to a joint end rather than supplanting human creativity.

## AI as a Facilitator for Social Activism

AI is being used not only for personal and creative growth but also as the essence that enables youth to take social action. It enables young activists to analyze and synthesize big data, based on which one can anticipate trends, make predictions, and draw up better strategies. At the same time, AI-powered platforms will help these organizations to raise their voices; ultimately organizations can do more than ever before by reaching an even larger audience and encouraging support for their views from afar. This is the AI application that allows young people to use technology to contribute more effectively to social causes--for change using technology and simultaneously addressing global issues.

Combining AI and creativity, education and social engagement makes for a heartwarming tale of technology completely serving young people. AI personalizes learning experiences, fosters creativity, and boosts the effectiveness of social activism. Somewhat it could be said as an indispensable tool for young people who are to inhabit the new age and mold it in any direction that they wish. Consequently, a more thorough exploration and application of AI in these domains is essential to unleash all their potential in the digital age.

## Democratization of Information and Opportunities

AI can make information membranes interface directly. This is an important step toward eliminating the digital gap. To reduce unevenness in development prospects for young people from a variety of starting points, artificial intelligence technologies by extension necessarily encourage inclusivity and access. Either this entails opening up access to the educational system or it means guiding different groups of students along their educational paths in such a manner that they benefit equally from available resources.

## Bridging Digital Divides

AI has immense potential for improving digital equity. By leveraging its capabilities to process vast amounts of information, technology can help identify and address gaps in access to educational resources. As Vassilakopoulou and Hustad (2021) rightfully point out, digital divides are multifaceted, stemming not just from a lack of connectivity but also from divergences in abilities, applications, and benefits garnered. Artificial intelligence can assist in bridging these fissures by delivering personalized instructional material. In so doing, AI affords all youth, regardless of socioeconomic background, increased opportunities to learn efficiently and fairly. Advanced analytical tools also help pinpoint population segments facing inequalities, allowing for targeted interventions and customized support. Overall, with care and oversight, machine learning shows promise for leveling long-standing educational inequities and establishing more inclusive learning landscapes for communities of all kinds.

## Enhancing Digital Literacy

While artificial intelligence platforms present numerous opportunities to enhance digital proficiency, a crucial element for thriving in today's technology-driven society, judiciously incorporating AI into educational curricula can help maximize its benefits. Tailoring lesson plans and content to match individual learning preferences, paces, and needs allows for customizing academic experiences. Such personalization has the power to boost engagement among students by addressing diverse backgrounds, skills, and challenges, reducing barriers that a uniform approach risks exacerbating, particularly for those who struggle most with conventional methodologies. Meanwhile, AI-assisted guidance accommodates varied learning curves, keeping all students moving together towards shared goals through flexible, supportive strategies attuned to each person's requirements.

## Creative Expression and Social Activism Development

While AI shows promise in fostering youthful ingenuity and social progress, ensuring ethical development and oversight remains paramount. Emergent generative technologies grant budding creators avenues to experiment with novel expressions, challenging preconceived boundaries of imaginative works and original contributions. Diversely, AI equips budding reformers with tools to amplify oft-muted voices, affords insights into systemic interplays rarely perceived, cultivates unity strengthens advocacy, and eases efforts to seed societal evolution from within. Nevertheless, guiding principles must govern each tool's application and evolution, safeguarding equity and well-being for all.

## CHALLENGES AND CONSIDERATIONS

Challenges that lie ahead despite getting widening AI access to knowledge and opportunities from concentrated access to AI is fraught with several hurdles. This includes getting around ethical data protection and security issues, matters of fairness and transparency in AI algorithm behavior, as well ensuring that AI technologies are available to everyone regardless of where they live. Overcoming these challenges will require joint efforts among governments, educators, and developers of artificial intelligence technology. They will have to make sure that AI technologies are put on the path of nurturing the next generation instead of enlarging existing gaps.

AI has the potential to be transformative in bringing information and opportunity to young people, so it is essential for closing the digital chasm. AI can improve digital literacy, foster the creativity of individuals, and empower social activism, thus AI may well play an important role also in creating an inclusive and fair digital society ahead. During this year, we will need to meet all these challenges and questions, especially as regards the place of AI in society. We should aim for universal redistribution of its benefits

With AI technologies, the youth do have a uniqueness in creativity and interaction that never existed before. For example, generative AI systems allow users with only very little effort (such as voice input) to create a medium of digitized digital content types such as text, images, and videos (Solaiman et al.,

2023). The democratization of content creation could produce a wider array of voices and perspectives in social networking media. Also, with AI-powered personalization algorithms helping to serve up just what people like, technically speaking it enables better user experience on websites. Mid-November 2013 Google now has a ranking in real-time of quality scores for your website which cannot be faked thereby enforcing high standards and making entering downtime superfluous.

The development of AI can fill a gap that existed long before digital. AI can democratize information and opportunities by providing personalized learning experiences (as described later) or translating languages. Moreover, it makes accessibility for people who have disabilities easier (Vinuesa et al., 2021). It may well be that all of the above mentioned points apply to young people from various backgrounds who have been left out so far and can take a full part in digital societies and get access to the resources and communities found online.

Nevertheless, while AI has brought positive effects, it also presents many challenges for society. Considering the huge number of AI-based personalization and recommendation algorithms, it seems difficult to know whether a new era will be created in which niche views are conveyed through big data analysis for oneself and echoed among like-minded listeners (Tomašev et al., 2020; Boyd & Crawford, 2012). Moreover, the issues regarding privacy and data integrity are getting more complex as AI systems tend to use large quantities of personal information for their proper operation.

Additionally, given the potential for AI to automate a large range of environmentally, physically, or cognitively strenuous tasks and the large slice of future employment this is likely to take, it could mean disaster for young people today. With the development of an AI-driven world, it becomes essential to discern what kind of skills will be needed in tomorrow's workforce and what effects these technologies will bring to labor force portability (Dwivedi et al., 2019).

AI, youth, and social media present a complex system of technological change, societal change, and personal adaptation. AI does offer tremendous possibilities for enhancing connectivity, creativity, and access to information. But at the same time, it brings risks that require careful management. Access, inclusion, and fairness in the design and implementation of AI technologies will be crucial if they are to serve the common good. In so far as mapping the future trajectory for AI, it is essential to engage youth in this conversation, thus granting them the power to create digital realms that suit them.

## ETHICAL IMPERATIVE OF AI DEVELOPMENT: THE INCLUSIVE PERSPECTIVE

In the ever-changing world of AI, ethical development that weighs the requirements of getting married and having children for both men and women alike seems necessary. With "AI+" services becoming ever more embedded in digital platforms, which are also the main access channels of youth Weibo and like Products of Tencent, people should behave responsibly in their use and applications This section underlines the necessity for a framework that supports ethical AI development, is inclusive of all people and considers how the multiple dimensions of AI interact with youth culture and society. The contemporary discussion of AI ethics emphasizes an agreement on matters basic in essence: transparency, justice or righteousness, fairness, responsibility, and privacy (Jobin et al., 2019). However, translating these high-level principles down into a practical sequence of actions that properly reflect the specific needs and challenges that young people have to face is hard. AI ethics involves turning these principles into two parties 'practices. It means that any interests of or harm to the children are well protected. (Mittelstadt, 2019)

## Prioritizing Inclusivity and Diversity

AI's ethical development needs to be inclusive and receptive to diversity. Lurie, et al. (2021) point out that research shows diverse teams do better at recognizing and eliminating bias in AI systems than non-divorced ones, resulting in fairer outcomes For another, Else carefully selected groups of young people from different backgrounds who contributed to work on AI technology batted forth first-hand viewpoints from their perspectives as well as those responsible for other work and benefited from this kind widespread attention to what real users – however quietly or subtly only when applicable may always have wanted. AI effects on young users are the result of biased algorithms and exposure to privacy leaks, and harmful or irrelevant media. The ethical development of AI requires identifying these risks so that children can enjoy their day in virtual reality while we do not help them get trafficked by cybercriminals (Bano et al., 2023).

## Ethical AI in Education Implementation

In the AI-enhanced digital world, to deal responsibly with younger generations of internet users, education is needed. It's important to instill principles of ethical AI into the curriculum and to make sure that young people receive the knowledge and skills needed for them to evaluate technologies and their effects on society (Taggart, 2020). The objective of this education should be to prepare young people to participate in the creation of fair and ethical AI systems. These are important steps to take toward a brighter future in AI policing social media. If one makes inclusiveness, vulnerability reduction, and ethical AI education the goal, AI technologies will be able to serve as a multiplier of young men's diversified criteria for success. In the future era of AI, a commitment to incorporate an ethical perspective that supports the fullness of living species - including people from all races, nationalities, and religions - must be made. So regardless of s age, sex, and gender, the youth cohort will benefit more generally from our digital advancements

## CONCLUSION AND WAY FORWARD

The analysis of artificial intelligence usage in social media reveals a complex situation with both opportunities and risks present especially regarding youth involvement. The knowledge extracted from the aforementioned sections confirms the intricate interplay between AI, social networking platforms, and young people in the context of technology's transformative power and the urgent need for inclusive, ethical development practices. AI-driven empowerment emerges as one of the main trends, underscoring AI's capabilities to enhance educational processes, foster creativity, and amplify voices in social activism. The role of AI in customizing learning and information accessibility on an individual level while making information available to all demonstrates AI's ability to reduce digital divides and provide unprecedented opportunities for growth and participation to young people.

The ethical evolution of AI technologies remains an ongoing concern while the importance of privacy, data security, and how AI is applied is highlighted. Youth participation in AI advancement, coupled with a focus on diversity and inclusion, is significant when it comes to preventing biases and creating technologies that address a wide variety of needs and perspectives. Digital literacy assumes a pioneering role in empowering young citizens to behave responsibly in AI-enhanced environments. Proficiency with technology and critical thinking are essential skills for youth to safely and productively engage with AI, assessing implications and impacts on society.

The future relationship between AI, social media, and new generations will continue evolving as technology advances. As AI increasingly shapes social dynamics and youth culture, proactively studying its ethical development and societal effects becomes imperative to inclusive progress. Approaches addressing diverse youth needs and vulnerabilities will be key to ensuring AI augmentation benefits all. The intersection of AI, digital communication, and young users represents both prospects and concerns. Throughout our journey into this changing landscape, collaboration between experts, designers, leaders, educators, and youth themselves remains crucial to prevent the degradation of young lives online. Adopting principles of equity and participation in developing digital wisdom and civic engagement can help youthfully navigate challenges while cultivating opportunities in an AI-influenced digital era.

While artificial intelligence brings both promise and peril, focusing now on nurturing its benefits while guarding against potential harms is crucial. This is especially true for today's digitally-native youth, who readily turn to online spaces as portals of expression, education, and social change. AI has formidable potential to reshape how information is accessed and learning occurs, transitioning from a communal effort into personalized experiences tailored to each individual. But with opportunity comes responsibility. From birth, young minds will develop immersed in a globally connected digital world, underscoring the need for judicious safeguards that respect privacy and data security as technologies increasingly mediate social connections. Progress demands weighing AI's capacity to spur ecological stewardship against ensuring systems reflect diversity, not bias. Answering questions around these ethical dilemmas requires inclusive, multivocal governance that includes youth perspective as a founding principle. Moving forward will mean navigating innovation's possibilities and pitfalls together.

The inclusion and diversity of advanced computational systems must consider ethical implications. Developing digital literacy in youth presents opportunities to critically assess emerging technologies and their wide-ranging societal impacts. It falls upon the next generation, not through resistance but innovation, to ensure an ethically aligned future. As we stand at a crossroads to an AI-transformed world, promoting fair governance over these policies remains ever more pressing. If advocating progress while safeguarding all, technology may serve as a tool for enlightenment and harmony. This vision of technology empowering humanity has long been embraced by many groups seeking joint solutions that responsibly fulfill our potential in the digital era.

# REFERENCES

Acemoglu, D., & Restrepo, P. (2019). Automation and new tasks: How technology displaces and reinstates labor. *The Journal of Economic Perspectives*, 33(2), 3–30. 10.1257/jep.33.2.3

Bhutoria, A. (2022). Personalized education and artificial intelligence in the United States, China, and India: A systematic review using a human-in-the-loop model. *Computers and Education: Artificial Intelligence*, 3, 100068. 10.1016/j.caeai.2022.100068

Bottaro, R., & Faraci, P. (2022). The use of social networking sites and its impact on adolescents' emotional well-being: A scoping review. *Current Addiction Reports*, 9(4), 518–539. 10.1007/s40429-022-00445-436185594

Buhmann, A., & Fieseler, C. (2021). Towards a deliberative framework for responsible innovation in artificial intelligence. *Technology in Society*, 64, 101475. 10.1016/j.techsoc.2020.101475

Capan, G., Bozal, Ö., Gündoğdu, İ., & Cemgil, A. T. (2020). Towards fair personalization by avoiding feedback loops. *arXiv preprint arXiv*:2012.12862.

Cipolletta, S., Malighetti, C., Cenedese, C., & Spoto, A. (2020). How can adolescents benefit from the use of social networks? The iGeneration on Instagram. *International Journal of Environmental Research and Public Health*, 17(19), 6952. 10.3390/ijerph1719695232977532

Dos Santos Melicio, B. C., Xiang, L., Dillon, E., Soorya, L., Chetouani, M., Sarkany, A., & Lorincz, A. (2023, October). *Composite AI for Behavior Analysis in Social Interactions*. In *Companion Publication of the 25th International Conference on Multimodal Interaction* (pp. 389-397). ACM. 10.1145/3610661.3616237

Dwivedi, Y. K., Hughes, L., Ismagilova, E., Aarts, G., Coombs, C., Crick, T., & Williams, M. D. (2021). Artificial Intelligence (AI): Multidisciplinary perspectives on emerging challenges, opportunities, and agenda for research, practice and policy. *International Journal of Information Management*, 57, 101994. 10.1016/j.ijinfomgt.2019.08.002

Hasse, A., Cortesi, S., Lombana-Bermudez, A., & Gasser, U. (2019). *Youth and artificial intelligence: Where we stand*. Berkman Klein Center Research Publication.

Jobin, A., Ienca, M., & Vayena, E. (2019). The global landscape of AI ethics guidelines. *Nature Machine Intelligence*, 1(9), 389–399. 10.1038/s42256-019-0088-2

Keles, B., McCrae, N., & Grealish, A. (2019). A systematic review: The influence of social media on depression, anxiety and psychological distress in adolescents. *International Journal of Adolescence and Youth*, 25(1), 79–93. 10.1080/02673843.2019.1590851

King, J. (2023). An Innovative Exploration of Psychological Research Methods Driven by Artificial Intelligence: A Case Study Using Facial Expression Technique to Improve Teenagers' Self Awareness. *International Journal of Education and Humanities*, 11(1), 212–215. 10.54097/ijeh.v11i1.13155

Lewis, D., & Moorkens, J. (2020). A rights-based approach to trustworthy AI in social media. *Social Media + Society*, 6(3), 2056305120954672. 10.1177/2056305120954672

Lozano-Blasco, R., Mira-Aladrén, M., & Gil-Lamata, M. (2023). Social media influence on young people and children: Analysis on Instagram, Twitter and YouTube. *Comunicar*, 31(74), 125–137. 10.3916/C74-2023-10

Nesi, J. (2020). The Impact of Social Media on Youth Mental Health. *North Carolina Medical Journal*, 81(2), 116–121. 10.18043/ncm.81.2.11632132255

Ntoutsi, E., Fafalios, P., Gadiraju, U., Iosifidis, V., Nejdl, W., Vidal, M. E., Ruggieri, S., Turini, F., Papadopoulos, S., Krasanakis, E., Kompatsiaris, I., Kinder-Kurlanda, K., Wagner, C., Karimi, F., Fernandez, M., Alani, H., Berendt, B., Kruegel, T., Heinze, C., & Staab, S. (2020). Bias in data-driven artificial intelligence systems—An introductory survey. *Wiley Interdisciplinary Reviews. Data Mining and Knowledge Discovery*, 10(3), e1356. 10.1002/widm.1356

Pasquinelli, M. (2023). *The eye of the master: A social history of artificial intelligence*. Verso Books.

Sands, S., Campbell, C. L., Plangger, K., & Ferraro, C. (2022). Unreal influence: Leveraging AI in influencer marketing. *European Journal of Marketing*, 56(6), 1721–1747. 10.1108/EJM-12-2019-0949

Stray, J. (2023). The AI learns to lie to please you: Preventing biased feedback loops in machine-assisted intelligence analysis. *Analytics*, 2(2), 350–358. 10.3390/analytics2020020

Vinuesa, R., Azizpour, H., Leite, I., Balaam, M., Dignum, V., Domisch, S., & Nerini, F. F. (2020). The role of artificial intelligence in achieving the Sustainable Development Goals. *Nature Communications*, 11(1), 1–10. 10.1038/s41467-019-14108-y31932590

Zhang, E., & Lu, X. (2023). Social AI Improves Well-Being Among Female Young Adults. arXiv e-prints, arXiv-2311.

Zhang, Z., Xu, Y., Wang, Y., Yao, B., Ritchie, D., Wu, T., & Li, T. J. J. (2022, April). Storybuddy: A human-AI collaborative chatbot for parent-child interactive storytelling with flexible parental involvement. In *Proceedings of the 2022 CHI Conference on Human Factors in Computing Systems* (pp. 1-21). ACM. 10.1145/3491102.3517479

# Chapter 21
# Youth Identity Formation in the Age of Digitalization:
## Exploring Digital Dilemmas in the North Macedonian Context

**Avni Avdiu**
*Mother Teresa University, North Macedonia*

**Agron Kurtishi**
iD https://orcid.org/0000-0002-0430-0380
*Mother Teresa University, North Macedonia*

**Arta Xhelili**
iD https://orcid.org/0000-0001-5345-9948
*Mother Teresa University, North Macedonia*

**Agron Vrangalla**
iD https://orcid.org/0000-0001-9621-0229
*Mother Teresa University, North Macedonia*

## ABSTRACT

*The use of digital display devices has grown and continues to expand significantly over the past few years. Since contents in online media are numerous, more intense, and without space and time limitations, compared to face to face interactions, their influence is much greater than other social agents'. Taking into consideration that youth use digital media frequently and for a longer duration, they have a considerable contribution to the formation of new generations' identities. This study analyzes the impact of digital media use on youth in terms of identity formation. A quantitative study was conducted based on 312 respondents' self-reports. The findings showed that a positively significant relationship exists between social media exposure and identity formation. The stronger the social media exposure, the less certain respondents are in regard to themselves and their values and beliefs.*

DOI: 10.4018/979-8-3693-3350-1.ch021

# INTRODUCTION

Social networks are no longer something exceptional. On the contrary, they are the most common thing for many users in the world. We already engage more into online surfing than in the process of thinking. With the massive boom of the Internet and social media, knowledge has taken on a completely different form. Critical thinking among young people is fading. Most of them live with the idea that information does not need to be memorized, it is enough to search for it in one of the search engines, or recently also by various Artificial Intelligence chatbots. In this sense, learning has taken a completely new form from the traditional one. No one memorizes anything anymore, no one worries that one day they may need information. In this case, critical thinking has been lost too. Young people do not engage in creating critical views on events and phenomena since they all think they can find them readily available on the web. In line with this logic, it can rightly be said that knowledge as a concept is no longer what was known before. Perhaps in any other case, it would be extremely worthwhile to conduct research about the redefinition of knowledge in the digital age.

Based on some statistics that Forbes Magazine has published in 2024, about 5.35 billion people use social media worldwide. On average, a person spends about 6.5 hours on the Internet every day (GWI, 2017). The most attractive type of content on social media are short videos, or shorts, or reels. The most common way people access social media is through mobile devices (78%). Research shows that there is a correlation between social media use and depression in teenagers. 67% of teens report feeling worse about their lives as a result of using social media. Teens who spend over three hours a day on social media platforms have an increased risk of mental health (Wong, 2023). In Germany over six percent of children and young people are addicted to social media. According to a study published in the spring of 2023 by the German Health Foundation DAK, this affects over 600,000 boys and girls. Media consumption is a serious issue for more than two million teenagers. They spend three to four hours a day in front of the screen, significantly more than before the coronavirus pandemic (DAK, 2023).

The Republic of North Macedonia (RNM) is not an exception and its statistics are as disturbing as those at the global level. According to Kemp (2024), by January 2024 there were 944.6 thousand active social media user identities, equivalent to 45.4% of the total population. Kepio's analysis reveals that social media users in RNM have grown by 150 thousand (+12.5 percent) between 2021 and 2022, and 30 thousand between early 2023 and the beginning of 2024 (Kemp, 2024). At the beginning of 2022 Facebook had 945.1 thousand users, Instagram had 809.4 thousand users, LinkedIn had 280.0 thousand members and Twitter had 93.8 thousand users from North Macedonia (Vrabotuvanje, 2022) (Table1).

*Table 1. Data on internet and social media usage in North Macedonia*

| Year | Internet users (in Mio) | Social media users (in Mio) | Mobile connections (in Mio) | did not use the internet | Facebook users | Instagram | Tik Tok | Facebook Messenger | LinkedIn | X (twitter) |
|------|------|------|------|------|------|------|------|------|------|------|
| 2024 | 1.82 | 1.40 | 2.55 | 267.000 | 944.600 | 811.500 | 754.000 | 816.200 | 370.000 | 133.100 |
| 2023 | 1.82 | 1.20 | 2.32 | 267.800 | 914.200 | 711.500 | / | 767.300 | 320.000 | 131.600 |
| 2022 | 1.75 | 1.35 | 2.25 | 333.100 | 945.100 | 809.400 | / | 814.600 | 280.000 | 93.800 |

continued on following page

*Table 1. Continued*

| Year | Internet users (in Mio) | Social media users (in Mio) | Mobile connections (in Mio) | did not use the internet | Facebook users | Instagram | Tik Tok | Facebook Messenger | LinkedIn | X (twitter) |
|------|------|------|------|------|------|------|------|------|------|------|
| **2021** | 1.71 | 1.20 | 2.10 | / | / | / | / | / | / | / |
| **2020** | 1.69 | 1.10 | 2.24 | / | / | / | / | / | / | / |

Research data from a study delivered by the International Foundation for Electoral Systems (IFES) - "Youth digital privacy in North Macedonia" reveal that young people in Macedonia use the Internet mostly for social media (92.3 percent), for communication (89.2 percent), and for listening to music (74.2 percent). Almost half of young people in the country use the Internet for entertainment, watching movies or TV shows, while only 17.1 percent of young people use the Internet for research and learning (Radiomof, 2023).

In the digital age, new questions and challenges arise regarding identity. The use of online platforms and social media can lead to a digital identity consisting of personal data, online activities and social behavior. But also, a very major problem we face in modern times is the loss of privacy and the possibility of identity theft. Moreover, the online media provide opportunity for construction of (multi)identity online. The possibility to present oneself online anonymously or under different pseudonyms can have an impact on the way individuals (mainly children) construct and present their identity. They can create different profiles for different purposes, which can result in a multifaceted and complex identity. Digital media plays an important role in the formation of political identities. People use social media and online platforms to discuss political issues, organize and fight for changes that reflect their identity and values. Despite the positive aspects of digital technology, their intensive use also presents risks and challenges to identity. These include issues such as cyberbullying, online bullying, internet addiction and distorted self-image through social comparison.

Through digital media we are given many opportunities for identity formation, but this also comes with problems, risks and challenges. Teenagers can be victims of cyberbullying, online bullying, and unhealthy comparisons, which can affect their self-esteem and identity.

The Council of the European Union referring to online media has concluded that: "besides their many positive advantages and effects, they have also led to increasing amounts of misinformation, manipulation and hate speech" (Rat der Europäischen Union, 2020). Cybermobbing is also part of the challenges of the new digital era.

The Federal Ministry of Family Affairs, Elderly and Youth in Germany, on its official website, defined Cybermobbing as "Cyberbullying, insulting, threatening, shaming or harassing people using communication media, for example through smartphones, emails, websites, forums, chats and communities" (BMFSFJ, 2021). According to this ministry, Cybermobbing can happen, for example, in chats, forums and through email, but also in social communities such as Facebook and Instagram and in video platforms such as YouTube, even if the operators of these sites make every effort to undertake actions against harassing, attacks and quickly deletes defamation (BMFSFJ, 2021). It only takes a few seconds to share a photo or even a comment to a very large number of people. Digital media has facilitated and multiplied the spread and forms of mobbing. Since young people are in the process of constructing their identity, often sharing a photo or a comment on the network can negatively affect the formation of identity in young people, and the reasons at this age can be very banal, e.g. (temporary) destruction of society, some personal revenge, emotional load, but there are cases when Cybermobbing is done just for fun. In the digital age, depending on the way of using the digital media, the formation of the identity can be positive, but it only takes one spark for all this positivity to result in the closure of the personality and introduction into some paths and worlds completely different from those of the former, i.e., from one moment to the next, the individual can lose his personality and change it with another. The identity in this case will have to be re-constructed, maybe partially, but the important thing is that there will be deviations and consequences. This means that "media-related change […] has a broad social significance for people's social relations, for the formation of their identity and worldview" (Breiter, Welling & Stolpmann, 2010, p. 13). The state and political actors are responsible to respond to all these social challenges among young people and initiate analyses, debates and discussions and implement changes in the relevant areas.

Thus, it appears that the use of media in all generations is very intensive, and the time spent with them (media) is very long. All this use of the media brings new opportunities to young people, but at the same time the use is also associated with many different risks that come from not knowing the media and not being aware of them. Both the opportunities and the dangers faced by the new generations have an impact on the construction of the identity of young people, but also significant impacts in the mental and physical aspect.

This study examines the identity of young people in the era of digitalization, through the prism of identity theory and dramaturgical theory. Identity develops within different stages of life, starting from early childhood through social learning. It is important to understand how social networks influence the formation of identity among young people. Through searching, communication, interaction, exchange of different experiences, gaming, consumption of audio, photo and video materials, use of Artificial Intelligence, and so on, young people unconsciously enter a new dimension of life. This directly affects the formation of their personal, cultural and social identity. Online media create virtual lives, therefore virtual people.

Young people, through their interaction in the virtual world, at the end of the day, are looking for a new identity. Since the Internet is an endless ocean, the rules and norms of its fair use are far from the knowledge of young people. In this case, it often happens that they lose their orientation during the mysterious swimming in this endless ocean. The paper deals with the idea of the well-known sociologist Erving Goffman, who, through his subtle approach, helps us to understand that the individual is in a big theatrical performance and in front of him is an entire audience that follows him. According to Goffman (1996) our personality is not that unique, but that it is built on the basis of the different experiences we experience during life.

The study is based on empirical research and draws conclusions from a survey administered to youth in North Macedonia. The surveys contain specific questions that make it possible to understand the general panorama of online media consumption and their effect on identity construction. Suffice to state that for 97% of teenagers in RNM, the Internet is the most important source of information. You will be able to learn the other details, both interesting and disturbing, while reading the chapter.

The challenge of examining and monitoring the new dynamics of the use of online media by young people remains an imperative of the time and an obligation for all researchers in the multidisciplinary fields. Also, parents, teachers and other agents of socialization have a key role in improving the situation created by the 'frightening' presence of the Internet in our lives.

## LITERATURE REVIEW

### Conceptualization of Identity

Identity is not born nor given by nature, but the individual builds it through communication and interaction with his environment. Sociologically it is described as "the uniqueness of an individual" (in relation to others) (Krappmann, 2000, p.9), while psychologically, referring to Wirtz (2016), in the Dorsch lexicon of psychology identity is represented as "the experienced enduring unity of the person himself". Erikson (1973, p.18) defined identity as "the immediate perception of one's own similarity and continuity in time and the accompanying perception that others also recognize this similarity and continuity". According to Abels (2019) identity is the awareness of being a distinctive individual with one's life history, to show a certain consistency in one's actions and to find a balance between individual demands and social expectations in relation to others. In sum, as stated by Keupp (2017) identity is the permanent process of adapting a person to create a balance between internal processes (own personal experiences, abilities, goals and values) and external changes (expectations and values of the social environment).

### Identity Theories

There are various theories of identity that deal with how individuals form, develop and understand their identity. Digital media has brought new challenges in regard to the construction of identity among the new generations, because the formation of identity is inevitably related to the consumption of digital media.

Ivan Petrovich Pavlov (1849-1936), based on the stimulus-response principle, saw people as a black box, whose personality was constructed as a reaction to external stimuli. According to Jean Piages (1896-1980) identity develops through different stages over time, from childhood by exploring the environment and new experiences. Sigmund Freud (1856-1939) sees identity as closely related to needs and drives (such as food, love and erotic pleasure) and their satisfaction. Their non-fulfillment leads to tensions. Erik Homburger Erikson (1902-1994) was in line with Freud, but he paid special attention to the so-called latent period during adolescence. Here, the feeling of being needed is important, while failures lead to feelings of inferiority (Erikson, 1973). For George Herbert Mead (1863-1931), identity is not innate but consists exclusively of communication with other people. A common language and a system of symbols is required to be able to communicate meaningfully while interacting with people (Mead, 1973).

In the same line, according to Erving Goffman (1922-1982), identity can only be formed through interaction with the social environment. Of special importance is the ability to present the ego identity, which according to Goffman is called identity representation, a feeling that an individual has about his or her identity. "The dramaturgy of life" develops the personal identity, the way we portray ourselves to the outside world. In terms of their social identity, individuals will "feel what kind of behavior they should adopt as the right thing to do" (Goffman, 1956, p. 268). Likewise, Lothar Krappmann (1936-...), emphasized the importance of interactions as an essential prerequisite for the socialization process and the formation of the ego identity.

The study of identity formation is grounded in Erikson's (1968) theory. The theory looks at three dimensions of identity formation: the psychological dimension (ego identity), personal dimension and the social component which comprises community roles.

## The Role of Media on Identity Formation

The discussion of identity and its changes in the digital age is very complex and requires an interdisciplinary approach that takes into account psychological, sociological, philosophical and technological perspectives. At a time when technology has a rapid development, the issue of identity becomes more and more important and current.

The process of identity formation is never ending, and it faces various issues. Especially in childhood and adolescence, these issues of identity formation are more intense and full of contradictions, confusions, instability and uncertainty. This is exactly where the media comes into play, with their role in providing children and teenagers with (strong) support in their path of identity formation. The role of the media, especially the digital ones, helps children and teenagers to exchange important information related to their presentation. Children and adolescents find different models to present themselves in digital media.

In the digital transformation we are experiencing, many processes have moved to the virtual world. In particular, the Internet conveys important socio-cultural patterns and lays the initial foundations for identity, due to the very fact that young people use it to a large extent. Social networks play a very important role in the construction and development of identity.

The phase of adolescence requires the construction of a certain system of values which will later serve as an orientation for the behavior itself. In the course of Internet navigation, young people often choose as model people who appear in their immediate world and the new generations (digital natives)[1], or as Eichenberg & Auersperg, (2018, p.7) calls them "Childhood 2.0". They do not distinguish whether these people are real, mediatic or virtual (Hoffmann, 2006:3329). Considering the large range of media available to young people today, they have many opportunities to see many different roles but also to imitate many roles, which they cannot try in real life. With this they are able to see which role is well received (by others) and which is not. These roles can have both positive and negative effects. Media platforms are a good basis for identity formation for young people as through these platforms they can present what they want and what they don't want, and they may not present at all (publish).

Online platforms often are not only used to get information, but also to make a comparison in many areas such as: clothing, presentation (appearance), society, environment, occasion, place, status, property, standard, experience, etc. which then influence certain social behaviors and identifications. These comparisons sometimes become a kind of standard for measurement and evaluation. The problem is that the measuring standard is becoming more and more visual and with this the intellectual values are the ones that suffer. When used actively, digital media constantly confronts us with the lives of others. This makes young people more sensitive. According to Bergmann (2021) those young people have an increased sensitivity to stress, a tendency to be depressed and anxious, uncertain and with a negative self-concept. Moreover, using the media for a long time, the fact that it is virtual is often forgotten and seems to become more real than real. According to Jarosz (2020), digital media "cannot be divided into 'good' or 'bad' and should not be blamed only for the negative effects of its use. If we deal with them, it is important to remain critical, question and address them in a reflective manner."

In modern times, the dynamics of identity development are characterized by new processes, and identity becomes a task for which we must redefine ourselves very often, perhaps every day. With the development and widespread spread of technology, opportunity and freedom take on new meanings, but they also bring with them new issues, risks, stresses and challenges as people feel under pressure to position themself. Young people especially have orientation issues.

In the time of such rapid technological development and transformation processes, children are using digital media more and more often, even from an early age. Thus, media education for the younger age is very important. According to Leopold and Ullmann (2018) the acquisition and correct handling of digital media are essential for the development of children in kindergarten.

A hallmark of the digitized society is a new combination of technical and social processes that structure our everyday life. This modern society has all the possibilities for generating and distributing multimedia products in as many media as possible, including the use of chat worlds and AI to improve performance. The offer of the media is very large and their use without space and time limitation, especially by the new generations, brings with it certain problems that have not been researched before. New generations are growing up between reality (poor) on the one hand and virtuality (rich) on the other. A very important feature of the new generations, who use the media without any time and space limitations, is that they are in search of their identity, which also floats between reality and virtuality.

The whole problem of such a large number of swimmers in this endless ocean, which every day tends to expand, will be the loss of the compass (orientation) of the participants in the future. If earlier, the identity of one generation was not much different from the identity of the next generation, it seems that in the digital age one can no longer speak of one identity, but of more identities at the same time. Therefore the process of identity development is fundamentally influenced by the media (Schorb, 2014, p.178).

Ruß-Mohl (2017, p. 52) states that "in the media society [...] mediatized with its massive overflow of information and the consequences of a new disinformation economy in times of fake news and alternative facts, conflicts of values, orientation and identity may further intensify".

Various studies have been conducted in order to study the impact of social media in identity formation. Social media provided a place where youth can share information, express ideas, expand their network and entertain (Song, 2023). In these platforms youth can also interact and participate in discussions that form and maintain values, ideas and beliefs. Research focusing on Facebook usage among college students and high school adolescents in Western cultures has established that online and offline identities are fluidly intertwined rather than dichotomous (Wilson, Gosling, & Graham, 2012; Valkenburg & Peter, 2011). A study conducted by Ophir et al. (2009) on social media use revealed that social media had an effect on youth cognition, since it offers an opportunity for multitasking and poorer memory and filtering necessary information. Another study looked at the impact that social media use and multiple identities have on conflicts with parents. Kidwell et al. (1995) found that youth that explore multiple identities are experiencing self-doubt, confusion and conflicts with their parents. Huang (2006) revealed that those that spent more hours online are significantly less likely to have an achieved identity compared to those that spent less time online. In another study, Vybiral et al. (2004) found that youth use the internet to explore their offline and online identity and clarify who they want to become. In sum, all these studies suggest that social media may be associated with identity formation.

## THEORETICAL FRAMEWORK

### Goffman's Dramaturgical Theory

Dramaturgy suggests that society is made up of individual performances put out by everyday actors. In a dramaturgical context, acting or dramatization takes place when people present themselves, collectively and individually, in a way that can create or destroy general understandings of reality held by others (Kivisto & Pittman, 2007). As put by Kivisto and Pittman (2017) Erving Goffman considered life as a theatrical scene and used the metaphor of life as theater. He saw human interactions as a theatrical play and the world as a stage. Erving Goffman's theory gives a great help to understand the individual surrounded by digital media. According to him, in every social interaction we participate in, consciously or unconsciously we try to project a concrete image of ourselves. Goffman spoke of human interaction as a performance where the individual performs in front of an audience on a certain stage. This is the dramaturgical approach he derived in the late 1950s. For Goffman, our personality is not an internal phenomenon. Moreover, personality is a selection of different masks that we put on, and this is called social dramaturgy. Our social interactions with others can be analyzed like theatrical and dramaturgical scenes. Interactionism was a "typical Goffman mask" and was heavily influenced by the Durkheimian anthropologists Warner and Radcliffe-Brown (Collins, 1986; Becker, 1999; Williams, 1986; Cahill, 2004).

The term "symbolic interaction" refers to a particular property, specific to human interactions, which is the ability of human beings to interpret or "define" mutual actions. Also, an essential part of symbolic interaction is the human capacity for self-reflective behavior. Society influences a person so that he builds his external personality in order to be suitable in society. Social interaction is seen as a theatrical performance involving actors, social actors and the audience, the actors towards whom the interaction is directed.

Dramaturgical analysis is important for the social sciences in general. Social dramaturgy is a micro-sociological approach that focuses on the study of human behavior and the rules that govern everyday human interactions. In Goffman's model, there are three stages in which dramaturgy occurs. "Stage" is the forum where dramaturgy is performed in front of the public. The scene begins to build from the moment we project our self-image to others. In the setting of the scene, the characters, their points of view, and the rhetoric about the "plot" are apparently transparent. However, most of the practical negotiation of power between actors takes place elsewhere: "offstage" and "backstage." Behind the scenes is our private life, which can also be another mask we wear. In the offstage environment, the range of acceptable discourse can differ significantly from that on stage, as the actors use a language that is not intended for the audience. Knowing the backstage activity is essential to understanding the power relations that an audience later observes. Backstage dramaturgy doesn't necessarily mean that actors "get out of their role," but they are more likely to do so in this forum. Social dramaturgy consists in recognizing the movement between stage and backstage.

Erving Goffman's dramaturgical approach shows us how the individual performs and manages his impression in order to be accepted in society. Theater actors in society have the same goal: to adapt their interactions with those around them. To convey a good impression, we must have dramaturgical (social) skills, the necessary costumes and props. However, all of this is irrelevant if the stage actors fail to agree on the expectations and limitations of their performance. In other words, their interpretation implicitly shows how to act in a certain social environment.

In addition, expertly transitioning from one group to another and "having" the right costume at all times are essential requirements for social success. Therefore, anyone who does not know how to act during the show is a danger to the other "actors" and can be expelled. As we perform an action, comments and expressions of surprise, approval, irony, or disgust shape what others think of us. Aware of this, we control what we say, what gestures we use and how we convey our reactions. We are always performing, interpreting, and acting. Further, in order to adapt we define our roles based on the environment in which we find ourselves. We always adapt to our role.

Just like actors in television shows, we can start the first episode with our personality and our work, our education, and our relationships, which are not well defined. We can start to change and define these aspects when we hear the reaction of our audience. Hereafter we devote our lives to the adaptation of the role. We do this until they (audience) give up on our show and we have to take off that mask.

For Goffman, in this social dramaturgy, whenever they interact people try to present an ideal image of themselves. This is because they believe it is useful or desirable to hide certain parts of themselves. We hide the process of exercising our role. We are like a teacher who lectures after a few hours of preparation, pretending to understand the topic he is talking about. In other words, we would rather show others only the final result of our test. We don't show others our "efforts" or how many times we have practiced what needs to be remembered. All this happens behind the scenes.

We hide all the hard work and effort it took us to get where we are. Our character may be inconsistent with all that we have done to earn praise. For example, imagine a politician who wins a political campaign by selling his integrity. He would have to fight tooth and nail to make it to the top. We hide everything that can prevent us from continuing our acting. To do this, we criticize ourselves. Further, we avoid reacting to insults so as to prevent it from affecting the image we have chosen to project. In their capacity as performers, individuals will be concerned with maintaining the impression that they live by the standards by which they and their productions are judged. Since these standards are numerous and so widespread, individuals who are performers live longer than we think in the moral world. However, in order to achieve these standards, individuals are not concerned with moral issues, but rather with the amoral ones of creating convincing impressions that these standards are being met. Hence, our activity largely deals with moral issues, but as performers we have no moral concerns about this. As performers, people are merchants of morality.

One of the central concepts in Goffman's theory is that of impression management, by seeing ourselves as an object, as others see us. Our performance should not fall under human impulses but should embody all the values expected by society. However, when an individual is presented to others, his performance will tend to embody and serve as an example of society's officially accredited values, in fact more than his behavior as a whole. Thus, when the individual presents himself before others, his performance will tend to incorporate and exemplify the officially accredited values of the society, more so, in fact, than does his behavior as a whole (Goffman, 1978, p.57).

The main goal of the individual according to Goffman is to be accepted in society, but for this he needs a front plan, which he formulates in a way that would be acceptable to others. The concept of image is one of the reasons why individuals see interaction with others as a kind of obligation, and Goffman also asserted that self-image and image of others are constructs of the same order: "group rules and situational definitions that determine how much feeling should be attached to one's image and how that feeling is distributed among the parties involved' (Goffman, 1967, p.6).

Physical proximity is of particular importance to ritual, and this is demonstrated in (at least) two cases: first, observers are entitled to infer how persons who are in physical proximity are in a social relationship, and second, individuals who are in a position of apparent physical proximity are entitled to initiate a conversation (Goffman 1963, p.102–103). When individuals are in physical (co)presence, they become available to each other in various ways - from physical to unwanted conversations - resulting in the creation of so-called "rules of peace" or mutual respect (Goffman, 1967, p.147).

Goffman argued that shame and embarrassment are essential for the normal functioning of social interaction (Goffman, 1956, p.270), while in the digital age, shame appears only through some emoticons. According to Goffman an individual builds his social identity on the basis of self-affirmations which if denied, entitle the individual to feel "rightfully" or "morally" irritated.

Goffman's dramaturgical analysis can find extension in the control of information by and between the actors and the "audience". The website or social networking app becomes a new stage with new props and new tools for the performer to use. Facebook sets the stage for interaction primarily through registration and filling out the profile with essential information about the user. The social network Facebook limits the audience to the number of "friends" an individual has. From Goffman's point of view, social media is close to the realm of self-expression to make a good impression on others. In his performance in social networks, the individual incorporates his knowledge and performs differently, in accordance with expectations and what is considered acceptable in social networks. In order to create images and desired impressions of self, people use selective posting online. They have the option to post what they want about themselves so they can create an understanding about who they are: interests, hobbies, movies they watched, books they have read etc. Through this they can present themselves in the most acceptable picture, in other words they take e role to perform.

Goffman's views of front stage and backstage are applied to social networking in order to understand the impact social media have on youths' identity. While online people do perform, the question is what's the impact of media offline when the person is no longer performing.

When analyzing the connection, role and influence of the media in general on the individual and society, this whole theory of Goffman translated into the language of comparison and analogy of today's social sciences, is associated with the anticipation of artificial intelligence (ChatGPT) by the British mathematician and scientist Alan Turing (1912-1954), who made a big splash when he floated the idea that would come the day when machines would be able to teach themselves (Burgess, 2021,12).

Regarding this theory, the current study proposes that social media, combined with Goffman dramaturgical theory concepts may create a ground for better understanding of the youths' identity formation in the digital era.

Based on Goffman's Dramaturgical theory and literature review on social media and identity formation, it is clear that there is a link between youths' social media usage and identity formation in the digital age. Despite the pervasiveness of technology in society, the implications of social media usage on identity development remain unknown.

Therefore, the following research questions and hypothesis are offered:

Research question 1: How is social media used by the North Macedonian youth?
1.1 What is youths' perception about their social media usage?
Research question 2: What are the relationships between social media use and youth's identity formation?
The above hypothesis will provide an answer to this research question:
H1. There will be a statistically significant relationship between social media use and youths' identity formation in North Macedonia.
Research question 3: How would sex, age, parent's level of education and time spent communicating within family moderate the relationship between perceived social media usage and identity formation among North Macedonian youth?
H2: Social media identity formation is moderated by age, sex, parent's level of education, time exposure with social media.

H3. There will be significant differences within social media identity formation when controlled by sex.

H4. There will be significant differences between social media use and identity formation when controlled by age.

H5. There will be significant differences between social media use and identity formation when controlled by a parent's level of education.

H6. Youth that spend more time online will be more influenced by social media in their identity formation.

H7. Youth that spend more time with their parent's will be less influenced by social media in their identity formation.

## METHOD

### Participants

The study used a non-probability sample by employing the Snowball technique to collect data. Participation in the survey was voluntary and anonymous. The response rate was 100%, resulting in a sample of 312 participants, of which 75.6% (n=236) females and 24.4% (n=76) males. The age range was from 13 to 25, with a mean of 18.9 years old and mode 16 years old. The highest percentage of respondents reside in rural places (52.6%), followed by respondents from urban places (47.4%). The majority of the respondents were from nuclear families (49.7%), extended family (46.2%) followed by a small percentage of single parent families (4.2%).

### Survey Instruments

The study used a close-ended questionnaire, consisting of three sections: *demographic information, The Functions of Identity scale and Social Media Scale*. Perceptions on identity formation were operationalized by a 20-item scale, divided into five subscales (structure, harmony, future, self and control), adapted from the Functions of Identity scale developed by Serafini and Adams (2002). In this scale participants indicate how well each statement described them by responding on a 5-point Likert scale ranging from 1 (Never) to 5 (Always). Social media use questionnaire was created to examine adolescents' social media usage. The questionnaire consisted of questions in regard to the time adolescents' spend on social media, which are the platforms they use the most, what's the main reason they use social media, Likert scale alternatives in regard to social media use and their self-perception in regard to social media addiction.

### Data Analysis

Surveys were coded and then entered into SPSS 20.00 data system. Data entries were coded in the affirmative direction (items were reverse coded). After inserting the data in the system, tests were run for reliability, descriptive statistics, and inferential statistics.

## Reliability

The reliability of the items was initially tested for all the cases. Cronbach's Alpha for identity formation was .764, while the reliability test for social media usage indicated .84, which indicates that the instrument has high internal consistency. After the reliability test, two new scales were computed for perceived social media identity formation and social media usage based on the mean of all related items. Subscales in regard to each identity formation factor were created: structure, harmony, future, self, and control.

## RESULTS

## Descriptive Statistics

Research question 1: How is social media used by the North Macedonian youth?
Descriptive statistics on the items measuring social media usage answers these research questions.

## What is Youths' Perception About Their Social Media Usage?

Asked from what age they own a smartphone, respondents' mean age was 12.1, with a mode 12, and with a minimum reported age 3 and maximum 25 years old. These numbers show that on average North Macedonian youth gets equipped with smartphones very early in their childhood.

In regard to social media profiles, 82.7% of the respondents declared that they own a social media profile. Of those that did not own a profile (17.3%), 12.2% were not interested, 3.2% did not have time, and 1.6% parents did not allow them to open a profile.

The social media they use the most were Tik Tok (24.7%), followed by Snapchat (24%) and Instagram (20.5%), and WhatsApp (17%). Only 2.2% of the respondents used Facebook (Table 2).

*Table 2. Descriptives in regard to social media platforms*

| Which social media do you use the most? | | | | | |
|---|---|---|---|---|---|
| | | Frequency | Percent | Valid Percent | Cumulative Percent |
| Valid | Facebook | 7 | 2.2 | 2.2 | 2.2 |
| | WhatsApp | 53 | 17.0 | 17.0 | 19.2 |
| | Instragram | 64 | 20.5 | 20.5 | 39.7 |
| | Youtube | 26 | 8.3 | 8.3 | 48.1 |
| | Tik Tok | 77 | 24.7 | 24.7 | 72.8 |
| | Viber | 4 | 1.3 | 1.3 | 74.0 |
| | Snapchat | 75 | 24.0 | 24.0 | 98.1 |
| | Google Classroom | 6 | 1.9 | 1.9 | 100.0 |
| | Total | 312 | 100.0 | 100.0 | |

The majority of the respondents reported spending 2-4 hours online (30.1%), followed by 20.8% spending 4-6 hours, 20.2% up to 6 hours, 19.2% 30 minutes -2 hours and only 9.6% reported spending 10-30 minutes per day (Graph 1). The prevailing reasons for using social media were for communication (39.1%), being informed (35.6%), and entertainment (17.6%).

*Figure 1. Sample measurement of time spent online*

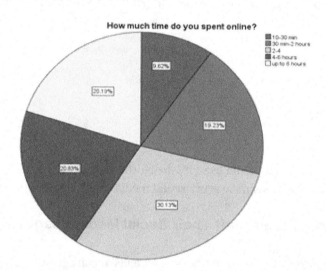

The table above provides descriptive statistics for each item of social media use:

*Table 3. Descriptive statistics of social media use items*

| Social Media use items | Strongly disagree | Disagree | Neutral | Agree | Strongly agree | Mean | Std. D |
|---|---|---|---|---|---|---|---|
| Use social media 15 minutes before going to sleep | 5.4 | 2.9 | 16.0 | 27.9 | 47.8 | 4.0962 | 1.11 |
| Use social media while eating breakfast/lunch/dinner | 20.2 | 19.6 | 20.5 | 18.9 | 20.8 | 3.0064 | 1.42 |
| Use social media within the first 15 minutes of waking up | 9.6 | 15.7 | 13.1 | 29.8 | 31.7 | 3.5833 | 1.33 |
| Feeling anxious if you don't have access to social media | 28.8 | 25.3 | 19.9 | 14.7 | 11.2 | 2.5417 | 1.34 |
| Feeling annoyed when you don't have access to social media | 15.1 | 18.9 | 20.8 | 26.0 | 19.2 | 3.1538 | 1.34 |
| Neglecting lessons due to the use of social media | 27.2 | 21.5 | 23.4 | 17.9 | 9.9 | 2.6186 | 1.32 |
| Use social media more than you planned | 10.3 | 18.9 | 18.6 | 29.5 | 22.8 | 3.3558 | 1.29 |
| Your parents complain about the time spent on social media | 21.5 | 17.6 | 24.7 | 20.5 | 15.7 | 2.9135 | 1.37 |
| Don't feel the need for social media | 18.9 | 22.8 | 29.2 | 16.0 | 13.1 | 2.8173 | 1.28 |

continued on following page

*Table 3. Continued*

| Social Media use items | Strongly disagree | Disagree | Neutral | Agree | Strongly agree | Mean | Std. D |
|---|---|---|---|---|---|---|---|
| Socia media are an important part of the daily routine | 6.7 | 14.7 | 23.4 | 29.8 | 25.3 | 3.5224 | 1.20 |
| Your life is unsatisfied compared to other people online | 33.7 | 25.3 | 17.9 | 14.7 | 8.3 | 2.3878 | 1.30 |
| Feel pressure in regard to social media likes | 45.2 | 25.3 | 16.0 | 7.1 | 6.4 | 2.0417 | 1.21 |
| Use a false age when interacting with others | 60.6 | 19.2 | 9.6 | 5.4 | 5.1 | 1.7532 | 1.15 |
| Use different identities depending on the situation | 59.6 | 21.8 | 6.7 | 6.4 | 5.4 | 1.7628 | 1.16 |
| Present yourself differently than you are offline | 58.7 | 18.9 | 11.9 | 6.7 | 3.8 | 1.7821 | 1.13 |

The percentage examination for each item shows that the greatest agreement has been reached in these items: use social media 15 minutes before going to sleep (75.7%), use social media within 15 minutes of waking up (61.5%), social media considered as an important part of the daily routine (55.1%), and use social media more than you planned (52.3%). The greatest disagreement was detected on items: use different identities depending on the situation (81.4%), presenting differently online (77.6%), using false age when online (79.8%) and feel pressure in regard to social media likes (70.5%). It can be concluded that in regard to social media usage respondents were reporting having issues with social media addiction but not being involved in manipulative behavior such as falsifying their identity online (Table 3).

## Inferential Statistics

Research question 2: What are the relationships between social media use and youth's identity formation?
The above hypothesis will provide an answer to this research question:

H1. There will be a statistically significant correlation between social media use and youths' identity formation in North Macedonia.

A correlation matrix showing the relationships between all variables, including the correlation of a variable with itself is presented in Table 4. The output data reveal that the relationship is statistically significant ($p < .005$) and positive for social media use and identity formation ($r = 0.128$, $p < 0.05$). This suggests that social media use correlates with adolescents' identity formation. Thus, social media usage matters in adolescents' identity formation. Changes in social media usage will be accompanied with changes in identity formation. The more social media usage the more it will reflect identity formation.

*Table 4. Correlation matrix showing interrelationships for social media use and identity formation*

| Correlations | | Social Media Scale | Identity Formation Scale |
|---|---|---|---|
| Social Media Scale | Pearson Correlation | 1 | .128* |
| | Sig. (2-tailed) | | .024 |
| | N | 312 | 312 |

*continued on following page*

*Table 4. Continued*

| Correlations | | Social Media Scale | Identity Formation Scale |
|---|---|---|---|
| Identity Formation Scale | Pearson Correlation | .128* | 1 |
| | Sig. (2-tailed) | .024 | |
| | N | 312 | 312 |

*. Correlation is significant at the 0.05 level (2-tailed).

A detailed examination of the correlation between social media perceptions and identity formation subscales is provided in Table 5.

*Table 5. Correlation matrix showing interrelationships of social media use and identity subscales*

| Correlations Subscale | | Social_media_identity | Structure | Future | Harmony | Control | Self |
|---|---|---|---|---|---|---|---|
| Social_media_identity | Pearson Correlation | - | | | | | |
| | Sig. (2-tailed) | | | | | | |
| Structure | Pearson Correlation | -.176** | | | | | |
| | Sig. (2-tailed) | .002 | - | | | | |
| Future | Pearson Correlation | .171** | -.036 | - | | | |
| | Sig. (2-tailed) | .002 | .529 | | | | |
| Harmony | Pearson Correlation | -.122* | .405** | -.091 | - | | |
| | Sig. (2-tailed) | .031 | .000 | .107 | | | |
| Control | Pearson Correlation | .023 | .256** | .143* | .408** | - | |
| | Sig. (2-tailed) | .689 | .000 | .011 | .000 | | |
| Self | Pearson Correlation | .015 | .148** | .337** | .267** | .411** | - |

**. Correlation is significant at the 0.01 level (2-tailed). *. Correlation is significant at the 0.05 level (2-tailed).

An inspection of the correlation coefficients (Table 5.) revealed that there is not a statistically significant relationship between social media identity and identity control (r=.023, p>.05) and self-subscales (r=.015, p>.05). On the other hand, the results show that there is a strong positive relationship with identity future subscale (r=.171, p<0.05) and strong negative correlation with identity structure subscale (r=-.176, p<.05) and identity harmony subscale (r=-.122, p<.05). The stronger the social media exposure the stronger will be the uncertainty in direction to the future. On the other hand there is a negative correlation between social media exposure and being certain of identity (structure subscale) and values and beliefs being in harmony with self (harmony subscale). Thus the stronger the social media exposure, the less certain respondents are in regard to themselves and their values and beliefs are not consistent with who they are.

<u>Research question 3:</u> How would sex, age, parent's level of education and time spent communicating within family moderate the relationship between perceived social media usage and identity formation among North Macedonian youth?

H2: Social media identity formation is moderated by age, sex, parent's level of education, time exposure with social media.

A social media identity scale was computed and multiple regression results are provided in Table 6. The multiple R(.245) and R square (.060) show that the independent variables explain 6% of the variance in social media identity scale and this result is statistically significant with ANOVA (Sig.=.002). The slopes (B) indicate that social media identity increases with social media exposure (.174), followed by father's education (.126) and decreases for gender (-.143). Since a male is coded as 1 and a female as 2, this indicates that the frequency of sex is greater for men. In other words, the rate of social media identity is more associated with males than females. The beta for social media usage time (.174) is greater than the beta for parent's education, age group and gender, thus social media time exposure is the most important independent variable.

*Table 6. Regression analysis with social media identity as dependent variable*

**Model Summary**

| Model | R | R Square | Adjusted R Square | Std. Error of the Estimate | | | |
|---|---|---|---|---|---|---|---|
| 1 | .245[a] | .060 | .044 | .93954 | | | |

**ANOVA[a]**

| Model | | Sum of Squares | df | Mean Square | F | Sig. |
|---|---|---|---|---|---|---|
| 1 | Regression | 16.662 | 5 | 3.332 | 3.775 | .002[b] |
| | Residual | 260.405 | 295 | .883 | | |
| | Total | 277.066 | 300 | | | |

a. Dependent Variable: Social_media_identity

b. Predictors: (Constant), Time spent online, Mother's educ, Age_group, Gender, Father's educ

**Coefficients[a]**

| Model | | Unstandardized Coefficients | | Standardized Coefficients | t | Sig. |
|---|---|---|---|---|---|---|
| | | B | Std. Error | Beta | | |
| 1 | (Constant) | 1.608 | .418 | | 3.847 | .000 |
| | Gender | -.323 | .133 | -.143 | -2.438 | .015 |
| | Age_group | .065 | .106 | .036 | .612 | .541 |
| | Mother's education | -.049 | .066 | -.053 | -.750 | .454 |
| | Father's education | .109 | .062 | .126 | 1.774 | .077 |
| | Time spent online | .136 | .045 | .174 | 3.034 | .003 |

a. Dependent Variable: Social_media_identity

H3. There will be significant differences within social media identity formation when controlled by sex.

Based on the ANOVA test, with the value of significance <.04, sex is significantly related to social media identity formation (Table 7.). Therefore the hypothesis is accepted and it is in line with the previous regression analysis in regard to hypothesis 2. Mean inspection shows that males score higher on social media identity formation (2.03) compared to females (1.77) and these differences are statistically significant. According to these results, there is a significant difference in social media identity formation by sex.

*Table 7. Mean comparison with social media identity as dependent and sex as independent variable*

| Descriptives | | | | | | | | |
|---|---|---|---|---|---|---|---|---|
| Social_media_identity | | | | | | | | |
| | N | Mean | Std. Deviation | Std. Error | 95% Confidence Interval for Mean | | Min | Max |
| | | | | | Lower Bound | Upper Bound | | |
| Male | 76 | 2.0296 | 1.13869 | .13062 | 1.7694 | 2.2898 | 1.00 | 5.00 |
| Female | 236 | 1.7722 | .87900 | .05722 | 1.6595 | 1.8850 | 1.00 | 5.00 |
| Total | 312 | 1.8349 | .95329 | .05397 | 1.7287 | 1.9411 | 1.00 | 5.00 |
| ANOVA | | | | | | | | |
| Social_media_identity | | | | | | | | |
| | Sum of Squares | df | Mean Square | F | Sig. | | | |
| Between Groups | 3.808 | 1 | 3.808 | 4.233 | .040 | | | |
| Within Groups | 278.817 | 310 | .899 | | | | | |
| Total | 282.624 | 311 | | | | | | |

H4. There will be significant differences between social media use and identity formation when controlled by age.

Based on the ANOVA test, with the value of significance >.05, the age groups are homogeneous (Table 8). These results indicate that age is not significantly related to social media identity formation. The differences in means are not statistically significant. Therefore, the hypothesis is rejected.

*Table 8. Mean comparison with social media identity as dependent and age as independent variable*

| Descriptives | | | | | | | | |
|---|---|---|---|---|---|---|---|---|
| Social_media_identity | | | | | | | | |
| Age | N | Mean | Std. Deviation | Std. Error | 95% Confidence Interval for Mean | | Minimum | Maximum |
| | | | | | Lower Bound | Upper Bound | | |
| 12-15 | 21 | 1.7143 | .85982 | .18763 | 1.3229 | 2.1057 | 1.00 | 3.75 |
| 16-20 | 205 | 1.8939 | .97739 | .06826 | 1.7593 | 2.0285 | 1.00 | 5.00 |
| 21-25 | 75 | 1.7500 | .94351 | .10895 | 1.5329 | 1.9671 | 1.00 | 5.00 |
| Total | 301 | 1.8455 | .96102 | .05539 | 1.7365 | 1.9545 | 1.00 | 5.00 |
| ANOVA | | | | | | | | |
| Social_media_identity | | | | | | | | |
| | Sum of Squares | df | Mean Square | F | Sig. | | | |
| Between Groups | 1.526 | 2 | .763 | .825 | .439 | | | |
| Within Groups | 275.541 | 298 | .925 | | | | | |
| Total | 277.066 | 300 | | | | | | |

H5. There will be significant differences between social media use and identity formation when controlled by a parent's level of education.

An ANOVA test revealed that for social media identity formation and parents' level of education the value of significance is > .05 which explains that the groups are homogeneous (Table 9). These results indicate that a parent's level of education is not significantly related to social media identity formation. There are group mean differences, but these differences are not statistically significant. Thus, the hypothesis is rejected.

*Table 9. Mean comparison with social media identity as dependent and age as independent variable*

**Descriptives**

Social_media_identity

| | N | Mean | Std. Deviation | Std. Error | 95% Confidence Interval for Mean | | Minimum | Maximum |
|---|---|---|---|---|---|---|---|---|
| | | | | | Lower Bound | Upper Bound | | |
| Uneducated | 1 | 2.2500 | . | . | . | . | 2.25 | 2.25 |
| Primary education | 69 | 1.6449 | .89772 | .10807 | 1.4293 | 1.8606 | 1.00 | 5.00 |
| Middle school | 124 | 1.8306 | .97507 | .08756 | 1.6573 | 2.0040 | 1.00 | 5.00 |
| Bachelor | 74 | 1.8851 | .84114 | .09778 | 1.6903 | 2.0800 | 1.00 | 4.50 |
| Master | 28 | 2.0804 | 1.06513 | .20129 | 1.6673 | 2.4934 | 1.00 | 5.00 |
| PhD | 12 | 1.9583 | 1.05977 | .30593 | 1.2850 | 2.6317 | 1.00 | 4.00 |
| Other | 4 | 2.1250 | 1.93111 | .96555 | -.9478 | 5.1978 | 1.00 | 5.00 |
| Total | 312 | 1.8349 | .95329 | .05397 | 1.7287 | 1.9411 | 1.00 | 5.00 |

**ANOVA**

Social_media_identity

| | Sum of Squares | df | Mean Square | F | Sig. |
|---|---|---|---|---|---|
| Between Groups | 5.058 | 6 | .843 | .926 | .476 |
| Within Groups | 277.566 | 305 | .910 | | |
| Total | 282.624 | 311 | | | |

H6. Youth that spend more time online will be less influenced by social media in their identity formation.

According to ANOVA test results there is a statistically significant difference among the dependent variable and the social media time exposure (p < .05). The F Ratio (2.738) and Sig. (.029) indicate a significant difference at the .05 level (Table 10). An inspection of the group shows that as time exposure in social media increases, social media identity formation scores will also increase. Based on these results, evidence was sufficient to reject the null hypothesis.

*Table 10. Mean comparison with social media identity as dependent and social media time exposure as independent variable*

| Descriptives | | | | | | | | |
|---|---|---|---|---|---|---|---|---|
| Social_media_identity | | | | | | | | |
| Social media Time exposure | N | Mean | Std. Deviation | Std. Error | 95% Confidence Interval for Mean | | Minimum | Maximum |
| | | | | | Lower Bound | Upper Bound | | |
| 10-30 min | 30 | 1.7250 | .91997 | .16796 | 1.3815 | 2.0685 | 1.00 | 5.00 |
| 30 min-2 hours | 60 | 1.6792 | .87466 | .11292 | 1.4532 | 1.9051 | 1.00 | 4.75 |
| 2-4 | 94 | 1.7048 | .89425 | .09223 | 1.5216 | 1.8879 | 1.00 | 5.00 |
| 4-6 hours | 65 | 1.9231 | .88490 | .10976 | 1.7038 | 2.1423 | 1.00 | 5.00 |
| up to 6 hours | 63 | 2.1389 | 1.12682 | .14197 | 1.8551 | 2.4227 | 1.00 | 5.00 |
| Total | 312 | 1.8349 | .95329 | .05397 | 1.7287 | 1.9411 | 1.00 | 5.00 |

| ANOVA | | | | | | | | |
|---|---|---|---|---|---|---|---|---|
| Social_media_identity | | | | | | | | |
| | Sum of Squares | df | Mean Square | F | Sig. | | | |
| Between Groups | 9.736 | 4 | 2.434 | 2.738 | .029 | | | |
| Within Groups | 272.888 | 307 | .889 | | | | | |
| Total | 282.624 | 311 | | | | | | |

H7. Youth that spent more time with their parent's will be less influenced by social media in their identity formation.

An ANOVA test revealed that for social media identity formation and time spent with the parents the value of significance is > .05 which explains that the groups are homogeneous (Table 11). These results indicate that time spent with parents is not significantly related to social media identity formation. Thus, the hypothesis is rejected.

*Table 11. Mean comparison with social media identity as dependent and family time as independent variable*

| ANOVA | | | | | |
|---|---|---|---|---|---|
| Social_media_identity and family time | | | | | |
| | Sum of Squares | df | Mean Square | F | Sig. |
| Between Groups | 1.272 | 3 | .424 | .464 | .707 |
| Within Groups | 281.352 | 308 | .913 | | |
| Total | 282.624 | 311 | | | |

## DISCUSSION

Internet use is growing rapidly amongst members of the overall population, specifically among youth. The study revealed that youth use the media mainly for identity search, identity construction, mutual communication, presence (on the network) and mutual recognition. Young people, through their interaction in the virtual world, at the end of the day, are looking for a new identity. The study found that youth are having issues with social media addiction but not being involved in manipulative behavior such as using multiple identities online. Even though multiple identities were not present the study found that social media usage matters in adolescent's identity formation. Changes in social media usage will be reflected with changes in identity formation. The more social media usage the more it will reflect identity formation. Specifically, the stronger the social media exposure, the less certain respondents are in regard to themselves and their values and beliefs are not consistent with who they are. The time exposure in social media was recognized as the most important variable in explaining the impact social media has on identity formation. As time exposure in social media increased, youths' identity became higher.

## Limitations

They study has certain limitations. First of all, the research might be questioned in regard to threats to external validity. The sample was based on a small non-random sample, so the research results may not be applicable to the whole population. Other than that, being a convenience sample, it does not reflect the ethnic diversity of North Macedonia. Having a larger sample would allow for more diverse and reliable results. Also, taking into consideration that social media are an integral part of youth life, it was difficult to find a control group of adolescents who do not use social media and compare data in regard to social media impact to identity formation. The study might also be subject to social desirability bias when discussing issues such as social media use and perception of their identity and self. Using an online survey might be considered as a limitation since respondents may be distracted and/or the survey not taken seriously. In the end, using only a quantitative approach does not allow one to deeply understand the impact of social media on identity. A method of triangulation would yield richer results.

## CONCLUSION

Communication, information gathering, entertainment, etc. are already dominated by digital media (Eichenberg & Auersperg, 2018, p. 8). The excessive use of digital media has a wide range of impacts on society and especially on future generations. Digital media not only affects mental and physical health, but also has a major impact on interpersonal behavior and social identity.

Based on this study we can conclude that the use of digital media can have a number of effects, especially for the youth of a society, who are in search of themselves, of defining themselves, in search of different models of identity and self-identity. The virtual world gives young people a variety of opportunities and models regarding their identity, and it is the youth who are highly influenced by online role models. They use them as inspiration to develop their own identity. The more models they have, it may result that they (adolescents) often change their identity and thus have large fluctuations in the formation of identity, i.e. it is no longer about one identity, but about multi-identities. The tasks of identity development in youth and adolescents are the same as before, although their implementation has changed significantly in modern times.

# REFERENCES

Abels, H. (2019). Identität. In: *Einführung in die Soziologie*. Studientexte zur Soziologie. Wiesbaden: Springer VS.c

Becker, H. C. (1999). The Chicago school, so-called. *Qualitative Sociology*, 22(1), 3–12. 10.1023/A:1022107414846

Bergemann, W. (2021). *Soziale Medien und Jugendliche. Massenexperiment mit offenem Ausgang.* Deutschlandfunk. https://www.deutschlandfunk.de/soziale-medien-und-jugendliche-massenexperiment -mit-offenem-100.html

BMFSFJ [Bundesministerium für Familie, Senioren, Frauen und Jugend] (2021). *Was ist Cybermobbing?* BMFSFJ. https://www.bmfsfj.de/bmfsfj/themen/kinder-und-jugend/medienkompetenz/was-ist -cybermobbing--86484

Breiter, A., Welling, S., & Stolpmann, B. E. (2010). *Medienkompetenz in der Schule. Integration von Medien in den weiterführenden Schulen in Nordrhein-Westfalen (Schriftenreihe Medienforschung der LfM, Bd. 64).* Berlin: Vistas Verl.

Burgess, M. (2021). *Inteligjenca artificiale – si do të përcaktohet dekada e ardhshme nga zhvillimi i sistemeve kompjuterike.* WIRED, Dukagjini, Prishtinë.

Cahill, S. E. (2004). Erving Goffman. In Charon, J. M. (Ed.), *Symbolic Interactionism: An Introduction, An Interpretation, An Integration* (pp. 175–188). Pearson Prentice Hall.

Collins, R. (1986). The passing of intellectual generations: Reflections on the death of Erving Goffman. *Sociological Theory*, 4(1), 106–113. 10.2307/202109

DAK. (2023). *DAK-Studie: In pandemie hat sich mediiensucht verdoppelt.* DAK. https://www.dak.de/ presse/bundesthemen/kinder-jugendgesundheit/dak-studie-in-pandemie-hat-sich-mediensucht-verdoppelt _48672#/

Eichenberg, C., & Auersperg, F. (2018). *Chancen und Risiken digitaler Medien für Kinder und Jugendliche: Ein Ratgeber für Eltern und Pädagogen.* Hogrefe. 10.1026/02647-000

Erikson, E. (1973). Identität und Lebenszyklus. Auflage. Frankfurt a. M.: Suhrkamp Verlag.

Goffman, E. (1956). Embarrassment and social organization. *American Journal of Sociology*, 62(3), 264–271. 10.1086/222003

Goffman, E. (1959). *The Presentation of Self in Everyday Life.* Doubleday Anchor Books.

Goffman, E. (1961/1973). *Asylums: Essays on the Social Situation of Mental Patients and Other Inmates.* Penguin.

Goffman, E. (1963). *Behavior in Public Places: Notes on the Social Organization of Gatherings.* The Free Press.

Goffman, E. (1963/1976). *Stigma: Notes on the Management of Spoiled Identity.* Penguin.

Goffman, E. (1967). *Interaction Ritual: Essays on Face-to-face Behavior.* Anchor Books and Doubleday.

Goffman, E. (1971). *Relations in Public: Microstudies of the Public Order*. Basic Books.

Goffman, E. (1978) The presentation of self in everyday life. London: Harmondsworth.

Goffman, E. (1996). *Wir alle spielen Theater: Die Selbstdarstellung im Alltag* (5th ed.). Piper.

GWI. (2017). *Digital vs. traditional media consumption: Analyzing time devoted to online and traditional forms of media at a global level, as well as by age and across countries*. Insight report. https://www.gwi .com/hubfs/Digital_vs_Traditional_Media_Consumption.pdf

Huang, Y. (2006). Identity and intimacy crises and their relationship to Internet dependence among college students. *Cyberpsychology & Behavior*, 9(5), 571–576. 10.1089/cpb.2006.9.57117034324

Jarosz, D. (2020). *Wie Soziale Medien das Selbstbild Jugendlicher beeinflussen*. Apomio.de. Gesundheits- blog. https://www.apomio.de/blog/artikel/wie-soziale-medien-das-selbstbild-jugendlicher-beeinflussen #perfektion, e hapur se fundmi ne date 10.03.2024.

Kemp, S. (2024). *Digital 2024: North Macedonia*. Datareportal. https://datareportal.com/reports/digital -2024-north-macedonia

Keupp, H. (2017). Identitätsarbeit als Balance von Eigenem und Fremden und die fatale Sehnsucht nach Reinheit. Evangelische Akademie Tutzing. https://www.ev-akademie-tutzing.de/static/media/attachments/ V201703-D84D461B18224264B796AE3A59240066/Beitrag%20Keupp%202017.pdf

Kidwell, J. S., Dunham, R. M., Bacho, R. A., Pastorino, E., & Portes, P. R. (1995). Adolescent identity exploration: A test of Erikson's theory of transitional crisis. *Adolescence*, 30, 785–793.8588516

Kivisto, P., & Pittman, D. (2007). Goffman's dramaturgical sociology. In *Illuminating social life: Classical and contemporary theory revisited* (pp. 271–290). SAGE Publications., https://www.sagepub.com/ sites/default/files/upm-binaries/16569_Chapter_10.pdf

Krappmann, L. (2000). *Soziologische Dimensionen der Identität. Strukturelle Bedingungen für die Teilnahme an Interaktionsprozessen*. Stuttgart: Klett-Cotta.

Leopold, M., & Ullmann, M. (2018). *Digitale Medien in der Kita. Alltagsintegrierte Medienbildung in der pädagogischen Praxis*. Herder Verlag.

Mead, G. H. (1973). Geist, Identität und Gesellschaft aus der Sicht des Sozialbehaviorismus. Frank- furt/M.: Suhrkamp.

Ophir, E., Nass, C., & Wagner, A. D. (2009). Cognitive control in media multitaskers. *Proceedings of the National Academy of Sciences of the United States of America*, 106(37), 15583–15587. 10.1073/ pnas.0903620106 19706386

Radiomof. (2023). *Младите ги користат социјалните мрежи за четување и видеа, ама не и за општествен активизам*. Radiomof. https://www.radiomof.mk/mladite-gi-koristat-socijalnite-mrezhi -za-chetuvanje-i-videa-ama-ne-i-za-opshtestven-aktivizam/

Rat der Europäischen Union. (2020). Schlussfolgerungen des Rates zur Medienkompetenz in einer sich ständig wandelnden *Welt: Official journal of EU*.https://eur-lex.europa.eu/legalcontent/DE/TXT/PDF/ ?uri=CELEX:52020XG0609(04)&from=EN, e hapur se fundmi ne date 04.03.2024.

Ruß-Mohl, S. (2017). Journalismus und Gemeinwohl in der Desinformationsökonomie. Plädoyer für eine „Alliance for Enlightenment" zwischen Wissenschaft und Journalismus. [ComSoc]. *Communicatio Socialis*, 50(1), 50–63. 10.5771/0010-3497-2017-1-50

Schorb, B. (2014). *Identität und Medien*. In A. Tillmann, S. Fleischer & K.-U. Hugger (Hrsg.), *Digitale Kultur und Kommunikation: Bd. 1. Handbuch Kinder und Medien* (f. 172–182). Springer VS. 10.1007/978-3-531-18997-0_13

Serafini, T. E., & Adams, G. R. (2002). Functions of identity: Scale construction and validation. *Identity*, 2(4), 363–391. 10.1207/S1532706XID0204_05

Song, J. (2023). Social media and it's impact on college students identity. *Communications in Humanities Research*, 10(1), 286–295. 10.54254/2753-7064/10/20231346

Valkenburg, P. M., & Peter, J. (2011). Online communication among adolescents: An integrated model of its attraction, opportunities, and risks. *The Journal of Adolescent Health*, 48(2), 121–127. 10.1016/j.jadohealth.2010.08.02021257109

Vrabotuvanje. (2022). *Колку македонци користат Facebook, Instagram, Twitter и LinkedIn*. Vrabotuvanje. https://www.vrabotuvanje.com.mk/Vest/22267/Kolku-makedonci-koristat-Facebook-Instagram-Twitter-i-LinkedIn/2/

Vybiral, Z., Smahel, D., & Divinova, R. (2004). Growing up in virtual reality - Adolescents and the Internet. In P. Mares (Ed.), *Society, reproduction and contemporary challenges* (pp. 169-188). Bnro: Barrister and Principal Publishing.

Williams, S. J. (1986). Appraising Goffman. *The British Journal of Sociology*, 37(3), 348–369. 10.2307/590645

Wilson, R. E., Gosling, S. D., & Graham, L. T. (2012). A review of Facebook research in the social sciences. *Perspectives on Psychological Science*, 7(3), 203–220. 10.1177/1745691612442904261684 59

Wirtz, M. (2016): *Identität, entwicklungspsychologische Perspektive*. Dorsch Lexikon der Psychologie. Hogrefe. https://dorsch.hogrefe.com/stichwort/identitaetentwicklungspsychologische-perspektive

Wong, B. (2023). Top social media statistics and trends of 2024. *Forbes advisor*. https://www.forbes.com/advisor/business/social-media-statistics/

## ENDNOTE

[1]    Digital native is a person who is very familiar with digital technology, computers, etc. because they have grown up with them (https://dictionary.cambridge.org/dictionary/english/digital-native)

# Chapter 22
# Youth Studes in the AI Era:
## Navigating Uncharted Territory

**Vijay Bhutani**
*Amity University, Greater Noida, India*

**Preeti Singh Bahadur**
*Amity University, Greater Noida, India*

**Sunil K. Sansaniwal**
 https://orcid.org/0000-0002-0997-5096
*The Energy and Resources Institute, New Delhi, India*

**Pratima Bais**
*Dr. C.V. Raman University, India*

## ABSTRACT

*The rapid advancement of Artificial Intelligence (AI) has significantly transformed various facets of contemporary society, and the impact on youth is particularly profound. The chapter will delve into the impact of AI on social interaction and identity formation among youth. Social media platforms powered by AI algorithms have revolutionized the way young people connect, communicate, and express themselves, shaping not only their social interactions but also their sense of self and identity. Furthermore, the chapter will explore the ethical implications of AI for youth, examining questions of privacy, autonomy, and agency in an increasingly data-driven world. With AI systems capable of collecting, analyzing, and interpreting vast amounts of personal data, concerns about surveillance, manipulation, and control loom large, raising profound questions about the rights and freedoms of young people in the digital age.*

## UNDERSTANDING YOUNG PEOPLE IN A TECHNOLOGICAL AGE

This section delves into the fascinating world of youth studies, laying the groundwork for examining how Artificial Intelligence (AI) is impacting the lives of young people today. By exploring the core concepts of youth studies, we gain a deeper understanding of the unique experiences, perspectives, and challenges faced by this dynamic generation. This knowledge becomes crucial as we investigate the ever-growing influence of AI on their lives. (Darvin, 2019)

DOI: 10.4018/979-8-3693-3350-1.ch022

*Figure 1. Youth and AI*

## WHAT ARE YOUTH STUDIES?

Youth studies is a vibrant interdisciplinary field dedicated to understanding the complexities of young people's lives. It encompasses various social sciences, including sociology, psychology, anthropology, and education. (Woodman, 2012) This field examines a broad spectrum of topics relevant to youth, such as:

- **Identity formation:** How young people develop their sense of self, navigate social pressures, and explore their place in the world.
- **Education and career trajectories:** The educational pathways young people take, their career aspirations, and the challenges they face in the job market.
- **Social and cultural influences:** The impact of family, peers, media, and technology on shaping young people's values, beliefs, and behaviours.
- **Health and well-being:** The physical and mental health concerns affecting young people, including issues like mental health disorders, substance abuse, and access to healthcare.
- **Civic engagement and political participation:** The ways young people engage with their communities, participate in activism, and influence social change.

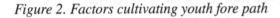

*Figure 2. Factors cultivating youth fore path*

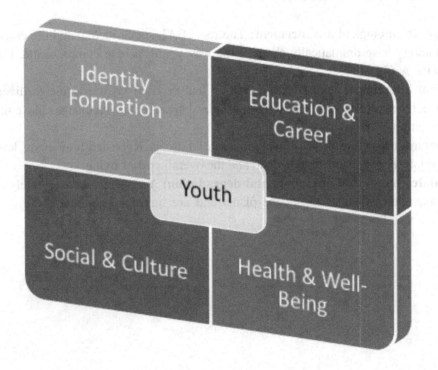

## WHY IS STUDYING YOUTH IMPORTANT?

Youth are not simply a passive demographic group; they are active agents of change. Understanding their experiences allows us to:

- **Develop effective policies and support systems:** By recognizing the needs and challenges young people face, we can create policies that promote their well-being, educational attainment, and economic opportunities.
- **Bridge the communication gap:** The knowledge gained from youth studies helps adults – educators, policymakers, parents – better understand and connect with young people.
- **Empower young people:** Youth studies can empower young people by acknowledging their perspectives and encouraging their participation in shaping their own future. (Woodman, 2012)

## THE UNIQUENESS OF THE YOUTH EXPERIENCE

Young people today are navigating a world vastly different from that of previous generations. Several factors contribute to this unique experience:

- **Rapid technological advancement:** The rise of AI, social media, and the constant presence of technology have dramatically changed the way young people communicate, learn, and interact with the world.
- **Global interconnectedness:** Globalization has exposed young people to diverse cultures and perspectives, broadening their horizons while also presenting challenges like cultural clashes and information overload.
- **Economic uncertainty:** The global economic landscape is constantly evolving, leading to concerns about job security, student loan debt, and the overall cost of living.
- **Climate change and environmental degradation:** Young people are acutely aware of the environmental challenges facing the planet and are increasingly vocal about demanding action. (Woodman, 2012)

*Figure 3. Youth studies architecture*

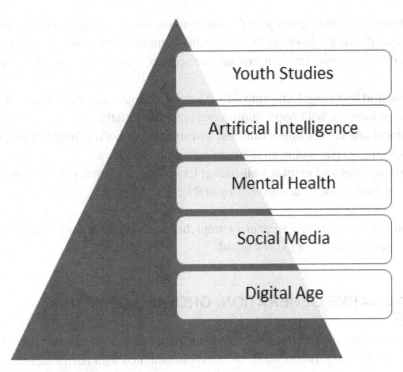

## EXAMPLES OF HOW YOUTH STUDIES INFORMS OUR UNDERSTANDING

Let's consider a few specific examples of how youth studies inform our understanding of young people and the impact of AI:

- **The Impact of Social Media on Mental Health:** Research in youth studies has explored the complex relationship between social media use and mental health concerns like anxiety and depression among young people. This understanding allows for the development of interventions and strategies to promote responsible social media use and enhance online safety. (Zhou et al., 2021)
- **The Rise of "Cyberbullying":** Youth studies have shed light on the phenomenon of cyberbullying and its detrimental effects on young people's emotional well-being. This knowledge informs the development of educational programs to combat cyberbullying and promote online empathy and respect.
- **The Potential of AI in Education:** AI-powered educational tools like personalized learning platforms and intelligent tutoring systems hold immense promise for creating more engaging and effective learning experiences. However, youth studies research helps ensure that these tools are implemented ethically and with a focus on human-centred learning. (Chen et al., 2020)

## THE STAGE IS SET: EXAMINING AI AND THE YOUTH LANDSCAPE

By understanding the core concepts of youth studies, we have established a strong foundation for exploring the multifaceted role of AI in shaping the contemporary youth landscape. In the following sections, we will delve deeper into this crucial intersection, examining how AI is impacting

- **Education and learning:** Exploring how AI-powered tools are influencing the way young people learn, with a focus on both opportunities and potential pitfalls.
- **Employment and career opportunities:** Investigating how AI is transforming the workforce and the skills young people will need to be successful in the future.
- **Social interactions and mental well-being:** Examining the impact of AI on young people's social interactions, online safety, and overall mental health.

By analyzing these areas, we can gain a comprehensive understanding of the complex relationship between young people and AI in today's world.

## THE DIGITAL NATIVE GENERATION: GROWING UP WITH AI

Today's youth, frequently referred to as "digital natives," have never known a world without the constant presence of technology. Born into an environment saturated with Artificial Intelligence (AI)-driven tools, their experiences, perspectives, and challenges are fundamentally shaped by this digital immersion. This chapter explores the multifaceted impact of this reality on three key aspects of their development: identity formation, social relationships, and critical thinking skills.(Garcia et al., 2015)

### Identity in the Digital Age

Digital immersion presents both opportunities and challenges for young people as they navigate the complex process of identity formation. Here's a closer look:

- **Curating the Self:** Social media platforms provide young people with a platform to explore and express their identities. However, a 2021 Pew Research Center survey found that 71% of teens feel pressure to project a perfect online image, potentially leading to feelings of inadequacy and anxiety.
- **The "Highlight Reel" Effect:** Social media feeds often showcase the best moments of others' lives, creating a distorted comparison and impacting self-esteem. A 2018 University of Pennsylvania study found that increased social media use correlated with decreased life satisfaction among young adults.
- **Exploration and Experimentation:** On the other hand, digital spaces offer avenues for young people to explore diverse identities and connect with like-minded communities. Platforms like online gaming communities can foster a sense of belonging and acceptance, particularly for those who may feel marginalized in traditional social settings. (Garcia et al., 2015)

## Social Relationships in a Wired World

The way young people build and maintain social relationships is also being significantly influenced by the digital world:

- **Rise of Online Communication:** Platforms like social media and messaging apps have become primary tools for communication among young people. A 2022 study by the Center for Generational Kinetics found that 80% of Gen Z report using social media daily, blurring the lines between online and offline interactions.
- **Benefits of Connectivity:** These digital platforms facilitate connection with friends and family geographically dispersed, fostering a sense of community and belonging. Social media can also serve as a valuable tool for organizing activities and events, strengthening social bonds.
- **Challenges of Digital Disconnect:** Overreliance on digital communication can negatively affect face-to-face social skills. A 2019 study published in Computers in Human Behavior found a correlation between increased social media use and decreased empathy and emotional intelligence. (Kumar Paur et al., n.d.)

## Critical Thinking in the Information Age

The development of critical thinking skills – the ability to analyze information, identify bias, and form independent judgments – is crucial in today's information-saturated world. Here's how the digital environment impacts this development:

- **Information Overload:** Young people are bombarded with information from a multitude of sources, both reliable and unreliable. A 2020 report by Stanford University's History Education Project found that students struggle to distinguish between credible and fabricated information online.
- **The Rise of "Fake News":** The spread of misinformation and "fake news" on social media platforms presents a significant challenge. A 2023 study by the MIT Media Lab found that AI-generated synthetic media, like deepfakes, can further exacerbate the spread of misinformation.
- **Potential for AI-powered Learning Tools:** AI-powered tools like personalized learning platforms and intelligent tutoring systems have the potential to enhance critical thinking skills by encouraging analysis and evaluation of information. However, these tools must be designed to cultivate critical thinking rather than simply providing pre-packaged answers. (Rubin, 2012)

## Quantitative Data Insights

Several studies offer quantitative data highlighting the impact of digital immersion on young people:

- **Screen Time:** A 2023 report by Common Sense Media found that on average, teenagers in the US spend over 8 hours per day using digital media.
- **Social Media Usage:** According to a 2022 Statista report, 90% of teens aged 13-17 in the US have used social media at least once.

- **Mental Health Concerns:** A 2021 report by the Centers for Disease Control and Prevention (CDC) found that rates of depression and anxiety among adolescents have increased significantly in recent years. While a causal link with digital technology use cannot be definitively established, research suggests a correlation. (Threadgold, 2020)

## The Way Forward

Understanding the complexities of digital immersion on the development of young people is vital. Parents, educators, and policymakers need to work together to create a balanced approach:

- **Promoting Digital Literacy:** Equipping young people with critical thinking skills and media literacy is crucial for navigating the digital world effectively. Educational programs should focus on identifying bias, evaluating information sources, and responsible online behavior.
- **Harnessing the Potential of AI:**

  - AI-powered tools can be used to personalize learning experiences, promoting critical thinking through interactive exercises and problem-solving activities.
  - However, it's important to ensure these tools are designed ethically, with a focus on human-centered learning that encourages curiosity, exploration, and independent thought.

- **Creating Supportive Environments:**

  - Parents and educators can foster open communication about challenges faced online, creating a safe space for young people to seek help and guidance.
  - Encouraging participation in extracurricular activities and hobbies can provide opportunities for social development and foster a sense of belonging beyond the digital world. (France & Roberts, 2015)

The digital native generation is growing up in a world fundamentally shaped by AI-driven technologies. While digital immersion presents both opportunities and challenges for their development, a proactive approach can ensure that young people are well-equipped to navigate the complexities of the digital age. By promoting digital literacy, harnessing the potential of AI for learning, and creating supportive environments, we can empower young people to thrive in this rapidly evolving technological landscape.

The future holds immense possibilities for the relationship between AI and young people. As AI continues to evolve, future chapters will explore topics like:

- The rise of AI-powered companionship tools and their potential impact on social development.
- The ethical considerations surrounding AI use in education, including issues of bias and data privacy.
- The potential of AI for fostering creativity, innovation, and problem-solving skills in young people. (Wyn & Woodman, 2007)

By fostering an ongoing conversation about these issues, we can ensure that AI serves as a force for positive change in the lives of young people and the world they will inherit.

# EDUCATION IN THE AI ERA: REIMAGINING LEARNING WITH ARTIFICIAL INTELLIGENCE

The educational landscape is undergoing a significant transformation fuelled by the rise of Artificial Intelligence (AI). This chapter delves into how AI is influencing both formal and informal learning environments, exploring its potential benefits and challenges.

## The Promise of AI in Education

AI holds immense potential to personalize and enhance learning experiences for young people:

- **Personalized Learning:** AI-powered platforms can analyze student data to identify strengths, weaknesses, and learning styles. This allows for the creation of personalized learning paths, catering to individual needs and fostering self-directed learning.
- **Intelligent Tutoring Systems:** AI-powered tutors can provide students with real-time feedback, answer questions, and offer guidance throughout the learning process. These systems can be particularly beneficial for students who may need extra support or those in geographically isolated areas.
- **Adaptive Learning Tools:** AI can be used to create adaptive learning environments that adjust the difficulty of learning materials based on a student's performance. This ensures a constant challenge and promotes deeper understanding.
- **Skill Development for the Future:** AI can be utilized to develop critical skills required in the AI era, such as coding, data analysis, and problem-solving. Interactive AI tools can create engaging learning experiences that equip young people for the future workforce. (Wood, 2017)

*Figure 4. AI market size in youth studies*

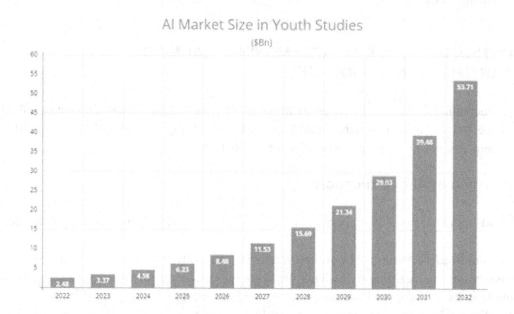

## Examples of AI in Action

- **DreamBox Learning:** This AI-powered platform uses adaptive learning techniques to personalize math instruction for students.
- **Duolingo:** This popular language learning app utilizes AI to personalize learning paths and provide targeted feedback to users.
- **IBM SkillsBuild:** This program offers free online courses on AI, cloud computing, and other in-demand skills, leveraging AI-powered learning tools to enhance the user experience. (McGarry, 2016)

## Quantitative Data on AI's Impact

- A 2022 study by the McKinsey Global Institute found that AI-powered personalized learning has the potential to increase student learning gains by up to 50%.
- A 2021 report by the World Economic Forum projects that by 2030, AI could create 5 million new jobs in the education sector, highlighting the increasing demand for AI-skilled educators.

## Challenges and Considerations

While AI offers exciting possibilities for education, there are also challenges that need to be addressed:

- **Privacy Concerns:** The use of student data in AI-powered educational tools raises concerns about student privacy and data security. Ensuring transparency and robust data protection measures are crucial.
- **Access and Equity:** Not all schools and students have equal access to technology and high-speed internet connectivity. This could exacerbate the existing digital divide, creating educational disparities.
- **The Role of the Teacher:** AI should not replace educators but rather augment their role. Teachers will need training and support to effectively integrate AI tools into their teaching practices.
- **The Potential for Bias:** AI algorithms can inherit biases from the data they are trained on. Careful design and monitoring are essential to avoid perpetuating biases in education. (Roll & Wylie, 2016)

## Moving Forward with Responsibility

To fully realize the potential of AI in education, a responsible and ethical approach is necessary:

- **Investment in Digital Infrastructure:** Bridging the digital divide requires investment in ensuring all students have access to high-speed internet and digital devices.
- **Developing Ethical Guidelines:** Clear ethical guidelines are needed regarding data collection, use, and student privacy in AI-powered education platforms.
- **Teacher Training and Support:** Educators need training on integrating AI tools into their teaching practices effectively while fostering human-centred learning environments.
- **Continuous Evaluation and Improvement:** Ongoing evaluation of AI tools is crucial to ensure their effectiveness, mitigate potential biases, and adapt them to changing educational needs. (Greenwald et al., 2021a)

The integration of AI into education is an ongoing journey. By embracing the potential benefits while addressing the existing challenges, AI can become a powerful tool for promoting personalized learning, equipping young people with the skills they need to thrive in the AI era, and creating a more equitable and effective education system for all.

# YOUTH EMPLOYMENT AND THE GIG ECONOMY: NAVIGATING WORK IN THE AGE OF AI

The landscape of work is undergoing a significant transformation driven by Artificial Intelligence (AI). This chapter explores how young people are navigating this evolving landscape, specifically focusing on the rise of the gig economy and the increasing reliance on AI-driven tools within traditional workplaces. We will also examine the critical role of education in preparing young people for success in an AI-centric job market. (McLeod, 2009)

## The Rise of the Gig Economy and Youth

The gig economy, characterized by temporary or freelance work arrangements, has emerged as a prominent feature of the modern workforce. Young people, often seeking flexibility and autonomy, are drawn to the gig economy in significant numbers:

- **Statistics:** A 2023 study by the International Labour Organization (ILO) found that young people (aged 16-24) represent a disproportionate share of the gig economy, with an estimated global prevalence rate of 29.1%.
- **Motivations:** Factors like the ability to set their own hours, work remotely, and potentially earn higher incomes compared to traditional entry-level jobs make the gig economy attractive to young people.
- **Examples:** Popular gig economy platforms like Uber, Lyft, Fiverr, and Upwork provide opportunities for young people to engage in freelance work like driving, content creation, and graphic design. (Mukhopadhyay & Chakrabarti, 2023)

However, the gig economy also presents challenges for young workers:

- **Job Insecurity and Lack of Benefits:** Gig workers often lack the stability and benefits associated with traditional employment, such as health insurance, paid sick leave, and unemployment benefits.
- **Uncertain Income Streams:** Earnings in the gig economy can be unpredictable and fluctuate depending on demand.
- **Lack of Training and Development:** Gig work typically provides limited opportunities for professional development and skill-building.

## AI in the Workplace and its Impact on Youth

AI is rapidly transforming traditional workplaces, impacting the nature of work and the skills required for success:

- **Automation and Job Displacement:** Some tasks traditionally performed by humans are being automated by AI, raising concerns about potential job displacement, particularly for young people entering the workforce with limited experience.

- **Demand for New Skills:** AI is creating a demand for new skills, such as data analysis, coding, and the ability to work effectively with AI tools.
- **Upskilling and Reskilling:** Young people need to be adaptable and willing to continuously learn and develop new skills to remain competitive in the AI-driven job market. (D'Alfonso et al., 2017)

Examples of AI in the Workplace:

- **Customer Service Chatbots:** AI-powered chatbots are increasingly used to answer customer queries and provide basic customer service, potentially impacting entry-level customer service jobs traditionally filled by young people.
- **AI-powered Recruitment Tools:** Companies are using AI to automate resume screening and candidate evaluation processes, potentially creating new opportunities for young people with the right skillsets.
- **Augmented Reality (AR) Training Tools:** AR technology powered by AI can create immersive training experiences for young workers, enhancing their skill development and knowledge acquisition. (Hasse et al., 2019)

## The Role of Education in Preparing Youth

Education plays a crucial role in equipping young people with the skills and knowledge necessary to thrive in the AI era:

- **STEM Education (Science, Technology, Engineering, and Math):** A strong foundation in STEM education is essential for young people to understand the principles of AI and its applications across various industries.
- **Critical Thinking and Problem-Solving Skills:** The ability to critically analyze information, solve complex problems, and think creatively is vital for success in an AI-driven world.
- **Adaptability and Lifelong Learning:** The rapid pace of technological change necessitates an emphasis on lifelong learning and the ability to adapt to new skills and challenges.
- **Entrepreneurship and Innovation:** As the gig economy continues to grow, fostering entrepreneurial skills and encouraging innovation will be crucial for young people to create their own opportunities. (Feldman-Barrett, 2018)

Quantitative Data on Education and AI:

- A 2022 report by the World Economic Forum estimates that by 2030, AI could create 85 million new jobs globally, highlighting the need for education systems to adapt and prepare young people for these new roles.
- A 2021 study by the Pew Research Center found that 73% of Americans believe that colleges and universities should be doing more to prepare students for the future of work.

The gig economy and AI are reshaping the world of work for young people. While challenges exist, there are also immense opportunities. By equipping themselves with the necessary skills and knowledge through a robust and adaptable education system, young people can be empowered to navigate the evolving landscape of work and thrive in the AI era. (Frey et al., 2020)

*Figure 5. Elemental share of AI in education*

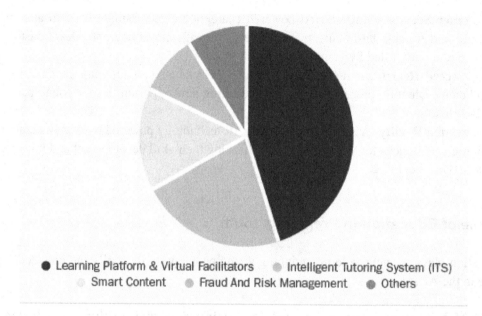

● Learning Platform & Virtual Facilitators    ● Intelligent Tutoring System (ITS)
    ● Smart Content    ● Fraud And Risk Management    ● Others

## SOCIAL MEDIA, MENTAL HEALTH, AND DIGITAL WELL-BEING: NAVIGATING THE ALGORITHMIC AGE

Social media platforms, increasingly powered by AI algorithms, have become a ubiquitous feature of young people's lives. While they offer avenues for connection, self-expression, and information sharing, these platforms can also have a significant impact on mental health and digital well-being. This chapter examines the complex relationship between young people, social media, and mental well-being, focusing on the potential pitfalls of AI-driven algorithms and strategies for promoting digital well-being. (Zhou et al., 2021)

### Algorithmic Biases and the "Filtered Reality"

AI algorithms curate social media feeds, potentially creating a distorted sense of reality for young people:

- **Echo Chambers and Confirmation Bias:** Algorithms can personalize content based on past interactions and preferences, creating echo chambers where users are primarily exposed to information and perspectives that reinforce their existing beliefs. This can limit their exposure to diverse viewpoints and hinder critical thinking.

- **The "Highlight Reel" Effect:** Social media feeds often showcase the best moments of others' lives, creating an unrealistic portrayal of happiness and success. This can foster feelings of inadequacy and social comparison among young people, potentially leading to anxiety and depression. (Frey et al., 2020)

## Examples of Algorithmic Bias

- A 2021 study by the Algorithmic Justice League found that social media algorithms can amplify negative stereotypes and discriminatory content, impacting young people's perceptions of themselves and others based on race, gender, or sexual orientation.
- A 2022 report by the Wall Street Journal revealed how Instagram algorithms can prioritize content that promotes unrealistic beauty standards, potentially contributing to body image issues and negative self-esteem among young users. (Greenwald et al., 2021b)

## Quantitative Data on Social Media and Mental Health

- A 2022 study published in the Journal of Youth and Adolescence found a positive correlation between increased social media use and symptoms of depression and anxiety among teenagers.
- A 2021 survey by the Pew Research Center found that nearly a third (32%) of teenagers in the US report feeling overwhelmed or anxious due to the pressures of social media.

## The Role of Technology in Shaping Perceptions

Social media platforms, with their constant notifications and pressure to maintain an online presence, can negatively impact young people's self-perception and relationships:

- **Cyberbullying and Online Harassment:** The anonymity offered by online platforms can embolden cyberbullying and harassment, leading to emotional distress and social isolation for young people.
- **Fear of Missing Out (FOMO):** The constant stream of updates about others' activities can create a fear of missing out (FOMO), leading to feelings of inadequacy and anxiety about social exclusion.
- **Addiction and Sleep Disruption:** Social media platforms can be highly addictive, leading to excessive screen time and sleep disruptions, further impacting mental health and well-being.

Examples of the Impact on Relationships:

- A 2020 study by the University of Pennsylvania found that increased social media use was associated with a decline in empathy and emotional intelligence among young adults, potentially hindering their ability to build and maintain healthy social relationships.
- A 2023 report by the Kaiser Family Foundation found that teenagers who spend more time on social media report feeling more lonely or isolated than their peers who use social media less frequently.

## Strategies for Promoting Digital Well-Being

Promoting digital well-being among young people in the age of AI-powered social media requires a multifaceted approach:

- **Mindful Social Media Use:** Encouraging young people to be mindful of their social media use, setting boundaries on screen time, and prioritizing face-to-face interactions can promote mental well-being.
- **Media Literacy Education:** Equipping young people with critical thinking skills and media literacy is crucial for them to evaluate information online, identify bias, and be discerning consumers of social media content.
- **Promoting Positive Online Communities:** Supporting young people in finding positive online communities that foster self-expression and interaction based on shared interests rather than social comparison can enhance their online experiences.
- **Parental Support and Open Communication:** Open communication between parents and children about online experiences and potential pitfalls is essential for promoting responsible social media use and emotional well-being.

Social media can be a powerful tool for young people, but it is essential to be aware of its potential downsides and actively promote digital well-being. By fostering critical thinking skills, encouraging mindful social media use, and creating supportive online and offline environments, we can empower young people to navigate the complexities of social media platforms and prioritize their mental health in a world increasingly driven by AI. (Zhang et al., 2024)

## ETHICAL CONSIDERATIONS AND EMPOWERMENT: SHAPING THE FUTURE WITH AI

While AI holds immense potential for young people, its integration raises significant ethical concerns. This chapter delves into these concerns, focusing on data privacy, algorithmic bias, and the empowering role of digital literacy. Additionally, it explores how young people can actively participate in shaping the responsible development and use of AI technologies. (Memmedova & Selahattin, 2018)

## Data Privacy and the "Digital Footprint"

The ubiquitous presence of AI necessitates careful consideration of data privacy:

- **Data Collection and Use:** AI systems rely on vast amounts of data, raising concerns about how young people's data is collected, stored, and used. Transparency and consent are crucial to protect privacy rights.
- **The "Digital Footprint":** Every online interaction creates a "digital footprint" that can follow young people throughout their lives. Ensuring young people understand how their data is used and have control over it is essential.

Examples of Data Privacy Concerns:

- A 2022 report by the Center for Democracy & Technology found that popular social media platforms often collect and share vast amounts of user data, including teenagers, raising concerns about potential misuse or breaches.
- A 2021 investigation by The New York Times revealed how facial recognition technology, powered by AI, is increasingly used in schools, raising privacy concerns and ethical questions about student surveillance.

Quantitative Data on Data Privacy:

- A 2023 survey by ExpressVPN found that 72% of teenagers globally are concerned about how companies use their personal data online.
- A 2022 study by Pew Research Center showed that 81% of parents in the US are either very or somewhat concerned about the amount of personal information their teenagers share online.

## Algorithmic Bias and Fairness

Algorithmic bias, when algorithms perpetuate existing societal biases based on the data they are trained on, can have a significant impact on young people:

- **Unfair Outcomes:** Biased algorithms can lead to unfair outcomes for young people in areas like education, job opportunities, and access to resources.
- **Limited Diversity in AI Development:** The lack of diversity among AI developers can further exacerbate algorithmic bias if the perspectives and experiences of young people from diverse backgrounds are not adequately represented in the development process.

Examples of Algorithmic Bias:

- A 2020 study by ProPublica revealed that an AI-powered risk assessment tool used in the criminal justice system showed racial bias, disproportionately flagging Black defendants as high risk.
- A 2022 report by Algorithmic Justice League found that AI-powered facial recognition software had higher error rates when identifying people of color, highlighting the potential for biased outcomes impacting young people.

## Empowering Youth through Digital Literacy

By promoting digital literacy and critical thinking skills, we can empower young people to navigate the ethical complexities of AI:

- **Understanding AI Systems:** Educating young people about how AI systems function, their limitations, and potential biases equips them to be discerning users of AI-powered technologies.
- **Advocacy and Participation:** Encouraging young people to voice their concerns and participate in discussions about the ethical development and use of AI ensures their perspectives are heard.
- **Innovation and Problem-Solving:** Young people can be powerful agents of positive change by using their creativity and technical skills to develop AI solutions that address social challenges and promote equitable outcomes.

Examples of Youth-Led AI Initiatives:

- The AI Youth Summit is a global initiative that empowers young people to explore AI responsibly, encouraging innovation, ethical thinking, and participation in shaping the future of AI.
- The #YouControlYourData campaign is led by young activists advocating for stronger data privacy regulations and user control over personal data collection and use.

AI is rapidly transforming the world around young people. While ethical concerns require careful consideration, empowering young people with digital literacy skills and encouraging their active participation are crucial for shaping the future of AI in a way that is responsible, inclusive, and promotes the well-being of all. By working together, we can ensure that AI becomes a force for positive change in the lives of young people.

## SHAPING THE FUTURE OF YOUTH IN THE AGE OF AI

This chapter has explored the multifaceted impact of Artificial Intelligence (AI) on today's youth, the "digital native" generation. We have delved into the influence of AI on identity formation, social relationships, critical thinking development, education, employment prospects, mental health, and ethical considerations.

Key Insights:

- **The digital environment presents both opportunities and challenges for young people.** AI offers tools for self-expression, learning, and connection, but also carries risks of social comparison, information overload, and privacy concerns.
- **Education plays a pivotal role in equipping young people for the AI era.** Promoting digital literacy, critical thinking skills, and adaptability will be crucial for success in the evolving job market.
- **The rise of the gig economy necessitates a focus on lifelong learning and upskilling.** Young people need to be adaptable and prepared to acquire new skills as AI continues to shape the workplace.

- **Mental health and well-being must be prioritized in the age of AI.** Social media platforms can have a significant impact on self-esteem and social connection. Promoting mindful technology use and fostering supportive environments are essential.
- **Ethical considerations around data privacy, algorithmic bias, and transparency are paramount.** Young people deserve to have control over their data and participate in discussions about the responsible development and use of AI.

Considerations for the Future:

- **Researchers:** Continued research is crucial to understand the long-term impact of AI on young people's development, both positive and negative.
- **Educators:** Integrating AI literacy into curriculum, fostering critical thinking, and promoting responsible technology use are essential components of preparing young people for the future.
- **Policymakers:** Developing policies that protect children's data privacy, promote algorithmic fairness, and encourage responsible AI development are necessary safeguards.
- **Parents and Guardians:** Open communication about online experiences, setting healthy boundaries for technology use, and fostering digital well-being are crucial for supporting young people in the digital age.

## A Nuanced Understanding

This exploration contributes to the ongoing dialogue about youth and AI. By acknowledging the challenges and opportunities presented by AI, we can create a more nuanced understanding of its impact. This, in turn, will inform initiatives and discussions that empower young people to thrive in the ever-evolving landscape of the digital era.

## Fostering Discussions and Initiatives

This chapter serves as a call to action. By fostering open discussions across sectors – researchers, educators, policymakers, parents, and young people themselves – we can create a collaborative environment. Through these collaborative efforts, we can ensure that AI becomes a force for positive change in the lives of young people, empowering them to become responsible digital citizens, innovators, and active participants in shaping the future. The journey of integrating AI into the lives of young people has just begun. By working together, we can create a future where AI serves as a powerful tool for learning, growth, and positive change for all.

# REFERENCES

Bahadur, P. S. (2024). Analysis on Various Aspects of Internet of Nano-Things (IoNT), Its Integration in Machine Learning, and Its Diverse Applications. In *Next Generation Materials for Sustainable Engineering* (pp. 297-315). IGI Global.

Bahadur, P. S., Singh, S., Bais, P., & Jaiswal, S. Laser in textile industry and its application, (2023) *Asian Textile Journal, 32* (3-4), pp. 50-54. https://www.atjournal.com/current-issues.html

Bais, P., Bahadur, P. S., & Sharma, S. (2023). Production and market development of sericulture. *Asian Textile Journal*, 32(7), 46–52.

Bhutani, V., Bahadur, P. S., & Sansaniwal, S. K. (2024). Next Generation Materials for Sustainable Development. In *Harnessing High-Performance Computing and AI for Environmental Sustainability* (pp. 236-265). IGI Global. 10.4018/979-8-3693-1794-5.ch011

Chen, L., Chen, P., & Lin, Z. (2020). Artificial Intelligence in Education: A Review. *IEEE Access : Practical Innovations, Open Solutions*, 8, 75264–75278. 10.1109/ACCESS.2020.2988510

D'Alfonso, S., Santesteban-Echarri, O., Rice, S., Wadley, G., Lederman, R., Miles, C., Gleeson, J., & Alvarez-Jimenez, M. (2017). Artificial intelligence-assisted online social therapy for youth mental health. *Frontiers in Psychology*, 8(JUN), 796. 10.3389/fpsyg.2017.0079628626431

Darvin, R. (2019). Youth, Technology, and the Hidden Curriculum of the 21st Century. *Youth and Globalization*, 1(2), 210–229. 10.1163/25895745-00102002

Feldman-Barrett, C. (2018). Back to the future: Mapping a historic turn in youth studies. *Journal of Youth Studies*, 21(6), 733–746. 10.1080/13676261.2017.1420150

France, A., & Roberts, S. (2015). The problem of social generations: A critique of the new emerging orthodoxy in youth studies. *Journal of Youth Studies*, 18(2), 215–230. 10.1080/13676261.2014.944122

Frey, W. R., Patton, D. U., Gaskell, M. B., & McGregor, K. A. (2020). Artificial Intelligence and Inclusion: Formerly Gang-Involved Youth as Domain Experts for Analyzing Unstructured Twitter Data. *Social Science Computer Review*, 38(1), 42–56. 10.1177/0894439318788831436061240

Garcia, A., Mirra, N., Morrell, E., Martinez, A., & Scorza, D. (2015). The Council of Youth Research: Critical Literacy and Civic Agency in the Digital Age. *Reading & Writing Quarterly*, 31(2), 151–167. 10.1080/10573569.2014.962203

Greenwald, E., Leitner, M., & Wang, N. (2021a). *Learning Artificial Intelligence: Insights into How Youth Encounter and Build Understanding of AI Concepts.* AAAI. www.aaai.org

Greenwald, E., Leitner, M., & Wang, N. (2021b). *Learning Artificial Intelligence: Insights into How Youth Encounter and Build Understanding of AI Concepts.* AAAI. www.aaai.org

Hasse, A., Cortesi, S., Lombana-Bermudez, A., & Gasser, U. (2019). *Youth and Artificial Intelligence: Where We Stand.* Harvard Press. https://cyber.harvard.edu/publication/2019/youth-and-

Kumar Paur, S., Das, K., Kumar Paul, S., & Professor, A. (n.d.). Technological Advancement: A Study on the Changing Scenario among Tribal Youth. In *Journal of the Anthropological Survey of India, 64(2).*

McGarry, O. (2016). Repositioning the research encounter: Exploring power dynamics and positionality in youth research. *International Journal of Social Research Methodology*, 19(3), 339–354. 10.1080/13645579.2015.1011821

McLeod, J. (2009). Youth Studies, Comparative Inquiry, and the Local/Global Problematic. *Review of Education, Pedagogy & Cultural Studies*, 31(4), 270–292. 10.1080/10714410903132840

Memmedova, K., & Selahattin, E. L. (2018). Effects of the technology use on anxiety and aggression levels of youth conducting their higher education studies abroad. *Quality & Quantity*, 52(S1), 501–507. 10.1007/s11135-017-0630-4

Mukhopadhyay, S., & Chakrabarti, A. (2023). A Review on the Impacts of Artificial Intelligence (AI) on Youth. In *Handbook of Youth Development* (pp. 195–207). Springer Nature Singapore. 10.1007/978-981-99-4969-4_11

Roll, I., & Wylie, R. (2016). Evolution and Revolution in Artificial Intelligence in Education. *International Journal of Artificial Intelligence in Education*, 26(2), 582–599. 10.1007/s40593-016-0110-3

Rubin, J. (2012). Technology's Impact on the Creative Potential of Youth. *Creativity Research Journal*, 24(2–3), 252–256. 10.1080/10400419.2012.677370

Threadgold, S. (2020). Figures of youth: On the very object of Youth Studies. *Journal of Youth Studies*, 23(6), 686–701. 10.1080/13676261.2019.1636014

Wood, B. E. (2017). Youth studies, citizenship and transitions: Towards a new research agenda. *Journal of Youth Studies*, 20(9), 1176–1190. 10.1080/13676261.2017.1316363

Woodman, D. (2012). *Youth Studies*. Routledge. 10.4324/9780203862094

Wyn, J., & Woodman, D. (2007). Researching Youth in a Context of Social Change: A Reply to Roberts. *Journal of Youth Studies*, 10(3), 373–381. 10.1080/13676260701342624

Zhang, H., Chai, J., & Li, C. (2024). On innovative strategies of youth sports teaching and training based on the internet of things and artificial intelligence technology from the perspective of humanism. *Learning and Motivation*, 86, 101969. 10.1016/j.lmot.2024.101969

Zhou, X., Edirippulige, S., Bai, X., & Bambling, M. (2021). Are online mental health interventions for youth effective? A systematic review. *Journal of Telemedicine and Telecare*, 27(10), 638–666. 10.1177/1357633X21104728534726992

# Chapter 23
# Screen Time and Identity Formation:
## A Digital Dilemma

**Ismail Baydili**
*Firat University, Turkey*

## ABSTRACT

*Artificial intelligence, one of the significant developments of our era, has a profound impact on many areas. These new companions frequently encountered in our daily lives facilitate many aspects of our lives. However, beyond the conveniences they provide, they also affect our identity and personality. The impact of digital tools is particularly significant for 'digital natives,' who were born in the digital age and have grown up using them. It is more inevitable and crucial for them than for other individuals. Young people who lack sufficient life experience and have not had enough human-to-human interaction may develop a communication pattern devoid of emotions and empathy by transitioning to human-machine experiences. This could have a profound impact on both individuals and society. Rather than creating machines that think and feel like humans, we may end up with humans who think and live like machines. This study examines the effects of artificial intelligence on human interaction, identity, and personality.*

## INTRODUCTION

By their very nature, humans are social beings and require other individuals to sustain their sociability. Indeed, in developmental processes that we can express as self-completion, especially for young individuals, the importance of human-to-human interaction is even more significant. The "social identity theory" argues that a part of human identity consists of connections within social groups. According to the theory, when an individual is aware of belonging to a social group, they experience various positive emotions, such as trust and value, more intensely (Tajfel & Turner, 1978). However, the human-to-human impact underlined by the theory has been decreasing recently due to digitalization. Considering the developments brought about by artificial intelligence, it has been observed that human-machine interaction is increasing instead of human-to-human interaction. This change particularly affects the identity and personality formation of young individuals. The socialization activities and spaces experienced by previous generations during childhood have started to disappear today. Childhood playmates and the

DOI: 10.4018/979-8-3693-3350-1.ch023

sharing of experiences with them have been replaced by digital tools, taking away the opportunities for children to socialize with their peers. Therefore, it has become inevitable for today's children, who are described as digital natives, to grow up in loneliness. However, contemporary children also need both peer and child-adult interactions because, through these interactions, they can become individuals who think, feel, and act according to certain values. The "symbolic interactionist approach" also expresses this view. According to this approach, social interaction is necessary for individuals to make evaluations regarding the meaning of a symbol (Wallace & Wolf, 2012). Institutions such as family, religion, economy, and school have critical importance in terms of behavior patterns (Gönç Şavran, 2011). Symbolic interactionism emphasizes that meaning is not universal and that individuals interpret symbols in the context of daily relationships, indicating that the interpretation process is dynamic.

Today's digital life offers us a world supported by artificial intelligence. In this world, there are values that are more generalized and claimed to be universal. However, it is distant from values such as family, friendship, religion, and culture. This distance leads to the disappearance of characteristics that would allow young people to shape their identities as "subjects" during their developmental stages. Young individuals whose subjective values are destroyed will not have the chance to go beyond having general identities in their later years. A "homogenized" youth will be constructed, playing the same digital games, spending their days with the same digital tools, and naturally growing in the same direction. The problem of machines becoming human-like due to the development of artificial intelligence will result in human beings becoming standardized and mechanized, turning mechanization into an evolution. The idealized images presented by artificial intelligence create standards that are incompatible with people's realities. These discrepancies will lead to the existence of individuals who have lost their self-esteem. As a result of all these evaluations, the situation we can express is not "the demand to return to old lives by leaving aside artificial intelligence-supported applications". We should continue to benefit from the advantages of artificial intelligence. However, we should not increase the time spent in front of screens due to artificial intelligence or any other reason. This way, we should maintain sufficient interaction with our environment and social environment, and we should not deprive ourselves of the opportunity to evaluate the symbols in our lives with the data we acquire from our social surroundings. Human-to-human interaction should be an indispensable value for us. Looking at this concept from Gerbner's "cultivation theory" perspective helps us understand why it is important. Gerbner's theory examines mass communication tools, especially television, and human relationships. According to Gerbner, mass communication tools, especially television, are very little subjective. They mostly convey contents that represent the desires of the dominant ideology. According to Gerbner, no matter which program we watch on television, there are various directions that influence our attitudes, beliefs, and behaviors. Mass communication tools aim to create public opinion through these directions. Gerbner also emphasizes that there are significant differences between the world presented on television and the real world, and these differences can only be revealed through strong analysis. One of the important claims of the theory is that television and other mass communication tools do not necessarily have to change individuals' attitudes. On the contrary, sometimes these tools can provide directions to strengthen attitudes. In other words, attitude reinforcement is also among the goals of mass communication tools. The theory fundamentally describes the needs created in individuals and offers formulas for meeting these needs (Özkan, 2017). When we adapt Gerbner's view on mass communication tools to today's AI-supported digital tools, we can say that these digital tools, just like mass communication tools, confine individuals to certain attitudes. Considering that many tools surrounding our lives are equipped with artificial intelligence nowadays, it is clear that we do not have the chance to perform our daily tasks without passing through the artificial intelligence filter. Although artificial intelligence has taken a significant place in our lives, we still cannot detach ourselves from the reality of needing human-to-human interaction.

The study focuses on the effects of artificial intelligence on the formation of young individuals' identities, particularly within the context of identity formation and artificial intelligence. It addresses the services and potential dangers of artificial intelligence, which has become one of the most important concepts in recent times, in the areas we encounter most frequently. The topics also include the examination of how digital natives' use of these tools could lead to changes in their identities.

## DIGITAL NATIVE AND DIGITAL IMMIGRANT

In recent years, two commonly encountered concepts have been digital natives and digital immigrants. The scope of these concepts is highly debatable because they do not have a clear boundary. Prensky (2001a, 2001b) first introduced the concept of digital natives based on age, suggesting that individuals born in the late 1980s to the early 2000s are considered digital natives. However, subsequent studies have shown that being a digital native requires more than just age. The most important requirement is exposure to and the ability to use information and communication technologies (ICT). Additionally, education and prior experiences play a significant role in defining digital natives. Digital natives can be defined as individuals who are born and raised in an environment with technological possibilities, thus possessing the ability to use technological resources effectively. Building on the definition of digital natives, digital immigrants can be described as individuals who were not born into a technological environment but later became inclined or compelled to use these technological tools (Arabacı & Polat, 2013). As evident from the definitions, we cannot solely categorize individuals as digital immigrants or digital natives based on age because proficiency in using technology is also a crucial criterion. Given that individuals within the same age group may have varying technology usage skills, the rates of digitalization will also differ. Despite this understanding, age is still used as a criterion in delineating the scope of these two concepts. One significant aspect highlighted by the age-based perspective in distinguishing digital natives and digital immigrants is the differences in "accent." According to this perspective, some digital immigrants may efficiently use digital tools compared to their peers, but they may still face an "accent" problem. For example, let's consider a scenario where both a digital native and a digital immigrant conduct the same research. While the digital immigrant may prefer going to the library and relying on written sources as their primary source, the digital native will choose to utilize online platforms (Tonta, 2009). Some argue that these two concepts can also be evaluated disregarding the age factor by emphasizing digital skills. Prensky is among those who belong to this group of thinkers. This is because Prensky, considering later studies (taking criticisms into account), began using the concept of "digital wisdom" (Prensky, 2011). This concept categorizes digital skills based on individuals' digital abilities and knowledge. Additionally, the concepts of digital natives and digital immigrants have led to the emergence of the "digital hybrid" concept. Digital hybrids are individuals who possess certain characteristics of both groups, as the name suggests. Although digital hybrids benefit from the opportunities of the digital world like digital natives, they are not as proficient in effective usage as digital natives. Moreover, they are not as resistant to technology as digital immigrants. The sharp differences between digital natives and digital immigrants necessitate the presence of an intermediate society. Digital hybrids are crucial in facilitating this transition (Karabulut, 2015).

The distinguishing characteristic of digital natives is their proficiency in learning technology. Digital natives easily adapt to technology and are not hesitate to use it. Having compatible experiences with technology, they are unafraid of breaking or using it incorrectly (Günüç, 2011). Digital natives are the generation that benefits from all the advantages of technology. In Prensky's terms, they are the generation whose native language is digital. Their digital habits influence their identities and personalities, providing them with a distinctive perspective. Digital natives are accustomed to quickly acquiring information. They are inclined to multitask and perform multiple tasks simultaneously. They use multimedia (versatile) posts more often than one-way posts. They can socialize comfortably on online platforms and do not hesitate to exchange data in digital environments (Karabulut, 2015). However, this generation also exhibits some negative traits. For example, individuals may prefer playing computer games over completing a task. This generation desires more independence and prefers to handle their tasks independently rather than relying on others. As a result, they are distant from some traditional concepts such as solidarity and cooperation. However, due to the constant need to take care of themselves, they are also inclined to learn with the assistance of digital tools (Oblinger & Oblinger, 2005). Digital natives also have some deficiencies compared to other generations. Growing up in front of screens, children may develop negative attitudes towards traditional communication methods and activities. They have the potential to develop screen addiction and display various antisocial behaviors as a consequence of this addiction. Digital natives, who are accustomed to multitasking, may also experience reluctance and distraction when faced with long and complex tasks. They are more likely to fail to focus on such tasks, which may lead to potential failures.

## ARTIFICIAL INTELLIGENCE AND DAILY LIFE

Is the development of artificial intelligence[1] positive or negative? The answer to this question depends on how AI will affect society and individuals. Many experts almost unanimously agree that, without posing a threat to human existence, AI can increase human productivity and happiness if used to benefit humans. However, it should be remembered that AI is just a tool. While this tool can bring new opportunities, it can also lead to new risks. Especially with the development of AI technology, the possibility of various machines replacing humans has long been a debated risk. This risk transforms AI into a subject of discussion. To fully understand AI, it is necessary to have a grasp of its details and be able to interpret information about AI. This way, it will be easier to take societal measures against the risks posed by AI. However, effective literature has not yet been produced regarding the contribution or harm of AI to human life. The majority of existing studies interpret the results of AI's technological advancements. Changes brought about by AI in social areas beyond software, electronics, computer engineering, or the healthcare field should also be examined. This is because all these changes collectively impact human beings.

The concept of AI was first mentioned in a proposal letter presented at the Dartmouth Conference in 1956 by John McCarthy, Marvin L. Minsky, Nathaniel Rochester, and Claude E. Shannon, with John McCarthy being considered the founder of this concept (Alpaydın, 2013). John McCarthy (2004) explains intelligence as follows: "It is a computational part of the ability to achieve goals in the world. Varying kinds and degrees of intelligence occur in people, many animals, and some machines." McCarthy explains artificial intelligence as "the science and engineering of making intelligent machines, especially intelligent computer programs." These definitions imply that machines can perform tasks such as problem-solving, generalization, inference, and reasoning, which are typically associated with humans. In other words, as Nils Nilsson (1990) puts it, we can describe artificial intelligence as an imitation of natural intelligence. Artificial intelligence is fundamentally built upon two values: "intelligent programming" and "human-like responses." The combination of these two values explains machines equipped with software that mimics human behavior. The significant milestone that brought AI into the spotlight occurred in 1997 when IBM developed the "Deep Blue" program, which faced off against world chess champion Gary Kasparov in a chess match. In this chess match, an AI application called "Deep Blue" emerged as the winner. Up until that point, artificial intelligence research had been progressing quietly, but this chess match captured the attention of the world because it demonstrated the existence of machines that could outperform humans in certain tasks. From 1997 to the present day, there have been many significant developments in the field of artificial intelligence. Therefore, in today's era of "Big Data," the rapid development of artificial intelligence and its almost universal application in various fields have become possible. Today, AI is used in many fields such as banking, technology, entertainment, enabling innovations like real-time language translations, autonomous vehicles, virtual classrooms, robotics, strategic planning, patient monitoring systems, and many others (Arslan, 2020).

While there have been significant developments in AI in recent years, some studies argue that AI cannot behave like a human. According to views based on the "Chinese Room"[2] experiment, even if AI performs a task, it does not do so consciously like a human would. In other words, it completes the task without truly understanding it. Therefore, the development of AI's predictive abilities does not necessarily mean an understanding of what real consciousness is (Cárdenas, 2023). However, contrary to this view, there are more people who believe that artificial intelligence will achieve much more significant feats in the future and have a profound impact on humanity. Although we do not know what the future holds, it is evident that AI technology is already impacting human life in many areas today. These impacts involve intervening in human nature and naturally leading to some changes in humans. It is beneficial to look at some examples of AI to better understand its impact on humans.

For many people, the first tangible impact of AI in our lives began with mobile phones. With the widespread use of mobile phones in the 1990s, people started to communicate instantly, independent of time and space. However, with the introduction of smartphones in the 2000s, it became apparent that mobile phones would have benefits beyond being a tool for voice and written communication in human life. Today, mobile phones are used actively as mini-computers in almost all our tasks. Modern smart-phones using artificial intelligence technology serve users with various functions such as internet access, calendar, voice assistant, task organizer, prediction tool, and more. They also have the ability to connect with various devices and infrastructures, access data about the user's daily life (health, sports, finance, etc.), store private user data, and present this data to the user when needed. The fundamental reason for this change in mobile phones is their integration with artificial intelligence. Although humanity had previously tested and embraced artificial intelligence with computers (with applications like Deep Blue), the widespread adoption of artificial intelligence by a large part of the population almost simultaneously occurred with the advent of smartphones.

One of the most popular examples of artificial intelligence is personal assistant programs like Siri, Google Assistant, and Alexa. These programs are software that interprets sentences spoken by people in various languages into commands that computers can understand. Thanks to these software applications, communication between humans and AI-based machines is made possible. Voice command systems are widely used today, especially in areas such as customer service in companies (Pehlivan Yirci, 2023). These software applications provide support for people in their daily lives. Individuals use these applications as assistants to obtain information and carry out their activities. In fact, in some cases, they are thought to be used for emotional support for users as well. According to research, these AI-based assistant applications will expand the boundaries of life over time.

Another development where artificial intelligence is heavily utilized and users constantly interact with it is seen in cameras. AI-powered cameras have significantly expanded their capabilities compared to traditional cameras (Tominaga et al., 2021). These cameras have made great strides in image processing, scene recognition, and improving image quality. They have also become part of security systems. AI-powered cameras used for identity verification in facial recognition and biometric security systems have become fundamental components of security systems. These systems have made access to sensitive information more secure. By automatically recognizing individuals (Jain et al., 2004) and allowing processing, these software applications have gone beyond traditional security systems. Other technologies used in security systems (such as keystroke dynamics, fingerprint recognition, or iris authentication) are also examples of artificial intelligence applications (Kumar & Singh, 2015). These methods have significantly strengthened the security of stored data.

Artificial intelligence is also heavily utilized in personalized systems that analyze user behaviors and provide recommendations based on their interests. In these systems, user behavior patterns are identified, and various recommendations are generated (Chen et al., 2020). This means that data obtained from user experiences is analyzed and interpreted to increase user satisfaction with new recommendations (Kumar & Singh, 2015). This AI-supported application not only presents new recommendations that users would find appealing but also creates a marketing strategy for the recommending entity (organization, company, etc.) (Davenport et al., 2019). Through systems that offer targeted recommendations, companies aim to sell more products. This method is widely used today. We can encounter this application while shopping for clothes, examining an electronic product on an online shopping page, watching a movie on an online platform, or searching for a product on a search engine. The working principle is entirely based on data input. In other words, the user must first enter data. For example, a user searches for sports shoe models on the internet. This search is for data for artificial intelligence. AI begins to show ads that are suitable for the keyword the user is searching for. As the data becomes more detailed, the displayed products will be more relevant. So, if a person searching on a search engine types in "sports shoes," they will start seeing recommendations for sports shoes. If they open and view the black-colored shoes from the recommendations, the suggestions will now be tailored to black-colored shoes. If they further refine their search for black slip-on sports shoes, the recommendations will adjust accordingly. In summary, the more data input provided, the more suitable recommendations will be generated.

AI-based translation platforms developed for understanding foreign languages are also widely used by users today. In earlier times, language translation was quite challenging. Apart from searching for words in printed dictionaries, it required significant mental gymnastics to place the sentence in context. Nowadays, translation is quite practical, thanks to AI technology. Translation platforms, while performing the translation of a given text, not only focus on the meaning of each word but also evaluate the meaning of the sentence by considering the context. Thus, they carry out a translation of the text that is termed meaningful translation. This means that the translation includes cultural elements and specific usages (Lihua, 2022). Consequently, the translation capability in the digital environment with AI has started to offer an assistant service that facilitates daily tasks. Moreover, thanks to AI technology, translation applications also show synonyms, antonyms, and general uses of a word in different sentences. These applications, capable of pronouncing pronunciations and contributing to travel or speaking practice, greatly facilitate language learning.

Another innovation that has emerged and provided us with significant contributions due to the entry of AI into our lives is the dictation feature. Thanks to this technology, a speaker's sentences can be accurately converted into text. The system provides ease of use through language processing and voice recognition. In some cases, programs that analyze emotions and feelings (Dwivedi et al., 2022) also provide users with detailed results. So, AI-supported voice messaging and dictation features offer users many advantages, such as enhanced communication efficiency, personalized interactions, increased user engagement, and facilitation of daily tasks.

In summary, artificial intelligence has shown its impact in nearly every field today. The standout features of this technology are its learning capacity and its ability to constantly improve and transform itself. Every piece of data entered into AI-based platforms contributes to the further development of these systems, playing a crucial role. Many AI-based applications, initially thought to be ineffective, have become indispensable tools today due to their ability to evolve over time. Looking at the wide range of uses of artificial intelligence today, it is evident that it is effective in many areas, from the healthcare sector to the automotive industry, financial analysis to educational processes. In the field of medicine, the utilization of AI-supported systems in disease diagnosis and treatment processes is particularly significant. Additionally, in many sectors where automation is increasing, AI-based systems contribute to enhancing efficiency and improving business processes. The future potential of artificial intelligence is also significant. Rapid advancements in areas such as deep learning and artificial neural networks will make AI technologies more complex and effective. However, in this process, special attention must be given to ethical and security issues. For instance, issues such as data privacy and security related to AI usage need to be carefully addressed.

## ARTIFICIAL INTELLIGENCE AND SCREEN TIME

The advancement in information and communication technologies, combined with artificial intelligence, has significantly intensified the use of digital tools in daily life. Considering the benefits brought by AI-based digital tools to human life, it is almost impossible to imagine giving up these new tools in the future (Gökel, 2020). The 2023 report from "We Are Social" is an important indicator for understanding the role of digital tools in our lives. According to the report, out of the world's population of 8.01 billion, 5.44 billion (68%) are mobile phone users, 5.16 billion (64.4%) are internet users, and 4.76 billion (59.4%) are active social media users. As can be understood from the numbers, a significant portion of the world's population is connected to the global network. To illustrate the rate of increase, consider this example: in the last three months of 2022 alone, the number of internet users surged by approximately 90 million, and this upward trend persists daily. However, there is not an equal distribution of internet usage worldwide. In other words, while certain parts of the world have the infrastructure and means to actively use the internet, some countries face a situation of deprivation. For instance, in India, according to data from early 2023, around 730 million people still do not have access to the internet. A similar situation exists in China, where a population of 375 million lives without internet access (www.wearesocial.com).

According to We Are Social's report, there has been a 20-minute decrease in internet usage per user 2023. The 2022 data indicates that an average user spent 7 hours a day on the internet, while the 2023 data shows that people spent 6 hours and 37 minutes on the internet. These numbers are quite close to the

2019 figures from the pre-Covid era. However, it is important to note that the decline in internet usage time does not imply that people are moving away from digital environments. On the contrary, there is data indicating that people's activities in the online environment are more purposeful (www.wearesocial .com). One of the significant reasons why people spend so much time in digital environments is AI technology. For example, artificial intelligence predicts users' needs, desires, interests, and preferences based on the digital footprints they leave in the virtual environment and makes recommendations to users accordingly. The data used to create these recommendations is also sold to companies for commercial purposes, such as advertising.

By targeting individuals with personalized ads, encouraging them to explore more products, and influencing purchase decisions, the trend towards personalized advertisements has been on the rise. Advertisements created using this method have the ability to generate personalized ads by integrating real-time data (Hairong, 2019). In other words, artificial intelligence strengthens the sales channel and attracts individuals' attention through personalized ads, encouraging them to explore products and ultimately increasing the time spent in front of the screen. Personalized recommendation systems are not only used in advertising and marketing but are also actively utilized in various online domains. For example, platforms recognized as some of the world's largest entertainment providers, such as Netflix, Amazon Prime, Tencent, iQIYI, Disney+, and Apple TV+, utilize a similar algorithm to assist their users. The algorithm primarily used creates viewing protocols. When a user starts watching something on TV, the algorithm begins to work based on the traces left by the user in the system, collecting clues that can be used to make recommendations to the user. Each viewing protocol restructuring leads to more data being gathered about the user. As a result, the recommendations made to the user are met with more approval (Varela, 2019). In short, the algorithms used measure users' viewing habits and make recommendations accordingly. These recommendations impact the time spent in front of the screen and encourage users to stay on the platform longer.

Tristan Harris, a former engineer at Google, has stated that similar practices are also used by Google. Harris admits that it is easy to control the human mind and that algorithms work similarly to slot machines, ensuring numerous methods to ensure that people spend more time in front of screens. Whether it's Google or other platforms, the working principle of algorithms is the same. First, the existing data is introduced, and then new information is organized based on this data. Whether Amazon recommends products or Netflix suggests movies, they utilize the same logic. This method is called deep learning. As computers continue to learn from our personal data, they can influence us based on the information they gather. Artificial intelligence not only determines what we buy or watch but also has the power to influence how we think and live. In other words, it also influences the cultural and personal characteristics of its users. According to the information conveyed in the documentary "The Social Dilemma," NBA player Kyrie Irving came to believe that the world was flat as a result of the direction of videos he watched on YouTube. Similarly, 'The Great Hack' documentary showed how data can be used to influence attitudes and behaviors. In another example, Facebook, by sharing data with Cambridge Analytica, influenced people's opinions using elements that would impact them (Manas, 2021). In summary, systems developed with screen-based artificial intelligence algorithms play a crucial role in human life. Although companies have developed these algorithms for commercial purposes, the consequences are not solely commercial. Particularly in terms of directing users' perceptions to increase screen time, they lead to significant issues. There are significant studies in the literature concerning prolonged screen time and its impact on individuals.

Many studies on screen time have criticized and provided recommendations based on scientific data regarding the extended hours users spend in front of screens. Particularly in the medical field, there are serious concerns about the harms of excessive screen time. Evidence shows that prolonged screen time contributes to issues such as sleep problems (Magee et al., 2014) and physical activity problems (Ballard et al., 2009). Additionally, scientific studies also examine the psychological effects of excessive screen time. These studies indicate that excessive screen time can negatively impact well-being (Twenge et al., 2018). The data obtained from studies on well-being is highly significant. Excessive use of various platforms, particularly social media, not only harms individuals but also poses a threat to public health. When analyzing usage that reaches addictive levels, significant distortions are observed in individuals. For example, body image perception changes in women[3]. Some female users may objectify themselves by turning their bodies into a means of gratification. Women who try to identify with the individuals they come across in social media feeds often find themselves in a competition to appear more beautiful, fit, and ideal and are exposed to negative psychological effects (Jabłońska & Zajdel, 2020). According to research, spending more time on social media applications during the day leads to a significant increase in social comparison and anxiety levels (Tütar & Kahraman, 2018). In fact, a different study has proven that spending long periods on these platforms increases anxiety symptoms. These two studies clearly demonstrate a relationship between anxiety disorders and screen time (Vannucci, 2017). When considering young female individuals, the potential dire consequences of this effect become even more critical. Young individuals who lack life experience and act based on limited information may face irreversible damage to their identities and personalities during their journey of self-realization.

The issues stemming from screen use are not only relevant to female users but also present dangerous addictions for males. One of the most prevalent issues among these addictions is digital gaming addiction. The new generations, who are natives of the digital world, are in constant interaction with digital tools from the moment they open their eyes. Therefore, digital natives enter the world of digital games without spending time on traditional games. The distinction between traditional game formats and digital game formats (Hazar, 2018) also poses potential risks for children. Addiction ranks among the significant risks. This type of addiction, more commonly encountered in adolescents who have not fully developed decision-making abilities, also includes high levels of internet usage. While well-developed self-regulation skills in adolescents often mitigate this problem, serious issues are observed in those who lack self-regulation. Gaming habits that consume 8-10 hours per day can lead to problems such as disruptions in family and peer relationships, anger management issues, and neglect of basic needs and activities (Köroğlu, 2013). In addition to these negatives, inadequate nutrition, decreased academic achievement, and even issues extending to suicide have been identified (Hagedorn & Young, 2011). Depending on the nature of the game being played, the normalization of negative emotions such as violence, murder, and war is sometimes observed. This type of addiction, which can lead to a spiritual collapse, necessitates taking precautions in adolescents. Although gaming addiction is frequently discussed among young males, it is also a concern for girls and even adults. Many games developed by artificial intelligence are in use today. In fact, Slattery (2023) suggests that we can develop a game using artificial intelligence to play with friends in the evening. In this context, we can assert that artificial intelligence has a significant impact on the gaming world and is a major factor in the prolongation of screen time.

Another significant issue greatly affected by screen time is obesity. As screen time increases, excessive snacking leads to nutritional imbalance and a decrease in metabolic rate. Furthermore, the influential impact of food advertisements on young individuals increases their cravings for food, which poses a significant risk. Unhealthy food consumption, irregular meal times, and a lack of portion control while in front of screens also contribute to the increase in obesity. A study conducted with adolescents aged 14–18 found a positive correlation between increased screen time and higher body mass index (BMI). Additionally, studies indicate that increased screen time leads to sleep problems in children (Muslu & Gökçay, 2019). Individuals who are dependent on screens often continue to monitor them until late hours, depriving themselves of sufficient sleep at night. This results in shortened daily sleep durations and a shift in sleep patterns. Increased arousal can lead to issues like nightmares and frequent awakenings during the night. Insufficient nighttime sleep can lead to daytime drowsiness, irritability, and attention deficits (Walters & Rye, 2009). Sleep disorders also contribute to obesity because sleep quality affects hormone balance in the body. A decrease in sleep disrupts hormone levels, leading to a reduction in energy expenditure but an increase in appetite, thereby increasing the likelihood of obesity.

## THE IMPACT OF ARTIFICIAL INTELLIGENCE ON YOUNG INDIVIDUALS

The innovations introduced into our lives with AI provide significant benefits in daily life for users; however, these beneficial applications also reshape an individual's structure and construct a new identity. Especially individuals born in the digital age exhibit significant influences of artificial intelligence in their identities and personalities. This is because these generations spend most of their day immersed in a network surrounded by AI-based algorithms, often disconnected from life outside of this network.

Social media platforms, one of the crucial AI application areas we constantly interact with in our daily lives, organize personalization, content suggestions, friend recommendations, and news feeds based on user experiences (Bell et al., 2022). Research indicates that AI-supported social media platforms increase user engagement and contribute to the development of trust in the platform (Kang & Lou, 2022). However, the continuous stream of different lives presented by social media also leads to an increase in feelings of envy among people. These platforms, which portray richer, more glamorous, and happier lives, can make individuals feel inadequate and lead to dissatisfaction with their own lives. In a social media system centered around likes and follows, individuals who want to appear as happy as the people they encounter in their feeds often start to "pretend" after a while. In other words, they begin to act as if they were rich or knowledgeable about a topic, even if they are not, by concealing certain aspects they lack and presenting themselves as possessing them. This situation eventually evolves from a voluntary action into a habit, resulting in changes in the individual's identity and personality. These changes lead to unhappiness because they create a gap between an individual's real life and their life on social media. Individuals caught between their real-world identity and their virtual-world identity experience an identity crisis (Baydili, 2023). Individuals who use social media platforms more frequently are driven by a stronger desire for likes and followers. The possibility of individuals comparing their lives to those presented in their social media feed and becoming unhappy increases the likelihood of developing depression. Therefore, while AI-equipped social media platforms technically facilitate people's lives (Sukhorukov et al., 2019), they also harm their moral, religious, social, and emotional aspects (Vinichenko et al., 2020). Even young people who struggle to resist data bombardment on screens may experience erosion in their identities, potentially leading to the emergence of a new type of identity (Awad & Feinstein 2020). Hence, everyone, especially young individuals, should be aware that the content in these platforms' feeds is selected through algorithms generated by artificial intelligence. More importantly, individuals who frequently use these platforms should practice digital detox at certain times to experience mental and psychological cleansing without disconnecting from the real world. This practice allows them to grasp the existence and meaning of the virtual world more comfortably.

Since the dawn of humanity, humans have lived as social beings, constantly needing other people throughout their lives. This need has brought about a desire for coexistence since the early days of history, with even primitive humans and nearly all human groups living together as communities. Over time, the desire for coexistence evolved, giving rise to the concept of family and allowing for closer relationships to develop. Humans have also defined people outside their families, creating categories such as relatives, friends, and companions based on the degree of closeness. The point being made here is that humans have always come together as social beings, from the past to the present. Socialization has helped humans meet many physiological and psychological needs. However, in the past few centuries, living conditions have changed, and the pace of transformation in human life has accelerated. Relaxations in the closeness of extended family and close kinship have led to increasing isolation among individuals. This isolation, described as a modern-era ailment, has intensified in the postmodern era, prompting people to seek different ways to satisfy their emotions. In this context, AI technologies have been used in recent decades to help meet the socialization needs of humans that they may not be able to fulfill due to the demands of modern life. New tools produced with AI technologies have been effective in satisfying feelings of loneliness and forming emotional connections for some users. Human-machine interaction has been attempted to cope with loneliness and stress. Additionally, AI is being used to provide companionship, enhance security, and improve social skills for elderly adults. However, despite AI and human communication being somewhat satisfying, they will never be as fulfilling as human-to-human interaction. It's important not to forget society's real need for human relationships and community. While artificial intelligence can alleviate social isolation to some extent, it cannot replace genuine human connections. Therefore, technology users should be cautious when interacting with artificial intelligence and continue to prioritize real human relationships (Zimmerman, Janhonen, & Beer, 2023).

One important question that may arise is why AI cannot replace humans. While AI can mimic human expressions, tones of voice, and emotions, it cannot truly understand humans. Therefore, it is not capable of providing emotional responses. While AI can mimic human expressions, tones of voice, and emotions, it cannot truly understand humans. Technology companies may equip AI models with 'human-like' features. However, due to the dissimilarity between the working principles of artificial intelligence and the human brain, AI cannot fully comprehend human emotions. For instance, artificial intelligence lacks the ability to perceive cultural differences and social norms. Therefore, AI applications carry the risk of misinterpreting emotions. In AI-human interactions, mutual pleasure and admiration are not central. Rather, artificial intelligence only mimics friendly behavior (Brandtzaeg, Skjuve & Følstad, 2022). Another question that arises is whether AI and human interaction have a positive impact on socialisation. Undoubtedly, they do. When interacting with artificial intelligence, individuals may feel at ease because they are not subject to the same judgments (such as appearance) that humans make. In communicating with artificial intelligence, people can express their anger or vulnerability without concealing it. AI can support the socialization process, but it cannot experience pain, mourn, or feel emotions. As a result, the communication established will be one-sided in terms of conveying meaning, which is a significant limitation in human development. It is important to consider the effects of young individuals spending time with AI applications on their identities. Furthermore, young individuals who lack sufficient human interaction and instead heavily rely on artificial intelligence may develop a one-dimensional perspective, as highlighted by Marcuse (1975), that is disconnected from alternative realities. This poses a significant risk of creating a society of one-dimensional individuals in the future. When considering AI, it is important to examine its impact on human development. The constant flow of information in the digital world, where AI is prevalent, can impose a certain perspective and lifestyle on individuals, potentially limiting them. The constant flow of information in the digital world, where AI is prevalent, can impose a certainperspective and lifestyle on individuals, potentially limiting them. The integration of AI into various areas, from household appliances to social media, can shape and restrict human experiences (Shneiderman, 2020). The use of intensive AI in relation to human creativity may impede the creativity of young individuals who are not accustomed to life without artificial intelligence. While there are applications designed to enhance human potential through artificial intelligence, such as therapy sessions and creative efforts (Szalai, 2020), it is important to consider the potential limitations. If this situation is ignored, it is possible for the problem of an 'echo chamber[4]' to arise (Valtonen et al., 2019). In other words, being consistently exposed to the same viewpoints can result in individuals being closed off to other perspectives.[5]

Another important point that needs to be emphasized is artificial intelligence's data storage capability. It is important to consider the potential consequences of using such applications. AI-based applications collect various data and have the ability to commercialise this data, potentially intruding into individuals' privacy. Despite being aware of this privacy issue, young individuals continue to use AI applications and may compromise their privacy with increasing usage. The concept of privacy centres around an individual's right to control the sharing of their personal information (Westin, 1968). Artificial intelligence applications pose a threat to this right by constantly monitoring individuals and collecting their digital footprints, contributing to the formation of big data. However, it is unclear where and how this data is used. Privacy is crucial in the formation of an individual's identity and is a fundamental aspect of being human (Dedeoğlu, 2004). The violation of privacy not only affects individuals but also disrupts social structure. It is not just a desire to live away from prying eyes. Privacy involves avoiding observing others, and reciprocity is essential (Lokke, 2018). The first fundamental point in protecting privacy is for individuals to take ownership of this concept. Nowadays, discussions about privacy generally focus on external factors. However, the issue of privacy primarily arises from individuals who choose to make their personal data public in the digital realm, resulting in a loss of privacy. Therefore, individuals must respect their own privacy to initiate the process. The increase in individuals disregarding privacy, and even the perspectives of new generations born in the digital age considering privacy as insignificant, pose challenges to social structures. Individuals who share personal information, such as details about their family, work, and personal life, for the purpose of gaining likes or followers on social media, are more likely to experience emotional satisfaction problems.

## CONCLUSION

In an era where artificial intelligence touches almost every aspect of our lives, it is difficult and unnecessary to escape from this technology. However, blindly trusting and surrendering to this technology is also not the right approach. Those who have grown up in traditional society and later adapted to the digital age (digital immigrants) may more openly see some of the problems of this era, whereas the (digital) natives of this age, who have not experienced a different way of life, may more quickly embrace the indispensability of technological advancements. Technological advancements bring innovations that enhance our lives, but we must not forget the existence of risks along with these innovations. When we can understand and evaluate these risks correctly, we can ensure the versatility of future generations, guarantee human-to-human interaction, and show that happiness can be found beyond a focus on instant gratification. Otherwise, there is a high likelihood of encountering a future generation that is one-dimensional, selfish, and perhaps a bit wounded.

It is important to remember that AI is not human. While technological advancements may enable artificial intelligence to exhibit human-like behaviours, and perhaps in the future, robots with many human-like characteristics could be developed, ultimately these tools are all machines. Even if they possess superior intelligence to humans, they do not have the ability to mimic human emotions. Emotions cannot be mathematically quantified in computer systems, and their relativity is high. Furthermore, predicting intentions is challenging for artificial intelligence. Machines without social intelligence are unlikely to predict intentions successfully. Therefore, the possibility of machines replacing humans decreases as they cannot comprehend human desires or wants.

The role of artificial intelligence in our lives must be evaluated objectively, considering the following facts. AI-supported social media platforms, personalized content recommendations, and digital assistants are tools that can shape young people's self-perception and influence their identity construction. These technologies can have a decisive impact on young people's preferences, interests, thought patterns, and values. However, it is important to note that further research is required to fully understand the effects of AI-powered machines on young individuals. The study's results emphasise the necessity for more comprehensive and in-depth research to comprehend the impact of AI technologies on the development of young people's identity and personality. These studies are crucial for comprehending the impact of AI technologies on the emotional, social, and cognitive development of young people, and for assessing how these technologies can either facilitate or impede healthy identity formation processes.

## REFERENCES

Alpaydın, E. (2013). *Yapay öğrenme (4. Baskı)*. Boğaziçi Üniversitesi Yayınevi.

Arabacı, İ. B., & Polat, M. (2013). Dijital yerliler, dijital göçmenler ve sinif yönetimi. *Elektronik Sosyal Bilimler Dergisi*, 12(47), 11–20.

Arslan, K. (2020). Eğitimde yapay zekâ ve uygulamaları. *Batı Anadolu Eğitim Bilimleri Dergisi*, 11(1), 71–88.

Awad, S. W. M. og Feinstein, K. A. (2020). Hybrid identity: A study of the development of self-identity with digital media and artificial intelligence. *PÓS: Revista do Programa de Pós-graduação em Artes da EBA/UFMG, 10*(19), 59-68.

Ballard, M., Gray, M., Reilly, J., & Noggle, M. (2009). Correlates of video game screen time among males: Body mass, physical activity, and other media use. *Eating Behaviors*, 10(3), 161–167. 10.1016/j.eatbeh.2009.05.00119665099

Baydili, İ. (2023). *Dijital kültürde kimlik İnşası ve bedenin sunumu: Instagram orneği. İ Y. Argın (ritstj.), Güncel yaklaşımlarla geleneksel ve yeni medyada beden (bls.* Nobel.

Bell, A. R., Tennfjord, M. K., Tokovska, M., & Eg, R. (2023). Exploring the role of social media literacy in adolescents' experiences with personalization: A norwegian qualitative study. *Journal of Adolescent & Adult Literacy*, 66(4), 239–248. 10.1002/jaal.1273

Brandtzaeg, P. B., Skjuve, M., & Følstad, A. (2022). My ai friend: How users of a social chatbot understand their human–ai friendship. *Human Communication Research*, 48(3), 404–429. 10.1093/hcr/hqac008

Cárdenas, P. O. R. (2023). What kind of "intelligence" is artificial intelligence? *Metafísica y Persona*, (30), 39–48.

Chen, L., Chen, P., & Lin, Z. (2020). Artificial intelligence in education: A review. *IEEE Access : Practical Innovations, Open Solutions*, 8, 75264–75278. 10.1109/ACCESS.2020.2988510

Cinelli, M., Morales, G. D. F., Galeazzi, A., Quattrociocchi, W., & Starnini, M. (2020). Echo chambers on social media: A comparative analysis. *arXiv preprint arXiv:2004.09603*.

Davenport, T., Guha, A., Grewal, D., & Bressgott, T. (2020). How artificial intelligence will change the future of marketing. *Journal of the Academy of Marketing Science*, 48(1), 24–42. 10.1007/s11747-019-00696-0

Dedeoğlu, G. (2004). Gözetleme, mahremiyet ve insan onuru. *TBD Bilişim*, 89, 36.

Dwivedi, A. K., Virmani, D., Ramasamy, A., Acharjee, P. B., & Tiwari, M. (2022). Modelling and analysis of artificial intelligence approaches in enhancing the speech recognition for effective multi-functional machine learning platform–a multi regression modelling approach. *Journal of Engineering Research-ICMET*, 04-06(Special Issue). 10.36909/jer.ICMET.17161

Gökel, Ö. (2020). Teknoloji bağımlılığının çeşitli yaş gruplarındaki çocuklara etkileri hakkındaki ebeveyn görüşleri. *Kıbrıs Türk Psikiyatri ve Psikoloji Dergisi*, 2(1), 41–47.

Gönç-Şavran, T. (2011). İşlevselcilik-i: Talcot parsons. *Modern sosyoloji tarihi*, 2-29.

Günüç, S. (2011). Türkiye, dijital yerlilerde çalışan bellek ve çoklu görev. İ *5th International Computer & Instructional Technologies Symposium, Fırat Üniversitesi, ELAZIĞ.*

Hagedorn, W. B. og Young, T. (2011). Identifying and intervening with students exhibiting signs of gaming addiction and other addictive behaviors: Implications for professional school counselors. *Professional School Counseling, 14*(4), 2156759X1101400401.

Hazar, Z. (2018). *Çağın vebası dijital oyun bağımlılığı ve başa çıkma yöntemleri.* Gazi Kitabevi.

Herbert, M. (1975). *Tek boyutlu İnsan,(çev. Afşar timuçin ve teoman tunçdoğan).* May Yayınları.

Jabłońska, M. R., & Zajdel, R. (2020). Artificial neural networks for predicting social comparison effects among female instagram users. *PLoS One, 15*(2), e0229354. 10.1371/journal.pone.022935432097446

Jain, A. K., Ross, A., & Prabhakar, S. (2004). An introduction to biometric recognition. *IEEE Transactions on Circuits and Systems for Video Technology, 14*(1), 4–20. 10.1109/TCSVT.2003.818349

Kang, H., & Lou, C. (2022). Ai agency vs. Human agency: Understanding human–ai interactions on tiktok and their implications for user engagement. *Journal of Computer-Mediated Communication, 27*(5), zmac014. 10.1093/jcmc/zmac014

Karabulut, B. (2015). Bilgi toplumu çağinda dijital yerliler, göçmenler ve melezler. *Pamukkale Üniversitesi Sosyal Bilimler Enstitüsü Dergisi,* (21), 11–23.

Köroğlu, E. (2013). *Dsm-v: Tanı ölçütleri başvuru kitabı,(e. Köroğlu. Çev.).* Amerikan Psikiyatri Birliği.

Kumar, S., & Singh, M. (2015). Biometric security based intelligent e-voting system. *International Journal of Computer Applications, 117*(4), 33–41. 10.5120/20546-2918

Li, H. (2019). Special section introduction: Artificial intelligence and advertising. *Journal of Advertising, 48*(4), 333–337. 10.1080/00913367.2019.1654947

Lihua, Z. (2022). Analysis of english translation model based on artificial intelligence attention mechanism. *Mathematical Problems in Engineering, 2022,* 2022. 10.1155/2022/9669152

Løkke, E. (2020). *Mahremiyet: Dijital toplumda özel hayat.* Koç Üniversitesi.

Magee, C. A., Lee, J. K., & Vella, S. A. (2014). Bidirectional relationships between sleep duration and screen time in early childhood. *JAMA Pediatrics, 168*(5), 465–470. 10.1001/jamapediatrics.2013.418324589672

McCarthy, J. (2004). *What is Artificial Intelligence?* Stanford. http://www-formal.stanford.edu/jmc/whatisai/. (Accessed:30.03.2024).

Muslu, M., & Gökçay, G. F. (2019). Teknoloji bağımlısı çocuklarda obeziteye neden olan risk faktörleri. *Gümüşhane Üniversitesi Sağlık Bilimleri Dergisi, 8*(2), 72–79.

Nilsson, N. J. (1990). *The mathematical foundations of learning machines.* Morgan Kaufmann Publishers Inc.

Oblinger, D. og Oblinger, J. (2005). Is it age or it: First steps toward understanding the net generation. *Educating the net generation, 2*(1-2), 20.

Özkan, S. (2017). Gerbner'in kültürel göstergeler kuramı bağlamında televizyon haber içeriklerine ilişkin bir araştırma. *Abant Kültürel Araştırmalar Dergisi*, 2(4), 129–141.

Pehlivan Yirci, N. (2023). *Pazarlamada yapay zeka uygulamaları, marka yolculuğu. İ N. Ç. Çetinkaya (ritstj.), Dijital dönüşüm ve sürdürülebilirlik (bls.* Bidge Yayınları.

Prensky, M. (2001). Digital Natives, digital immigrants. Marc Prensky. https://www.marcprensky.com/writing/Prensky.

Prensky, M. (2001b). Digital natives, digital immigrants part 2: Do they really think differently? *On the Horizon*, 9(6), 1–6. 10.1108/10748120110424843

Prensky, M. (2011). *Digital wisdom and homo sapiens digital. İ Deconstructing digital natives (bls.* Routledge.

Pulurluoğlu, T. (2022). *Sosyal medyaya eleştirel bir bakış: Sosyal ikilem (social dilemma) netflix belgesel filminin analizi.*

Shneiderman, B. (2020). Human-centered artificial intelligence: Three fresh ideas. *AIS Transactions on Human-Computer Interaction*, 12(3), 109–124. 10.17705/1thci.00131

Slattery, P. (n.d.). Understanding AI's impact on behaviour and Society. *Psychology Today*. http://www.Psychologytoday.Com/us/blog/transformative-ai/202311/understanding-ais-impact-on-behaviour-and-society.

Sukhorukov, A., Eroshkin, S., Vanyurikhin, P., Karabahciev, S. og Bogdanova, E. (2019). Robotization of business processes of enterprises of housing and communal services. *İ E3S Web of Conferences.*

Szalai, J. (2021). The potential use of artificial intelligence in the therapy of borderline personality disorder. *Journal of Evaluation in Clinical Practice*, 27(3), 491–496. 10.1111/jep.1353033368981

Tajfel, H. og Turner, J. C. (1978). Intergroup behavior. *Introducing social psychology, 401*, 466.

Tominaga, S., Nishi, S., & Ohtera, R. (2021). Measurement and estimation of spectral sensitivity functions for mobile phone cameras. *Sensors (Basel)*, 21(15), 4985. 10.3390/s2115498534372223

Tonta, Y. (2009). Dijital yerliler, sosyal ağlar ve kütüphanelerin geleceği. *Türk Kütüphaneciliği*, 23(4), 742–768.

Tütar, R., & Kahraman, S. (2018). *Sosyal medya kullanıcılarının sosyal görünüş kaygısı ve mutluluk açısından incelenmesi. III.* International Dmitri Yavoronitski Europeancongress On Social Sciences.

Twenge, J. M., Martin, G. N., & Campbell, W. K. (2018). Decreases in psychological well-being among american adolescents after 2012 and links to screen time during the rise of smartphone technology. *Emotion (Washington, D.C.)*, 18(6), 765–780. 10.1037/emo000040329355336

Valtonen, T., Tedre, M., Mäkitalo, K., & Vartiainen, H. (2019). Media literacy education in the age of machine learning. *The Journal of Media Literacy Education*, 11(2), 20–36. 10.23860/JMLE-2019-11-2-2

Vannucci, A., Flannery, K. M., & Ohannessian, C. M. (2017). Social media use and anxiety in emerging adults. *Journal of Affective Disorders*, 207, 163–166. 10.1016/j.jad.2016.08.04027723539

Varela, D. og Kaun, A. (2019). *The netflix experience: A user-focused approach to the netflix recommendation algorithm.*

Varol, S. F. (2022). Yankı odası: Kavramsal bir çerçeve. *Journal of Academic Social Science Studies*, 15(91).

Vinichenko, M. V., Rybakova, M. V., Nikiporets-Takigawa, G. Y., Chulanova, O., & Lyapunova, N. (2020). The influence of artificial intelligence on the human potential development: The views of orthodox clergy and parishioners. *Cuestiones Políticas*, 37(65), 400–418. 10.46398/cuestpol.3865.27

Wallace, R., & Wolf, A. (2012). *Çağdaş sosyoloji kuramları: Klasik geleneğin geliştirilmesi (3. Bs.). L. Elburuz ve MR Ayas, Çev.* Doğu Batı Yayınları.

Walters, A. S., & Rye, D. B. (2009). Review of the relationship of restless legs syndrome and periodic limb movements in sleep to hypertension, heart disease, and stroke. *Sleep*, 32(5), 589–597. 10.1093/sleep/32.5.58919480225

Washington School of Law. (1984). *Washington and lee law review* (41 bindi). School of Law, Washington and Lee University.

Zimmerman, A., Janhonen, J., & Beer, E. (2023). Human/ai relationships: Challenges, downsides, and impacts on human/human relationships. *AI and Ethics*, 1–13. 10.1007/s43681-023-00348-8

## ENDNOTES

[1]    In the study, the term "AI" is sometimes used interchangeably with "artificial intelligence."

[2]    The Chinese Room experiment is a thought experiment proposed by American philosopher John Searle. This experiment is an important argument used to understand artificial intelligence and consciousness issues. According to this theory, a person can translate Chinese texts through a computer even if they don't understand Chinese. However, in this case, the person is obligated to translate the Chinese characters sent by the computer. This implies that the computer does not actually understand Chinese but only operates with symbols. According to this experiment, a person who does not know Chinese responds to texts conveyed in Chinese in a room with the help of a computer. The responses given by this person are in Chinese. To the observer outside the room, the person inside appears to have perfect knowledge of Chinese because their responses to the texts are very good. However, in reality, the person in the room does not understand Chinese; they only process symbols. This experiment has triggered debates in the fields of philosophy of mind and artificial intelligence. Searle, using this experiment, argued that processing symbols does not convey true meaning and consciousness. According to him, computers can process symbols but cannot express real meaning and understanding. Therefore, the Chinese Room Experiment has emerged as a critique of claims that artificial intelligence systems can mimic real mental processes.

[3]    Male users are also influenced by social media's portrayal of body image, although the assumption is often that women are more affected. This is why the example of the "female body" is frequently used.

[4]    An echo chamber is an environment where an individual's thoughts, opinions, and political inclinations are reinforced due to constant interaction with like-minded individuals (Cinelli et al., 2020).

5      Another concept similar to an echo chamber is the "filter bubble." Highlighting the bias in content exposure due to digitalization, this concept suggests that individuals encounter content on the internet that aligns with their past searches rather than being exposed to new content. This situation affects an individual's development and leads to a one-sided upbringing on digital platforms (Varol, 2022). All of these described situations contribute to significant deficiencies in the development of young individuals, ultimately leading to one-dimensional growth in the children of the digital age.

# Compilation of References

. Dwivedi, D. N., & Anand, A. (2021). The Text Mining of Public Policy Documents in Response to COVID-19: A Comparison of the United Arab Emirates and the Kingdom of Saudi Arabia. *Public Governance / Zarządzanie Publiczne, 55*(1), 8-22. 10.15678/ZP.2021.55.1.02

Aadit, T., Deepak, J., Janhavi, P., & Jyoti, D. (2021). Video Chat Application for Mutes. *IEEE International Conference on Emerging Smart Computing and Informatics (ESCI).* IEEE. 10.1109/ESCI50559.2021.9397044

Abbasi, N. (2016). Adolescent identity formation and the school environment. In *The translational design of schools* (pp. 81–103). Brill. 10.1007/978-94-6300-364-3_4

Abdullah, N., Hassan, I., Ahmad, M., Hassan, N., & Ismail, M. (2021). Social media, youths and political participation in malaysia: A review of literature. *International Journal of Academic Research in Business & Social Sciences, 11*(4). 10.6007/IJARBSS/v11-i4/9578

Abels, H. (2019). Identität. In: *Einführung in die Soziologie.* Studientexte zur Soziologie. Wiesbaden: Springer VS.c

Abi-Jaoude, E., Naylor, K. T., &Pignatiello, A. (2020). Smartphones, social media use and youth mental health. *CMAJ: Canadian Medical Association journal = journal de l'Association medicale canadienne, 192*(6), E136–E141. 10.1503/cmaj.190434

Abreu, J. F., Almeida, P., Velhinho, A., & Varsori, E. (2019). Returning to the TV screen: the potential of content unification in iTV. In *Managing Screen Time in an Online Society* (pp. 146–171). IGI Global. 10.4018/978-1-5225-8163-5.ch007

Abubakari, M. S., Shafik, W., & Hidayatullah, A. F. (2024). Evaluating the Potential of Artificial Intelligence in Islamic Religious Education: A SWOT Analysis Overview. In *AI-Enhanced Teaching Methods* (pp. 216-239). IGI Global. 10.4018/979-8-3693-2728-9.ch010

Abulibdeh, A., Zaidan, E., & Abulibdeh, R. (2024). Navigating the confluence of artificial intelligence and education for sustainable development in the era of industry 4.0: Challenges, opportunities, and ethical dimensions. *Journal of Cleaner Production, 437,* 140527. 10.1016/j.jclepro.2023.140527

Acemoglu, D., & Restrepo, P. (2019). Automation and new tasks: How technology displaces and reinstates labor. *The Journal of Economic Perspectives, 33*(2), 3–30. 10.1257/jep.33.2.3

Acquisti, A., & Gross, C. L. (2006). The value of information privacy: Evidence from a field experiment. *Management Science, 52*(2), 190–200.

Adams, H. R. (2024). Bring Your Own Device (BYOD) and Equitable Access to Technology. In *Intellectual Freedom Issues in School Libraries.* 10.5040/9798400670886.ch-034

Adams, B., & Khomh, F. (2020). The diversity crisis of software engineering for artificial intelligence. *IEEE Software, 37*(5), 104–108. 10.1109/MS.2020.2975075

Aggarwal, D. (2023). Integration of innovative technological developments and AI with education for an adaptive learning pedagogy. *China Petroleum Processing and Petrochemical Technology*, 23(2), 709–714.

Aguboshim, F. C., Udobi, J. I., & Otuu, O. O. (2023). Security Issues Associated with Bring Your Own Device (BYOD): A Narrative Review. In *Research Highlights in Science and Technology, 2*. https://doi.org/10.9734/bpi/rhst/v2/19215D

Ahmad Tarmizi, S., Mutalib, S., Abdul Hamid, N., Abdul-Rahman, S., & Md Ab Malik, A. (2019). A Case Study on Student Attrition Prediction in Higher Education Using Data Mining Techniques. *Soft Computing in Data Science*. Springer. doi:10.1007/978-981-15-0399-3_15. (181-192). http://link.springer.com/10.1007/978-981-15-0399-3_1510.1007/978-981-15-0399-3_15

Ahmad, S., Rahmat, M., Mubarik, M., Alam, M., & Hyder, S. (2021). Artificial Intelligence and Its Role in Education. *Sustainability (Basel)*, 13(22), 12902. 10.3390/su132212902

Ahmed, Z., Mohamed, K., Zeeshan, S., & Dong, X. (2020). Artificial intelligence with multi-functional machine learning platform development for better healthcare and precision medicine. *Database (Oxford)*, 2020, baaa010. 10.1093/database/baaa01032185396

AI Now Institute. (2019). *Artificial intelligence and society: A framework for accountability and regulation*. AI Now Institute.

Aishwarya, G., Satyanarayana, V., Singh, M., & Kumar, S. (2022). *Contemporary evolution of artificial intelligence (ai): an overview and applications*. 10.3233/ATDE220731

Ajzen, I. (1991). The theory of planned behavior. *Organizational Behavior and Human Decision Processes*, 50(2), 179–211. 10.1016/0749-5978(91)90020-T

Akgun, S., & Greenhow, C. (2022). Artificial intelligence in education: Addressing ethical challenges in K-12 settings. *AI and Ethics*, 2(3), 431–440. 10.1007/s43681-021-00096-734790956

Akkök, F., Hughes, D., & CareersNet, U. K. (2021). *Career chat: The art of AI and the human interface in career development* (*Working Paper Series 2*, p. 91). European Centre for the Development of Vocational Training. https://www.cedefop.europa.eu/files/6202_en_0.pdf#page=93

Alam, A. (2023). Harnessing the Power of AI to Create Intelligent Tutoring Systems for Enhanced Classroom Experience and Improved Learning Outcomes. In *Intelligent Communication Technologies and Virtual Mobile Networks* (pp. 571–591). Springer Nature Singapore. https://link.springer.com/chapter/10.1007/978-981-99-1767-9_4210.1007/978-981-99-1767-9_42

Alamry, G. A., & Elwakeel, L. M. (2024). User-Centered Smart Environments: Advanced Research on the Integration of User Preferences and Artificial Intelligence for Personalized Residential Interior Design Solutions. *Kurdish Studies*, 12(1), 4870–4880.

Al-Dajani, A., Al-Hawamdeh, M., & Al-Dajani, S. (2020). The impact of AI-powered chatbots on student engagement in higher education. In *Proceedings of the 12ᵗʰ International Conference on Educational Data Mining* (pp. 35-44). ACM.

Aleven, V., Baraniuk, R., Brunskill, E., Crossley, S., Demszky, D., Fancsali, S., & Xing, W. (2023, June). Towards the Future of AI-Augmented Human Tutoring in Math Learning. In *International Conference on Artificial Intelligence in Education* (pp. 26–31). Springer Nature Switzerland. https://link.springer.com/chapter/10.1007/978-3-031-36336-8_310.1007/978-3-031-36336-8_3

Ali, M., Siddique, A., Aftab, A., Abid, M. K., & Fuzail, M. (2024). AI-Powered customized learning paths: Transforming data administration for students on digital platforms. *Journal of Computing & Biomedical Informatics*, 6(02), 195–204.

Alkaissi, H., & McFarlane, S. I. (2023). Artificial hallucinations in ChatGPT: Implications in scientific writing. *Cureus*, 15(2), 1–4. 10.7759/cureus.3517936811129

Alpaydın, E. (2013). *Yapay öğrenme (4. Baskı)*. Boğaziçi Üniversitesi Yayınevi.

Alrusaini, O., & Beyari, H. (2022). The Sustainable Effect of Artificial Intelligence and Parental Control on Children's Behavior While Using Smart Devices' Apps: The Case of Saudi Arabia. *Sustainability (Basel)*, 14(15), 9388. 10.3390/su14159388

Al-Said, K. (2023). Effect of _Bring Your Own Device' (BYOD) on Student Behavior, Well-Being, and Learning Economic Disciplines. *International Journal of Information and Education Technology (IJIET)*, 13(4), 658–663. 10.18178/ijiet.2023.13.4.1850

AlShebli, B., Cheng, E., Waniek, M., Jagannathan, R., Hernández-Lagos, P., & Rahwan, T. (2022). Beijing's central role in global artificial intelligence research. *Scientific Reports*, 12(1), 21461. 10.1038/s41598-022-25714-036509790

Alter, A. (2017). *Irresistible: The Rise of Addictive Technology and the Business of Keeping Us Hooked*. Penguin Books.

American Psychological Association. (2023). *Health Advisory on Social Media Use in Adolescence*. American Psychological Association.

Amurskaya, O., Gimaletdinova, G., & Khalitova, L. (2017). Multimedia Sanako study 1200 for TEFL in institution of higher education. *Xlinguae*, 10(3), 229–236. 10.18355/XL.2017.10.03.18

Anderson, R. (2001). *Security engineering: A guide to building dependable distributed systems*. Wiley.

Annese, S. (2004). Mediated identity in the parasocial interaction of TV. *Identity*, 4(4), 371–388. 10.1207/s1532706xid0404_5

Annie E. Casey Foundation. (2024, January 19) *What is generation alpha?* AECF. https://www.aecf.org/blog/what-is-generation-alpha

Anorue, L. I., ETUMNU, E. W., Onyebuchi, C. A., & Obayi, P. M. (2022). Effectiveness of the use of ICT by media practitioners in modern day broadcasting. *International Journal of Communication and Social Sciences*, 1, 43–59.

Arabacı, İ. B., & Polat, M. (2013). Dijital yerliler, dijital göçmenler ve sinif yönetimi. *Elektronik Sosyal Bilimler Dergisi*, 12(47), 11–20.

Arcelay, I., Goti, A., Oyarbide-Zubillaga, A., Akyazi, T., Alberdi, E., & Garcia-Bringas, P. (2021). Definition of the future skills needs of job profiles in the renewable energy sector. *Energies*, 14(9), 2609. 10.3390/en14092609

Archives of Disease in Childhood. (2019). Screentime and child health. *Archives of Disease in Childhood, 104*(4), 380-380.

Armstrong-Carter, E., & Telzer, E. (2021). Advancing measurement and research on youths' prosocial behavior in the digital age. *Child Development Perspectives*, 15(1), 31–36. 10.1111/cdep.12396

Arslan, K. (2020). Eğitimde yapay zekâ ve uygulamaları. *Batı Anadolu Eğitim Bilimleri Dergisi*, 11(1), 71–88.

Astriani, M. S., Rizqi, D., & Kurniawan, A. (2023). Bring your own device (BYOD) restaurant: Self-service dining ordering system. *AIP Conference Proceedings*, 2510(1), 030012. 10.1063/5.0128353

Astro Awani. (2019). *Diambil dari: Selangor catat jumlah tertinggi laporang pencemaran*. https://www.astroawani.com/beritamalaysia/selangor-catat-jumlah-tertinggilaporan-pencemaran-223806

Atie, E., Ivanova, O., & Švagždienė, M. (2022). Kardiogeninio šoko etiologija ir diagnostika. Sveikatos mokslai= Health sciences in Eastern Europe. *Vilnius:Sveikatos mokslai, 32*, Nr. 1.

Awad, S. W. M. og Feinstein, K. A. (2020). Hybrid identity: A study of the development of self-identity with digital media and artificial intelligence. *PÓS: Revista do Programa de Pós-graduação em Artes da EBA/UFMG, 10*(19), 59-68.

Awad, S. W. M., & Feinstein, K. A. (2020). Hybrid identity: A study of the development of self-identity with digital media and artificial intelligence. PÓS: Revista do Programa de Pós-graduação em Artes da EBA/UFMG, 10(19), 59-68.

Aydın, O., Obuća, F., Boz, C., & Ünal-Aydın, P. (2020). Associations between executive functions and problematic social networking sites use. *Journal of Clinical and Experimental Neuropsychology, 42*(6), 634–645. 10.1080/138033 95.2020.179835832781930

Ayub, S., Hassim, N., Yahya, A., Hamzah, M., & Bakar, M. (2019). Exploring the characteristics of healthy lifestyle campaign on social media: A case study on fit malaysia. *Jurnal Komunikasi Malaysian Journal of Communication, 35*(4), 322–336. 10.17576/JKMJC-2019-3504-20

Azamatova, A., Bekeyeva, N., Zhaxylikova, K., Sarbassova, A., & Ilyassova, N. (2023). The effect of using artificial intelligence and digital learning tools based on project-based learning approach in foreign language teaching on students' success and motivation. [IJEMST]. *International Journal of Education in Mathematics, Science, and Technology, 11*(6), 1458–1475. 10.46328/ijemst.3712

Bahadur, P. S. (2024). Analysis on Various Aspects of Internet of Nano-Things (IoNT), Its Integration in Machine Learning, and Its Diverse Applications. In *Next Generation Materials for Sustainable Engineering* (pp. 297-315). IGI Global.

Bahadur, P. S., Singh, S., Bais, P., & Jaiswal, S. Laser in textile industry and its application, (2023) *Asian Textile Journal, 32* (3-4), pp. 50-54. https://www.atjournal.com/current-issues.html

Baidoo-Anu, D., & Owusu Ansah, L. (2023). Education in the era of generative Artificial Intelligence (AI): Understanding the potential benefits of ChatGPT in promoting teaching and learning. *Journal of AI, 7*(1), 52–62. 10.61969/jai.1337500

Bais, P., Bahadur, P. S., & Sharma, S. (2023). Production and market development of sericulture. *Asian Textile Journal, 32*(7), 46–52.

Bajraktarov, S., Kunovski, I., Raleva, M., Kalpak, G., Novotni, A., Stefanovski, B., & Hadzihamza, K. (2023). *Mental health of adolescents and their caregivers during the Covid-19 pandemic in North Macedonia.* University Clinic of Psychiatry.

Baker, M. B., Schwartz, M. Z., & Hogue, K. (2019). Empathetic: A web-based social skills training program for adolescents with an autism spectrum disorder. *Journal of Autism and Developmental Disorders, 49*(10), 3461–3473.31201578

Baker, M. B., Yudelson, P. J., & Means, B. (2018). Artificial intelligence in education: A review of the literature. *Educational Researcher, 47*(2), 60–69.

Ballard, M., Gray, M., Reilly, J., & Noggle, M. (2009). Correlates of video game screen time among males: Body mass, physical activity, and other media use. *Eating Behaviors, 10*(3), 161–167. 10.1016/j.eatbeh.2009.05.00119665099

Ballestar, M. T., García-Lazaro, A., Sainz, J., & Sanz, I. (2022). Why is your company not robotic? The technology and human capital needed by firms to become robotic. *Journal of Business Research, 142*, 328–343. 10.1016/j.jbusres.2021.12.061

Baltezarevic, B. (2023). Decoding identity and representation in the age of AI. *Megatrend revija, 20*(2), 141-146.

Bano, M., Zowghi, D., Gervasi, V., & Shams, R. (2023). AI for All: Operationalising Diversity and Inclusion Requirements for AI Systems. *arXiv preprint arXiv:2311.14695.*

Bâra, A. (2024). Enabling coordination in energy communities: A Digital Twin model. *Energy Policy.* Elsevier.

Bareis, J., & Katzenbach, C. (2022). Talking AI into Being: The Narratives and Imaginaries of National AI Strategies and Their Performative Politics. *Science, Technology & Human Values*, 47(5), 855–881. 10.1177/01622439211030007

Barker, P., & Manji, K. (1992). Computer-based training: An institutional approach. *Education and Computing*, 8(3), 229–237. 10.1016/0167-9287(92)92766-S

Baroudi, J. J., & Orlikowski, W. J. (1988). A Short-Form Measure of User Information Satisfaction: A Psychometric Evaluation and Notes on Use. *Journal of Management Information Systems*, 4(4), 44–59. 10.1080/07421222.1988.11517807

Barr, N., Pennycook, G., Stolz, J. A., & Fugelsang, J. A. (2015). The brain in your pocket: Evidence that Smartphones are used to supplant thinking. *Computers in Human Behavior*, 48, 473–480. 10.1016/j.chb.2015.02.029

Basu, R. (2019). Impact of digital detox on individual performance of the employees. *International Journal of Research and Analytical Reviews*, 6(2), 378–381.

Bauer, G. R., Churchill, S. M., Mahendran, M., Walwyn, C., Lizotte, D., & Villa-Rueda, A. A. (2021). Intersectionality in quantitative research: A systematic review of its emergence and applications of theory and methods. *SSM - Population Health*, 14, 100798. 10.1016/j.ssmph.2021.10079833997247

Bauer, G. R., & Scheim, A. I. (2019). Advancing quantitative intersectionality research methods: Intracategorical and intercategorical approaches to shared and differential constructs. *Social Science & Medicine*, 226, 260–262. 10.1016/j.socscimed.2019.03.01830914246

Baumrind, D. (1971). Current patterns of parental authority. *Developmental Psychology*, 4(1, Pt.2), 1–103. 10.1037/h0030372

Baydili, İ. (2023). *Dijital kültürde kimlik İnşası ve bedenin sunumu: Instagram orneği. İ Y. Argın (ritstj.), Güncel yaklaşımlarla geleneksel ve yeni medyada beden (bls.* Nobel.

Bean, J. P. (1980). Dropouts and turnover: The synthesis and test of a causal model of student attrition. *Research in Higher Education*, 12(2), 155–187. 10.1007/BF00976194

Becht, A., Nelemans, S., Branje, S. J. T., Vollebergh, W., Koot, H., Denissen, J. J. A., & Meeus, W. (2016). The quest for identity in adolescence: Heterogeneity in daily identity formation and psychosocial adjustment across 5 years. *Developmental Psychology*, 52(12), 2010–2021. 10.1037/dev000024527893245

Becker, H. C. (1999). The Chicago school, so-called. *Qualitative Sociology*, 22(1), 3–12. 10.1023/A:1022107414846

Bektaş, F., Dereli, B., Hayta, F., Şahin, E., Ali, U., & Eryiğit, G. (2022). Towards a Multilingual Platform for Gamified Morphology Learning. *2022 7th International Conference on Computer Science and Engineering (UBMK)*. IEEE. https://ieeexplore.ieee.org/abstract/document/9919484/

Bell, G. (2021). Talking to AI: An anthropological encounter with artificial intelligence. *The SAGE Handbook of Cultural Anthropology*. SAGE Publications Ltd.

Bell, A. R., Tennfjord, M. K., Tokovska, M., & Eg, R. (2023). Exploring the role of social media literacy in adolescents' experiences with personalization: A norwegian qualitative study. *Journal of Adolescent & Adult Literacy*, 66(4), 239–248. 10.1002/jaal.1273

Bellantuono, L. (2023). Detecting the socio-economic drivers of confidence in government with eXplainable Artificial Intelligence. *Scientific Reports* 13. Nature Publishing Group UK London.

Benus, S. (2014). *Social aspects of entrainment in spoken interaction*. Cognitive Computation.

Bereményi, B. Á. (2023). Between choices and "going with the flow". Career guidance and Roma young people in Hungary. *International Journal for Educational and Vocational Guidance*, 23(3), 555–575. 10.1007/s10775-022-09536-0

Bergemann, W. (2021). *Soziale Medien und Jugendliche. Massenexperiment mit offenem Ausgang.* Deutschlandfunk. https://www.deutschlandfunk.de/soziale-medien-und-jugendliche-massenexperiment-mit-offenem-100.html

Berghe, R., Verhagen, J., Oudgenoeg-Paz, O., Ven, S., & Leseman, P. (2019). Social bobots for language learning: A Review. *Review of Educational Research*, 89(2), 259–295. 10.3102/0034654318821286

Berman, M. G., Jonides, J., & Kaplan, S. (2008). The Cognitive Benefits of Interacting With Nature. *Psychological Science*, 19(12), 1207–1212. 10.1111/j.1467-9280.2008.02225.x19121124

Bers, M. (2014). *Tinkering: Kids, technology, and power tools.* The MIT Press.

Betts, L. R., Spenser, K. A., & Gardner, S. E. (2017). Adolescents' Involvement in Cyber Bullying and Perceptions of School: The Importance of Perceived Peer Acceptance for Female Adolescents. *Sex Roles*, 77(7–8), 471–481. 10.1007/s11199-017-0742-228979061

Betz, N. E. (1994). Self-Concept Theory in Career Development and Counseling. *The Career Development Quarterly*, 43(1), 32–42. 10.1002/j.2161-0045.1994.tb00844.x

Beyens, I., Keijsers, L., & Coyne, S. M. (2022). Social media, parenting, and well-being. *Current Opinion in Psychology*, 47, 101350. 10.1016/j.copsyc.2022.10135035561563

Beyens, I., Pouwels, J. L., van Driel, I. I., Keijsers, L., & Valkenburg, P. M. (2020). The effect of social media on well-being differs from adolescent to adolescent. *Scientific Reports*, 10(1), 10763. 10.1038/s41598-020-67727-732612108

Beyers, W., & Goossens, L. (2008). Dynamics of perceived parenting and identity formation in late adolescence. *Journal of Adolescence*, 31(2), 165–184. 10.1016/j.adolescence.2007.04.00317629552

Bhat, S., D'Souza, R., Suresh, E. S. M., Bhat, S., Raju, R., & Bhat, V. S. (2021). Dynamic classroom strategies to address learning diversity. *Journal of Engineering Education Transformations*, 34(0), 694–702. 10.16920/jeet/2021/v34i0/157168

Bhutani, V., Bahadur, P. S., & Sansaniwal, S. K. (2024). Next Generation Materials for Sustainable Development. In *Harnessing High-Performance Computing and AI for Environmental Sustainability* (pp. 236-265). IGI Global. 10.4018/979-8-3693-1794-5.ch011

Bhutoria, A. (2022). Personalized education and artificial intelligence in the United States, China, and India: A systematic review using a human-in-the-loop model. *Computers and Education: Artificial Intelligence*, 3, 100068. 10.1016/j.caeai.2022.100068

Bimrose, J., & Brown, A. (2014). Mid-Career Progression and Development: The Role for Career Guidance and Counseling. In Arulmani, G., Bakshi, A. J., Leong, F. T. L., & Watts, A. G. (Eds.), *Handbook of Career Development* (pp. 203–222). Springer New York. 10.1007/978-1-4614-9460-7_11

Birk, S., Kremers, S. P. J., & Janssen, I. (2019). The impact of technology on children's physical activity: A systematic review. *International Journal of Environmental Research and Public Health*, 16(12), 1–20.

Blancaflor, E. B., & Hernandez, J. R. (2023). A Compliance Based and Security Assessment of Bring Your Own Device (BYOD) in Organizations. *Communications in Computer and Information Science, 1823 CCIS*. 10.1007/978-3-031-35299-7_10

BMFSFJ [Bundesministerium für Familie, Senioren, Frauen und Jugend] (2021). *Was ist Cybermobbing?* BMFSFJ. https://www.bmfsfj.de/bmfsfj/themen/kinder-und-jugend/medienkompetenz/was-ist-cybermobbing--86484

Bonab, A. B., Rudko, I., & Bellini, F. 2021. A Review and a Proposal About Socio-economic Impacts of Artificial Intelligence. In *Business Revolution in a Digital Era*. Cham: Springer International Publishing. 10.1007/978-3-030-59972-0_18

Bonnardel, N., & Zenasni, F. (2010). The impact of technology on creativity in design: An enhancement? *Creativity and Innovation Management*, 19(2), 180–191. 10.1111/j.1467-8691.2010.00560.x

Bostrom, N. (1998). How long before superintelligence. *International Journal of Futures Studies*, 2(1), 1–9.

Bostrom, N., & Sandberg, A. (2009). Cognitive enhancement: Methods, ethics, regulatory challenges. *Science and Engineering Ethics*, 15(3), 311–341. 10.1007/s11948-009-9142-519543814

Bottaro, R., & Faraci, P. (2022). The use of social networking sites and its impact on adolescents' emotional well-being: A scoping review. *Current Addiction Reports*, 9(4), 518–539. 10.1007/s40429-022-00445-436185594

Bowler, D. E., Buyung-Ali, L. M., Knight, T. M., & Pullin, A. S. (2010). A systematic review of evidence for the benefits of exposure to natural environments to health. *BMC Public Health*, 10(1), 456. 10.1186/1471-2458-10-45620684754

Boyd, D. M., & Ellison, N. B. (2007). Social network sites: Definition, history, and scholarship. *Journal of Computer-Mediated Communication*, 13(1), 210–230. 10.1111/j.1083-6101.2007.00393.x

Bozkurt, A., Karadeniz, A., Baneres, D., Guerrero-Roldán, A. E., & Rodríguez, M. E. (2021). Artificial intelligence and reflections from educational landscape: A review of AI Studies in half a century. *Sustainability (Basel)*, 13(2), 800. 10.3390/su13020800

Bozkurt, A., & Tu, C. (2016). Digital identity formation: Socially being real and present on digital networks. *Educational Media International*, 53(3), 153–167. 10.1080/09523987.2016.1236885

Bradley, J. (2023, Jan 7). *Embracing Change: Transforming Your Life One Step at a Time*. Medium. https://medium.com/lampshade-of-illumination/embracing-change-transforming-your-life-one-step-at-a-time-63781bd0f63b

Brandtzaeg, P. B., Skjuve, M., & Følstad, A. (2022). My ai friend: How users of a social chatbot understand their human–ai friendship. *Human Communication Research*, 48(3), 404–429. 10.1093/hcr/hqac008

Bratman, G. N., Daily, G. C., Levy, B. J., & Gross, J. J. (2015). The benefits of nature experience: Improved affect and cognition. *Landscape and Urban Planning*, 138, 41–50. 10.1016/j.landurbplan.2015.02.005

Braun, B. J., Histing, T., Menger, M. M., Platte, J., Grimm, B., Hanflik, A. M., Richter, P. H., Sivananthan, S., Yarboro, S. R., Gueorguiev, B., Pokhvashchev, D., & Marmor, M. T. (2023). "Bring Your Own Device"—A New Approach to Wearable Outcome Assessment in Trauma. *Medicina (Lithuania)*, 59(2). 10.3390/medicina59020403

Breiter, A., Welling, S., & Stolpmann, B. E. (2010). *Medienkompetenz in der Schule. Integration von Medien in den weiterführenden Schulen in Nordrhein-Westfalen (Schriftenreihe Medienforschung der LfM, Bd. 64)*. Berlin: Vistas Verl.

Brey, P. (2017). *Robot ethics 2.0: An expanded perspective*. Cambridge University Press.

Brockmann PE., Diaz B., Damiani F., &Villarroel L., Núñez F., & Bruni, O. (2016). Impact of television on the quality of sleep in preschool children. *Sleep Med.* .10.1016/j.sleep.2015.06.005

Brodić, D., & Amelio, A. (2015). Classification of the Extremely Low Frequency Magnetic Field Radiation Measurement from the Laptop Computers. *Measurement Science Review*, 15(4), 202–209. 10.1515/msr-2015-0028

Bronfenbrenner, U. (1979). Contexts of child rearing: Problems and prospects. *American psychologist,34*. American Psychological Association.

Brown, J. S., & Valkenburg, P. M. (2012). Parental mediation of children's media use: A meta-analysis. *Communication Research*, 39(3), 318–341.

Brown, L., & Kuss, D. J. (2020). Fear of missing out, mental wellbeing, and social connectedness: A seven-day social media abstinence trial. *International Journal of Environmental Research and Public Health*, 4566(12), 4566. 10.3390/ijerph1712456632599962

Brynjolfsson, E., & McAfee, A. (2014). *The second Machine Age: Work, progress, and Prosperity in a time of brilliant technologies*. W. W. Norton & Company.

Buchanan, L., & Beer, D. (2018). Age Invaders: A game to bridge generations. In *Proceedings of the 2018 CHI Conference on Human Factors in Computing Systems* (pp. 1–14). New York, NY, USA: ACM Press.

Buhmann, A., & Fieseler, C. (2021). Towards a deliberative framework for responsible innovation in artificial intelligence. *Technology in Society*, 64, 101475. 10.1016/j.techsoc.2020.101475

Bujang, S. D. A., Selamat, A., & Krejcar, O. (2021). Decision Tree (J48) Model for Student's Final Grade Prediction: A Machine Learning Approach. *IOP Conference Series. Materials Science and Engineering*, 1051(1), 012005. 10.1088/1757-899X/1051/1/012005

Bukralia, R., Deokar, A. V., & Sarnikar, S. (2015). *Using academic analytics to predict dropout risk in e-Learning courses*. Springer International Publishing. 10.1007/978-3-319-11575-7_6

Buolamwini, J., & Gebru, T. (2018). Gender shades: Intersectional accuracy disparities in commercial gender classification. In *Proceedings of the 2018 ACM Conference Extended Abstracts on Human Factors in Computing Systems (Lecture Notes in Computer Science, Vol. 10791)*. Association for Computing Machinery.

Buolamwini, J., & Gebru, T. (2018). Gender Shades: Intersectional Accuracy Disparities in Commercial Gender Classification. *Proceedings of Machine Learning Research*, 81, 1–15.

Burgess, M. (2021). *Inteligjenca artificiale – si do të përcaktohet dekada e ardhshme nga zhvillimi i sistemeve kompjuterike*. WIRED, Dukagjini, Prishtinë.

Burke, J. G. (2017). WoeBot: A randomized controlled trial of a conversational AI system for depression. *Journal of Medical Internet Research Mental Health*, 6(1), e24.

Cahill, S. E. (2004). Erving Goffman. In Charon, J. M. (Ed.), *Symbolic Interactionism: An Introduction, An Interpretation, An Integration* (pp. 175–188). Pearson Prentice Hall.

Cameron Guthrie, S. F.-W. (2021). Online consumer resilience during a pandemic: An exploratory study of e-commerce behavior before, during and after a COVID-19 lockdown. *Journal of Retailing and Consumer Services*, 61, 102570. 10.1016/j.jretconser.2021.102570

Cantos, K. F. S., Giler, R. C. V., & Magayanes, I. E. C. (2023). Artifical intelligence in language teaching and learning. *Ciencia Latina Revista Cientifica Multidisciplinar*, 7(4), 5629–5638. 10.37811/cl_rcm.v7i4.7368

Capan, G., Bozal, Ö., Gündoğdu, İ., & Cemgil, A. T. (2020). Towards fair personalization by avoiding feedback loops. *arXiv preprint arXiv*:2012.12862.

Caraway, B. R. (2018). Literal media ecology: Crisis in the conditions of production. *Television & New Media*, 19(5), 486–503. 10.1177/1527476417712459

Cárdenas, P. O. R. (2023). What kind of "intelligence" is artificial intelligence? *Metafísica y Persona*, (30), 39–48.

Cardona, M. A., Rodríguez, R. J., & Ishmael, K. (2023). *Artificial intelligence and the future of teaching and learning: Insights and recommendations*.https://policycommons.net/artifacts/3854312/ai-report/4660267/

Carpenter, J., & Bithell, J. (2000). Bootstrap confidence intervals: When, which, what? A practical guide for medical statisticians. *Statistics in Medicine*, 19(9), 1141–1164. 10.1002/(SICI)1097-0258(20000515)19:9<1141::AID-SIM479>3.0.CO;2-F10797513

Carr, N. (2011). *The Shallows: What the Internet Is Doing to Our Brains*. W. W. Norton & Company.

Carter, J. A., & Palermos, S. O. (2019). The ethics of extended cognition: Is having your computer compromised a personal assault? *Journal of the American Philosophical Association*.

Cathrin, S., & Wikandaru, R. (2023) *The future of character education in the era of artificial intelligence*. Humanika, Kajian Ilmiah Mata Kuliah Umum10.21831/hum.v23i1.59741

Cavanagh, T., Chen, B., Lahcen, R. A. M., & Paradiso, J. R. (2020). Constructing a design framework and pedagogical approach for adaptive learning in higher education: A practitioner's perspective. *International Review of Research in Open and Distance Learning*, 21(1), 173–197. 10.19173/irrodl.v21i1.4557

Cave, S. J., Nyrup, R., Vold, K., & Weller, A. (2018). Motivations and Risks of Machine Ethics. *Proceedings of the IEEE*, 99, 1–13.

CEFR. (2018). *Common european framework of reference for languages: learning, teaching, assessment companion volume with new descriptors*. Council of Europe.

Chabris, C., & Simons, D. (2010). *The invisible gorilla: And other ways our intuitions deceive us*. Harmony.

Chaka, C. (2023). Fourth industrial revolution—A review of applications, prospects, and challenges for artificial intelligence, robotics and blockchain in higher education. *Research and Practice in Technology Enhanced Learning*, 18, 1–39.

Chakraborty, U. (2020). *Artificial Intelligence for All: Transforming Every Aspect of Our Life*. Bpb publications. https://books.google.com/books?hl=en&lr=&id=J-_QDwAAQBAJ&oi=fnd&pg=PT18&dq=a+new+generation+of+academics+is+investigating+how+AI-powered+mobile+apps+might+transform+sectors+including+banking,+agriculture,+transportation,+and+entertainment&ots=uxHLvq7Yk-&sig=rP6WItgTh2EZwK_T3HEmNukmJr4

Chan, C., & Lee, K. (2023). *The AI generation gap: Are Gen Z students more interested in adopting generative AI such as ChatGPT in teaching and learning than their Gen X and millennial generation teachers?* Smart Learning Environment., 10.1186/s40561-023-00269-3

Chang, A. M., Aeschbach, D., Duffy, J. F., & Czeisler, C. A. (2015). Evening use of light-emitting eReaders negatively affects sleep, circadian timing, and next-morning alertness. *Proceedings of the National Academy of Sciences of the United States of America*, 112(4), 1232–1237. 10.1073/pnas.141849011225535358

Chang, Y., & Zhao, Y. (2020). The Proposal, Connotation and Significance of the Concept of Content-Language Integration (CLI)—From content-based instruction to content-language integration education. *Foreign Lang. Educ. China*, 41, 49–54.

Chao, J., Ellis, R., Jiang, S., Rosé, C., Finzer, W., Tatar, C., Fiacco, J., & Wiedemann, K. (2023). Exploring artificial intelligence in english language arts with storyQ. *The Thirty-Seventh AAAI Conference on Artificial Intelligence (AAAI-23)*. AAAI. 10.1609/aaai.v37i13.26899

Charmaraman, L. (2020). Social and behavioral health factors associated with violent and mature gaming in early adolescence. *International journal of environmental research and public health,17*.

Chassiakos, Y. L. R., & Stager, M. (2020). Current trends in digital media: How and why teens use technology. In *Technology and adolescent health* (pp. 25–56). Elsevier. 10.1016/B978-0-12-817319-0.00002-5

Chen, S., & She, W. (2023) Values and Ethics- How artificial intelligence will better serve humanity. B. Majoul et al. (Eds.): ICLAHD 2022, ASSEHR 726, pp. 296–300, 2023. https://doi.org/10.2991/978-2-494069-97-8_37

Chen, C.-H., & Yeh, Y.-C. (2018). The impact of technology acceptance on students' learning motivation and achievement in a digital learning environment. *Computers & Education*, 122, 160–171.

Chen, L., Chen, P., & Lin, Z. (2020). Artificial intelligence in education: A review. *IEEE Access : Practical Innovations, Open Solutions*, 8, 75264–75278. 10.1109/ACCESS.2020.2988510

Chen, M., & Decary, M. (2020). Artificial intelligence in healthcare: An essential guide for health leaders. *Healthcare Management Forum*, 33(1), 10–18. 10.1177/0840470419873123311550922

Chen, X., Zou, D., Cheng, G., & Xie, H. (2021). Artificial intelligence-assisted personalized language learning: systematic review and co-citation analysis. *International Conference on Advanced Learning Technologies (ICALT)*, (pp. 241–245). IEEE. 10.1109/ICALT52272.2021.00079

Chen, Y., Chen, Y., & Chen, Y. (2019). Virtual communities and collaboration: Enhancing social connections through AI-driven platforms. In *Proceedings of the 2019 CHI Conference on Human Factors in Computing Systems* (pp. 1-10). New York, NY, USA: ACM Press.

Chen, Y.-W., Wang, C.-H., & Chao, C.-H. (2019). A survey on voice assistants. *IEEE Transactions on Affective Information and Social Computing*, 1(1), 1–17.

Chen, Y., Zhang, J., & Zhang, Y. (2019). AI-assisted language learning: A review of the literature. *Language Learning & Technology*, 24(2), 1–24.

Chi, N., Lurie, E., & Mulligan, D. K. (2021, July). Reconfiguring diversity and inclusion for AI ethics. In *Proceedings of the 2021 AAAI/ACM Conference on AI, Ethics, and Society* (pp. 447-457). ACM. 10.1145/3461702.3462622

Chisega, N. (2023). The new revolution language learning: The power of artificial intelligence and education 4.0. *Bulletin*, 2, 16–27.

Choudrie, A., & Kaur, H. (2019). Parental mediation of children's digital media use: A systematic review. *International Journal of Human-Computer Interaction*, 35(1), 1–20.

Chu, Y.-H., & Kim, Y. (2005). The effects of website design and consumer involvement on online shopping behavior. *Journal of Business Research*, 57(5), 571–580.

Cinelli, M., Morales, G. D. F., Galeazzi, A., Quattrociocchi, W., & Starnini, M. (2020). Echo chambers on social media: A comparative analysis. *arXiv preprint arXiv:2004.09603*.

Cipolletta, S., Malighetti, C., Cenedese, C., & Spoto, A. (2020). How can adolescents benefit from the use of social networks? The iGeneration on Instagram. *International Journal of Environmental Research and Public Health*, 17(19), 6952. 10.3390/ijerph1719695232977532

Cirillo, D. (2020). Sex and gender differences and biases in artificial intelligence for biomedicine and healthcare. *NPJ digital medicine*. Nature Publishing Group.

Ciston, S. (2019). Intersectional AI Is Essential. *Journal of Science and Technology of the Arts*, 11(2), 3–8. 10.7559/citarj.v11i2.665

Clark, A., & Chalmers, D. (1998). The extended mind. *Analysis*, 58(1), 7–19. 10.1093/analys/58.1.7

Clarke, B. (2009). Early Adolescents' Use of Social Networking Sites to Maintain Friendship and Explore Identity: Implications for Policy. *Policy and Internet*, 1(1), 55–89. 10.2202/1944-2866.1018

Clark, L. S. (2021). Parenting in a digital age: Challenges and opportunities. *The Future of Children*, 31(2), 119–140.

Cockburn, I. M., Henderson, R., & Stern, S. (2018). *The impact of artificial intelligence on innovation (Vol. 24449)*. National bureau of economic research Cambridge, MA, USA.

Collins, P. H. (2020). Defining black feminist thought. In *Feminist theory reader* (pp. 278–290). Routledge.

Collins, R. (1986). The passing of intellectual generations: Reflections on the death of Erving Goffman. *Sociological Theory*, 4(1), 106–113. 10.2307/202109

Correa, C. H. (2019). Screen Time and the Logic of Identification in the Networked Society. In *Managing Screen Time in an Online Society* (pp. 99-121). IGI Global. 10.4018/978-1-5225-8163-5.ch005

Cotton, D. R. E., Cotton, P. A., & Shipway, J. R. (2024). Chatting and cheating: Ensuring academic integrity in the era of ChatGPT. *Innovations in Education and Teaching International*, 61(2), 228–239. 10.1080/14703297.2023.2190148

Craig-Bray, L., Adams, G., & Dobson, W. R. (1988). Identity formation and social relations during late adolescence. *Journal of Youth and Adolescence*, 17(2), 173–187. 10.1007/BF0153796624277583

Crawford, K., & Ferri, R. (2019). An algorithmic approach to algorithmic accountability. *AI & Society*, 34(1), 145–159.

Crenshaw, K. (1989). Demarginalizing the intersection of race and sex: A black feminist critique of antidiscrimination doctrine, feminist theory, and antiracist politics. *University of Chicago Legal Forum*, 1989(1), 139–167.

Crenshaw, K. (1991). Mapping the margins: Intersectionality, identity politics, and violence against women of color. *Stanford Law Review*, 43(6), 1241–1299. 10.2307/1229039

Crocetti, E., Klimstra, T., Hale, W.III, Koot, H., & Meeus, W. (2013). Impact of Early Adolescent Externalizing Problem Behaviors on Identity Development in Middle to Late Adolescence: A Prospective 7-Year Longitudinal Study. *Journal of Youth and Adolescence*, 42(11), 1745–1758. 10.1007/s10964-013-9924-623385617

Croeser, S., & Eckersley, P. (2019, January). Theories of parenting and their application to artificial intelligence. In *Proceedings of the 2019 AAAI/ACM Conference on AI, Ethics, and Society* (pp. 423–428). ACM. 10.1145/3306618.3314231

Csikszentmihalyi, M. (1990). *Flow: The Psychology of Optimal Experience*. Harper & Row.

Csikszentmihalyi, M. (1997). *Finding Flow: The Psychology of Engagement with Everyday Life*. Basic Books.

Csikszentmihalyi, M., & Csikzentmihaly, M. (1990). *Flow: The psychology of optimal experience* (Vol. 1990). Harper & Row.

Cunningham, N. R., & Eastin, M. S. (2017). Second screen and sports: A structural investigation into team identification and efficacy. *Communication & Sport*, 5(3), 288–310. 10.1177/2167479515610152

D'Alfonso, S., Santesteban-Echarri, O., Rice, S., Wadley, G., Lederman, R., Miles, C., Gleeson, J., & Alvarez-Jimenez, M. (2017). Artificial intelligence-assisted online social therapy for youth mental health. *Frontiers in Psychology*, 8(JUN), 796. 10.3389/fpsyg.2017.0079628626431

Dabingaya, M. (2022). Analyzing the Effectiveness of AI-Powered Adaptive Learning Platforms in Mathematics Education. *Interdisciplinary Journal Papier Human Review*, 3(1), 1–7. 10.47667/ijphr.v3i1.226

Dahdal, S. (2019). Cultural educating of palestinian youth through collaborative digital storytelling. *E-Learning and Digital Media*, 16(2), 136–150. 10.1177/2042753019828354

Dai, Z., Sun, C., Zhao, L., & Zhu, X. (2023). The Effect of Smart Classrooms on Project-Based Learning: A Study Based on Video Interaction Analysis. *Journal of Science Education and Technology*, 32(6), 858–871. 10.1007/s10956-023-10056-x

DAK. (2023). *DAK-Studie: In pandemie hat sich mediiensucht verdoppelt.* DAK. https://www.dak.de/presse/bundesthemen/kinder-jugendgesundheit/dak-studie-in-pandemie-hat-sich-med+ 沒得-sucht-verdoppelt_48672#/

Dalton, T. (2019). *The Joy of Missing Out: Live More by Doing Less.* Thomas Nelson.

Danaher, J. (2018). Toward an Ethics of AI Assistants: An Initial Framework. *Philosophy & Technology*, 31(4), 1–25. 10.1007/s13347-018-0317-3

Darling, N., & Steinberg, L. (1993). Parenting style as context: An integrative model. *Psychological Bulletin*, 113(3), 487–496. 10.1037/0033-2909.113.3.487

Darvin, R. (2019). Youth, Technology, and the Hidden Curriculum of the 21st Century. *Youth and Globalization*, 1(2), 210–229. 10.1163/25895745-00102002

Davenport, T., Guha, A., Grewal, D., & Bressgott, T. (2020). How artificial intelligence will change the future of marketing. *Journal of the Academy of Marketing Science*, 48(1), 24–42. 10.1007/s11747-019-00696-0

Davis, C. H. (2019). Student activism, resource mobilization, and new tactical repertoires in the 'digital age. In *Student activism, politics, and campus climate in higher education* (pp. 112–124). Routledge. 10.4324/9780429449178-7

Davis, K. (2013). Young people's digital lives: The impact of interpersonal relationships and digital media use on adolescents' sense of identity. *Computers in Human Behavior*, 29(6), 2281–2293. 10.1016/j.chb.2013.05.022

Davis, K., & Weinstein, E. (2017). Identity development in the digital age: An Eriksonian perspective. In *Identity, sexuality, and relationships among emerging adults in the digital age* (pp. 1–17). IGI Global. 10.4018/978-1-5225-1856-3.ch001

De Angelis, L., Baglivo, F., Arzilli, G., Privitera, G. P., Ferragina, P., Tozzi, A. E., & Rizzo, C. (2023). ChatGPT and the rise of large language models: The new AI-driven infodemic threat in public health. *Frontiers in Public Health*, 1–8.37181697

De Felice, F., Iovine, G., & Petrillo, A. (2023). Reflections on Metaverse. In *Concepts in Smart Societies: Next-generation of Human Resources and Technologies* (p. 72). CRC Press. https://books.google.com/books?hl=en&lr=&id=0STcEAAAQBAJ&oi=fnd&pg=PA72&dq=De+Felice+et+al.,+2022+%2B+fear+of+missing+out+(FOMO)&ots=sr4_m3Klt_&sig=WuB8RWrPOO5ZAteuxbmwmijczyA10.1201/9781003251507-5

de Hond, A. A., van Buchem, M. M., & Hernandez-Boussard, T. (2022). Picture a data scientist: A call to action for increasing diversity, equity, and inclusion in the age of AI. *Journal of the American Medical Informatics Association : JAMIA*, 29(12), 2178–2181. 10.1093/jamia/ocac15636048021

de Queiroz, F. S., & Andersen, M. B. (2020). Psychodynamic approaches. In *Applied Sport, Exercise, and Performance Psychology* (pp. 12–30). Routledge. https://www.taylorfrancis.com/chapters/edit/10.4324/9780429503702-2/psychodynamic-approaches-fernanda-serra-de-queiroz-mark-andersen

De Witte, N. A. J., Joris, S., Van Assche, E., & Van Daele, T. (2021, December 23). Technological and Digital Interventions for Mental Health and Wellbeing: An Overview of Systematic Reviews. *Frontiers in Digital Health*, 754337, 754337. 10.3389/fdgth.2021.75433735005695

Dedeoğlu, G. (2004). Gözetleme, mahremiyet ve insan onuru. *TBD Bilişim*, 89, 36.

Delacroix, E., Parguel, B., & Benoit-Moreau, F. (2019). Digital subsistence entrepreneurs on Facebook. *Technological Forecasting and Social Change*, 146, 887–899. 10.1016/j.techfore.2018.06.018

Deshpande, V., Srivastava, A., & Terveen, L. (2019). *Recommender systems handbook.* MIT Press.

Dey, S. K., & Dey, A. (2021). Digital Pedagogical Paradigm in Language Lab-Based English Teaching for Higher Technical Education. In Deyasi, A., Mukherjee, S., Mukherjee, A., Bhattacharjee, A. K., & Mondal, A. (Eds.), *Computational Intelligence in Digital Pedagogy* (Vol. 197, pp. 251–275). Springer Singapore. 10.1007/978-981-15-8744-3_13

Di Paolo, E. (2009). Extended life. *Topoi*, 28(1), 9–21. 10.1007/s11245-008-9042-3

Di Vaio, A., Palladino, R., Hassan, R., & Escobar, O. (2020). Artificial intelligence and business models in the sustainable development goals perspective: A systematic literature review. *Journal of Business Research*, 121, 283–314. 10.1016/j.jbusres.2020.08.019

Dienlin, T. J. N., & Johannes, N. (2020). The impact of digital technology use on adolescent well-being. *Dialogues in Clinical Neuroscience*, 22(2), 135–142. 10.31887/DCNS.2020.22.2/tdienlin32699513

Dimitriadis, Y., Lithari, E., & Koutsabasis, P. (2018). *A systematic literature review of learning analytics research in higher education. Computers & education*, *125*, 170–185.

Divya, T. V., & Manikandan, K. (2013). *Perceived Parenting Style Scale*. Department of Psychology, University of Calicut.

Dixon, J., Hong, B., & Wu, L. (2021). The robot revolution: Managerial and employment consequences for firms. *Management Science*, 67(9), 5586–5605. 10.1287/mnsc.2020.3812

Dos Santos Melicio, B. C., Xiang, L., Dillon, E., Soorya, L., Chetouani, M., Sarkany, A., & Lorincz, A. (2023, October). *Composite AI for Behavior Analysis in Social Interactions*. In *Companion Publication of the 25th International Conference on Multimodal Interaction* (pp. 389-397). ACM. 10.1145/3610661.3616237

Dresp-Langley, B., & Hutt, A. (2022). Digital Addiction and Sleep. *International Journal of Environmental Research and Public Health*, 19(11), 6910. 10.3390/ijerph1911691035682491

Duan, Y. (2019). Artificial intelligence for decision making in the era of Big Data–evolution, challenges and research agenda. *International journal of information management,48*. Elsevier.

Duerager, A., & Livingstone, S. (2012). *How can parents support children's internetsafety?* EU Kids Online.

Du, Y. (2021). systematic review of artificial intelligence in language learning. advances in engineering and applied science research. *Proceedings of the 2021 International Conference on Intelligent Manufacturing Technology and Information Technology*. IEEE.

Dwairy, M. (2004). Parenting Styles and Mental Health of Palestinian–Arab Adolescents in Israel. *Transcultural Psychiatry*, 41(2), 233–252. 10.1177/136346150404356615446722

Dwijendra, N. (2022). Benchmarking of traditional and advanced machine Learning modelling techniques for forecasting in book. *Visualization Techniques for Climate Change with Machine Learning and Artificial Intelligence*. Elsevier. 10.1016/B978-0-323-99714-0.00017-0

Dwivedi, D. N., Mahanty, G., & Pathak, Y. K. (2023). AI Applications for Financial Risk Management. In M. Irfan, M. Elmogy, M. Shabri Abd. Majid, & S. El-Sappagh (Eds.), *The Impact of AI Innovation on Financial Sectors in the Era of Industry 5.0* (pp. 17-31). IGI Global. 10.4018/979-8-3693-0082-4.ch002

Dwivedi, D. N., Mahanty, G., & Vemareddy, A. (2023). Sentiment Analysis and Topic Modeling for Identifying Key Public Concerns of Water Quality/Issues. In: Harun, S., Othman, I.K., Jamal, M.H. (eds) *Proceedings of the 5th International Conference on Water Resources (ICWR) – Volume 1. Lecture Notes in Civil Engineering*. Springer, Singapore. 10.1007/978-981-19-5947-9_28

Dwivedi, D. N., Pandey, A. K., & Dwivedi, A. D. (2023). Examining the emotional tone in politically polarized Speeches in India: An In-Depth analysis of two contrasting perspectives. *SOUTH INDIA JOURNAL OF SOCIAL SCIENCES, 21*(2), 125-136. https://journal.sijss.com/index.php/home/article/view/65

Dwivedi, Y. (2021). Artificial Intelligence (AI): Multidisciplinary perspectives on emerging challenges, opportunities, and agenda for research, practice and policy. *International Journal of Information Management, 57*. Elsevier.

Dwivedi, A. K., Virmani, D., Ramasamy, A., Acharjee, P. B., & Tiwari, M. (2022). Modelling and analysis of artificial intelligence approaches in enhancing the speech recognition for effective multi-functional machine learning platform–a multi regression modelling approach. *Journal of Engineering Research-ICMET*, 04-06(Special Issue). 10.36909/jer.ICMET.17161

Dwivedi, D. N. (2024). The Use of Artificial Intelligence in Supply Chain Management and Logistics. In Sharma, D., Bhardwaj, B., & Dhiman, M. (Eds.), *Leveraging AI and Emotional Intelligence in Contemporary Business Organizations* (pp. 306–313). IGI Global. 10.4018/979-8-3693-1902-4.ch018

Dwivedi, D. N., & Anand, A. (2021). Trade Heterogeneity in the EU: Insights from the Emergence of COVID-19 Using Time Series Clustering. *Zeszyty Naukowe Uniwersytetu Ekonomicznego w Krakowie*, 3(993), 9–26. 10.15678/ZNUEK.2021.0993.0301

Dwivedi, D. N., & Anand, A. (2022). A Comparative Study of Key Themes of Scientific Research Post COVID-19 in the United Arab Emirates and WHO Using Text Mining Approach. In Tiwari, S., Trivedi, M. C., Kolhe, M. L., Mishra, K., & Singh, B. K. (Eds.), *Advances in Data and Information Sciences. Lecture Notes in Networks and Systems* (Vol. 318). Springer. 10.1007/978-981-16-5689-7_30

Dwivedi, D. N., & Batra, S. (2024). Case Studies in Big Data Analysis: A Novel Computer Vision Application to Detect Insurance Fraud. In Darwish, D. (Ed.), *Big Data Analytics Techniques for Market Intelligence* (pp. 441–450). IGI Global. 10.4018/979-8-3693-0413-6.ch018

Dwivedi, D. N., Batra, S., & Pathak, Y. K. (2024). Enhancing Customer Experience: Exploring Deep Learning Models for Banking Customer Journey Analysis. In Sharma, H., Chakravorty, A., Hussain, S., & Kumari, R. (Eds.), *Artificial Intelligence: Theory and Applications. AITA 2023. Lecture Notes in Networks and Systems* (Vol. 843). Springer. 10.1007/978-981-99-8476-3_39

Dwivedi, D. N., & Gupta, A. (2022). Artificial intelligence-driven power demand estimation and short-, medium-, and long-term forecasting. In *Artificial Intelligence for Renewable Energy Systems* (pp. 231–242). Woodhead Publishing. 10.1016/B978-0-323-90396-7.00013-4

Dwivedi, D. N., & Khashouf, S. (2024). Tackling Customer Wait Times: Advanced Techniques for Call Centre Optimization. In Bansal, S., Kumar, N., & Agarwal, P. (Eds.), *Intelligent Optimization Techniques for Business Analytics* (pp. 255–267). IGI Global. 10.4018/979-8-3693-1598-9.ch011

Dwivedi, D. N., & Mahanty, G. (2024). AI-Powered Employee Experience: Strategies and Best Practices. In Rafiq, M., Farrukh, M., Mushtaq, R., & Dastane, O. (Eds.), *Exploring the Intersection of AI and Human Resources Management* (pp. 166–181). IGI Global. 10.4018/979-8-3693-0039-8.ch009

Dwivedi, D. N., & Mahanty, G. (2024). Guardians of the Algorithm: Human Oversight in the Ethical Evolution of AI and Data Analysis. In Kumar, R., Joshi, A., Sharan, H., Peng, S., & Dudhagara, C. (Eds.), *The Ethical Frontier of AI and Data Analysis* (pp. 196–210). IGI Global. 10.4018/979-8-3693-2964-1.ch012

Dwivedi, D. N., & Mahanty, G. (2024). Unmasking the Shadows: Exploring Unethical AI Implementation. In Dadwal, S., Goyal, S., Kumar, P., & Verma, R. (Eds.), *Demystifying the Dark Side of AI in Business* (pp. 185–200). IGI Global. 10.4018/979-8-3693-0724-3.ch012

Dwivedi, D. N., Mahanty, G., & Dwivedi, V. N. (2024). The Role of Predictive Analytics in Personalizing Education: Tailoring Learning Paths for Individual Student Success. In Bhatia, M., & Mushtaq, M. (Eds.), *Enhancing Education With Intelligent Systems and Data-Driven Instruction* (pp. 44–59). IGI Global. 10.4018/979-8-3693-2169-0.ch003

Dwivedi, D. N., Mahanty, G., & Vemareddy, A. (2022). How Responsible Is AI?: Identification of Key Public Concerns Using Sentiment Analysis and Topic Modeling. [IJIRR]. *International Journal of Information Retrieval Research*, 12(1), 1–14. 10.4018/IJIRR.298646

Dwivedi, D. N., & Pathak, S. (2022). Sentiment Analysis for COVID Vaccinations Using Twitter: Text Clustering of Positive and Negative Sentiments. In Hassan, S. A., Mohamed, A. W., & Alnowibet, K. A. (Eds.), *Decision Sciences for COVID-19. International Series in Operations Research & Management Science* (Vol. 320). Springer. 10.1007/978-3-030-87019-5_12

Dwivedi, D. N., Tadoori, G., & Batra, S. (2023). Impact of women leadership and ESG ratings and in organizations: A time series segmentation study. *Academy of Strategic Management Journal*, 22(S3), 1–6.

Dwivedi, D. N., Wójcik, K., & Vemareddyb, A. (2022). Identification of Key Concerns and Sentiments Towards Data Quality and Data Strategy Challenges Using Sentiment Analysis and Topic Modeling. In Jajuga, K., Dehnel, G., & Walesiak, M. (Eds.), *Modern Classification and Data Analysis. SKAD 2021. Studies in Classification, Data Analysis, and Knowledge Organization*. Springer. 10.1007/978-3-031-10190-8_2

Dwivedi, D., Batra, S., & Pathak, Y. K. (2023). A machine learning based approach to identify key drivers for improving corporate's esg ratings. *Journal of Law and Sustainable Development*, 11(1), e0242. 10.37497/sdgs.v11i1.242

Dwivedi, D., Kapur, P. N., & Kapur, N. N. (2023). Machine Learning Time Series Models for Tea Pest Looper Infestation in Assam, India. In Sharma, A., Chanderwal, N., & Khan, R. (Eds.), *Convergence of Cloud Computing, AI, and Agricultural Science* (pp. 280–289). IGI Global. 10.4018/979-8-3693-0200-2.ch014

Dwivedi, D., Mahanty, G., & Dwivedi, A. D. (2024). Artificial Intelligence Is the New Secret Sauce for Good Governance. In Ogunleye, O. (Ed.), *Machine Learning and Data Science Techniques for Effective Government Service Delivery* (pp. 94–113). IGI Global. 10.4018/978-1-6684-9716-6.ch004

Dwivedi, D., & Vemareddy, A. (2023). Sentiment Analytics for Crypto Pre and Post Covid: Topic Modeling. In Molla, A. R., Sharma, G., Kumar, P., & Rawat, S. (Eds.), Lecture Notes in Computer Science: Vol. 13776. *Distributed Computing and Intelligent Technology. ICDCIT 2023*. Springer. 10.1007/978-3-031-24848-1_21

Dwivedi, Y. K., Hughes, L., Ismagilova, E., Aarts, G., Coombs, C., Crick, T., Duan, Y., Dwivedi, R., Edwards, J., Eirug, A., Galanos, V., Ilavarasan, P. V., Janssen, M., Jones, P., Kar, A. K., Kizgin, H., Kronemann, B., Lal, B., Lucini, B., & Williams, M. D. (2021). Artificial Intelligence (AI): Multidisciplinary perspectives on emerging challenges, opportunities, and agenda for research, practice and policy. *International Journal of Information Management*, 57, 101994. 10.1016/j.ijinfomgt.2019.08.002

Dziadosz, J. (2018). *The potential of AI in education*. Education Dive. https://www.educationdive.com/news/the-potential-of-ai-in-education/536385/

Eduljee, N. B., Murphy, L., & Croteau, K. (2022). Digital Distractions, Mindfulness, and Academic Performance With Undergraduate College Students. In S. Gupta (Ed.), Handbook of Research on Clinical Applications of Meditation and Mindfulness-Based Interventions in Mental Health (pp. 319-336). IGI Global. https://doi.org/10.4018/978-1-7998-8682-2.ch02010.4018/978-1-7998-8682-2.ch020

Eichenberg, C., & Auersperg, F. (2018). *Chancen und Risiken digitaler Medien für Kinder und Jugendliche: Ein Ratgeber für Eltern und Pädagogen.* Hogrefe. 10.1026/02647-000

Eid, A. (2023). Visual Static Hand Gesture Recognition Using Convolutional Neural Network. *Algorithm MDPI,16*(8), 1-19.

El Asmar, W. (2022). *The Effectiveness of AI-Powered Digital Educational Platforms: Students' Attainment and Teachers' Teaching strategies in a private high school in Dubai* [PhD Thesis, The British University in Dubai]. https://search.proquest.com/openview/a0fbb2f4cebaed07810cb3970f96fcbf/1?pq-origsite=gscholar&cbl=2026366&diss=y

Engelbart, D. C. (1962). *Augmenting human intellect: a conceptual framework. Summary Report AFOSR-3233.* Stanford Research Institute, Menlo Park, CA.

Engelbrecht, J. M., Michler, A., Schwarzbach, P., & Michler, O. (2024). Bring Your Own Device - Enabling Student-Centric Learning in Engineering Education by Incorporating Smartphone-Based Data Acquisition. *Lecture Notes in Networks and Systems, 900 LNNS.* 10.1007/978-3-031-52667-1_36

Erikson, E. (1973). Identität und Lebenszyklus. Auflage. Frankfurt a. M.: Suhrkamp Verlag.

Erikson, E. H. (1950). *Childhood and Society.* Norton.

Esteva, A., Kuprel, P., Shiraishi, K., Delange, F., Sabe, A., Li, Z, & Szolovits, P. (2019). Dermatologist-level classification of skin cancer with deep neural networks. *Nature*, 542(5895), 115–118.28117445

Evans, C., & Erickson, N. (2019). Intersectionality and depression in adolescence and early adulthood: A MAIHDA analysis of the national longitudinal study of adolescent to adult health, 1995-2008. *Social Science & Medicine*, 220, 1–11. 10.1016/j.socscimed.2018.10.01930390469

Eysenbach, G. (2023). The role of chatgpt, generative language models, and artifical intelligence in medical education: A conversation with chatgpt and a call for paper. *JMIR Medical Education*, 9, 1–13. 10.2196/4688536863937

Fasanya, B. K., & Strong, J. D. (2019). Younger Generation Safety: Hearing Loss and Academic Performance Degradation Among College Student Headphone Users. In *Advances in Safety Management and Human Factors*. Springer International Publishing. 10.1007/978-3-319-94589-7_51

Fast, N. (2020). Power and decision making: new directions for research in the age of artificial intelligence. *Current opinion in psychology*. Elsevier.

Faul, F., Erdfelder, E., Buchner, A., & Lang, A. G. (2009). Statistical power analyses using G*Power 3.1: Tests for correlation and regression analyses. *Behavior Research Methods*, 41(4), 1149–1160. 10.3758/BRM.41.4.114919897823

Feldman-Barrett, C. (2018). Back to the future: Mapping a historic turn in youth studies. *Journal of Youth Studies*, 21(6), 733–746. 10.1080/13676261.2017.1420150

Fernández-Gutiérrez, M., Gimenez, G., & Calero, J. (2020). Is the use of ICT in education leading to higher student outcomes? Analysis from the Spanish Autonomous Communities. *Computers & Education*, 157, 103969. 10.1016/j.compedu.2020.103969

Festinger, L. (1954). A theory of social comparison processes. *Human Relations*, 7(2), 117–140. 10.1177/001872675400700202

Fetzer, J. H., & Fetzer, J. H. (1990). *What is artificial intelligence?* Springer.

Fink, L., Shao, J., Lichtenstein, Y., & Haefliger, S. (2020). The ownership of digital infrastructure: Exploring the deployment of software libraries in a digital innovation cluster. *Journal of Information Technology*, 35(3), 251–269. 10.1177/0268396220936705

Fioravanti, G., Prostamo, A., & Casale, S. (2019). Taking a short break from Instagram: The effects on subjective well-being. *Cyberpsychology, Behavior, and Social Networking.* 10.1089/cyber.2019.040031851833

Fiske, S. T., & Taylor, S. E. (1984). *Social cognition: From brains to culture.* McGraw-Hill.

Floridi, L. (2013). *The philosophy of information.* Oxford University Press.

Floridi, L. (2014). *The fourth revolution: How the infosphere is reshaping human reality.* Oxford University Press.

Floridi, L., Taddeo, M., & Woods, J. (2018). Responsible AI: An agenda. *AI & Society, 33*(3), 331–344.

Ford, L. (2018). *Artificial intelligence and children's rights: A framework for policy and practice.* UNICEF Office of Research - Innocenti.

Fox, J., & Ralston, R. (2016). Queer identity online: Informal learning and teaching experiences of LGBTQ individuals on social media. *Computers in Human Behavior, 65,* 635–642. 10.1016/j.chb.2016.06.009

France, A., & Roberts, S. (2015). The problem of social generations: A critique of the new emerging orthodoxy in youth studies. *Journal of Youth Studies, 18*(2), 215–230. 10.1080/13676261.2014.944122

Fredricks, J. A., Bohnert, A. M., & Burdette, K. (2019). Moving beyond attendance: Lessons learned from assessing engagement in afterschool contexts. *Journal of Youth Development.*

Frey, C. B., & Osborne, M. A. (2013). *The future of employment: How susceptible are jobs to computerization?* IZA Discussion Papers.

Frey, W. R., Patton, D. U., Gaskell, M. B., & McGregor, K. A. (2020). Artificial Intelligence and Inclusion: Formerly Gang-Involved Youth as Domain Experts for Analyzing Unstructured Twitter Data. *Social Science Computer Review, 38*(1), 42–56. 10.1177/089443931878831436061240

Frischmann, B., & Selinger, E. (2018). *Re-engineering humanity.* Cambridge University Press. 10.1017/9781316544846

Fuchs, K. (2023). Exploring the opportunities and challenges of NLP models in higher education: is Chat GPT a blessing or a curse?. *Frontiers in Education (Vol. 8,* p. 1166682). 10.3389/feduc.2023.1166682

Fuentes, M., Garcia, O., & Garcia, F. (2020). Special Issue Psychosocial Risk and Protective Factors for Sustainable Development in Childhood and Adolescence. *Sustainability (Basel), 12*(15), 5962. 10.3390/su12155962

Ganatra, N. J., & Pandya, J. D. (2023). The transformative impact of artificial intelligence on hr practices and employee experience: A review. *Journal of Management Research and Analysis, 10*(2), 106–111. 10.18231/j.jmra.2023.018

Gani, N., Dom, N., Dapari, R., & Precha, N. (2023). Spatial and temporal analysis of 2019 novel coronavirus (2019-ncov) cases in selangor, malaysia. *The Indonesian Journal of Geography, 55*(1), 148. 10.22146/ijg.73633

Gao, Y., Wang, Y., & Tang, X. (2018). *AICAN: An artificial intelligence system for creating art.* arXiv preprint arXiv:1805.06997.

Garcia, A., Mirra, N., Morrell, E., Martinez, A., & Scorza, D. (2015). The Council of Youth Research: Critical Literacy and Civic Agency in the Digital Age. *Reading & Writing Quarterly, 31*(2), 151–167. 10.1080/10573569.2014.962203

Garcia-Hernandez, J. A., Arroyo-Morales, M. J., & Gomez-Skarmeta, J. F. (2020). Artificial intelligence for assistive technology: A systematic review. *International Journal of Environmental Research and Public Health, 17*(14), 4829.

Gati, I., Levin, N., & Landman-Tal, S. (2019). Decision-Making Models and Career Guidance. In Athanasou, J. A., & Perera, H. N. (Eds.), *International Handbook of Career Guidance* (pp. 115–145). Springer International Publishing. 10.1007/978-3-030-25153-6_6

Gawande, V., Al Badi, H., & Al Makharoumi, K. (2020). An Empirical Study on Emerging Trends in Artificial Intelligence and its Impact on Higher Education. *International Journal of Computer Applications*, 175(12), 43–47. 10.5120/ijca2020920642

Gedrimiene, E., Celik, I., Kaasila, A., Mäkitalo, K., & Muukkonen, H. (2024). Artificial Intelligence (AI)-enhanced learning analytics (LA) for supporting Career decisions: Advantages and challenges from user perspective. *Education and Information Technologies*, 29(1), 297–322. 10.1007/s10639-023-12277-4

Gellert, M. J., Chan, K. H., & Selinger, E. M. (2018). Facial recognition technology: A review of ethics, policy, and social implications. *IEEE Security and Privacy*, 16(3), 50–58.

Gervasio, M. A., Riedl, J. C., & Swartout, B. (2019). Interactive storytelling: An introduction. In *Interactive Storytelling: An introduction* (pp. 1–22). Springer.

Ghiglino, D., Floris, F., De Tommaso, D., Kompatsiari, K., Chevalier, P., Priolo, T., & Wykowska, A. (2023). Artificial scaffolding: Augmenting social cognition by means of robot technology. *Autism Research*, 16(5), 997–1008. 10.1002/aur.290636847354

Ghosh, S., & Singh, A. (2020). The scope of Artificial Intelligence in mankind: A detailed review. *Journal of Physics: Conference Series*, 1531(1), 012045. https://iopscience.iop.org/article/10.1088/1742-6596/1531/1/012045/meta. 10.1088/1742-6596/1531/1/012045

Giedd, J. (2012). The digital revolution and adolescent brain evolution. *The Journal of adolescent health: official publication of the Society for Adolescent Medicine, 51*(2), 101-105.

Gill, A., & Mathur, A. (2023). Exploring the futuristic landscape of artificial intelligence for alpha generation: A comprehensive study. *World Journal of Advanced Research and Reviews*, 20(2), 1250–1264. 10.30574/wjarr.2023.20.2.2369

Gill, S. S., Xu, M., Patros, P., Wu, H., Kaur, R., Kaur, K., Fuller, S., Singh, M., Arora, P., Parlikad, A. K., Stankovski, V., Abraham, A., Ghosh, S. K., Lutfiyya, H., Kanhere, S. S., Bahsoon, R., Rana, O., Dustdar, S., Sakellariou, R., & Buyya, R. (2024). Transformative effects of ChatGPT on modern education: Emerging Era of AI Chatbots. *Internet of Things and Cyber-Physical Systems*, 4, 19–23. 10.1016/j.iotcps.2023.06.002

Gkountara, D. N., & Prasad, R. (2022). A review of artificial intelligence in foreign language learning. *International Symposium on Wireless Personal Multmedia Commun, Cations (WPMC)*. IEEE. 10.1109/WPMC55625.2022.10014767

Glanz, K., Rimer, B. K., & Viswanath, K. (2015). *Health behavior: Theory, research, and practice*. John Wiley & Sons.

Glassman, J., Humphreys, K., Yeung, S., Smith, M., Jauregui, A., Milstein, A., & Sanders, L. (2021). Parents' perspectives on using artificial intelligence to reduce technology interference during early childhood: Cross-sectional online survey. *Journal of Medical Internet Research*, 23(3), e19461. 10.2196/1946133720026

Goffman, E. (1978) The presentation of self in everyday life. London: Harmondsworth.

Goffman, E. (1956). Embarrassment and social organization. *American Journal of Sociology*, 62(3), 264–271. 10.1086/222003

Goffman, E. (1959). *The Presentation of Self in Everyday Life*. Doubleday Anchor Books.

Goffman, E. (1961/1973). *Asylums: Essays on the Social Situation of Mental Patients and Other Inmates*. Penguin.

Goffman, E. (1963). *Behavior in Public Places: Notes on the Social Organization of Gatherings*. The Free Press.

Goffman, E. (1963/1976). *Stigma: Notes on the Management of Spoiled Identity*. Penguin.

Goffman, E. (1967). *Interaction Ritual: Essays on Face-to-face Behavior*. Anchor Books and Doubleday.

Goffman, E. (1971). *Relations in Public: Microstudies of the Public Order*. Basic Books.

Goffman, E. (1996). *Wir alle spielen Theater: Die Selbstdarstellung im Alltag* (5th ed.). Piper.

Gökel, Ö. (2020). Teknoloji bağımlılığının çeşitli yaş gruplarındaki çocuklara etkileri hakkındaki ebeveyn görüşleri. *Kıbrıs Türk Psikiyatri ve Psikoloji Dergisi*, 2(1), 41–47.

Goldberg, D., & Williams, P. (1991). *General health questionnaire (GHQ)*. NferNelson.

Golubeva, N. A. (2020). *Digital Identity Features of Teenagers and Youth in Modern Technological Society*.

Gonçalves LL, Nardi AE, King ALS. Digital Dependence in Organizations: Impacts on the Physical and Mental Health of Employees. Clin Pract Epidemiol Ment Health. 2023 Jan 25;19:e174501792212300. doi: 10.2174/17450179-v19 -e230109-2022-17. PMID: 37275437; PMCID: PMC10161397.10.2174/17450179-v19-e230109-2022-1737275437

Gönç-Şavran, T. (2011). İşlevselcilik-i: Talcot parsons. *Modern sosyoloji tarihi*, 2-29.

González-Nucamendi, A., Noguez, J., Neri, L., Robledo-Rella, V., & García-Castelán, R. M. (2023). Predictive analytics study to determine undergraduate students at risk of dropout. *Frontiers in Education*, 8, 1244686. 10.3389/feduc.2023.1244686

Good, B. (2021). Digital pathways to wellness among youth in residential treatment: An exploratory qualitative study. *Journal of Adolescent Research*, 38(5), 803–841. 10.1177/07435584211014884

Gopinath, V., Hitt, M. A., & Lee, D. (2004). The impact of e-commerce on traditional retailing: A study of the US retail industry. *Journal of Retailing*, 80(3), 315–333.

Górriz, J. M., Ramírez, J., Ortíz, A., Martinez-Murcia, F. J., Segovia, F., Suckling, J., Leming, M., Zhang, Y.-D., Álvarez-Sánchez, J. R., Bologna, G., Bonomini, P., Casado, F. E., Charte, D., Charte, F., Contreras, R., Cuesta-Infante, A., Duro, R. J., Fernández-Caballero, A., Fernández-Jover, E., & Ferrández, J. M. (2020). Artificial intelligence within the interplay between natural and artificial computation: Advances in data science, trends and applications. *Neurocomputing*, 410, 237–270. 10.1016/j.neucom.2020.05.078

Goswami, P., & Parekh, V. (2023). The impact of screen time on child and adolescent development: A review. *International Journal of Contemporary Pediatrics*, 10(7), 1161–1165. 10.18203/2349-3291.ijcp20231865

Gowda, A. A., Su, H. K., Kuo, W. K., & Santoso, H. D. (2022, February). Monitoring and Alerting Panic Situations in Students Using Artificial Intelligence. In *2022 IEEE 5th Eurasian Conference on Educational Innovation (ECEI)* (pp. 35–38). IEEE.

Granic, I., Morita, H., & Scholten, H. (2020). Beyond screen time: Identity development in the digital age. *Psychological Inquiry*, 31(3), 195–223. 10.1080/1047840X.2020.1820214

Green, L. (2020). Digital technologies and family life. *International Journal of Child-Computer Interaction, 23*, 100–105.

Greenfield, P. M. (2019). Communication technologies and social transformation: Their impact on human development. *Children in changing worlds: Sociocultural and temporal perspectives*, pp. 235–273. APA.

Greenfield, S. (2017). *Cognitive development and screen time in children*.

Greenwald, E., Leitner, M., & Wang, N. (2021a). *Learning Artificial Intelligence: Insights into How Youth Encounter and Build Understanding of AI Concepts*. AAAI. www.aaai.org

Greenwald, E., Leitner, M., & Wang, N. (2021b). *Learning Artificial Intelligence: Insights into How Youth Encounter and Build Understanding of AI Concepts.* AAAI. www.aaai.org

Griffee, K., Martin, R., Chory, A., & Vreeman, R. (2022). A systematic review of digital interventions to improve art adherence among youth living with hiv in sub-saharan africa. *AIDS Research and Treatment, 2022*, 1–7. 10.1155/2022/988630636199816

Grimalda, G., Buchan, N., & Brewer, M. (2015). *Globalization, social identity, and cooperation: An experimental analysis of their linkages and effects,* (No. 10). Global Cooperation Research Papers.

Grimalda, G., Buchan, N., & Brewer, M. (2018). *Social identity mediates the positive effect of globalization on individual cooperation: Results from international experiments.* PloS.

Grinin, L., & Grinin, A. (2023). Technologies: Limitless Possibilities and Effective Control. In Sadovnichy, V., Akaev, A., Ilyin, I., Malkov, S., Grinin, L., & Korotayev, A. (Eds.), *Reconsidering the Limits to Growth* (pp. 139–154). Springer International Publishing., 10.1007/978-3-031-34999-7_8

Gulati, R., West, M., Zilles, C., & Silva, M. (2024). Comparing the Security of Three Proctoring Regimens for Bring-Your-Own-Device Exams. *SIGCSE 2024 - Proceedings of the 55th ACM Technical Symposium on Computer Science Education, 1.* https://doi.org/10.1145/3626252.3630809

Günüç, S. (2011). Türkiye, dijital yerlilerde çalışan bellek ve çoklu görev. İ *5th International Computer & Instructional Technologies Symposium, Fırat Üniversitesi, ELAZIĞ.*

Gupta, A. (2021). Understanding Consumer Product Sentiments through Supervised Models on Cloud: Pre and Post COVID. *Webology, 18*(1). .10.14704/WEB/V18I1/WEB18097

Gupta, A., Dwivedi, D. N., & Shah, J. (2023). Applying Artificial Intelligence on Investigation. In: *Artificial Intelligence Applications in Banking and Financial Services.* Springer, Singapore. 10.1007/978-981-99-2571-1_9

Gupta, A., Dwivedi, D. N., & Shah, J. (2023). Applying Machine Learning for Effective Customer Risk Assessment. In: *Artificial Intelligence Applications in Banking and Financial Services. Future of Business and Finance.* Springer, Singapore. 10.1007/978-981-99-2571-1_6

Gupta, A., Dwivedi, D. N., & Shah, J. (2023). Artificial Intelligence-Driven Effective Financial Transaction Monitoring. In: *Artificial Intelligence Applications in Banking and Financial Services.* Springer, Singapore. 10.1007/978-981-99-2571-1_7

Gupta, A., Dwivedi, D. N., & Shah, J. (2023). Data Organization for an FCC Unit. In: *Artificial Intelligence Applications in Banking and Financial Services. Future of Business and Finance.* Springer, Singapore. 10.1007/978-981-99-2571-1_4

Gupta, A., Dwivedi, D. N., & Shah, J. (2023). Ethical Challenges for AI-Based Applications. In: *Artificial Intelligence Applications in Banking and Financial Services.* Springer, Singapore. 10.1007/978-981-99-2571-1_10

Gupta, A., Dwivedi, D. N., & Shah, J. (2023). Financial Crimes Management and Control in Financial Institutions. In: *Artificial Intelligence Applications in Banking and Financial Services.* Springer, Singapore. 10.1007/978-981-99-2571-1_2

Gupta, A., Dwivedi, D. N., & Shah, J. (2023). Machine Learning-Driven Alert Optimization. In: *Artificial Intelligence Applications in Banking and Financial Services.* Springer, Singapore. 10.1007/978-981-99-2571-1_8

Gupta, A., Dwivedi, D. N., & Shah, J. (2023). Overview of Money Laundering. In: *Artificial Intelligence Applications in Banking and Financial Services. Future of Business and Finance.* Springer, Singapore. 10.1007/978-981-99-2571-1_1

Gupta, A., Dwivedi, D. N., & Shah, J. (2023). Overview of Technology Solutions. In: *Artificial Intelligence Applications in Banking and Financial Services. Future of Business and Finance.* Springer, Singapore. 10.1007/978-981-99-2571-1_3

Gupta, A., Dwivedi, D. N., & Shah, J. (2023). Planning for AI in Financial Crimes. In: *Artificial Intelligence Applications in Banking and Financial Services. Future of Business and Finance.* Springer, Singapore. 10.1007/978-981-99-2571-1_5

Gupta, A., Dwivedi, D. N., & Shah, J. (2023). Setting up a Best-In-Class AI-Driven Financial Crime Control Unit (FCCU). In: *Artificial Intelligence Applications in Banking and Financial Services.* Springer, Singapore. 10.1007/978-981-99-2571-1_11

Gupta, A., Dwivedi, D.N. & Jain, A. (2021). Threshold fine-tuning of money laundering scenarios through multi-dimensional optimization techniques. *Journal of Money Laundering Control.* 10.1108/JMLC-12-2020-0138

Gupta, A., Dwivedi, D.N., Shah, J. & Jain, A. (2021). Data quality issues leading to sub optimal machine learning for money laundering models. *Journal of Money Laundering Control.* 10.1108/JMLC-05-2021-0049

Gupta, M., Parra, C. M., & Dennehy, D. (2022). Questioning Racial and Gender Bias in AI-based Recommendations: Do Espoused National Cultural Values Matter? *Information Systems Frontiers,* 24(5), 1465–1481. 10.1007/s10796-021-10156-234177358

Gupta, M., & Sharma, A. (2021). Fear of missing out: A brief overview of origin, theoretical underpinnings and relationship with mental health. *World Journal of Clinical Cases,* 9(19), 4881–4889. 10.12998/wjcc.v9.i19.488134307542

GWI. (2017). *Digital vs. traditional media consumption: Analyzing time devoted to online and traditional forms of media at a global level, as well as by age and across countries.* Insight report. https://www.gwi.com/hubfs/Digital_vs_Traditional_Media_Consumption.pdf

Haddock A, Ward N, Yu R, O'Dea N. Positive Effects of Digital Technology Use by Adolescents: A Scoping Review of the Literature. Int J Environ Res Public Health. 2022 Oct 27;19(21):14009. doi: 10.3390/ijerph192114009. PMID: 36360887; PMCID: PMC9658971.10.3390/ijerph19211400936360887

Hagedorn, W. B. og Young, T. (2011). Identifying and intervening with students exhibiting signs of gaming addiction and other addictive behaviors: Implications for professional school counselors. *Professional School Counseling, 14*(4), 2156759X1101400401.

Hale, L., & Guan, S. (2015). Screen time and sleep among school-aged children and adolescents: A systematic literature review. *Sleep Medicine Reviews,* 21, 50–58. 10.1016/j.smrv.2014.07.00725193149

Halim, I. I. A., Buja, A. G., Idris, M. S. S., & Mahat, N. J. (2024). Implementation of BYOD Security Policy in Malaysia Institutions of Higher Learning (MIHL): An Overview. *Journal of Advanced Research in Applied Sciences and Engineering Technology,* 33(2), 1–14. 10.37934/araset.33.2.114

Halim, M., Ibrahim, M., Adib, N., Hashim, H., & Omar, R. (2023). Exploring hazard of social media use on adolescent mental health. https://doi.org/10.21203/rs.3.rs-2961547/v1

Hand, G., & Giacobbi, P. R.Jr. (2020). A Review of Small Screen and Internet Technology–Induced Pathology as a Lifestyle Determinant of Health and Illness. *American Journal of Lifestyle Medicine,* 14(2), 122–125. 10.1177/15598 2761989094732231474

Handong, W. (2017). Institutional arrangement and legal regulation in the era of artificial intelligence. [Journal of Northwest University of Political Science and Law]. *Science of Law,* 5, 128–136.

Hanna-Pladdy, B., & Mackay, A. (2011). The relation between instrumental musical activity and cognitive aging. *Neuropsychology,* 25(3), 378–386. 10.1037/a002189521463047

Han, Y. (2020). Research on the Reform of Education and Teaching Methods in the Era of Artificial Intelligence. *Advances in Social Science, Education and Humanities Research,* 505. Advance online publication. 10.2991/assehr.k.201214.065

Hardey, M. (2002). Life beyond the screen: Embodiment and identity through the internet. *The Sociological Review*, 50(4), 570–585. 10.1111/1467-954X.00399

Har, F., & Ma, B. W. L. (2023). The Future of Education Utilizing an Artificial Intelligence Robot in the Centre for Independent Language Learning: Teacher Perceptions of the Robot as a Service. In Hong, C., & Ma, W. W. K. (Eds.), *Applied Degree Education and the Shape of Things to Come. Lecture Notes in Educational Technology*. Springer. 10.1007/978-981-19-9315-2_3

Harris, T. (2020). Tech companies must rethink the 'fear of missing out' they have created. *The Guardian*.

Hartig, T., Mitchell, R., de Vries, S., & Frumkin, H. (2014). Nature and Health. *Annual Review of Public Health*, 35(1), 207–228. 10.1146/annurev-publhealth-032013-18244324387090

Hashiguti, S. T., Brito, C. C. P., & Ângelo, R. C. (2021). Meaning making in the context of EFL teaching and learning with an artificial intelligence. *European Scientific Journal*, 17(22), 19. 10.19044/esj.2021.v17n22p19

Hasnine, M. N., Nguyen, H. T., Tran, T. T. T., Bui, H. T., Akçapınar, G., & Ueda, H. (2023). A real-time learning analytics dashboard for automatic detection of online learners' affective states. *Sensors (Basel)*, 23(9), 4243. 10.3390/s2309424337177447

Hasse, A., Cortesi, S., Lombana-Bermudez, A., & Gasser, U. (2019). *Youth and artificial intelligence: Where we stand.* Berkman Klein Center Research Publication.

Hasse, A., Cortesi, S., Lombana-Bermudez, A., & Gasser, U. (2019). *Youth and Artificial Intelligence: Where We Stand.* Harvard Press. https://cyber.harvard.edu/publication/2019/youth-and-

Hasse, A., Cortesi, S., Lombana-Bermudez, A., & Gasser, U. (2019). Youth and artificial intelligence: Where we stand. Youth and Media, Berkman Klein Center for Internet & Society. Retrieved from https://cyber.harvard.edu/publication/2019/youth-andartificial- intelligence/where-we-stand

Hazar, Z. (2018). *Çağın vebası dijital oyun bağımlılığı ve başa çıkma yöntemleri.* Gazi Kitabevi.

Heersmink, R. (2017). Extended mind and cognitive enhancement: Moral aspects of cognitive artifacts. *Phenomenology and the Cognitive Sciences*, 16(1), 17–32. 10.1007/s11097-015-9448-5

Hellas, A., Ihantola, P., Petersen, A., Ajanovski, V., Gutica, M., Hynninen, T., Knutas, A., Leinonen, J., Messom, C., & Liao, S. Predicting academic performance: a systematic literature review. *Proceedings Companion of the 23rd Annual ACM Conference on Innovation and Technology in Computer Science Education*, (pp. 175-199). ACM. 10.1145/3293881.3295783

Herbert, M. (1975). *Tek boyutlu İnsan,(çev. Afşar timuçin ve teoman tunçdoğan).* May Yayınları.

Hernández-Orallo, J., & Vold, K. (2019, January). AI extenders: the ethical and societal implications of humans cognitively extended by AI. In *Proceedings of the 2019 AAAI/ACM Conference on AI, Ethics, and Society* (pp. 507-513). ACM. 10.1145/3306618.3314238

Hernández-Saca, D., Gutmann Kahn, L., & Cannon, M. (2018). Intersectionality Dis/ability Research: How Dis/ability Research in Education Engages Intersectionality to Uncover the Multidimensional Construction of Dis/abled Experiences. *Review of Research in Education*, 42(1), 286–311. 10.3102/0091732X18762439

Hincks, R. (2003). Speech technologies for pronunciation feedback and evaluation. *ReCALL*, 15(1), 3–20. 10.1017/S0958344003000211

Hinduja, S., & Patchin, J. W. (2010). Bullying, Cyberbullying, and Suicide. *Archives of Suicide Research*, 14(3), 206–221. 10.1080/13811118.2010.49413320658375

Hinkley, T., & McCann, J. R. (2018). Mothers' and father's perceptions of the risks and benefits of screen time and physical activity during early childhood: A qualitative study. *BMC Public Health*, 18(1), 1–8. 10.1186/s12889-018-6199-630453927

Hogenhout and Takahashi. (2022). *A future with AI: Voice of Global Youth*. Final report, United Nations office of information and communication technology. https://unite.un.org/news/future-ai-voices-global-youth-report-launched

Holland, J. L., Fritzsche, B. A., & Powell, A. B. (1994). *The Self-Directed Search Technical Manual*. Psychological Assessment Resources.

Hollis, C., Livingstone, S., & Sonuga-Barke, E. (2020). Editorial: The role of digital technology in children and young people's mental health - a triple-edged sword? *Journal of Child Psychology and Psychiatry, and Allied Disciplines*, 61(8), 837–841. 10.1111/jcpp.1330232706126

Holloway, D., & Green, L. (2019). The importance of digital literacy in the digital age. *New Media & Society*, 21(7), 1563–1582.

Hongmei, C., Chuan, W., & Kaur, N. (2023). *International University Students' Cognition of a Community of Shared Future for Mankind*.

Howley, R. (2019) *The effect of artificial intelligence on the youth*. https://www.proquest.com/openview/d84a86cf41d62229ab84860328e20c92/1.pdf?pq-origsite=gscholar&cbl=18750&diss=y

Huang, S., Lai, X., Ke, L., Li, Y., Wang, H., Zhao, X., Dai, X., & Wang, Y. (2024). AI Technology panic-is AI Dependence Bad for Mental Health? A Cross-Lagged Panel Model and the Mediating Roles of Motivations for AI Use among Adolescents. *Psychology Research and Behavior Management*, 17, 1087–1102. 10.2147/PRBM.S44088938495087

Huang, X., Zou, D., Cheng, G., & Xie, H. (2021). A systematic review of AR and VR enhanced language learning. *Sustainability (Basel)*, 13(9), 4639. 10.3390/su13094639

Huang, Y. (2006). Identity and intimacy crises and their relationship to Internet dependence among college students. *Cyberpsychology & Behavior*, 9(5), 571–576. 10.1089/cpb.2006.9.57117034324

Huang, Y.-C., Hsieh, Y.-C., & Lin, C.-Y. (2019). The effects of educational technology on students' social skills: A meta-analysis. *Computers & Education*, 139, 103195.

Hung, J. (2022, June). Digitalisation, Parenting, and Children's Mental Health: What Are the Challenges and Policy Implications? *International Journal of Environmental Research and Public Health*, 19(11), 6452. 10.3390/ijerph1911645235682037

Hunt, M. G., Marx, R., Lipson, C., & Young, J. (2018). NO MORE FOMO: LIMITING SOCIAL MEDIA DECREASES LONELINESS AND DEPRESSION. *Journal of Social and Clinical Psychology*, 37(10), 751–768. 10.1521/jscp.2018.37.10.751

Hunt, V., Layton, D., & Prince, S. (2015). *Why Diversity Matters*. McKinsey & Company.

Hu, T., & Lu, H. (2020). Study on the influence of artificial intelligence on legal profession. *5th International Conference on Economics, Management, Law and Education (EMLE 2019)*, (pp. 964–968) IEEE.

Hutchins, E. (1999). Cognitive artifacts. *The MIT Encyclopedia of the Cognitive Sciences, 126*(1999), 127.

Ide, N. M., & Véronis, J. (1990). Artificial intelligence and the study of literary narrative. *Poetics*, 19(1–2), 37–63. 10.1016/0304-422X(90)90030-9

Igbokwe, I. C. (2023). Application of artificial intelligence (AI) in educational management. *International Journal of Scientific and Research Publications*, 13(3), 300–307. 10.29322/IJSRP.13.03.2023.p13536

Ihmeideh, F. M., & Shawareb, A. A. (2014). The Association Between Internet Parenting Styles and Children's Use of the Internet at Home. *Journal of Research in Childhood Education*, 28(4), 411–425. 10.1080/02568543.2014.944723

Indeks Belia Malaysia. (2015). *Institut Penyelidikan Pembangunan Belia Malaysia*. IYRES.

Ironsi, C. S. (2023). Investigating the use of virtual reality to improve speaking skills: insights from students and teachers. *Smart Learning Environments, 10*(1), 53.Panjeti-Madan, V. N., & Ranganathan, P. (2023). Impact of screen time on children's development: cognitive, language, physical, and social and emotional domains. *Multimodal Technologies and Interaction*, 7(5), 52. 10.3390/mti7050052

Ismail, M., Hassan, N., Nor, M., Zain, M., & Samsu, K. (2021). The influence of political socialization among educated youth at universiti putra malaysia. *International Journal of Academic Research in Business & Social Sciences*, 11(12). 10.6007/IJARBSS/v11-i12/11941

Ito, M., Horst, H., & Bittani, M (2008). Living and learning with new media: Summary of findings from the digital youth project. *Catherine T. MacArthur Foundation Reports on Digital Media and Learning*. MacArthur Foundation.

Ito, M., Horst, H., Bittanti, M., Boyd, D., Herr-Stephenson, B., Lange, P., Nardi, B., Pascoe, T., Robinson, L., & Wesch, M. (2010). *Living and learning with new media: Summary of findings from the Digital Youth Project*. MIT Press.

Jabłońska, M. R., & Zajdel, R. (2020). Artificial neural networks for predicting social comparison effects among female instagram users. *PLoS One*, 15(2), e0229354. 10.1371/journal.pone.022935432097446

Jackaria, P. M., Hajan, B. H., & Mastul, A. R. H. (2024). A Comparative Analysis of the Rating of College Students' Essays by ChatGPT versus Human Raters. *International Journal of Learning, Teaching and Educational Research, 23*(2).

Jacko, J. A. (Ed.). (2012). *Human-computer interaction handbook: Fundamentals, evolving technologies, and emerging applications*. CRC Press. 10.1201/b11963

Jaelani, A., & Umam, A. (2021). Preparing EFL pre-service teachers for curriculum 2013 through authentic materials and assessment integration. [Journal of English Educators Society]. *JEES*, 6(1), 171–177. 10.21070/jees.v6i1.829

Jago, R., Davison, K.K., Brockman, R., Page, A.S., Thompson, J.L., & Fox K.R. (2011). Parenting styles, parenting practices, and physical activity in 10- to 11-year olds. *Prev Med. Jan;52*(1), 44-7. 10.1016/j.ypmed.2010.11.001

Jagoda, P. (2023). Artificial Intelligence in Video Games. *American Literature*, 95(2), 435–438. 10.1215/00029831-10575246

Jain, A. K., Ross, A., & Prabhakar, S. (2004). An introduction to biometric recognition. *IEEE Transactions on Circuits and Systems for Video Technology*, 14(1), 4–20. 10.1109/TCSVT.2003.818349

Jaleniauskienė, E., Lisaitė, D., & Brazaitė, L. D. (2023). Artificial Intelligence Language Education: A Bibliometric Analysis. *Sustainable Multilingualism*, 23(1), 156–193. 10.2478/sm-2023-0017

Jamil, H., Raza, S. H., & Naqvi, S. G. (2023). Artificial Intelligence and Grand Challenges for Education. *Journal of Policy Research*, 9(1). 10.5281/zenodo.7951651

Janssen, I., & LeBlanc, A. G. (2010). A systematic review of the health benefits of physical activity and fitness in school-aged children and youth. *The International Journal of Behavioral Nutrition and Physical Activity*, 7(1), 40. 10.1186/1479-5868-7-4020459784

Jarosz, D. (2020). *Wie Soziale Medien das Selbstbild Jugendlicher beeinflussen*. Apomio.de. Gesundheitsblog. https://www.apomio.de/blog/artikel/wie-soziale-medien-das-selbstbild-jugendlicher-beeinflussen#perfektion, e hapur se fundmi ne date 10.03.2024.

Jaspers, E. D., & Pearson, E. (2022). Consumers' acceptance of domestic Internet-of-Things: The role of trust and privacy concerns. *Journal of Business Research*, 142, 255–265. 10.1016/j.jbusres.2021.12.043

Jensen, L. A., & Dost-Gözkan, A. (2015). Adolescent-parent relations in Asian Indian and Salvadoran immigrant families: A cultural-developmental analysis of autonomy, authority, conflict, and cohesion. *Journal of Research on Adolescence*, 25(2), 340–351. 10.1111/jora.12116

Jensen, M. M., Vaidya, N. P., & Wiggins, C. (2019). Artificial intelligence and information literacy: A review and research agenda. *The Journal of Documentation*, 75(4), 965–992.

Jeunemaître, A. M. (2023). The Future of Wellbeing: Value Creation in Digital Mental Health Services. *The Future of Consumption*, 233–249. 10.1007/978-3-031-33246-3_15

Jia, C., Hew, K., Bai, S., & Huang, W. (2021). Adaptation of a conventional flipped course to an online flipped format during the Covid-19 pandemic: Student learning performance and engagement. *Journal of Research on Technology in Education*. 10.1080/15391523.2020.1847220

Jiao, W., Wang, W., Huang, J., Wang, X., & Tu, Z. (2023). Is ChatGPT a good translator? yes with GPT-4 as the engine. *arxiv:2301.08745*, 1-10.

Jobin, A., Ienca, M., & Vayena, E. (2019). The global landscape of AI ethics guidelines. *Nature Machine Intelligence*, 1(9), 389–399. 10.1038/s42256-019-0088-2

Johnson, J. (2019). Artificial intelligence & future warfare: Implications for international security. *Defense & Security Analysis*, 35(2), 147–169. 10.1080/14751798.2019.1600800

Johnson, J. (2021). Enhancing childhood education with AI tools. *Educational Technology Research and Development*, 69(1), 45–63.

Johnston, R., Pattie, C., Jones, K., & Manley, D. (2020). Intersectionality and English Voting Behaviour: And Was There a 2017 Youthquake. *Political Studies Review*, 18(2), 294–303. 10.1177/1478929919875055

Kabat-Zinn, J. (2003). Mindfulness-based interventions in context: Past, present, and future. *Clinical Psychology : a Publication of the Division of Clinical Psychology of the American Psychological Association*, 10(2), 144–156. 10.1093/clipsy.bpg016

Kahrimanis, G., & Dimitriadis, Y. (2019). Digital ageism and the need for inclusive technology: A review and future directions. *International Journal of Human-Computer Interaction*, 35(1), 1–16.

Kanapathipillai, K., & Kumaran, S. (2022). An empirical study on the influence of social capital on the digital entrepreneurs' performance during the omicron variant wave (sars-cov-2: b.1.1.529). *European Journal of Management and Marketing Studies*, 7(2). 10.46827/ejmms.v7i2.1227

Kang, B. & Kang, S. (2022). Construction of chinese language teaching system model based on deep learning under the background of artificial intelligence. *Hindawi Scientiifc Programming*, 1-10.

Kang, H., & Lou, C. (2022). Ai agency vs. Human agency: Understanding human–ai interactions on tiktok and their implications for user engagement. *Journal of Computer-Mediated Communication*, 27(5), zmac014. 10.1093/jcmc/zmac014

Kang, K., & Wang, S. (2018). Analyze and predict student dropout from online programs. In *Proceedings of the 2nd International Conference on Compute and Data Analysis* (pp. 6-12). 10.1145/3193077.3193090

Karabulut, B. (2015). Bilgi toplumu çağinda dijital yerliler, göçmenler ve melezler. *Pamukkale Üniversitesi Sosyal Bilimler Enstitüsü Dergisi*, (21), 11–23.

Karakose, T. Y. B., Yıldırım, B., Tülübaş, T., & Kardas, A. (2023, February 8). comprehensive review on emerging trends in the dynamic evolution of digital addiction and depression. *Frontiers in Psychology*, 14, 1126815. 10.3389/fpsyg.2023.112681536844332

Kardefelt-Winther, D. (2014). A conceptual and methodological critique of internet addiction research: Towards a model of compensatory internet use. *Computers in Human Behavior*, 31, 351–354. 10.1016/j.chb.2013.10.059

Kashchey, N., Spornik, A., & Shipulin, V. (2020). Personal And Collective Identity: Transformations. *European Proceedings of Social and Behavioural Sciences*. Research Gate.

Kashif, A. (2024). Examining the Impact of AI-Enhanced Social Media Content on Adolescent Well-being in the Digital Age. *Kurdish Studies*, 12(2), 771–789.

Kavun, N. (2019). Mango Languages. *CALICO Journal*, 36(3), 256–265. 10.1558/cj.38302

Keles, B., McCrae, N., & Grealish, A. (2019). A systematic review: The influence of social media on depression, anxiety and psychological distress in adolescents. *International Journal of Adolescence and Youth*, 25(1), 79–93. 10.1080/02673843.2019.1590851

Kelly, K. (2016). *The inevitable: Understanding the 12 technological forces that will shape our future*. Penguin.

Kelly, M. A., Barnert, E., & Bath, E. (2018). Think, Ask, Act: The Intersectionality of Mental and Reproductive Health for Judicially Involved Girls. *Journal of the American Academy of Child and Adolescent Psychiatry*, 57(10), 715–718. 10.1016/j.jaac.2018.07.87030274642

Kemp, S. (2024). *Digital 2024: North Macedonia*. Datareportal. https://datareportal.com/reports/digital-2024-north-macedonia

Kern, M. L., Williams, P., Spong, C., Colla, R., Sharma, K., Downie, A., Taylor, J. A., Sharp, S., Siokou, C., & Oades, L. G. (2020). Systems informed positive psychology. *The Journal of Positive Psychology*, 15(6), 705–715. 10.1080/17439760.2019.1639799

Kern, M. R., Duinhof, E. L., Walsh, S. D., Cosma, A., Moreno-Maldonado, C., Molcho, M., Currie, C., & Stevens, G. (2020). Intersectionality and Adolescent Mental Well-being: A Cross-Nationally Comparative Analysis of the Interplay Between Immigration Background, Socioeconomic Status and Gender. *The Journal of Adolescent Health*, 66(6, 6S), S12–S20. 10.1016/j.jadohealth.2020.02.01332446604

Keupp, H. (2017). Identitätsarbeit als Balance von Eigenem und Fremden und die fatale Sehnsucht nach Reinheit. Evangelische Akademie Tutzing. https://www.ev-akademie-tutzing.de/static/media/attachments/V201703-D84D461B18224264B796AE3A59240066/Beitrag%20Keupp%202017.pdf

Khalaf, A., Alubied, A., Khalaf, A., & Rifaey, A. (2023). The Impact of Social Media on the Mental Health of Adolescents and Young Adults. *Systematic Reviews*. 10.7759/cureus.4299037671234

Khin, S., & Ho, T. C. (2018). Digital technology, digital capability and organizational performance: A mediating role of digital innovation. *International Journal of Innovation Science*, 11(2), 177–195. 10.1108/IJIS-08-2018-0083

Kidwell, J. S., Dunham, R. M., Bacho, R. A., Pastorino, E., & Portes, P. R. (1995). Adolescent identity exploration: A test of Erikson's theory of transitional crisis. *Adolescence*, 30, 785–793.8588516

Kilduff, C. L. S., Deshmukh, M., Guevara, G., Neece, J., Daniel, C., Thomas, P. B. M., Lovegrove, C., Sim, D. A., & Timlin, H. M. (2023). Creating a secure clinical 'Bring Your Own Device' BYOD photography service to document and monitor suspicious lesions in the lid oncology clinic. *Eye (London, England)*, 37(4), 744–750. 10.1038/s41433-022-02049-835379923

Kim, S., Yoo, E., & Kim, S. (2023). *A Study on the Prediction of University Dropout Using Machine Learning*. arXiv preprint arXiv:2310.10987. DOI:/arXiv.2310.1098710.48550

Kim, N. Y., Cha, Y., & Kim, H. S. (2019). Future english learning: Chatbots and artificial intelligence. *Multimedia-Asisted Language Learning*, 22(3), 32–53.

King, J. (2023). An Innovative Exploration of Psychological Research Methods Driven by Artificial Intelligence: A Case Study Using Facial Expression Technique to Improve Teenagers' Self Awareness. *International Journal of Education and Humanities*, 11(1), 212–215. 10.54097/ijeh.v11i1.13155

Kivisto, P., & Pittman, D. (2007). Goffman's dramaturgical sociology. In *Illuminating social life: Classical and contemporary theory revisited* (pp. 271–290). SAGE Publications., https://www.sagepub.com/sites/default/files/upm-binaries/16569_Chapter_10.pdf

Klimstra, T. (2013). Adolescent Personality Development and Identity Formation. *Child Development Perspectives*, 7(2), 80–84. 10.1111/cdep.12017

Koli, R. R. (2020). Human Action Recognition Using Deep Neural Networks. *IEEE Fourth World Conference on Smart Trends in Systems, Security and Sustainability (WorldS4)*. IEEE.

Konca, A. (2021). Digital Technology Usage of Young Children: Screen Time and Families. *Early Childhood Education Journal*, 50(7), 1097–1108. 10.1007/s10643-021-01245-7

Konrath, S., O'Brien, E. H., & Hsing, C. (2011). Changes in dispositional empathy in American college students over time: A meta-analysis. *Personality and Social Psychology Review*, 15(2), 180–198. 10.1177/1088868310377395 20688954

Köroğlu, E. (2013). *Dsm-v: Tanı ölçütleri başvuru kitabı,(e. Köroğlu. Çev.)*. Amerikan Psikiyatri Birliği.

Koufaris, S. (2002). The impact of website design on consumer effect, cognition, and behavior: An empirical investigation. *Journal of Retailing*, 78(2), 177–195.

Krappmann, L. (2000). *Soziologische Dimensionen der Identität. Strukturelle Bedingungen für die Teilnahme an Interaktionsprozessen*. Stuttgart: Klett-Cotta.

Kraut, R., Patterson, M., Lundmark, V., Kiesler, S., Mukopadhyay, T., & Scherlis, W. (1998). Internet paradox. A social technology that reduces social involvement and psychological well-being? *The American Psychologist*, 53(9), 1017–1031. 10.1037/0003-066X.53.9.10179841579

Krumshteyn, A., Weng, S., & Kautz, J. (2019). MoodScanner: A mobile application for rapid screening of mood disorders. *Journal of Affective Disorders*, 240, 32–38.

Ku, Y.-J., Chen, M.-J., & King, C.-T. (2019). A Virtual Sign Language Translator on Smartphones. *Seventh International Symposium on Computing and Networking Workshops (CANDARW)*. IEEE.

Kukulska-Hulme, A., & Shield, L. (2007). An overview of mobile assisted language learning: Can mobile devices support collaborative practice in speaking and listening. *ReCALL*, 20(3), 1–20.

Kulkarni, A. (2019). Artificial intelligence in education: A review of current research and future directions. *International Journal of Artificial Intelligence in Education*, 29(1), 1–20.

Kulkarni, A., Kulkarni, S., & Washburn, J. (2017). Adaptive and personalized learning: A survey. *IEEE Transactions on Education*, 60(1), 62–73.

Kulkarni, S., Liu, Y., & Barr, R. (2017). AI in education: A review of the literature. *Computers & Education*, 148, 103927.

Kulkarni, S., Liu, Y., & Barr, R. (2017). The impact of intelligent tutoring systems on student learning: A meta-analysis. *Educational Psychologist*, 52(3), 197–210.

Kumar Paur, S., Das, K., Kumar Paul, S., & Professor, A. (n.d.). Technological Advancement: A Study on the Changing Scenario among Tribal Youth. In *Journal of the Anthropological Survey of India, 64*(2).

Kumar, S., & Singh, M. (2015). Biometric security based intelligent e-voting system. *International Journal of Computer Applications*, 117(4), 33–41. 10.5120/20546-2918

Kumar, V., Kautz, J., & Liu, Z. (2018). News recommendation at scale. *Communications of the ACM*, 61(10), 84–91.

Kung, T. H., Cheatham, M., Medenilla, A., Sillos, C., De Leon, L., Elepaño, C., Madriaga, M., Aggabao, R., Diaz-Candido, G., Maningo, J., & Tseng, V. (2023). Performance of ChatGPT on USMLE: Potential for AI-assisted medical education using large language models. *PLOS Digital Health*, 2(2), 1–12. 10.1371/journal.pdig.000019836812645

Kurtz, G., & Kohen-Vacs, D. (2024). Humanoid robot as a tutor in a team-based training activity. *Interactive Learning Environments*, 32(1), 340–354. 10.1080/10494820.2022.2086577

Kurzweil, R. (2005). The singularity is near. In *Ethics and emerging technologies* (pp. 393–406). Springer.

Kushlev, K., Proulx, J., & Dunn, E. W. (2016). "Silence Your Phones": Smartphone Notifications Increase Inattention and Hyperactivity Symptoms. *Proceedings of the 2016 CHI Conference on Human Factors in Computing Systems*. ACM. 10.1145/2858036.2858359

Kushwaha, A. K., Pharswan, R., Kumar, P., & Kar, A. K. (2023). How Do Users Feel When They Use Artificial Intelligence for Decision Making? A Framework for Assessing Users' Perception. *Information Systems Frontiers*, 25(3), 1241–1260. 10.1007/s10796-022-10293-2

Kuzu, Y., & Kozan, T. (2019). An adaptive learning system using artificial intelligence for personalized learning. *International Journal of Artificial Intelligence in Education*, 29(1), 4–21.

Lainjo, B. (2023). Mitigating Academic Institution Dropout Rates with Predictive Analytics Algorithms. *International Journal of Education, Teaching, and Social Sciences*.

Lainjo, B., & Tsmouche, H. (2023). Impact of Artificial Intelligence On Higher Learning Institutions. *International Journal of Education, Teaching, and Social Sciences*.

Lam, H., Beckman, T., Harcourt, M., & Shanmugam, S. (2024). Bring Your Own Device (BYOD): Organizational Control and Justice Perspectives. *Employee Responsibilities and Rights Journal*. 10.1007/s10672-024-09498-1

Lanier, J. (2018). *Ten Arguments for Deleting Your Social Media Accounts Right Now*. Henry Holt and Co.

Lau, K. (2018). *Duolingo's AI-powered approach to language learning*. TechCrunch. https://techcrunch.com/2018/05/23/duolingos-ai-powered-approach-to-language-learning/

Law, B. (1981). Community interaction: A 'mid-range' focus for theories of career development in young adults. *British Journal of Guidance & Counselling*, 9(2), 142–158. 10.1080/03069888108258210

Leahy, S. M., Holland, C., & Ward, F. (2019). The digital frontier: Envisioning future technologies impact on the classroom. *Futures*, 113, 102422. 10.1016/j.futures.2019.04.009

Lee, C., & Kim, H. (2020). Groundwork of artificial intelligence humanities. Jahr. *Europski Časopis Za Bioetiku*, 11(1), 189–207.

Lee, H. E., Ji Young, K., & Changsook, K. (2022). The Influence of Parent Media Use, Parent Attitude on Media, and Parenting Style on Children's Media Use. *Children (Basel, Switzerland)*, 9(37), 1–12. 10.3390/children901003735053662

Lee, J., & Kim, Y. (2021). AI tutors in the home: Parental mediation of AI-assisted learning. *Computers & Education*, 164, 104385.

Lee, J., Suh, T., Roy, D., & Baucus, M. (2019). Emerging Technology and Business Model Innovation: The Case of Artificial Intelligence. *Journal of Open Innovation*, 5(3), 44. 10.3390/joitmc5030044

Lee, S. (2018). Autonomous vehicles: A review of the state-of-the-art and future directions. *IEEE Transactions on Intelligent Transportation Systems*, 20(1), 1–15.

Lehtimaki, S., Martic, J., Wahl, B., Foster, K., & Schwalbe, N. (2020). Evidence on Digital Mental Health Interventions for Adolescents and Young People: Systematic Overview. *JMIR Mental Health*, 8(1), e25847.33913817

Lent, R. W., & Brown, S. D. (2019). Social cognitive career theory at 25: Empirical status of the interest, choice, and performance models. *Journal of Vocational Behavior*, 115, 1–25. 10.1016/j.jvb.2019.06.004

Leopold, M., & Ullmann, M. (2018). *Digitale Medien in der Kita. Alltagsintegrierte Medienbildung in der pädagogischen Praxis*. Herder Verlag.

Lérida-Ayala, V. (2022). Internet and video games: Causes of behavioral disorders in children and teenagers. *Children, 10*.

Levenson, J. C., Shensa, A., Sidani, J. E., Colditz, J. B., & Primack, B. A. (2017). The association between social media use and sleep disturbance among young adults. *Preventive Medicine*, 85, 36–41. 10.1016/j.ypmed.2016.01.00126791323

Lewis, D., & Moorkens, J. (2020). A rights-based approach to trustworthy AI in social media. *Social Media + Society*, 6(3), 2056305120954672. 10.1177/2056305120954672

Li, S. (2021). Research on the exploration and reflection of foreign language teaching based on "artificial intelligence +education" in the big data ear. *2021 2nd International Conference on Big Data Economy and Information Management (BDEIM)*, (pp. 354-357). IEEE.

Li, W. (2022). Analysis of piano performance characteristics by deep learning and artificial intelligence and its application in piano teaching. *Frontiers in Psychology, 12*, 751406.

Liang, J. C., Hwang, G. J., Chen, M. R. A., & Darmawansah, D. (2021). Roles and research foci of artificial intelligence in language education: An integrated bibliographic analysis and systematic review approach. *Interactive Learning Environments*, 1–27.

Lichtwarck-Aschoff, A., van Geert, P., Bosma, H., & Kunnen, S. (2008). Time and identity: A framework for research and theory formation. *Developmental Review*, 28(3), 370–400. 10.1016/j.dr.2008.04.001

Licklider, J. C. R. (1960). Man-computer symbiosis. *IRE Transactions on Human Factors in Electronics*, 1(1), 4–11. 10.1109/THFE2.1960.4503259

Liesa-Orús, M., Latorre-Cosculluela, C., Vázquez-Toledo, S., & Sierra-Sánchez, V. (2020). The technological challenge facing higher education professors: Perceptions of ICT tools for developing 21st century skills. *Sustainability (Basel)*, 12(13), 5339. 10.3390/su12135339

Li, H. (2019). Special section introduction: Artificial intelligence and advertising. *Journal of Advertising*, 48(4), 333–337. 10.1080/00913367.2019.1654947

Lihua, Z. (2022). Analysis of english translation model based on artificial intelligence attention mechanism. *Mathematical Problems in Engineering*, 2022, 2022. 10.1155/2022/9669152

Limtrakul, N., Louthrenoo, O., Narkpongphun, A., Boonchooduang, N., & Chonchaiya, W. (2017). Media use and psychosocial adjustment in children and adolescents. *Journal of Paediatrics and Child Health*, 54(3), 296–301. 10.1111/jpc.1372528948669

Lin, C.-Y., & Liu, C.-H. (2018). Parental mediation of children's digital media use in Taiwan: A qualitative study. *Computers in Human Behavior*, 81, 262–270.

Linden, D., Stern, L., & Kulikowich, M. (2019). Artificial intelligence and education: A review of the literature. *Educational Research Review*, 26, 100650.

Linden, L., Pactwa, S., & Simard, R. (2019). Duolingo: The freemium language-learning service. *Journal of Digital Media Arts and Practices*, 3(1), 3–16.

Lin, L. Y., Sidani, J. E., Shensa, A., Radovic, A., Miller, E., Colditz, J. B., Hoffman, B. L., Giles, L. M., & Primack, B. A. (2016). Association between social media use and depression among U.S. young adults. *Depression and Anxiety*, 33(4), 323–331. 10.1002/da.2246626783723

Lin, Y.-H., Lin, Y.-C., Lee, Y.-H., Lin, P.-H., Lin, S.-H., Chang, L.-R., Tseng, H.-W., Yen, L.-Y., Yang, C. C. H., & Kuo, T. B. J. (2016). Time distortion associated with smartphone addiction: Identifying smartphone addiction via a mobile application (App). *Journal of Psychiatric Research*, 65, 139–145. 10.1016/j.jpsychires.2015.04.00325935253

Lipps, G., Lowe, G. A., Gibson, R. C., Halliday, S., Morris, A., Clarke, N., & Wilson, R. N. (2012). Parenting and depressive symptoms among adolescents in four Caribbean societies. *Child and Adolescent Psychiatry and Mental Health*, 6(1), 31. 10.1186/1753-2000-6-3122998793

Li, R. (2020). Using artificial intelligence in learning english as a foreign language: An examination of IELTS LIULISHUO as an online platform. *Journal of Higher Education Research*, 1(2), 85–89. 10.32629/jher.v1i2.178

Lissak, G. (2018). Adverse physiological and psychological effects of screen time on children and adolescents: Literature review and case study. *Environmental Research*, 164, 149–157. 10.1016/j.envres.2018.01.01529499467

Liu, Y., Chen, Y., & Barr, R. (2020). AI in education: A review of the literature. *Computers & education*.

Liu, C.-H., Liu, C.-Y., & Hsieh, C.-H. (2016). A survey on chatbots: Technologies, applications, and challenges. *IEEE Transactions on Knowledge and Data Engineering*, 28(10), 2143–2160.

Liu, J., Chang, H., Forrest, J. Y. L., & Yang, B. (2020). Influence of artificial intelligence on technological innovation: Evidence from the panel data of china's manufacturing sectors. *Technological Forecasting and Social Change*, 158, 120142. 10.1016/j.techfore.2020.120142

Liu, X., & He, J. (2020). Artificial intelligence in youth mental health: A systematic review. *Journal of Affective Disorders*, 269, 243–252. 10.1016/j.jad.2019.11.099

Liu, Y., Han, T., Ma, S., Zhang, J., Yang, Y., Tian, J., He, H., Li, A., He, M., Liu, Z., Wu, Z., Zhu, D., Li, X., Qiang, N., Shen, D., Liu, T., & Ge, B. (2023). Summary of ChatGPT-related research and perspective towards the future of large language models. *Meta-Radiology*, 1(2), 1–21. 10.1016/j.metrad.2023.100017

Livberber, T. (2023). Toward non-human-centered design: Designing an academic article with ChatGPT. *El Profesional de la Información*, 32(5), e320512. 10.3145/epi.2023.sep.12

Livingstone, S., & Blum-Ross, A. (2020). Digital parenting in a globalized world. *Global Studies of Childhood*, 10(1), 85–99.

Livingstone, S., & Haddon, L. (2009). *Managing online risk: Parenting for a digital future*. Oxford University Press.

Livingstone, S., & Haddon, L. (2009). *Managing online risks for children and young people*. Macmillan Children's Books.

Livingstone, S., & Haddon, L. (2016). Media, risk, and safety in the digital age. In Livingstone, S. (Ed.), *Media, risk, and safety in the digital age* (pp. 1–18). Palgrave Macmillan.

Lo, C. K. (2023). What Is the impact of ChatGPT on education? A rapid review of the literature. *Education Sciences*, 13(410), 2–15. 10.3390/educsci13040410

Loh, K. K., & Kanai, R. (2016). *How digital screen time affects attention spans.*

Løkke, E. (2020). *Mahremiyet: Dijital toplumda özel hayat.* Koç Üniversitesi.

Lourens, A., & Bleazard, D. (2016). Applying predictive analytics in identifying students at risk: A case study. *South African Journal of Higher Education*, 30(2), 129–142. 10.20853/30-2-583

Lozano-Blasco, R., Mira-Aladrén, M., & Gil-Lamata, M. (2023). Social media influence on young people and children: Analysis on Instagram, Twitter and YouTube. *Comunicar*, 31(74), 125–137. 10.3916/C74-2023-10

Luckin, R. (2017). Towards artificial intelligence-based assessment systems. *Nature Human Behaviour, 1*(3), 0028.

Luger, G. F. (2021). Modern AI and How We Got Here. In G. F. Luger, *Knowing our World: An Artificial Intelligence Perspective* (pp. 49–74). Springer International Publishing. 10.1007/978-3-030-71873-2_3

Lund, B. D., & Wang, T. (2023). *Chatting about ChatGPT: How may AI and GPT impact academia and libraries?* Social Science Research Network.

Lund, B. D., Wang, T., Mannuru, N. R., Nie, B., Shimray, S., & Wang, Z. (2023). ChatGPT and a new academic reality: Artificial intelligence-written research papers and the ethics of the large language models in scholarly publishing. *Journal of the Association for Information Science and Technology*, 74(5), 570–581. 10.1002/asi.24750

Luyckx, K., Lens, W., Smits, I., & Goossens, L. (2010). Time perspective and identity formation: Short-term longitudinal dynamics in college students. *International Journal of Behavioral Development*, 34(3), 238–247. 10.1177/0165025409350957

Maaz, M., Rasheed, H. A., Khan, S. H., & Khan, F. S. (2023). *Video-ChatGPT: Towards detailed video understanding via large vision and language models. ArXiv.* I-XVI.

Machin, M., Sanguesa, J. A., Garrido, P., & Martinez, F. J. (2018). On the use of artificial intelligence techniques in intelligent transportation systems. *2018 IEEE Wireless Communications and Networking Conference Workshops (WCNCW)*, (pp. 332–337). IEEE. 10.1109/WCNCW.2018.8369029

Magee, C. A., Lee, J. K., & Vella, S. A. (2014). Bidirectional relationships between sleep duration and screen time in early childhood. *JAMA Pediatrics*, 168(5), 465–470. 10.1001/jamapediatrics.2013.418324589672

Magis-Weinberg, L., Suleiman, A. B., & Dahl, R. (2021). Context, Development, and Digital Media: Implications for Very Young Adolescents in LMICs. *Frontiers in Psychology*, 12, 12. 10.3389/fpsyg.2021.63271333967899

Mahanty, G., Dwivedi, D. N., & Gopalakrishnan, B. N. (2021). The Efficacy of Fiscal Vs Monetary Policies in the Asia-Pacific Region: The St. Louis Equation Revisited. *Vision (Basel)*, (November). 10.1177/09722629211054148

Makeleni, S., Mutongoza, B. H., & Linake, M. A. (2023). Language education and artificial intelligence: An exploration of challenges confronting academics in global south universities. *Journal of Culture and Values in Education*, 6(2), 158–171. 10.46303/jcve.2023.14

Makridakis, S. (2017). The forthcoming Artificial Intelligence (AI) revolution: Its impact on society and firms. In *Futures* (Vol. 90, pp. 46–60). Elsevier. https://www.sciencedirect.com/science/article/pii/S0016328717300046

Manago, A. M. (2015). Media and the Development of Identity. In Scott, R. A., & Kosslyn, S. M. (Eds.), *Emerging Trends in the Social and Behavioral Sciences*. Wiley. 10.1002/9781118900772.etrds0212

Manyika, J., Lund, S., Chui, M., Bughin, J., Woetzel, L., Batra, P., Ko, R., & Sanghvi, S. (2017) *Jobs lost, jobs gain: What the future of work will mean for jobs, skills, and wages*. McKinsey and Company. https://www.mckinsey.com/featured-insights/future-of-work/jobs-lost-jobs-gained-what-the-future-of-work-will-mean-for-jobs-skills-and-wages

Manyika, J., Bughin, J., Dobbs, R., Roxburgh, C., & Stirling, A. (2019). *Employment, education, entertainment, and economic growth*. McKinsey Global Institute.

Maras, D., Flament, M., Murray, M., Buchholz, A., Henderson, K., Obeid, N., & Goldfield, G. (2015). Screen time is associated with depression and anxiety in Canadian youth. *Preventive Medicine*, 73, 133–138. 10.1016/j.ypmed.2015.01.02925657166

Marcia, J. E. (1966). Development and validation of ego-identity status. *Journal of Personality and Social Psychology*, 3(5), 551 558. 10.1037/h00232815939604

Marciano, L., Camerini, A., & Morese, R. (2021). The Developing Brain in the Digital Era: A Scoping Review of Structural and Functional Correlates of Screen Time in Adolescence. *Frontiers in Psychology*, 12, 671817. 10.3389/fpsyg.2021.67181734512437

Marco, J. (2019). Artificial Intelligence and Children's Privacy: A Review and Future Directions. *International Journal of Human-Computer Interaction*, 35(1), 1–16.

Markauskaite, L., Marrone, R., Poquet, O., Knight, S., Martinez-Maldonado, R., Howard, S., Tondeur, J., De Laat, M., Shum, S. B., & Gašević, D. (2022). Rethinking the entwinement between artificial intelligence and human learning: What capabilities do learners need for a world with AI? *Computers and Education: Artificial Intelligence*, 3, 100056. 10.1016/j.caeai.2022.100056

Martins, J., & Mota, L. (2022). *Innovative board game design in an academic environment during the Covid-19 pandemic*. DS 117: Proceedings of the 24th International Conference on Engineering and Product Design Education (E&PDE 2022), London South Bank University in London, UK. https://www.designsociety.org/download-publication/45838/INNOVATIVE+BOARD+GAME+DESIGN+IN+AN+ACADEMIC+ENVIRONMENT+DURING+THE+COVID-19+PANDEMIC

Marwick, A. E., & Boyd, D. (2014). Networked privacy: How teenagers negotiate context in social media. *New Media & Society*, 16(7), 1051–1067. 10.1177/1461444814543995

Mas, I., & Porteous, D. (2015). Minding the Identity Gaps. *Innovations*. MIT Press.

Mauthner, N. S. (2019). Toward a posthumanist ethics of qualitative research in a big data era. *The American Behavioral Scientist*, 63(6), 669–698. 10.1177/0002764218792701

Mayhew, A., & Weigle, P. (2018). Media engagement and identity formation among minority youth. *Child and Adolescent Psychiatric Clinics of North America*, 27(2), 269–285. 10.1016/j.chc.2017.11.01229502751

Mbambala, T. P., & Abdullah, H. (2023). Promoting Bring Your Own Device (BYOD) Information Privacy Protection Awareness among Public Libraries in Gauteng. *Proceedings - International Conference on Advanced Computer Information Technologies, ACIT*. ACIT.10.1109/ACIT58437.2023.10275501

McAdams, D. P., & Zapata-Gietl, C. (2015). Three strands of identity development across the human life course: Reading Erik Erikson in full. *The Oxford handbook of identity development*, 81-94.

McCall, B. (2020). COVID-19 and artificial intelligence: Protecting health-care workers and curbing the spread. *The Lancet. Digital Health*, 2(4), e166–e167. 10.1016/S2589-7500(20)30054-632289116

McCarthy, J. (2004). *What is Artificial Intelligence?* Stanford. http://www-formal.stanford.edu/jmc/whatisai/. (Accessed:30.03.2024).

McGarry, O. (2016). Repositioning the research encounter: Exploring power dynamics and positionality in youth research. *International Journal of Social Research Methodology*, 19(3), 339–354. 10.1080/13645579.2015.1011821

McLeod, J. (2009). Youth Studies, Comparative Inquiry, and the Local/Global Problematic. *Review of Education, Pedagogy & Cultural Studies*, 31(4), 270–292. 10.1080/10714410903132840

McLuhan, M. (1964). *Understanding media*. McGraw-Hill.

McReynolds, E. (2017). *Toys that listen: A study of parents, children, and internet-connected.*

McStay, A., & Rosner, G. (2021). Emotional artificial intelligence in children's toys and devices: Ethics, governance and practical remedies. *Big Data & Society*, 8(1), 2053951721994877. 10.1177/2053951721994877

Mead, G. H. (1973). Geist, Identität und Gesellschaft aus der Sicht des Sozialbehaviorismus. Frankfurt/M.: Suhrkamp.

Memmedova, K., & Selahattin, E. L. (2018). Effects of the technology use on anxiety and aggression levels of youth conducting their higher education studies abroad. *Quality & Quantity*, 52(S1), 501–507. 10.1007/s11135-017-0630-4

Menary, R. (2007). *Cognitive integration: Mind and cognition unbounded.* Palgrave Macmillan. 10.1057/9780230592889

Meshi, D. (2019). Excessive social media users demonstrate impaired decision making in the Iowa Gambling Task. *Journal of behavioral addictions,8.* Akadémiai Kiadó Budapest: 169–173.

Mijwil, M. M., Aggarwal, K., Doshi, R., Hiran, K. K., & Gök, M. (2022). The distinction between R-CNN and Fast R-CNN in image analysis: A Performance Comparison. *Asian Journal of Applied Sciences*, 10(5), 429–437. 10.24203/ajas.v10i5.7064

Mikhaylov, S. J., Esteve, M., & Campion, A. (2018). Artificial intelligence for the public sector: Opportunities and challenges of cross-sector collaboration. *Philosophical Transactions. Series A, Mathematical, Physical, and Engineering Sciences*, 376(2128), 20170357. 10.1098/rsta.2017.035730082303

Minsky, M. L. (Ed.). (1968). *Semantic Information Processing.* MIT Press.

Mirbabaie, M., Stieglitz, S., & Marx, J. (2022). Digital Detox. *Business & Information Systems Engineering*, 64(2), 239–246. 10.1007/s12599-022-00747-x

Misra, N. N., Dixit, Y., Al-Mallahi, A., Bhullar, M. S., Upadhyay, R., & Martynenko, A. (2020). IoT, big data, and artificial intelligence in agriculture and food industry. *IEEE Internet of Things Journal*, 9(9), 6305–6324. 10.1109/JIOT.2020.2998584

Mohammad Hossein Jarrahi, D. L. (2023). Mindful work and mindful technology: Redressing digital distraction in knowledge work. *Digital Business*, 3(1), 100051. 10.1016/j.digbus.2022.100051

Mohassel, P., & Zhang, L. (2017). Everlasting cookies: Long-term tracking using browser fingerprints. In *Proceedings of the 2017 ACM SIGSAC Conference on Computer and Communications Security* (pp. 1511-1525). ACM.

Mohd Shukry, A. I., Mohamad Rosman, M. R., Nik Rosli, N. N. I., Alias, N. R., Razlan, N. M., & Alimin, N. A. (2023). "Bring-Your-Own-Device" (BYOD) and Productivity. [IJIM]. *International Journal of Interactive Mobile Technologies*, 17(11), 83–100. 10.3991/ijim.v17i11.38139

Moir, C.-L., Tzani, C., Ioannou, M., Lester, D., Synnott, J., & Thomas, J. V. W. (2023). Cybersuicide: Online-Assisted Suicide. *Journal of Police and Criminal Psychology*, 38(4), 879–891. 10.1007/s11896-023-09602-5

Mokona, H., Yohannes, K., & Ayano, G. (2020). Youth unemployment and mental health: Prevalence and associated factors of depression among unemployed young adults in Gedeo zone, Southern Ethiopia. *International Journal of Mental Health Systems*, 14(1), 1–11. 10.1186/s13033-020-00395-232782471

Montgomery, K. (2000). Youth and digital media: A policy research agenda. *The Journal of Adolescent Health*, 27(2, Suppl), 61–68. 10.1016/S1054-139X(00)00130-010904209

Moon, M.-H., & Kim, G. (2023). Predicting University Dropout Rates Using Machine Learning Algorithms. *Journal of Economics and Finance Education*, 32(2), 57–68. 10.46967/jefe.2023.32.2.57

*Most popular social networks worldwide as of April 2024, ranked by number of monthly active users (in millions)*. (2022). Statista. https://www.statista.com/statistics/272014/global-social-networks-ranked-by-number-of-users/

Muehlhauser, L., & Salamon, A. (2013). Intelligence explosion: Evidence and import. In *Singularity hypotheses: A scientific and philosophical assessment* (pp. 15–42). Springer.

Muggleton, S. (2014). Alan Turing and the development of Artificial Intelligence. *AI Communications*, 27(1), 3–10. 10.3233/AIC-130579

Muhammad, R. (2023). Barriers and effectiveness to counselling careers with Artificial Intelligence: A systematic literature review. *Ricerche Di Pedagogia e Didattica.Journal of Theories and Research in Education*, 18(3), 143–164.

Mukhopadhyay, S., & Chakrabarti, A. (2023). A Review on the Impacts of Artificial Intelligence (AI) on Youth. In *Handbook of Youth Development* (pp. 195–207). Springer Nature Singapore. 10.1007/978-981-99-4969-4_11

Muppalla, S. K., Vuppalapati, S., Reddy Pulliahgaru, A., & Sreenivasulu, H. (2023). Effects of Excessive Screen Time on Child Development: An Updated Review and Strategies for Management. *Cureus*, 15(6), e40608. 10.7759/cureus.4060837476119

Murphy, K. (2019). *Carnegie Learning's Mika: AI-powered math instruction*. EdTech Magazine. https://edtechmagazine.com/k12/article/2019/

Muslu, M., & Gökçay, G. F. (2019). Teknoloji bağımlısı çocuklarda obeziteye neden olan risk faktörleri. *Gümüşhane Üniversitesi Sağlık Bilimleri Dergisi*, 8(2), 72–79.

Nadeem, A. (2022). Gender bias in AI-based decision-making systems: a systematic literature review. *Australasian Journal of Information Systems,26*. Australian Computer Society.

Nagata, J. M., Cortez, C. A., Cattle, C. J., Ganson, K. T., Iyer, P., Bibbins-Domingo, K., & Baker, F. (2021). Screen Time Use Among US Adolescents During the COVID-19 Pandemic: Findings from the Adolescent Brain Cognitive Development (ABCD) Study. *JAMA Pediatrics*.

Nagy, V., Kovács, G., Földesi, P., & Sándor, Á. P. (2023). Car Simulator Study for the Development of a Bring-Your-Own-Device (BYOD) Dashboard Concept. *Chemical Engineering Transactions*, 107. Advance online publication. 10.3303/CET23107070

Nair, K., James, J. K., & Santhosh, K. (2015). Identity Crisis among Early Adolescents in Relations to Abusive Experiences in the Childhood, Social Support, and Parental Support. *Journal of Psychosomatic Research*, 10, 167.

Nakshine VS, Thute P, Khatib MN, Sarkar B. Increased Screen Time as a Cause of Declining Physical, Psychological Health, and Sleep Patterns: A Literary Review. Cureus. 2022 Oct 8;14(10):e30051. doi: 10.7759/cureus.30051. PMID: 36381869; PMCID: PMC9638701.10.7759/cureus.3005136381869

Nalepa, G. J., Costa, A., Novais, P., & Julian, V. (2018). Cognitive Assistants. *International Journal of Human-Computer Studies*, 117, 1–68. 10.1016/j.ijhcs.2018.05.008

Nalin, M., Baroni, I., Kruijff-Korbayová, I., Canamero, L., Lewis, M., Beck, A., & Sanna, A. (2012, September). Children's adaptation in multi-session interaction with a humanoid robot. In *2012 IEEE RO-MAN: The 21st IEEE International Symposium on Robot and Human Interactive Communication* (pp. 351-357). IEEE. 10.1109/ROMAN.2012.6343778

Nam, V. H. (2021). Youth Identity in the Digital Age. *Asia Journal of Theology*, 35(1), 58–82. 10.54424/ajt.v35i1.4

Nasar, I., Uzer, Y., & Purwanto, M. B. (2023). Artificial Intelligence in Smart Classrooms: An Investigative Learning Process for High School. [AJAE]. *Asian Journal of Applied Education*, 2(4), 547–556. 10.55927/ajae.v2i4.6038

National Education Association. (2021). *AI in education: A guide for educators*. National Education Association. https://www.nea.org/advocating-for-change/resources/ai-education-guide-educators

Ndovela, S., & Mutanga, B. (2024). Academic Factors Influencing Students Career Choices in the IT Field: Insights from South African IT Students. *Indonesian Journal of Information Systems*, 6(2), 107–116. 10.24002/ijis.v6i2.8293

Neophytou, E., Manwell, L. A., & Eikelboom, R. (2019). Effects of Excessive Screen Time on Neurodevelopment, Learning, Memory, Mental Health, and Neurodegeneration: A Scoping Review. *International Journal of Mental Health and Addiction*, 19(3), 724–744. 10.1007/s11469-019-00182-2

Nesi, J. (2020). The Impact of Social Media on Youth Mental Health. *North Carolina Medical Journal*, 81(2), 116–121. 10.18043/ncm.81.2.11632132255

Newell, A., & Card, S. K. (1985). The prospects for psychological science in human-computer interaction. *Human-Computer Interaction*, 1(3), 209–242. 10.1207/s15327051hci0103_1

Newport, C. (2016). *Deep Work: Rules for Focused Success in a Distracted World*. Grand Central Publishing.

Newport, C. (2019). *Digital Minimalism: Choosing a Focused Life in a Noisy World*. Portfolio.

Nga, P. T. (2022). Artificial intelligence (AI) Application in foreign language teaching and learning. *European Journal of Applied Sciences*, 10(5), 89–93.

Nguyen, V. T. (2022). The perceptions of social media users of digital detox apps considering personality traits. *Education and Information Technologies*, 27(7), 9293–9316. 10.1007/s10639-022-11022-735370441

Nicosia, J., Wang, B., Aschenbrenner, A. J., Sliwinski, M. J., Yabiku, S. T., Roque, N. A., Germine, L. T., Bateman, R. J., Morris, J. C., & Hassenstab, J. (2023). To BYOD or not: Are device latencies important for bring-your-own-device (BYOD) smartphone cognitive testing? *Behavior Research Methods*, 55(6), 2800–2812. 10.3758/s13428-022-01925-135953659

Niese, B. (2019). *Making good decisions: an attribution model of decision quality in decision tasks*. Kennesaw State University.

Nikitas, A., Michalakopoulou, K., Njoya, E. T., & Karampatzakis, D. (2020). Artificial intelligence, transport and the smart city: Definitions and dimensions of a new mobility era. *Sustainability (Basel)*, 12(7), 2789. 10.3390/su12072789

Nikolaidis, P., Ismail, M., Shuib, L., Khan, S., & Dhiman, G. (2022). *Predicting Student Attrition in Higher Education through the Determinants of Learning Progress: A Structural Equation Modelling Approach. Sustainability*. https://www.mdpi.com/2071-1050/14/20/1358410.3390/su142013584

Nilsson, N. J. (1990). *The mathematical foundations of learning machines*. Morgan Kaufmann Publishers Inc.

Niyozov, N., Bijanov, A., Ganiyev, S., & Kurbonova, R. (2023). The pedagogical principles and effectiveness of utilizing ChatGPT for language learning. *E3S Web of Conferences, 461*, 01093. E3S. https://www.e3s-conferences.org/articles/e3sconf/abs/2023/98/e3sconf_rses23_01093/e3sconf_rses23_01093.html

Nowak, A., Lukowicz, P., & Horodecki, P. (2018). Assessing artificial intelligence for humanity: Will ai be the our biggest ever advance? or the biggest threat [opinion]. *IEEE Technology and Society Magazine, 37*(4), 26–34. 10.1109/MTS.2018.2876105

Nowland, R., Necka, E. A., & Cacioppo, J. T. (2018). Loneliness and Social Internet Use: Pathways to Reconnection in a Digital World? *Perspectives on Psychological Science, 13*(1), 70–87. 10.1177/174569161771305228937910

Ntoutsi, E., Fafalios, P., Gadiraju, U., Iosifidis, V., Nejdl, W., Vidal, M., Ruggieri, S., Turini, F., Papadopoulos, S., Krasanakis, E., Kompatsiaris, I., Kinder-Kurlanda, K., Wagner, C., Karimi, F., Fernandez, M., Alani, H., Berendt, B., Kruegel, T., Heinze, C., & Staab, S. (2020). Bias in data-driven artificial intelligence systems—An introductory survey. *Wiley Interdisciplinary Reviews. Data Mining and Knowledge Discovery, 10*(3), e1356. 10.1002/widm.1356

Nurillah, R. A., & Trihandoyo, A. (2024). Analisis Faktor-Faktor Keamanan Informasi Perusahaan Dalam Penerapan Bring Your Own Device (BYOD). *IKRA-ITH Informatika : Jurnal Komputer Dan Informatika, 8*(2), 136–145. 10.37817/ikraith-informatika.v8i2.2973

Nurmalitasari, A. (2023). The Predictive Learning Analytics for Student Dropout Using Data Mining Technique: A Systematic Literature Review. *Advances in Technology Transfer Through IoT and IT Solutions*. Springer. doi:10.1007/978-3-031-25178-8_2. https://link.springer.com/10.1007/978-3-031-25178-8_210.1007/978-3-031-25178-8_2

Nushi, M., & Eqbali, M. H. (2018). Babbel: A mobile language learning app. *TESL Reporter, 51*, 13–13.

O'Connor, E., & Madge, N. (2019). The impact of AI on health monitoring in family settings. *Health Communication, 34*(12), 1425–1434.

O'Connor, S., & Liu, H. (2023). Gender bias perpetuation and mitigation in AI technologies: Challenges and opportunities. *AI & Society*, 1–13. 10.1007/s00146-023-01675-4

O'Keeffe, G. S., & Clarke-Pearson, K. (2011). The impact of social media on children, adolescents, and families. *Pediatrics, 127*(4), 800–804. 10.1542/peds.2011-005421444588

O'Reilly, M., Dogra, N., Whiteman, N., Hughes, J., Eruyar, S., & Reilly, P. (2018). Is social media bad for mental health and wellbeing? Exploring the perspectives of adolescents. *Clinical Child Psychology and Psychiatry, 23*(4), 601–613. 10.1177/135910451877515429781314

Oblinger, D. og Oblinger, J. (2005). Is it age or it: First steps toward understanding the net generation. *Educating the net generation, 2*(1-2), 20.

Odgers, C. L., & Jensen, M. R. (2020). Annual research review: Adolescent mental health in the digital age: Facts, fears, and future directions. *Journal of Child Psychology and Psychiatry, and Allied Disciplines, 61*(3), 336–348. 10.1111/jcpp.1319031951670

Odgers, C., & Jensen, M. R. (2020). Annual Research Review: Adolescent mental health in the digital age: facts, fears, and future directions. Journal of child psychology and psychiatry, and allied disciplines. *One, 13*(12), e0206819.

Oh, J., Capezzuto, L., Kriara, L., Schjodt-Eriksen, J., van Beek, J., Bernasconi, C., Montalban, X., Butzkueven, H., Kappos, L., Giovannoni, G., Bove, R., Julian, L., Baker, M., Gossens, C., & Lindemann, M. (2024). Use of smartphone-based remote assessments of multiple sclerosis in Floodlight Open, a global, prospective, open-access study. *Scientific Reports, 14*(1), 122. 10.1038/s41598-023-49299-438168498

Onwubere, C., & Osuji, H. (2021). Utilisation des données géospatiales et des technologies d'intelligence artificielle et évolution des pratiques sociales chez les jeunes nigérians. *Communication Technologies Et Développement*, (10). 10.4000/ctd.5525

Ophir, E., Nass, C., & Wagner, A. D. (2009). Cognitive control in media multitaskers. *Proceedings of the National Academy of Sciences of the United States of America*, 106(37), 15583–15587. 10.1073/pnas.090362010619706386

Oqaidi, K., Aouhassi, S., & Mansouri, K. (2022). A Comparison between Using Fuzzy Cognitive Mapping and Machine Learning to Predict Students' Performance in Higher Education. *2022 IEEE 3rd International Conference on Electronics, Control, Optimization and Computer Science (ICECOCS)*. IEEE. https://ieeexplore.ieee.org/document/9983470/10 .1109/ICECOCS55148.2022.9983470

Orben A. (2020). The Sisyphean Cycle of Technology Panics. *Perspectives on psychological science: a journal of the Association for Psychological Science, 15*(5), 1143–1157. 10.1177/1745691620919372

Osama, M., Ali, S., & Malik, R. J. (2018). Posture related musculoskeletal discomfort and its association with computer use among university students. *JPMA. The Journal of the Pakistan Medical Association*, 68, 639–641.29808057

Oskotsky, T., Maric, I., Tang, A., & Lituiev, D. (2021). *Nurturing Diversity and Inclusion in Biomedicine Through an AI Summer Program for High School Students*. ArXiv. 10.1101/2021.03.06.434213

Osuji, C. I. (2021). Artificial Intelligence and Literary Analyses: Challenges and Prospects. *Unilag Journal of Humanities*, 9(2), 43–58.

Ovalle, A., Ovalle, A., Gautam, V., Gee, G., & Chang, K. W. (2023, August). Factoring the matrix of domination: A critical review and reimagination of intersectionality in ai fairness. In *Proceedings of the 2023 AAAI/ACM Conference on AI, Ethics, and Society* (pp. 496-511). ACM. 10.1145/3600211.3604705

Owens, J. N., Beevers, S. C., & Townsend, M. E. (2019). Woebot: A conversational AI agent for delivering cognitive behavioral therapy. *Journal of Affective Disorders*.

Özkan, S. (2017). Gerbner'in kültürel göstergeler kuramı bağlamında televizyon haber içeriklerine ilişkin bir araştırma. *Abant Kültürel Araştırmalar Dergisi*, 2(4), 129–141.

Padilla-Walker, L. M., & Coyne, S. M. (2011). "Turn that thing off!" parent and adolescent predictors of proactive media monitoring. *Journal of Adolescence, 34*(4), 705–715. https://doi.org/10.1016/j.adolescence.2010.09.002

Palanisamy, R., Norman, A. A., & Mat Kiah, M. L. (2024). Employees' BYOD Security Policy Compliance in the Public Sector. *Journal of Computer Information Systems*, 64(1), 62–77. 10.1080/08874417.2023.2178038

Pappamihiel, N. E., & Walser, T. M. (2009). English Language Learners and Complexity Theory: Why Current Accountability Systems Do Not Measure Up. *The Educational Forum*, 73(2), 133–140. 10.1080/00131720902739544

Parsons, F. (1909). *Choosing a vocation*. University of California.

Pasquinelli, M. (2023). *The eye of the master: A social history of artificial intelligence*. Verso Books.

Patchin, J. W., & Hinduja, S. (2017). Digital Self-Harm Among Adolescents. *The Journal of Adolescent Health*, 61(6), 761–766. 10.1016/j.jadohealth.2017.06.01228935385

Patnaik, S., Sen, S., & Mahmoud, M. S. (Eds.). (2020). *Smart Village Technology: Concepts and Developments* (Vol. 17). Springer International Publishing. 10.1007/978-3-030-37794-6

Patton, W., & McMahon, M. (2014). Lifelong Career Development Learning: A Foundation for Career Practice. In *Career Development and Systems Theory* (pp. 277–296). Brill. https://brill.com/downloadpdf/book/9789462096356/BP000011.pdf

Paulich, K. N., Ross, J. M., Lessem, J., & Hewitt, J. (2021). *Screen time and early adolescent mental health, academic, and social outcomes in 9- and 10- year old children: Utilizing the Adolescent Brain Cognitive Development (ABCD) Study.* PLoS ONE.

Paulich, K. N., Ross, J. M., Lessem, J., & Hewitt, J. (2021). Screen time and early adolescent mental health, academic, and social outcomes in 9- and 10- year old children: Utilizing the Adolescent Brain Cognitive Development (ABCD) Study. *PLoS One*, 16(4), e0247868. 10.1371/journal.pone.025659134496002

Pawluczuk, A., & erban, A. M. (2022). *Technology and the new power dynamics: limitations of digital youth work.* EU andCoE Youth Partnership. https://pjpeu.coe.int/documents/42128013/116591216/Limits+of+digital+youth+work.pdf/732ddd6a-15cb-02a6-c336-efa9aa8154c0

Pedro, F., Subosa, M., Rivas, A., & Valverde, P. (2019). *Artificial intelligence in education: Challenges and opportunities for sustainable development.* https://repositorio.minedu.gob.pe/handle/20.500.12799/6533

Pehlivan Yirci, N. (2023). *Pazarlamada yapay zeka uygulamaları, marka yolculuğu. İ N. Ç. Çetinkaya (ritstj.), Dijital dönüşüm ve sürdürülebilirlik (bls.* Bidge Yayınları.

Peinado, I., de Lera, E., Usero, J. M., Clark, C. B., Treviranus, J., & Vanderheiden, G. C. (2021). Digital Inclusion at the Workplace Post Covid19. In *IJCCI* (pp. 460–467). 10.5220/0010722900003063

Peltola, L. (2019). *Making sense of the relationship between social media influencers on Instagram and the consumers who follow them* [Master's Thesis, Hanken School of Economics]. https://helda.helsinki.fi/bitstream/10227/261590/1/Peltola.pdf

Pendy, B. (2023). From traditional to tech-infused: The evolution of education. *BULLET: Jurnal Multidisiplin Ilmu*, 2(3), 767–777.

Perkins, M. (2023). Academic integrity considerations of AI large language models in the post-pandemic era: ChatGPT and beyond. *Journal of University Teaching & Learning Practice*, 20(2), 6–24. 10.53761/1.20.02.07

Petihakis, G., Kiritsis, D., Farao, A., Bountakas, P., Panou, A., & Xenakis, C. (2023). A Bring Your Own Device security awareness survey among professionals. *ACM International Conference Proceeding Series*. 10.1145/3600160.3605072

Petticrew, M., & Roberts, H. (2006). *Systematic reviews in the social sciences: A practical guide.* Blackwell Publishing., 10.1002/9780470754887

Pfeifer, J. H., & Berkman, E. T. (2018). The development of self and identity in adolescence: Neural evidence and implications for a value-based choice perspective on motivated behavior. *Child Development Perspectives*, 12(3), 158–164. 10.1111/cdep.1227931363361

Pflügner, K., Maier, C., Mattke, J., & Weitzel, T. (2020). Personality profiles that put users at risk of perceiving technostress. *Business & Information Systems Engineering*, 63(4), 389–402. 10.1007/s12599-020-00668-7

Philippe Doneys, K. K. (2024). Gender, technology and development: reflections on the past, and provocations for the future. *Technology and Development*, 285-294. 10.1080/09718524.2022.2153459

Pohlan, L. (2019). Unemployment and social exclusion. *Journal of Economic Behavior & Organization*, 164, 273–299. 10.1016/j.jebo.2019.06.006

Pokrivcakova, S. (2019). Preparing teachers for the application of AI-powered technologies in foreign language education. *Journal of Language and Cultural Education*, 7(3), 135–153. 10.2478/jolace-2019-0025

Porter, A. K., Matthews, K. J., Salvo, D., & Kohl, H. W. (2017). Associations of physical activity, sedentary time, and screen time with cardiovascular fitness in United States adolescents: Results from the NHANES National Youth Fitness Survey. *Journal of Physical Activity & Health*, 14(7), 506–512. 10.1123/jpah.2016-016528290741

Post, B., Badea, C., Faisal, A., & Brett, S. J. (2023). Breaking bad news in the era of artificial intelligence and algorithmic medicine: An exploration of disclosure and its ethical justification using the hedonic calculus. *AI and Ethics*, 3(4), 1215–1228. 10.1007/s43681-022-00230-z36338525

Pozzi, F. A., & Dwivedi, D. (2023). ESG and IoT: Ensuring Sustainability and Social Responsibility in the Digital Age. In Tiwari, S., Ortiz-Rodríguez, F., Mishra, S., Vakaj, E., & Kotecha, K. (Eds.), *Artificial Intelligence: Towards Sustainable Intelligence. AI4S 2023. Communications in Computer and Information Science* (Vol. 1907). Springer. 10.1007/978-3-031-47997-7_2

Pradhan, I. P., & Saxena, P. (2023). Reskilling workforce for the Artificial Intelligence age: Challenges and the way forward. In *The adoption and effect of artificial intelligence on human resources management, Part B* (pp. 181–197). Emerald Publishing Limited. 10.1108/978-1-80455-662-720230011

Prasanth, A., & Alqahtani, H. (2023). Predictive Models for Early Dropout Indicators in University Settings Using Machine Learning Techniques. In *2023 IEEE International Conference on Emerging Technologies and Applications in Sensors (ICETAS)*. IEEE. 10.1109/ICETAS59148.2023.10346531

Prensky, M. (2001). Digital Natives, digital immigrants. Marc Prensky. https://www.marcprensky.com/writing/Prensky.

Prensky, M. (2001b). Digital natives, digital immigrants part 2: Do they really think differently? *On the Horizon*, 9(6), 1–6. 10.1108/10748120110424843

Prensky, M. (2011). *Digital wisdom and homo sapiens digital. Í Deconstructing digital natives (bls.* Routledge.

Price, C. (2018). *How to Break Up With Your Phone*. Trapeze.

Przybylski, A. K., Murayama, K., DeHaan, C. R., & Gladwell, V. (2013). Motivational, emotional, and behavioral correlates of fear of missing out. *Computers in Human Behavior*, 29(4), 1841–1848. 10.1016/j.chb.2013.02.014

Przybylski, A. K., Murayama, K., DeHaan, C. R., & Gladwell, V. (2013). The motivational value of digital games: A uses and gratification perspective. *Psychology of Popular Media Culture*, 2(2), 90–109.

Pulurluoğlu, T. (2022). *Sosyal medyaya eleştirel bir bakış: Sosyal ikilem (social dilemma) netflix belgesel filminin analizi.*

Puspitaningsih, S., Irhadtanto, B., & Puspananda, D. R. (2022). The Role of Artificial Intelligence in Children's Education for A Digital Future. *KnE Social Sciences*, 642-647.

Putnam, H. (1960). Minds and Machines. In Hook, S. (Ed.), *Dimensions of Mind*. New York University Press.

Putnam, H. (1967). *The Nature of Mental States*. University of Pittsburgh Press.

Putnam, R. D. (2000). *Bowling Alone: The Collapse and Revival of American Community*. Simon & Schuster.

PwC. (2018). Artificial intelligence: The economic impact. *PwC's Global Artificial Intelligence Study*. PwC.

Qi, C. (2023). Effects of Bring Your Own Device (BYOD) Attributes on Work-to-life Conflict. *Asia Pacific Journal of Information Systems*, 33(3), 831–862. 10.14329/apjis.2023.33.3.831

Qin, C., Zhang, A., Zhang, Z., Chen, J., Yasunaga, M., & Yang, D. (2023). Is ChatGPT a general-purpose natural language processing task solver? *Proceedings of the 2023 Conference on Empirical Methods in Natural Language Processing*, (pp. 1339-1384). IEEE. 10.18653/v1/2023.emnlp-main.85

Radesky, J. S., Schumacher, J., & Zuckerman, B. (2015). Mobile and interactive media use by young children: The good, the bad, and the unknown. *Pediatrics*, 135(1), 1–3. 10.1542/peds.2014-225125548323

Radiomof. (2023). *Младите ги користат социјалните мрежи за четување и видеа, ама не и за општествен активизам.* Radiomof. https://www.radiomof.mk/mladite-gi-koristat-socijalnite-mrezhi-za-chetuvanje-i-videa-ama-ne-i-za-opshtestven-aktivizam/

Radtke, T. A., Apel, T., Schenkel, K., Keller, J., & von Lindern, E. (2022). Digital detox: An effective solution in the smart-phone era? A systematic literature review. *Mobile Media & Communication*, 10(2), 190–215. 10.1177/20501579211028647

Ragnedda, M., & Muschert, G. W. (2013). *The digital divide: The internet and social inequality in international perspective*. Routledge. 10.4324/9780203069769

Rahman, M. A., Duradoni, M., & Guazzini, A. (2022). Identification and prediction of phubbing behavior: A data-driven approach. *Neural Computing & Applications*, 34(5), 3885–3894. 10.1007/s00521-021-06649-5

Rainie, L., & Wellman, B. (2012). *Networked*. MIT Press. 10.7551/mitpress/8358.001.0001

Rajesh, P., Sreekanksha, G., Miralee, K., Govind, R., & Deepak, R. (2022). Smart classroom robot. *International Journal of Advance Scientific Research And Engineering Trends*, 7(4). https://ijasret.com/VolumeArticles/FullTextPDF/1303_9.SMART_CLASSROOM_ROBOT.pdf

Rakowski, R., Polak, P., & Kowalikova, P. (2021). Ethical aspects of the impact of AI: The status of humans in the era of artificial intelligence. *Society*, 58(3), 196–203. 10.1007/s12115-021-00586-8

Ramdani, B., Raja, S., & Kayumova, M. (2022). Digital innovation in SMEs: A systematic review, synthesis and research agenda. *Information Technology for Development*, 28(1), 56–80. 10.1080/02681102.2021.1893148

Ramesh, N., Vijay, C., &Gonsalves, K. (2022). Parenting styles and mental health of adolescents: A cross-sectional study in South India. *Journal of Mental Health and Human Behaviour*. 10.4103/jmhhb.jmhhb_176_20

Rana, S. A., Azizul, Z. H., & Awan, A. A. (2023). A step toward building a unified framework for managing AI bias. *PeerJ Computer Science, 9*, e1630.Riley, J. (2023). AI Powers the Digital Economy. *Ubiquity.*

Rat der Europäischen Union. (2020). Schlussfolgerungen des Rates zur Medienkompetenz in einer sich ständig wandelnden *Welt: Official journal of EU.*https://eur-lex.europa.eu/legalcontent/DE/TXT/PDF/?uri=CELEX:52020XG0609(04)&from=EN, e hapur se fundmi ne date 04.03.2024.

Razzak, A., & Yousaf, S. (2022). Perceived resilience and vulnerability during the pandemic-infused panic buying and the role of COVID conspiracy beliefs. Evidence from Pakistan. *Journal of Global Marketing*, 35(5), 368–383. 10.1080/08911762.2022.2051156

Reid Chassiakos, Y. L., Radesky, J., Christakis, D., Moreno, M. A., Cross, C., Hill, D., Ameenuddin, N., Hutchinson, J., Levine, A., Boyd, R., Mendelson, R., & Swanson, W. S. (2016). Children and adolescents and digital media. *Pediatrics*, 138(5), e20162593. 10.1542/peds.2016-259327940795

Reid, G. G., & Boyer, W. (2013). Social Network Sites and Young Adolescent Identity Development. *Childhood Education*, 89(4), 243–253. 10.1080/00094056.2013.815554

Reinecke, L., Aufenanger, S., Beutel, M. E., Dreier, M., Quiring, O., Stark, B., Wölfling, K., & Müller, K. W. (2017). Digital Stress over the Life Span: The Effects of Communication Load and Internet Multitasking on Perceived Stress and Psychological Health Impairments in a German Probability Sample. *Media Psychology*, 20(1), 90–115. 10.1080/15213269.2015.1121832

Reiss, M. J. (2021). The Use of AI in Education: Practicalities and Ethical Considerations. *London Review of Education*, 19(1). https://eric.ed.gov/?id=EJ1297682. 10.14324/LRE.19.1.05

Ren, Y., & Lan, L. (2021). Application and Development Prospect of Artificial Intelligence in Quality Education. *2021 3rd International Conference on Internet Technology and Educational Informization (ITEI)*, (pp. 172–175). IEEE.

Repetskaya, A. I. (2021). *Modern Sociocultural Practices in the Field of Fashion Consumption: The Main Youth Trends*. KnE Social Sciences.

Resnick, M., Maloney, K., Eastwood, T., Rusk, R., Rosenbaum, S., Dahl, P., & Silverman, B. (2009). Scratch: Programming for all. *Communications of the ACM*, 52(8), 78–85.

Ribble, M. S. (2009). Raising a Digital Child: A Digital Citizenship *Handbook for Parents*.

Ricci, M., Masthoff, J., & Cunningham, P. (2015). Personalized recommendations for music playlists. *ACM Computing Surveys*, 48(3), 1–32.

Richards, R., McGee, R., Williams, S. M., Welch, D., & Hancox, R. (2010). Adolescent screen time and attachment to parents and peers. *Archives of Pediatrics & Adolescent Medicine*, 164(3), 258. 10.1001/archpediatrics.2009.28020194259

Rich, E. (1985). Artificial intelligence and the humanities. *Computers and the Humanities*, 19(2), 117–122. 10.1007/BF02259633

Risko, E. F., & Gilbert, S. J. (2016). Cognitive offloading. *Trends in Cognitive Sciences*, 20(9), 676–688. 10.1016/j.tics.2016.07.00227542527

Riva, G., Chrysanthou, A., & Coulson, C. (2020). The role of virtual reality in social interaction and communication. In *Proceedings of the 2020 CHI Conference on Human Factors in Computing Systems* (pp. 1-14). New York, NY, USA: ACM Press.

Rodríguez-García, J. D., Moreno-León, J., Román-González, M., & Robles, G. (2021). Evaluation of an Online Intervention to Teach Artificial Intelligence with LearningML to 10-16-Year-Old Students. *Proceedings of the 52nd ACM Technical Symposium on Computer Science Education*, (pp. 177–183). ACM. 10.1145/3408877.3432393

Rogers, E. M. (1995). *Diffusion of Innovations* (4th ed.). Free Press.

Rogers, Y., Sharp, H., & Preece, J. (2011). *Interaction design: Beyond human-computer interaction*. John Wiley & Sons.

Roll, I., & Wylie, R. (2016). Evolution and Revolution in Artificial Intelligence in Education. *International Journal of Artificial Intelligence in Education*, 26(2), 582–599. 10.1007/s40593-016-0110-3

Romero-Acosta, K., Gómez-de-Regil, L., Lowe, G. A., Garth, E. L., & Gibson, R. C. (2021). Parenting Styles, Anxiety and Depressive Symptoms in Child/Adolescent. *International Journal of Psychological Research*, 14(1), 12–32. 10.21500/20112084.470434306576

Rosenfield, M. (2020). A double-blind test of blue-blocking filters on symptoms of digital eye strain. *Work* 65. IOS Press.

Rosen, L. D. (2013). Media use in early childhood: What we know and do not know. *Pediatrics*, 132(5), e1259–e1269.

Rosenmann, A., Reese, G., & Cameron, J. (2016). *Social Identities in a Globalized World*.

Roslan, S., Arsyad, M., Hos, J., Supiyah, R., Anggraini, D., & Ridwan, H. (2023, May 17). Pelatihan Pendampingan Orangtua terhadap Kecerdasan Anak di Era Modernisasi di Desa Wawatu Kecamatan Moramo Utara Kabupaten Konawe Selatan. *Indonesian Journal of Community Services.*, 2(1), 35–44. 10.47540/ijcs.v2i1.837

Rouse, W. B., & Spohrer, J. C. (2018). Automating versus augmenting intelligence. *Journal of Enterprise Transformation*, 1-21.

Rowlands, M. (2010). *The new science of the mind: From extended mind to embodied phenomenology*. MIT. 10.7551/mitpress/9780262014557.001.0001

Rubin, J. (2012). Technology's Impact on the Creative Potential of Youth. *Creativity Research Journal*, 24(2–3), 252–256. 10.1080/10400419.2012.677370

Ruß-Mohl, S. (2017). Journalismus und Gemeinwohl in der Desinformationsökonomie. Plädoyer für eine „Alliance for Enlightenment" zwischen Wissenschaft und Journalismus. [ComSoc]. *Communicatio Socialis*, 50(1), 50–63. 10.5771/0010-3497-2017-1-50

Saçan, S., Yarali, K. T., & Kavruk, S. Z. (2022). Investigation of Metaphorical Perceptions of Children on the Concept of "Artificial Intelligence. *Mehmet Akif Ersoy Üniversitesi Eğitim Fakültesi Dergisi*, (64), 274–296.

Salah, K., Rehman, M. H. U., Nizamuddin, N., & Al-Fuqaha, A. (2019). Blockchain for AI: Review and open research challenges. *IEEE Access : Practical Innovations, Open Solutions*, 7, 10127–10149. 10.1109/ACCESS.2018.2890507

Salehi, H., & Burgueño, R. (2018). Emerging artificial intelligence methods in structural engineering. *Engineering Structures*, 171, 170–189. 10.1016/j.engstruct.2018.05.084

Samek, W., Wiegand, T., & Müller, K. R. (2017). Explainable artificial intelligence: Understanding, visualizing and interpreting deep learning models. *arXiv preprint arXiv:1708.08296*

Sandrasegaran, K., & Huang, X. (2009). Digital Identity in Current Networks. In *Encyclopedia of Information Science and Technology*, Second Edition (pp. 1125-1132). IGI Global. 10.4018/978-1-60566-026-4.ch179

Sands, S., Campbell, C. L., Plangger, K., & Ferraro, C. (2022). Unreal influence: Leveraging AI in influencer marketing. *European Journal of Marketing*, 56(6), 1721–1747. 10.1108/EJM-12-2019-0949

Sandstrom, G. M., & Dunn, E. W. (2014). Social interactions and well-being: The surprising power of weak ties. *Personality and Social Psychology Bulletin*, 40(7), 910–922. 10.1177/0146167214529799 24769739

Sangeetha, S. R., Singh, P., & Jahagirdar, S. R. (2023). Estimation of Distance to Empty of Small Commercial EVs for BYOD (Bring Your Own Device) Application using EKF and ANN. *2023 IEEE Renewable Energy and Sustainable E-Mobility Conference. RESEM*, 2023, 1–5. 10.1109/RESEM57584.2023.10236430

Santos, F. C. C. (2023). Artificial intelligence in automated detection of disinformation: A thematic analysis. *Journalism and Media*, 4(2), 679–687. 10.3390/journalmedia4020043

Sarker, I. H. (2022). AI-Based Modeling: Techniques, Applications and Research Issues Towards Automation, Intelligent and Smart Systems. *SN Computer Science*, 3(2), 158. 10.1007/s42979-022-01043-x35194580

Saura, J. R., Palos-Sanchez, P. R., & Correia, M. B. (2019). Digital marketing strategies based on the e-business model: Literature review and future directions. *Organizational transformation and managing innovation in the fourth industrial revolution*, 86-103.

Schiff, D. (2021). Out of the laboratory and into the classroom: The future of artificial intelligence in education. *AI & Society*, 36(1), 331–348. 10.1007/s00146-020-01033-832836908

Schiff, D. S., & Rosenberg-Kima, R. B. (2023). AI in education: landscape, vision and critical ethical challenges in the 21st century. In *Handbook of Critical Studies of Artificial Intelligence* (pp. 804–814). Edward Elgar Publishing. 10.4337/9781803928562.00081

Schmidt, T., & Strasser, T. (2022). Artificial intelligence in foreign language learning and teaching: *A CALL for Intelligent Practive. Anglistik. International Journal of English Studies*, 33(1), 165–184.

Schnell, S. M. (2013). *Deliberate identities: becoming local in America in a global age.*

Schorb, B. (2014). *Identität und Medien.* In A. Tillmann, S. Fleischer & K.-U. Hugger (Hrsg.), *Digitale Kultur und Kommunikation: Bd. 1. Handbuch Kinder und Medien* (f. 172–182). Springer VS. 10.1007/978-3-531-18997-0_13

Schwartz, S., & Petrova, M. (2018). Fostering healthy identity development in adolescence. *Nature Human Behaviour*, 2(2), 110–111. 10.1038/s41562-017-0283-2

Scott, D. A., Valley, B., & Simecka, B. A. (2017). Mental Health Concerns in the Digital Age. *International Journal of Mental Health and Addiction*, 15(3), 604–613. 10.1007/s11469-016-9684-0

Scully-Russ, E., & Torraco, R. (2020). The Changing Nature and Organization of Work: An Integrative Review of the Literature. *Human Resource Development Review*, 19(1), 66–93. 10.1177/1534484319886394

Seidel, E., & Kutieleh, S. (2017). Using predictive analytics to target and improve first year student attrition. *Australian Journal of Education*, 61(2), 200–218. 10.1177/0004944117712310

Selwyn, N. (2018). The digital child's dilemma: Navigating the uncertainties of childhood in the age of algorithms. *British Journal of Sociology of Education*, 39(4), 531–544.

Senyo, P. K., Liu, K., & Effah, J. (2019). Digital business ecosystem: Literature review and a framework for future research. *International Journal of Information Management*, 47, 52–64. 10.1016/j.ijinfomgt.2019.01.002

Serafini, T. E., & Adams, G. R. (2002). Functions of identity: Scale construction and validation. *Identity*, 2(4), 363–391. 10.1207/S1532706XID0204_05

Setiawati, Y., Hartanti, D. T., Husada, D., Irwanto, I., Ardani, I. G. A. I., & Nazmuddin, M. (2021). Relationship between Paternal and Maternal Parenting Style with Internet Addiction Level of Adolescents. *Iranian Journal of Psychiatry*, 16(4), 438–443. 10.18502/ijps.v16i4.723135082856

Seyed Amin Mirlohi Falavarjani, F. Z. (2019). The reflection of offline activities on users' online social behavior: An observational study. *Information Processing & Management*, 56(6), 102070. 10.1016/j.ipm.2019.102070

Shafik, W. (2024e). Mobile Learning and Bring Your Own Device (BYOD): Enhancing Education in the Digital Age. In *Integrating Cutting-Edge Technology into the Classroom* (pp. 240-267). IGI Global. 10.4018/979-8-3693-3124-8.ch012

Shafik, W. (2024a). Introduction to ChatGPT. In *Advanced Applications of Generative AI and Natural Language Processing Models* (pp. 1–25). IGI Global. 10.4018/979-8-3693-0502-7.ch001

Shafik, W. (2024b). An Overview of Artificial Intelligence-Enhanced Teaching Methods. In *AI-Enhanced Teaching Methods* (pp. 132–159). IGI Global. 10.4018/979-8-3693-2728-9.ch006

Shafik, W. (2024c). Data Privacy and Security Safeguarding Customer Information in ChatGPT Systems. In *Revolutionizing the Service Industry with OpenAI Models* (pp. 52–86). IGI Global. 10.4018/979-8-3693-1239-1.ch003

Shafik, W. (2024d). *The Role of Artificial Intelligence in the Emerging Digital Economy Era. Artificial Intelligence Enabled Management: An Emerging Economy Perspective.* De Gruyter. 10.1515/9783111172408-003

Shafiq, D. A., Marjani, M., Habeeb, R. A. A., & Asirvatham, D. (2022). Predictive Analytics in Education: A Machine Learning Approach. In *2022 3rd International Multidisciplinary Conference on Computer and Energy Science (SpliTech)* (pp. 1-6). IEEE. [DOI:10.1109/MACS56771.2022

Shankar, V. (2023). *Disconnect to Reconnect: Guide to Digital Detoxificatiom.* Independently published.

Sheahan, G., Reznick, R., Klinger, D., Flynn, L., & Zevin, B. (2019). Comparison of Personal Video Technology for Teaching and Assessment of Surgical Skills. *Journal of Graduate Medical Education,* 11(3), 328–331. 10.4300/JGME-D-18-01082.131210866

Sheppard, A. L., & Wolffsohn, J. S. (2018). Digital eye strain: Prevalence, measurement and amelioration. *BMJ Open Ophthalmology,* 3(1), e000146. 10.1136/bmjophth-2018-00014629963645

Shifflet-Chila, E. D., Harold, R., Fitton, V. A., & Ahmedani, B. (2016). Adolescent and family development: Autonomy and identity in the digital age. *Children and Youth Services Review,* 70, 364–368. 10.1016/j.childyouth.2016.10.005

Shihepo, E., Bhunu-Shava, F., & Chitauro, M. (2023). Designing A Real-Time Bring your Own Device Security Awareness Model for Mobile Device Users within Namibian Enterprises. *2023 6th International Conference on Information Systems and Computer Networks, ISCON 2023.* IEEE.10.1109/ISCON57294.2023.10112191

Shiohira, K. (2021). Understanding the Impact of Artificial Intelligence on Skills Development. Education 2030. *UNESCO-UNEVOC International Centre for Technical and Vocational Education and Training.* UNESCO. https://eric.ed.gov/?id=ED612439

Shneiderman, B. (2020). Human-centered artificial intelligence: Three fresh ideas. *AIS Transactions on Human-Computer Interaction,* 12(3), 109–124. 10.17705/1thci.00131

Shuqfa, Z., & Harous, S. (2019). Data Mining Techniques Used in Predicting Student Retention in Higher Education: A Survey. *2019 International Conference on Electrical and Computing Technologies and Applications (ICECTA).* IEEE. . https://ieeexplore.ieee.org/document/8959789/10.1109/ICECTA48151.2019.8959789

Shurid, S. A., & Amin, K. H. (2020). Bangla Sign Language Recognition and Sentence Building Using Deep Learning. *IEEE AsiaPacific Conference on Computer Science and Data Engineering (CSDE).* IEEE.

Siamack Zahedi, R. J. (2021). A systematic review of screen-time literature to inform educational policy and practice during COVID-19. *International Journal of Educational Research Open,* 2, 100094. 10.1016/j.ijedro.2021.10009435059672

Sima, V., Gheorghe, I. G., Subić, J., & Nancu, D. (2020). Influences of the industry 4.0 revolution on the human capital development and consumer behavior: A systematic review. *Sustainability (Basel),* 12(10), 4035. 10.3390/su12104035

Sittig, D. B., & Singh, H. (2017). Health care provider use of social media and mobile health technologies: A cross-sectional survey. *JAMA Internal Medicine,* 177(12), 1790–1792.29059277

Slattery, P. (n.d.). Understanding AI's impact on behaviour and Society. *Psychology Today.* http://www.Psychologytoday.Com/us/blog/transformative-ai/202311/understanding-ais-impact-on-behaviour-and-society.

Smart, P. R. (2018). Human-extended machine cognition. *Cognitive Systems Research,* 49, 9–23. 10.1016/j.cogsys.2017.11.001

Smith, J. (2021). *Our journey with AI-enhanced home-schooling: Lessons learned and strategies for success.* HomeSchooling. https://www.homeschooling.com/ai-enhanced-homeschooling-lessons-learned-strategies-success/

Smith, J. (2019). AI and parenting: Opportunities and challenges. *Journal of Child and Family Studies,* 28(2), 327–338.

Snezhana, D. (2023). Applying artificial intelligence (AI) for mitigation climate change consequences of the natural disasters. *Dineva, S.(2023). Applying Artificial Intelligence (AI) for Mitigation Climate Change Consequences of the Natural Disasters.Research Journal of Ecology and Environmental Sciences,* 3(1), 1–8.

Solove, D. (2011). Conceptualizing privacy. *University of Pennsylvania Law Review,* 160(2), 477–565.

Song, J. (2023). Social media and it's impact on college students identity. *Communications in Humanities Research*, 10(1), 286–295. 10.54254/2753-7064/10/20231346

Son, J., Ružić, N. K., & Philpott, A. (2023). Artifical intelligence technilogies and applications for language learning and teaching. *Journal of China Computer-Assisted Language Learning*, 1–19.

Sonnenberg, B., Riediger, M., Wrzus, C., & Wagner, G. G. (2019). Me, myself, and my mobile: A segmentation of youths based on their attitudes towards the mobile phone as a status instrument. *Computers in Human Behavior*, 93, 252–262.

Soubhagyalakshmi, P., & Reddy, K. S. (2023). An efficient security analysis of bring your own device. *IAES International Journal of Artificial Intelligence*, 12(2), 696. 10.11591/ijai.v12.i2.pp696-703

Sparrow, B., Liu, J., & Wegner, D. M. (2011). Google effects on memory: Cognitive consequences of having information at our fingertips. *Science*, 333(6043), 776–778. 10.1126/science.120774521764755

Spohrer, J., & Banavar, G. (2015). Cognition as a service: An industry perspective. *AI Magazine*, 36(4), 71–86. 10.1609/aimag.v36i4.2618

Squire, K., & Steinkuehler, C. (2017). The Problem with Screen Time. *Teachers College Record*, 119(1), 1–24. 10.1177/016146811711901207

Stahl, B. C., Andreou, A., Brey, P., Hatzakis, T., Kirichenko, A., Macnish, K., Shaelou, S. L., Patel, A., Ryan, M., & Wright, D. (2021). Artificial intelligence for human flourishing–Beyond principles for machine learning. *Journal of Business Research*, 124, 374–388. 10.1016/j.jbusres.2020.11.030

Stangl, F. J., Riedl, R., Kiemeswenger, R., & Montag, C. (2023, August 3). Negative psychological and physiological effects of social networking site use: The example of Facebook. *Frontiers in Psychology*, 14, 1141663. 10.3389/fpsyg.2023.114166337599719

Stathoulopoulos, K., & Mateos-Garcia, J. C. (2019). Gender diversity in AI research. *SSRN* 3428240.

Stefano Za, R. W. (2021). *Sustainable Digital Transformation: Paving the Way Towards Smart Organizations and Societies*. Springer International Publishing.

Steinberg, L., & Morris, A. S. (2001). Adolescent Development. *Annual Review of Psychology*, 52(1), 83–110. 10.1146/annurev.psych.52.1.8311148300

Stenslie, S. (2011). *Virtual touch: A study of the use and experience of touch in artistic, multimodal and computer-based environments*. Oslo School of Architecture and Design. https://aho.brage.unit.no/aho-xmlui/bitstream/handle/11250/93049/Virtual%20Touch%20PhD%20Stenslie%20withCover.pdf

Stevens, R., Gilliard-Matthews, S., Dunaev, J., Woods, M., & Brawner, B. (2016). The digital hood: Social media use among youth in disadvantaged neighborhoods. *New Media & Society*, 19(6), 950–967. 10.1177/1461444815625941286944736

Stiglic, N., & Viner, R. (2019). Effects of screentime on the health and well-being of children and adolescents: A systematic review of reviews. *BMJ Open*, 9(1), e023191. 10.1136/bmjopen-2018-02319130606703

Stray, J. (2023). The AI learns to lie to please you: Preventing biased feedback loops in machine-assisted intelligence analysis. *Analytics*, 2(2), 350–358. 10.3390/analytics2020020

Stunden, C., Zasada, J., VanHeerwaarden, N., Hollenberg, E., Abi-Jaoudé, A., Chaim, G., Cleverley, K., Henderson, J., Johnson, A., Levinson, A., Lo, B., Robb, J., Shi, J., Voineskos, A., & Wiljer, D. (2020). Help-seeking behaviors of transition-aged youth for mental health concerns: Qualitative study. *Journal of Medical Internet Research*, 22(10), e18514. 10.2196/1851433016882

Sturm, S. (2010). *Social networking psych studies: research shows teen Facebook users prone to depression*. Trend Hunter.

Subrahmanyam, K., & Smahel, D. (2011). *Digital Youth: The Role of Media in Development*.

Subrahmanyam, K., & Smahel, D. (2011). Constructing Identity Online: Identity Exploration and Self-Presentation. In *Digital Youth: The Role of Media in Development*. Springer. 10.1007/978-1-4419-6278-2_4

Su, J., & Yang, W. (2023). Artificial Intelligence (AI) literacy in early childhood education: An intervention study in Hong Kong. *Interactive Learning Environments*, 1–15. Advance online publication. 10.1080/10494820.2023.2217864

Sukhorukov, A., Eroshkin, S., Vanyurikhin, P., Karabahciev, S. og Bogdanova, E. (2019). Robotization of business processes of enterprises of housing and communal services. Í *E3S Web of Conferences*.

Sushil, G. S., Deshmukh, R. K., & Junnarkar, A. A. (2024). A Security Framework Design for Generating Abnormal Activities Report of Bring Your Own Devices (BYODs). *Lecture Notes in Electrical Engineering*, 1106, 429–441. Advance online publication. 10.1007/978-981-99-7954-7_39

Sutton, J. (2006). Distributed cognition: Domains and dimensions. *Pragmatics & Cognition*, 14(2), 235–247. 10.1075/pc.14.2.05sut

Syvertsen, T. (2020). *Digital detox: The politics of disconnecting*. Emerald Publishing Limited. 10.1108/9781787693395

Syvertsen, T., & Enli, G. (2020). Digital detox: Media resistance and the promise of authenticity. *Convergence (London)*, 26(5-6), 1269–1283. 10.1177/1354856519847325

Szalai, J. (2021). The potential use of artificial intelligence in the therapy of borderline personality disorder. *Journal of Evaluation in Clinical Practice*, 27(3), 491–496. 10.1111/jep.1353033368981

T, J. V., & Amala Bai, V. M. (2024). Evaluation of security framework for BYOD device in cloud environment. *Automatika*, 65(3). 10.1080/00051144.2024.2310458

Taecharungroj, V. (2023). "What Can ChatGPT Do?" analyzing early reactions to the Innovative AI Chatbot on Twitter. *Big Data and Cognitive Computing*, 7(35), 1–10. 10.3390/bdcc7010035

Tajfel, H. og Turner, J. C. (1978). Intergroup behavior. *Introducing social psychology, 401*, 466.

Tajfel, H., & Turner, J. C. (1979). An integrative theory of intergroup conflict. In Austin, W. G., & Worchel, S. (Eds.), *The social psychology of intergroup relations* (pp. 33–47). Brooks/Cole.

Tambe, S., Galphat, Y., Rijhwani, N., Goythale, A., & Patil, J. (2020). *Analyzing and Enhancing Communication Platforms available for a Deaf-Blind user*. IEEE. 10.1109/iSSSC50941.2020.9358823

Taneja, A., Nair, G., Joshi, M., Sharma, S., Sharma, S., Jambrak, A. R., Roselló-Soto, E., Barba, F. J., Castagnini, J. M., Leksawasdi, N., & Phimolsiripol, Y. (2023). Artificial intelligence: Implications for the agri-food sector. *Agronomy (Basel)*, 13(5), 1397. 10.3390/agronomy13051397

Technostress, B. C. (1984). *The human cost of the computer revolution*. Addison Wesley Publishing Company.

Thagard, P. (1996). *Mind: Introduction to cognitive science* (Vol. 4). MIT Press Cambridge.

Thomée, S., Dellve, L., Härenstam, A., & Hagberg, M. (2010). Perceived connections between information and communication technology use and mental symptoms among young adults - a qualitative study. *BMC Public Health*, 10(1), 66. 10.1186/1471-2458-10-6620152023

Threadgold, S. (2020). Figures of youth: On the very object of Youth Studies. *Journal of Youth Studies*, 23(6), 686–701. 10.1080/13676261.2019.1636014

Thulin, E., & Vilhelmson, B. (2019). More at home, more alone? Youth, digital media and the everyday use of time and space. *Geoforum*, 100, 41–50. 10.1016/j.geoforum.2019.02.010

Tian, S., Jin, Q., Yeganova, L., Lai, P., Zhu, Q., Chen, X., Yang, Y., Chen, Q., Kim, W., Comeau, D. C., Islamaj, R., Kapoor, A., Gao, X., & Lu, Z. (2024). Opportunities and challenges for ChatGPT and large language models in biomedicine and health. *Briefings in Bioinformatics*, 25(1), 1–9.38168838

Tinto, V. (1975). Dropout from Higher Education: A Theoretical Synthesis of Recent Research. *Review of Educational Research*, 45(1), 89–125. 10.3102/00346543045001089

Toh, W., & Lim, F. (2020). Using video games for learning: Developing a metalanguage for digital play. *Games and Culture*, 16(5), 583–610. 10.1177/1555412020921339

Toma, C. L., Hancock, J. T., & Ellison, N. B. (2008). Separating fact from fiction: An examination of deceptive self-presentation in online dating profiles. *Personality and Social Psychology Bulletin*, 34(8), 1023–1036. 10.1177/01 46167208318067185938866

Tominaga, S., Nishi, S., & Ohtera, R. (2021). Measurement and estimation of spectral sensitivity functions for mobile phone cameras. *Sensors (Basel)*, 21(15), 4985. 10.3390/s2115498534372223

Tonini, L. (2024). *"Talk to me, Hal": A Study of Player Experience and Interaction in a Voice Interaction VR Game Featuring AI-driven Non-player Characters* [Master's Thesis, University of Twente]. http://essay.utwente.nl/98788/

Tonta, Y. (2009). Dijital yerliler, sosyal ağlar ve kütüphanelerin geleceği. *Türk Kütüphaneciliği*, 23(4), 742–768.

Topol, E. J. (2019). *Deep medicine: How artificial intelligence can transform healthcare*. Basic Books.

Trabelsi, Z., Alnajjar, F., Parambil, M. M. A., Gochoo, M., & Ali, L. (2023). Real-time attention monitoring system for classroom: A deep learning approach for student's behavior recognition. *Big Data and Cognitive Computing*, 7(1), 48. 10.3390/bdcc7010048

Tremblay, M. S., Colley, R. C., Saunders, T. J., Healy, G. N., & Owen, N. (2010). Physiological and health implications of a sedentary lifestyle. *Applied Physiology, Nutrition, and Metabolism*, 35(6), 725–740. 10.1139/H10-07921164543

Tremblay, M. S., LeBlanc, A. G., Kho, M. E., Saunders, T. J., Larouche, R., Colley, R. C., Goldfield, G., & Connor Gorber, S. (2011). A systematic review of sedentary behaviour and health indicators in school-aged children and youth. *The International Journal of Behavioral Nutrition and Physical Activity*, 8(1), 98. 10.1186/1479-5868-8-9821936895

Tuah, F. F., & Abd Rahim, N. A. (2023). The Implementation of Bring Your Own Device (BYOD) at School through Actor-Network Theory (ANT). *International Journal of Academic Research in Progressive Education and Development*, 12(2). 10.6007/IJARPED/v12-i2/17434

Tucker, C. M., Roncoroni, J., & Buki, L. P. (2019). Counseling Psychologists and Behavioral Health: Promoting Mental and Physical Health Outcomes. *The Counseling Psychologist*, 47(7), 970–998. 10.1177/0011000019896784

Tucker, L. B., Velosky, A. G., Fu, A. H., & McCabe, J. T. (2019). Chronic Neurobehavioral Sex Differences in a Murine Model of Repetitive Concussive Brain Injury. *Frontiers in Neurology*, 10, 509. 10.3389/fneur.2019.0050931178814

Tung, T. M. (2024). A Systematic Analysis Of Artificial Intelligence's Usage In Online Advertising. *Migration Letters : An International Journal of Migration Studies*, 21(S6), 892–900.

Turkle, S. (2011). *Alone Together: Why We Expect More from Technology and Less from Each Other*. Basic Books.

Turkle, S. (2015). *Reclaiming Conversation: The Power of Talk in a Digital Age*. Penguin Press.

Turner, G., van Zoonen, L., & Harvey, J. (2014). Confusion, control and comfort: Premediating identity management in film and television. *Information Communication and Society*, 17(8), 986–1000. 10.1080/1369118X.2013.870592

Turner, J. C. (1985). Social categorization and the self-concept: A social cognitive theory of group behavior. In Lawler, E. J. (Ed.), *Advances in Group Processes: Theory and Research* (Vol. 2, pp. 77–122). JAI Press.

Tur-Porcar, A. (2017). Parenting styles and Internet use. *Psychology and Marketing*, 34(11), 1016–1022. 10.1002/mar.21040

Tütar, R., & Kahraman, S. (2018). *Sosyal medya kullanıcılarının sosyal görünüş kaygısı ve mutluluk açısından incelenmesi. III.* International Dmitri Yavoronitski Europeancongress On Social Sciences.

Twenge, J. M. (2017). Have smartphones destroyed a generation? *The Atlantic*.https://www.theatlantic.com/magazine/archive/2017/09/has-the-smartphone-destroyed-a-generation/534198/

Twenge, J. M., & Campbell, W. K. (2018). *Psychological effects of screen time on children and adolescents*. Science Direct.

Twenge, J., Martin, G. N., & Spitzberg, B. H. (2019). Trends in U.S. Adolescents' media use, 1976–2016: The rise of digital media, the decline of TV, and the (near) demise of print. *Psychology of Popular Media Culture*.

Twenge, J. M. (2017, September). Have smartphones destroyed a generation? *Atlantic (Boston, Mass.)*.

Twenge, J. M., & Campbell, W. K. (2018). Associations between screen time and lower psychological well-being among children and adolescents: Evidence from a population-based study. *Preventive Medicine Reports*, 12, 271–283. 10.1016/j.pmedr.2018.10.00330406005

Twenge, J. M., Martin, G. N., & Campbell, W. K. (2018). Decreases in psychological well-being among american adolescents after 2012 and links to screen time during the rise of smartphone technology. *Emotion (Washington, D.C.)*, 18(6), 765–780. 10.1037/emo000040329355336

Twenge, J., & Campbell, W. K. (2018). *Associations between screen time and lower psychological well-being among children and adolescents*. Preventive Medicine Reports.

Udayanan, A. R., Bargavi, N., Awasthi, S., Deshmukh, S. V., & Jadhav, D. Y. (2024). Determinants Influencing the Adoption of Artificial Intelligence in Driving Effective Human Resource Management. *Journal of Informatics Education and Research*, 4(2). http://jier.org/index.php/journal/article/view/828

Ugur, N. G., & Koc, T. (2015, July 3). Time for Digital Detox: Misuse of Mobile Technology and Phubbing. *Procedia: Social and Behavioral Sciences*, 195, 1022–1031. 10.1016/j.sbspro.2015.06.491

Uhls, Y. T., Michikyan, M., Morris, J., Garcia, D., Small, G. W., Zgourou, E., & Greenfield, P. M. (2014). Five days at outdoor education camp without screens improves preteen skills with nonverbal emotion cues. *Computers in Human Behavior*, 39, 387–392. 10.1016/j.chb.2014.05.036

UNICEF. (2021) *Policy guidelines on AI for children*. UNICEF. https://www.unicef.org/globalinsight/media/2356/file/UNICEF-Global-Insight-policy-guidance-AI-children-2.0-2021.pdf

United Nations International School of Hanoi. (2024) *What is generation alpha? 8 characteristics of generation alpha*. https://articles.unishanoi.org/characteristics-of-generation-alpha/

Valkenburg, P. M., & Peter, J. (2011). Online communication among adolescents: An integrated model of its attraction, opportunities, and risks. *The Journal of Adolescent Health*, 48(2), 121–127. 10.1016/j.jadohealth.2010.08.02021257109

Valkenburg, P. M., Peter, J., & Schouten, A. P. (2016). Friend networking sites and their relationship to adolescents' well-being and social self-esteem. *Cyberpsychology & Behavior*, 9(5), 584–590. 10.1089/cpb.2006.9.58417034326

Valkenburg, P. M., Schouten, B. M., & Peter, J. (2015). Parental mediation of children's media use: A review of the literature. *International Journal of Communication*, 9, 1682–1698.

Valtonen, T., Tedre, M., Mäkitalo, K., & Vartiainen, H. (2019). Media literacy education in the age of machine learning. *The Journal of Media Literacy Education*, 11(2), 20–36. 10.23860/JMLE-2019-11-2-2

Van den Branden, K. (2016). Task-based language teaching. In *The Routledge handbook of English language teaching* (pp. 238–251). Routledge. https://www.taylorfrancis.com/chapters/edit/10.4324/9781315676203-21/task-based-language -teaching-kris-van-den-branden10.4324/9781315676203-21

Van der Lely, S., Frey, S., Garbazza, C., Wirz-Justice, A., Jenni, O., Steiner, R., Wolf, S., Cajochen, C., Bromundt, V., & Schmidt, C. (2015). Blue blocker glasses as a countermeasure for alerting effects of evening light-emitting diode screen exposure in male teenagers. *The Journal of Adolescent Health*, 56(1), 113–119. 10.1016/j.jadohealth.2014.08.00225287985

Vanden Abeele, M. M. (2021). Digital well-being as a dynamic construct. *Communication Theory*, 31(4), 932–955. 10.1093/ct/qtaa024

Vannucci, A., Flannery, K. M., & Ohannessian, C. M. (2017). Social media use and anxiety in emerging adults. *Journal of Affective Disorders*, 207, 163–166. 10.1016/j.jad.2016.08.04027723539

Varadarajan, S., Venguidesvarane, A. G., Ramaswamy, K., Rajamohan, M., Krupa, M., & Christadoss, S. B. (2021). Prevalence of excessive screen time and its association with developmental delay in children aged <5 years: A population-based cross-sectional study in India. *PLoS One*, 16(7), 16. 10.1371/journal.pone.025410234228768

Varela, D. og Kaun, A. (2019). *The netflix experience: A user-focused approach to the netflix recommendation algorithm.*

Varma, A. (2023). Artificial intelligence and people management: A critical assessment through the ethical lens. *Human Resource Management Review,33*. Elsevier.

Varol, S. F. (2022). Yankı odası: Kavramsal bir çerçeve. *Journal of Academic Social Science Studies*, 15(91).

Varsori, E., & Pereira, S. (2019). A Critical Review of Social Screen Time Management by Youngsters in Formal Educational Contexts. *Managing Screen Time in an Online Society*, 172-191.

Varsori, E., & Pereira, S. (2019). A Critical Review of Social Screen Time Management by Youngsters in Formal Educational Contexts. Managing Screen Time in an Online Society, 172-191. 10.4018/978-1-5225-8163-5.ch008

Vaterlaus, J. M., Aylward, A., Tarabochia, D., & Martin, J. D. (2021). "A smartphone made my life easier": An exploratory study on age of adolescent smartphone acquisition and well-being. *Computers in Human Behavior*, 114.

Velez, G., & Spencer, M. B. (2018). Phenomenology and intersectionality: Using PVEST as a frame for adolescent identity formation amid intersecting ecological systems of inequality. *New Directions for Child and Adolescent Development*, 2018(161), 75–90. 10.1002/cad.2024729969194

Vemuri, N. V. N. (2023). Enhancing Human-Robot Collaboration in Industry 4.0 with AI-driven HRI. *Power System Technology*, 47(4), 341–358. 10.52783/pst.196

Vesselinov, R., & Grego, J. (2012). Duolingo effectiveness study. *City University of New York, USA, 28*(1–25). https:// www.languagezen.com/pt/about/english/Duolingo_Efficacy_Study.pdf

Vicsek, L. (2021). Artificial intelligence and the future of work–lessons from the sociology of expectations. *The International Journal of Sociology and Social Policy*, 41(7/8), 842–861. 10.1108/IJSSP-05-2020-0174

Vigneshwaran, S. (2019). *Hand Gesture Recognition and Voice Conversion System for Dump People*. IEEE.

Vijayakumar, M. (2018). Assessment of co-morbid factors associated with text-neck syndrome among mobile phone users. *International Journal of Scientific Research in Science and Technology*, 4, 38–46.

Villanti, A. C., Johnson, A. L., Ilakkuvan, V., Jacobs, M. A., Graham, A. L., & Rath, J. M. (2017). Social media use and access to digital technology in US young adults in 2016. *Journal of Medical Internet Research*, 19(6), e196. 10.2196/jmir.730328592394

Vinichenko, M., Narrainen, G. S., Melnichuk, A., & Chalid, P. (2021). *The influence of artificial intelligence on human activities*. Frontier Information Technology and Systems Research in Cooperative Economics.

Vinichenko, M. V., Rybakova, M. V., Nikiporets-Takigawa, G. Y., Chulanova, O., & Lyapunova, N. (2020). The influence of artificial intelligence on the human potential development: The views of orthodox clergy and parishioners. *Cuestiones Políticas*, 37(65), 400–418. 10.46398/cuestpol.3865.27

Vinuesa, R., Azizpour, H., Leite, I., Balaam, M., Dignum, V., Domisch, S., & Nerini, F. F. (2020). The role of artificial intelligence in achieving the Sustainable Development Goals. *Nature Communications*, 11(1), 1–10. 10.1038/s41467-019-14108-y31932590

Vogel, E. A., Rose, J. P., Okdie, B. M., Eckles, K., & Franz, B. (2015). Who compares and despairs? The effect of social comparison orientation on social media use and its outcomes. *Personality and Individual Differences*, 86, 249–256. 10.1016/j.paid.2015.06.026

Vold, K. (2018). Overcoming Deadlock: Scientific and Ethical Reasons to Embrace the Extended Mind Thesis. *Philosophy and Society, 29*, 475.

Vorderer, P., Krömer, N., & Schneider, F. M. (2016). Permanently online, connected: Explorations into university students' use of social media and mobile smart devices. *Computers in Human Behavior*, 63, 694–703. 10.1016/j.chb.2016.05.085

Vosoughi, S., Roy, D., & Aral, S. (2018). The spread of true and false news online. *Science*, 359(6380), 1146–1151. 10.1126/science.aap955929590045

Vrabotuvanje. (2022). *Колку македонци користат Facebook, Instagram, Twitter и LinkedIn*. Vrabotuvanje. https://www.vrabotuvanje.com.mk/Vest/22267/Kolku-makedonci-koristat-Facebook-Instagram-Twitter-i-LinkedIn/2/

Vybiral, Z., Smahel, D., & Divinova, R. (2004). Growing up in virtual reality - Adolescents and the Internet. In P. Mares (Ed.), *Society, reproduction and contemporary challenges* (pp. 169-188). Bnro: Barrister and Principal Publishing.

Waelen, R., & Wieczorek, M. (2022). The Struggle for AI's Recognition: Understanding the Normative Implications of Gender Bias in AI with Honneth's Theory of Recognition. *Philosophy & Technology*, 35(2), 53. 10.1007/s13347-022-00548-w

Wallace, R., & Wolf, A. (2012). *Çağdaş sosyoloji kuramları: Klasik geleneğin geliştirilmesi (3. Bs.)*. L. Elburuz ve MR Ayas, *Çev*. Doğu Batı Yayınları.

Walters, A. S., & Rye, D. B. (2009). Review of the relationship of restless legs syndrome and periodic limb movements in sleep to hypertension, heart disease, and stroke. *Sleep*, 32(5), 589–597. 10.1093/sleep/32.5.58919480225

Wang, X., Lu, Z., & Yin, M. 2022. Will You Accept the AI Recommendation? Predicting Human Behavior in AI-Assisted Decision Making. In *Proceedings of the ACM Web Conference 2022*. Virtual Event, Lyon France: ACM. 10.1145/3485447.3512240

Wang, R., Yin, Y., Zhang, H., Pan, L., Zhu, Y., Wang, M., Huang, Z., Wang, W., & Deng, G. (2023). Risk factors associated with the prevalence of neck and shoulder pain among high school students: A cross-sectional survey in China. *BMC Musculoskeletal Disorders*, 24(1), 641–649. 10.1186/s12891-023-06656-837559076

Wang, Y. F., & Petrina, S. (2013). Using learning analytics to understand the design of an intelligent language tutor–Chatbot lucy. *Editorial Preface*, 4(11), 124–131.

Wang, Y., Wu, L., Wang, L., Zhang, Y., Du, X., & Dong, G. (2017). Impaired decision-making and impulse control in Internet gaming addicts: Evidence from the comparison with recreational Internet game users. *Addiction Biology*, 22(6), 1610–1621. 10.1111/adb.1245827687019

Warburton, D. E., Nicol, C. W., & Bredin, S. S. (2006). Health benefits of physical activity: The evidence. [CMAJ]. *Canadian Medical Association Journal*, 174(6), 801–809. 10.1503/cmaj.05135116534088

Washington School of Law. (1984). *Washington and lee law review* (41 bindi). School of Law, Washington and Lee University.

Weiser, E. B. (2001). The Functions of Internet Use and Their Social and Psychological Consequences. *Cyberpsychology & Behavior*, 4(6), 723–743. 10.1089/109493101753337667811800180

Weizenbaum, J. (1966). ELIZA: A computer program for the study of natural language communication between man and machine. *Communications of the ACM*, 9(1), 36–45. 10.1145/365153.365168

Westman, S., Kauttonen, J., Klemetti, A., Korhonen, N., Manninen, M., Mononen, A., Niittymäki, S., & Paananen, H. (2021). Artificial Intelligence for Career Guidance–Current Requirements and Prospects for the Future. *IAFOR Journal of Education*, 9(4), 43–62. 10.22492/ije.9.4.03

Whitebread, D. (2012). *The Importance of Play*. Cambridge Primary Review Trust.

White, R. E., & Pillemer, D. B. (2012). Childhood memory and self-description in young adults: The role of family context and autobiographical memory strategies. *Memory (Hove, England)*, 20(4), 445–457.

Wiederhold, B. K. (2020). Forging Stronger Bonds Through Technology: How Virtual Reality Can Instill Empathy. *Cyberpsychology, Behavior, and Social Networking*, 577-578(9), 577–578. 10.1089/cyber.2020.29193.bkw32845732

Wies B, Landers C, Ienca M. Digital Mental Health for Young People: A Scoping Review of Ethical Promises and Challenges. Front Digit Health. 2021 Sep 6;3:697072. doi: 10.3389/fdgth.2021.697072. PMID: 34713173; PMCID: PMC8521997.10.3389/fdgth.2021.69707234713173

Williams, R., Ali, S., Devasia, N., DiPaola, D., Hong, J., Kaputsos, S. P., Jordan, B., & Breazeal, C. (2023). AI+ ethics curricula for middle school youth: Lessons learned from three project-based curricula. *International Journal of Artificial Intelligence in Education*, 33(2), 325–383. 10.1007/s40593-022-00298-y35935456

Williams, S. J. (1986). Appraising Goffman. *The British Journal of Sociology*, 37(3), 348–369. 10.2307/590645

Wilson, R. E., Gosling, S. D., & Graham, L. T. (2012). A review of Facebook research in the social sciences. *Perspectives on Psychological Science*, 7(3), 203–220. 10.1177/174569161244290426168459

Windley, P. J. (2005). *Digital Identity: Unmasking identity management architecture (IMA)*. O'Reilly Media, Inc.

Wirtz, M. (2016): *Identität, entwicklungspsychologische Perspektive*. Dorsch Lexikon der Psychologie. Hogrefe. https://dorsch.hogrefe.com/stichwort/identitaetentwicklungspsychologische-perspektive

Wong, B. (2023). Top social media statistics and trends of 2024. *Forbes advisor*. https://www.forbes.com/advisor/business/social-media-statistics/

Wong, M. (2020). Hidden youth? a new perspective on the sociality of young people 'withdrawn' in the bedroom in a digital age. *New Media & Society*, 22(7), 1227–1244. 10.1177/1461444820912530

Wood, S., & Scott, J. (2015). Parental mediation of children's media use: A review of the literature. *International Journal of Communication, 9*, 1682–1698.

Wood, B. E. (2017). Youth studies, citizenship and transitions: Towards a new research agenda. *Journal of Youth Studies*, 20(9), 1176–1190. 10.1080/13676261.2017.1316363

Woodman, D. (2012). *Youth Studies*. Routledge. 10.4324/9780203862094

World Economic Forum. (2018). *The future of jobs report 2018*. World Economic Forum.

Wu, Y. (2022). Loneliness behind live streaming: Exploration of alone together in live streaming in the version of interactive ritual chain. *2022 8th International Conference on Humanities and Social Science Research (ICHSSR 2022)*. Research Gate.

Wyn, J., & Woodman, D. (2007). Researching Youth in a Context of Social Change: A Reply to Roberts. *Journal of Youth Studies*, 10(3), 373–381. 10.1080/13676260701342624

Xiaoyong, H. U., Shuo, S. U. N., Wenjie, Y., & Geying, D. (2023). Artificial Intelligence Empowering the High-Quality Development of Education: Demands, Visions, and Paths. *Frontiers of Education in China*, 18(1).

Xie, L., Housni, A., Nakhla, M., Cianci, R., Leroux, C., Costa, D., & Brazeau, A. (2023). Adaptation of an adult web application for type 1 diabetes self-management to youth using the behavior change wheel to tailor the needs of health care transition: Qualitative interview study. *JMIR Diabetes*, 8, e42564. 10.2196/4256437121571

Yang, W., Hu, X., Yeter, I. H., Su, J., Yang, Y., & Lee, J. C. K. (2023). Artificial intelligence education for young children: A case study of technology-enhanced embodied learning. *Journal of Computer Assisted Learning*. Advance online publication. 10.1111/jcal.12892

Yan, M., Filieri, R., & Gorton, M. (2021). Continuance intention of online technologies: A systematic literature review. *International Journal of Information Management*, 58, 102315. 10.1016/j.ijinfomgt.2021.102315

Yan-Ping, L., & Ai-Qin, Q. (2022). Replace or create: Analysis of the Relationship between the Artificial Intelligence and Youth Employment in Post Epidemic Era. *Procedia Computer Science*, 202, 217–222. 10.1016/j.procs.2022.04.029

Yeo, Y. H., Samaan, J. S., Ng, W. H., Ting, P. S., Trivedi, H., Vipani, A., Ayoub, W., Yang, J. D., Liran, O., Spiegel, B., & Kuo, A. (2023). Assessing the performance of ChatGPT in answering questions regarding cirrhosis and hepatocellular carcinoma. *Clinical and Molecular Hepatology*, 29(3), 721–732. 10.3350/cmh.2023.008936946005

Yin, N. (2021). Research on the impacts of artificial intelligence technology on language teaching innovation. *Frontiers in Educational Research*, 4(7), 25–31.

Yip, J., Lee, K., & Lee, J. (2019). Design partnerships for participatory librarianship: A conceptual model for understanding librarians co designing with digital youth. *Journal of the Association for Information Science and Technology*, 71(10), 1242–1256. 10.1002/asi.24320

Yongmou, L., & Taicheng, T. (2023). Cognitive reconstruction and action orientation of digital governance. *Engineering Research*, 15(4), 280–289.

Yousif, J. (2023). Social and Telepresence Robots a future of teaching. *Authorea Preprints*. https://www.techrxiv.org/doi/full/10.36227/techrxiv.15152073.v1

Yuan, C., Xie, Q., & Ananiadou, S. (2023). Zero-shot temporal relation extraction with ChatGPT. *Workshop on Biomedical Natural Language Processing*. IEEE.

Zamborsky, R., Kokavec, M., Simko, L., & Bohac, M. (2017). Carpal tunnel syndrome: Symptoms, causes and treatment options. Literature reviev. *Ortopedia, Traumatologia, Rehabilitacja*, 19(1), 1–8. 10.5604/15093492.123262928436376

Zaremohzzabieh, Z., Abdullah, H., Ahrari, S., Abdullah, R., & Siti, M. M. N. (2024). Exploration of vulnerability factors of digital hoarding behavior among university students and the moderating role of maladaptive perfectionism. *Digital Health*, 10, 1–16. 10.1177/20552076241226962238298527

Zhang, D., Mishra, S., Brynjolfsson, E., Etchemendy, J., Ganguli, D., Grosz, B., Lyons, T., Manyika, J., Niebles, J. C., & Sellitto, M. (2021). *The AI index 2021 annual report*. ArXiv Preprint ArXiv:2103.06312.

Zhang, E., & Lu, X. (2023). Social AI Improves Well-Being Among Female Young Adults. arXiv e-prints, arXiv-2311.

Zhang, Y., & Khare, A. (2009). *The Impact of Accessible Identities on the Evaluation of Global versus Local Products*.

Zhang, H., Chai, J., & Li, C. (2024). On innovative strategies of youth sports teaching and training based on the internet of things and artificial intelligence technology from the perspective of humanism. *Learning and Motivation*, 86, 101969. 10.1016/j.lmot.2024.101969

Zhang, H., Lee, I., Ali, S., DiPaola, D., Cheng, Y., & Breazeal, C. (2023). Integrating Ethics and Career Futures with Technical Learning to Promote AI Literacy for Middle School Students: An Exploratory Study. *International Journal of Artificial Intelligence in Education*, 33(2), 290–324. 10.1007/s40593-022-00293-335573722

Zhang, X. (2019). Memrise. *CALICO Journal*, 36(2), 152–161. 10.1558/cj.37857

Zhang, Y., Ren, G., & Wang, D. (2022). Ethical challenges and strategies of artificial intelligence applications. *2022 Eleventh International Conference of Educational Innovation through Technology (EITT)*, (pp. 110–113). IEEE. 10.1109/EITT57407.2022.00025

Zhang, Z., Xu, Y., Wang, Y., Yao, B., Ritchie, D., Wu, T., & Li, T. J. J. (2022, April). Storybuddy: A human-AI collaborative chatbot for parent-child interactive storytelling with flexible parental involvement. In *Proceedings of the 2022 CHI Conference on Human Factors in Computing Systems* (pp. 1-21). ACM. 10.1145/3491102.3517479

Zhao, J., Zhang, Y., Jiang, F., Ip, P., Ho, F., Zhang, Y., & Huang, H. (2018). Excessive Screen Time and Psychosocial Well-Being: The Mediating Role of Body Mass Index, Sleep Duration, and Parent-Child Interaction. *The Journal of Pediatrics*, 202, 157–162.e1. 10.1016/j.jpeds.2018.06.02930100232

Zhenjun Yan, L. J. (2023). Intelligent urbanism with artificial intelligence in shaping tomorrow's smart cities: Current developments, trends, and future directions. *Journal of Cloud Computing (Heidelberg, Germany)*, 197(1), 179. 10.1186/s13677-023-00569-6

Zhou, X., Edirippulige, S., Bai, X., & Bambling, M. (2021). Are online mental health interventions for youth effective? A systematic review. *Journal of Telemedicine and Telecare*, 27(10), 638–666. 10.1177/1357633X21104728534726992

Zimmerman, A., Janhonen, J., & Beer, E. (2023). Human/ai relationships: Challenges, downsides, and impacts on human/human relationships. *AI and Ethics*, 1–13. 10.1007/s43681-023-00348-8

Zohuri, B., & Mossavar-Rahmani, F. (2023). The Symbiotic Relationship Unraveling the Interplay between Technology and Artificial Intelligence (An Intelligent Dynamic Relationship). *Journal of Energy and Power Engineering*, 17, 63–68.

Zohuri, B., & Rahmani, F. M. (2023). Artificial intelligence driven resiliency with machine learning and deep learning components. *Japan Journal of Research*, 1, 1–7.

Zou, R., Zeb, S., Nisar, F., Yasmin, F., Poulova, P., & Haider, S. A. (2022). The Impact of Emotional Intelligence on Career Decision-Making Difficulties and Generalized Self-Efficacy Among University Students in China. *Psychology Research and Behavior Management*, 15, 865–874. 10.2147/PRBM.S35874235422664

Zowghi, D., & da Rimini, F. (2023). Diversity and inclusion in artificial intelligence. *arXiv preprint arXiv:2305.12728*.

Zuraina, A. (2020). Artifical intelligence (AI): a review of its uses in language teaching and learning. *The 6th International Conference on Software Engieering & Computer Systems*. IEEE.

Министерство за здравство (2018). Националнастратегија за унапредување на менталнотоздравје во РепубликаМакедонијасептември 2018 - 2025 година со акциски план (септември 2018 – 2025).

Национален младински совет на Македонија (2021). *Застапувачко-нормативен документ за менталноздравјекајмлади.*

# About the Contributors

**Zeinab Zaremohzzabieh** is a Research Fellow at the Women and Family Studies Research Center, University of Religions and Denominations, Qom, Iran. Her research background includes recent studies on young Malaysian's participation in the agricultural industry, preparation readiness for natural disasters, internet addiction, and subjective well-being among different ethnic groups. Her methodological expertise includes both quantitative and qualitative research methods, with a focus on structural equation modelling and meta-analysis.

**Rusli Abdullah** is a distinguished academic and researcher renowned for his significant contributions in the field of Information Technology. Currently serving as a Professor at the Department of Software Engineering & Information System within the Faculty of Computer Science & Information Technology at the esteemed University Putra Malaysia, Prof. Rusli has played a pivotal role in advancing knowledge and innovation within his areas of expertise. With an extensive academic background and professional experience, Prof. Rusli Abdullah has become a prominent figure in the realms of Knowledge Management, Computer Science, Information Systems, and Software Engineering. His commitment to academic excellence is reflected in his numerous scholarly publications and research endeavors, which have significantly enriched the academic landscape. Throughout his career, Prof. Rusli has not only excelled in teaching and mentorship but has also made substantial contributions to the body of knowledge through his research. His work has not only broadened the horizons of understanding in his specialized fields but has also impacted the practical applications of Information Technology in various sectors. Beyond his academic pursuits, Prof. TS. Dr. Rusli Abdullah is recognized for his leadership in fostering collaboration and interdisciplinary research initiatives. His visionary approach and dedication to advancing the frontiers of technology have made him a respected authority within the academic community. As a Professor at the forefront of his field, Prof. Rusli continues to inspire and guide the next generation of professionals and researchers. His legacy is marked by a commitment to excellence, a passion for knowledge dissemination, and a lasting impact on the fields of Knowledge Management, Computer Science, Information Systems, and Software Engineering.

**Seyedali Ahrari** currently works at the Women and Family Studies Research Center, University of Religions and Denominations, Qom, Iran. Seyedali Ahrari does research in Educational Policy, Curriculum Theory and Adult Education. Their current project is 'Environmental Citizenship.

**Haslinda Abdullah** is currently a Director at Institute for Social Science Studies, (IPSAS) UPM and a Professor of Applied Psychology at the Department of Social and Development Sciences, Faculty of Human Ecology, University Putra Malaysia. Currently her works are more focused on youth and development especially on youth wellbeing and mental health. Her credentials and knowledge on the Malaysian youth is reflected in her role as a member of the think tank for the Institute for Youth Research Malaysia 2018-2020 (IYRES), a statutory body acting as the National youth development research center under Ministry of Youth and Sports. She has wide experience as a reviewer for International as well as National Journal. She has also act as Chief Editor for several Special Edition under Pertanika Journal, UPM.

**Seyedali Ahrari** is a Postdoctoral Fellow in faculty of educational studies, Universiti Putra Malaysia. His research interests include youth development, higher education, and social entrepreneurship.

**Mahmoud Y. Al.Faress** is a seasoned professional in computer engineering and data science. He holds a Ph.D. in distributed databases in real-time systems from Aleppo University, Syria with partnership with London Metropolitan University in UK, and has extensive experience spanning over two decades. His expertise includes project management, data mining and data analyzing, service-oriented architecture, and TOGAF certification. Mahmoud has made significant contributions to academia through book translations, journal publications, and impactful industry projects, particularly in Riyadh, Saudi Arabia. His skills in data analysis, business intelligence tools, and programming languages make him a valuable asset in driving data-driven insights and innovation.

*About the Contributors*

**Omar Al Jadaan** is a prominent computer scientist, specializing in artificial intelligence, algorithms, software engineering, and information technology. Hailing from Syria, he earned his Bachelor's degree in Engineering, followed by a Master's in Computer and Information Sciences from Hyderabad University. His academic journey culminated in a Ph.D. from Osmania University, focusing on multi-objective optimization using genetic algorithms. Prof. Jadaan has been working as an academician at Ras Al Khaimah Medical and Health Sciences University since 2010, imparting knowledge in computer science. His extensive research contributions span various fields, from health studies to sports motivation, solidifying his scholarly reputation.

**Mohd Mursyid Arshad** received his early education at Sekolah Kebangsaan Tunku Ismail, Sungai Petani and furthering his studies at Sekolah Menengah Kebangsaan Ibrahim, Sungai Petani and Penang Matriculation College (KMPP). He received a Bachelor's 1st Class Degree in Human Resource Development in 2008, Master of Science (Extension Education) in 2010 and Doctor of Philosophy (Extension Education- Youth Development) in 2016. He started his career as a Human Resource Executive (Head of Training and Development Section) at Honda Malaysia Sdn. Bhd. His association with UPM dates back to 2008, when he joined the Department of Profesional Development and Continuing Education, Faculty of Educational Studies, Universiti Putra Malaysia. He was received Vice Chancellor Award 2008, Best Academic Award (HRD) 2008.

**Avni Avdiu** was born on January 10, 1973 in Kumanovo. He completed primary school in his hometown, and secondary school in Gjilan, Republic of Kosovo, with exemplary success. Graduated from Pristina in philosophy, journalism and sociology. He completed his master's degree in media sociology in Tirana, Albania. He received his doctorate in political philosophy in Skopje and his doctorate in media sociology in Tirana. He lectured at the University of Pristina and several private colleges in the Republic of Kosovo, and currently is a professor at the Department of Media and Intercultural Communication at "Mother Teresa" University in Skopje, Republic of North Macedonia. He has worked for over 30 years in the field of journalism as an announcer, journalist, reporter, translator on radio, TV, newspapers and magazines in Kosovo and North Macedonia. He has written five books, 3 of which on the field of media.

**Elisabeta Bajrami Ollogu** is a lecturer of Social Policy at the Faculty of Social Sciences, "Mother Teresa" University – Skopje and a civil society activist. Her academic background is a combination of Social and Law studies (holding Bachelor and Master Degrees in each of the fields). She has a PhD in Social Policy and her research interests include welfare studies; social policy; social protection, migration and family policy in the context of South East European countries. Additionally, she has conducted research in youth migration, youth participation and youth policies, issues in which she is active in media and other related public activities. She has considerable experience in teaching in higher Education institutions of Albania and North Macedonia. In addition to her work as a lecturer, she has been part of the implementation of many projects and researches and has published several research works. She is an active member of several civil society initiatives whose main goal is fostering women social participation and enhancing their leading and decision-making capacity as a way to increase their public presence in policymaking. Currently she is also the deputy director of Women in Science Network/Rrjeti i Grave në Shkencë (NGO) in North Macedonia.

**Ruqia Safdar Bajwa** is an Assistant Professor in the Department of Applied Psychology at Bahauddin Zakariya University, Multan, Pakistan. With a PhD from the University of Putra Malaysia, She has established herself as a leading researcher in the fields of social psychology, cyberpsychology, behavioural addiction, health psychology, organizational behaviour, educational psychology, and youth studies. Dr. Bajwa combines academic excellence with practical applications, addressing critical issues in mental health and psychological well-being. Her work not only advances theoretical knowledge but also offers practical insights into improving mental health outcomes.

**Nita Beluli Luma** boasts an impressive academic and professional background, having served as a lecturer for over 11 years across various universities in North Macedonia. For the past 5 years, Nita works as an Associate Professor at Mother Teresa University, where she also serves as the Head of the Department of Psychology. Upon obtaining a doctoral degree in Clinical Psychology and receiving extensive training as a Cognitive Behavioral Therapy (CBT) therapist, she aims to merge her knowledge and skills in both academia and psychotherapy. Nita's research studies are focused on the mental health of children and adolescents. Her work has been published in several reputable academic journals such as Routledge, the European Journal of Psychology Research, European Journal of Medicine and Natural Sciences, Journal of Sleep Disorders and Management, etc.

**Vijay Bhutani** is an Assistant Professor of Mechanical Engineering at Amity University Greater Noida, He teaches and mentors undergraduate and diploma students, conduct and supervise research projects, and publish papers in peer-reviewed journals. His main areas of interest and expertise are thermal engineering, renewable energy, solar energy, and automobile industry. He is pursuing my PhD in Renewable and Sustainable Energy where he is working on Energy saving in conventional buildings. He has a master's degree in mechanical engineering from GJUS&T, and a bachelor's degree in mechanical engineering from the same Institute. He is passionate about applying knowledge and skills to solve real-world problems and contribute to the advancement of science and technology.

**Nur Raihan Che Nawi** is a senior lecturer at the Department of Professional Development & Continuing Education at the Faculty of Educational Studies, Universiti Putra Malaysia. Her expertise lies in human resource development, youth, and social entrepreneurship.

**Dwijendra Nath Dwivedi** is a professional with 20+ years of subject matter expertise creating right value propositions for analytics and AI. He currently heads the EMEA+AP AI and IoT team at SAS, a worldwide frontrunner in AI technology. He is a post-Graduate in Economics from Indira Gandhi Institute of Development and Research and is PHD from crackow university of economics Poland. He has presented his research in more than 20 international conference and published several Scopus indexed paper on AI adoption in many areas. As an author he has contributed to more than 8 books and has more than 25 publications in high impact journals. He conducts AI Value seminars and workshops for the executive audience and for power users.

**Ismi Arif Ismail** is the Head of Professional Development and Continuing Education Department, taking office on November 1, 2008. Dr. Ismi started his teaching career in 1993 at Methodist English School, Banting, Selangor. His association with UPM dates back to 1995, when he joined the Department of Extension Education as a postgraduate student and eventually as a faculty member in 2000. He has been widely published, as author or co-author of a book, book chapters, monographs, proceedings, and scores of scholarly papers, abstracts and related materials in areas such as continuing education, extension education, leadership, youth development and human resource development. Dr. Ismi received a bachelor's degree in TESL (Hons) from National University of Malaysia in 1993, a master's degree in Extension Education from UPM in 1999 and a doctorate in Continuing Education from the University of Warwick, United Kingdom in 2005. He is married to Ms. Azlina Yacob, an English Language lecturer of a teacher training institute in Bangi, and they are blessed with four children.

**Diturije Ismaili** holds a PhD degree on EU project management from Faculty of Law at "St Cyril and Methodius" in Skopje. She is Dean of the Faculty of Social Sciences, lecturer at Faculty of Social Sciences at Mother Teresa University and Academic Coordinator for EU Projects. She has gained international experience while she has been working as Head of Research at South East European University for 12 years where she has leaded several TEMPUS, FP7, COST, and other internal and external projects. She worked in Tirana-Albania as well for four years where she leaded the Research and Projects Office at Epoka University with high susses rate on EU projects. She has been member in many projects' development boards and currently she is working in three COST Actions and a capacity building project of Erasmus Plus. Diturije is Higher Education expert and she has been engaged with the National Accreditation Agency for Albanian Institutional accreditation and currently as an external expert for evaluation of the Erasmus+ projects. She has published several papers in international journals with impact factor. Diturije currently is involved in ongoing support for grant proposal development at Mother Teresa University. She participated in different International conferences and trainings.

**Ahmad Jabas**, a Ph.D. holder in Cloud Computing from Osmania University, is an esteemed professional in computer science and engineering. His leadership at Shaqra University includes pivotal projects in ERP and mobile app development. Ahmad's expertise in algorithms and network systems is evident through his authored book chapters and impactful research activities. Proficient in Arabic, English, and Turkish, he stands as a driving force in technological innovation and academic scholarship, showcasing exceptional skills in academia, administration, and research.

**Sowmiya KC**, an accomplished Ph.D. scholar at Sri Vasavi College in Erode, emerges as a dynamic and vibrant researcher with a rich educational background. Having laid the foundation with a B.Ed. degree and furthered her academic pursuits with post-graduation at PSGR Krishnammal College for Women, she has adeptly positioned herself at the forefront of scholarly exploration.Her commitment to advancing knowledge is exemplified through her proactive involvement in two conferences in 2023, where she not only showcased her research prowess but also actively engaged with peers and experts, fostering meaningful discussions. Notably, the recognition garnered from presenting her research findings at these conferences has resulted in the acceptance of her journal article for publication later this year.This noteworthy achievement not only underscores Sowmiya's dedication to the academic realm but also highlights her impactful contributions to the scholarly discourse. As a Ph.D. scholar, she stands as a vibrant and influential contributor to the ever-evolving landscape of research and academic exploration, leaving an indelible mark on her field.

**Agron Kurtishi**, Associate Professor Lecturer & Head of the Department for Media and Intercultural Communication Faculty of Social Sciences University "Mother Teresa" - Skopje Basic and master studies in the field of planning, of media development and consulting at the University of Siegen (Germany), second masters studies at the Viadrina European University in Frankfurt (Germany) and at the University of Sofia (Bulgaria) in the field of Media and Intercultural Communication. Dissertation in the field of Media, Journalism and Communication massive in Sofia. Lecturer at the University of Southeast Europe (RNM), State University of Tetovo (RNM), AAB College (Pristina, Kosovo) and currently at the University "Mother Tereza" in Skopje in the field of Media, Journalism and Communication. Publications: The change of social reality from facts and fictions in the Media, Grafoden, Skopje. ISBN: 9786086676117. Media transition and their democratization processes in Macedonia, Grafoden, Skpoje. ISBN: 9786086676100 Participant in many scientific, national and international conferences in the field of media, communication and journalism. Publisher of a series of scientific articles in various international scientific journals.

**Aini Azeqa Ma'rof** is a distinguished social psychology researcher, having earned a Ph.D. from Sheffield University with a specialization in intergroup contact intervention and prosocial behavior. Her work is dedicated to fostering psychosocial well-being, encouraging prosocial behavior, facilitating attitude change, and improving intergroup relations within communities. With a focus on developing social-psychological interventions that promote unity, Dr. Azeqa investigates how positive actions and attitudes can be nurtured among diverse groups to enhance community dynamics. Dr. Azeqa has contributed significantly to the field through various publications, focusing on the role of intergroup contact in diverse communities, promoting positive attitude changes through community-based interventions, and enhancing psychosocial well-being. Dr. Azeqa continues to influence the field through research that bridges gaps between groups and cultivates a more inclusive and supportive society.

**Mahboobeh Moosivand** holds PhD in Philosophy of Education from Kharazmi University in Tehran. She is a faculty member at Alzahra University. My research interests include Gender differences in education, Women empowerment, and Adolescent issues during puberty. She would like to collaborate internationally with other researchers in the following areas: Collaborative research studies and papers, Participation in writing research proposals, Invitation to participate in international webinars at Alzahra University, Invitations to researchers and professors to take part in research opportunities offered by Alzahra University.

**Shahzad Khaver Mushtaq** is working as Assistant Professor at the University of Sargodha (UOS) since 2009. Specializing in an array of subjects, Shahzad imparts knowledge on sociological theory, medical sociology, social research methods, gender issues and community development. His academic journey is marked by a profound commitment to teaching and fostering research that navigates the complexities of diversity and interdisciplinary approaches. Before his tenure at UOS, Shahzad garnered extensive experience in the development sector, working with local, national, and international organizations across Pakistan. His work primarily focused on community development, human rights, democratic governance, research and monitoring, showcasing his dedication to creating impactful social change. As a teacher and researcher, Shahzad's scholarly pursuits are deeply rooted in exploring the theoretical foundations of Youth relations, medical sociology, gender, religion and politics. His expertise and dedication to his fields of study have made him a respected figure among his peers and students alike.

**Fakhroddin Noorbehbahani** received his BSc and MSc in Computer and IT Engineering from, respectively, Isfahan University of Technology and Amirkabir University of Technology, Iran, in 2007 and 2010. He is currently the Ph.D. student at the Department of Electrical and Computer Engineering in Isfahan University of Technology, Iran. His research interests include Data Mining, Pattern Recognition and Information Security.

**Hina Saeed**, a multifaceted, accomplished and a dedicated scholar is currently pursuing her Ph.D. in her field of expertise while excelling as the Lecturer at the esteemed University of Multan. Her unwavering commitment to academia and passion for knowledge have been the driving forces behind her success.

**Fatima Zahra Sali** is an Assistant Professor in the College of Education.

**Sunil K. Sansaniwal** brings a wealth of experience in research and academia in the energy and environment sector. He holds a doctorate in enhancing indoor environmental quality through occupants' adaptive actions from Malaviya National Institute of Technology, Jaipur. He is a qualified Mechanical Engineer from the reputed university in India. Dr. Sansaniwal 's expertise shines through his adept science communication skills and his affiliations with various internationally recognized journals. His contributions have earned him numerous accolades from both national and international organizations. He has authored over 30 research articles, accumulating more than 2050 citations. Dr. Sansaniw has also served as an editor and reviewer for multiple publishers, keeping him abreast of the latest developments in his field. He has been instrumental in several research projects focusing on sustainable cooling in India, the development of green procurement guides for cooling appliances, sectorial energy efficiency, building energy demand reduction and the implementation of building and environmental codes. Currently, he serves as an Associate Fellow at the Centre for Climate Change Research at The Energy and Resources Institute, New Delhi, India, where he continues to contribute significantly to the field.

**SC Vetrivel** is a faculty member in the Department of Management Studies, Kongu Engineering College (Autonomous), Perundurai, Erode Dt. Having experience in Industry 20 years and Teaching 16 years. Awarded with Doctoral Degree in Management Sciences in Anna University, Chennai. He has organized various workshops and Faculty Development Programmes. He is actively involved in research and consultancy works. He acted as a resource person to FDPs & MDPs to various industries like, SPB ltd, Tamilnadu Police, DIET, Rotary school and many. His areas of interest include Entrepreneurship, Business Law, Marketing and Case writing. Articles published more than 100 International and National Journals. Presented papers in more than 30 National and International conferences including IIM Bangalore, IIM Kozhikode, IIM Kashipur and IIM Indore. He was a Chief Co-ordinator of Entrepreneurship and Management Development Centre (EMDC) of Kongu Engineering College, he was instrumental in organizing various Awareness Camps, FDP, and TEDPs to aspiring entrepreneurs which was funded by NSTEDB – DST/GoI.

**Wasswa Shafik** (Member, IEEE) received a Bachelor of Science degree in information technology engineering with a minor in mathematics from Ndejje University, Kampala, Uganda, a Master of Engineering degree in information technology engineering (MIT) from Yazd University, Iran, and a Ph.D. degree in computer science with the School of Digital Science, Universiti Brunei Darussalam, Brunei Darussalam. He is also the Founder and a Principal Investigator of the Dig Connectivity Research Laboratory (DCRLab) after serving as a Research Associate at Network Interconnectivity Research Laboratory, Yazd University. Prior to this, he worked as a Community Data Analyst at Population Services International (PSI-Uganda), Community Data Officer at Programme for Accessible Health Communication (PACE-Uganda), Research Assistant at the Socio-Economic Data Centre (SEDC-Uganda), Prime Minister's Office, Kampala, Uganda, an Assistant Data Officer at TechnoServe, Kampala, IT Support at Thurayya Islam Media, Uganda, and Asmaah Charity Organization. He has more than 60 publications in renowned journals and conferences. His research interests include Computer Vision, AI-enabled IoT/IoMTs, Smart Cities.

**Preeti Singh Bahadur**, Amity University, Greater Noida (U. P.) is working as an Associate Professor in Applied Science Department. She completed her B.Sc. in (Electronics), M.Sc. (Physics) and Ph.D. (Physics) degree from Barkatullah University, Bhopal, (M.P.). She has a total of 21 years of research and teaching experience. Her current areas of interest are condensed matter physics, Laser, optics, optoelectronics Thermal and Dynamical properties of Alkali halides, cyanides, superoxide and fullerene materials. She has guided M.Phil., Ph.D. scholars and many UG/PG students in their dissertation work. She handled one research projects funded by the University Grant Commission, Government of India. She has published 90+ research articles in various journal of repute, indexed in SCI/SCIE/SCOPUS. She has also presented more than 25 research papers in various international and national conferences in India and abroad. She is a persistent reviewer of leading national and international journals. She is a program committee member of various IEEE conferences and a member of Journal of Advances in Physics, Member of Scientific, Technical Committee & Editorial Review Board on Engineering and Physical Sciences, World Academy of Science, Engineering and Technology (WASET), Editorial Board Member of various Journals. She is a life member of Amity University Network (AUN) Research lab. She has chaired many sessions from different conferences, head of the session of various international conferences. Also, she has attended various FDP's on teaching pedagogy, ICT teaching and learning tools, LaTeX from various governing bodies like M.A.N.I.T, IIT Bombay, MHRD government of India. Also attended various Workshop on Virtual Labs, held at amity University, Greater Noida in collaboration with IIT Delhi Virtual Labs, and MHRD Govt. of India under the Mission on Education through Information and Communications Technology (ICT). She is an active reviewer of many journals. She is a good learner and listener and contributed greatly to society through academics and research. She has been awarded an employee of the quarter from Amity University, Greater Noida also awarded Shiksha rattan saman by Nayya Foundation in recognition of Sterling Merit, Excellent Performance and outstanding contribution in the Field of Education and for the Progress of the Nation Individual Achievement, Intellectual Excellence and National Development at Asansol, West Bengal. Dr. Preeti has taught many engineering subjects at UG and PG level. Few subjects like Engineering Physics, Lasers and Research Methodologies are the key subject of interest.

**Arun VP** is a driven and accomplished professional with a diverse educational background and extensive hands-on experience across various industries. Graduating with honors, Arun earned his Master of Business Administration (M.B.A) with a specialization in Human Resources and Marketing from the renowned Sona School of Management in Salem in 2018, where he excelled academically with an impressive 8.3 Cumulative Grade Point Average (CGPA). Before pursuing his MBA, Arun laid a solid foundation by obtaining a Bachelor of Engineering degree from Kongu Engineering College in 2014. Throughout his academic journey, Arun displayed an unwavering commitment to learning and personal growth, actively seeking opportunities to expand his knowledge and skills beyond the confines of traditional education. He sought practical experiences to complement his theoretical understanding, such as a 45-day summer internship focused on conducting a feasibility study for R-Doc Sustainability in the market.

**Agron Vragalla**, born on 3 July 1989 in Kichevo, North Macedonia. PhD candidate in South East European University, Phd Studies in Faculty of Languages, Cultures and Communication, Profile: Media and Communication. Former Assistant professor at The State University of Tetova, Faculty of Law, branch – Journalism. I am currently an Assistant – professor University of Mother Teresa in Skopje, Faculty of Social Sciences, Department of Media and Intercultural Communication.

**Xiaodan Wang** is a PhD candidate at Universiti Putra Malaysia, and her supervisor is Dr. Aini Azeqa Ma'rof. Her current work focuses more on youth and development, especially the study of youth online gaming intentions and behaviors, as well as the relationship between social media and social anxiety. Have published articles on relevant research.

**Wei Wang** is a PhD student, Universiti Putra Malaysia, Malaysia; Lecturer, Business School, Huaihua College, China.

**Arta Xhelili** is a lecturer at "Mother Teresa" University, in the Faculty of Social Sciences, Media and Intercultural Communication study program. She received her Ph.D. degree in social sciences with an emphasis in communication from the University of "St. Kriil and Methodi" in Skopje and the M.A. degree from Ball State University, Indiana, in Organizational and Professional Communication and Training Development. Her research interests lie in the broad areas of communication, gender studies and media. Arta Xhelili can be reached at arta.xhelili@unt.edu.mk .

**Asma Yunus** is an Assistant Professor in the Department of Sociology and Criminology at the University of Sargodha, Punjab, Pakistan. .

**Huma Zaidi** holds the position of Associate Professor within the Department of General Education at RAK Medical & Health Sciences University. Her educational journey includes earning Bachelor's and Master's degrees in English from Aligarh Muslim University, India, followed by her Ph.D. in Language and Literature from the same institution in 2003. Dr. Zaidi's expertise lies in teaching English and Health Sciences Communication, and she has facilitated numerous workshops both in India and the UAE. Her academic portfolio boasts a wealth of research articles, showcasing her significant contributions to the field.

# Index

## A

Accountability 35, 50, 59, 60, 61, 94, 213, 216, 288, 299, 301, 305, 306, 310, 312, 321, 324, 325, 340

adolescents 1, 2, 3, 4, 5, 6, 9, 10, 11, 14, 15, 17, 18, 19, 20, 21, 22, 23, 24, 31, 33, 41, 51, 52, 60, 65, 67, 68, 70, 71, 72, 73, 74, 75, 76, 77, 78, 79, 80, 81, 82, 83, 84, 85, 86, 87, 95, 100, 107, 116, 117, 125, 126, 245, 246, 247, 319, 336, 337, 338, 339, 341, 342, 343, 344, 345, 346, 347, 348, 349, 368, 371, 375, 376, 380, 383, 389, 392, 400, 422, 423, 427, 429

AI 3, 4, 23, 25, 28, 34, 37, 44, 45, 46, 47, 48, 49, 50, 51, 52, 53, 54, 55, 56, 57, 58, 59, 60, 61, 62, 63, 64, 65, 66, 68, 81, 82, 88, 89, 90, 91, 92, 93, 94, 95, 96, 107, 108, 129, 130, 131, 132, 133, 134, 135, 136, 137, 138, 139, 140, 141, 144, 146, 164, 165, 166, 167, 168, 169, 170, 171, 172, 174, 175, 176, 177, 178, 179, 180, 181, 182, 183, 184, 185, 197, 198, 200, 203, 204, 205, 206, 207, 208, 209, 210, 211, 212, 213, 214, 215, 216, 217, 218, 221, 222, 224, 225, 226, 227, 228, 235, 236, 237, 238, 239, 240, 243, 244, 245, 246, 251, 254, 255, 256, 257, 258, 259, 260, 261, 263, 264, 265, 266, 267, 268, 269, 273, 274, 275, 277, 278, 283, 285, 287, 288, 289, 298, 299, 300, 301, 302, 303, 304, 305, 306, 307, 308, 309, 310, 311, 312, 313, 314, 315, 316, 317, 318, 319, 320, 321, 322, 323, 324, 325, 326, 327, 328, 329, 330, 331, 332, 333, 334, 335, 336, 337, 338, 339, 340, 341, 342, 343, 344, 345, 346, 347, 348, 349, 351, 352, 353, 354, 355, 356, 357, 358, 359, 360, 361, 362, 363, 364, 365, 366, 367, 368, 369, 376, 393, 396, 397, 398, 399, 400, 401, 402, 403, 404, 405, 406, 408, 409, 410, 411, 412, 413, 415, 417, 418, 419, 420, 421, 423, 424, 425, 426, 427, 428, 429, 430

AI literacy 45, 55, 57, 139, 174, 175, 180, 181, 305, 309, 311, 312, 411

AI on loss in decision-making 254, 256, 258, 259

Algorithmic Bias 55, 56, 307, 407, 408, 409, 411

Artificial Intelligence 3, 4, 37, 42, 44, 45, 46, 47, 48, 49, 51, 52, 53, 55, 59, 60, 61, 62, 63, 64, 65, 67, 68, 82, 88, 92, 107, 108, 129, 138, 139, 141, 164, 171, 172, 173, 174, 175, 176, 177, 178, 180, 181, 182, 183, 184, 185, 197, 198, 199, 200, 201, 203, 221, 222, 223, 224, 225, 226, 227, 228, 229, 231, 236, 237, 238, 239, 240, 242, 243, 244, 245, 246, 248, 251, 254, 255, 263, 264, 265, 266, 267, 274, 278, 285, 287, 288, 289, 298, 299, 301, 302, 305, 306, 308, 309, 310, 312, 313, 314, 315, 316, 317, 320, 321, 322, 323, 324, 325, 326, 327, 328, 329, 330, 333, 334, 335, 336, 337, 340, 342, 343, 344, 345, 346, 348, 349, 350, 351, 352, 353, 354, 355, 356, 357, 361, 362, 363, 364, 366, 367, 368, 369, 371, 373, 379, 393, 398, 401, 404, 410, 412, 413, 414, 415, 416, 417, 418, 419, 420, 421, 422, 423, 424, 425, 426, 427, 428, 429, 430

## B

Bring Your Own Device 140, 141, 160, 171, 172, 173

## C

Career Guidance 129, 130, 131, 132, 133, 134, 135, 136, 138, 139

Challenges 1, 2, 23, 25, 33, 35, 37, 38, 42, 44, 45, 46, 47, 50, 52, 54, 55, 56, 61, 63, 65, 68, 70, 71, 72, 73, 75, 76, 77, 78, 79, 80, 81, 88, 89, 90, 91, 92, 96, 97, 104, 107, 109, 120, 121, 129, 135, 136, 138, 139, 141, 142, 144, 151, 152, 155, 158, 164, 174, 175, 176, 178, 179, 181, 182, 183, 184, 190, 199, 200, 204, 211, 218, 221, 222, 225, 227, 228, 239, 242, 255, 263, 264, 285, 287, 290, 298, 299, 300, 301, 303, 304, 308, 309, 310, 311, 312, 313, 320, 323, 324, 325, 329, 333, 335, 336, 337, 338, 340, 344, 347, 348, 351, 352, 353, 354, 356, 357, 364, 365, 367, 368, 372, 373, 374, 375, 392, 393, 395, 396, 398, 399, 400, 401, 403, 404, 405, 406, 410, 411, 425, 430

ChatGPT 108, 172, 173, 182, 183, 184, 223, 225, 226, 227, 228, 229, 230, 231, 232, 233, 234, 235, 236, 237, 238, 239, 240, 379

children 2, 3, 4, 5, 7, 10, 14, 15, 17, 19, 20, 22, 23, 24, 27, 30, 31, 33, 38, 44, 45, 46, 47, 48, 49, 51, 52, 55, 56, 57, 58, 59, 60, 61, 63, 64, 65, 66, 74, 75, 77, 79, 84, 85, 86, 105, 115, 117, 123, 124, 125, 126, 127, 152, 154, 174, 175, 179, 180, 183, 184, 185, 188, 232, 246, 264, 303, 355, 356, 358, 359, 361, 365, 366, 369, 371, 372, 375, 376, 408, 411, 415, 417, 422, 423, 431

Child well-being 47

Cutting-Edge Technology 173

## D

Deep Learning 63, 144, 146, 184, 198, 208, 209, 210, 211, 226, 227, 238, 265, 290, 291, 292, 294, 297,

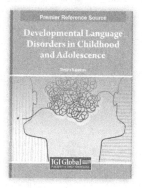

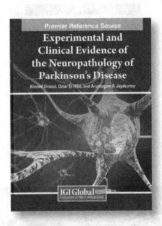
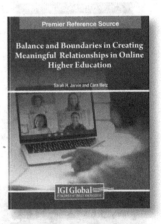